Second Canadian Edition

Cultural ANTHROPOLOGY

William A. Haviland
University of Vermont

Shirley A. Fedorak
University of Saskatchewan

Gary W. Crawford
University of Toronto

Richard B. Lee
University of Toronto

THOMSON
NELSON

Australia   Canada   Mexico   Singapore   Spain   United Kingdom   United States

THOMSON

✳

NELSON

Cultural Anthropology
Second Canadian Edition

by William A. Haviland, Shirley A. Fedorak,
Gary W. Crawford, and Richard B. Lee

Editorial Director and Publisher:
Evelyn Veitch

Executive Editor:
Joanna Cotton

Acquisitions Editor:
Cara Yarzab

Marketing Manager:
Lenore Taylor

Senior Developmental Editor:
Katherine Goodes

Photo Researcher:
Mary Rose MacLachlan

Permissions Coordinator:
Mary Rose MacLachlan

Production Editor:
Carrie McGregor

Copy Editor:
Marcia Miron de Gallego

Proofreader:
June Trusty

Indexer:
Belle Wong

Production Coordinator:
Hedy Sellers

Creative Director:
Angela Cluer

Interior Design Modifications:
Katherine Strain

Cover Design:
Katherine Strain

Cover Image:
"Cycle of Life" by Jane Ash Poitras,
RCA, courtesy of the artist.
Copyright © 2002, Jane Ash Poitras

Compositor:
Nelson Gonzalez

Printer:
Quebecor World

**National Library of Canada
Cataloguing in Publication Data**

Cultural anthropology / William A. Haviland ... [et al.]. — 2nd Canadian ed.

First Canadian ed. written by William A. Haviland, Gary W. Crawford and Shirley A. Fedorak

Includes bibliographical references and index.

ISBN 0-17-641665-X

1. Ethnology. I. Haviland, William A. II. Haviland, William A. Cultural anthropology.

GN316.C84 2004   306
C2004-900746-7

PREFACE

PURPOSE OF THE BOOK

Comprehensive, readable, and written for the student, Haviland/Fedorak/Crawford/Lee's market-leading text, *Cultural Anthropology*, is a highly relevant, high-quality teaching tool for introductory anthropology courses at colleges and universities. This new second Canadian edition is a truly exciting and unique examination of the field of sociocultural anthropology, its insights, its relevance, and the continuing role of cultural survival issues. Although focusing on sociocultural anthropology, the text also relates to the other fields of anthropology: biological anthropology, archaeology, and linguistics. *Cultural Anthropology* has two goals for introductory anthropology courses: to provide an overview of principles and processes of sociocultural anthropology, and to plant a seed of cultural awareness in Canadian students that will continue to grow and to challenge ethnocentrism long past the end of the semester.

The first and foremost aim of the text is to give students a comprehensive introduction to sociocultural anthropology. Because it draws from the research and ideas of a number of schools of anthropological thought, the text exposes students to a mix of such approaches as evolutionism, historical particularism, diffusionism, functionalism, French structuralism, structural functionalism, and others. The second aim of the text is to open students' eyes to the true complexity and breadth of human behaviour and the human condition. The questioning aspect of sociocultural anthropology is perhaps the most relevant gift we can pass on to our students. *Cultural Anthropology* is a tool to enable students to think both in and out of context.

Cultural Anthropology's invigorated writing, comprehensive coverage, lavish illustrations, and relevant and engaging ethnographic examples stimulate comprehension of the material. The text continues to discuss early research, key findings, and influential anthropologists, while adding original research on culture change and updating coverage of current controversies. Gender, ethnicity, and stratification concepts and terminologies are in accordance with contemporary thinking, and the narrative has been streamlined using more fully developed, balanced, and global examples. Students will also find interesting such relevant topics as body piercing, body art, and culture shock.

Many Messages, Many Media

The cover image chosen for this edition reflects several key themes in the study of cultural anthropology. The image is by Jane Ash Poitras, a well-known First-Nations Canadian artist from Edmonton, Alberta. We chose this work for several reasons: first, it is a compelling image that speaks to the history and diversity of anthropology with the "snapshots" of peoples from different culture groups; second, because of the artist's personal history as a First-Nations Canadian artist from a Cree background; and third, because Jane Ash Poitras is well known for using multimedia on her canvases.

Anthropology is arguably among the most naturally "multimedia" of all studies, and we find sociocultural anthropologists working within numerous guises of human behaviour, ranging from music to oral narrative, ritual dancing, weaving, and spray-paint graffiti. Since anthropology has been an archive of human behaviour, it is important that the discipline show the richness and diversity of humanity through appropriate media. This second Canadian edition of *Cultural Anthropology* continues to recognize both the level of comfort with non-print media of students as well as the many potential paths to exploring the techniques, processes, and findings of sociocultural anthropology. The art program is an important part of this text's narrative. The video cases show culture in motion and provide visual images of real people to supplement the ideas and concepts presented here. PowerPoint slides bring the ideas and art of the textbook into the classroom. The textbook's website holds a wealth of information and quizzes in a virtual setting. And, of course, the suggested readings, featuring many Canadian authors, and the bibliography continue to show the rich library of anthropological texts available to students. Thus, *Cultural Anthropology* allows instructors to draw upon a broad set of instructional tools to expand their classroom.

SPECIAL FEATURES OF THE BOOK

Chapter Openers

Well-designed chapter openers provide previews that summarize the major concepts to be learned in each chapter. New to this edition is the inclusion of chapter outlines to prepare students for the chapter's content.

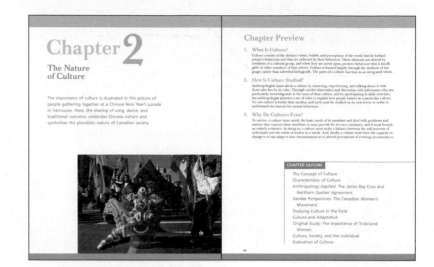

Maps, Photographs, and Illustrations

Colourful and eye-catching visuals are used to make important anthropological points and to clarify anthropological concepts. These also have proved to be valuable and memorable teaching aids.

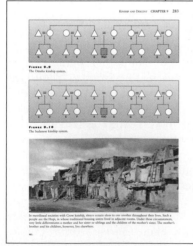

New Chapter

Chapter 14, "The Anthropology of Health," is a new and valuable addition to the text. Beginning with an overview of medical anthropology, topics range from its history to the disparity between nations, from HIV/AIDS in Africa to Vancouver's Downtown Eastside homeless and drug culture, and much more!

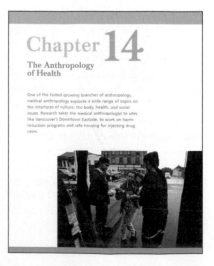

Original Studies

The Original Studies feature excerpts, integrated within the flow of the text, are from case studies and other original works by women and men in the field. Found throughout the text, they illustrate important anthropological concepts and show students how anthropologists study human behaviour, past and present.

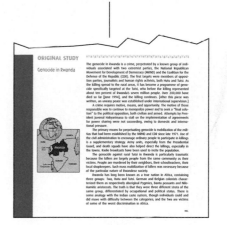

Anthropology Applied

These features focus on applications of anthropology in a wide variety of social contexts, as well as career opportunities outside of academia. New are features on Asen Balikci's work with the Netsilik Inuit, and Dara Culhane's ongoing applied research projects with formerly homeless women in Vancouver's Downtown Eastside.

Gender Perspectives

Along with integrated text coverage of gender, these features delve into specific gender-related issues.

Anthropologist Profiles

Each chapter contains a profile of an eminent Canadian anthropologist who works in a field relevant to the chapter.

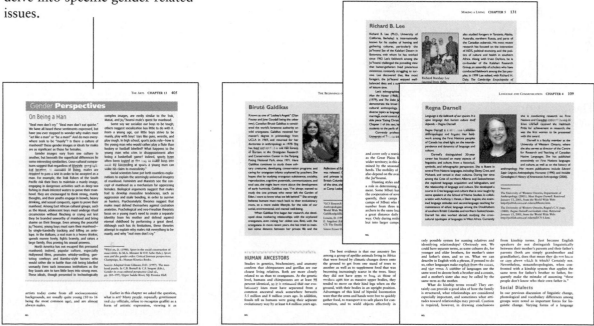

Glossary

A running glossary is provided in each chapter, which, along with the cumulative glossary at the back of the textbook, aids student mastery of the language of the field.

...of classes: lower lower, middle lower, upper lower, lower middle, and so forth. Canada is a class society, with labels such as upper, middle, and lower class generally tied to income levels. Thus, the class people belong to is earned through endeavour and is know as **achieved status.** Based on gender, ethnicity, and even age, Canadians

Despite their close association, the clothing worn by these two individuals and the way they interact clearly indicate they are of different social classes.

Social class.   A category of individuals who enjoy equal or nearly equal prestige according to the evaluation system.
> Achieved status.   Status an individual earns.

NEL

Chapter Summary

These review sections summarize the chapter's content and are designed to help students master the material.

Questions for Critical Thought

The Questions for Critical Thought are designed to encourage students to think critically and apply important concepts to contemporary issues.

THE NATURE OF ANTHROPOLOGY   CHAPTER 1   31

CHAPTER SUMMARY

Throughout human history, people have needed to know who they are, where they came from, and why they behave as they do. Traditionally, myths and legends provided the answers to these questions. Anthropology, as it has emerged over the past 200 years, offers another approach to answering the questions people ask about themselves.

Anthropology is the study of humankind. In employing a scientific approach, anthropologists seek to produce a reasonably objective understanding of both human diversity and those aspects all humans have in common. The five major branches of anthropology are biological anthropology, archaeology, linguistic anthropology, applied anthropology, and sociocultural anthropology. Biological anthropology focuses on humans as biological organisms. Biological anthropologists trace the evolutionary development of the human animal and study biological variation within the species today. Linguistic anthropologists, who study human languages, may deal with descriptions of languages, with histories of languages, or with how languages are used in particular social settings. Applied anthropologists put to practical use the knowledge and expertise of anthropology. Sociocultural anthropologists study humans in terms of their cultures in the present and recent past. Ethnographers go into the field to observe and

describe human behaviour; ethnologists do comparative studies of particular facets of a culture, such as religion or economic practices; and ethnohistorians study cultures of the recent past using oral histories and written accounts left by explorers, missionaries, and traders.

Anthropology is unique among the social and natural sciences in that it is concerned with formulating explanations of human diversity based on a study of all aspects of human biology and behaviour in all known societies, rather than in European and North American societies alone. Thus anthropologists have devoted much attention to the study of non-Western peoples.

Anthropologists are concerned with the objective and systematic study of humankind. The data sociocultural anthropologists use may be from a single society or from numerous societies that are compared.

In anthropology, the humanities and sciences come together into a genuinely human science. Anthropology's link with the humanities can be seen in its concern with people's values, languages, arts, and literature, but above all in its attempt to convey the experience of living as other people do. As both a science and a humanity, anthropology has essential skills to offer the modern world, where understanding the other people with whom we share the globe has become a matter of survival.

QUESTIONS FOR CRITICAL THOUGHT

1. Think about movies you have seen and novels you have read that feature anthropologists as characters. How are they portrayed? How do these characterizations contrast with the discipline as presented in this chapter?
2. Respond to the question, "What good is anthropology, anyway?"
3. Identify your future career. How might anthropological knowledge help you understand and interact with people in your chosen career (e.g., teacher, doctor, police officer, bank teller, lawyer)?
4. If an anthropologist chose your community, college dorm, or organization to study, what information would you willingly share? What information would you be more hesitant to share? How would the anthropologist's presence interfere with your everyday life?
5. Think about how Richard Lee's Christmas gift was received by the Ju/'hoansi. How would you or your family react if you received an extremely expensive or very personal gift from an acquaintance? Have you ever received an unexpected Christmas gift and not been able to, or wanted to, give one in return? How would you handle such a situation?

NEL

Internet Resources and Suggested Readings

These sections provide classical, contemporary, and web-based resources to further explore the concepts within the chapter.

414   PART IV   THE SEARCH FOR ORDER: SOLVING THE PROBLEM OF DISORDER

INTERNET RESOURCES

Paul Kane's Great Nor-West
http://www.umanitoba.ca/cm/vol2/no26/kane.html
A comprehensive examination of Paul Kane's life and work, displaying some of his paintings.

The Group of Seven and Their Contemporaries
http://www.mcmichael.com/group.htm
A good presentation of the Group of Seven's lives and work. Includes links to sites on each artist, which display some of their work in vivid colour.

Important Moments in the History of Canadian Visual Culture
http://www.ouc.bc.ca/fiar/1918_45.html
This site provides a timeline of visual art in Canada.

Modern and Contemporary Art at the McMichael
http://www.mcmichael.com/modern.htm
This site provides a brief examination of modern and contemporary art in Canada.

Inuit Art Background
http://www.harrisinuitgallery.com/artinfo.htm
This site provides a brief sketch of Inuit art and its history. The site also includes photos of Inuit sculpture.

Manitoba Aboriginal Artist Archive
http://aboriginalcollections.ic.gc.ca/artist/artists/006/index.html
This site features several Manitoba artists and provides descriptions and photos of their work.

Music and Anthropology
http://www.muspe.unibo.it/period/ma/index/ma_ind.htm
The *Journal of Musical Anthropology* of the *Mediterranean* presents several journal articles reflecting on music. Two recent additions: "Relating the present to the past: Thoughts on the study of musical change and culture change in ethnomusicology" and "Music, ceremony and self-identity in Renaissance Venice."

Professional Weeping
http://www.research.umbc.edu/eol/5/greene
A study of professional weeping: music, affect, and hierarchy in a south Indian folk performance by Paul D. Greene. Some of the topics include funerals, oppari, and performance analysis.

Urban Expression
http://www.graffiti.org/faq/pamdennant.html
A comprehensive examination by Pamela Dennant of the roots of New York graffiti. Provides a good historical overview set within the social and political context of inner-city New York.

SUGGESTED READINGS

Dundes, A. (1980). *Interpreting folk lore.* Bloomington: Indiana University Press.
A collection of articles that assess the materials folklorists have amassed and classified, this book seeks to broaden and refine traditional assumptions about the proper subject matter and methods of folklore.

Hannah, J.L. (1988). *Dance, sex and gender.* Chicago: University of Chicago Press.

Like other art forms, dances are social acts that contribute to the continuation and emergence of culture. One of the oldest—if not the oldest—art forms, dance shares the same instrument, the human body, with sexuality. This book, written for a broad nonspecialist audience, explicitly examines sexuality and the construction of gender identities as they are played out in the production and visual imagery of dance.

NEL

POLITICAL ORGANIZATION AND THE MAINTENANCE OF ORDER   CHAPTER 11   351

McGlynn, F., & Tuden, A. (Eds.). (1991). *Anthropological approaches to political behavior.* Pittsburgh, PA: Pittsburgh Press.
A diverse collection of essays taken from previous editions of the journal *Ethnology.* These articles serve to highlight various theoretical concerns in political anthropology, and provide valuable insight into political behaviour, power, and action.

McRoberts, K. (1997). *Misconceiving Canada: The struggle for national unity.* Toronto: Oxford University Press.
A very readable examination of the struggle for national unity in Canada. In addition to providing political analysis, McRoberts examines from a historical perspective the issues of unity facing Canadians.

CNN TODAY VIDEOS

The Politics of Reconciliation: Cambodia and the Khmer Rouge (CNN Cultural Anthropology, vol. 3, 2:30)
This segment examines how the Cambodian people are attempting to come to a civil resolution of the harsh period of dominance by the Khmer Rouge.

Russian Social Protest (CNN Cultural Anthropology, vol. 2, 1:38)
In a provincial northern Russian city, citizens face economic and social upheaval since the breakup of the old Soviet Union.

Yugoslavia History (CNN Cultural Anthropology, vol. 2, 2:12)
This segment follows the development of the multiethnic Yugoslavia from World War II through the death of its postwar leader Tito. It provides background for the tragic recent developments in the Balkans.

A Glimpse Inside Afghanistan (CNN Cultural Anthropology, vol. 3, 1:26)
This short, offbeat clip of a motorcycle stuntman inside Afghanistan throws light on the restriction on public display imposed by the Muslim fundamentalist rulers of the country.

The Promising Future of a Central American Nation: Guatemala (CNN Cultural Anthropology, vol. 3, 1:53)
Democracy and freedom are slowly taking root inside Guatemala, a Central American country that has known mostly dictatorship and civil unrest until recently.

Caste Killings in India (CNN Cultural Anthropology, vol. 6, 2:10)
A boyfriend and girlfriend are hanged because their families are from different castes. Few people in and around the village condemn the killings. Social activists in India say a global forum must act now.

CNN Today Videos

New to this edition, these video cases are suggested for further study of a particular culture. The set of videos is available to instructors for use in the classroom and for lending.

NEL

ORGANIZATION OF THE BOOK

A Unifying Theme

To provide students with a sense of the big picture, *Cultural Anthropology* uses a theme that allows students to contextualize each part and each chapter, regardless of the order in which they are read. Accordingly, each part, as well as each chapter within the part, has been developed as a self-contained unit of study that may be used in any sequence by the instructor. There are five parts in *Cultural Anthropology*:

Part I: Anthropology and the Study of Culture introduces students to the development of anthropology, the nature of culture in general, and the beginnings of human culture.

Part II: Culture and Survival discusses language and communication, patterns of subsistence and adaptation, and economic systems.

Part III: The Foundation of Groups examines sex and marriage, family and household, kinship and descent, and grouping by sex, age, common interest, and class.

Part IV: The Search for Order explains political organization and the maintenance of order, religion and the supernatural, and the arts.

Part V: Exploring Health and Illness Factors, Cultural Change, and the Future of Humanity discusses the anthropology of health as well as cultural change and the future of humanity.

WHAT'S NEW IN THE SECOND CANADIAN EDITION

This Canadian revision continues to offer a holistic perspective of an integrated, four-fields approach for understanding human behaviour. Each chapter has been thoroughly revised and updated with Canadian content. Canada's First Nations, Inuit, and Métis peoples are featured in this second edition, as well as Asian-Canadian groups who have played such a vital role in building this country. Major changes to the second Canadian edition include:

CHAPTER I Extensive revisions to the introduction to anthropology. Two major sections added: "New Directions in Ethnographic Fieldwork" and "Anthropology's Contributions to Other Disciplines." Revised Gender Perspectives feature, "The Anthropology of Gender," which includes archaeological interpretations of gender. Research of contemporary and early Canadian anthropologists highlighted throughout the chapter. This chapter emphasizes the significance of anthropology in the study of contemporary human cultures and the contributions toward this goal made by Canadian anthropologists.

CHAPTER 2 New information provided on culture shock as experienced by Canadian immigrants. Expanded and revised section on the Hutterite subculture, and added material on punk subcultures and the struggle of Acadians to retain their culture. Examination of the ways Asian Canadians have adapted to life in Canada using their traditional culture. A new biography of anthropologist Marius Barbeau. The pluralistic nature of Canada is emphasized in this chapter.

CHAPTER 3 New Gender Perspectives feature, "Gender Bias in Primatology." Revised early evolution scheme. This chapter provides a brief synopsis of human biological evolution and the beginnings of cultural behaviour.

CHAPTER 4 New Anthropology Applied feature, "Visual Anthropology and Ethnographic Film." New information provided on language retention, featuring Canadian Buddhists and French Canadians, and a discussion of language loss worldwide. Revised Gender Perspectives feature, "Gender in Language." Explanation of language diversity in China. A comprehensive discussion of language and communication and its role in human culture is provided in this chapter.

CHAPTER 5 Revised introduction to patterns of subsistence. New material on Blackfoot First Nations as a hunter-gatherer group. Extensive reorganization of the discussion on the characteristics of food foragers. A discussion of Inuit seal sharing. Expanded discussion of the division of labour on Canadian family farms. Diverse ways of making a living are featured in this chapter.

CHAPTER 6 New section on resource depletion, featuring cod fisheries in Canada. Expanded discussion of First Nations involvement in the fur trade. New section on Chinese-Canadian economic contributions to Canadian society. Major new section on food consumption, including behaviour, taboos, and ritual. New section on the global economy and the process of globalization. This chapter examines contemporary small-scale and industrial societies' economic practices.

CHAPTER 7 New section on human sexuality and updated material on adolescent sexuality. New discussion of homosexuality and anthropological research. Revised material on the Nayar marriage system. Updated material on same-sex marriages in Canada. A comprehensive and cross-cultural overview of issues related to sex and marriage is presented in this chapter.

CHAPTER 8 New sections on defining the family and same-sex families. New discussion of eldercare and China's one-child policy. Expanded discussion of childrearing practices among the Inuit. This chapter offers insight into the complexities of family and household organization.

CHAPTER 9 New section on contemporary Chinese-Canadian kinship. Revised and updated kinship terminologies and diagrams. The discussion of social organization is continued in this chapter.

CHAPTER 10 Revised social stratification section, with the addition of theories of stratification. New section on the concept of race and racial stratification, presenting a historical and anthropological discussion of racism experienced by Chinese Canadians. Revised section on gender stratification and an added section on ethnic stratification. The emphasis in this chapter is on social stratification in its many forms.

CHAPTER 11 New Gender Perspectives feature, "Minority Women in Canadian Politics." New biography of anthropologist Bernard Saladin d'Anglure. Added discussion of global terrorism. This chapter considers political organization from a cross-cultural perspective.

CHAPTER 12 Expanded discussion of mythology. New section on neo-paganism, featuring Wicca and Reconstructionist religions. The features and functions of religion are examined from a cross-cultural perspective in this chapter.

CHAPTER 13 Revised Gender Perspectives feature, "On Being A Man." New section on body art, including body painting, tattooing, piercing, and adornment. Highlighted in this chapter are the various forms of artistic expression found in human cultures, including contemporary Western cultures.

CHAPTER 14 New chapter on the anthropology of health. Includes an overview of medical anthropology and biocultural and biomedical perspectives on health and illness; health and the human condition; disparities between rich and poor nations; the history of human health; a case study featuring the Ju/'hoansi; shamanism; critical medical anthropology; poverty and health; Vancouver's Downtown Eastside homeless and drug culture; women and health; environmental health and justice; HIV/AIDS in Africa; the youth in a southern Africa secondary school; and contemporary biomedicine and its discontents.

CHAPTER 15 Chapters 15 and 16 of the previous edition of this text have been merged into one chapter. New and revised material on Nunavut. New Gender Perspectives feature, "Reproductive Rights in Canada." This chapter synthesizes the issues facing contemporary cultures, including culture change and sociocultural adaptation challenges.

SUPPLEMENTS TO THE BOOK

Cultural Anthropology recognizes that anthropology is arguably among the most naturally "multimedia" of all studies. The selection of ancillaries accompanying this text reflects this need for teaching and learning tools to also be of many media.

For the Student

Cultural Anthropology Student Resources Website (http://www.cultural2e.nelson.com)

Available free to students, this powerful web-based supplement provides:

- Chapter-related true/false questions
- Chapter-related multiple-choice questions
- Chapter-related short questions
- Chapter-related Internet activities
- Chapter-related key term glossary
- Chapter summaries
- Crossword puzzles
- Pronunciation guide
- Anthropology web links
- PowerPoint lecture notes
- Videos

- Anthropological research on the Internet
- *Earthwatch Journal*, including questions
- *Anthropology News* link

Researching Anthropology on the Internet

This useful guide is designed to assist anthropology students with all their needs when doing research on the Internet. Part One contains general information necessary to get started. Part Two looks at each main discipline of anthropology and refers students to sites where the most enlightening research can be obtained. Offered free through the textbook's website.

PowerPoint Lecture Notes

Chapter-by-chapter slide show providing an overview of chapter content, available as a download on the website.

Anthropology Online: Wadsworth's Anthropology Resource Centre

This resource centre contains a wealth of additional resources, quizzes, and exercises for both students and instructors. Included on this website is "A Virtual Tour of Applying Anthropology," a special section where students can find anthropologists at work, graduate student information, job boards, internships and fieldwork, and an essay on careers with video.

For the Instructor

Instructor's Manual

Revised by Ara Murray, Camosun College, this manual offers teaching objectives and lecture and class activity suggestions that correspond to each chapter of the textbook. Available in both print and electronic formats.

Test Bank

Revised by Marjorie Mitchell, University of Victoria, the test bank contains more than 1200 true/false and multiple-choice questions, 30 per-cent of them new or revised from the last edition. Available in both print and electronic formats from your local sales representative.

Cultural Anthropology Instructor Resources Website (http://www.cultural2e.nelson.com)

Instructor supplements are available on the password-protected instructor resource centre on the textbook's general website:

- Instructor's Manual
- PowerPoint lecture notes

Also accessible to instructors are the student resources of extra quizzes, crossword puzzles, Internet activities, and so forth. Explore such resources as web links to the Canadian Museum of Civilization, the Smithsonian Institute, The Archaeology Channel, and many more! Stay in touch using the *Earthwatch Journal* and the *Anthropology News* links.

PowerPoint Lecture Slides

Chapter-by-chapter slide show providing an overview of chapter content, available as a download on the website.

CNN Today Cultural Anthropology and Physical Anthropology Video Series

The *CNN Today* anthropology video series is an exclusive series jointly created by Thomson and CNN for cultural anthropology courses. Each video in the series consists of approximately 45 minutes of footage originally broadcast on CNN within the last several years. The videos are broken into short two- to seven-minute segments, which are perfect for classroom use as lecture launchers or to illustrate key anthropological concepts. In *Cultural Anthropology*, chapter-related video segments are noted at the end of each chapter. Order your set of videos from your local sales representative.

ACKNOWLEDGMENTS

Second Canadian Edition

We are indebted to many people for their assistance, patience, and encouragement throughout the development of this second "Canadianized" edition of William A. Haviland's *Cultural Anthropology*. First, a special thanks goes to Dr. William A. Haviland for his continued uncanny insight into what first-year students really need from an introductory anthropology course. It has been our inspiration for many years.

We are also grateful to the numerous reviewers for their comments and feedback on the first Canadian edition and on the draft manuscripts of this second edition. Without exception, their suggestions were thoughtful and relevant, and the second edition is much better as a result. Although we were not able to address all the comments, we did our best. Individuals who read and commented on portions of the manuscript include:

Naomi Adelson, *York University*

Janice Boddy, *University of Toronto*

Laird Christie, *Wilfrid Laurier University*

Constance Deroche, *University College of Cape Breton*

Douglass Drozdow-St Christian, *University of Western Ontario*

Nadia Ferrara, *McGill University*

Mathais Guenther, *Wilfrid Laurier University*

Doreen Klassen, *Sir Wilfred Grenfell College*

Harriet Lyons, *University of Waterloo*

Bruce Miller, *University of British Columbia*

Lisa Mitchell, *University of Victoria*

Ara Murray, *Camosun College*

Josephine Smart, *University of Calgary*

Angele Smith, *University of Northern British Columbia*

Canada is graced with gifted applied anthropologists, several of whom generously consented to have their work featured in our Anthropology Applied boxes: James B. Waldram, John O'Neil, Michael Asch, and Edward J. Hedican. We also owe a special debt to anthropologist Monica Keller and folklorist Michael Taft, who were contributing writers. Thanks also to Laurel Bossen, who contributed her expertise to a Gender Perspectives feature, and to colleagues at the University of Toronto in Mississauga who provided further thoughts and ideas.

We also must thank the many people who helped us locate information on leading Canadian anthropologists. We learned, the hard way, that not only are Canadian anthropologists generous with their time, but they are also much too modest. We hope this text will, in some small way, publicize the many accomplishments of our homegrown and adopted anthropologists. Special thanks are extended to research assistants Lindsay Stokalko and Maureen Murney who tirelessly searched for resources and checked Internet sites. Their efforts were greatly appreciated.

We also extend our gratitude to several friends, family members, and colleagues for cheerfully searching through their photo albums for photos: Herbert Bear, Clayton Bear, Dr. Debra Bear, Betty Fedorak, John Fedorak, Annie Fedorak, Jeremy and Sinead van Olst, Dr. Ernest Walker, and Dr. Josephine Smart.

For their support, patience, and expertise, we wish to thank our families: Robert, Lisa, Kris, and Cory Fedorak; Karen Bauman and Kyle Crawford; David, Miriam, and Louise Lee; and Dr. Harriet Rosenberg.

To the staff of Thomson Nelson, we are grateful for your diligence, kindness, and enthusiasm for this project, with special thanks to acquisitions editor Cara Yarzab, who brought us together for this project, and to Katherine Goodes, our developmental editor, for her patient guidance and unswerving enthusiasm. Our gratitude to Nelson photo editor Mary Rose MacLachlan, who instinctively knew what we were looking for, and heartfelt thanks to Carrie McGregor, production editor; Marcia Miron de Gallego, copy editor; and June Trusty, proofreader, for their hard work in polishing this text. We also wish to express our appreciation to the skilled editorial, design, and production team, who have produced a visually striking text. We feel privileged to have worked with each one of you.

And, finally, thank you to our anthropology and medical anthropology students, past and present, at the University of Saskatchewan, University of Toronto, and University of Toronto at Mississauga who enthusiastically offered their unique perspectives. Many of their comments and words of wisdom have found their way into this text. We know what anthropology can mean to students—its value not only as an academic endeavour but as a resource for real life. Anthropology can make a difference and we must instill in our students a cultural awareness that will greatly assist them in their future endeavours.

Shirley A. Fedorak
Gary W. Crawford
Richard B. Lee

ABOUT THE AUTHORS

Dr. William A. Haviland, Professor Emeritus at the University of Vermont, earned his B.A., M.A., and Ph.D. degrees at the University of Pennsylvania. He has published widely on archaeological, ethnological, and physical anthropological research carried out in Guatemala, Maine, and Vermont. Dr. Haviland is a member of many professional societies, including the American Anthropological Association and the American Association for the Advancement of Science.

One of Dr. Haviland's greatest loves is teaching, which originally prompted him to write *Cultural Anthropology*. He says he learns something new every year from his students about what they need from a first college course in anthropology. In addition to writing *Cultural Anthropology*, Dr. Haviland has authored several other popular works for anthropology students.

Shirley A. Fedorak is a sessional lecturer in cultural anthropology and archaeology at the University of Saskatchewan, where she has taught since 1991. During the 1990s, she worked on several curriculum projects, including "People in Their World: A Study of First Nations Peoples on the Plains," sponsored by the Saskatchewan Public School Board. She has also written and developed multimedia courses in anthropology and archaeology for the University of Saskatchewan Extension Division. Recently, Professor Fedorak discovered the value of web-based resources, and has designed her own web page entitled *Anthropology and You* at http://www.members.shaw.ca/sfedorak1. In addition to writing the First Canadian Edition of William Haviland's *Cultural Anthropology*, Professor Fedorak co-authored the Canadian supplement *Canadian Perspectives on Archaeology and Biological Anthropology* (2002), and is currently writing a collection of Canadian ethnographic studies.

Like Dr. Haviland, one of Professor Fedorak's greatest loves is teaching, which played a role in her agreeing to "Canadianize" *Cultural Anthropology*. She too has learned a great deal from her students over the years, and readily shares her views on the importance and value of an anthropological education in today's rapidly changing world: "Of all the disciplines, cultural anthropology is the one where students actually learn about what it means to be citizens of the world."

Dr. Gary W. Crawford is a professor of anthropology at the University of Toronto at Mississauga, where he has been based since 1979. He is also a research associate at the Royal Ontario Museum in Toronto. Dr. Crawford received his doctorate in anthropology from the University of North Carolina at Chapel Hill. He has published and lectured on the archaeology and paleoethnobotany of Japan, China, Korea, the Great Lakes region, and Kentucky. Dr Crawford also co-authored the Canadian supplement *Canadian Perspectives on Archaeology and Biological Anthropology*. Among his professional memberships are affiliations with the Society for American Archaeology, the Society for Economic Botany, and the Society for Archaeological Sciences.

Introductory anthropology has been one of Dr. Crawford's key teaching interests over the years. He has been gratified by the success of many of his students, whose life and career choices have been influenced by their study of anthropology.

Dr. Richard Borshay Lee (B.A. and M.A., University of Toronto; Ph. D., University of California, Berkeley) is a professor of anthropology at the University of Toronto and a member of the faculty of the Centre for International Health. He has held academic appointments at Harvard, Rutgers, and Columbia Universities, and research positions at Stanford, The Australian National University, and Kyoto University. His current research interests include the social and cultural aspects of HIV/AIDS, human rights and indigenous peoples, critical medical anthropology, gender relations, and the politics of culture. He is internationally known for his studies of hunting-and-gathering societies, particularly the Ju/'hoansi–!Kung San of Botswana. His book *The !Kung San* (1979) was honoured by inclusion on a list of the 100 most important works of science of the 20th century by the journal *American Scientist* (1999, November). A Fellow of the Royal Society of Canada and past president of the Canadian Anthropology Society, Dr. Lee has been awarded honorary doctorates by the University of Alaska and Guelph University for his research and advocacy on behalf of indigenous peoples.

BRIEF CONTENTS

PART I   Anthropology and the Study of Culture

CHAPTER 1   The Nature of Anthropology   2

CHAPTER 2   The Nature of Culture   34

CHAPTER 3   The Beginnings of Human Culture   60

PART II   Culture and Survival: Communicating and Staying Alive

CHAPTER 4   Language and Communication   90

CHAPTER 5   Making a Living   122

CHAPTER 6   Economic Systems   152

PART III   The Formation of Groups: Solving the Problem of Cooperation

CHAPTER 7   Sex and Marriage   196

CHAPTER 8   Family and Household   232

CHAPTER 9   Kinship and Descent   260

CHAPTER 10 Social Stratification and Groupings   288

PART IV   The Search for Order: Solving the Problem of Disorder

CHAPTER 11 Political Organization and the Maintenance of Order   316

CHAPTER 12 Religion and the Supernatural   352

CHAPTER 13 The Arts   384

PART V   Exploring Health and Illness Factors, Cultural Change, and the Future of Humanity

CHAPTER 14 The Anthropology of Health   416

CHAPTER 15 Cultural Change and the Future of Humanity   452

CONTENTS

Preface iii
Acknowledgments x
About the Authors xii
Putting the World in Perspective xxii

PART I
ANTHROPOLOGY AND THE STUDY OF CULTURE

CHAPTER 1
The Nature of Anthropology 2

Chapter Preview 3
The Development of Anthropology 4
Father Joseph-François Lafitau,
  Sir Daniel Wilson 5
  Canadian Anthropology 5
  A Note about Terminology 6
The Discipline of Anthropology 7
  Biological Anthropology 8
  Archaeology 8

Anthropology Applied:
Forensic Anthropology 9

  Linguistic Anthropology 11
  Applied Anthropology 12
  Sociocultural Anthropology 12
    Ethnography 13

Original Study: **Eating Christmas
in the Kalahari** 15

      New Directions in Ethnographic
        Fieldwork 22
      Ethnology 23
      Ethnohistory 24
Anthropology and Science 24

Gender Perspectives: **The Anthropology
of Gender** 26

Anthropology and the Humanities 28
Anthropology's Contributions to Other
  Disciplines 28
Questions of Ethics 29
Relevance of Anthropology in
  Contemporary Life 30

Chapter Summary 31
Questions for Critical Thought 31
Internet Resources 32

Suggested Readings 33
***CNN Today* Videos** 33

CHAPTER 2
The Nature of Culture 34

Chapter Preview 35
The Concept of Culture 36
Characteristics of Culture 36
  Culture Is Shared 36

Anthropology Applied: **The James Bay
Cree and Northern Quebec Agreement** 38

Gender Perspectives: **The Canadian
Women's Movement** 42

  Culture Is Learned 43
  Culture Is Based on Symbols 44
  Culture Is Integrated 44
Marius Barbeau 46
Studying Culture in the Field 46
Culture and Adaptation 47

Original Study: **The Importance of
Trobriand Women** 48

  Functions of Culture 51
  Culture and Change 51
Culture, Society, and the Individual 52
Evaluation of Culture 53

Chapter Summary 56
Questions for Critical Thought 57
Internet Resources 57
Suggested Readings 58
***CNN Today* Videos** 59

CHAPTER 3
The Beginnings of Human Culture 60

Chapter Preview 61
Humans and the Other Primates 62
  Evolution through Adaptation 62
  Anatomical Adaptation 63
    Primate Dentition 63
    Sense Organs 64
    The Primate Brain 65
    The Primate Skeleton 65
  Adaptation through Behaviour 66
    Chimpanzee Behaviour 66
Biruté Galdikas 69
Human Ancestors 69

The First Hominines   70
Homo habilis   73

Gender Perspectives: **Gender Bias in
Primatology?**   74

Tools, Meat, and Brains   74
Homo erectus   76
Homo sapiens   79
   Archaic *Homo sapiens*   79
Anatomically Modern Peoples and
   the Upper Paleolithic   82
   Peopling the New World   83

Anthropology Applied: **Stone Tools
for Modern Surgeons**   84

Chapter Summary   86
Questions for Critical Thought   87
Internet Resources   87
Suggested Readings   88
CNN Today **Videos**   89

PART II
CULTURE AND SURVIVAL:
COMMUNICATING AND STAYING ALIVE

CHAPTER 4
Language and Communication   90

Chapter Preview   91
The Nature of Language   93
   The Sound and Shape of Language   94
      Phonology   94
      Morphology   94
      Grammar and Syntax   95
The Gesture-Call System   96
   Kinesics   96
   Touch   98
   Proxemics   99
   Paralanguage   99
      Voice Qualities   99
      Vocalizations   100
Linguistic Change   100

Anthropology Applied: **Visual
Anthropology and Ethnographic Film**   104

Language in Its Cultural Setting   106
   Language and Thought   107
      Kinship Terms   108
Regna Darnell   109
   Social Dialects   109

Gender Perspectives: **Gender in Language**   111

Original Study: **Speak *bilingue*?**   112

Pidgin and Creole Languages   115
The Origins of Language   115

Chapter Summary   118
Questions for Critical Thought   119
Internet Resources   119
Suggested Readings   120
CNN Today **Videos**   121

CHAPTER 5
Making a Living   122

Chapter Preview   123
Adaptation   124
The Food-Foraging Way of Life   128
   Characteristics of Food Foragers   130
      Mobility and Technology   130
Richard B. Lee   131
      Camp Organization   132
      Division of Labour   133

Gender Perspectives: **Gender Autonomy
in Foraging Groups**   135

Food Sharing   136
Egalitarian Society   137
The Food-Producing Way of Life   138
   The Settled Life of Farmers   139
   Pastoralism: The Bakhtiari   140
   Intensive Agriculture and
      Nonindustrial Cities   143

Anthropology Applied: **Agricultural
Development and the Anthropologist**   144

Aztec City Life   145
Mechanized Agriculture   147
   The Canadian Family Farm   147

Chapter Summary   148
Questions for Critical Thought   149
Internet Resources   149
Suggested Readings   150
CNN Today **Videos**   151

CHAPTER 6
Economic Systems   152

Chapter Preview   153
Economic Anthropology   154
Richard F. Salisbury   156
Resources   157
   Patterns of Labour   157
      Sexual Division of Labour   157

Age Division of Labour 158
Cooperation 160
Craft Specialization 161
Control of Land 162
Technology 162
Resource Depletion 163
Distribution and Exchange 164
Reciprocity 164

Original Study: **Reciprocity on Skid Row** 166

Barter and Trade 174
The Kula Ring 175
Redistribution 176
Distribution of Wealth 177
Market Exchange 180
Chinese-Canadian Contributions to the
Canadian Economy 183
Consumption 184
Consumption Behaviour 185
Food Taboos 185
Food as Ritual and Social Interaction 185
Economics, Culture, and the World of
Business 186
The Global Economy 187

Gender Perspectives: **Women and
Economic Development** 189

Anthropology Applied: **Anthropology
and the World of Business** 190

Chapter Summary 191
Questions for Critical Thought 192
Internet Resources 193
Suggested Readings 193
***CNN Today* Videos** 194

PART III
THE FORMATION OF GROUPS:
SOLVING THE PROBLEM OF
COOPERATION

CHAPTER 7
Sex and Marriage 196

Chapter Preview 197
Human Sexuality 199
Homosexuality 199
Control of Sexual Relations 200

Anthropology Applied: **Anthropology
and AIDS** 201

Rules of Sexual Access 203
The Incest Taboo 205

Gender Perspectives: **Female Genital
Mutilation** 206

Endogamy and Exogamy 209
The Distinction between Marriage
and Mating 210
Common-Law Marriages 211
Same-Sex Marriages 211
Forms of Marriage 213
Janice Boddy 214
The Levirate and the Sororate 216
Serial Monogamy 217
Choice of Spouse 217

Original Study: **Arranging Marriage
in India** 218

Cousin Marriage 223
Marriage Exchanges 224
Divorce 226

Chapter Summary 227
Questions for Critical Thought 228
Internet Resources 229
Suggested Readings 229
***CNN Today* Videos** 230

CHAPTER 8
Family and Household 232

Chapter Preview 233
The Family Defined 234

Original Study: **The Ephemeral
Modern Family** 236

Functions of the Family 239
Nurturance of Children 239

Gender Perspectives: **The Motherhood
Mandate** 241

Economic Cooperation 241
Family and Household 242
Laurel Bossen 243
Form of the Family 244
The Nuclear Family 244
The Extended Family 245
Same-Sex Families 247
Residence Patterns 248
Problems of Family and Household
Organization 250
Polygamous Families 250
Extended Families 251
Nuclear Families 252
Female-Headed Families 253

Anthropology Applied: **Public Health
Surveillance and First Nations Self-
Government**   254

Chapter Summary   255
Questions for Critical Thought   256
Internet Resources   256
Suggested Readings   257
CNN Today **Video**   258

CHAPTER 9
Kinship and Descent   260

Chapter Preview   261
Why We Study Kinship   263
Urban Kinship Systems in Canada   263
Descent Groups   264
    Unilineal Descent   264
        Patrilineal Descent and Organization   265

Original Study: **Coping as a Woman
in a Man's World**   266

        Matrilineal Descent and Organization   268
        Double Descent   269

Gender Perspectives: **The Kinkeepers**   270

    Ambilineal Descent   270
Forms and Functions of Descent Groups   271
    The Lineage   271
    The Clan   272
    Phratries and Moieties   272
    Bilateral Descent and the Kindred   273

Anthropology Applied: **Federal
Recognition for Native Americans**   274

    The Descent Group   276
Parin Dossa   277
Contemporary Chinese-Canadian Kinship   278
Kinship Terminology and Kinship Groups   279
    Eskimo System   279
    Hawaiian System   280
    Iroquois System   281
    Crow System   281
    Omaha System   282
    Sudanese or Descriptive System   282

Chapter Summary   284
Questions for Critical Thought   285
Internet Resources   285
Suggested Readings   286
CNN Today **Videos**   286

CHAPTER 10
Social Stratification and Groupings   288

Chapter Preview   289
Grouping by Gender   290
Age Grouping   291
Bonnie McElhinny   292
Common-Interest Associations   293
    Kinds of Common-Interest Associations   294
        Men's and Women's Associations   294
Social Stratification   295
    Theories of Stratification   297
    The Concept of Race   298
    Racial Stratification   298

Anthropology Applied: **Social Impact
Assessment: The Berger Report**   301

    Class and Caste   302
    Mobility   305
    Gender Stratification   306

Gender Perspectives: **Purdah**   307

    Ethnic Stratification   308

Original Study: **Genocide in Rwanda**   310

Chapter Summary   312
Questions for Critical Thought   313
Internet Resources   313
Suggested Readings   314
CNN Today **Videos**   315

PART IV
THE SEARCH FOR ORDER: SOLVING
THE PROBLEM OF DISORDER

CHAPTER 11
Political Organization and the Maintenance
of Order   316

Chapter Preview   317
Kinds of Political Systems   318
    Uncentralized Political Systems   318
        Band Organization   318
        Tribal Organization   320
        Kinship Organization   323
        Age-Grade Organization   324
        Association Organization   324
    Centralized Political Systems   324
        Chiefdoms   324
        State Systems   326
    Political Leadership and Gender   328

Gender Perspectives: **Minority Women in Canadian Politics** 330

Political Organization and the
   Maintenance of Order 331
   Internalized Controls 332
   Externalized Controls 332

Original Study: **Limits on Power in Bedouin Society** 334

Bernard Saladin d'Anglure 337
Social Control through Law 337
   Definition of Law 338
   Functions of Law 338
   Crime 339

Anthropology Applied: **Dispute Resolution and the Anthropologist** 341

Political Organization and External
   Affairs 342
   War 342
   Canada's Role in International
      Peacekeeping 345
Political Systems and the Question
   of Legitimacy 346
Religion and Politics 347

Chapter Summary 348
Questions for Critical Thought 349
Internet Resources 349
Suggested Readings 350
CNN *Today* **Videos** 351

CHAPTER 12
Religion and the Supernatural 352

Chapter Preview 353
The Anthropological Approach to
   Religion 356
The Practice of Religion 357
   Supernatural Beings and Powers 357
      Gods and Goddesses 358
      Ancestral Spirits 359
      Animism 360
      Animatism 360
   Robin Ridington 361
      Myths 362
   Religious Specialists 363
      Priests and Priestesses 363
      Shamans 363

Original Study: **Healing among the Ju/'hoansi of the Kalahari** 364

   Rituals and Ceremonies 366

   Rites of Passage 366

Gender Perspectives: **Menstrual Taboo** 368

   Rites of Intensification 369
Religion, Magic, and Witchcraft 370
   Witchcraft 371
      Ibibio Witchcraft 371
   The Functions of Witchcraft 372
      Psychological Functions of Witchcraft
         among the Navajo 373

Anthropology Applied: **Aboriginal Men and Traditional Healing in Canadian Prisons** 374

   Neo-Paganism 375
The Functions of Religion 377
Religion and Cultural Change 378
   Revitalization Movements 379

Chapter Summary 381
Questions for Critical Thought 382
Internet Resources 382
Suggested Readings 383
CNN *Today* **Videos** 383

CHAPTER 13
The Arts 384

Chapter Preview 385
The Anthropological Study of Art 389
Verbal Arts 389

Anthropology Applied: **Protecting Cultural Heritages** 390

   Myths 391
   Legends 392
   Tales 393
   Other Verbal Arts 394

Original Study: **The Mock Wedding: Folk Drama in the Prairie Provinces** 396

The Art of Music 400
Julie Cruikshank 401
   Functions of Music 401
Visual Art 404

Gender Perspectives: **On Being a Man** 405

   Canadian Visual Art 406
Body Art 409
   Body Painting 409
   Tattooing 410
   Body Adornment 411
Censorship 412

Chapter Summary   412
Questions for Critical Thought   413
Internet Resources   414
Suggested Readings   414
CNN Today Videos   415

PART V
EXPLORING HEALTH AND ILLNESS
FACTORS, CULTURAL CHANGE, AND
THE FUTURE OF HUMANITY

CHAPTER 14
The Anthropology of Health   416

Chapter Preview   417
The Biocultural Approach   418
The Cultural Interpretive Approach   420
  The Three Bodies: An Approach to
    Culture and Health   420
  Shamanism   422
Margaret Lock   423
  Does Shamanism Work?   424
Critical Medical Anthropology   426
  Culture and Health through History   427
    Band Societies   428
    Tribal Societies and Chiefdoms   429
    State Societies and the Rise of Cities   430
    The Industrial Revolution and the
      Modern World System   431
  Health Outcomes of Modernity   432

Original Study: Health and Disease in
One Culture: The Ju/'hoansi   434

  Poverty   436
    Homelessness   437

Anthropology Applied: Vancouver's
Downtown Eastside   438

    Lethal but Legal: Alcohol, Tobacco,
      and Health   439

Gender Perspectives: Women and Health   440

    Environmental Health and Justice   442
Contemporary Biomedicine   443
  Medical Anthropology in Canada   445

Chapter Summary   446
Questions for Critical Thought   448
Internet Resources   448
Suggested Readings   449
CNN Today Videos   450

CHAPTER 15
Cultural Change and the Future of Humanity   452

Chapter Preview   453
Mechanisms of Change   454
  Innovation   454
  Diffusion   456
  Cultural Loss   457
Forcible Change   459
  Acculturation   459
  Genocide   460
Directed Change and Applied Anthropology   462
Sally Weaver   463
  Revitalization Movements   464
Rebellion and Revolution   464

Gender Perspectives: Reproductive
Rights in Canada   465

Modernization   467
  Skolt Lapps and the Snowmobile
    Revolution   468
  The Shuar Solution   469
  Modernization and the Developing World   469
  Modernization: Must It Always Be
    Painful?   470
The Cultural Future of Humanity   471
  One-World Culture?   471
  Nunavut   473
  The Rise of the Multinational
    Corporation   473
  Ethnic Resurgence   476
  Cultural Pluralism   477
  Ethnocentrism   478
  Global Apartheid   478
Problems of Structural Violence   478

Anthropology Applied: Aboriginal
Rights in Canada   479

  World Hunger   480
  Pollution   482
  Population Control   483
  The Culture of Discontent   485
Humanity's Future   486

Chapter Summary   486
Questions for Critical Thought   488
Internet Resources   488
Suggested Readings   489
CNN Today Videos   490

Bibliography   B-1
Index   I-1
Photo Permissions   P-1
Text Permissions   T-1

To our students,
past, present, and future

PUTTING THE WORLD IN PERSPECTIVE

Cartography (the craft of mapmaking as we know it today) had its beginnings in 13th-century Europe, and its subsequent development is related to the expansion of Europeans to all parts of the globe. From the beginning, there have been two problems with maps: the technical one of how to depict a three-dimensional spherical object on a two-dimensional, flat surface, and the cultural one of whose worldview they reflect. In fact, the two issues are inseparable, for any projection inevitably makes a statement about how one views one's own people and their place in the world. Indeed, maps often shape our perception of reality as much as they reflect it.

In cartography, a projection refers to the system of intersecting lines (of longitude and latitude) by which part or all of the globe is represented on a flat surface. There are more than 100 different projections in use today, ranging from polar perspectives to interrupted "butterflies" to rectangles to heart shapes. Each projection causes distortion in size, shape, or distance in some way or another. A map that shows the shape of land masses correctly will of necessity misrepresent the size. A map that is accurate along the equator will be deceptive at the poles.

Perhaps no projection has had more influence on the way we see the world than that of Gerhardus Mercator, who devised his map in 1569 as a navigational aid for mariners. So well suited was Mercator's map for this purpose that it continues to be used for navigational charts today. At the same time, the Mercator projection became a standard for depicting land masses, something for which it was never intended. Although an accurate navigational tool, the Mercator projection greatly exaggerates the size of land masses in higher latitudes, giving about two-thirds of the map's surface to the northern hemisphere. Thus, the lands occupied by Europeans and European descendants appear far larger than those of other people. For example, North America (19 million square kilometres) appears almost twice the size of Africa (30 million square kilometres), while Europe is shown as equal in size to South America, which actually has nearly twice the land mass of Europe.

A map developed in 1805 by Karl B. Mollweide was one of the earlier equal-area projections of the world. Equal-area projections portray land masses in correct relative size, but, as a result, distort the shape of continents more than other projections. They most often compress and warp lands in the higher latitudes and vertically stretch land masses close to the equator. Other equal-area projections include the Lambert Cylindrical Equal-Area Projection (1772), the Hammer Equal-Area Projection (1892), and the Eckert Equal-Area Projection (1906).

The Van der Grinten Projection (1904) was a compromise aimed at minimizing both the distortion of size in the Mercator and the distortion of shape in equal-area maps such as the Mollweide. Although this projection is an improvement, the lands of the northern hemisphere are still emphasized at the expense of the southern. For example, in the Van der Grinten, the Commonwealth of Independent States (the former Soviet Union) and Canada are shown at more than twice their relative sizes.

The Robinson Projection, which was adopted by the National Geographic Society in 1988 to replace the Van der Grinten, is one of the best compromises to date between the distortion of size and shape. Although an improvement over the Van der Grinten, the Robinson Projection still depicts lands in the northern latitudes as proportionally larger at the same time that it depicts lands in the lower latitudes (representing most developing nations) as proportionally smaller. Like European maps before it, the Robinson Projection places Europe at the centre of the map with the Atlantic Ocean and the Americas to the left, emphasizing the cultural connection between Europe and North America, while neglecting the geographical closeness of northwestern North America to northeast Asia.

The following pages show four maps that each convey quite different "cultural messages." Included among them is the Peters Projection, an equal-area map that has been adopted as the official map of UNESCO (the United Nations Educational, Scientific, and Cultural Organization), and a map made in Japan, showing us how the world looks from the other side.

MERCATOR

MOLLWEIDE

VAN DER GRINTEN

ROBINSON

INUIT

INUIT

INUIT

SCOT

TLINGIT

INUIT

TORY
ISLANDERS

BELLA COOLA
KWAKIUTL

WESTERN
ABENAKI

NASKAPI

MONTAGNAIS

OJIBWA

MALISEET

CROW

IROQUOIS

MI'KMAQ

N. PAIUTE
SHOSHONE

SIOUX

PENOBSCOT

POMO

UTE

PEQUOT

S. PAIUTE

NAVAJO

OMAHA
CHEYENNE

AMISH

NEW YORK CITY JEWS

PUEBLO (HOPI,
TEWA, ZUNI)

COMANCHE

CHEROKEE

APACHE

CANARY
ISLANDERS

AZTEC

MAYA

PUERTO RICANS

HAWAIIAN

ZAPOTEC

HAITIANS
CARIBBEAN

BAUL

MENDE

SHUAR

YANOMAMI

KPELLE

ASHANT

INCA

MUNDURUCU

SHERENTE

INCA

CINTA-LARGA

SAMOAN

AYMARA

KAYAPO

INCA

YAGHAN

THE ROBINSON PROJECTION   The map above is based on the Robinson Projection, which is used
today by the National Geographic Society and Rand McNally. Although the Robinson Projection distorts the relative size of land masses, it does so to a much lesser degree than most other projections.

NEL

SAAMI (SKOLT LAPPS)

INUIT

CROATS
SERBS
BOSNIANS

CHECHENS

JAPANESE

KURDS

ISRAELIS

BAKHTIARI

TIBETANS
MELEMCHI

CHINESE

AWLAD ALI
BEDOUINS

EGYPTIANS

CHENCHU

KAREN

TAIWANESE

TRUK

NUER

NAYAR

KAPAUKU

YORUBA

AFAR &
TEGREANS

KOTA AND
KURUMBA

WAPE
ENGA

BENIN

IBIBIO

AZANDE

TURKANA
NANDI

TSEMBAGA

U.

MONGO

MBUTI

SOMALI

TODA AND
BADAGA

MINANGKABAU

MELANESIANS

AKO

HUTU
AND TUTSI

GUSII
TIRIKI

MASAI

ARAPESH

TROBRIANDERS

BALINESE

DOBU

HADZA

JU/'HOANSI

ABORIGINES

SHMEN

SWAZI

TASMANIANS

Still, it places Europe at the centre of the map. This particular view of the world has been used to identify the location of many of the cultures discussed in this text.

GREENLAND

CZECHOSLOVAKIA
AUSTRIA
GERMANY
ICELAND DENMARK
NETHERLANDS
BELGIUM
UNITED
KINGDOM
IRELAND
SWITZERLAND
SLOVENIA FRAN
ITALY
PORTUGAL SPAIN
TUNI
MOROCCO
WESTERN ALGERI
SAHARA
MAURITANIA
MALI
NIGER
SENEGAL
GAMBIA
GUINEA-BISSAU
GUINEA
SIERRA LEONE
LIBERIA
IVORY COAST
BURKINA FASO
GHANA
TOGO
BENIN
EQUATORIAL GUINEA

CANADA

UNITED STATES

UNITED STATES

MEXICO

THE
BAHAMAS
HAITI
CUBA DOMINICAN REPUBLIC
JAMAICA
BELIZE
GUATEMALA HONDURAS
EL SALVADOR NICARAGUA
COSTA RICA
PANAMA VENEZUELA GUYANA
SURINAME
FRENCH
COLOMBIA GUIANA
ECUADOR

PERU BRAZIL

BOLIVIA

PARAGUAY
CHILE

ARGENTINA

URUGUAY

ANTARCTICA

THE PETERS PROJECTION   The map above is based on the Peters Projection, which has been adopted
as the official map of UNESCO. While it distorts the shape of continents (countries near the equator
are vertically elongated by a ratio of two to one), the Peters Projection does show all continents

according to their correct relative size. Though Europe is still at the centre, it is not shown as larger and more extensive than the developing countries.

GREENLAND

ICELAND

NORWAY

GERMANY
DENMARK
NETHERLANDS
BELGIUM

SWEDEN

FINLAND

RUSSIA

UNITED
KINGDOM

ESTONIA
LATVIA
LITHUANIA
POLAND BELARUS
HUNGARY

ARMENIA

IRELAND

CZECHOSLOVAKIA
AUSTRIA
SWITZERLAND

ITALY

GEORGIA AZERBAIJAN

KAZAKHSTAN

ROMANIA
UKRAINE
MOLDOVA

KIRGHIZSTAN

MONGOLIA

NORTH
KOREA

FRANCE

SERBIA

TAJIKISTAN

SOUTH
KOREA

PORTUGAL

SPAIN

SLOVENIA
CROATIA
BOSNIA-HERZEGOVINA

BULGARIA

MACEDONIA
TURKEY
GREECE
ALBANIA

UZBEKISTAN

PEOPLE'S REPUBLIC
OF CHINA

JAPAN

MONTE-
NEGRO

SYRIA
LEBANON
ISRAEL

IRAQ

IRAN

TURKMENISTAN

AFGHAN-
ISTAN

NEPAL BHUTAN

TAIWAN

MOROCCO

TUNISIA

KUWAIT
BAHRAIN

PAKISTAN

WESTERN
SAHARA

ALGERIA

LIBYA

EGYPT

JORDAN

SAUDI
ARABIA

QATAR

UNITED
ARAB
EMIRATES

INDIA

MYANMAR

MAURITANIA

MALI

NIGER

CHAD

SUDAN

YEMEN OMAN

BANGLA-
DESH

VIETNAM
LAOS

PHILIPPINES

SENEGAL
GAMBIA
GUINEA-BISSAU
GUINEA
SIERRA LEONE
LIBERIA

NIGERIA

CENTRAL
AFRICAN
REPUBLIC

ETHIOPIA

DJIBOUTI

SOMALIA

SRI LANKA

THAILAND
CAMBODIA

BRUNEI
MALAYSIA

SINGAPORE

INDONESIA

PAPUA
NEW
GUINEA

IVORY COAST
BURKINA FASO
GHANA
TOGO
BENIN

DEMOCRATIC
REPUBLIC OF
CONGO

KENYA

UGANDA

CAMEROON
EQUATORIAL
GUINEA
GABON

CONGO

RWANDA
BURUNDI

TANZANIA

MALAWI

ANGOLA

ZAMBIA

MADAGASCAR

NAMIBIA

ZIMBABWE

AUSTRALIA

BOTSWANA

MOZAMBIQUE
SWAZILAND
LESOTHO

SOUTH
AFRICA

ANTARCTICA

JAPANESE MAP Not all maps place Europe at the centre of the world, as this Japanese map illustrates. Besides reflecting the importance the Japanese attach to themselves in the world, this map has

the virtue of showing the geographic proximity of North America to Asia, a fact easily overlooked when maps place Europe at their centre.

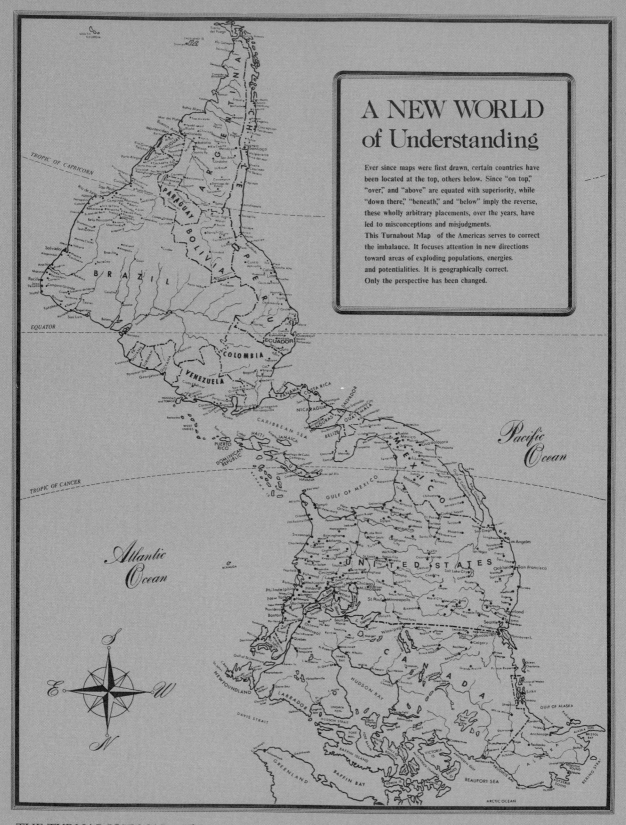

THE TURNABOUT MAP The way maps may reflect (and influence) our thinking is exemplified by the "Turnabout Map," which places the South Pole at the top and the North Pole at the bottom. Words and phrases such as "on top," "over," and "above" tend to be equated by some people with superiority. Turning things upside down may cause us to rethink the way North Americans regard themselves in relation to the people of Central America. © 1982 by Jesse Levine Turnabout Map™ —Dist. by Laguna Sales, Inc., 7040 Via Valverde, San Jose, CA 95135

Cultural ANTHROPOLOGY

Chapter 1

The Nature of Anthropology

A depiction of early contact between Jacques Cartier and First Nations. Such encounters sparked interest in other peoples and led to the development of sociocultural anthropology.

Chapter Preview

1. What Is Anthropology?

Anthropology, the study of humankind everywhere, throughout time, seeks to produce reliable knowledge about people and their behaviour, about what makes them different and what they all share in common.

2. What Do Anthropologists Do?

Biological anthropologists trace the evolutionary development of humans as biological organisms and look at biological variations within the species, past and present. They also study the physical and behavioural nature of our closest biological relatives: nonhuman primates such as monkeys and apes. Archaeologists seek to explain human behaviour by studying material culture of past cultures. Linguistic anthropologists study the way language is used as a resource for practising, developing, and transmitting a culture. Sociocultural anthropologists are concerned with recent and contemporary human cultures, as they have been observed, experienced, and discussed with people whose culture they seek to understand.

3. How Do Anthropologists Do What They Do?

Anthropologists, in common with other scientists, are concerned with explaining observed phenomena. Most anthropological investigation involves fieldwork. Biological anthropologists and archaeologists most often conduct excavations of sites where evidence of human activity is found. Linguistic anthropologists study how people use language to relate to one another, usually living for brief periods with the people whose language they are studying. Sociocultural anthropologists immerse themselves in a contemporary culture by living with the people, participating in their daily activities, and observing, firsthand, how they live.

CHAPTER OUTLINE

The Development of Anthropology

The Discipline of Anthropology

Anthropology Applied: Forensic Anthropology

Original Study: Eating Christmas in the Kalahari

Anthropology and Science

Gender Perspectives: The Anthropology of Gender

Anthropology and the Humanities

Anthropology's Contributions to Other Disciplines

Questions of Ethics

Relevance of Anthropology in Contemporary Life

For as long as they have lived on earth, people have needed answers to questions about who they are, where they come from, and why they act as they do. Throughout most of their history, though, people relied on myth and folklore for their answers to these questions, rather than the systematic testing of data obtained through careful observation. Anthropology, over the past 200 years, has emerged as a scientific approach to answering these questions. Simply stated, **anthropology is the study of humankind in all places and in all times.**

Other disciplines also are concerned with human beings. Some, such as anatomy and physiology, study humans as biological organisms. The social sciences are concerned with the distinctive forms human relationships can take, while the humanities examine the great achievements of human cultures. Anthropologists are interested in all of these aspects of humanity; the difference is they are concerned with *everything* that has to do with humans. It is this unique, broad perspective that equips anthropologists to deal with that elusive thing called human nature.

Anthropology is the most liberating of all the sciences. Not only has it exposed the fallacies of racial and cultural superiority, but its devotion to the study of all peoples, regardless of where and when they live, has cast more light on human nature than all the reflections of sages or the studies of laboratory scientists. Indeed, anthropological knowledge and understanding of the past and the present may even help humankind deal with its future.

▲▽▲▽▲▽▲▽▲▽▲▽▲▽▲▽▲▽▲▽▲▽▲▽▲▽

THE DEVELOPMENT OF ANTHROPOLOGY

Although works of anthropological significance have a considerable antiquity—two examples are the accounts of other peoples by Herodotus the Greek and by the Arab Ibn Khaldun, written in the 5th century B.C. and 14th century A.D., respectively—anthropology as a distinct field of inquiry is a relatively recent product of Western society. In Canada, for example, under the guidance of Sir Daniel Wilson, the University of Toronto offered the first anthropology course in North America in 1860.

If people have always been concerned about themselves and others and their origins, why then did it take such a long time for the systematic discipline of anthropology to appear? The answer to this question is as complex as human history. In part, it relates to the limits of human technology. Throughout most of history, people have been restricted in their geographical horizons. Without the means to travel to distant places, observation of cultures far from home was a difficult—if not impossible—venture. Extensive travel was usually the exclusive domain of a few elite; the study of foreign peoples and cultures was not likely to flourish until adequate modes of transportation and communication could be developed.

This is not to say people were unaware of the existence of others in the world who looked and acted differently from themselves. The Old and New Testaments of the Bible, for example, are full of references to diverse peoples, among them Jews, Egyptians, Hittites, Babylonians, Ethiopians, Romans, and so forth. However, the differences among these peoples pale by comparison with those between any of them and (for example) aboriginal peoples of Australia, the Amazon forest, or the Canadian Arctic. With the means to travel to truly faraway places, people found it possible to meet and observe, for the first time, radically different people. It was the massive encounter with hitherto unknown peoples, which came as Europeans sought to extend their trade and political domination to all parts of the world, that focused attention on human differences in all their glory.

Another significant element that contributed to the slow growth of anthropology was the failure of Europeans to recognize that beneath all the differences, they shared a basic "humanity" with people everywhere. Cultural groups that did not share the fundamental cultural values of Europeans were labelled as "savage" or "barbarian." Not until the late 18th century did a

---

Anthropology. The study of humankind in all times and places.

Father Joseph-François Lafitau   *(1681–1746)*
Sir Daniel Wilson   *(1816–1892)*

In Canada, anthropological studies began in the 18th and 19th centuries with the help of dedicated scholars interested in the study of human culture. Two early contributors to Canadian anthropology, neither of whom were academic anthropologists, were Father Joseph-François Lafitau and Sir Daniel Wilson.

Father Lafitau was a Jesuit missionary who lived with the Iroquois near Montreal from 1715 to 1720. Although Father Lafitau is most often credited with discovering wild ginseng in North America, his firsthand observations and scholarly writings provided valuable insight into the plants, animals, and people of the region. He noted a possible connection between Asian peoples, who used ginseng over 15 000 years ago, and North American aboriginal peoples. Among his literary works, Father Lafitau wrote *Customs of the American Indians Compared with the Customs of Primitive Times* (Toronto: Champlain Society, 1974).[1]

Sir Daniel Wilson was born in Edinburgh, Scotland, and educated at the University of Edinburgh. He moved to Canada in 1853, to become the first professor of history and English literature at the University of Toronto, and in 1881 he became the first president of the University of Toronto. Wilson's contributions to science and education are many; he is described as an educator and administrator, archaeologist, artist, and anthropologist. Most notably, he recognized the importance of cultural studies, and is credited with founding the first anthropology courses at a Canadian university, nearly 150 years ago. Among his scholarly works, Wilson wrote *The Archaeology and Prehistoric Annals of Scotland*, which laid the groundwork for scientific inquiry in archaeology and introduced the term "prehistoric" to the scientific community.[2] Wilson was a significant influence on the development of professional anthropology and archaeology in Canada.

---

[1]Progenix Corporation. (1998). *The history of ginseng in the United States*. Retrieved March 12, 2001, from the World Wide Web: http://progenixcorp.com/ushistory.html.

[2]Kelley, J. H., & Williamson, R. F. (1996, January). The positioning of archaeology within anthropology: A Canadian historical perspective. *American Antiquity*, 61 (1), 5–20.

---

significant number of Europeans consider the behaviour of such people at all relevant to an understanding of themselves. This growing interest in human diversity, coming when efforts to explain reality in terms of natural laws were increasing, cast doubts on the traditional biblical mythology, which no longer adequately "explained" human diversity.

Although anthropology originated within the context of Western society, it has long since gone global. Today, it is an exciting international discipline whose practitioners are drawn from diverse societies in all parts of the world. Even cultures that have long been studied by European and North American anthropologists—First Nations peoples of Canada, for example—have produced anthropologists who continue to make their mark on the discipline. Their distinctive perspectives help shed new light not only on their own cultures but on others (including Western societies) as well.

Canadian Anthropology

Canadian anthropology owes its development and continued growth to several noteworthy individuals, many of whom are profiled in this book, and the institutions in which they worked. Three main influences are evident in the development of Canadian anthropology: museums, academic departments, and applied research. The National Museum of Canada in Ottawa played a major role in the direction of early Canadian anthropology. Anthropologists with the museum, such as Edward Sapir, head of the anthropology division of the Geological Survey of the National Museum of Canada (now the Museum of Civilization), French-Canadian Marius Barbeau, David Boyle, and Diamond Jenness conducted ethnographic, linguistic, and archaeological research into aboriginal cultures. Besides their academic pursuits, these scholars, along with other staff at the museum, were early advocates for aboriginal rights to religious and cultural freedom. This tradition of advocacy has remained an integral component of Canadian anthropology to the present day.[1]

In 1925 Thomas F. McIlwraith was appointed lecturer in anthropology at the University of Toronto.[2] Under McIlwraith's guidance, anthropology at the University of Toronto continued to grow in importance until, in 1936, the first academic department of anthropology at a Canadian university was created. After World War II, academic departments of anthropology were established at other universities, most notably McGill and the University of British Columbia. Academic departments became the second stronghold for Canadian anthropology, and remain so today.

A major source of strength and growth in Canadian anthropology has been applied anthropology. By the 1960s Canadian anthropologists, such as Harry Hawthorn at the University of British Columbia, were actively involved in aboriginal policy issues. Among many applied studies, Hawthorn examined the sociocultural reasons for tensions between local residents and the Doukhobors who had moved to British Columbia from Saskatchewan. As you will see in the following chapters, Canadian applied anthropologists have worked diligently in the areas of advocacy for First Nations self-government and land claims, policy issues, First Nations health, social impact, and Quebec nationalism. In recent years applied anthropology has evolved into a more participatory-action research or collaborative approach whereby aboriginal groups have become active participants in research projects concerning their communities.

In the latter part of the 20th century, expansion of academic departments continued across the country. Although anthropological and archaeological interest in the aboriginal peoples of Canada (First Nations, Inuit, and Métis) has remained paramount, Canadian anthropologists have also turned their attention to other issues, such as multiculturalism, ethnicity, immigration, health, and gender.[3] Many Canadian anthropologists, such as Richard B. Lee (see Chapter 5) and Bernand Arcand have embraced a global perspective, conducting international as well as national research. In keeping with the applied and advocacy influences of Canadian anthropology, French-Canadian anthropologists, such as Marc-Adélard Tremblay, helped shape government policies that have strengthened Quebec's identity and self-determination.

By the closing years of the 20th century, Canadian anthropology had matured into a multifaceted, comprehensive, and intrepid discipline. The future of Canadian anthropology in the 21st century remains unclear. However, the discipline is alive with potential, poised to provide valuable insight into Canada's future role in the global community. For further discussion of the development of anthropological thought, visit the textbook's website at http://www.cultural2e.nelson.com.

A Note about Terminology

Many of the names assigned to aboriginal peoples, usually by European explorers and colonial governments, were not the terms used by the people to refer to themselves. Often these European names had derogatory connotations, such as Eskimo, which means "eaters of raw meat." Today, concerted efforts are being made to

---

[1]Hedigan, E.J. (1995). *Applied anthropology in Canada: Understanding aboriginal issues.* Toronto: University of Toronto Press.

[2]University of Toronto. (2001). *A brief history of anthropology at the University of Toronto.* Retrieved June 20, 2001, from the World Wide Web: http://www.chass.utoronto.ca/anthropology/history.htm.

[3]For a detailed discusssion of the development of Canadian anthropology, see Erwin, A.M. (2000). *Canadian perspectives in cultural anthropology.* Scarborough, ON: Nelson Thomson Learning.

use the names actually chosen by the people. In Canada we use the terms First Nations, Inuit, and Métis to identify aboriginal peoples collectively, and their chosen names to identify distinctive cultural groups (e.g., Kwakwaka'wakw instead of Kwakiutl and Dane-zaa instead of Beaver).

In a text such as this one, where we refer to indigenous peoples around the world, the issue becomes even more problematic. In the United States, Native American or Indian are the preferred terms, and in South and Central America, Indian is used. From a Canadian perspective none of these labels seem appropriate; therefore, the term aboriginal peoples will be used to refer to all the North and South American indigenous groups. For other regions of the world, every effort will be made to use the people's preferred name. For example, the Ju/'hoansi of the Kalahari Desert in Africa, a cultural group discussed extensively in this text, used to be called the pejorative

"bushmen," later they were called the !Kung, and today we use their own name, Ju/'hoansi (meaning "genuine people"). Yet whichever terms are used, the decision will not satisfy everyone; indeed, the whole issue of terminology is complicated and highly sensitive, especially since even within aboriginal groups a consensus regarding appropriate labels has not been achieved, and some confusion remains among nonaboriginal peoples as to which names are preferred. Nonetheless, this attempt to use sensitive, culturally appropriate terms is one small step in the right direction.

THE DISCIPLINE OF ANTHROPOLOGY

Anthropology is traditionally divided into four fields: biological anthropology, archaeology, linguistic anthropology, and sociocultural anthropology. Biological anthropology is concerned primarily with humans as biological organisms, while sociocultural anthropology deals with humans as cultural animals. A number of Canadian anthropologists received their training at British schools, while others were educated at American institutions. In the British tradition, the term social anthropology is preferred to cultural anthropology. To accommodate both traditions we use the term sociocultural anthropology. Archaeology, too, is interested in cultural behaviour, by reconstructing the lives of people who lived in the past. Linguistic anthropology is the study of human languages of the past and present, as a means for people to relate to each other and to develop and communicate ideas about each other and the world. These fields are closely related; we cannot understand what people do unless we know what people are. And we want to know how biology does and does not influence culture, as well as how culture affects biology. Applied anthropology has become increasingly important, and today is often considered a fifth field that intersects with the other fields of anthropology (see Figure 1.1). Applied anthropologists attempt to use their expertise to solve the practical problems of humanity, using the methods and knowledge of anthropology.

Not only are all anthropologists not male, neither are they all of European descent. Mamphela Ramphele, vice-chancellor of the University of Cape Town, is a South African anthropologist who has studied the migrant labour hostels of Cape Town.

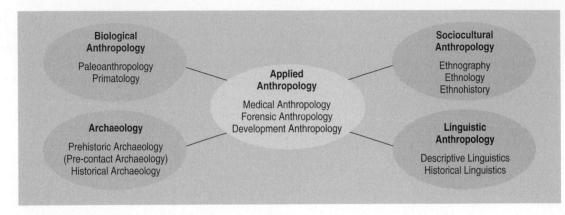

FIGURE 1.1 The subfields of anthropology.

Biological Anthropology

Biological anthropology is the branch of anthropology that focuses on humans as biological organisms. Within biological anthropology, the subfield of **paleoanthropology** studies fossil remains of our ancient ancestors, in an attempt to reconstruct the course of human biological evolution. Whatever distinctions people may claim for themselves, they are mammals—specifically, primates—and, as such, they share a common ancestry with other primates, most specifically apes and monkeys. **Primatology** is the study of the biological and social nature of our closest relatives: prosimians, monkeys, and apes. Well-known primatologists Dian Fossey (gorillas), Jane Goodall (chimpanzees), and Canadian primatologists Biruté Galdikas (orangutans) and Linda Fedigan (Japanese macaques and capuchins) have provided us with startling new insights into the complex social behaviour of nonhuman primates. Through the analysis of fossils and observation of living primates, biological anthropologists try to trace the ancestry of the human species in order to understand how, when, and why we became the kind of animal we are today. **Forensic anthropology**, as described in the box on page 9, is a relatively new and exciting field within biological

anthropology and archaeology with an applied concentration. It is also a leading specialization in the field of forensic science.

Biological anthropologists also study present-day human variation. Although we are all members of a single species, we differ from each other in many obvious and not so obvious ways. We differ not only in such visible traits as the colour of our skin and the shape of our noses but also in such biochemical factors as our blood types and our susceptibility to certain diseases. The biological anthropologist applies all the techniques of modern molecular biology to achieve a fuller understanding of human variation and the ways it relates to the different environments people have lived in.

Archaeology

Archaeology is the study of material remains in order to describe and explain human behaviour. Traditionally, archaeologists have focused on people who lived before us, for material products of behaviour, rather than behaviour itself, are all that survive of the past. Archaeologists study the tools, pottery, and other enduring relics that remain as the legacy of extinct cultures, some of them as old as 2.5 million years. Such objects, and the way they

---

Biological anthropology.   The systematic study of humans as biological organisms. **> Paleoanthropology.**   The study of fossil remains with the goal of reconstructing human biological evolution. **> Primatology.**   The study of nonhuman primates, their biology, adaptation, and social behaviour. **> Forensic anthropology.**   A field of applied biological anthropology and archaeology that specializes in the identification of human skeletal remains for legal purposes. **> Archaeology.**   The study of material remains, usually from the past, to describe and explain human behaviour.

Anthropology **Applied**

Forensic Anthropology

In the public mind, anthropology often is identified with the recovery of the bones of remote human ancestors, the unearthing of ancient campsites and "lost cities," or the study of present-day indigenous peoples whose way of life is erroneously seen as something "out of the past." People often are unaware of the many practical applications of anthropological knowledge. One field of applied anthropology—known as forensic anthropology—specializes in the identification of human skeletal remains for legal purposes. Forensic anthropologists are routinely called on by police and other authorities to identify the remains of murder victims, missing persons, or people who have died in disasters such as plane crashes or terrorist attacks. From skeletal remains, the forensic anthropologist can establish the age, sex, race, and stature of the deceased and often whether the person was right- or left-handed, exhibited any physical abnormalities, or has evidence of trauma (broken bones and the like). Even some details of an individual's health and nutritional history can be read from the bones.

One well-known Canadian forensic anthropologist is Owen Beattie. Beattie has conducted more than 100 forensic investigations for coroners, police departments, and medical examiners across Canada in the past 20 years. Currently, Beattie teaches biological and forensic anthropology at the University of Alberta in Edmonton and serves as consultant in Physical Anthropology for the Office of the Chief Medical Examiner in Alberta. As a forensic anthropologist, Beattie has become increasingly involved in the investigation of human rights violations around the world. In the mid-1990s, he served as part of a United Nations international team that exhumed and analyzed victims of the 1994 Rwandan massacres.

Beattie also has used his considerable forensic expertise to help solve some of the most fascinating mysteries of the Arctic north. He is most famous for his work on the remains of members of the doomed 1845–48 Franklin Expedition to find the Northwest Passage. His two award-winning books, *Frozen in Time* and *Buried in Ice,* examine the mysterious fate of Sir John Franklin's crew. In 1999, Beattie supervised removal of the frozen

Shown here is Dr. Owen Beattie from the University of Alberta, whose specialty is forensic anthropology. Dr. Beattie is widely known for his work on the fate of the 1845–48 Franklin Expedition.

remains of a 15th-century hunter discovered in a remote glacier in Tatshenshini-Alsek National Wilderness Park, British Columbia. The ancient hunter and the artifacts associated with the body have elicited great interest within the scientific and First Nations communities.

Presently, Beattie is completing a project on the 1719 disappearance of Captain James Knight's ships, the *Albany* and *Discovery,* on their way to explore Hudson Bay.

Young Alberta Book Society. (1998). *Owen Beattie.* Retrieved October 16, 2000, from the World Wide Web: http://www.culturenet.ucalgary.ca/yabs/beattieo.html.

8th Annual Young Scientist Conference. (n.d.). *Owen Beattie.* Retrieved October 16, 2000, from the World Wide Web: http://ftp.ei.educ.ab.ca/dept/ins/beattie/html.

were left in the ground, reflect certain aspects of human behaviour. For example, shallow, restricted concentrations of charcoal that include oxidized earth, bone fragments, and charred plant remains and nearby pieces of fire-cracked rock, pottery, and tools suitable for food preparation are indicative of cooking and associated food processing at a First Nations site. From such remains much can be learned about a people's diet and subsistence activities. Thus **prehistoric archaeologists** can find out about human behaviour in the distant past, far beyond the mere 5000 years historians are limited to by their dependence on written records. In Canada we tend to use the term "pre-contact" rather than prehistoric when referring to the ancestors of contemporary First Nations, Inuit, and Métis cultures, to avoid the suggestion that people living in North America before Europeans arrived did not have a history. This, of course, is not true; aboriginal peoples possess diverse and vibrant cultural histories spanning thousands of years before Europeans arrived in Canada. Archaeologists are not limited to the study of prehistoric societies; **historic archaeologists** study those cultures with historic documents available in order to supplement the material remains people left behind. In most literate societies, written records are associated with governing elites, rather than with people at the "grass-roots." Thus, although documents can tell archaeologists much they might not know from archaeological evidence alone, it is equally true that archaeological remains can tell historians much about a cultural group that is not apparent from its written records.

Although archaeologists have concentrated on the human past, significant numbers of them are concerned with the study of material objects in contemporary settings. One example is William Rathje, director of the University of Arizona's Garbage Project, which, by a carefully controlled study of household waste, continues to produce information about contemporary social issues. One aim of this project has been to test the validity of interview-survey techniques, on which sociologists, economists, other social scientists,

William Rathje, director of the University of Arizona's Garbage Project, holds a newspaper retrieved from deep in a landfill, a vivid demonstration that biodegradables in compacted landfills do not biodegrade as expected.

and policymakers rely heavily for their data. The tests clearly show a significant difference between what people say they do and what garbage analysis shows they actually do. In 1973, a questionnaire was administred to determine the rate of alcohol consumption in Tucson. In one part of town, 15 percent of respondent households affirmed consumption of beer, but no household reported consumption of more than eight cans a week. Analysis of garbage from the same area,

Wanuskewin Heritage Park, located outside Saskatoon, Saskatchewan, contains virtually every type of archaeological site common to the Northern Plains, spanning some 6000 years. These sites help archaeologists reconstruct the history of pre-contact Plains peoples in this region.

Prehistoric/pre-contact archaeology. The study of ancient cultures that did not possess writing systems to record their history. **> Historic archaeology.** The study of past cultures that possessed written records of their history.

however, demonstrated that beer was consumed in more than 80 percent of households, and 50 percent discarded more than eight empty cans a week. Another interesting finding of the Garbage Project is that when beef prices reached an all-time high in 1973, so did the amount of beef wasted by households (not just in Tucson, but other parts of the country as well). Although common sense would lead us to suppose just the opposite, high prices and scarcity correlate with more, rather than less, waste. Such findings suggest that ideas about human behaviour based on conventional interview-survey techniques alone can be seriously in error.

The previous discussion should not lead students to believe that archaeologists are concerned only with material culture—the physical evidence of past cultures. The artifacts are merely a means to interpret and reconstruct human history. Robert McGhee, curator of Arctic archaeology at the Canadian Museum of Civilization, dismisses the value of artifacts as objects themselves; rather, he uses these artifacts to learn about the people who used and then discarded them. Using archaeological evidence, McGhee has highlighted the important role the Arctic has played in human history and how the Inuit have interacted with other cultures, such as Norsemen, Basques, and Asians.

Linguistic Anthropology

Perhaps the most distinctive feature of humanity is language. Language is what allows us to preserve and transmit our culture from generation to generation. Humans are not alone in the use of symbolic communication. Studies have shown that the sounds and gestures some other animals make—especially apes—may serve functions comparable to those of human language; yet no other animal has developed a system of symbolic communication as complex as that of humans.

The branch of anthropology that studies human languages is called **linguistic anthropology.**

Linguistic anthropologists study the way language is used as a resource for practising, developing, and transmitting culture. They examine how people use language and other means of expression to develop relationships with one another and to maintain social distinctiveness.

Descriptive linguists deal with the description of a language (the way a sentence is formed or a verb conjugated), and **historical linguists** deal with the history of languages (the way languages develop and influence each other with the passage of time). Both approaches yield valuable information, not only about the ways people communicate both verbally and nonverbally, but also about the ways they understand the world around them. The everyday language of North Americans, for example, includes a number of slang words, such as *dough, loonies, dust, loot, cash, change,* and *bread,* to identify what a person of Papua New Guinea would recognize only as *money.* Such phenomena help identify items considered especially important to a culture. Through the study of language in its social setting, known as **sociolinguistics,** anthropologists can understand how people perceive themselves and the world around them.

Linguistic anthropologists also make a significant contribution to our understanding of the human past. As an example, Horatio Hale was the first ethnographer to discover the linguistic link between Siouan languages and the Tutelos of Ontario.[4] Hale also recorded Iroquoian oral traditions, and in 1883 he published the *Iroquois Book of Rites.* By working out the genealogical relationships among languages and examining the distributions of those languages, linguistic anthropologists may estimate how long the speakers of those languages have lived where they do. By identifying words in related languages that have survived from an ancient ancestral tongue, they also

---

[4]Hale, H. (1883). The Tutelo tribe and language. *Proceedings of the American Philosophical Society, 21* (114).

Linguistic anthropology. The study of how people use language to relate to each other and how they develop and transmit culture. **> Descriptive linguistics.** The study of patterns and structure in language. **> Historical linguistics.** The study of language origins, language change, and the relationships between languages. **> Sociolinguistics.** The study of language within its social setting.

can suggest both where and how the speakers of the ancestral language lived.

Applied Anthropology

Applied anthropology is a veritable gold mine of cultural knowledge that, when put to practical use, can help solve or at least alleviate some of the social problems that humans in many cultures experience. The Anthropology Applied boxes found throughout this book feature some of the specialized services applied anthropologists provide. Besides academic settings, applied anthropologists often work within government bureaux, private corporations, and international development agencies. More often than not, they function as mediators between the members of a cultural group and some government or private agency. Canadian applied anthropologists provide fundamental background information for First Nations land claims negotiations. Indeed, as mentioned earlier, applied anthropologists have played a prominent role in the development of Canadian anthropology as a discipline.

Applied research is extremely important in sociocultural anthropology, but it also affects the other fields of anthropology. Applied archaeologists work in cultural resource management (CRM), assessing and, at times, excavating archaeological sites threatened by human activity, such as dam building. In Canada CRM archaeology is the main type of archaeology conducted. Public archaeologists, as part of the applied nature of CRM, have also worked alongside First Nations groups to develop cultural awareness programs that introduce the public to the value of heritage sites and the history they recount. As you have already seen, forensic anthropology is an excellent example of applied research in biological anthropology. Applied linguistic anthropologists are becoming increasingly involved in language retention among First Nations groups and serve as advisers for bilingual education. Applied medical anthropologists (featured in Chapter 14) work closely with traditional healers to reconcile traditional medical practices with modern medicine.

Sociocultural Anthropology

While archaeologists have traditionally concentrated on past cultures, the field of **sociocultural anthropology** examines contemporary or recent cultures. And unlike archaeologists, who focus on material objects to learn about human behaviour, sociocultural anthropologists concentrate on the study of human behaviour as it can be seen, experienced, and even discussed with those whose culture is to be understood.

Sociocultural anthropology is closely related to the other social sciences, especially sociology, since both anthropology and sociology attempt to describe and explain the behaviour of people within social contexts. Sociologists, however, have concentrated heavily on studies of people living in modern North American and European societies, thereby increasing the probability that their theories of human behaviour will be **culture bound**: that is, based on assumptions about the world and reality that are part of the sociologists' Western culture. Since sociocultural anthropologists, too, are products of the culture they grew up in, they also are vulnerable to culture-bound theorizing. However, they constantly seek to minimize the problem by drawing together corroborating information from many different cultures before attempting to explain human behaviour. We will return to a discussion of the comparative method later in this chapter.

The emphasis sociocultural anthropologists place on studies of contemporary non-Western cultures has often led to findings that dispute existing beliefs derived from Western studies. Sociocultural anthropologists were the first to demonstrate

> that the world does not divide into the pious and the superstitious; that there are sculptures in jungles and paintings in deserts; that political order is possible without centralized power and principled justice without codified rules; that the norms of reason were not fixed in Greece, the evolution of morality not consummated in England. . . . We have, with no little success, sought to keep the

---

Applied anthropology. Applied anthropologists attempt to solve or alleviate some of the social problems that humans experience using the knowledge and expertise of anthropology. **> Sociocultural anthropology.** The study of human behaviour in contemporary cultures. **> Culture bound.** Theories about the world and reality based on the assumptions and values of one's own culture.

world off balance; pulling out rugs, upsetting tea tables, setting off firecrackers. It has been the office of others to reassure; ours to unsettle."[5]

Sociocultural anthropologists seek to understand the ways diverse cultural groups live their lives—to explain similarities and differences found among human cultures. They seek to understand the interrelatedness of sociocultural systems, the way our economies, religions, and social and political organization influence each other. Sociocultural anthropologists are also interested in culture change—the ways cultures everywhere continue to change as they adapt to new situations. Throughout this book we will be highlighting the value of sociocultural anthropology in solving practical problems; however, the greatest value of sociocultural anthropology in today's global community is to serve as a medium for promoting cultural awareness and appreciation of our incredible cultural diversity.

Sociocultural anthropology is both comparative and descriptive. **Ethnography** involves the collection of descriptive material on a specific culture. The information collected provides a descriptive account (or ethnography) of the people. **Ethnology** is the comparative study of patterns in contemporary cultures. Ethnologists attempt to develop generalizations or rules to explain human behaviour. **Ethnohistory** is a method of studying cultures of the recent past using oral histories; archaeological sites; the accounts of explorers, missionaries, and traders; and documents such as land titles, birth and death records, and other archival materials.

Ethnography

Whenever possible, the anthropologist becomes an ethnographer by going to live among the people under study. Through **participant observation**—eating a people's food, speaking their language,

and personally experiencing their habits and customs—the ethnographer can understand their way of life to a far greater extent than any nonparticipant anthropologist or other social scientist ever could; anthropologists learn a culture best by learning how to behave acceptably in the society where they are doing fieldwork. An early example of ethnography was the groundbreaking yet often ignored work of James A. Teit in the 1890s. Teit, an associate of American anthropologist Franz Boas, spent much of his career documenting the lives of the Nlaka'pamux First Nations of south central British Columbia[6] (for further discussion of Franz Boas's work, visit the textbook's website at http://www.cultural2e.nelson.com). Teit collected numerous oral narratives and songs, as well as material on ethnobotany, face painting, body tattooing, basketry, and the rituals of womanhood: puberty, marriage, pregnancy, and childbirth. Significant as those contributions remain, Teit's most noteworthy contribution to early ethnography was his determination to present the voice and experience of women; in fact, his accounts are some of the only Native-based ethnographic interpretations from the 1800s. His focus on the experiences of women, as seen through their eyes, challenged 19th- and 20th-century male-centredness in ethnographic research, and thus his work is more typical of the contemporary ethnography discussed later in this chapter.

Participant observation of the culture under study does not mean the ethnographer must join in a people's battles in order to study a culture where warfare is prominent; but by living among a warlike people, the ethnographer should be able to understand the role of warfare in the overall cultural scheme. He or she must be a meticulous observer to get a broad overview of a culture without placing undue emphasis on one of its parts at the expense of another. Only by discovering how

---

[5]Geertz, C. (1984). Distinguished lecture: Anti anti-relativism. *American Anthropologist, 86,* 275.

[6]Wickwire, W. (1993, fall). Women in ethnography: The research of James A. Teit. *American Society for Ethnohistory, 40* (4), 539–567.

Ethnography. The collection of descriptive material on a culture. **> Ethnology.** The comparative study of cultures to explain human behaviour. **> Ethnohistory.** The study of cultures from the recent past using oral histories, archaeological sites, and written accounts left by explorers, missionaries, and traders. **> Participant observation.** A method of learning a people's culture through direct participation in their everyday life.

all cultural institutions—social, political, economic, religious—relate to one another can ethnographers begin to understand cultural systems. Anthropologists refer to this as the **holistic perspective,** and it is one of the fundamental principles of anthropology. Robert Gordon, an anthropologist from Namibia, speaks of it in this way: "Whereas the sociologist or the political scientist might examine the beauty of a flower petal by petal, the anthropologist is the person that stands on the top of the mountain and looks at the beauty of the field. In other words, we try and go for the wider perspective."[7]

When participating in unfamiliar cultures, ethnographers do not just blunder about blindly but enlist the assistance of individual **informants.** These are members of the society the ethnographer is working in, with whom she or he develops close relationships and who help interpret whatever activities are occurring. As a child learns proper behaviour from its parents, so do anthropologists in the field need help from informants to

unravel the "mysteries" of what is, at first, a strange culture.

The importance of fieldwork is conveyed by the experiences of Richard B. Lee, who lived with the Ju/'hoansi of the Kalahari Desert. The following Original Study illustrates the impossibility of going into the field free of all naiveté, biases, and assumptions; the importance of expecting the unexpected; and the necessity of establishing a rapport with the people being studied.

The popular image of ethnographic fieldwork is that it takes place among far-off, exotic peoples. To be sure, much ethnographic work has occurred in places such as Africa, the islands of the Pacific Ocean, the deserts of Australia, and so on. One very good reason for this is that non-Western peoples have been ignored too often by other social scientists. Still, anthropologists have recognized from the start that an understanding of human behaviour depends on knowledge of all cultures and peoples, including their own. In the 1950s and 1960s many Canadian anthropologists turned their attention to social issues facing Canadian society. One of the landmark projects of this period was Harry Hawthorn's 1955 report on the impact of providing First Nations peoples

---

[7]Gordon, R. (1981, December). [Interview for Coast Telecourses, Inc.] Los Angeles.

In Cartagena, Colombia, an ethnographer interviews local fishermen.

Holistic perspective. A fundamental principle of anthropology, that the various parts of culture must be viewed in the broadest possible context to understand their interconnections and interdependence. **> Informants.** Members of a society the ethnographer works in who help interpret what she or he sees taking place.

ORIGINAL STUDY

Eating Christmas in the Kalahari

Richard B. Lee

The Ju/'hoan knowledge of Christmas is thirdhand. The London Missionary Society brought the holiday to the southern Tswana tribes in the early nineteenth century. Later, native catechists spread the idea far and wide among the Bantu-speaking pastoralists, even in the remotest corners of the Kalahari Desert. The Ju idea of the Christmas story, stripped to its essentials, is "praise the birth of White Man's god-chief"; what keeps their interest in the holiday high is the Tswana-Herero custom of slaughtering an ox for their Ju neighbors as an annual goodwill gesture. Since the 1930s, part of the San's annual round of activities has included a December congregation at the cattle posts for trading, marriage brokering, and several days of trance-dance feasting at which the local Tswana headman is host.

As a social anthropologist working with the Ju/'hoansi, I found that the Christmas ox custom suited my purposes. I had come to the Kalahari to study the hunting and gathering subsistence economy of the Ju/'hoansi, and to accomplish this it was essential not to provide them with food, share my own food, or interfere in any way with their food-gathering activities. While liberal handouts of tobacco and medical supplies were appreciated, they were scarcely adequate to erase the glaring disparity in wealth between the anthropologist, who maintained a two-month inventory of canned goods, and the Ju, who rarely had a day's supply of food on hand. My approach, while paying off in terms of data, left me open to frequent accusations of stinginess and hard-heartedness. By their lights, I was a miser.

The Christmas ox was to be my way of saying thank you for the cooperation of the past year; and since it was to be our last Christmas in the field, I was determined to slaughter the largest, meatiest ox that money could buy, insuring that the feast and trance dance would be a success.

Through December I kept my eyes open at the wells as the cattle were brought down for watering. Several animals were offered, but none had quite the grossness that I had in mind. Then, 10 days before the holiday, a Herero friend led an ox of astonishing size and mass up to our camp. It was solid black, stood five feet high at the shoulder, had a five-foot span of horns, and must have weighed 1200 pounds on the hoof. Food consumption calculations are my specialty, and I quickly figured that bones and viscera aside, there was enough meat—at least four pounds—for every man, woman, and child of the 150 Ju/'hoansi in the vicinity of /Xai/ xai who were expected at the feast.

Having found the right animal at last, I paid the Herero £20 ($56) and asked him to keep the beast with his herd until Christmas Day. The next morning word spread among the people that the big solid-black one was the ox chosen by /Tontah for the Christmas feast. That afternoon I received the first delegation. Ben!a, an outspoken 60-year-old mother of five, came to the point slowly.

"Where were you planning to eat Christmas?"

"Right here at /Xai/ xai," I replied.

"Alone or with others?"

"I expect to invite all the people to eat Christmas with me."

"Eat what?"

"I have purchased Yehave's black ox, and I am going to slaughter and cook it."

"That's what we were told at the well but refused to believe it until we heard it from yourself."

"Well, it's the black one," I replied expansively, although wondering what she was driving at.

"Oh, no!" Ben!a groaned, turning to her group. "They were right." Turning back to me she asked, "Do you expect us to eat that bag of bones?"

"Bag of bones! It's the biggest ox at /Xai/ xai."

"Big, yes, but old. And thin. Everybody knows there's no meat on that old ox. What did you expect us to eat off it, the horns?"

Everybody chuckled at Ben!a's one-liner as they walked away, but all I could manage was a weak grin.

That evening it was the turn of the young men. They came to sit at our evening fire. /Gaugo, about my age, spoke to me man-to-man.

"/Tontah, you have always been square with us. What has happened to change your heart? That sack of guts and bones of Yehave's will hardly feed one camp, let alone all the !Kung around /Xai/ xai." And he proceeded to enumerate the seven camps in the /Xai/ xai vicinity, family by family. "Perhaps you have forgotten that we are not few, but many. Or are you too blind to tell the difference between a proper cow and an old wreck? That ox is thin to the point of death."

"Look, you guys," I retorted, "that is a beautiful animal, and I'm sure you will eat it with pleasure at Christmas."

"Of course we will eat it; it's food. But it won't fill us up to the point where we will have enough strength to dance. We will eat and go home to bed with stomachs rumbling."

That night as we turned in, I asked my wife Nancy: "What did you think of the black ox?"

"It looked enormous to me. Why?"

"Well, about eight different people have told me I got gypped; that the ox is nothing but bones."

"What's the angle?" Nancy asked. "Did they have a better one to sell?"

"No, they just said that it was going to be a grim Christmas because there won't be enough meat to go around. Maybe I'll get an independent judge to look at the beast in the morning."

Bright and early, Halingisi, a Tswana cattleowner, appeared at our camp. But before I could ask him to give me his opinion on Yehave's black ox, he gave me the eye signal that indicated a confidential chat. We left the camp and sat down.

"/Tontah, I'm surprised at you; you've lived here for three years and still haven't learned anything about cattle."

"But what else can a person do but choose the biggest, strongest animal one can find?" I retorted.

"Look, just because an animal is big doesn't mean that it has plenty of meat on it. The black one was a beauty when it was younger, but now it is thin to the point of death."

"Well, I've already bought it. What can I do at this stage?"

"Bought it already? I thought you were just considering it. Well, you'll have to kill and serve it, I suppose. But don't expect much of a dance to follow."

My spirits dropped rapidly. I could believe that Ben!a and /Gaugo just might be putting me on about the black ox, but Halingisi seemed to be an impartial critic. I went around that day feeling as though I had bought a lemon of a used car.

In the afternoon it was ≠Tomazho's turn. ≠Tomazho is a fine hunter, a top trance performer, and one of my most reliable informants. He approached the subject of the Christmas cow as part of my continuing education.

"My friend, the way it is with us Ju/'hoansi," he began, "is that we love meat. And even more than that, we love fat. When we hunt we always search for the fat ones, the ones dripping with layers of white fat: fat that turns into a clear, thick oil in the cooking pot, fat that slides down your gullet, fills your stomach and gives you a roaring diarrhea," he rhapsodized.

"So, feeling as we do," he continued, "it gives us pain to be served such a scrawny thing as Yehave's black ox. It is big, yes, and no doubt its giant bones are good for soup, but fat is what we really crave, and so we will eat Christmas this year with a heavy heart."

The prospect of a gloomy Christmas now had me worried, so I asked ≠Tomazho what I could do about it.

"Look for a fat one, a young one ... smaller, but fat. Fat enough to make us / / gom ('evacuate the bowels'); then we will be happy."

My suspicions were aroused when ≠Tomazho said that he happened to know of a young, fat, barren cow that the owner was willing to part with. Was ≠Tomazho working on commission, I wondered? But I dispelled this unworthy thought when we approached the Herero owner of the cow in question and found that he had decided not to sell.

The scrawny wreck of a Christmas ox now became the talk of the /Xai/xai waterhole and was the first news told to the outlying groups as they began to come in from the bush for the feast. What finally convinced me that real trouble might be brewing was the visit from/N!au, an old conservative with a reputation for fierceness. His nickname meant "spear" and referred to an incident 30 years ago in which he had speared a man to death. He had an intense manner; fixing me with his eyes, he said in clipped tones:

"I have only just heard about the black ox today, or else I would have come here earlier. /Tontah, do you honestly think you can serve meat like that to people and avoid a fight?" He paused, letting the implications sink in. "I don't mean fight you, /Tontah; you are a White man. I mean a fight between Ju/'hoansi. There are many fierce ones here, and with such a small quantity of meat to distribute, how can you give everybody a fair share? Someone is sure to accuse another of taking too much or hogging all the choice pieces. Then you will see what happens when some go hungry while others eat."

The possibility of at least a serious argument struck me as all too real. I had witnessed the tension that surrounds the distribution of meat from a kuku or gemsbok kill, and had documented many arguments that sprang up from a real or imagined slight in meat distribution. The owners of a kill may spend up to two hours arranging and rearranging the piles of meat under the gaze of a circle of recipients before handing them out. And I also knew that the Christmas feast at /Xai/ xai would be bringing together groups that had feuded in the past.

Convinced now of the gravity of the situation, I went in earnest to search for a second cow; but all my inquiries failed to turn one up.

The Christmas feast was evidently going to be a disaster, and the incessant complaints about the meagerness of the ox had already taken the fun out of it for me. Moreover, I was getting bored with the wisecracks, and after losing my temper a few times, I resolved to serve the beast anyway. If the meat fell short, the hell with it. In the Ju/'hoan idiom, I announced to all who would listen:

"I am a poor man and blind. If I have chosen one that is too old and too thin, we will eat it anyway and see if there is enough meat there to quiet the rumbling of our stomachs."

On hearing this speech, Ben!a offered me a rare word of comfort. "It's thin," she said philosophically, "but the bones will make a good soup."

At dawn Christmas morning, instinct told me to turn over the butchering and cooking to a friend and take off with Nancy and spend Christmas alone in the bush. But curiosity kept me from retreating. I wanted to see what such a scrawny ox looked like on butchering, and if there was going to be a fight, I wanted to catch every word of it. Anthropologists are incurable that way.

The great beast was driven up to our dancing ground, and a shot in the forehead dropped it in its tracks. Then, freshly cut branches were heaped around the fallen carcass to receive the meat. Ten men volunteered to help with the cutting. I asked /Gaugo to make the breast bone cut. This cut, which begins the butchering process for most large game, offers easy access for removal of the viscera. But it also allows the hunter to spot-check the amount of fat on the animal. A fat game animal carries a white layer up to an inch thick on the chest, while in a thin one, the knife will quickly cut to bone. All eyes fixed on his hand as /Gaugo, dwarfed by the great carcass, knelt to the breast. The first cut opened a pool of solid white in the black skin. The second and third cut widened and deepened the creamy white. Still no bone. It was pure fat; it must have been two inches thick.

"Hey /Gau," I burst out, "that ox is loaded with fat. What's this about the ox being too thin to bother eating? Are you out of your mind?"

"Fat?" /Gau shot back, "You call that fat? This wreck is thin, sick, dead!" And he broke out laughing. So did everyone else. They rolled on the ground, paralyzed with laughter. Everybody laughed except me; I was thinking.

I ran back to the tent and burst in just as Nancy was getting up. "Hey, the black ox. It's fat as hell! They were kidding about it being too thin to eat. It was a joke or something. A put-on. Everyone is really delighted with it!"

"Some joke," my wife replied. "It was so funny that you were ready to pack and leave /Xai/ xai."

If it had indeed been a joke, it had been an extraordinarily convincing one, and tinged, I thought, with more than a touch of malice, as many jokes are. Nevertheless, that it was a joke lifted my spirits considerably, and I returned to the butchering site, where the shape of the ox was rapidly disappearing under the axes and knives of the butchers. The atmosphere had become festive. Grinning broadly, their arms covered with blood well past the elbow, men packed chunks of meat into the big cast-iron cooking pots, 50 pounds to the load, and muttered and chuckled all the while about the thinness and worthlessness of the animal and /Tontah's poor judgement.

We danced and ate that ox for two days and two nights; we cooked and distributed 14 potfuls of meat, and no one went home hungry and no fights broke out.

But the "joke" stayed in my mind. I had a growing feeling that something important had happened in my relationship with the Ju/'hoansi, and that the clue lay in the meaning of the joke. Several days later, when most of the people had dispersed back to the bush camps, I raised the question with Hakekgose, a Tswana man who had grown up among the Ju, married a Ju girl, and who probably knew their culture better than any other non-Ju/'hoan.

"With us Whites," I began, "Christmas is supposed to be the day of friendship and brotherly love. What I can't figure out is why the Ju went to such lengths to criticize and belittle the ox I had bought for the feast. The animal was perfectly good, and their jokes and wisecracks practically ruined the holiday for me."

"So it really did bother you," said Hakekgose. "Well, that's the way they always talk. When I take my rifle and go hunting with them, if I miss, they laugh at me for the rest of the day. But even if I hit and bring one down, it's no better. To them, the kill is always too small or too old or too thin; and as we sit down on the kill site to cook and eat the liver, they keep grumbling, even with their mouths full of meat. They say things like, 'Oh this is awful! What a worthless animal! Whatever made me think that this Tswana rascal could hunt!'"

"Is this the way outsiders are treated?" I asked.

"No, it is their custom; they talk that way to each other too. Go and ask them."

/Gaugo had been one of the most enthusiastic in making me feel bad about the merit of the Christmas ox. I sought him out first.

"Why did you tell me the black ox was worthless, when you could see that it was loaded with fat and meat?"

"It is our way," he said, smiling. "We always like to fool people about that. Say there is a Ju/'hoan who has been hunting. He must not come home and announce like a braggart, 'I have killed a big one in the bush!' He must first sit down in silence until I or someone else comes up to his fire and asks, 'What did you see today?' He replies quietly, 'Ah, I'm no good for hunting. I saw nothing at all [pause] just a little tiny one.' Then I smile to myself," /Gaugo continued, "because I know he has killed something big.

"In the morning we make up a party of four or five people to cut up and carry the meat back to the camp. When we arrive at the kill we examine it and cry out, 'You mean to say you have dragged us all the way out here in order to make us cart home your pile of bones? Oh, if I had known it was this thin I wouldn't have come.' Another one pipes up, 'People, to think I gave up a nice day in the shade for this. At home we may be hungry, but at least we have nice cool water to drink.' If the horns are big, someone says, 'Did you think that somehow you were going to boil down the horns for soup?'

"To all this you must respond in kind. 'I agree,' you say, 'this one is not worth the effort; let's just cook the liver for strength and leave the rest for the hyenas. It is not too late to hunt today, and even a duiker or a steenbok would be better than this mess.'

"Then you set to work nevertheless, butcher the animal, carry the meat back to the camp, and everyone eats," /Gaugo concluded.

Things were beginning to make sense. Next, I went to ≠Tomazho. He corroborated /Gaugo's story of the obligatory insults over a kill and added a few details of his own.

"But," I asked, "why insult a man after he has gone to all that trouble to track and kill an animal and when he is going to share the meat with you so that your children will have something to eat?"

"Arrogance," was his cryptic answer.

"Arrogance?"

"Yes, when a young man kills much meat he comes to think of himself as a chief or a big man, and he thinks of the rest of us as his servants or inferiors. We can't accept this. We refuse one who boasts, for someday his pride will make him kill somebody. So we always speak of his meat as worthless. This way we cool his heart and make him gentle."

"But why didn't you tell me this before?" I asked ≠Tomazho with some heat.

"Because you never asked me," said ≠Tomazho, echoing the refrain that has come to haunt every field ethnographer.

The pieces now fell into place. I had known for a long time that in situations of social conflict with Ju/'hoansi I held all the cards. I was the only source of tobacco in a thousand square miles, and I was not incapable of cutting an individual off for noncooperation. Though my boycott never lasted longer than a few days, it was an indication of my strength. People resented my presence at the waterhole, yet simultaneously dreaded my leaving. In short, I was a perfect target for the charge of arrogance and for the Ju tactic of enforcing humility.

I had been taught an object lesson by the Ju/'hoansi; it had come from an unexpected corner and had hurt me in a vulnerable area. For the big black ox was to be the one totally generous, unstinting act of my year at /Xai/ xai, and I was quite unprepared for the reaction I received.

As I read it, their message was this: There are no totally generous acts. All "acts" have an element of calculation. One black ox slaughtered at Christmas does not wipe out a year of careful manipulation of gifts given to serve your own ends. After all, to kill an animal and share the meat with people is really no more than Ju/'hoansi do for each other every day and with far less fanfare.

In the end, I had to admire how the Ju had played out the farce—collectively straight-faced to the end. Curiously, the episode reminded me of the Good Soldier Schweik and his marvelous encounters with authority. Like Schweik, the Ju/'hoansi had retained a thoroughgoing skepticism of good intentions. Was it this independence of spirit, I wondered, that had kept them culturally viable in the face of generations of contact with more powerful societies, both Black and White? The thought that the Ju/'hoansi were alive and well in the Kalahari was strangely comforting. Perhaps, armed with that independence and with their superb knowledge of their environment, they might yet survive the future.

Source: From "Eating Christmas in the Kalahari," by Richard Borshay Lee, with permission from *Natural History*, December 1969; Copyright the American Museum of Natural History, 1969.

with old age pensions. This study is an early example of applied anthropology. Hawthorn continued his research, studying social and economic conditions among First Nations peoples of British Columbia. Canadian anthropologists have not only focused on First Nations peoples. Marius Barbeau actively promoted the folk culture of French Canada—their arts and crafts, literature, and song and dance. In the early 1960s, Marc-Adélard Tremblay, along with Paul Charest and Yvan Breton, conducted a community study of Saint Augustin, a Quebec fishing village on the Gulf of St. Lawrence. Along with its ethnographic value, this study is notable for being one of the first to trace the social changes experienced by a traditional community as it became a modern community over the course of 65 years.

This trend toward focusing on contemporary domestic issues continues today. Often, Canadian anthropologists find themselves studying people they have studied in other settings. Thus, as people from the Pacific Rim, India, and the Middle East have moved to Canada, or as refugees have arrived from Africa, Central America, Asia, and other places, anthropologists have been there not just to study them but also to help them adjust to their new circumstances. Anthropologists are applying the same research techniques that served them so well in the study of non-Western peoples to the study of such diverse subjects as First Nations self-government and land claims; English–French relations; Asian immigrants; motorcycle gangs; health care delivery systems; and ethnic, age, and gender issues.

Though it has much to offer, the anthropological study of our own culture is not without its own special problems. Sir Edmund Leach, a major figure in British anthropology, put it in the following way:

> Surprising though it may seem, fieldwork in a cultural context of which you already have intimate first-hand experience seems to be much more difficult than fieldwork which is approached from the naive viewpoint of a total stranger. When anthropologists study facets of their own society their vision seems to become distorted by prejudices which derive from private rather than public experience."[8]

[8]Leach, E. (1982). *Social anthropology* (p. 124). Glasgow, Scotland: Fontana Paperbacks.

Anthropologists carry out fieldwork at home as well as abroad. Shown here is anthropologist Dr. Josephine Smart (centre) of the University of Calgary, with her daughter Jasmine Smart and anthropologist Dr. Judith Nagata of York University, outside an Indian restaurant owned and operated by Chinese from Bombay. The visit to this restaurant is related to a broader project on the globalization and localization of Chinese immigrant cuisine in Canada.

Although ethnographers strive to get inside views of other cultures, they do so as outsiders. And the most successful anthropological studies of their own culture by North Americans have been done by those who also worked in other cultures. As an example, Parin Dossa (see Chapter 9) has studied Muslim women in Canada and on the coast of Kenya. Her current work examines the mental health and displacement of Iranian women. Like other contemporary Canadian anthropologists, Parin Dossa conducts her research using the narratives of the people she studies. The more we learn of other cultures, the more we gain a different perspective on our own. Put another way, as other cultures are seen as less exotic, the more exotic our own becomes. In addition to Canadian ethnographers going outside their own culture before trying to study it themselves (so that they may see themselves as *others* see them), much is to be gained by encouraging anthropologists from Europe, Africa, Asia, and Central and South America to do fieldwork in North America. For example, Yvon Csonka, who is a research associate at the Prehistory Department, University of Neuchatel, Switzerland, has studied the Caribou Inuit of the west coast of Hudson Bay. Her 1995 study supplements the findings of earlier, classic ethnography by Birket-Smith (1929) and Rasmussen (1930).[9] From their outsiders' perspective come insights all too easily overlooked by an insider. This does not mean the special difficulties of studying our own culture cannot be overcome; what is required is an acute awareness of those difficulties.

New Directions in Ethnographic Fieldwork

The vitality and worth of any science is dependent on its ability to evolve and mature as a discipline. Ethnographic fieldwork, in particular participant observation, has been considered the hallmark of anthropological research for more than a century. Moreover, remaining scientifically objective, unbiased, and detached from the "study group" has long been the basis of ethnographic research. In the late 20th century, anthropologists such as J. Clifford, E. Marcus, and M.J. Fischer began asking some difficult questions about ethnographic research. Just how objective can ethnographers be, and do ethnographers have the ability to remain uninfluenced by circumstances, personal biases, and emotions? (For further discussion of the postmodernist perspective, visit the textbook's website at http://www.cultural2e.nelson.com.)

Anthropologists are also considering the dynamics of power and authority. Whose voice should be heard in the ethnographic record, the ethnographer's or the informant's, or is there a way to blend the two? And who has the authority to represent the ideology of the study group? Many anthropologists now believe it is impossible for Western ethnographers to completely understand indigenous ideology or point of view; indeed, there are multiple points of view and voices within any cultural group.[10]

Indigenous groups are now representing themselves to the world, and the ethnographer is only one of many voices. Anthropologists like Judith Abwunza acknowledge the value of presenting multiple voices: In studying female power and resistance among Kenyan women, Abwunza recorded the women's experiences in their own words. In this way, ethnographers are no longer the only authority responsible for interpreting anthropological data, and the ethnographer's knowledge is not the only knowledge presented. Leslie Main Johnson recognized this potential when she examined indigenous knowledge with the Gitksan people of northern British Columbia. She asked the question: When Gitksan people look at the environment, what do they see?[11]

Anthropologists also are paying closer attention to living histories, through narratives and oral histories. Robin Ridington (see Chapter 12) typifies this new ethnography in his work with the Dane-zaa. Employing a collaborative approach, and recording oral histories and unedited narratives, Ridington set out to tell the story of the Dane-zaa in their own words and using their voices.

An offshoot of this re-evaluation of the ethnographer's role is a closer look at the process of fieldwork—ethnographers are writing about *their* experiences in the field. An example of this type of writing is Richard B. Lee's "Eating Christmas in the Kalahari," excerpted on pages 15–20. Lee demonstrates one of the pitfalls of anthropologists living in a very different cultural milieu, and in doing so, he also helps us understand the worldview of the Ju/'hoansi.

As indigenous groups around the world have taken ownership of their history and ideology, ethnographers have begun to work in partnership with these groups. Participatory-action research means that the study groups are involved in the actual research and interpretation of the ethnographic data. A new and exciting approach is the team-research model, whereby each ethnographer does research in his or her own area of specialization (e.g., political and legal issues, ritual, demographics, subsistence strategies, and so on). Thus, the field of ethnography is evolving, in an attempt to better meet the needs and wishes of the cultural groups under study and to provide a

[9]Lee, R.B., & Daly, R. (Eds.). (1999). *The Cambridge encyclopedia of hunters and gatherers.* Cambridge, UK: Cambridge University Press.

[10]Conaty, G.T. (1995, May). Economic models and Blackfoot ideology. *American Ethnologist, 22* (2), 403–409.

[11]Johnson, L.M. (2002). Indigenous knowledge as a basis for living in local environments. In R.B. Morrison & C.R. Wilson (Eds.), *Ethnographic essays in cultural anthropology: A problem-based approach.* Itasca, IL: F.F. Peacock.

richer, more comprehensive presentation of indigenous worldviews. Throughout this text, you will encounter many examples of these new approaches.

Ethnology

Although ethnographic fieldwork is basic to sociocultural anthropology, it is not the sole occupation of anthropologists. Largely descriptive in nature, ethnography provides the basic data the ethnologist, who is more theoretically oriented, then may use to study one particular aspect of a culture by comparing it with that same aspect in others. Anthropologists constantly make such **cross-cultural comparisons,** which, like holism, are another hallmark of sociocultural anthropology. Interesting insights into our own practices may come from cross-cultural comparisons, such as comparing the time people devote to what we consider housework. In North American society, a widespread belief is that the ever-increasing output of household appliance consumer goods has resulted in a steady reduction in housework, with a consequent increase in leisure time. Thus, consumer appliances have become principal indicators of a high standard of living. Anthropological research among food foragers (people who rely on wild plant and animal resources for subsistence), however, has shown that they work far less at household tasks, and indeed less at all subsistence pursuits, than do people in industrialized societies. Aboriginal Australian women, for example, devote approximately 20 hours per week to collecting and preparing food, as well as other domestic chores. By contrast, women in the rural United States in the 1920s, without the benefit of labour-saving appliances, devoted approximately 52 hours per week to their housework. We might suppose this has changed in the decades since, yet some 50 years later urban U.S. women (and this finding can be applied to Canadian women as well), who were not working for wages outside their homes were putting 55 hours per week into their housework—this in spite of all their "labour-saving" dishwashers, washing machines, clothes dryers, vacuum cleaners, food processors, and microwave ovens.[12]

More than any other feature, the cross-cultural perspective distinguishes sociocultural anthropology from other social sciences. It provides anthropology with far richer data than those of any other social science, and it also can be applied to any current issue. As a case in point, consider the way infants in the United States and Canada are routinely made to sleep apart from their parents, their mothers in particular. To European North Americans, this seems normal, but cross-cultural studies show that "co-sleeping" is the rule in most cultural groups. Only in the past 200 years, generally in Western industrialized societies, has it been considered proper for mother and infant to sleep apart. In fact, it amounts to a cultural experiment in childrearing.

Recent studies have shown that this unusual degree of separation of mother and infant in Western societies has important consequences. For one, it increases the length of the infant's crying bouts, which may last in excess of three hours a day in the child's second and third months. The benefits of co-sleeping go beyond significant reductions in crying: Infants also nurse more often and three times as long per feeding; they receive more stimuli (important for neurological development); and they are apparently less susceptible to sudden infant death syndrome. The mother benefits as well if frequent nursing delays the return of ovulation after childbirth, and she gets at least as much sleep as mothers who sleep without their infants.[13]

Cross-cultural studies were facilitated by the work of George Peter Murdock, who in 1937 established the Cross Cultural Survey in Yale's Institute of Human Relations, which later became the Human Relations Area Files (HRAF), a catalogue of cross-indexed ethnographic data. The

---

[12]Bodley, J.H. (1985). *Anthropology and contemporary human problems* (2nd ed., p. 69). Palo Alto, CA: Mayfield.
[13]Barr, R.G. (1997, October). The crying game. *Natural History*, 47. Also McKenna, J.J. (1997, October). Bedtime story. *Natural History*, 50.

Cross-cultural comparison.   Comparing one particular aspect of a culture with that same aspect in others.

HRAF is now available at many colleges and universities (e.g., University of Toronto). The file facilitates searches for causal relationships by using statistical techniques to provide testable generalizations. The HRAF is not without its own set of problems; the searches do not provide cause-and-effect analysis, nor are the sources always reliable. Most problematic of all, the information is taken out of context and tends to negate the holistic mandate of sociocultural anthropology.

Cross-cultural comparisons highlight alternative ways of doing things, so they have much to offer North Americans, large numbers of whom, opinion polls show, continue to doubt the effectiveness of their own ways of doing things. In this sense, we may think of ethnology as the study of alternative ways of doing things. Also, by making systematic cross-cultural comparisons of cultures, ethnologists seek to arrive at valid conclusions concerning the nature of culture in all times and places.

Ethnohistory

Ethnohistorians study cultures of the recent past using oral histories and written accounts left by explorers, missionaries, and traders, and by analyzing data such as archaeological records, land titles, birth and death records, and other archival materials. The ethnohistorical analysis of cultures, in partnership with archaeological research, is a valuable means for understanding culture change. Canadian ethnohistorians have explored the economic, social, and political changes experienced by First Nations when they joined the colonial fur trade.

Ethnohistoric research is also valuable for assessing the reliability of data used for making cross-cultural comparisons. Anthropologists using resources such as the Human Relations Area Files have sometimes concluded that among food foragers it is (and was) the practice for married couples to live in or near the household of the husband's parents (known as patrilocal residence). To be sure, this is what many ethnographers reported. Most such ethnographies were done among food foragers whose traditional practices had been severely altered by pressures emanating from the expansion of Europeans to all parts of the globe. For example, the Western Abenaki people of northwestern New England are believed to have practised patrilocal residence prior to the actual invasion of their homeland by English colonists. Ethnohistoric research, however, shows that their participation in the fur trade with Europeans, coupled with increasing involvement in warfare to stave off foreign incursions, led to the increased importance of men's activities and a change from more flexible to patrilocal residence patterns.[14] Upon close examination, other cases of patrilocal residence among food foragers turn out to be similar responses to circumstances associated with the rise of colonialism. Rather than wives regularly going to live with their husbands in proximity to the latter's male relatives, food-foraging peoples originally seem to have been far more flexible in their postmarital residence arrangements.

Although a valuable research tool, ethnohistory is not without its own set of problems and limitations. Early explorers, traders, and missionaries came to Canada with preconceived notions about First Nations peoples; many of the early accounts reflect these biases and suffer from inaccuracies, misinterpretations, and distortions. As an example, ignorance and personal biases are rife in early accounts of practices such as the Sun Dance and potlatch ceremonies. Ethnohistorians must take into consideration the reliability and objectivity of their sources, and often rely on several forms of information to validate their findings.

▲▽▲▽▲▽▲▽▲▽▲▽▲▽▲▽▲▽▲▽▲▽▲▽▲▽▲▽▲▽▲

ANTHROPOLOGY AND SCIENCE

The primary concern of all anthropologists, regardless of specialization, is the careful and systematic study of humankind. Anthropology has been called a social or a behavioural science by some, a natural science by others, and one of the humanities by still others. Anthropology displays many of the characteristics of a science, including designing hypotheses or tentative explanations for certain observable phenomena, collecting data to test and prove or disprove these hypotheses, and developing a theory to explain

---

[14]Haviland, W.A., & Power, M.W. (1994). *The original Vermonters* (Rev. and exp. ed., pp. 174–175, 215–216, 297–299). Hanover, NH: University Press of New England.

the phenomena. The scientific methodology of such a broad discipline can cause difficulties. In order to arrive at useful theories concerning human behaviour, anthropologists must begin with hypotheses that are as objective and as minimally culture bound as possible. And herein lies a major—some people would say insurmountable—problem: It is difficult for someone who has grown up in one culture to develop hypotheses about others that are not culture bound.

As one example of this sort of problem, consider the attempts by archaeologists to understand the nature of settlement in the Classic period of Maya civilization. This civilization flourished between A.D. 250 and 900 in what is now northern Guatemala, Belize, and adjacent portions of Mexico and Honduras. Today much of this region is covered in a dense tropical forest that people of European background find difficult to deal with. In recent times this forest has been inhabited by a few people who sustain themselves through slash-and-burn farming. (After cutting and burning the natural vegetation, they grow crops for two years or so before fertility is exhausted, and a new field must be cleared.) Yet numerous archaeological sites have been found there, featuring temples sometimes as tall as modern 20-storey buildings; other sorts of monumental architecture; and carved stone monuments. Because of their cultural bias against tropical forests as places to live, and against slash-and-burn farming as a means of raising food, North American and European archaeologists asked this question: How could the Maya have maintained large, permanent settlements on the basis of slash-and-burn farming? The answer seemed self-evident: They could not; therefore, the great archaeological sites must have been ceremonial centres inhabited by few, if any, people. Periodically a rural peasantry, living scattered in small hamlets over the countryside, must have gathered in these centres for rituals or to provide labour for their construction and maintenance.

This view dominated for several decades, and not until 1960 did archaeologists, working at Tikal, one of the largest of all Maya sites, decide to ask the simplest and least biased questions they could think of: Did anyone live at this particular site on a permanent basis? If so, how many, and how were they supported? Working intensively for the next decade, with as few preconceived notions

as possible, the archaeologists were able to establish that Tikal was a large settlement inhabited on a permanent basis by tens of thousands of people who were supported by forms of agriculture more productive than slash-and-burn agriculture alone. This work at Tikal invalidated the older culture-bound ideas and paved the way for a new understanding of Classic Maya civilization.

By recognizing the potential problems of framing explanations that are not culture bound, anthropologists have relied heavily on a technique that has proved successful in other fields of the natural sciences. As did the archaeologists working at Tikal, they immerse themselves in the data to the fullest extent possible. By doing so, they become so thoroughly familiar with the minute details that they can begin to see patterns inherent in the data, many of which might otherwise have been overlooked. These patterns allow anthropologists to propose explanations, which then may be subjected to further testing.

This approach is most easily seen in ethnographic fieldwork, but it is just as important in archaeology. Unlike many social scientists, the ethnographer usually does not go into the field armed with prefigured questionnaires; rather, the ethnographer recognizes that probably various unguessed factors exist, to be found out only by maintaining as open a mind as possible. This does not mean anthropologists never use questionnaires, for sometimes they do. Generally, though, they use them as a means of supplementing or clarifying information gained through other methods. As the fieldwork proceeds, ethnographers sort their complex observations into a meaningful whole, sometimes by formulating and testing hypotheses, but often as not by making use of intuition and playing hunches. What is important is that the results are constantly scrutinized for consistency, for if the parts fail to fit together in an internally consistent manner, then the ethnographer knows a mistake has been made and further work is necessary.

Two studies of a village in Peru illustrate the contrast between anthropological and other social science approaches. In the first study, a sociologist conducted a survey and concluded that people in the village worked together on one another's individually owned plots of land. By contrast, an anthropologist who lived in the village for over a year (during which time the sociologist carried out

Gender **Perspectives**

The Anthropology of Gender

Although gender permeates virtually every aspect of our lives, the term **gender** as opposed to sex is a somewhat elusive concept. Sex refers to the biological and anatomical differences between men and women; humans belong to one of two sexes—male or female. Gender, on the other hand, is a social or cultural construct that provides us with guidelines for our social identity, status, and behaviour, and may include more than the feminine and masculine genders, such as the *berdache,* or "two spirits," of some North American aboriginal cultures and the *hijra* of India, who are neither man nor woman.

Gender is learned; through enculturation we learn the gender roles of our culture. Thus, gender is culturally defined. If gender is culturally defined, then it stands to reason that we will find differences in roles and expectations assigned to each gender from one culture to another. Anthropologists examine how gender roles influence and are influenced by such factors as subsistence strategies, marriage practices, political organization, religious beliefs, and kinship, and how these roles affect the status of each gender. Because gender roles differ from culture to culture, levels of status and power relations also vary, leading to what anthropologists call gender stratification.

Anthropologists generally agree that some form of gender stratification exists within all present-day societies. Even in so-called egalitarian cultures, such as traditional food-foraging groups, where there is little or no ranking, slight differences between male and female status are evident. Studies of gender stratification invariably focus on female inequality; some anthropologists have gone so far as to suggest a "universal male dominance." Examples of female inequality are readily available: exclusion from participating in or leading religious services; a dichotomy between purity and pollution, good and bad, authority and submission; differential value placed on production activities, as when hunted meat is more valued than gathered plants and male labour is compensated at a higher rate than female labour; lack of control over reproductive decisions, such as birth control; and health and safety issues.

The study of gender from an anthropological perspective is fairly recent and has been fraught with difficulties and barriers, most notably the anthropologist's inability to see beyond his or her own society's perceptions of gender. Even in archaeological interpretations, determining gender identity is mired in androcentric (male-centred) notions. Tomb 7 at Monte Alban, located in the centre of the Valley of Oaxaca in the highlands of southern Mexico, is a good example. The rich artifacts and obvious power of the primary individual buried in the tomb led archaeologists to identify the remains as male even though the skeletal evidence was ambiguous and many of the artifacts were spinning and weaving implements. Years later, when anthropologists reinterpreted the material culture from a gender-neutral perspective, they found that the individual was at least gender-female, even if biological sex could not be absolutely determined. This new interpretation also opened up discussions of power relations and gender ideologies in ancient Mesoamerica, where women may have held stations of honour deserving of lavish burials.

In the following chapters, we will examine many issues of gender, from women's movements resisting gendered power to gender bias in language, gendered pressures on men, and examples of contemporary gender inequality, such as female genital mutilation and *purdah.*

Sources:

Goulet, J.A. (1996, December). The 'berdache'/'two-spirit': A comparison of anthropological and native constructions of gendered identities among the northern Athapaskans. *Journal of Royal Anthropological Institute,* 2, 683–701.

McCafferty, S.D., & McCafferty, G.G. (1994, April). Engendering tomb 7 at Monte Alban: Respinning an old yarn. *Current Anthropology, 35* (2), 143–166.

Gender. A set of standards and behaviours attached to individuals, usually, but not always, based on biological sex.

his study) observed the practice only once. Although a belief in exchange relations was important for the people's understanding of themselves, it was not an economic fact.[15]

This does not mean that all sociological research is bad and all anthropological research is good, but merely that reliance on questionnaire surveys is a risky business, no matter who does it.

Yet another problem in scientific anthropology is the matter of replication. In the other physical and natural sciences, replication of observations and/or experiments is a major means of establishing the reliability of a researcher's conclusions. However in anthropology, observational access is far more limited. In particular, access to a non-Western culture is constrained by the difficulty of getting there and being accepted; by the limited number of ethnographers; by often inadequate funding; by the fact that cultures change, so what is observable at one time may not be at another; and so on. Thus, researchers cannot easily see for themselves whether the ethnographer "got it right." For this reason, an ethnographer bears a special responsibility for accurate reporting.

The result of archaeological or ethnographic fieldwork, if properly carried out, is a coherent account of a culture, which provides an explanatory framework for understanding the behaviour of the people who have been studied. And this framework, in turn, is what permits anthropologists to frame broader hypotheses about human behaviour. Plausible though such explanations may be, however, the consideration of a single society is generally insufficient for their testing. As discussed earlier, without some basis for comparison, the hypotheses grounded in a single case may be no more than historical coincidence. Yet a single case may be enough to cast doubt on, if not refute, a theory that previously had been held valid. The discovery in 1948 that Aborigines living in Australia's Arnhem Land put in an average workday of less than six hours, while living well above a level of bare sufficiency, was enough to call into question the widely accepted notion that food-foraging peoples are so preoccupied with finding food that they lack time for any of life's more pleasurable activities. Even today,

Development schemes in nonindustrial countries have traditionally favoured projects like dam building that more often than not fail to deliver the expected benefits, owing to the developers' lack of understanding of local peoples' practices and needs.

economists are prone to label such peoples as "backward," even though the observations made in the Arnhem Land study have since been confirmed many times over in various parts of the world.

Explanations of cultural phenomena may be tested by the comparison of archaeological and/or ethnographic data for several societies found in a particular region. Carefully controlled comparison provides a broader context for understanding cultural phenomena than does the study of a single culture. The anthropologist who undertakes such a comparison may be more confident that the conditions believed to be related really are related, at least within the region under investigation; however, a valid explanation in one region is not necessarily so in another.

Ideally, theories in sociocultural anthropology are generated from worldwide comparisons. The cross-cultural researcher examines a worldwide sample of societies in order to discover whether or not explanations of cultural phenomena seem to be universally applicable. Ideally, the sample should be selected at random, thereby increasing the probability that the conclusions of the cross-cultural researcher will be valid. However, the greater the number of societies compared, the less likely the investigator is to have a detailed understanding of all the societies encompassed by the study. The cross-cultural researcher depends on other ethnographers for data. It is impossible for any individual

---

[15]Chambers, R. (1983). *Rural development: Putting the last first* (p. 51). New York: Longman.

personally to perform in-depth analyses of a broad sample of human cultures throughout the world.

▲▽▲▽▲▽▲▽▲▽▲▽▲▽▲▽▲▽▲▽▲▽▲▽▲▽▲

ANTHROPOLOGY AND THE HUMANITIES

Although the sciences and humanities are often thought of as mutually exclusive approaches to learning, they both come together in anthropology. That is why, for example, anthropological research is funded not only by "hard science" agencies such as the Medical Research Council of Canada, but also by organizations such as the Social Science and Humanities Research Council.

The humanistic side of anthropology is perhaps most immediately evident in its concern with other cultures' languages, values, and achievements in the arts and literature (including oral literature among peoples without writing systems). Beyond this, anthropologists remain committed to the proposition that they cannot fully understand another culture by simply observing it; as the term *participant observation* implies, they must *experience* it as well. Thus, ethnographers spend prolonged periods living with the people they study, sharing their joys and suffering their deprivations, including sickness and, sometimes, premature death. They are not so naive as to believe they can be, or even should be, dispassionate about the people whose trials and tribulations they share. Nor do they believe that they can ever know the culture the way a native does. Nor are anthropologists so self-deceived as to believe they can avoid dealing with the moral and political consequences of their findings. Indeed, anthropology has a long tradition of advocacy for the rights of indigenous peoples, a topic we shall return to in later chapters of this textbook.

The humanistic side of anthropology is evident as well in its emphasis on qualitative (detailed description) as opposed to quantitative (numerical measurement) research. This does not mean anthropologists are unaware of the value of quantification and statistical procedures; they do make use of them for various purposes. However, reducing people and what they do to numbers has a definite "dehumanizing" effect (it is easier to ignore the concerns of "impersonal" numbers than it is those of flesh-and-blood human beings) and ignores important issues not susceptible to numeration. For all these reasons, anthropologists tend to place less emphasis on numerical data than do other social scientists.

Given anthropologists' intense encounters with other groups of people, it should come as no surprise that they have amassed as much information about human frailty and nobility—stuff of the humanities—as any other discipline. Small wonder, too, that above all they intend to avoid allowing a "coldly" scientific approach to blind them to the fact that human groups are made up of individuals with a rich assortment of emotions and aspirations that demand respect. Anthropology sometimes has been called the most human of the sciences, a designation anthropologists embrace with considerable pride.

▲▽▲▽▲▽▲▽▲▽▲▽▲▽▲▽▲▽▲▽▲▽▲▽▲▽▲

ANTHROPOLOGY'S CONTRIBUTIONS TO OTHER DISCIPLINES

Students often ask, "Why should we study anthropology?" To answer this question we need to examine the personal, academic, and professional benefits of an education in anthropology. For those of us who have ever wondered why people behave the way they do, believe in what they do, or look the way they do, anthropology can help answer these questions. Anthropologists can teach us about the different ways in which people organize their lives and can go a long way toward explaining human behaviour.

Regardless of their field of study, students can benefit academically from an anthropological education. For example, from an economic anthropology course, a student can learn about the myriad ways that people around the world organize their production, exchange, and consumption activities and will come to understand that there are many meanings associated with economic activities. Anthropology also contributes to disciplines outside the social sciences; archaeological and ethnohistorical research has much to offer history and geology, and biological anthropology both benefits from and contributes to the science of biology. Thus, any student who studies anthropology, even briefly, receives a broader, more well-rounded education.

For those students who decide to major in anthropology, there are numerous areas of specialization that prepare them for future careers. For example, urban anthropologists often work in areas of policy, planning, and development in urban settings. Medical anthropologists work alongside other health specialists to identify the beliefs, attitudes, and behaviours that affect health and illness.

Professionally, anthropologists are not the only scholars who study people, nor are their findings set apart from those of psychologists, economists, sociologists, or biologists; rather, these disciplines (and many more) contribute to the common goal of understanding humanity, and anthropologists gladly offer their findings for the benefit of these other disciplines. Anthropologists do not expect, for example, to know as much about the structure of the human eye as anatomists or as much about the perception of colour as psychologists. As synthesizers, however, they are better prepared than other scientists to understand how these subjects relate to colour-naming behaviour in different human groups. As a case in point, the Coast Salish languages of southwestern British Columbia do not have separate words to distinguish blue from green, while Russian has a separate word for pale blue and another word for dark blue.[16] Since anthropologists look for broad explanations of human behaviour without limiting themselves to any single social or biological aspect of that behaviour, they can acquire an especially extensive overview of humans as complex biological and cultural organisms.

Researchers outside the field of anthropology are beginning to recognize the value of anthropology's unique methodology—that of immersion in a culture. Participant observation provides a research model for other disciplines, such as education, geography, and psychology. Thus, anthropology enhances the research and experience of

other disciplines, disciplines that would be diminished if not for the knowledge and research methods of anthropology.

QUESTIONS OF ETHICS

The kinds of research anthropologists carry out and the settings they work within raise a number of important questions concerning ethics. Who will make use of the findings of anthropologists, and for what purposes? In the case of a militant minority, for example, will others use anthropological data to suppress that minority? And what of traditional communities around the world? Who is to decide what changes should, or should not, be introduced for community "betterment"? By whose definition is it betterment—the community's, some remote national government's, or an international agency's (e.g., the World Bank)? Then consider the problem of privacy. Anthropologists deal with people's private and sensitive matters, including things that people would not care to have generally known about them. How do anthropologists write about such matters and at the same time protect the privacy of informants? Not surprisingly, because of these and other questions, anthropologists must carefully consider the subject of ethics.

Anthropologists recognize they have obligations to three sets of people: those they study, those who fund the research, and those in the profession who expect them to publish their findings so that they may be used to further knowledge. Because fieldwork requires a relationship of trust between fieldworker and informants, the anthropologist's first responsibility clearly is to his or her informants and their people. Everything possible must be done to protect their physical, social, and psychological welfare and to honour their dignity and privacy. In other words, *do no harm*. Although early ethnographers often provided the kind of information colonial administrators needed to control the "natives," they have long since ceased to be comfortable with such work and regard as basic a people's right to their own culture.

As an example of how the sometimes conflicting interests of the people studied, of the

---

[16]For further discussion see Bonvillain, N. (2000). *Language, culture, and communication: The meaning of messages* (3rd ed.). Upper Saddle River, NJ: Prentice Hall.

profession, and of funding agencies may be dealt with, we turn to a 1981 interview given by Laura Nader:

> In the case of the Zapotec, I was dealing with very sensitive materials about law and disputes and conflicts and so forth. And I was very sensitive about how much of that to report while people were still alive and while things might still be warm, so I waited on that. . . . I feel comfortable now releasing that information. With regard to a funder in that case, it was the Mexican government, and I feel that I have written enough to have paid off the [money] which they gave me to support that work for a year. So, I've not felt particularly strained for my Zapotec work in those three areas. On energy research that I've done, it's been another story. Much of what people wanted me to do energy research for was . . . to tell people in decision-making positions about American consumers in such a way that they could be manipulated better, and I didn't want to do that. So what I said was I would be willing to study a vertical slice. That is, I would never study the consumer without studying the producer. And once you take a vertical slice like that, then it's fair because you're telling the consumer about the producer and the producer about the consumer. But just to do a study of consumers for producers, I think I would feel uncomfortable.[17]

ture, language retention, sovereignty, immigration policies, First Nations land claims, and Canada's place in the international community. Anthropology can lend its unique perspective to these ongoing issues.

Equally important is anthropology's role as an educator—providing the general public with the knowledge and understandings of anthropology. Canada is a multicultural society, composed of numerous aboriginal peoples and immigrants from all corners of the world. As citizens of Canada and the global community, it is important for us to learn to live in peace and harmony, to avoid misunderstandings and condemnations based on ignorance, fear, and an unwillingness to accept different ways of living. Just as Franz Boas exhorted his colleagues to recognize the uniqueness and validity of every culture, contemporary anthropologists must pass along this ideology to the people of their own societies. What anthropology has to contribute to contemporary life, then, is a conceptual framework for promoting understanding, acceptance, and appreciation of the incredible cultural diversity of our global community. In other words, sociocultural anthropology is in an excellent position to promote global cultural awareness. Anthropology is also an examination of our identity—who we are and where we come from. Perhaps, in the end, our satisfaction with our own identities comes from this fundamental understanding. These are nothing less than basic skills for survival in the modern world.

▲▽▲▽▲▽▲▽▲▽▲▽▲▽▲▽▲▽▲▽▲▽▲▽▲▽▲▽▲

RELEVANCE OF ANTHROPOLOGY IN CONTEMPORARY LIFE

Like all disciplines, anthropology is increasingly called upon to justify its existence and to demonstrate its relevance to contemporary life. Anthropologists attempt to link the exotic nature of anthropological research to the everyday lives of people—to the issues that confront us and challenge our identity and well-being. For instance, Canadians continue to grapple with complex issues such as defining Canadian cul-

Failure to respect the needs of diverse cultural groups can lead to serious consequences, such as the armed confrontation on the Kahnesatake Reserve in Oka, Quebec, in September 1990. Shown here is a Canadian soldier and a member of the Mohawk Warriors society, coming face to face in a tense standoff.

---

[17]Nader, L. (1981, December). [Interview for Coast Telecourses, Inc.]. Los Angeles.

CHAPTER SUMMARY

Throughout human history, people have needed to know who they are, where they came from, and why they behave as they do. Traditionally, myths and legends provided the answers to these questions. Anthropology, as it has emerged over the past 200 years, offers another approach to answering the questions people ask about themselves.

Anthropology is the study of humankind. In employing a scientific approach, anthropologists seek to produce a reasonably objective understanding of both human diversity and those aspects all humans have in common. The five major branches of anthropology are biological anthropology, archaeology, linguistic anthropology, applied anthropology, and sociocultural anthropology. Biological anthropology focuses on humans as biological organisms. Biological anthropologists trace the evolutionary development of the human animal and study biological variation within the species today. Archaeologists study material objects usually from past cultures in order to explain human behaviour. Linguistic anthropologists, who study human languages, may deal with descriptions of languages, with histories of languages, or with how languages are used in particular social settings. Applied anthropologists put to practical use the knowledge and expertise of anthropology. Sociocultural anthropologists study humans in terms of their cultures in the present and recent past. Ethnographers go into the field to observe and describe human behaviour; ethnologists do comparative studies of particular facets of a culture, such as religion or economic practices; and ethnohistorians study cultures of the recent past using oral histories and written accounts left by explorers, missionaries, and traders.

Anthropology is unique among the social and natural sciences in that it is concerned with formulating explanations of human diversity based on a study of all aspects of human biology and behaviour in all known societies, rather than in European and North American societies alone. Thus anthropologists have devoted much attention to the study of non-Western peoples.

Anthropologists are concerned with the objective and systematic study of humankind. The data sociocultural anthropologists use may be from a single society or from numerous societies that are then compared.

In anthropology, the humanities and sciences come together into a genuinely human science. Anthropology's link with the humanities can be seen in its concern with people's values, languages, arts, and literature, but above all in its attempt to convey the experience of living as other people do. As both a science and a humanity, anthropology has essential skills to offer the modern world, where understanding the other people with whom we share the globe has become a matter of survival.

QUESTIONS FOR CRITICAL THOUGHT

1. Think about movies you have seen and novels you have read that feature anthropologists as characters. How are they portrayed? How do these characterizations contrast with the discipline as presented in this chapter?

2. Respond to the question, "What good is anthropology, anyway?"

3. Identify your future career. How might anthropological knowledge help you understand and interact with people in your chosen career (e.g., teacher, doctor, police officer, bank teller, lawyer)?

4. If an anthropologist chose your community, college dorm, or organization to study, what information would you willingly share? What information would you be more hesitant to share? How would the anthropologist's presence interfere with your everyday life?

5. Think about how Richard Lee's Christmas gift was received by the Ju/'hoansi. How would you or your family react if you received an extremely expensive or very personal gift from an acquaintance? Have you ever received an unexpected Christmas gift and not been able to, or wanted to, give one in return? How would you handle such a situation?

6. In light of the September 11, 2001, terrorist attacks on New York City and Washington, D.C., many people are unsure of how to deal with the new reality of our Western world. How might anthropology help ease tensions, fears, and misunderstandings that can arise between cultural groups? What future roles do you see for anthropology in our global community?

INTERNET RESOURCES

Anthropology and Ethics
http://library.lib.binghamton.edu/subjects/
anthro/ethics.html

This site provides numerous links to anthropology associations, including the Canadian Archaeology Association. In each link the associations present their codes of professional ethics and address issues such as professional responsibility.

Careers in Anthropology
http://www.iupui.edu/it/anthropo/careers.htm

Answers questions on what students can do with a degree in anthropology, and provides links to several related pages. This site is a valuable resource for students who are thinking about majoring in anthropology or who will soon graduate with an anthropology degree.

About Anthropology
http://www.anthropology.about.com/mlibrary
.htm

This site is an excellent general source for studying anthropology, offering information on a wide range of topics, with links to related sites.

Field School Opportunities
http://www.aaanet.org/ar/fs/fschool.htm

Provides links to field school opportunities throughout the world.

Anthropologists at Work
http://anthap.oakland.edu/~dow/napafaq.htm

This site responds to students' questions about anthropology careers and the type of work anthropologists do, and provides some excellent practical advice for newly graduated students.

Tel Dor
http://www.sas.upenn.edu/~ekondrat/Dor.html

An interesting website featuring Tel Dor, an ancient city in Israel. Visit the site to learn about Dor's history and the archaeology of the region.

See beautiful photographs and maps of the site. Learn how archaeologists conduct a huge, multi-year excavation.

Forensic Anthropology
http://medstat.med.utah.edu/kw/osteo/index2
.html

This website provides links to newsworthy discoveries in forensic anthropology, for example, "More remains uncovered from Confederate submarine."

Franz Boas 1858–1942
http://www.mnsu.edu/emuseum/information/
biography/abcde/boas_franz.html

A small site featuring the life of Franz Boas, perhaps the most famous North American anthropologist. Also provides links to other famous anthropologists: Louis Henry Morgan and Edward Tylor.

Dancing, Language, and Racism—The Passions of Franz Boas
http://www.utexas.edu/ftp/courses/wilson/
ant304/biography/arybios97/airaudibio.html

An extensive description of Franz Boas's life and career, including discussion of his influence on Canadian anthropology.

What Is Anthropology?
http://www.louisville.edu/a-s/anthro/whatis.htm

A fairly comprehensive explanation of anthropology and its subdisciplines.

Ju'hoansi
http://www.ling.ohio-state.edu/~amiller

An audio example of Ju'hoansi speech.

SUGGESTED READINGS

Bonvillain, N. (1998). *Women and men: Cultural constructs of gender* (2nd ed.). Upper Saddle River, NJ: Prentice Hall.

This book presents a comprehensive examination of gender notes from an ethnographic and historical perspective. Some topics considered are gender and the body, gender and religion, and gender roles within several cultural groups discussed in this textbook (e.g., Ju/'hoansi, Inuit, Yanomamo).

Cole, S. (2000). Reflections on anthropology in Canada. *Anthropologica, 42,* (2), 23–30.

A review of current trends in anthropology in Canada, including the persistence of psychological anthropology and the importance of political economy, gender, and changing relationships with First Nations people.

DeVita, P.R. (Ed.). (1992). *The naked anthropologist: Tales from around the world.* Belmont, CA: Wadsworth.

This collection of personal accounts from anthropologists teaches us about the trials and tribulations, as well as the joys, of ethnographic fieldwork.

Lett, J. (1987). *The human enterprise: A critical introduction to anthropological theory.* Boulder, CO: Westview.

Part 1 examines the philosophical foundations of anthropological theory, paying special attention to the nature of scientific inquiry and the mechanisms of scientific progress. Part 2 deals with the nature of social science as well as the particular features of anthropology.

Peacock, J.L. (1986). *The anthropological lens: Harsh light, soft focus.* New York: Cambridge University Press.

This lively and innovative book manages to give readers a good understanding of the diversity of activities anthropologists undertake while identifying the unifying themes that hold the discipline together.

Ruggiero, V.R. (2001). *Thinking critically about ethical issues* (5th ed.). Mountain View, CA: Mayfield.

A refreshing look at ethical issues from a practical or applied stance rather than a theoretical perspective. Each chapter ends with a collection of ethical or moral questions relevant to anthropologists and the general public.

Spradley, J.P. (1970). *The ethnographic interview.* New York: Holt, Rinehart and Winston.

Although somewhat dated, this book contains one of the best available discussions on the nature and value of ethnographic research. The bulk of the book is devoted to a step-by-step, easy-to-understand account of how to conduct ethnographic research with the assistance of "informants." Numerous examples drawn from the author's own research in such diverse settings as skid row, courtrooms, and bars make for interesting reading. A companion volume, *Participant Observation,* also is highly recommended.

CNN TODAY VIDEOS

Ancient Pueblos (CNN Cultural Anthropology, vol. 3, 4:24)
This segment looks at ancient sites of the ancestors of modern-day Pueblo Indians.

Life on the Edge: The Town of Churchill (CNN Cultural Anthropology, vol. 3, 5:00)
Seventeenth-century English explorers founded the town of Churchill on Hudson Bay. The town, mainly inhabited by native peoples, is enjoying new prosperity thanks to a large influx of tourists and a growing appreciation of native arts and crafts.

China's Last Remaining Shamans (CNN Cultural Anthropology, vol. 3, 2:44)
Traditional languages and customs of China's many ethnic minorities were virtually wiped out during the Cultural Revolution of the 1960s. Today the Chinese government is attempting to preserve the traditions of some of its ethnic minorities.

Chapter 2
The Nature of Culture

The importance of culture is illustrated in this picture of people gathering together at a Chinese New Year's parade in Vancouver. Here, the sharing of song, dance, and traditional costumes celebrates Chinese culture and symbolizes the pluralistic nature of Canadian society.

Chapter Preview

1. What Is Culture?

Culture consists of the abstract values, beliefs, and perceptions of the world that lie behind people's behaviour and that are reflected by their behaviour. These elements are shared by members of a cultural group, and when they are acted upon, produce behaviour that is intelligible to other members of that culture. Culture is learned largely through the medium of language, rather than inherited biologically. The parts of a culture function as an integrated whole.

2. How Is Culture Studied?

Anthropologists learn about a culture by observing, experiencing, and talking about it with those who live by its rules. Through careful observation and discussion with informants who are particularly knowledgeable in the ways of their culture, and by participating in daily activities, the anthropologist abstracts a set of rules to explain how people behave in a particular culture. No one culture is better than another, and each must be studied on its own terms in order to understand the reasons for certain behaviour.

3. Why Do Cultures Exist?

To survive, a culture must satisfy the basic needs of its members and deal with problems and matters that concern these members, it must provide for its own continuity, and it must furnish an orderly existence. In doing so, a culture must strike a balance between the self-interests of individuals and the needs of society as a whole. And, finally, a culture must have the capacity to change so it can adapt to new circumstances or to altered perceptions of existing circumstances.

CHAPTER OUTLINE

The Concept of Culture

Characteristics of Culture

Anthropology Applied: The James Bay Cree and
    Northern Quebec Agreement

Gender Perspectives: The Canadian Women's
    Movement

Studying Culture in the Field

Culture and Adaptation

Original Study: The Importance of Trobriand
    Women

Culture, Society, and the Individual

Evaluation of Culture

Students of anthropology are bound to find themselves studying a seemingly endless variety of human cultures, each with its own distinctive system of politics, social organization, economics, and religion. Yet for all this variation, these cultures have one thing in common: Each is a collection of people cooperating to ensure their collective survival and well-being. For this to work, some degree of predictable behaviour is required of each individual within the culture, for group living and cooperation are impossible unless individuals know how others are likely to behave in any given situation. For humans, it is culture that sets the limits of behaviour and guides it along predictable paths.

THE CONCEPT OF CULTURE

Anthropologists first introduced the concept of **culture** near the end of the 19th century. In 1871 British anthropologist Sir Edward Burnett Tylor defined culture as "that complex whole which includes knowledge, belief, art, law, morals, custom and any other capabilities and habits acquired by man as a member of society." Since Tylor's time, definitions of culture have proliferated; by the early 1950s North American anthropologists A.L. Kroeber and Clyde Kluckhohn were able to collect more than a hundred definitions of culture from the literature. Recent definitions tend to distinguish between actual behaviour on the one hand and the abstract values, beliefs, and perceptions of the world that lie behind that behaviour on the other. To put it another way, culture is not only observable behaviour but the shared ideals, values, and beliefs people use to interpret experience and generate behaviour and that are reflected by their behaviour.

CHARACTERISTICS OF CULTURE

Although each culture is unique, anthropologists also recognize that all cultures display remark-

able similarities in fulfilling the needs of their members. Through the comparative study of many different cultures, anthropologists have arrived at an understanding of the basic characteristics all cultures share. A careful study of these characteristics helps us to see the importance and the function of culture itself.

Culture Is Shared

As stated earlier, culture is a set of shared ideals, values, and standards of behaviour; it is the common denominator that makes the actions of individuals intelligible to other members of the same culture. They share a cultural identity, separate from other cultures. Because they share a common culture, people can predict how others are most likely to behave in a given circumstance and can react accordingly. When people move to another country, they lose the ability to predict other people's behaviour, creating a sense of uncertainty. The shock, confusion, and insecurity that many people feel when living in an unfamiliar culture is known as **culture shock**. Anthropologists in the field may experience bouts of culture shock until they become familiar with the customs and language and learn the appropriate behaviour in the new culture. Anthropologists tend to be highly motivated to learn the new culture as quickly as possible. The surprise comes when they must put aside all they have learned and readjust to their home culture.

Culture shock especially affects people immigrating to a multicultural country like Canada. New arrivals must deal with a confusing array of conflicting social, cultural, and religious values. This is particularly true when considering women's roles in contemporary Canadian society. Immigrants from more traditional cultures may have difficulty accepting that women in Canada have considerable control over their lives. A recent case in North York, Ontario, illustrates this point: A Sri Lankan Tamil man abducted a 16-year-old girl and held her captive for four days, hoping to shame her family into accepting

---

Culture.   The shared ideals, values, and beliefs that people use to interpret experience and generate behaviour and that are reflected by their behaviour. **> Culture shock.**   The shock, confusion, and insecurity that many people feel when living in an unfamiliar culture.

him as a suitor.[1] In Sri Lanka arranged marriages are the norm, but when Tamil families immigrate to Canada, the young people want to date, choose their own spouses, and be like their fellow students, causing clashes with the older, more conservative members of the Tamil community. In this case, traditional members of the Tamil community felt that since the young girl had spent time alone with the man, she should marry him.

From a Canadian perspective, culture differs from society. A **society** is a group of people who live in the same geographical region, speak the same language, and are interdependent to a certain extent. A society may, and often does, contain more than one cultural group. In Canada we have many distinct cultures: First Nations peoples, Inuit, Métis, and English- and French-speaking Canadians, including immigrants from around the world. The way people within a society depend on one another can be seen in such things as their economic systems and their family relationships; moreover, members of a society are held together by a sense of common identity. The relationships that hold a society together are known as its **social structure.**

---

[1]Culture shock: Immigrants come to Canada with the hope of improving life for themselves and future generations but fitting into an entirely new culture isn't easy. (1998, January). *Canada and the World Backgrounder, 63* (4), 20–24.

Although a culture is shared by its members, we must realize that it is not entirely uniform. For one thing, no member has the exact same version of his or her culture as another. Beyond such individual variation, however, some further variation is bound to occur within a given culture. At the very least, differences between the roles of men and women exist. These differences stem from the fact that women give birth, men do not, and male and female anatomy and physiology differ in obvious ways. Every culture gives meaning to these differences by explaining them and specifying what to do about them. Every culture, as well, specifies how the two kinds of people resulting from the differences should relate to one another and to the world at large. Like culture, we learn these gender roles from birth. Since each culture teaches gender roles in its own way, tremendous variation occurs from one culture to another even as variation occurs within each culture.

In addition to cultural variation along lines of gender, cultural variation related to age occurs. In any society, children are not expected to behave as adults, and the reverse is equally true. Other examples of cultural variation include ethnicity, occupation, social class, sexual orientation, geographical distribution (e.g., eastern Canada–western Canada, rural–urban), physical or mental challenges, and special-interest groups such as skateboarders. Even within these smaller groups,

In all human cultures, children's play is used both consciously and unconsciously to teach gender roles.

Society. A group of people who live in the same region, speak the same language, and are interdependent. **> Social structure.** The relationships of groups within a society that hold it together.

Anthropology **Applied**

The James Bay Cree and Northern Quebec Agreement

In a pluralistic country such as Canada, where a number of distinct cultural groups exist side by side, members of these groups may have difficulty understanding each other's needs and aspirations. For this reason anthropologists, with their special understanding of culture, are frequently employed as go-betweens in situations requiring interaction between peoples of differing cultural traditions. In Canada, this often means using their knowledge and unique perspectives to serve as advocates for aboriginal rights.

For example, in 1972 when the James Bay Cree launched their opposition to construction of a hydroelectric project on their traditional hunting lands, the Grand Council called on anthropologist Harvey A. Feit, who, as a graduate student in 1968, had studied the James Bay Cree ecological practices. The Cree were able to use Feit's doctoral research in their court case against the Quebec and federal governments.

Twelve thousand James Bay Cree live east and southeast of James Bay, in subarctic northern Quebec. The people fish and hunt small game, geese, moose, and beaver on approximately 380 000 square kilometres of land. They have always maintained a special relationship with the land and its resources; their subsistence strategy revolves around a system of hunting-territory stewardships. The Cree strive to maintain a balance between resources and hunting. This balance was threatened in the 1970s when the Quebec government began building a massive hydroelectric project on the Cree hunting lands without consulting the people.

Feit served as an adviser to the James Bay Cree from 1973 to 1978. With his assistance, the Cree opposition to large-scale exploitation of natural resources on their land eventually led to the negotiation of the first modern treaty and one of the most comprehensive land claims settlements in Canada: the James Bay Cree and Northern Quebec Agreement. This settlement entitles the Cree to hunting rights; authority over education, health, social services, policing, housing, and municipal affairs; guaranteed income programs; and a voice in future development projects and environmental management. This successful negotiation illustrates the power aboriginal groups can wield against centralized governments and corporations when they utilize resources such as an anthropologist-advocate.

Sources:

Feit, H.A. (1995). Hunting and the quest for power: The James Bay Cree and Whitemen in the 20th century. In R.B. Morrison & C.R. Wilson (Eds.), *Native peoples: The Canadian experience* (2nd ed.). Toronto: McClelland & Stewart.

Feit, H.A. (1999). James Bay Cree. In R.B. Lee & R. Daly (Eds.), *The Cambridge encyclopedia of hunters and gatherers*. Cambridge, UK: Cambridge University Press.

which may appear, at least on the surface, culturally uniform, there are many differences. A case in point is the Chinese Buddhist community in Toronto, which is composed of immigrants from Hong Kong, mainland China, and Taiwan and refugees from Southeast Asia. Although they are all Chinese Buddhists, they come from different countries and thus exhibit cultural and linguistic diversity, as well as a wide range of socio-economic statuses.

When there are such groups within a society, each functioning by its own distinctive standards of behaviour while at the same time sharing some common standards, we speak of **subcultures**. The word *subculture,* it should be noted, carries no connotation of lesser status relative to the word *cultural.*

Hutterites are an example of an ethnic subculture found within Canada and the United States. Hutterites are one of four surviving groups (the others being the Amish, Mennonites, and Brethren) descended from 16th-century Anabaptists in Austria and Moravia. They fled Europe to escape religious persecution. Today more than 35 000[2] Hutterites live in 400 communities spread across Montana, Washington, the Dakotas, Minnesota, and the western Canadian provinces: Manitoba, Saskatchewan, Alberta, and British Columbia. The Hutteries branched into three groups named after their leaders: Schmiedeleut, Dariusleut, and Lehrerleut.

The Hutterites are a pacifist, agrarian people, and their lives revolve around deep religious beliefs. They value simplicity, hard work, and a close-knit communal lifestyle, mingling as little as possible with non-Hutterites. They dress in a distinctive modest garb and, even today, own little personal property. The colonists live a communal lifestyle, eating in the common dining hall and sharing laundry facilities, although each family has its own private apartment. Unlike the Amish or Mennonites, Hutterites do not shun modern conveniences, such as tractors and combines, appliances, and even computers.

Their children attend school within their communities, taught by Hutterite teachers committed to Hutterite values. In recent years, more emphasis has been placed on higher education, with some children completing grade 12, some taking vocational training, and still others attending university, especially teacher-training programs.

Hutterite colonies are stratified, based on gender and age. Men hold positions of authority in the colony; women cannot sit on the council or vote in colony matters, although they can express their opinions to their husbands. Children and young people are highly valued in Hutterite colonies, but they do not have any official say in the running of the colony until they are baptized in their early to mid-20s.

Although Hutterite nonconformity to many of the standards of Canadian society, such as choosing to live in self-sufficient, closed communities, has caused occasional misunderstandings with their neighbours, most informed people recognize that Hutterites do contribute to Canadian society—they purchase farm equipment; visit dentists, doctors, and optometrists and use banks in nearby urban centres; buy household appliances and goods; sell turkeys, chickens, hogs, and cattle to markets; and offer services such as repairing equipment in nearby communities. In today's multicultural Canadian society, Hutterites are accepted and respected for their successful agricultural enterprise. For the most part, the Hutterite subculture lives in peace, isolated from and yet a part of Canadian society.

The experience of the Hutterites is one example of the way a subculture may fit within the larger society. Different as they are, Hutterites actually practise many of the values that citizens of Canada respect in the abstract: thrift, hard work, independence, and a close family life. The degree of tolerance accorded to them is also due in part to the fact that Hutterites descend from white-skinned Europeans. Canadian aboriginal groups were treated very differently by Europeans, who came to North America as conquerors and who defined aboriginal values as "savage." Europeans and their descendants in what is now Canada generally accepted the

---

[2]Together they stay a world apart (1998). *Smithsonian Magazine,* 29 (8).

Subculture. A group of people within a larger society who have distinctive standards and patterns of behaviour.

notion that aboriginal cultures would gradually assimilate into Euro-Canadian culture. Despite assimilation programs, such as residential schools, just the opposite has happened: First Nations, Métis, and Inuit cultures continue to flourish as distinct entities, even as they take their place in Canadian society.

The Acadians of New Brunswick and Nova Scotia are another example of a subculture that has sought a new life in Canada, and despite serious political and economic challenges they have managed to retain their language, customs, and beliefs for centuries. The Acadians are descendants of approximately 100 French families who settled on the banks of the Bay of Fundy in the 17th century.[3] They were fishers and farmers with a strong sense of community and independence, living peaceful, prosperous lives and raising large families.

In 1755 the British government demanded that the Acadians sign an oath of allegiance to the Crown. Those who refused (about 8000 people) were deported to New England, the American colonies, and Europe. This expulsion had a dramatic effect on the Acadian sense of security and community; it also had a lasting effect on their economic well-being. Even though the Acadians were allowed to return to Canada in 1764, they found their fertile lands in the hands of new settlers. The Acadians were forced into small settlements scattered along the remote coastal regions, thus breaking up their tight-knit communities.

Economic problems are the greatest threat to Acadian solidarity and cultural integrity in the 21st century. They live on poor farming land, their fishing grounds are nearly depleted, and the region has little economic or industrial development. Each year more young Acadians are forced to leave their communities in search of employment in other parts of Canada. Consequently, the Acadian subculture and way of life is once more in jeopardy, this time from economic rather than political causes.

Implicit in the discussion thus far is the fact that subcultures may develop in different ways. On the one hand, the Hutterite subculture emerged as the product of the way they have communicated and interacted in pursuit of their common goals within the wider society, and the Acadians, although still quite distinct, have undergone some assimilation owing to economic realities that have forced many to leave their communities. On the other hand, aboriginal subcultures are the result of once independent cultures having been forcibly brought under the control of the Canadian federal government. Although all aboriginal cultures have undergone change as a result, they have remained different enough from Canadian immigrant subcultures to be considered distinct cultures as opposed to subcultures. In this sense, *culture* and *subculture* represent opposite ends of a continuum, with no clear dividing line in the "grey area" between.

Sometimes a subculture appears to operate outside mainstream society, as in the case of punk subcultures. Young people, wearing unique clothing, hairstyles, and various body piercings,

This member of the punk subculture is proclaiming her unique identity through her distinctive clothing, makeup, and hairstyle.

[3]The Francophone Connection. (2002). *The Acadians of Nova Scotia*. Retrieved August 13, 2003, from the World Wide Web: http://www.francophonie.gc.ca/communit/ne_shtml.

join punk subcultures because of a feeling of alienation from mainstream adolescent culture and a need to be part of a meaningful group outside the norm. Punk subcultures tend to be male dominated; however, Dr. Lauraine Leblanc of McGill University refutes the male-centred view that females are passive participants in punk subcultures. Rather, she suggests that by joining punk groups, females are resisting the gender norms of mainstream society. Punk subcultures offer young women a place in the world, a place where they do not have to conform to typical gender roles and take on a "normal" gender identity, and where they can assert their independence and individuality.[4]

This examination of culture and subculture brings to light the pluralistic nature of Canadian society. **Pluralistic societies** contain several distinct cultures and subcultures. Although we define subculture as any group of people with a set of standards and behaviour distinct from the larger society, we are usually referring to ethnic subcultures when we say Canada is a pluralistic society. Canada is a cultural mosaic of these ethnic subcultures, as are most societies today (see Figure 2.1). For well over a century, people have been coming to Canada from virtually every corner of the world. These people have brought their ideals, beliefs, languages, and cultural customs and traditions to their new home. And although these traditional cultures have changed over time, today's Canadian identity owes much of its flavour to these intrepid immigrants.

The pluralistic nature of Canadian society is not without its own set of problems. Members of one cultural group may have difficulty understanding the needs and concerns of another. The separatist movement in Quebec is a case in point. French Canadians have always feared losing their language and culture and becoming assimilated into English Canada. These fears have created a strong Quebec nationalism and a vocal movement to maintain independence from the rest of Canada. French-Canadian alienation has led to

FIGURE 2.1

Shown here are a few of the ethnic groups of the Russian Federation. Contrary to popular belief, the ethnic conflicts that have broken out since the collapse of the Soviet Union stem not from the supposedly conflictive nature of ethnicity but from Stalin's policy of emphasizing ethnicity while preventing its expression and forcibly removing populations from their homelands to new localities.

two Quebec referendums on the question of separation from Canada: one in 1980 and the most recent in 1995, when separatism was narrowly defeated. Despite repeated attempts on both sides to develop a symbiotic relationship, the future of Quebec in Canada remains unclear.

However, most subcultures within Canadian society have found ways to adapt to the pluralistic nature of Canada. The Japanese, Tibetan, Vietnamese, Cambodian, and Chinese Buddhist communities in Toronto have relied on their religious institutions for support while adjusting to Canadian life. They have maintained many of their traditional ways, yet they have also responded to their young people's call for accommodation to Canadian society. For example, the Japanese Jodo Shinshu sect, one of the oldest Buddhist groups in Canada, has dealt with the issue of language by conducting services in English and Japanese.[5] Today, most Buddhist

---

[4]Rains, P. (2000). Review of *Pretty in punk: Girls' resistance in a boys' subculture,* by L. Leblanc. *The Canadian Review of Sociology and Anthropology, 37* (ii), 113.

[5]McLellan, J. (2002). *Many petals of the lotus: Five Asian Buddhist communities in Toronto.* Toronto: University of Toronto Press.

Pluralistic societies.   Societies that contain several distinct cultures and subcultures.

Gender **Perspectives**

The Canadian Women's Movement

Never doubt that a small group of thoughtful, committed citizens can change the world. Indeed, it's the only thing that ever has.

– Margaret Mead

The 150-year history of the women's movement in Canada, and indeed, North America, has been filled with small gains, disheartening setbacks, and far-reaching changes. Although the women's movement in Canada began when religious organizations attempted to improve the lot of women domestically (e.g., prohibition of alcohol to reduce abusive situations), eventually women realized they had little real power or influence if they could not vote. The suffragette movement set in motion years of demonstrations and petitions to gain women the right to vote, and despite misconceptions, outrage, and ridicule, in 1918 Canadian women who owned property were given the right to vote in federal elections.

In Canada, the Famous Five—Emily Murphy, Louise McKinney, Irene Parlby, Nellie McClung, and Henrietta Muir Edwards—fought to have Canadian women legally declared "persons." When all other avenues failed, they took their fight to the British Privy Council, which, in 1929, declared women to be persons under the law and eligible to serve in the senate.

During World War II, many women entered the workforce to replace men who were fighting in the war. This was a major step forward for women; they proved to themselves and to others that they could work outside the home and still be good mothers and wives. By the end of the war all Canadian provinces, except Quebec and Newfoundland, had granted women the right to vote provincially and to hold public office.

In the 1950s, despite a resurgence of "traditional" values, the number of women working outside the home continued to rise. Following close on the heels of the African–American civil rights movement, the second wave of feminism in the 1960s and 1970s demanded reproductive and sexual freedom and an end to discrimination and harass-

ment in the workplace. In the early 1980s, gender discrimination was included in the Canadian Charter of Rights and Freedoms, and in the 1990s gender persecution was added to the Canadian Immigration Act as a valid reason for a woman from another country to claim refugee status in Canada.

At the end of the 20th century, the women's movement suffered some predictable setbacks. Young women who had never experienced the restrictions of their mothers and grandmothers, who never had to fight for the right to attend university, work at well-paying, satisfying careers, or choose whether or not to have children, have turned their backs on the women's movement, afraid to acknowledge their feminism for fear of being labelled radical feminists, lesbians, or male-bashers. They ignored seven generations of women and men who fought for the everyday rights and freedoms they now took for granted. Today, it is difficult to envision a time when adult women could not vote, hold a credit card in their name, or

The struggle for women's rights is far from over. In 1996 over a thousand women and men participated in the International Women's Day March at the University of Toronto.

take out a bank loan without a male co-signer, when husbands could legally imprison or beat their wives, and when women were not allowed to enter professions such as medicine. Fortunately, concerted efforts by women's groups and the inclusion of women's studies in academia have reopened the channels of communication, and today we recognize a wide range of "feminisms."

The struggle for women's rights is far from over. The issues of equal pay for equal work, reproductive rights, adequate daycare and maternity leave, political and religious leadership roles, and archaic laws are still with us. And although young people of the early 21st century may be rejecting the feminist label, they are embracing the ideology of gender equality. In the words of Naomi Wolf, author of *Fire with Fire,* you are a feminist if you believe women matter as much as men do and women have the right to determine their lives.

Sources:

National Women's History Project. (1998a). *Living the legacy: The women's rights movement 1848–1998.* E. Eisenber & M. Ruthsdotter. Retrieved November 25, 2000, from the World Wide Web: http://www.legacy98.org/move-hist.html.

National Women's History Project. (1998b). *The women's movement in Canada.* Retrieved November 25, 2000, from the World Wide Web: http://130.15.62.164/Projects/squeezeboxdays/newfeminism.html.

communities, although still distinct subcultures, have embraced Canadian society and willingly contribute to Canada's well-being with their beliefs in social tolerance and harmony.

Culture Is Learned

All culture is learned rather than biologically inherited, which has prompted anthropologist Ralph Linton to refer to it as humanity's "social heredity." People learn their culture by growing up with it, and the process whereby culture is transmitted from one generation to the next is called **enculturation.**

Most animals eat and drink whenever the urge arises. Humans, however, do most of their eating and drinking at certain culturally prescribed times and feel hungry as those times approach. These eating times vary from culture to culture, as does what is eaten and how it is eaten. To add complexity, food is used to do more than merely satisfy nutritional requirements. When used to celebrate rituals and religious activities, food "establishes relationships of give and take, of cooperation, of sharing, of an emotional bond that is universal."[6]

[6]Caroulis, J. (1996). Food for thought. *Pennsylvania Gazette,* 95 (3), 16.

Even in politically stable countries like Canada, pluralism presents its own challenges. In Canada, the Quebec separatist movement continues to challenge Canadian unity.

Enculturation.   The process that transmits a society's culture from one generation to the next.

Through enculturation we learn the socially appropriate way to satisfy our biologically determined needs. The biological needs of humans are the same as those of other animals: Besides food and sleep, they include shelter, safety, and sexual gratification. We must distinguish between the needs themselves, which are not learned, and the learned ways they are satisfied. Thus, a Canadian's idea of a comfortable way to sleep may vary greatly from that of a Japanese person.

Enculturation not only serves to fulfill biological needs, it also teaches us how to "fit in" and be accepted by other members of our cultural group. Any society, and Canada is no exception, possesses many enculturative forces. Take, for example, a young child entering school. From the very first day of kindergarten, a child begins learning how to act and behave appropriately—at least in an educational environment. Other enculturative forces include family, peers, religious organizations, and the media (it should be noted that not all enculturative forces are positive all of the time). The enculturation process is never complete. Old patterns of behaviour are altered to meet the changing needs of society, and new patterns are developed. Although the older generation typically passes on knowledge to the younger generation, older people can also learn from the young, especially during times of rapid change.

To return to our earlier discussion of culture shock, once an individual living in a foreign country learns the customs, beliefs, and norms of the culture, he or she will no longer experience culture shock.

Culture Is Based on Symbols

When anthropologist Leslie White observed that human behaviour originates in the use of symbols, he expressed an opinion anthropologists share. Art, religion, and money involve symbols. We are all familiar with the fervour and devotion religion can elicit from a believer. A Christian cross, an Islamic crescent, a Jewish Star of David, or any object of worship may bring to mind centuries of struggle and persecution or may stand for a whole philosophy or creed. The most important symbolic aspect of culture is language—the substitution of words for objects.

This Inukshuk is a symbol of presence, left by Inuit people as they travelled their lands.

Through language, humans are able to transmit culture from one generation to another. Language makes it possible to learn from cumulative shared experience. Without it, we could not inform others about events they were not a party to. We shall consider the important relationship between language and culture in greater detail in Chapter 4.

Culture Is Integrated

For comparison and analysis, anthropologists customarily break a culture down into many seemingly discrete parts, even though such distinctions are arbitrary. The anthropologist who examines one aspect of a culture invariably finds it necessary to examine others as well. This tendency for all aspects of a culture to function as an interrelated whole is called **integration**.

The integration of the economic, political, and social aspects of a culture can be illustrated by the Kapauku Papuans, a mountain people of

---

Integration. The tendency for all aspects of a culture to function as an interrelated whole.

western New Guinea studied in 1955 by North American anthropologist Leopold Pospisil,[7] The Kapauku economy relies on plant cultivation, along with pig breeding, hunting, and fishing. Although plant cultivation provides most of the people's food, men achieve political power and positions of legal authority through the complex business of pig breeding.

Kapauku pig breeding relies on sweet potatoes grown in garden plots. Kapauku culture defines essential gardening activities as women's work. Furthermore, pigs must be cared for by women. So, to raise many pigs, a man must have many women in the household. He accomplishes this by marrying them. Multiple wives (polygyny) are not only permitted but are highly desired by the Kapauku. For each wife, however, a man must pay a bride price, which can be expensive. Furthermore, wives have to be compensated for their care of pigs. Put simply, it takes pigs, by which wealth is measured, to get wives, which are necessary to raise pigs in the first place. Needless to say, this requires considerable entrepreneurship. It is this ability that produces leaders in Kapauku society.

The interrelatedness of the various parts of Kapauku culture is even more complex than this. For example, one condition conducive to polygyny is a surplus of adult women. In the Kapauku case, warfare is endemic, regarded as a necessary evil. By the rules of Kapauku warfare, men get killed but women do not. This system works to promote the kind of imbalance of sexes that facilitates polygyny. Polygyny also tends to work best if wives come to live in their husband's village, rather than the other way around, and this is the case among the Kapauku. Thus, the men of a village are "blood" relatives of one another. Given this, a patrilineal (descent reckoned through men) emphasis in Kapauku culture is not unexpected.

These examples by no means exhaust the interrelationships found in Kapauku culture. For example, both patrilineality and endemic warfare tend to promote male dominance, so it is not surprising to find that positions of leadership in Kapauku society are held exclusively by men, who appropriate the products of women's labour in order to play their political "games." Despite assertions to the contrary, male dominance is by no means characteristic of all human societies. Rather, as with the Kapauku, it arises only under particular circumstances that, if changed, would alter the way men and women relate to one another.

From what has been said so far, we might suppose the various parts of a culture must operate in perfect harmony at all times. The analogy would be that of a machine: all parts must be compatible and complementary or it won't run. To a degree, this is true of all cultures. A change in one part of a culture usually will affect other parts, sometimes in rather dramatic ways. This point, which we will return to later in this chapter, is particularly important today as diverse agents seek to introduce changes of all sorts into societies around the world.

While we must recognize that a degree of harmony is necessary in any properly functioning culture, we should not assume complete harmony is required. Because no two individuals experience the enculturation process in precisely the same way, no two individuals perceive their culture in exactly the same way, so some potential for change always exists in any culture. We should speak, instead, of a strain to consistency in culture. So long as the parts are reasonably consistent, a culture will operate reasonably well. If, however, that strain to consistency breaks down, a situation of cultural crisis ensues.

---

[7]Pospisil, L. (1963). *The Kapauku Papuans of west New Guinea.* New York: Holt, Rinehart and Winston.

Marius Barbeau   *(1883–1969)*

Marius Barbeau is considered a pioneer in Canadian anthropology. His contributions to early Canadian ethnography are many, but he is best known as the founder of Canadian folklore studies.

Born in Sainte-Marie de Beauce, Quebec, Barbeau earned a law degree from Laval University and then became the first French-Canadian Rhodes scholar at Oxford University, where he earned a degree in anthropology. Returning to Canada in 1911, Barbeau accepted a position at the National Museum of Canada (then known as the Geological Survey of Canada). He worked for the museum until his retirement in 1948.[1]

At the urging of Edward Sapir, Barbeau recorded and preserved the oral histories of the Huron-Wendat of Quebec, Ontario, and Oklahoma. In 1914 he met Franz Boas, who persuaded him to record French-Canadian songs, dance, artwork, and folktales. The folktales were published in the *Journal of American Folklore*. In 1916 Barbeau was finally able to satisfy his long-time interest in totem poles by studying the craft in British Columbia and Alaska. He published a monograph on the totem poles of the Upper Skeena River in 1929. Barbeau's detailed notes and papers provide a rich source of information from a linguistic, ethnographic, sociocultural, and historic perspective of the political histories and social organization of West Coast First Nations peoples (the Haida, Nootka, Kwakiutl, Tsimshian, and Gitksan) before contact with Europeans and the conditions they faced after Europeans arrived.[2]

Barbeau has been praised by contemporary First Nations for his efforts to record the voices of the people and his attempts to understand their worldview. He once said, "I'm interested in what they think, in their own happiness, in their dirge songs, in their morality, in their art, in their curing."[3] Barbeau was also an advocate for aboriginal rights. Along with Diamond Jenness, curator of the National Museum of Canada, he criticized the federal government's unwillingness to consult aboriginal peoples on policy issues.

During his illustrious career, Barbeau managed to collect and record more than 400 French-Canadian folktales, 7000 songs, and 2000 artifacts. He wrote over 1000 books and articles, and even published a novel, *The Dream of Kamalmouk,* based on his work the *Downfall of Temlaham*. In honour of his contributions to Canadian studies, Barbeau received the prestigious Prix David award, as well as honorary doctorates from the University of Montreal and Oxford, and was named a Companion of the Order of Canada.

---

[1]Canadian Museum of Civilization Corporation. (2001). *Marius Barbeau: I was a pioneer*. Retrieved August 11, 2003, from the World Wide Web: http://www.civilization .ca/academ/barbeau/baineng.html.

[2]University of Toronto. (1988). *Barbeau, Marius. Barbeau Papers: Northwest Coast Files*. Retrieved August 11, 2003, from the World Wide Web: http://www.library .utoronto.ca/robarts/microtext/collection/pages/barbpaps .html.

[3]Canadian Museum of Civilization Corporation. (2001). *1965 CBC interview with Marius Barbeau*. Retrieved August 11, 2003, from the World Wide Web: http://www.civilization.ca/academ/barbeau/banaeng.html. Originally published in 1982 in the Oracle series (no. 44) of the National Museum of Man.

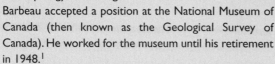

STUDYING CULTURE IN THE FIELD

Armed, now, with some understanding of what culture is, we next address this question: How does an anthropologist study culture in the field? Culture, being a set of standards, cannot itself be directly observed; only actual behaviour is observable. The anthropologist must abstract a set of standards from what is seen and heard in order to explain social behaviour, much as a linguist, from the way people speak a language, tries to determine the ways those speakers combine sounds into meaningful phrases.

To pursue this further, consider the following discussion of exogamy—marriage outside a group—among the Trobriand Islanders, as described by Bronislaw Malinowski.

Describing another culture is like trying to describe a new game. To describe basketball to someone unfamiliar with the sport would be at best a caricature of the game as Canadians know it. The problem in anthropology is how to describe another culture for an audience unfamiliar with it, so that the description is meaningful.

> If you were to inquire into the matter among the Trobrianders, you would find that . . . the natives show horror at the idea of violating the rules of exogamy and that they believe that sores, diseases, even death might follow clan incest. [But] from the viewpoint of the native libertine, *suvasova* (the breach of exogamy) is indeed a specially interesting and spicy form of erotic experience. Most of my informants would not only admit but did actually boast about having committed this offense.[8]

Malinowski himself determined that although such breaches did occasionally occur, they were much less frequent than gossip would have it. Had Malinowski relied solely on what the Trobrianders told him, his description of their culture would have been inaccurate. The same sort of discrepancy between cultural ideals and the way people really do behave can be found in any culture. Chapter 1 offered an example from contemporary North America in the Garbage Project discussion.

From these examples, it is obvious that anthropologists must be cautious if they are to provide a realistic description of a culture. To play it safe, data drawn in three different ways ought to be considered. First, the people's own understanding of the rules they share—that is, their notion of the way their society *ought* to be—must be examined. Second, the extent to which people believe they are observing those rules—that is, how they think they actually do behave—needs to be investigated. Third, the behaviour that can be directly observed should be considered. As shown in the Garbage Project discussion, the way people think they *should* behave, the way they think they *do* behave, and the way they *actually* behave may be three distinctly different versions. By carefully examining these elements, anthropologists can draw up a set of rules that may explain the acceptable behaviour within a culture.

Of course, the anthropologist is only human. As discussed in Chapter 1, it is difficult, if not impossible, for anthropologists to cast aside completely their personal feelings and biases, which have been shaped by their own culture. Yet it is important to make every effort to do just this, for otherwise anthropologists may seriously misinterpret what they see. As a case in point, consider how the male bias of the European culture anthropologist Bronislaw Malinowski came from caused him to miss important factors in his pioneering study of the Trobriand Islanders. (For further discussion of the pioneers of the development of anthropology, visit the textbook's website at http://www.cultural2e.nelson.com.)

CULTURE AND ADAPTATION

In the course of their evolution, humans, like all animals, have been continually faced with the problem of adapting to their environment. The term **adaptation** refers to a natural (rather than willful) process organisms undergo to achieve a beneficial adjustment to an available environment and the results of that process—the characteristics possessed by organisms that permit them to overcome hazards and secure the resources they need for the particular environments they live in. Humans have come to depend more and more on

---

[8]Malinowski, B. (1922). *Argonauts of the western Pacific.* New York: Dutton.

Adaptation. A process organisms undergo to achieve a beneficial adjustment to an available environment and the results of that process: characteristics that fit them to the particular conditions of the environment they are generally found in.

ORIGINAL STUDY

The Importance of Trobriand Women

Annette B. Weiner

Walking into a village at the beginning of fieldwork is entering a world without cultural guideposts. The task of learning values that others live by is never easy. The rigors of fieldwork involve listening and watching, learning a new language of speech and actions, and most of all, letting go of one's own cultural assumptions in order to understand the meanings others give to work, power, death, family, and friends. As my fieldwork in the Trobriand Islands of Papua New Guinea was no exception, I wrestled doggedly with each of these problems. Doing research in the Trobriand Islands created one additional obstacle. I was working in the footsteps of a celebrated anthropological ancestor, Bronislaw Kasper Malinowski. . . .

In 1971, before my first trip to the Trobriands, I thought I understood many things about Trobriand customs and beliefs from having read Malinowski's exhaustive writings. Once there, however, I found that I had much more to discover about what I thought I already knew. For many months I worked with these discordant realities, always conscious of Malinowski's shadow, his words, his explanations. Although I found significant differences in areas of importance, I gradually came to understand how he reached certain conclusions. The answers we both received from informants were not so dissimilar, and I could actually trace how Malinowski had analyzed what his informants told him in a way that made sense and was scientifically significant—given what anthropologists generally then recognized about such societies. Sixty years separate our fieldwork, and any comparison of our studies illustrates not so much Malinowski's mistaken interpretations but the developments in anthropological knowledge and inquiry from his time to mine.

This important point has been forgotten by those anthropologists who today argue that ethnographic writing can never be more than a kind of fictional account of an author's experiences. Although Malinowski and I were in the Trobriands at vastly different historical moments and there also are many areas in which our analyses differ, a large part of what we learned in the field was similar. From the vantage point that time gives to me, I can illustrate how our differences, even those that are major, came to be. Taken together, our two studies profoundly exemplify the scientific basis that underlies the collection of ethnographic data. Like all such data, however, whether researched in a laboratory or a village, the more we learn about a subject, the more we can refine and revise earlier assumptions. This is the way all sciences create their own historical developments. Therefore, the lack of agreement between Malinowski's ethnography and mine must not be taken as an adversarial attack against an opponent. Nor should it be read as an example of the writing of ethnography as "fiction" or "partial truths." Each of our differences can be traced historically within the discipline of anthropology.

My most significant point of departure from Malinowski's analyses was the attention I gave to women's productive work. In my original research plans, women were not the central focus of study, but on the first day I took up residence in a village I was taken by them to watch a distribution of their own wealth—bundles of banana leaves and banana fiber skirts—which they exchanged with other women in commemoration of someone who had recently died. Watching that event forced me to take women's economic

In the Trobriand Islands, women's wealth consists of skirts and banana leaves, large quantities of which must be given away on the death of a relative.

roles more seriously than I would have from reading Malinowski's studies. Although Malinowski noted the high status of Trobriand women, he attributed their importance to the fact that Trobrianders reckon descent through women, thereby giving them genealogical significance in a matrilineal society. Yet he never considered that this significance was underwritten by women's own wealth because he did not systematically investigate the women's productive activities. Although in his field notes he mentions Trobriand women making these seemingly useless banana bundles to be exchanged at a death, his published work only deals with men's wealth.

My taking seriously the importance of women's wealth not only brought women as the neglected half of society clearly into the ethnographic picture but also forced me to revise many of Malinowski's assumptions about Trobriand men. For example, Trobriand kinship as described by Malinowski has always been a subject of debate among anthropologists. For Malinowski, the basic relationships within a Trobriand family were guided by the matrilineal principle of "mother-right" and "father-love." A father was called "stranger" and had little authority over his own children. A woman's brother was the commanding figure and exercised control over his sister's sons because they were members of his matrilineage rather than their father's matrilineage.

According to Malinowski, this matrilineal drama was played out biologically by the Trobrianders' belief that a man has no role as genitor. A man's wife is thought to become pregnant when an ancestral spirit enters her body and causes conception. Even after a child is born, Malinowski reported, it is the woman's brother who presents a harvest of yams to his sister so that her child will be fed with food from its own matrilineage, rather than its father's matrilineage. In this way, Malinowski conceptualized matrilineality as an institution in which the father of a child, as a member of a different matrilineage, was excluded not only from participating in procreation but also from giving any objects of lasting value to his children, thus provisioning them only with love.

In my study of Trobriand women and men, a different configuration of matrilineal descent emerged. A Trobriand father is not a "stranger" in Malinowski's definition, nor is he a powerless figure as the third party to the relationship between a woman and her brother. The father is one of the most important persons in his child's life, and remains so even after his child grows up and marries. Even a father's procreative importance is incorporated into his child's growth and development. A Trobriand man gives his child many opportunities to gain things from his matrilineage, thereby adding to the available resources that he or she can draw upon. At the same time, this giving creates obligations on the part of a man's children toward him that last even beyond his death. Therefore, the roles that men and their children play in each other's lives are worked out through extensive cycles of exchanges, which define the strength of their relationships to each other and eventually benefit the other members of both their matrilineages. Central to these exchanges are women and their wealth.

That Malinowski never gave equal time to the women's side of things, given the deep significance of their role in societal and political life, is not surprising. Only recently have anthropologists begun to understand the importance of taking women's work seriously. In some cultures, such as the Middle East or among Australian aborigines, it is extremely difficult for ethnographers to cross the culturally bounded ritual worlds that separate women from men. In the past, however, both women and men ethnographers generally analyzed the societies they studied from a male perspective. The "women's point of view" was largely ignored in the study of gender roles, since anthropologists generally perceived women as living in the shadows of men—occupying the private rather than the public sectors of society, rearing children rather than engaging in economic or political pursuits.

Source: Weiner, A.B. (1988). *The Trobrianders of Papua New Guinea* (pp. 4–7). New York: Holt, Rinehart and Winston.

cultural adaptation. Biology has not provided them with built-in fur coats to protect them in cold climates, but it has provided them with the ability to make their own coats, build fires, and erect shelters to protect themselves against the cold. More than this, culture enables people to use a wide diversity of environments. By manipulating environments through cultural means, people have been able to move into the Arctic and the Sahara and have even set foot on the moon. Through culture the human species has secured not just its survival but its expansion as well.

This does not mean humans do everything *because* it is adaptive to a particular environment. For one, people do not just react to an environment as given; rather, they react to it as they perceive it, and different groups of people may perceive the same environment in radically different ways. They also react to things other than the environment: their own biological natures, for one, and their beliefs, attitudes, and the consequences of their own behaviour, for others. All of these present them with problems, and people maintain cultures to deal with problems or

What is adaptive at one time may not be at another. In the United States, the principal source of fruits, vegetables, and fibre is the Central Valley of California, where irrigation works have made the desert bloom. As happened in ancient Mesopotamia, evaporation concentrates salts in the water, but here pollution is made even worse by chemical fertilizers. These poisons are now accumulating in the soil and threaten to make the valley a desert in the near future.

matters that concern them. To be sure, their cultures must produce behaviour that is generally adaptive, or at least not maladaptive, but this is not the same as saying cultural practices necessarily arise because they are adaptive in a given environment. The fact is, current utility of a custom is an unreliable guide to its origin.

A further complication is the relativity of any given adaptation: What is adaptive in one context may be seriously maladaptive in another. For example, the sanitation practices of food-foraging peoples—their toilet habits and methods of garbage disposal—are appropriate in the context of low population levels and some degree of residential mobility. These same practices, however, become serious health hazards in the context of large, fully sedentary populations. Similarly, behaviour that is adaptive in the short run may be maladaptive in the long run. For example, the development of irrigation in ancient Mesopotamia (modern-day Iraq) made it possible in the short run to increase food production, but in the long run it favoured the gradual accumulation of salts in the soils. This, in turn, contributed to the collapse of civilization there after 2000 B.C. Similarly, the development of prime farmland today in places such as the eastern United States for purposes other than food production makes

us increasingly dependent on food raised in marginal environments. High yields are presently possible through the application of expensive technology, but continuing loss of topsoil, increasing salinity of soils from the evaporation of irrigation waters, and silting of irrigation works, not to mention impending shortages of water and fossil fuels, make high yields over the long term unlikely.

Functions of Culture

From what has been said so far, it is clear a culture cannot survive if it does not successfully meet the needs of its members. A culture must provide the means for the production and distribution of goods and services considered necessary for life. It must provide for biological continuity through the reproduction of its members. It must enculturate new members so that they can become functioning adults. It must maintain order among its members, as well as between them and outsiders. It must motivate its members to survive and to engage in activities necessary for survival. And it must encourage them to find meaning in their lives. On top of these roles, a culture must be able to change if it is to remain adaptive under changed conditions. We will be examining how culture fulfills these needs throughout the rest of this text.

Culture and Change

All cultures change over time, although not always as rapidly or as massively as many are doing today. Changes occur in response to events such as environmental crises, the intrusion of outsiders, or the modification of behaviour and values within the culture. In North American culture, clothing fashions change frequently. In the past few decades it has become culturally permissible for men and women alike to bare more of their bodies not just in swimming but in dress as well. Along with this has come greater permissiveness about the body in photographs and movies. Finally, the sexual attitudes and practices of North Americans have become less restrictive. Obviously, these changes are interrelated, reflecting an underlying change in attitudes toward cultural rules regarding sexuality.

Although cultures must be able to change to remain adaptive, culture change can bring unexpected and often disastrous results. A case in

Although pastoral nomads are often blamed for causing the sort of environmental degradation evident here, the fault is not theirs. Rather, it lies with the governments of countries that restrict their movements, thereby causing overgrazing.

point is the droughts that periodically afflict so many people living in Africa just south of the Sahara Desert. Native to this region are some 14 million pastoral nomadic people whose lives are centred on cattle and other livestock, which are herded from place to place as required for pasturage and water. For thousands of years these people went about their business, efficiently using vast areas of arid lands in ways that allowed them to survive severe droughts many times in the past. Unfortunately for them, their nomadic lifestyle, which makes it difficult to impose controls upon them and takes them across international boundaries at will, makes them a source of annoyance to the governments of the postcolonial states of the region. Seeing nomads as a challenge to their authority, these governments have gone all out to

convert them into sedentary villagers. Overgrazing has resulted from this loss of mobility, and the problem has been compounded by governmental efforts to involve the pastoralists in a market economy by encouraging them to raise many more animals than required for their own needs in order to have a surplus to sell. The resultant devastation, where previously no significant overgrazing or erosion had occurred, now makes droughts far more disastrous than they would otherwise be and places the former nomads' very existence in jeopardy.

Historically, First Nations peoples of Canada have undergone dramatic changes in their lifestyles, largely as a result of European (English, French, and Spanish) colonial expansion into North America. Many First Nations groups were encouraged to give up their traditional subsistence strategies in favour of commercial fur trade. When the fur trade collapsed they were faced with economic ruin. At the same time, bison populations were declining dramatically, and European settlers were coveting First Nations' traditional hunting territories. All of these factors left many First Nations peoples destitute. The government's response was to relocate (sometimes forcefully) First Nations peoples onto resource-poor reservations, and compel them to take up European-style agriculture. Government officials, aided by European missionary services, removed (again forcefully) First Nations children from their homes and settled them in residential schools where they were to be "civilized." These measures led to the disruption of First Nations cultures. Today, First Nations peoples are reclaiming their heritage and demanding that their needs be recognized. They are regaining control of their lives through land claims settlements, social healing programs, and self-government.

CULTURE, SOCIETY, AND THE INDIVIDUAL

Ultimately, culture and society are no more than a union of individuals, all of whom have their own special needs and interests. If a society is to survive, it must succeed in balancing the self-interests of its members, possibly from many cultural backgrounds, against the demands of the society as a whole. To accomplish this, a society offers rewards for adherence to its standards. In most cases, these rewards assume the form of social acceptance. In contemporary North American society, a woman who has a rewarding professional career, is a loving wife and mother, and volunteers in the community may be honoured with the YWCA Woman of the Year Award.

In order to ensure the survival of the group, each person must learn to postpone certain immediate satisfactions. Yet the needs of the individual cannot be suppressed too far, lest stress levels become too much to bear. Hence, a delicate balance always exists between personal interests and the demands the group makes on each individual.

Take the matter of sex, which is important in any culture, for it helps to strengthen cooperative bonds between men and women and ensures the perpetuation of the culture itself. Yet sex can be disruptive to social living; if who has sexual access to whom is not clearly spelled out, competition for sexual privileges can destroy the cooperative bonds human survival depends on. Uncontrolled sexual activity, too, can result in reproductive rates that cause a society's population to outstrip its resources. Hence, as they shape sexual behaviour, every culture must balance the needs of the whole against the need for sufficient individual gratification, lest frustration build until it causes disruption. Of course, cultures vary widely in the way they resolve this dilemma. Resolutions range all the way from the restrictive approach of British and Canadian society in the late 19th and early 20th century, which specified no sex out of wedlock, to practices among the Canela of eastern Brazil that guarantee that, sooner or later, everyone in a given village will have had sex with just about everyone of the opposite sex. Permissive though the latter situation may seem to Westerners, strict rules specify how the system operates.[9]

Not just in sex, but in all things, cultures must strike a balance between the needs of individuals and those of society. When the needs of society take precedence, people experience excessive

In Canada, First Nations peoples have exhibited symptoms of stress brought on by frustration and a sense of hopelessness when their needs are not met by society. Yet, aboriginal peoples of Canada have shown remarkable resilience. Shown here is a woman fishing from a canoe.

stress. Symptomatic of this stress are increased levels of mental illness and behaviour regarded as antisocial: violence, crime, abuse of alcohol and other drugs, suicide, and alienation. If not corrected, the situation can result in cultural breakdown. But just as problems develop if the needs of society take precedence over those of individuals, so do they develop if the balance is upset in the other direction.

EVALUATION OF CULTURE

Twenty-first-century humans are aware of the diverse cultural solutions to the problems of their existence. The question often arises: Which culture is best? In the 19th century, Europeans (and European North Americans) had few doubts about the answer—they saw their civilization as the peak of human development. At the same time, though, anthropologists were intrigued to find that all cultures they encountered saw themselves as the best of all possible worlds. Commonly, this point of view was reflected in peoples' names for their societies, which, roughly translated, usually meant "we human beings," as opposed to outsiders, who were called, essentially, "you subhumans." For example, the name Ju/'hoansi means "real people." Anthropologists

---

[9]Crocker, W.H., & Crocker, J. (1994). *The Canela: Bonding through kinship, ritual, and sex* (pp. 143–171). Fort Worth, TX: Harcourt Brace.

now know that any culture functioning adequately regards itself as the best, a view reflecting a phenomenon known as **ethnocentrism**. Hence, the 19th-century Europeans and Euro-Canadians were merely displaying their own ethnocentrism. Ethnocentrism is a deeply engrained attitude found in all stable cultures; to believe that our culture is functioning at optimum efficiency and that we are living a good life is a natural feeling. Problems arise when ethnocentrism is taken to extremes; then it becomes harmful and limiting to our human growth. Ethnocentrism can prevent us from questioning our customs, traditions, and even our beliefs, and perhaps developing new ways of doing things. Ethnocentrism can also stand in the way of understanding and appreciating other cultures and other ways of living. In its extreme form, ethnocentrism can lead to prejudice and racism—ethnic conflict is rampant around the world, in part as a result of extreme ethnocentrism.

Anthropologists have been engaged actively in the fight against ethnocentrism ever since they started to live among preindustrial peoples and discovered they were just as human as anyone else. As a consequence, anthropologists began to examine each culture on its own terms, asking whether or not the culture satisfied its people's needs and expectations. If a people practised human sacrifice, for example, anthropologists investigated the circumstances that made the taking of human life acceptable according to the culture's values. The idea that one must suspend judgement on other peoples' practices in order to understand them in their own cultural terms is called **cultural relativism**. Cultural relativism refutes ethnocentrism and, like holism and cross-cultural comparison, has become a hallmark of anthropological fieldwork. Anthropologists keep in mind their mission is not to transform a culture; rather, they attempt to determine the reasons for certain behaviour. Only through such an approach can we gain an undistorted view of another people's ways, as well as insights into the practices of our own culture.

Take, for example, the 16th-century Aztec practice of sacrificing humans for ritual purposes. Few (if any) North Americans today would con-

done such practices, but by suspending judgement we can get beneath the surface and understand how it functioned to reassure the populace that the Aztec state was healthy and that the sun would remain in the heavens. Beyond this, we can understand how the death penalty functions in the same way in countries such as the United States and China today. Numerous studies by a variety of social scientists have shown clearly that the death penalty does not deter violent crime, any more than Aztec sacrifice really provided sustenance for the sun. In fact, cross-cultural studies show that homicide rates mostly decline after its abolition.[10] Just like Aztec human sacrifice, capital punishment is an institutionalized magical response to perceived disorder. As anthropologists Anthony Parades and Elizabeth D. Purdum point out, it "reassures many that society is not out of control after all, that the majesty of the law reigns and that God is indeed in his heaven."[11]

Essential though cultural relativism is as a research tool, it does not require that we suspend judgement forever or that we defend the right of any cultural group to engage in any practice, no matter how reprehensible. All that is necessary is that we avoid *premature* judgement until we have a proper understanding of the culture we are interested in. Then, and only then, may we adopt a critical stance.

Cultural relativism is an extremely important approach in anthropology, but one that is not without controversy. Many anthropologists are questioning the distance and objectiveness they must maintain to be culturally relative. Furthermore, they are grappling with issues of human rights versus anthropological professionalism. Human rights advocates argue that cultural freedom does not give carte blanche to practices such as ethnic cleansing, political torture, or gender inequalities. Anthropologists struggle to reconcile their own sense of human

---

[10]Ember, C.J., & Ember, M. (1996). What have we learned from cross-cultural research? *General Anthropology, 2* (2), 5.

[11]Parades, J.A., & Purdum, E.D. (1990). Bye, bye Ted. . . . *Anthropology Today, 6* (2), 9.

Ethnocentrism.   The belief that one's own culture is superior to all others. **> Cultural relativism.**   The thesis that one must suspend judgement on other peoples' practices to understand them in their own cultural terms.

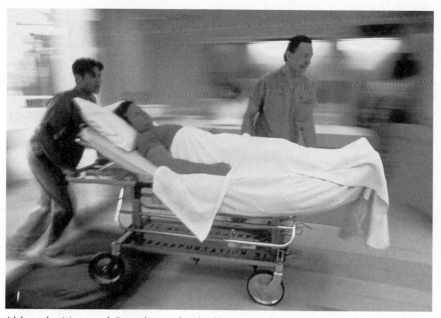

Although citizens of Canada are fond of boasting that theirs is the finest health care system in the world, they are merely reflecting the ethnocentrism of their own culture. Objective measures show that, while the Canadian system is better than many, it is far from perfect.

rights and morality with their responsibility as objective scientists.

While anthropologists avoid the "anything goes" position of cultural relativism pushed to absurdity, they also must avoid the pitfall of judging the practices of other cultures in terms of ethnocentric criteria. A still useful formula for measuring the success of a culture was devised more than 40 years ago by anthropologist Walter Goldschmidt.[12] In his view the important question to ask is: How well does a given culture satisfy the physical and psychological needs of those whose behaviour it guides? Specific indicators are found in the nutritional status and general physical and mental health of its population; the incidence of violence, crime, and delinquency; the demographic structure; the stability and tranquillity of domestic life; and the group's relationship to its resource base. The culture of a people who experience high rates of malnutrition, violence, crime, delinquency, suicide, emotional disorders and despair, and environmental degradation may be said to be operating less well than that of another

One sign that a culture is not adequately satisfying the needs and expectations of its members is a high incidence of crime and delinquency. It is, therefore, sobering to note that the United States has a higher percentage of its population in prison than any other country in the world, yet it still has insufficient space to hold all those convicted of crimes.

[12]Bodley, J.H. (1990). *Victims of progress* (3rd ed., p. 138). Mountain View, CA: Mayfield.

people who exhibit few such problems. In a well-working culture, people "can be proud, jealous, and pugnacious, and live a very satisfactory life without feeling 'angst,' 'alienation,' 'anomie,' 'depression,' or any of the other pervasive ills of our own inhuman and civilized way of living."[13] When people feel helpless to effect their own lives in their own societies and when traditional ways of coping no longer seem to work, the symptoms of cultural breakdown become prominent.

A culture is essentially a system to ensure the continued well-being of a group of people; there-

---

[13]Fox, R. (1968). *Encounter with anthropology* (p. 290). New York: Dell.

fore, it may be termed successful as long as it secures the survival of a society in a way that its members recognize as reasonably fulfilling. What complicates matters is that any society is made up of groups with different interests, raising the possibility that some peoples' interests may be served better than others. Therefore, a culture that is quite fulfilling for one group within a society may be less so for another. For this reason, anthropologists always must ask this: Whose needs, and whose survival, are best served by the culture in question? Only by examining the overall situation can a reasonably objective judgement be made as to how well a culture is working.

CHAPTER SUMMARY

Culture, to anthropologists, consists of the shared ideals, values, and beliefs members of a society use to interpret experience and to generate behaviour and that are reflected by their behaviour.

All cultures share certain basic characteristics; studying these sheds light on culture's nature and function. Culture cannot exist without society: a group of people sharing a common homeland who are dependent on each other for survival. Society is held together by relationships determined by social structure or social organization. Within any society, more than one culture can exist. All is not uniform within a culture; one reason is that some differences exist between male and female roles in any human society. Anthropologists use the term *gender* to refer to the elaborations or meanings cultures assign to the biological differences between men and women. Age variation is also universal, and in some cultures other subcultural variations occur as well. A subculture, such as the Hutterites or Acadians, shares certain overarching assumptions of the larger culture while observing a distinctively different set of rules. Pluralistic societies are those with particularly marked cultural variation, often containing several distinct cultural and subcultural groups operating under different sets of standards.

In addition to being shared, culture is learned. Individual members of a society learn the accepted norms of social behaviour through the process of enculturation. Another characteristic is that culture is based on symbols. It is transmitted

through the communication of ideas, emotions, and desires expressed in language. Finally, culture is integrated, so all aspects of a culture function as an integrated whole. In a properly functioning culture, though, total harmony of all elements is approximated, rather than completely achieved.

The job of anthropologists is to understand what they observe to explain the social behaviour of a people. To arrive at a realistic description of a culture free from personal and cultural biases, anthropologists must (1) examine a people's notion of the way their society ought to function; (2) determine how a people think they behave; and (3) compare these with how a people actually do behave. Anthropologists also must be as free as possible from their own cultural biases.

Cultural adaptation has enabled humans, in the course of evolution, to survive and expand in a variety of environments. Sometimes, though, what is adaptive in one set of circumstances, or in the short run, is maladaptive in another set of circumstances, or in the long run.

To survive, a culture must satisfy the basic needs of its members, provide for their continuity, and maintain order among them and between them and outsiders.

All cultures change over time, sometimes because the environment they must cope with has changed, sometimes as a result of the intrusion of outsiders, or sometimes because values within the culture have undergone modification. Although cultures must change to adapt to new circumstances, sometimes the unforeseen consequences of change are disastrous for a society.

A society must strike a balance between the self-interests of individuals and the needs of the group. If one or the other becomes paramount, the result may be cultural breakdown.

Ethnocentrism is the belief that our own culture is superior to all others. To avoid making ethnocentric judgements, anthropologists adopt the approach of cultural relativism, which requires examination of each culture in its own terms and according to its own standards. The least biased measure of a culture's success, however, employs criteria indicative of the culture's effectiveness at securing the survival of a society in a way its members see as reasonably fulfilling.

QUESTIONS FOR CRITICAL THOUGHT

1. Have you ever had an experience that made you aware of profound cultural differences between yourself and someone else? How did you react (e.g., feelings of uncomfortableness, stress, fear)? How did any other parties react? How did you attempt to overcome the cultural differences?

2. How would you respond to the question, "Which culture is best?"

3. To what extent have you ever felt yourself a member of a distinct subculture? Have you ever experienced negative feedback from other people because of your subcultural identity?

4. Write about your experiences with culture shock (perhaps as a first-year university student moving to an urban centre or while backpacking through Europe). How did this experience challenge your assumptions about the world around you? How did you feel, emotionally and physically? At what point did you make the adjustment to the new cultural environment—or did you? When you returned home, was there a period of readjustment to your own culture?

5. In the past two centuries, Europeans and North Americans have experienced a tension between preexisting cultural practices and changes prompted by new technology. What kinds of cultural traits seem to have become nonadaptive in recent decades in North America?

6. Enculturative forces within any society are not always positive. Can you identify any enculturative forces in Canadian society that may be perceived as negative (at least some of the time)?

7. If you immigrated to another country, would you attempt to adopt local behaviour as your own, or would you try to maintain your own traditions and identity? Which of your behaviours would you most likely try to preserve, and which would be most difficult to give up? What would be the basis for your choices?

INTERNET RESOURCES

Hutterites
http://www.in-forum.com/specials/awa/1117a.html
A discussion of contemporary Hutterites in Minnesota.
http://www.hutterites.org/groups.htm
An extensive site with many links to information on Hutterite history, social structure, education, and so on.

The Women's Rights Movement 1848–1998
http://www.legacy98.org/move-hist.html
A historical examination of the women's movement. Although this site focuses on American history, it is relevant to the study of the Canadian women's movement.

The Women's Movement in Canada
http://130.15.62.164/Projects/squeezeboxdays/canada.html

A brief examination of the history of the women's movement in Canada. This site also includes links to other sites, such as the suffragettes, the new feminism, and women in media.

Canadian Museum of Civilization
http://www.civilization.ca

This is an extensive site, providing significant information on Canadian history, including diverse topics such as postage stamps, glassmaking, religion and ritual, Inuit and folk art, social movements, and cultural traditions found within and outside Canada. An excellent resource for students from many disciplines.

Body Ritual among the Nacirema
http://www.msu.edu/~jdowell/miner.html

Read the classic article "Body Ritual among the Nacirema" for an enlightening and delightful

introduction to the many pitfalls of anthropological research.

What Is Culture?
http://www.wsu.edu:8001/vcwsu/commons/topics/culture/culture-index.html

An education site that explores the nature of culture. It provides links to several special aspects of culture, including women, culture, and power.

Anthropology and You
http://members.shaw.ca/sfedorak1

Geared to first-year anthropology students using this textbook, this site introduces the concepts of anthropology in an effort to make anthropology relevant to Canadians. Contains a selection of food for thought designed to challenge students to think beyond academia and bring anthropology into their everyday lives.

SUGGESTED READINGS

Brown, D.E. (1991). *Human universals*. New York: McGraw-Hill.

The message of this book is that we should not let our fascination with the diversity of cultural practices interfere with the study of those aspects all cultures share in spite of their differences. Important though the differences are, the universals have special relevance for our understanding of the nature of all humanity and raise issues that transcend the boundaries of biological and social science, as well as the humanities.

Ervin, A.M. (2001). *Canadian perspectives in cultural anthropology*. Toronto: Nelson Thomson Learning.

An excellent supplement to any introductory sociocultural anthropology textbook, this book contains 20 modules that expound on a variety of subjects relevant to Canadian students, from the development of Canadian anthropology to French-Canadian extended families and Vietnamese refugees in Montreal.

Hatch, E. (1983). *Culture and morality: The relativity of values in anthropology*. New York: Columbia University Press.

This book is about cultural relativism, often used as a cover term for the quite different concepts of relativity of knowledge, historical relativism, and ethical relativism. It traces the attempts of anthropologists to grapple with these concepts, beginning with the rise of the discipline in the 19th century.

Leblanc, L. (1999). *Pretty in punk: Girls' resistance in a boys' subculture*. New Brunswick, NJ: Rutgers University Press.

Labelled an "ethnography of gender resistance," this book provides an insider's look at the punk subculture. It examines females in punk groups, their power relations, and their ability to create an alternative gender norm. Written in a style that a general audience can enjoy and appreciate.

Lee, R.B., & Daly, R. (Eds.). (1999). *The Cambridge encyclopedia of hunters and gatherers*. Cambridge, UK: Cambridge University Press.

This impressive work presents the ethnographic research on diverse hunting-and-gathering peoples around the world, including several aboriginal groups in Canada. The book is divided into two parts, the first containing more than 50 case studies, written by experts on hunter gatherer peoples, the second containing essays on prehistory, social life, gender, music and art, health, religion, and indigenous knowledge.

Manning, F. (Ed.). (1983). *Consciousness and inquiry: Ethnology and Canadian realities.* No. 89E. Ottawa: National Museum of Canada.

This collection of essays provides an excellent opportunity for students to examine some of the issues unique to Canadian anthropology and Canadian society: multiculturalism, the anthropology of Quebec, applied anthropology in Canada, as well as reflections on anthropology as a discipline.

McLellan, J. (2002). *Many petals of the lotus: Five Asian Buddhist communities in Toronto.* Toronto: University of Toronto Press.

A very readable ethnography of five Buddhist communities in Toronto. McLellan provides readers with an honest account of the successes and difficulties faced by Asian immigrants and refugees in Canada.

Reasons, C.E., & Pavlich, D. (1995). The legal and social alienation of aboriginal peoples in Canada. *International Journal of Canadian Studies, 12.*

This article examines the struggles between aboriginal people and their colonizers, as well as the loss of their land, culture, and self-worth. It discusses the social, political, and legal attempts to reduce social alienation.

Women in Canadian society. (1995). *International Journal of Canadian Studies, 11.*

This is a collection of interdisciplinary essays, presenting an international perspective on contemporary issues. Many of the essays focus on the effects of gender construction.

CNN TODAY VIDEOS

Culture Crimes: Myanmar Stolen Artifacts (CNN Cultural Anthropology, vol. 3, 3:32)
A large black market exists around the world, dealing in stolen cultural artifacts and art. The segment also touches on the actions of former colonial rulers with regard to cultural artifacts.

Chocolate Cravings (CNN Cultural Anthropology, vol. 3, 1:38)
The preference for certain foods, such as chocolate in the West, are shown to be culturally acquired.

Papua New Guinea Tourism (CNN Cultural Anthropology, vol. 5, 6:57)
Tourists visiting Papua New Guinea get a glimpse of a colourful and fascinating culture that has survived into the 21st century.

Chapter 3

The Beginnings of Human Culture

From studying other primates related to us, we can discover which characteristics we share and which we do not. The former we owe to a common ancestry; the latter are what make us distinctly human.

Chapter Preview

1. To What Group of Animals Do Humans Belong?

Humans are classified by biologists as belonging to the Primate Order, a group that also includes lemurs, lorises, tarsiers, monkeys, and apes. By studying the anatomy and behaviour of monkeys and apes, the primates most closely related to us, we draw closer to understanding how and why humans developed as they did.

2. When and How Did Humans Evolve?

Present evidence suggests that humans evolved from small apelike primates that lived between 15 million and 8 million years ago. By 4.4 million years ago, human ancestors had become fully adapted for moving about on the open savanna on their hind legs in the distinctive human manner. Otherwise, the behaviour of these early hominines probably was comparable to that of modern-day chimpanzees.

3. When and How Did Human Culture Evolve?

Human culture appears to have developed as some populations of early hominines began making stone tools they could butcher animals with for their meat. Actually, the earliest stone tools and evidence of significant meat eating date to between 2.5 million and 2 million years ago, along with the appearance of the genus *Homo,* whose brain was significantly enlarged over that of any other early hominine. From then on the increasing importance of culture in human survival favoured the evolution of a better brain, which in turn made possible improvement in culture as the vehicle humans used to secure their survival. By about 200 000 years ago, the human brain had reached its modern size, but culture has continued to evolve and change down to the present.

CHAPTER OUTLINE

Humans and the Other Primates

Human Ancestors

Gender Perspectives: Gender Bias in
    Primatology?

Anthropology Applied: Stone Tools for Modern
    Surgeons

Early forerunners of humanity, like all other creatures, depended a great deal on physical attributes for survival. Although learned behaviour was certainly important to them, much of what they did was still dictated by their biological natures. In the course of evolution, however, humans came to rely increasingly on learned behaviour as an extremely effective way to adapt to the environment. They learned to manufacture and use tools; they organized into social units more proficient at foraging for food than their ancestors had been; and at some point they learned to preserve their traditions and knowledge to bridge the past and present through the use of symbols. In other words, humans became increasingly committed to culture as a vehicle for solving the problems they confronted.

This cultural ability has made humans unusual among the creatures on this planet. Humans do not merely adapt to the environment; they attempt to mould and manipulate it to suit the needs and desires they themselves define. If they manage to avoid self-destruction through misuse of their technology (and it is by no means certain they will), their medical technology eventually may enable them to control genetic inheritance and thus the future course of their biological evolution. Space technology may enable them to propagate their species in extraterrestrial environments. And computer technology enables them to correlate and organize an ever-increasing amount of knowledge as they themselves attempt to keep pace with the changes they have wrought.

Humans have gotten where they are today in an extraordinarily short period; human culture, as we know it, came into existence a mere 2.5 million years ago. By looking backward to see where we came from and how we became the way we are today, we gain insight into how human culture arose and how it increasingly took on the job of solving the problems of human existence. In the process, we gain a fuller understanding of the nature of culture itself.

HUMANS AND THE OTHER PRIMATES

Biologists classify humans as belonging to the **Primate Order,** a group of mammals that also includes lemurs, lorises, tarsiers, monkeys, and apes. We might properly question the value of studying primates other than humans, when humans and their distinctive cultural capacities are what concern us. Humans, however, did not start out as humans. Their roots, like those of the other living primates, lie in ancient times and in less specialized biological creatures; their development was influenced by the same evolutionary processes. By studying the environment of those times, the anatomical features that evolved in the context of that environment, and the rudimentary cultural adaptations of those primates we are related to, we may draw closer to an understanding of how and why humans developed as they did.

The first primates originated at a time when a new, mild climate favoured the spread of dense tropical and subtropical forests over much of the earth, including North and South America, Southeast Asia, the Middle East, and most of Africa. Forestation set the stage for the evolutionary development from a relatively inconspicuous ground existence to tree living.

Evolution through Adaptation

The term *adaptation* refers to both a process organisms undergo to achieve a beneficial adjustment to an available environment and the results of that process—the characteristics of organisms that fit them to the particular set of environmental conditions they generally are found in. The process of **natural selection** favours not just the survival of well-adapted individuals but also the propagation of their genetic traits. The well-adapted individuals produce the greater percentage of offspring for the next generation. Although some individuals less suited to the envi-

---

Primate Order.   The group of mammals that includes lemurs, lorises, tarsiers, monkeys, apes, and humans. **> Natural selection.**   The evolutionary mechanism by which individuals with characteristics best suited to a particular environment survive and reproduce with greater frequency than those without them.

Modern lemurs represent highly evolved variants of an early primate model. In them, primate characteristics are not as prominent as they are in monkeys, apes, and humans.

ronment may in fact survive, they often do not reproduce; they may be incapable of attracting mates, they may be sterile, or they may produce offspring that do not survive after birth.

By chance, the ancestral primates possessed certain characteristics that allowed them to adapt to life in the forests. Their relatively small size allowed them to use the small branches of trees; larger and heavier competitors and predators could not follow. The move to the small branches also opened up an abundant new food supply. The primates could gather leaves, flowers, fruits, insects, birds' eggs, and even nesting birds, rather than having to wait for them to fall to the ground.

The move to an arboreal existence brought a combination of the problems of earthbound existence and flight. In their move into space, birds developed highly stereotyped behavioural patterns keyed to the problems of flight. Animals living on the ground developed a slower-paced, more flexible relationship to the environment.

The tree-dwelling primates, however, were obliged to develop both flexible behaviour and virtually automatic mechanisms for moving through the trees, for if they were no longer limited to roaming on the ground, they also no longer had the certainty of a substantial surface directly beneath their feet. Initial forays into the trees must have included many errors in judgement and coordination, leading to falls that injured or killed those who were poorly adapted to arboreal life. Natural selection favoured those who judged depth correctly and gripped the branches tightly. Early primates who took to the trees had the potential for successful adaptation to another way of life merely by possessing characteristics adaptive to one way of life that, purely by chance, also were suitable for a different way of life. Thus, as ground dwellers they happened to possess features potentially useful to tree dwellers. Nevertheless, the transition to life in the trees required important physical adjustments. The way these early primates adapted has considerable relevance for their human descendants.

Anatomical Adaptation

From the study of both ancient and modern primates, anthropologists have worked out a list of characteristics common to them all.

Primate Dentition

The diet available to arboreal primates—shoots, leaves, insects, and soft fruits—required relatively unspecialized teeth, compared with those found in other mammals. Based on the evidence of comparative anatomy and the fossil record, the mammals ancestral to the primates possessed 3 incisors, 1 canine, 4 premolars, and 3 molars on each side of the jaw, top and bottom, for a total of 44 teeth. The incisors (in the front of the mouth) were used for gripping and cutting, canines (behind the incisors) were used for tearing and shredding, and molars and premolars (the "cheek teeth") were used for grinding and chewing food.

The evolutionary trend for primate dentition generally has been toward economy, with fewer smaller teeth doing more work (see Figure 3.1). In the early stages, one incisor on each side of the upper and lower jaws was lost, further

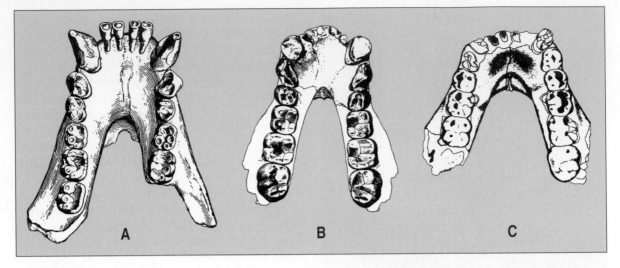

FIGURE 3.1

The fossil ape jaw on the left (A) shows the different kinds of teeth primates possessed: four incisors in front, two canines behind, followed by two premolars and three molars. B and C show variations on this pattern. They are the jaws of *Australopithecus* (C) and a more ancient, apelike ancestor (B) (see pp. 69–71).

differentiating primates from other mammals. The canines of most of the primates grew longer, forming daggerlike teeth that enabled them to rip open tough husks of fruit and other foods. Over the millennia, the first and second premolars became smaller and eventually disappeared altogether; the third and fourth premolars grew larger and added a second pointed projection, or cusp, thus becoming *bicuspid*. The molars also evolved from a three-cusp to a four- and even five-cusp pattern. Thus the functions of grasping, cutting, and grinding were served by different kinds of teeth.

Sense Organs

The primates' adaptation to life in the trees involved changes in the form and function of their sensory apparatus. To mammals living on the ground, the sense of smell is of great importance, for it enables them to operate at night, as well as to sense what is out of sight—to "see around corners," as it were. Not only can they sniff out their food, but they also can be warned of the presence of hidden predators. Up in the trees, though, primates are out of the way of most predators, and good vision is a better guide than smell for judging correctly where the next branch

is. Accordingly, the sense of smell declined in primates, while that of sight became highly developed.

Travelling through trees demands judgements concerning depth, direction, distance, and the relationships of objects hanging in space, such as vines or branches. In tarsiers, monkeys, apes, and humans, this is achieved through *stereoscopic colour vision*. The ability to see the world in the three dimensions of height, width, and depth requires two eyes set next to each other on the same plane so that the visual fields of the two eyes overlap. Stereoscopic colour vision appears to have led to increased brain size in the visual area in primates and a greater complexity at nerve connections.

A more acute sense of touch also characterized the arboreal primates. An effective feeling and grasping mechanism helped prevent them from falling and tumbling while speeding through the trees. The early mammals from which primates evolved possessed tiny hairs that gave them extremely sensitive tactile capacities. In primates these hairs were replaced by sensitive pads backed up by nails on the tips of the animals' fingers and toes.

The ability to judge depth correctly and grasp branches strongly is of obvious utility to animals as active in the trees as this South American squirrel monkey.

The Primate Brain

The most outstanding characteristic of primate evolution has been the great increase in brain size. The cerebral hemispheres—the areas of conscious thought—have grown dramatically, and in monkeys, apes, and humans they completely cover the *cerebellum,* the part of the brain that coordinates the muscles and maintains body equilibrium.

One of the main reasons for this change is probably the primates' arboreal existence. An animal living in the trees is constantly acting and reacting to the environment. Messages from the hands, feet, eyes, and ears, as well as from the sensors of balance, movement, heat, touch, and pain, are simultaneously relayed to the *cortex.* Obviously the cortex had to develop considerably to receive, analyze, and coordinate these impressions and transmit the appropriate responses back down the motor nerves to the proper receptors. The enlarged cortex not only made the primates more efficient in the daily struggle for survival but also prepared the way for heightened cerebration, or thought—an ability that played a decisive role in humanity's emergence.

The Primate Skeleton

The skeleton gives a vertebrate animal its basic shape or silhouette, supports the soft tissues, and helps protect vital internal organs. The opening of the skull through which the spinal cord passes and connects to the brain is an important clue to evolutionary relationships. In primates, the trend is for this opening to shift forward, toward the centre of the skull's base, so that it faces downward, rather than directly backward, as in dogs and other mammals. This shift enables the backbone to join the skull at the centre of its base, a more advantageous arrangement for an animal that assumes an upright posture at least occasionally. The head thus is balanced on the vertebral column, instead of projecting forward from it.

For most primates, the snout or muzzle portion of the skull was reduced as the sense of smell declined. The smaller snout offers less interference with stereoscopic vision and enables the eyes to be placed in a more frontal position. A solid wall of bone surrounds the eye in most primate species, affording them greater protection than seen in most mammals.

Below the primate skull and neck is the clavicle, or collarbone. It acts as a strut, placing the arms at the side rather than in front of the body, thus permitting them to swing sideways and outward from the trunk. Apes and humans especially can move their arms with great freedom. This enables apes to swing and hang vertically from tree branches.

The limbs end in hands and feet with five extremely flexible digits, reminiscent of those possessed by more ancient vertebrate ancestors. At the tips of the digits are sensitive pads backed up by flat nails, which provide an excellent grasping device for use when moving from branch to branch. The thumb and great toe are opposable to varying degrees (with full opposability, for example, the thumb tip can push against any other fingertip) so that food can be handled easily, branches grasped, and objects manipulated.

Hindsight shows that retention of the primitive primate hand proved a valuable asset to later primates. In part, unspecialized hands capable of grasping enabled our ancestors to manufacture and use tools and thus alter the course of their evolution.

Adaptation through Behaviour

Important though anatomical adaptation has been to the primates, it has not been the only way of coping with the environment. Studies of monkeys and apes living today indicate that learned social behaviour plays an important role in adaptation. The range of behaviour living primates show is great, but by looking at the behaviour of the species most closely related to humans—chimpanzees in particular and the other great apes as well—or of ones such as baboons that have adapted to environments somewhat similar to those our own ancestors faced millions of years ago, we may discover clues to patterns that contributed to the emergence of human cultural behaviour. Jane Goodall's pioneering study of wild chimpanzees in Tanzania has provided us with startling new insights into chimpanzee behaviour, even though we must realize that no living primate represents a precise analogue for the behaviour of our ancient ancestors.

Chimpanzee Behaviour

Like all primates, chimpanzees are social animals.[1] In their native haunts, the largest organizational unit is the community, composed of 50 or more individuals. Rarely, however, do all these animals gather at once. Instead, they usually are found ranging singly or in small subgroups consisting of adult males together, females with their young, or males and females together with young. In their travels, subgroups may join forces and forage together, but sooner or later these will break up again into smaller units. When they do, members are often exchanged, so the new subunits are composed differently from those that initially came together.

Although relationships between individuals within the community are relatively harmonious, dominance hierarchies, whereby some animals outrank and can dominate others, do exist. Generally, males outrank females, although high-ranking females may dominate low-ranking males. Physical strength and size play a role in determining an animal's rank, but what really counts is its mother's rank, how effective it is at creating alliances with other individuals, and, for males, how motivated they are to achieve high status.

Grooming, the ritual cleaning of another chimp's coat to remove parasites and other matter, is a common chimpanzee pastime. Besides being hygienic, it is a gesture of friendliness, submission, appeasement, and closeness. Group sociability, an important behavioural trait undoubtedly found among human precursors, is expressed by embracing, touching, and joyously welcoming other chimps. Group protection and coordination of group efforts are facilitated by visual and vocal communication, including warning, threatening, and gathering calls.

The sexes intermingle continually, and, as with humans, no fixed breeding season exists. Sexual activity, however—initiated by either the male or the female—occurs only during the period each month when the female is fertile. Once impregnated, females are not sexually receptive until their offspring are weaned, at about four years of age. To a degree, chimps are promiscuous in their

[1]Goodall, J. (1986). *The chimpanzees of Gombe: Patterns of behavior.* Cambridge, MA: Belknap Press.

sexual behaviour, and 12 to 14 males have been observed to have as many as 50 copulations in one day with a single female. Thus, not all offspring are fathered by dominant males. Nevertheless, dominant males try to monopolize females when the latter are most receptive sexually, although cooperation from the female is usually required for this to succeed. By making herself scarce, and even sneaking off to find a male in a neighbouring group, she may exercise some choice in the matter. An alpha male, however, can monopolize females to some extent, and some alphas have been seen to monopolize several females at the same time.

In most primate species, females and their offspring constitute the core of the social system. The mature females may well be the point where any evolutionary theory of behaviour should begin.[2] Among chimps the mother–infant bond is especially strong for the first five years, but a close association commonly continues after this. Although females sometimes leave the group they were born into (unlike most other primate species, with males normally transferring out of their natal group into one they will live in as adults), when they do so their young sons and daughters accompany them. Commonly, sons,

and often daughters, remain with their mothers for life. Unlike a human baby, the young chimp must be ready at birth to go everywhere with its mother, for its very survival depends on its ability to remain close to her. Males are generally attentive to juveniles and may share in parental responsibilities. However, they do wander off to forage by themselves. Thus, the females provide the group's stability.

Chimpanzees show a remarkable dependence on learned cultural behaviour. This behaviour is to some extent different from one chimpanzee group to another. Born without built-in responses that will dictate its behaviour in complex situations, the young chimp, like the young human, learns how to interact with others, and even to manipulate them for his or her own benefit, by trial and error, social facilitation, observation and imitation, and practice. Mistakes made along the way often result in reprimands from other group members.

Among the many things young chimpanzees learn from adults is how to make and use tools. Not only do they deliberately modify objects to make them suitable for particular purposes, but chimps also can to some extent modify them to regular and set patterns. They also can pick up, and even prepare, objects in anticipation of future use at some other location, and they can use objects as tools to solve new and novel problems. For example, chimps have been observed using

---

[2]Fedigan, L. (1982). *Primate paradigms; Sex roles and social bonds*. Montreal: Eden Press.

Among chimpanzees, as among most primates, grooming is an important part of social activity.

This bonobo (pygmy chimpanzee) figured out by himself how to make stone tools like those our own ancestors made 2.5 million years ago.

Chimpanzees are aware of themselves as individuals. A chimp knows, for example, that the animal in the mirror is him- or helfself and not some other chimp.

grass stalks, twigs they have stripped of leaves, and sticks up to three feet long to "fish" for termites. They insert the stick into a termite nest, wait a few minutes, pull the stick out, and eat the insects clinging to it.

Other examples of wild chimpanzee use of objects as tools involve leaves, used as wipes or as sponges to get water out of a tree hollow to drink. Stones and rocks also are used as hammers and anvils to open palm nuts and hard fruits. Such tool-using behaviour, which young animals learn from their mothers and other adults in their group, may reflect one of the preliminary adaptations that, in the past, led to human cultural behaviour.

Although fruits, other plant foods, and invertebrate animals constitute the bulk of the chimpanzee diet, chimps will kill and eat other small to medium-sized animals, an unusual behaviour among primates. Chimpanzee females sometimes hunt, but males do so far more frequently. When hunting, they may spend up to two hours watching, following, and chasing intended prey. Moreover, in contrast to the usual primate practice of each animal finding its own food, hunting among chimpanzees frequently involves teamwork to trap and kill prey. The most sophisticated example of this teamwork occurs when hunting baboons; once a potential victim has been partially isolated from its troop, three or more adults will carefully position themselves to block off escape routes while another climbs toward the prey for the kill. Once a kill has been made, the meat is shared in a strategic way to support male allies and females.

The more we learn about chimpanzees, the more we become aware of a degree of intelligence and capacity for conceptual thought hitherto unsuspected for any nonhuman primate. That chimpanzees are not alone in these capabilities has been confirmed by research such as Biruté Galdikas's study of the solitary orangutans of Borneo's rain forests.

Birutć Galdikas

Known as one of "Leakey's Angels" (Dian Fossey and Jane Goodall being the other two), Canadian Biruté Galdikas is considered the world's foremost authority on wild orangutans. Galdikas received her master's degree in primatology from UCLA in 1969, and returned for her doctorate in anthropology in 1978. She has lived and worked in the rain forests of Borneo, at the Orangutan Research and Conservation Center in the Tanjung Puting National Park, since 1971. Here Galdikas continues to study these solitary creatures, developing conservation programs and caring for orangutan infants orphaned by poachers. She hopes that by studying orangutan subsistence, sociality, reproduction, cognitive potentials, communications, and tool use, she might learn more about the development of early hominids. Galdikas says, "I've always wanted to study the one primate who never left the Garden of Eden. I want to know what we left behind."[1] She strongly believes humans must reach back to their evolutionary roots, to a more stable lifestyle, for the sake of our social, environmental, and mental well-being.

When Galdikas first began her research, she developed close mothering relationships with the orphaned orangutans, even raising her oldest son, Binti, with the orangutans. In more recent years, she has tried to maintain some distance between her private life and the

orangutans. Nonetheless, Galdikas has continued to act as an advocate for the protection of orangutans, establishing a nonprofit organization, the Orangutan Foundation International, with support groups around the world, and campaigning for the creation of a large wildlife preserve in Borneo.

In 1995 Galdikas received the Order of Canada for her work with endangered orangutans in the rain forests of Borneo. Earlier that year, her much anticipated autobiography, *Reflections of Eden: My Years with the Orangutans in Borneo,* was released. Galdikas currently teaches human origins and primate behaviour at Simon Fraser University in British Columbia for several months of the year. The rest of the time, she lives with her husband and two children at Camp Leakey, Borneo.

[1]GCS Research Society. (1996). *Biruté Galdikas: Anthropologist.* Retrieved November 25, 2000, from the World Wide Web: http://www.science.ca/scientists/Galdikas/galdikas.html.

Lessem, D. (1995–96). Interview with Biruté Galdikas. In E. Angeloni (Ed.), *Physical anthropology 95/96.* Guildford, CT: The Dushkin Publishing Group, Inc.

Simon Fraser University. (1995, June 30). Press release.

HUMAN ANCESTORS

Studies in genetics, biochemistry, and anatomy confirm that chimpanzees and gorillas are our closest living relatives. Both are more closely related to us than to orangutans. At the genetic level, humans and chimpanzees are at least 98 percent identical, so it is estimated that our evolutionary lines must have separated from a common ancestral stock somewhere between 5.5 million and 8 million years ago. In addition, fossils tell us humans were going their separate evolutionary way by at least 4.4 million years ago.

The best evidence is that our ancestry lies among a group of apelike animals living in Africa that were forced by climatic changes down onto the ground to get from one stand of trees to another as well as to supplement food that was becoming increasingly scarce in the trees. Since they did not have arms as long as those of modern apes nor as massive upper bodies, they tended to move on their hind legs when on the ground, with their bodies in an upright position. Advantages of this kind of bipedal locomotion were that the arms and hands were free to quickly gather food, to transport it to safe places for consumption, and to wield objects effectively in

A young baboon clings to its mother's back. The ability of apes as well as monkeys to carry their infants is limited by their need to use their arms in locomotion.

threat displays to protect themselves against ground-dwelling predators. Additionally, they could transport offspring more effectively than merely allowing the latter to hang on by themselves. Finally, erect posture on the ground minimized the body area exposed to the hot sun, thereby helping to avoid overheating.

Hominid or Hominine

The classification of organisms depends on one's perspective. In recent years, the close genetic relationship among humans, chimpanzees, and gorillas means to some scientists that all three are in the hominid family (hominidae), distinguished at the subfamily level (hominine). Others try to take behaviour into account as well. The distinct behavioural differences between humans on the one hand, and gorillas and chimpanzees on the other, suggests differences are too great to classify them all in the same family. In this case, chimpanzees and gorillas belong in the family of great apes.

The First Hominines

The first undoubted **hominines** (humans or, in this case, near humans) are represented by fossils from East Africa that go back 6 million to 4.4 million years. All are extremely fragmentary, although about 45 percent of one individual is known from a site in Ethiopia. Known as *Ardipithecus*, the fossil is 4.4 million years old. Although much smaller than a modern chimpanzee, it is more chimpanzee-like in its features than any other hominine. But unlike chimpanzees, and like all other hominines, it walked upright, on two feet in a fully human manner, that is, bipedally.

No potential hominine had been found to be older than 6 million years, at least not until 2001, when the substantial part of a cranium was reported. *Sahelanthropus tchadenisis,* found in northern Chad, dates to 7 million to 6.5 million years ago. It has a small brain case like an ape, but its canines are small and the face is human-like. For now, it is the only known candidate that could be ancestral to all hominines.

Hominine.   A subfamily of primates that includes humans and near humans.

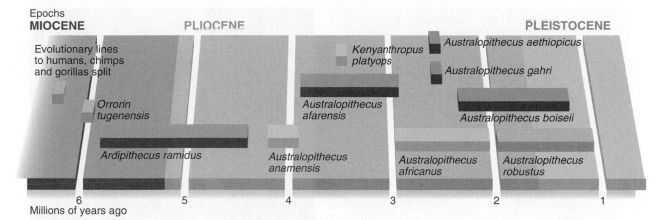

Epochs
MIOCENE   PLIOCENE   **PLEISTOCENE**

FIGURE 3.2

The earliest hominine fossils and the scientific names by which they have been known, arranged according to when they lived. *A. aethiopicus, A. boisei,* and *A. robustus* are all robust australopithecines; *A. afarensis, A. africanus,* and *A. anamensis* are gracile australopithecines. Recently, *Sahelanthropus tchadensis* was added to the record (7 million to 6.5 million years ago). Whether all the different species' names are warranted is hotly debated.

Descendants of *Ardipithecus* are assigned to one or another species of the genus *Australopithecus* (see Figure 3.2). Opinions vary on just how many species existed; for the sake of simplicity, it suffices for our purposes to refer to them simply as *australopithecines*. The earliest australopithecine fossils date back as many as 4.2 million years ago,[3] whereas the most recent ones are only about 1 million years old. They have been found along the length of eastern Africa from Ethiopia to South Africa and westward into Chad (see Figure 3.3).

None of these early hominines were as large as most modern people, although all were more muscular for their size. The structure and size of the teeth are more like those of modern people than those of apes, and the condition of the molars indicates food was chewed in hominine fashion: that is, with a grinding motion, rather than simple up and down movement of the jaws. Unlike the apes, no gap exists between the canines and the teeth next to them on the lower jaw, except in some of the earliest hominines. The australopithecines retain some other apelike features, but otherwise their jaws are very similar to those of early *Homo*. The brain/body ratio, which permits a rough estimate of australopithecine intelligence, suggests intelligence was comparable to that of modern chimpanzees or gorillas. Moreover, the outside appearance of the brain is more apelike than human, suggesting that cerebral organization toward a human condition had not yet occurred.[4]

Australopithecine fossils also have provided anthropology with two striking facts. First, by at least 4 million years ago, this hominine was bipedal, walking erect. Second, hominines acquired their erect bipedal posture long before they acquired their highly developed and enlarged brain. Where resources were dispersed, such as in the savanna environment, a biped could not run as fast as a quadruped but could travel long distances in search of food much more efficiently. It could carry food to safe places, it could carry infants (rather than relying on them to hang on for themselves), and it was exposed to less direct

---

[3]Wolpoff, M. (1996). *Australopithecus:* A new look at an old ancestor. *General Anthropology, 3* (1), 2.

[4]Falk, D. (1989). Ape-like endocast of "Ape Man Taung." *American Journal of Physical Anthropology, 80,* 339.

Australopithecus.   The earliest well-known hominine, who lived between 1 million and 4.2 million years ago and includes several species.

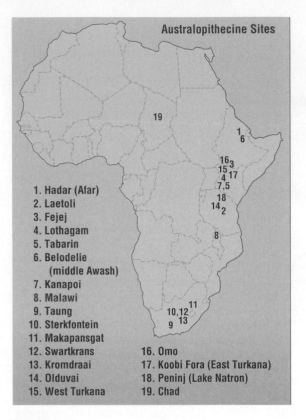

FIGURE 3.3

Australopithecus fossils have been found in South Africa, Malawi, Tanzania, Kenya, Ethiopia, and Chad.

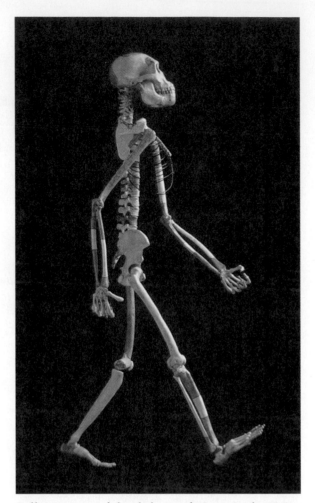

Sufficient parts of the skeleton of "Lucy," a hominine that lived between 2.6 million and 3.3 million years ago, survived to permit this reconstruction. Her hip and leg bones reveal that she moved around in a fully human manner.

heat from the sun than when in a quadrupedal position.

Although these hominines were accomplished bipeds, evidence from the arm, hand, and foot skeletons of australopithecines indicates they had not given up tree climbing altogether. One reason may be that trees, sparsely distributed though they were becoming on the savanna, continued to be important places of refuge in a land teeming with dangerous predatory animals. Another is that food was still to be found in trees. Dental and skeletal evidence suggests that the males, who were about twice the size of the females, fed more often on the ground and lower levels of trees than females, who had a higher proportion of fruit in the diet.[5] A similar pattern is seen today among orangutans, where it is a response to highly dis-

persed resources. As a consequence, food to which males have access is of lower quality than that eaten by females, and males must consume more of it. A major difference, of course, is that orangutan males still forage in the forest, whereas australopithecines did not. In such a situation, the latter may have been tempted to try out supplementary food sources on the ground, especially as existing sources became scarcer. This likely occurred: A cold, dry climate episode has been identified for the crucial period between 2.6 million and 2.3 million years ago. The major new food source was animal flesh, but, as we shall see, the activities

[5]Leonard, W.R., & Hegman, M. (1987). Evolution of P3 morphology in *Australopithecus afarensis*. *American Journal of Physical Anthropology, 73*, 61.

of females were every bit as important as those of males for increasing the amount of meat in the hominine diet.

Homo habilis

A number of the deposits in South and East Africa dating from 2.5 million to 1.5 million years ago have produced the fossil remains of a lightly built hominine with a body all but indistinguishable from that of the earlier australopithecines[6] except the teeth are smaller and the brain is significantly larger, relative to body size. Furthermore, the inside of the skull shows a pattern in the left cerebral hemisphere that, in people today, is associated with a speech area. Although this does not prove hominines could speak, it is clear that a marked advance in information-processing capacity over that of australopithecines occurred. Since a major brain-size increase and a tooth-size reduction are important trends in the evolution of the genus *Homo,* but not of any species of australopithecine, it looks as if these hominines, now known as ***Homo habilis*** (meaning "handy man"), were evolving in a more human direction.

The increased consumption of meat by evolving hominines is a point of major importance. The large human brain consumes 20 to 25 percent of an adult's energy, more than twice that of nonhuman primates.[7] Meat is more energy-dense than plant food and would have been important for enabling the maintenance of the evolving brain. Furthermore, the nutritive demands of nerve tissue, which the brain is made of, are high—higher, in fact, than the demands of the other types of tissue in the human body. One can meet these demands on a vegetarian diet, but the overall nutritive value of a given amount of such food is less than that of the same amount of meat. Thus, eating meat in addition to vegetable foods ensured that a reliable source of high-quality nutrition would be available to support a more highly developed brain, once it evolved. The most readily accessible plant sources would have been the proteins available in leaves and legumes (nitrogen-fixing plants; familiar modern examples are beans and peas). The problem is, these are hard for primates like humans to digest, unless they are cooked. The leaves and legumes available contain substances that cause the proteins to pass right through the gut without being absorbed. One view holds that cooking was begun by the first *Homo.*

Much has been written of a popular nature about the addition of meat to the hominine diet, often with numerous colourful references to "killer apes." Such references are quite misleading, not only because hominines are not apes, but also because they obtained their meat not by killing live animals but by scavenging, or even by stealing it from other predators. It is significant that teeth like those of australopithecines are poorly suited for meat eating. Even chimpanzees, whose canine teeth are far larger and sharper, frequently have trouble tearing through the skin of other animals. What hominines need for efficient use of meat, in the absence of teeth like those of carnivorous animals, are sharp tools for butchering. The earliest tools of this sort, found in Ethiopia, are about 2.5 million years old. The only tools used before this time were probably heavy sticks to dig up roots or ward off animals, unshaped stones to use as missiles for defence or to crack open nuts, and perhaps simple carrying devices made of knotted plant fibres.

The earliest *identifiable* tools consist of a number of implements made by striking flakes from the surface of a stone core, leaving either a uni- or bi-faced tool. The resultant *choppers,* flakes with sharp edges, and *hammerstones* were used for cutting meat and cracking bones to extract marrow. These, together with the cores they were struck from, are known as **Oldowan tools.** Their appearance marks the beginning of the **Paleolithic,** or Old Stone Age. It is significant that the earliest *Homo habilis* fossils to exhibit the trend toward modern human features

---

[6]Lewin, R. (1987). The earliest "humans" were more like apes. *Science, 236,* 1062.

[7]Leonard, W.R. (2003). Food for thought. *Scientific American, 13* (2), 62–71.

Homo habilis. The earliest species of the genus *Homo,* preceding and ancestral to *Homo erectus.* **> Oldowan tools.** The earliest identifiable stone tools that first appeared 2.5 million years ago. **> Paleolithic.** The Old Stone Age, characterized by chipped stone tools.

Gender **Perspectives**

Gender Bias in Primatology?

A popular but controversial view holds that, until female primatologists began to study primates, the importance of female primates was undervalued and misunderstood. Male scholars had apparently constructed theories, for example, about male dominance hierarchies through their filter of masculinity. Biruté Galdikas, Jane Goodall, and Dian Fossey are prominent primatologists in the public eye, reinforcing another view—that women are disproportionately drawn to, and qualified to conduct, primatology. In fact, there are probably as many male primatologists as there are female, many have studied with the same professors, and some of the earliest studies of monkeys by male scholars paid close attention to female roles. Yet the idea that male and female scientists approach issues differently persists. Naomi Quinn is a prominent feminist anthropologist who holds that academia in general is a male world and men produce male-biased theory and treat women as inherently inferior. In her view, a feminine approach considers cooperation, empathy, and holism, whereas a masculine approach does not. Linda Fedigan, though, raises questions about the issue of gender and research, the answers to which are not all that clear. What is gender and why is it relevant? Why would we want to know if the gender or sex of a researcher affects his or her research? We need to try to answer such questions in order to understand if gender has any impact on research.

Shirley Strum has studied baboons for many years and feels that being a female has had no impact on her work. One common suspicion, that fieldwork is biased physically toward men, is not true in her view. Strum points out that research funding has allowed marginalized women to continue their work. She also notes that "if I had to rank 'factors' (things that make interesting differences), theoretical framework seems the overarching one and there is not a gendered take on this."[1] Japanese primatologists, as a group of mainly men, appear to have approaches that fit the male stereotype described by Western female scholars. There is no agreement on how to evaluate gender and its effects in science, let alone primatology. Some support the ideas that men and women do science differently, others do not.

[1]Strum, S.C. (2000). E-mail exchanges. In S.C. Strum & L. Fedigan (Eds.), *Primate encounters: Models of science, gender, and society*. Chicago: University of Chicago Press.

Source: Strum, S.C., & Fedigan L. (2000). *Primate encounters: Models of science, gender, and society*. Chicago: University of Chicago Press.

---

appeared by 2.4 million years ago, soon after the earliest evidence of stone toolmaking and increased meat consumption.

Tools, Meat, and Brains

The significance of stone toolmaking and meat eating for future human evolution was enormous. Not only did they provide a secure source of high-quality protein, but also, as we have seen, they made possible the development of larger brains. Animals that live on plant foods must eat large quantities of vegetation, and this consumes much of their time. Meat eaters, by contrast, have no need to eat so much or so often. Consequently, meat-eating hominines may have had more leisure time available to explore and manipulate their environment; like lions and leopards, they would have time to lie around and play.

As already noted, *Homo habilis* got meat by scavenging from carcasses of dead animals, rather than hunting live ones. We know this because the marks of stone tools on the bones of butchered animals commonly overlie marks the teeth of carnivores made. Clearly, *Homo habilis* did not get to the prey first. Because carcasses are usually widely scattered, the only way these early hominines could have obtained a reasonably steady supply of meat would have been to do on the ground what vultures do in the air: range over vast areas in search of dead animals.[8] Bipedal

[8]Lewin, R. (1987). Four legs bad, two legs good. *Science, 235, 969.*

locomotion allowed them to do just that, without tiring, in an energetically efficient way. Thus bipedalism, which arose for reasons having nothing to do with scavenging, made it possible for our ancestors to take up a new mode of life on the savanna.

Although finding carcasses is one thing, it is quite another to get a portion of the meat. Since early hominines lacked the size and strength to drive off predators, or to compete directly with such formidable scavengers as hyenas, which are soon attracted to kills, they must have had to rely on their wit and cunning for success. We can imagine them lurking in the vicinity of a kill, sizing up the situation as the predator ate its fill while hyenas and other scavengers gathered, and devising strategies to outwit them all to grab a piece of the carcass. Hominines depending on stereotyped instinctual behaviour in such a situation would have been at a competitive disadvantage. In fact, their safest strategy would have been to seek out the carcasses of leopard kills.[9] We know *H. habilis* and leopards shared the same environment and that leopards, after satisfying their initial hunger, drag what is left of their kill into a tree where other predators cannot get at it. Such carcasses would have been accessible to *H. habilis*, who was good at climbing trees and who was active in daytime when leopards are more likely "sleeping it off" somewhere in the shade.

Several lines of evidence suggest it was probably males, rather than females, who scavenged for food. As already noted, somewhat different foraging patterns by the earlier australopithecines appear to have predisposed the males more than the females in this direction. Furthermore, without contraceptive devices and formulas to bottle feed to infants, females in their prime, when not pregnant, must have had infants to nurse. Although this would not have restricted their local mobility, any more than it does a female ape or monkey, it would have made it less easy for them than for males to range over the vast distances (on the order of 83 square kilometres) necessary to search out carcasses. Another necessity for the successful scavenger would have

been the ability to rapidly mobilize high bursts of energy to elude successfully the carnivorous competitors at the scavenging site. Although human anatomical and physiological differences between the sexes today are relatively insignificant compared with *Homo habilis* (whose males were about twice the size of females), as a general rule men can still run faster than women (even though some women can certainly run faster than some men). Finally, even for the smartest and swiftest individuals, scavenging would have been a risky business. To place *Homo habilis* females at risk would have been to place their offspring, actual and potential, at risk as well. Males, however, would have been relatively expendable, for, to put the matter bluntly, only a few males would be required to impregnate a large number of females. In evolutionary terms, the population that placed its males at risk was less likely to jeopardize its chances for reproductive success than one that placed its females at risk.

Although we should not assume *Homo habilis* had meat on a daily basis, a reasonably steady supply would have required devoting substantial amounts of time and energy to the search for carcasses, and food gathered by females and shared with males could have supplied the latter with both needs. Among modern apes and monkeys, food is rarely shared among adults, the one notable exception being the chimpanzee. Although they rarely share other foods, adult chimp males almost always share meat, frequently with females. Thus, increased consumption of meat by *Homo habilis* may have promoted the sharing of food between the sexes, although not necessarily between mated males and females; it could just as well have been between brothers and sisters or mothers and sons. On the other hand, the potential of females to be constantly receptive sexually may have promoted sharing between a male and one or more sex partners, for among most monkeys and apes, males attempt to monopolize females when the latter are at the height of sexual receptivity. As discussed in Chapter 7, the human female's ability, alone among the primates, to respond sexually at any time probably was an incidental by-product of bipedal locomotion; hence, it should have been characteristic of the earliest hominines.

---

[9]Cavallo, J.A. (1990, February). Cat in the human cradle. *Natural History*, 54–60.

For this new pattern of sharing to work, the females, no less than the males, had to "sharpen their wits." Although they continued to gather the same kinds of foods their ancestors had been eating all along, instead of consuming all this food themselves as they gathered it (as other primates do) they had to gather enough to share with the males, from whom they got a portion of the meat. To do this, they had to plan ahead to decide where food would be found in sufficient quantities; they had to figure out ways to transport it to some previously agreed-upon location for division, all the while taking precautions to prevent either spoilage or loss to animals such as rats and mice. These altered female activities, therefore, played a key role in the development of better brains.

Finally, toolmaking itself played a role in the evolution of the human brain, first by putting a premium on manual dexterity and fine manipulation, as opposed to hand use emphasizing power rather than precision. This in turn put a premium on improved organization of the nervous system. Second, the stone used to make the tools was procured at some distance from where the tools were used to process parts of carcasses. Thus, the fact that tooth marks of carnivores sometimes overlie butcher marks on bones, the incredible density of bones at some Oldowan sites, and weathering patterns indicate that, although the sites were repeatedly used over a period of years, the refuse from butchering served to attract other carnivores. Since they could have made short work of *Homo habilis*, it is unlikely the latter lingered at the site longer than necessary at any one time.

All of this is quite unlike the behaviour of historically known food-foraging peoples, who bring whole (rather than partial) carcasses back to camp, where they are completely processed; neither meat nor marrow is left (as they were at Oldowan sites), and the bones are broken in ways they were not at Oldowan sites to get at the marrow and to fabricate tools and other objects. Nor do historically known food foragers camp in the midst of so much garbage. Evidently, the Oldowan sites are places *H. habilis* took the spoils of their scavenging to, where tools and the raw materials for making them had been stockpiled in advance for butchering. At these places, the remains were quickly processed so that those doing the butchering could clear out before their lives were endangered by carnivores attracted by the meat. The advanced preparation for meat processing this implies attests to the growing importance of foresight and the ability to plan ahead.

In sum, a combination of factors, all associated in one way or another with the addition of more meat to the human diet, imposed strong selective pressures for better brains in *Homo habilis* for females as well as males. From this point on, the record shows increasing brain size relative to body size and increasing cultural development, each presumably acting to promote the other.

From fossils found in South Africa, Tanzania, Kenya, and Ethiopia, it is clear that *Homo habilis* was widespread in eastern Africa, while the remains of **Homo erectus** have been found not only in Africa and Southeast Asia but well into China and Europe.

Homo erectus

In spite of their broad distribution, fossils of *Homo erectus*, the oldest dating to about 2 million years ago, reveal no more significant physical variations than seen in modern human populations. These fossils indicate that *H. erectus* had a body much like our own, although with heavier musculature and a smaller birth canal. Differences in body size between the sexes were considerably reduced compared with early *Homo habilis*. The brain size was significantly larger than that of *H. habilis* and well within the lower range of modern brain size. The dentition was fully human, although relatively large by modern standards. As one might expect, given its larger brain, *H. erectus* outstripped its predecessors in cultural development. In Africa the Oldowan chopper was transformed into the more sophisticated hand axe (the Stone Age equivalent of "building a better mousetrap"). The teardrop-shaped hand axes characterize the **Acheulian tradition**, which lasted from about 1.5 million to 150 000 years ago. In parts of Europe chopper

---

Homo erectus.   The species of *Homo* preceding and ancestral to *Homo sapiens*. **> Acheulian tradition.**   A tool tradition associated with *Homo erectus* in Africa and Europe characterized by teardrop-shaped axes and flake tools. Named after the site where it was first defined, St. Acheul, France, it lasted from 1.5 million to about 150 000 years ago.

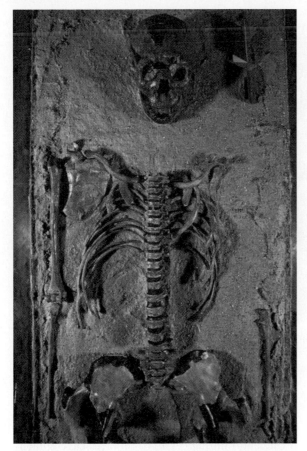

Shown here is a fossilized skeleton of an early human *(Homo erectus)*. Despite being less than 12 years old, this boy was already 168 centimetres in height. The skeleton, dated at 1.6 million years old, was found in Nariokotome in Kenya in 1984.

tools continued to be made, but, later, in both Africa and Europe, the hand axe appears further refined and developed.

During this time, tool kits also began to diversify, indicating the increased efficiency of *H. erectus* at adapting to diverse environments. At first the hand axes—shaped by regular blows that gave them a larger and finer cutting edge than chopper tools—were probably all-purpose implements, useful in food processing, hide scraping, and defence. But *H. erectus* then developed cleavers (like hand axes but without points), which could be used for killing as well as butchering; several different types of scrapers for processing hides for bedding and clothing; and flake tools to cut meat and process vegetables. Adaptation to the specific regions *H. erectus* inhabited is also indicated by different assortments of tools found in these regions.

The improved technological efficiency of *H. erectus* is also evident in the selection of raw materials. Instead of making a few large tools out of large pieces of stone, these hominines placed a new emphasis on smaller tools that were more economical with raw materials. Moreover, new techniques were developed to produce thinner, straighter, and sharper tools. A hard wooden baton for flaking produced shallow flake scars, rather than the crushed edge found on the older tools. By first preparing a flat platform on a core, from which flakes could be struck off, *H. erectus* could make even sharper and thinner implements. The toolmaker also could shape the core so that flake points 7.5 to 8.5 centimetres long could be struck off ready for use.

By 700 000 years ago—as attested by an identifiable hearth in a rock shelter in Thailand—*Homo erectus* learned how to use fire.[10] Studies of modern humans indicate they can remain reasonably comfortable down to 10°C with a minimum of clothing as long as they are active; below that temperature, the extremities cool to the point of pain. Thus, dispersal of early humans into regions where winter temperatures regularly went below 10°C, as they must have in China and most of Europe, was probably not possible without fires to keep warm. There is evidence that *H. erectus* had moved as far north as Dmanis, Russia, 1.8 million years ago, suggesting fire was used quite early in human history.

In addition to keeping warm, the use of fire enabled *H. erectus* to cook food, a significant step in human cultural adaptation. This development altered the forces of natural selection, which previously favoured individuals with heavy jaws and large, sharp teeth (food is tougher and needs more chewing when uncooked), thus paving the way for reduction in tooth size as well as supportive facial architecture. Cooking did more than this, though. Because it detoxifies a number of otherwise poisonous plants; alters digestion-inhibiting substances so that important vitamins, minerals, and proteins can be absorbed while in the gut, rather than just passing through unused; and makes complex carbohydrates such as starch—high-energy foods—digestible, cooking

---

[10]Pope, G. (1988, October). Bamboo and human evolution. *Natural History, 98*, 56.

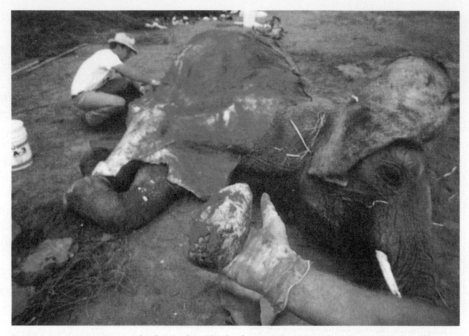

Experimentation on an elephant that died of natural causes demonstrates the effectiveness of Acheulian tools. Simple flakes of flint easily slice through the thick hide, while hand axes sever large muscles. With such tools, two men can butcher 45 kilograms of meat each in an hour.

substantially increased and made more secure the basic resources available to humans.

Like tools, then, fire gave people more control over their environment. It may have been used—if not by *Homo erectus,* then by subsequent hominines—to frighten away cave-dwelling predators so that the humans might live in the caves; it then could be used to provide warmth and light in these cold and dark habitations. Even more, it modified the natural succession of day and night, perhaps encouraging *H. erectus* to stay up after dark to review the day's events and plan the next day's activities. This, of course, implies at least rudimentary linguistic ability (see Chapter 4 for more on language origins). That *H. erectus* was capable of at least some planning is implied by the existence of populations in temperate climates, where the ability to anticipate needs for the winter season by preparing in advance to protect against the cold would have been crucial for survival.[11]

As *H. erectus* became technologically more proficient, hunting began to replace scavenging as the means for procuring meat, animal hides, and sinew. That these hominines were hunters by 400 000 years ago is attested by the recovery of sophisticated spears of this age that had been preserved in a bog in northern Germany. The complexity of hunting techniques by this time suggests, however, more than just greater technological capability; it also reflects an increased organizational ability. For example, excavations in Spain at Ambrona and Torralba indicate that group hunting techniques were used to drive a variety of large animals (including elephants) into a swamp so that they could be killed easily.[12]

With *Homo erectus,* then, we find a clearer manifestation than ever before of the interplay among cultural, physical, and environmental factors. Social organization and technology developed along with an increase in brain size and

[11]Goodenough, W.H. (1990). Evolution of the human capacity for beliefs. *American Anthropologist, 92,* 601.

[12]Freeman, L.G. (1992). Ambrona and Torralba: New evidence and interpretation. Paper presented at the 91st Annual Meeting, American Anthropological Association, Chicago, IL.

Shown here are wooden spears made by *Homo erectus* 400 000 years ago. Found in a bog in northern Germany, they are anything but crude, testifying to the sophisticated toolmaking and hunting skills developed by then.

complexity. Cultural adaptations such as cooking and more complex tool kits facilitated dental reduction; dental reduction in turn encouraged an even heavier reliance on tool development and facilitated language development. The improvements in communication and social organization that language brought undoubtedly contributed to improved methods for food gathering and hunting, to a population increase, and to territorial expansion. Evidence from tools and fossils indicates that just as *H. erectus* was able to move into areas previously uninhabited by hominines (Europe and Asia), *Homo sapiens*—our next subject—could live in areas previously uninhabited by *H. erectus*.

Homo sapiens.   The modern human species.

Homo sapiens

At various sites in Europe and Africa, a number of hominine fossils have been found that date between roughly 400 000 and 200 000 years ago. Some of these—most commonly the African fossils but also a skull from southern France—have been called *Homo erectus;* others—most commonly skulls from Steinheim, Germany, and Swanscombe, England—have been called **Homo sapiens.** In fact, all show a mixture of characteristics of both forms, which is what one would expect of remains transitional between the two. For example, skulls from Ethiopia, Steinheim, and Swanscombe had rather large brains for *Homo erectus.* Their overall appearance, however, is different from modern human skulls: They are large and robust, with their maximum breadth lower on the skull, and they had more prominent brow ridges, larger faces, and bigger teeth. Even a skull from Morocco, which had a rather small brain for *Homo sapiens,* looks surprisingly modern from the back. Finally, the various jaws from Morocco and France seem to combine features of *Homo erectus* with those of the European Neanderthals.

Whether to call these early humans "primitive" *H. sapiens* or "advanced" *H. erectus* seems a matter of taste; both labels are in keeping with their apparently transitional status.

Archaic *Homo sapiens*

The abundance of human fossils more recent than 200 000 years old is in marked contrast to the scarcity of more ancient ones. All of the younger fossils are assignable to *Homo sapiens,* although a distinction is made between archaic *H. sapiens* and anatomically modern *H. sapiens,* which by about 30 000 years ago had supplanted the former everywhere. Recently, 12 faceless skulls from near the Solo River on the island of Java have been cited as an exception. Just redated to between 53 000 and 27 000 years ago, they retain features of earlier Javanese *H. erectus,* leading some anthropologists to regard them as the same species. Earlier researchers, however, had labelled them "neanderthaloid,"[13] which would imply their inclusion in

[13]Clark, W.E. LeGros. (1955). *The fossil evidence for human evolution* (pp. 76–79). Chicago: University of Chicago Press.

archaic *H. sapiens*. Like the Neanderthals and other representatives of archaic *H. sapiens,* their brain size falls within the modern range, while the outside of the skull retains a somewhat "primitive" look. Viewing the Solo River skulls as *H. erectus* reflects a common tendency to think in terms of "typical" representatives, forgetting that a species always displays a range of variation. As paleontologist Stephen Jay Gould notes, "The history of any entity (a group, an institution, an evolutionary lineage) must be tracked by changes in the variation of all components . . . and not epitomized as a single item (. . . a supposedly typical example)."[14] Because the Solo River skulls fit within the normal range of variation for archaic *H. sapiens,* they probably are members of that species rather than of *H. erectus*.

No representatives of archaic *H. sapiens* are better known than the **Neanderthals,** whose fossils are confined to Europe and the Middle East, dating from 130 000 to 30 000 years ago. These extremely muscular people, while having brains of modern size, possessed faces distinctively different from those of modern humans. Midfacial projection of their noses and teeth formed a kind of prow, at least in part to sustain the large size of their front teeth. Over the eyes were prominent brow ridges, and on the back of the skull a bony mass provided for attachment of powerful neck muscles.

Living in other parts of the world were variants of archaic *H. sapiens* that lacked the extreme midfacial projection and massive muscle attachments on the back of the skull characteristic of the Neanderthals. The Solo River skulls from Java are a prime example. In them, features of *H. erectus* are combined with those of archaic, as well as more modern, *H. sapiens*. The fossils look like robust versions of some more recent Southeast Asian populations or, if one looks backward, somewhat less primitive versions of the *H. erectus* populations that preceded them in this region. Fossils from various parts of Africa, the most famous being a skull from Kabwe in

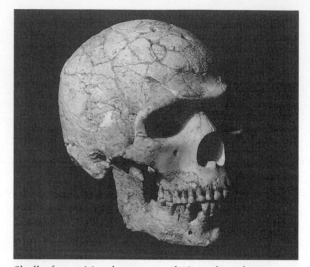

Skull of transition between archaic and modern *Homo sapiens*.

Zambia, show a similar combination of ancient and modern traits. Finally, equivalent remains have been found at several localities in China.

Adaptations to the environment by archaic *Homo sapiens* were, of course, both physical and cultural, but the capacity for cultural adaptation was predictably greater than it had been. The Neanderthal's extensive use of fire, for example, was essential to survival in an arctic climate such as that of Europe at the time. They lived in small bands or single-family units, both in the open and in caves, and undoubtedly communicated by speech (see Chapter 4). Evidence of deliberate burials seems to reflect complex ritual behaviour. Moreover, the remains of an amputee discovered in Iraq and an arthritic man unearthed in France imply that Neanderthals took care of the disabled, an unprecedented example of social concern.

Hunting techniques improved along with social organization and a more developed weapon and toolmaking technology. The toolmaking tradition of all but the latest Neanderthals (whose technology was comparable to that of anatomically modern *H. sapiens*)[15] is called **Mousterian** after a site

---

[14]Gould, S.J. (1996). *Full house: The spread of excellence from Plato to Darwin* (p. 72). New York: Crown.

[15]Mellars, P. (1989). Major issues in the emergence of modern humans. *Current Anthropology, 30,* 356–357.

Neanderthal. The representative group of archaic *Homo sapiens* living in Europe and the Middle East from about 130 000 years ago to about 30 000 years ago. **> Mousterian.** A toolmaking tradition of the Neanderthals and their contemporaries of Europe, southwestern Asia, and North Africa.

(Le Moustier) in France. Mousterian tools date from 100 000 to 40 000 years ago and characterized this period in Europe, North Africa, and southwestern Asia.

Mousterian tools are generally lighter and smaller than those of earlier traditions. Whereas previously only two or three flakes could be obtained from the entire core, Neanderthal toolmakers obtained many more smaller flakes, which they skillfully retouched and sharpened. Their tool kits also contained a greater variety of types than the earlier ones: hand axes, flakes, scrapers, borers, notched flakes for shaving wood, and many types of points that could be attached to wooden shafts to make spears. This variety of tools facilitated more effective use of food resources and enhanced the quality of clothing and shelter.

For archaic *H. sapiens,* improved cultural adaptation is no doubt related to the fact that the brain of archaic *H. sapiens* had achieved modern size. Such a brain made possible not only sophisticated technology but also conceptual thought of considerable complexity. Evidence of conceptual thought is provided by the ceremonial burial of the dead, as well as by objects of apparently symbolic significance. Among the latter are nonutilitarian items, such as pendants, and carved and engraved markings on objects that would have required some form of linguistic explanation. Other examples include the oldest known flute (made of bone) and the common use of red ochre (a red pigment).[16]

One of the great debates in anthropology today is whether one, some, or all populations of the archaic species played a role in the evolution of modern *H. sapiens.* With the possible exception of Neanderthals who coexisted between 40 000 and 30 000 years ago with anatomically modern humans in Europe and the Middle East, the fossil evidence suggests that local populations in eastern and southern Asia, as well as in Africa, made the transition from *Homo erectus* to modern *Homo sapiens* (the "multiregional hypothesis"). In contrast, a comparison of molecular data from modern human populations living in diverse geographic regions has led some anthropologists to argue that all modern people are derived from a single population of archaic *H. sapiens* that lived in Africa (although some have argued in favour of Asia). These modern people eventually replaced the Neanderthals, who left no descendants. This "Eve hypothesis" has been criticized on several grounds; one is that it conflicts with the fossil evidence for continuity between older and more recent populations not just in Africa but in China, Southeast Asia, and parts of the Middle East, even if not in western Europe. Another is a lack of archaeological evidence of an invasion of Asia by people possessing a different technology. Finally, these molecular data analyses have serious problems.[17] Even a recent analysis of DNA (deoxyribonucleic acid) extracted from a Neanderthal skeleton, said to relegate these hominines to a side branch of human evolution, is open to different interpretation.[18] Although the Eve hypothesis still has its champions, it has serious problems to overcome before its acceptance is warranted. New life has been breathed into the Eve hypothesis with the report in 2003 of near-modern human skulls, including one of a child, from Ethiopia. Dating to 160 000 years ago, the *Homo sapiens idaltu* fossils provide the first good evidence for near-modern human beings significantly older than the Neanderthals. The child's skull has evidence of long-term handling, suggesting ancestors were venerated.

Taking a cautious approach, all that can be said at the moment is that at least one population of archaic *Homo sapiens* evolved into modern humans. As noted earlier, the basic difference between the two types of *H. sapiens* is that the modern face is less massive, as is the bony architecture at the rear of the skull that provided the attachment needed for the neck musculature to compensate for the weight of a massive face.

---

[16]Bednarik, R.G. (1995). Concept-mediated marking in the Lower Paleolithic. *Current Anthropology, 36,* 606. Also Rice, P.C. (1997). Paleoanthropology 1996—Part II. *General Anthropology, 3* (2), 10.

[17]Cachel, S. (1997). Dietary shifts and the European Upper Paleolithic transition. *Current Anthropology, 38,* 590.

[18]Cooper, A., Poinar, H.N., Pääbo, S., Radovčić, J., Debénath, A., Caparros, M., Barroso-Ruiz, C., Bertranpetit, J., Nielsen-March, C., Hedges, R.E.M., & Sykes, B. (1997). Neanderthal genetics, *Science, 277,* 1021–1024.

Anatomically Modern Peoples and the Upper Paleolithic

Although populations of archaic and anatomically modern *Homo sapiens* managed to coexist for a time in Europe, by 30 000 years ago peoples whose physical appearance was similar to our own had the world to themselves. As is usual in human populations, these **Upper Paleolithic peoples** reveal considerable physical variability, but, generally speaking, they all had characteristically modern-looking faces. As suggested in our discussion of *Homo erectus*, specialized tools and cooking helped achieve this modernization by gradually assuming the chewing and softening functions once served by large teeth and heavy jaws. Selection seems to have favoured diminished muscles for chewing, and consequently the bones these muscles were attached to became less massive.

At this point in human evolution, culture had become a more potent force than biology. As the smaller features of Upper Paleolithic peoples suggest, physical bulk was no longer required for survival. New technological developments had contributed to the increasing complexity of the brain by the time of archaic *H. sapiens,* and this complexity now enabled people to create a still more sophisticated technology. Similarly, conceptual thought and symbolic behaviour seem to have developed beyond those of archaic *H. sapiens.* More than ever, intelligence henceforth provides the key to humanity's increased reliance on cultural rather than physical adaptation.

In Upper Paleolithic times, human intelligence enabled people to manufacture tools that surpassed the physical equipment of predators and to develop more efficient means of social organization and cooperation—all of which made them far more proficient at hunting and fishing as well as at gathering. Cultural adaptation also became highly specific and regional, thus increasing human chances for survival under a variety of environmental conditions. Instead of manufacturing crude all-purpose tools, Upper Paleolithic populations of the savanna, forest, and shore all developed specialized devices suited to the resources of their particular environment and to the different seasons. This versatility also permitted human habitation of new areas, most notably Australia (by 60 000 years ago) and the Americas (by 12 500 years ago at the very latest).

This degree of specialization naturally required improved manufacturing techniques. The blade method of manufacture (see Figure 3.4), invented by archaic *H. sapiens* and later used widely in Europe and western Asia, required less raw material than before and resulted in smaller and lighter tools with a better ratio between weight of flint and length of cutting edge. The pressure-flaking technique—in which a bone, antler, or a wooden tool was used to press off small flakes from a flint core—gave the toolmaker greater control over the tool's shape than was possible by simply striking it directly with another stone or piece of antler.

The *burin*—a stone tool with chisel-like edges—although invented earlier by Mousterian toolmakers, came into common use in the Upper Paleolithic. The burin provided an excellent means of carving bone and antler, used for tools such as fishhooks and harpoons. The *atlatl*, which consisted of a piece of wood with a groove in it for holding and throwing a spear, also appeared at this time. With the atlatl, hunters increased the force behind the spear throw. The bow and arrow went even beyond this. The bowstring increased the force on the arrow, enabling it to travel farther and with greater effectiveness than a spear thrown with an atlatl.

One important aspect of Upper Paleolithic culture is its art. As far as we know, humans had not produced artwork of this calibre before; therefore, the level of artistic proficiency is certainly amazing. In some regions, tools and weapons were decorated with engravings of animal figures; pendants were made of bone and ivory, as were female figurines; and sculptures were made of clay. More spectacular, and quite unlike anything the earlier Neanderthals created, are the cave paintings in Spain and France and the paintings and engravings on the walls of rock shelters in southern Africa. Made with mineral oxide pigments, these skillfully executed paintings depict humans and animals that coexisted

---

Upper Paleolithic peoples.   The first people of modern appearance, who lived in the last part (Upper Paleolithic) of the Old Stone Age.

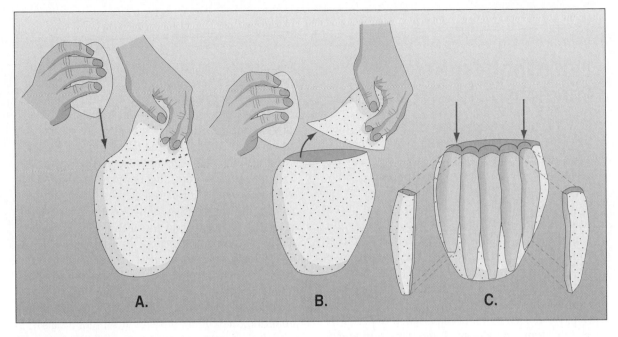

FIGURE 3.4
During the Upper Paleolithic, a new technique was used to manufacture blades. The stone was broken to create a striking platform, then vertical blades were flaked off the sides to form sharp-edged tools.

with Upper Paleolithic peoples. Because the southern African rock art tradition lasted a full 27 000 years into historic times, we have learned that it depicts visions of the artists when in trance. Along with the animals, the art also includes a variety of geometric motifs of a sort the human nervous system generates spontaneously when in trance. Australian rock art, some of it older than European cave art, is also associated with trancing and includes similar motifs. Since the same geometric designs occur in the cave art of Europe, it seems it, too, depicted images seen in altered states of consciousness. Just as the rock art of southern Africa and Australia is related to what we would label religious experiences, so too was the Stone Age art of Europe.

Peopling the New World

The Americas were among the last territories to be occupied by people. Genetic and linguistic evidence indicates that the process of peopling the New World was anything but simple. Aboriginal peoples of the Americas have the most diverse languages of any continent. At least five distinct

The intellectual capabilities of Upper Paleolithic peoples, whose skeletons differ in no significant way from our own, are reflected in the efficiency with which some of them hunted game far larger and more powerful than themselves, as well as in the sophistication of their art. The painting of animals like the one shown here attests not only to the artist's technical skill but also to his or her knowledge of the animal's anatomy.

Anthropology **Applied**

Stone Tools for Modern Surgeons

In 1975, Don Crabtree, then at the Idaho State University Museum, underwent heart surgery; in 1980, an anonymous patient in Boulder, Colorado, underwent eye surgery; and in 1986, David Pokotylo of the Museum of Anthropology at the University of British Columbia underwent reconstructive surgery on his hand. What these operations had in common was that the scalpels used were not surgical steel. Instead, they were made of obsidian (a naturally occurring volcanic "glass") by the same technique Upper Paleolithic people used to make blades. In all three cases, the scalpels were handmade by archaeologists who specialized in the study of ancient stone tool technology: Crabtree himself, Payson Sheets at the University of Colorado, and Pokotylo with his colleague Len McFarlane (who hafted the blades) of the Museum of Anthropology.

The reason these scalpels were modelled on ancient stone tools, rather than made of modern steel or even diamond, is that the obsidian blade is superior in almost every way: It is 210 to 1050 times sharper than surgical steel, 100 to 500 times sharper than a razor blade, and 3 times sharper than a diamond blade (which costs much more and cannot be made with more than 3 millimetres of cutting edge). Also, obsidian blades are easier to cut with and do less damage in the process (under a microscope, incisions made with the sharpest steel blades show torn, ragged edges and are littered with bits of displaced flesh).[1] As a consequence, the surgeon has better control over what he or she is doing, and the incisions heal faster with less scarring and pain.

To develop and market obsidian scalpels, Sheets formed a corporation in partnership with Boulder, Colorado, eye surgeon Dr. Firmon Hardenbergh. Together, they developed a means of producing cores of uniform size from molten glass, as well as a machine to detach blades from the cores. With the advent of laser surgery, however, the potential market for scalpels of any sort appears to be shrinking significantly.

---

[1]Sheets, P.D. (1987). Dawn of a new Stone Age in eye surgery. In R.J. Sharer & W. Ashmore (Eds.), *Archaeology: Discovering our past* (p. 231). Palo Alto, CA: Mayfield.

---

genetic groupings have been found among pre-contact and later aboriginal peoples. There may have been many migrations or there may have been a single one, lasting millennia. We are far from a clear answer. Most archaeologists agree, however, that the aboriginal peoples of the Americas have their roots in Siberian northeast Asia.

Upper Paleolithic cultures were so effective that Siberia presented few obstacles to skilled modern humans. They were widespread in the region by 18 000 to 14 000 years ago. Just how early they arrived there is unknown, but evidence suggests they were there at least 35 000 years ago. By 11 200 years ago, a Paleoindian tradition known as Clovis, unique to the New World, was centred in the southeastern United States, although the tradition is found over a much larger area. The origin of Clovis is debated, but because it is not found in the Old World or Alaska and Yukon Territory, many archaeologists feel that it developed from an as yet undefined earlier tradition. Linguistic diversification in the Americas would have needed far more than 11 000 years, according to language specialists. Evidence for people in the New World before 11 200 years ago is slowly growing.

Three times during the last glacial period, sea levels were low enough to make Siberia, Alaska, and Yukon Territory one contiguous land mass known as Beringia. Here, Upper Paleolithic people lived as they did elsewhere in Asia, following and hunting animals in their seasonal rounds and moving to collect plants when they were in season for food, teas, medicine, and other purposes. At the Bluefish Caves in Yukon Territory the discovery of bones and small tools indicates human presence there between 15 000

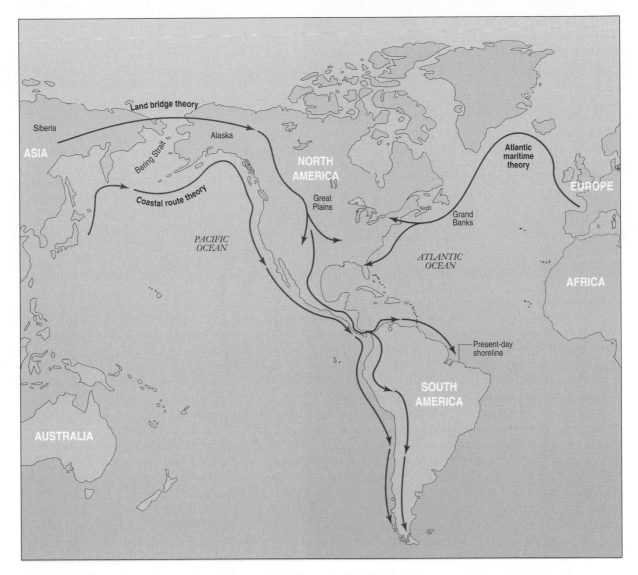

MAP 3.1
This map shows possible routes taken by Paleolithic people into the New World.

and 12 000 years ago. These easternmost Siberians were blocked from land access to the southern Americas by two continental glaciers. Even if the two glaciers occasionally separated during mild episodes, the corridor between them would have been inhospitable.

Nevertheless, people had spread to southern South America, where the Monte Verde site was occupied by 12 500 years ago. By 11 000 years ago non-Clovis peoples at the Quebrada Jaguay site in coastal Peru were exploiting maritime resources. For people to have reached Monte Verde so early, they would have had to circumvent the glacier barrier covering Canada. The most likely way was by boats, hopping down the west coast of the Americas from landfall to landfall. Evidence for this will be difficult to find because the ancient shoreline is now submerged. As the glaciers retreated, sites such as Debert in Nova Scotia, dating to 10 600 years ago, show that people moved quickly from the south to form the ancestral First Nations of Canada.

The Asian ancestry of the Clovis peoples is not actually confirmed by the evidence in the preceding discussion. The technology most closely resembling Clovis is found in the Upper Paleolithic of France and Spain, not in Asia. Dennis Stanford of the Smithsonian Institution hypothesizes that small numbers of Upper Paleolithic people could have easily made it to the Grand Banks, some of which was dry land because of lowered sea levels. From there, migration westward was almost inevitable. A recently documented genetic group found in about 20 000 indigenous North Americans, and in some pre-contact populations, is found only in Europe.

With people moving into the New World at the end of the Upper Paleolithic, we have reached a logical place to end our examination of the beginnings of human culture. This closure should not be taken to mean that human evolution stopped at the end of the Paleolithic. Since then, the human species has continued to change biologically, even though it remains the same species now as then. Culture, too, has continued to change, and revolutionary developments, such as the development of food production and, later, state-level societies, came after the Paleolithic. These developments will be touched on in subsequent chapters, especially Chapters 5 and 15.

CHAPTER SUMMARY

Anthropology includes the study of primates other than humans to explain why and how humans developed as they did. As the early primates became tree dwellers, various modifications occurred—in dental characteristics, sense organs, the brain, and skeletal structure—that helped them to adapt to their environment. In addition, learned social behaviour became increasingly important to them. By studying the behaviour of present-day primates, anthropologists seek clues for reconstructing behavioural patterns that may have characterized the apelike primates ancestral to both humans and present-day apes.

Like all monkeys and apes, chimpanzees live in structured social groups and express their sociability through communication by visual and vocal signals. They also exhibit learning, but unlike most other primates, they can make and use tools.

The earliest undoubted members of the human family were living in Africa by 4.2 million years ago. These hominines were fully bipedal (able to walk and run erect). Best known are the australopithecines, who were well equipped for generalized food gathering in a savanna environment. Although still strikingly apelike from the waist up, australopithecines had a fully human dentition with many features easily derivable from earlier apelike primates, some of whom lived under conditions that forced them to spend

considerable time on the ground and appear to have had the capacity for at least occasional bipedal locomotion.

It seems that an early form of australopithecine gave rise to an early form of the genus *Homo*. Of major significance is that members of this new genus were both meat eaters and makers of stone tools. Toolmaking enabled *Homo habilis* to process meat so that it could be eaten; because making tools from stone depended on fine manipulation of the hands, it put a premium on more developed brains.

Homo erectus, the next *Homo* species to develop, exhibited a nearly modern body, a brain close in size to the modern human brain, and fully human dental characteristics. This hominine's ability to use fire provided a further means of controlling the environment. The technological efficiency of *H. erectus* is evidenced in refined toolmaking, with the development of the hand axe and, later, specialized tools for hunting, butchering, food processing, hide scraping, and defence. In addition, hunting techniques ultimately developed by *H. erectus* reflected a considerable advance in organizational ability.

By 200 000 years ago, hominines possessed the brain capacity of true *Homo sapiens*. Apparently several local variations of archaic *H. sapiens*, including the Neanderthals, existed. Their capacity for cultural adaptation was considerable, doubtlessly because their fully modern brains made possible not only sophisticated technology but complex conceptual thought as well. Those who lived in Europe used fire extensively in their arctic climate, lived in small bands, and communicated by speech. Remains indicate the existence of ritual behaviour, and the aged and infirm were cared for.

Evidence indicates that at least one population of archaic *H. sapiens* evolved into modern humans. Upper Paleolithic peoples possessed physical features similar to those of present-day human populations as sheer physical bulk gave way to smaller features. Cave paintings found in Spain and France and rock art from southern Africa, which served a religious purpose, attest to a highly sophisticated aesthetic sensibility. By at least the end of the Upper Paleolithic, big-game hunters had crossed the Bering Strait and begun dispersing through North and later South America.

We thus have seen a close interrelation between developing culture and developing humanity. The critical importance of culture as the human adaptive mechanism is apparent because culture seems to have imposed selective pressures favouring a better brain, and a better brain, in turn, made possible improved cultural adaptation. Indeed, it seems fair to say that modern humans look the way they do today because cultural adaptation played such an important role in the survival of our ancient ancestors. Because cultural adaptation worked so well, human populations grew, probably very slowly, causing a gradual expansion into previously uninhabited parts of the world. And this, too, affected cultural adaptation, as humans made adjustments to meet new conditions.

QUESTIONS FOR CRITICAL THOUGHT

1. How does primatology help us understand human origins?

2. Should the genetic similarity of humans and chimpanzees lead to legislation to stop chimpanzee use in biomedical research? Why or why not? What about other less closely related primates? Supposing they possess a degree of self-awareness comparable to that of humans, what are the ethics of holding chimpanzees captive and carrying out laboratory research on them?

3. Why are the "invention" of human culture and tool use connected? What other activities, such as language or living in groups, could have affected the early evolution of human culture? What other kinds of tools might our human ancestors have developed that we might be unlikely to find now? Why wouldn't we find them today? What might such tools have told us about these peoples?

4. What methodological limitations hamper our understanding of early human culture? What aspects of the earliest human culture are so far invisible or difficult to ascertain?

5. The last major human migration into a pristine continent brought people to the New World from Asia. What factors may have been responsible for this event?

INTERNET RESOURCES

The Jane Goodall Institute
http://www.janegoodall.org/chimp_central/conservation
This site addresses the current situation in the Congo Basin, where wildlife is being threatened by new incursions into the land. For anyone who is interested in wildlife protection, environment, and cultural practices, this is a good site to visit.

Biographies of Primatologists
http://www.primate.wisc.edu/pin/bio.html

This site lists many well-known primatologists and provides a biography of each one, including the "greats" such as Dian Fossey (of *Gorillas in the Mist* fame), Jane Goodall, Biruté Galdikas, and Mary Leakey, as well as several primate biographies, such as one of Booee the chimpanzee.

Early Human Phylogeny
http://www.mnh.si.edu/anthro/humanorigins/ha/a_tree.html
A good site for students to examine the complexity of deciphering our ancient family tree;

presents new fossil evidence that further obscures the links between early humans.

Geological Time Scale

http://www.zoomdinosaurs.com/subjects/geologictime.html

This Enchanted Learning Software site offers students a superior geological time scale and an excellent discussion of plate tectonics and continental drift. Each epoch has further links to describe the nature of the earth and its inhabitants at that time. This is a highly recommended site for anthropology, biology, and geology students and instructors alike.

Homo habilis

http://citd.scar.utoronto.ca/antd15/shan/homo.html

In addition to a brief discussion of *Homo habilis*, this site offers some links to archaeological sites, such as Lake Turkana, and a profile of Louis Leakey.

Earliest Modern Humans

http:www.nature.com/cgi-taf/dynapage.taf?file=/nature/journal/v423/n6941/full/nature01669_fs.html

This is the original article reporting the oldest modern human remains so far discovered (in Ethiopia). The authors consider location, timing, and the circumstances of modern humans.

Neanderthal DNA

http://www.sciencemag.org/cgi/content/full/299/5612/1525

An article on Neanderthals exploring their physical form, behaviour, and disappearance, raising the question of the role that genes played in their failure to compete culturally.

Neanderthal DNA

http://www.nature.com/cgi-taf/dynapage.taf?file=/nature/journal/v404/n6777/full/404453a0_fs.html

The authenticity of ancient DNA from a Neanderthal in the northern Caucasus is corroborated in this study. Problems with ancient DNA analysis are briefly outlined, and the relationship between Neanderthal and modern humans is evaluated. Links are provided to related research.

Early Modern Human Culture

http://anthro.palomar.edu/homo2/sapiens_culture.htm

Detailed discussion of early modern human cultures, beginning around 100 000 years ago until approximately 17 000 years ago. Focuses on Cro-Magnons and their artwork.

SUGGESTED READINGS

de Waal, F. (1996). *Good natured: The origins of right and wrong in humans and other animals*. Cambridge, MA: Harvard University Press.

Primatologist Frans de Waal, although fully up on field studies of wild primates, has spent much of his career studying chimpanzees and other primates in captivity. In this book he argues that moral behaviour can be found in nonhuman animals, most clearly in apes but also in other primate and even nonprimate species. Written for a general audience, but with a strong scientific foundation, the book communicates its message in a clear and responsible way.

Fedigan L.M., & Strum, S.C. (2000). *Primate encounters: Models of science, gender, and society*. Chicago: University of Chicago Press.

Examines primatology in the context of social, cultural, and historical issues. International and gender perspectives on primate research are emphasized. E-mail exchanges among the authors are included and provide unparalleled access to the thought processes behind the essays.

Goodall, J. (1990). *Through a window*. Boston: Houghton Mifflin.

This fascinating book is a personal account of Goodall's 30 years of experience studying wild chimpanzees in Tanzania. A pleasure to read and a fount of information on the behaviour of these apes, the book is profusely illustrated as well.

Klein, R.G., & Edgar, B. (2002). *The dawn of human culture*. New York: Wiley.

How and when human culture came to be is the subject of this book, which proposes a new, genetically based theory. The account follows the record of human origins, focusing on technology, and includes some of the most recent fossil discoveries.

Shreeve, J. (1995). *The Neandertal enigma: Solving the mystery of modern human origins*. New York: Morrow.

Shreeve is a science writer who has written extensively about human evolution. This book is engagingly written and covers most of the major issues in the Neanderthal–Modern debate.

CNN TODAY VIDEOS

Early Hominid (CNN Physical Anthropology, vol. 3, 2:12)
Physical anthropologists discover fossils in northeast Ethiopia revealing one of the earliest known finds of a meat-eating hominid. Segment shows dating techniques.

Jane Goodall (CNN Physical Anthropology, vol. 3, 10:28)
An interview with the noted primatologist, Jane Goodall, discussing her breakthrough work with chimpanzees.

Mungo Man's New Age (CNN Physical Anthropology, vol. 3, 1:23)
Genetic research on Mungo Man results in interesting questions about human origins by challenging the Out of Africa theory, which states that all living people are descendants of homosapiens coming from Africa more than 100,000 years ago.

Chapter 4

Language and Communication

The richness of human culture is made possible by language, one of our most distinctive characteristics. Although we are genetically programmed to speak, what we speak is determined by our culture.

Chapter Preview

1. What Is Language?

Language is a system of sounds or gestures that, when put together according to certain rules, results in meanings intelligible to all speakers. Although humans rely primarily on language to communicate with one another, it is not their sole means of communication. Language is embedded in a gesture-call system that consists of paralanguage — extralinguistic noises that accompany language — and kinesics, body motions that convey messages. We also convey messages through use of space and touch.

2. How Is Language Related to Culture?

Languages are spoken by people who are members of distinctive cultures. Social variables, such as the history, class, gender, and status of the speaker, influence language use. Moreover, people communicate what is meaningful to them, and what is or is not meaningful is defined by their particular culture. In fact, our language use affects, and is affected by, our culture. Language retention in today's world is of particular concern to aboriginal cultures.

3. How Did Language Begin?

Many explanations have been proposed to account for the origin of language. Human language may have begun as a system of gestures with rudimentary structure. A key factor in its elaboration may have been the importance of planning ahead for future contingencies by our ancient ancestors. Since speech, like gestures, is a product of muscular movements, spoken language may have emerged as the muscles of the mouth and vocal tract were favoured so that people could use their hands for other things while they talked, allowing them to communicate with others without having to be in full view.

CHAPTER OUTLINE

The Nature of Language

The Gesture-Call System

Linguistic Change

Anthropology Applied: Visual Anthropology and Ethnographic Film

Language in Its Cultural Setting

Gender Perspectives: Gender in Language

Original Study: Speak *bilingue*?

The Origins of Language

Because culture is learned and not inherited biologically, its transmission from one person to another, and from one generation to the next, depends on an effective communication system that is far more complex than that of any other animal. Thus, a first requirement for any culture is providing a means of communication among individuals. All cultures do this through some form of language, one of the most distinctive of human characteristics.

All normal humans have the ability to speak, and they spend a considerable part of each day doing so. Indeed, **language** is so much a part of our lives that it permeates everything we do, and everything we do is reflected in our language. No one doubts that our ability to speak, whether it be through sounds or gestures (sign languages, such as American Sign Language used by the hearing impaired, are fully developed languages in their own right), rests squarely upon our biological organization. We are "programmed" to speak, although only in a general way. Beyond the cries of babies, which are not learned but which do communicate, humans must learn how to speak. We are taught to speak a particular language, and any normal child from anywhere in the world readily learns whatever language is spoken where he or she happens to be reared.

Language is a system for communicating in **symbols**. "Symbol," in our definition, means any kind of sound or gesture to which cultural tradition has assigned meaning, and not a symbol that has a natural or self-evident meaning, which language specialists call a **signal**. A tear is a signal of crying, and crying is a signal of some kind of emotional or physical state; the word *crying*, however, is a symbol, a group of sounds to which we have learned to assign the meaning of a particular action, and that we can use to communicate that meaning whether or not anyone around us is actually crying.

Currently, language experts are not certain how much credit to give to animals, such as dolphins or chimpanzees, for the ability to use symbols as well as signals, even though these animals

This example of animal communication shows a young domestic cat in a playful posture to the older cat.

and many others have been found to communicate in remarkable ways. Several apes have been taught American Sign Language. As an example, Chanteh the orangutan has learned 150 different signs, developing the communication skills of a two- to three-year-old child. Even among vervet monkeys, at least 10 different calls are used for communication, and these are not mere indexes for degree of arousal or fear. As primatologist Allison Jolly notes:

> They mean something in the outside world; they include which direction to look in or where to run. There is an audience effect: calls are given when there is someone appropriate to listen . . . monkey calls are far more than involuntary expressions of emotion.[1]

What are the implications of this nonhuman ability to communicate for our understanding of the nature and evolution of language? The answer lies in developing a better understanding of animal communication than we now have. What is clear is that animal communication cannot be dismissed as a set of simple reflexes or fixed action patterns, even though debate continues over just how human

---

[1]Jolly, A. (1991). Thinking like a vervet. *Science, 251,* 574.

Language.   A system of communication using sounds or gestures put together in meaningful ways according to a set of rules. **> Symbols.**   Sounds or gestures that stand for meanings among a group of people. **> Signal.**   A sound or gesture that has a natural or self-evident meaning.

and animal communication relate to each other.[2] The fact is, human culture, as we know it, is ultimately dependent on a system of communication far more complex than that of any other animal. Human cultures are so rich in content that they require communication systems that not only give precise labels to various classes of phenomena but also permit people to think and talk about their own and others' experiences in the past and future as well as the present. The central and most highly developed human system of communication is language. Knowledge of the workings of language, then, is essential to a full understanding of culture.

THE NATURE OF LANGUAGE

Any human language—French, English, Chinese, Swahili, Cree—is obviously a means of transmitting information and sharing with others both

cultural and individual experiences. Because we tend to take language for granted, it is perhaps not so obvious that language is also a system that enables us to translate our concerns, beliefs, and perceptions into symbols others can understand and interpret. In spoken language, this is done by taking a few sounds—no language uses more than about 50—and developing rules for putting them together in meaningful ways. Sign languages do the same thing but with gestures rather than sounds. The many languages that presently exist all over the world—some 6000 or so different ones—may well astound and mystify us by their great variety and complexity, but this should not blind us to the fact that all languages, as far back as we can trace them, are organized in the same basic way.

The roots of **linguistics,** the modern scientific study of language, go back a long way, to the works of ancient grammarians in India more than 2000 years ago. In the age of exploration and discovery, the scientific study of language was given impetus by the accumulation of facts: the collection of sounds, words, and sentences from all sorts of different languages, encountered by European

[2]Armstrong, D.F., Stokoe, W.C., & Wilcox, S.F. (1994). Signs of the origin of syntax. *Current Anthropology, 35,* 349–368. Burling, R. (1993). Primate calls, human language, and nonverbal communication. *Current Anthropology, 34,* 25–53.

For linguist Megan Biesele studying the Ju/'hoansi language in the field, the tape recorder has become an indispensable tool.

Linguistics.   The modern scientific study of all aspects of language.

explorers, invaders, and missionaries in exotic lands. In the 21st century, although researchers are still collecting data, they have made considerable progress in the reasoning process, testing and working from new and improved theories. Insofar as language theories and facts are verifiable by independent researchers looking at the same materials, a science of linguistics now exists. Linguistic anthropology focuses on the way humans use language to develop, practise, and transmit culture. Linguistic anthropologists also examine the way people use language, both verbal and nonverbal, to develop social relationships with each other, and to create, maintain, and reproduce social distinctions.

The Sound and Shape of Language

How can a linguistic anthropologist approach and make sense of a language that has not already been analyzed and described or that is not covered in immediately available materials? Hundreds of such languages exist in the world today; fortunately, some effective methods have been developed to help with the task. It is a painstaking process to unravel a language, but it is ultimately rewarding and often even fascinating for its own sake.

For a spoken language, the process requires first a trained ear and a thorough understanding of the way speech sounds are produced. Otherwise, it would be extremely difficult to write out or make intelligent use of any data. To satisfy this preliminary requirement, most people need special training in **phonetics,** or the systematic study of the production, transmission, and reception of speech sounds.

Phonology

To analyze and describe any new language, a researcher needs an inventory of all of its sounds and an accurate way of writing them down. Some sounds of other languages may be similar to the researcher's own; others (such as the "clicks" in San languages) may be sounds the researcher has never consciously produced. Once a researcher knows all the possible sounds in a language, he or she can study the patterns these sounds take as they are used to form words. From this, the person can discover the underlying rules that explain which combinations of sounds are permissible in the language and which are not.

The first step in studying any language, once a number of utterances have been collected, is to isolate the **phonemes,** or the smallest classes of sound that make a difference in meaning. This isolation and analysis is done by a process called the minimal-pair test: The linguist tries to find two short words that appear to be exactly alike except for one sound, such as *bit* and *pit* in English. If the substitution of *b* for *p* in this minimal pair makes a difference in meaning (which it does in English), then those two sounds are distinct phonemes of the language and will require two different symbols to record. If, however, the linguist finds two different pronunciations, as when *butter* is pronounced "budder," and then finds that their meaning is the same for a native speaker, the sounds represented are variants of the same phoneme. In such cases, only one of the two symbols will be used to record that sound. For greater accuracy and to avoid confusion with the various sounds of the researcher's language, the symbols of a phonetic alphabet, such as was developed by Edward Sapir for the American Anthropological Association, are used to distinguish the sounds of most languages in a way comprehensible to anyone who knows the system.

Morphology

The process of making and studying an inventory of sounds is a lengthy task; concurrently, the linguist may begin to work out all the combinations of sounds that seem to have meaning. These are called **morphemes,** and they are the smallest units that have meaning in a language. They may consist of words or parts of words. A linguist can abstract morphemes and their meanings from speakers of a language by pointing or gesturing to elicit words and their meanings, but the ideal situation is to have an informant, a person who knows enough of a common second language to help the linguist make approximate translations.

Phonetics.   The study of the production, transmission, and reception of speech sounds. **> Phonemes.**   In linguistics, the smallest classes of sound that make a difference in meaning. **> Morphemes.**   In linguistics, the smallest units of sound that carry meaning.

It is pointless to write down data without any suggestion of meaning for them. *Cat* and *dog* would, of course, turn out to be morphemes, or meaningful combinations of phonemes, in English. By pointing to two of either of these animals, the linguist could elicit *cats* and *dogs*. This indicates that another unit carries meaning, an *-s*, that may be added to the original morpheme to mean "plural." The *-s* that cannot occur in the language unattached is a **bound morpheme;** because *dog* and *cat* can occur unattached to anything, they are called **free morphemes.** Because the sound represented in writing as *s* is actually different in the two words (*s* in *cats* and *z* in *dogs*), the sounds *s* and *z* are two varieties of the same morpheme (even though they may be two different phonemes) occurring in different contexts but with no difference in meaning.

Grammar and Syntax

The next step is to put morphemes together to form phrases or sentences. This process is known as identifying the *syntactic units* of the language, or the way morphemes are combined into larger chains that have meaning. Linguists use a method called **frame substitution.** The linguist identifies strings such as *my cat, your cat, I see your cat,* and *she sees my cat.* This begins to establish the rules of phrase and sentence making, the **syntax** of the language.

Further success with this sort of linguistic study depends on individual ingenuity, tact, logic, and experience with language. A language may make extensive use of utterances that are not found in the linguist's language and that the linguist may not even think of asking for. Furthermore, some speakers may pretend they cannot say (or may truly not be able to say) certain words their culture considers impolite, taboo, or inappropriate for mention to outsiders.

The **grammar** of a language consists of all observations about its morphemes and syntax. Further work may include the establishment, by substitution frames, of all the **form classes** of the language: that is, the parts of speech or categories of words that work the same way in any sentence. For example, a linguist may establish a category called *nouns,* defined as anything that will fit the substitution frame "I see a. . . ." The researcher makes the frame, tries out a number of words in it, and has a native speaker indicate "yes" or "no" for whether the words work. In English, the words *house* and *cat* will fit this frame and can be said to belong to the same form class, but the word *think* will not. Another possible substitution frame for nouns might be "The _____ died," in which the word *cat* will fit, but not the word *house.* Thus the linguist can identify subclasses of English nouns: in this case, "animate" or "inanimate" subclasses. The same procedure can be followed for all the words of the language, using as many different frames as necessary, until a lexicon, or dictionary, can be created that accurately describes the possible uses of all the words in the language.

One of the strengths of modern descriptive linguistics is the objectivity of its methods. A descriptive linguist does not approach a language with the idea that it must have nouns, verbs, prepositions, or any other of the form classes identifiable in his or her own language. The linguist instead sees what turns up in the language and makes an attempt to describe it in terms of its own inner workings. For convenience, morphemes that behave approximately like nouns and verbs may be labelled as such, but if the terms would be misleading, the linguist instead might call them "x-words" and "y-words," or "form class A" and "form class B."

Bound morpheme.   A sound that can occur in a language only in combination with other sounds, as *s* in English does to signify the plural. **> Free morphemes.**   Morphemes that can occur unattached in a language; for example, *dog* and *cat* are free morphemes in English. **> Frame substitution.**   A method used to identify the syntactic units of language. For example, a category called *nouns* may be established as anything that will fit the substitution frame "I see a. . . ." **> Syntax.**   In linguistics, the rules or principles of phrase and sentence making. **> Grammar.**   The entire formal structure of a language consisting of all observations about the morphemes and syntax. **> Form classes.**   The parts of speech or categories of words that work the same way in any sentence.

THE GESTURE-CALL SYSTEM

Efficient though languages are at naming and talking about things, all are deficient to some degree in communicating certain kinds of information people need to know to understand what is being said. For this reason, human language is always embedded within a *gesture-call system* (also known as nonverbal communication). The various sounds and gestures of this system serve to "key" speech, providing listeners with the appropriate frame for interpreting what a speaker is saying. Through it, we learn information such as the age and gender of the speaker, as well as his or her individual identity if it is someone we already know. Moreover, subtle messages about emotions and intentions are conveyed. Is the speaker happy, sad, enthusiastic, tired, or in some other emotional state? Is he or she requesting information, denying something, reporting factually, or lying? Very little of this information is conveyed by spoken language alone. In English, for example, at least 90 percent of emotional information is transmitted not by the words spoken but by body language and tone of voice. No language communicates peoples' emotions and intentions as effectively as the gesture-call system.

As features we have inherited from our primate ancestors, many sounds and gestures of our nonverbal communication are subject to greater genetic determination than language. This accounts for the universality of various cries and facial expressions, as well as for the great difficulty people have bluffing or lying through gesture-calls. This does not mean the system is entirely immune to deliberate control, for it is not; it is merely less subject to control than spoken language.

Kinesics

The gestural component of the gesture-call system consists of postures, facial expressions, and bodily motions that convey messages. For example, humans use more than 250 000 facial expressions. The method for notating and analyzing this body language is known as **kinesics**. Kinesic messages may be communicated directly, such as gestures do. For example, in North

Humans talk, while much communication among other primates is done through gestures. Still, humans have not abandoned gestural communication, as we see here.

America scratching our scalp, biting our lip, or knitting our brows are ways of conveying doubt. Posture can provide clues about the social status, level of education, and mental acuity of the speakers, as well as their emotional state and interest in the conversation. More complex examples are the gender signals North American men and women send. Although some regional and class variation occurs, women when standing generally bring their legs together, at times even crossing them. Men, by contrast, hold their legs apart, with the upper legs at a 10° or 15° angle.

Such gender markers should not be mistaken for invitations to sexual activity. Rather, they are conventions inscribed on the body through imitation and subtle training. In any culture, as little girls grow up, they imitate their mothers or other older women; little boys do the same with their fathers or other older men. In North American culture, by the time individuals become adults,

---

Kinesics.   A system of notating and analyzing postures, facial expressions, and body motions that convey messages.

Nick Binder's body language clearly shows his disappointment after his team, the Almonte Thunderbirds, lost the game.

There is a great deal of similarity around the world in such basic expressions as smiling, laughing, crying, and anger, evident in the expressions of these children from Asia and the Canadian Artic.

they have acquired a host of gender markers that intrude into every moment of their lives, so much so that they are at a loss if they do not know the sex of someone they must interact with. This is easily verified, as the philosopher Marilyn Frye suggests:

> To discover the differences in how you greet a woman and how you greet a man, for instance, just observe yourself, paying attention to the following sorts of things: frequency and duration of eye contact, frequency and type of touch . . . physical distance maintained between bodies, how and whether you smile . . . whether your body dips into a shadow curtsey or bow. That I have two repertories for handling introductions to people was vividly confirmed for me when a student introduced me to his friend, Pat, and I really could not tell what sex Pat was. For a moment I was stopped cold, completely incapable of action. I felt myself helplessly caught between two paths—the one I would take if Pat were female and the one I would take if Pat were male. Of course the paralysis does not last. One is rescued by one's ingenuity and good will: one can invent a way to behave as one says "How do you do?" to a human being. But the habitual ways are not for humans: they are one way for women and another for men.[3]

[3]Frye, M. (1983). Sexism. *The politics of reality* (p. 20). New York: The Crossing Press.

Often, kinesic messages complement spoken messages, such as nodding the head while affirming something verbally or smiling to indicate appreciation and enjoyment. Other examples are punching the palm of the hand for emphasis, raising the head and brows when

Learned gestures that different cultures assign different meanings to are known as conventional gestures. An example is this sign, which in North America means "OK." In Brazil, it is an obscene gesture.

asking a question, or using the hands to illustrate the subject being talked about. Such gestures are rather like bound morphemes; they have meaning but do not stand alone, except in particular situations, such as a nodded response to a question.

Although little scientific notice was taken of body language prior to the 1950s, since then a great deal of research has occurred. Cross-cultural research has shown many similarities in such basic facial expressions as smiling, laughing, crying, and expressions of anger. Such smirks, frowns, and so forth that we have inherited from our primate ancestry require little learning and are harder to fake than learned gestures. Great similarity, too, exists around the world in the routine for greeting over a distance. Europeans, Balinese, Papuans, Samoans, Ju/'hoansi, and at least some South American aboriginals all smile and nod, and if the individuals are especially friendly, they will raise their eyebrows with a rapid movement, keeping them raised for a fraction of a second. By doing so, they signal a readiness for contact. The Japanese, however, suppress the eyebrow flash, regarding it as indecent, which shows that important differences, as well as similarities, occur cross-culturally. This point can be further demonstrated by gestural expressions for "yes" and "no." In North America, we nod our heads for "yes" or shake them for "no." The people of Sri Lanka, also, will nod to answer "yes" to a factual question, but if they are asked to do something, a slow sideways movement of the head means "yes." In Greece, the nodded head means "yes," but "no" is indicated by jerking the head back so as to lift the face, while the eyes are often closed and the eyebrows lifted. Body movements and gestures such as these, which vary cross-culturally and have to be learned, are known as **conventional gestures.**

Touch

Touch is an interesting form of body language. Through touch we express all sorts of messages—greetings, friendship, love, sympathy, and even angry threats. For example, North American businesspeople shake hands when they meet; men who are old friends may slap each other on the back, while women may embrace and kiss each other on the cheek. We hug family members or close friends as a sign of love and affection, while in sports, such as basketball, one player may grab another, in a show of force. All of these actions are transmitting messages. Like all forms of non-verbal communication, the use of touch to convey messages varies from one culture to another, with some non-Western cultures, such as Middle Easterners, much more touch-oriented than many North Americans.

Conventional gestures   Body movements that have to be learned and can vary cross-culturally.   **> Touch.**   A form of body language involving physical contact.

Proxemics

As with touch, the use of space is culturally defined. The way we arrange the space around us and the messages conveyed by this use of space may vary significantly from one culture to another. Canadians tend to avoid invading someone's "personal space," viewing this as a breach of good manners. In other regions of the world, however, activities such as standing in line to purchase tickets at a tourist site—for example, at the Acropolis in Greece—is uncommon. There, people crowd together, sometimes pushing and shoving toward the ticket window. Personal space appears irrelevant in such a situation. Even within a single culture, gender and degree of intimacy may influence how much personal space individuals maintain. Friends will likely stand closer to each other than students and their professor; men and women also tend to maintain more space than men do with other men or women do with other women. The study of the cultural use of space is known as **proxemics**.

The "in-your-face" form of communication appears to get the message across.

Paralanguage

Another important component of the gesture-call system is **paralanguage**, consisting of cries, laughs, groans, and other sounds that are not part of language but always accompany it. The importance of paralanguage is suggested by this remark: "It's not so much *what* was said as *how* it was said." Recent studies have shown that subliminal messages communicated by seemingly minor differences in phraseology, tempo, length of answers, and the like are far more important in courtroom proceedings than even the most perceptive trial lawyer may realize. Among other things, how a witness gives testimony alters the reception this evidence gets from jurors and bears on the witness's credibility where inconsistencies exist in testimony.[4]

Voice Qualities

Although it is not always easy for the linguist to distinguish between the sounds of language and paralinguistic noises, two different kinds of the latter have been identified. The first has to do with **voice qualities**, which operate as the background characteristics of a speaker's voice. These involve pitch range (from low to high pitched); lip control (from closed to open); glottis control (sharp to smooth transitions in pitch); articulation control (forceful and relaxed speech); rhythm control (smooth or jerky setting off of portions of vocal activity); resonance (from resonant to thin); and tempo (an increase or decrease from the norm).

Voice qualities are capable of communicating much about the speaker's state. An obvious example of this is slurred speech, which may indicate the speaker is intoxicated or ill. Or if someone says rather languidly, coupled with a restricted pitch range, that he or she is delighted

---

[4]O'Barr, W.M., & Conley, J.M. (1993). When a juror watches a lawyer. In W.A. Haviland & R.J. Gordon (Eds.), *Talking about people* (2nd ed., pp. 42–45). Mountain View, CA: Mayfield.

Proxemics. The study of the cultural use of space. **> Paralanguage.** The extralinguistic noises that accompany language, such as crying or laughing. **> Voice qualities.** In paralanguage, the background characteristics of a speaker's voice.

with something, it probably indicates the person is not delighted at all. The same words said more rapidly, with increasing pitch, might indicate the speaker is genuinely excited about the matter.

Vocalizations

The second kind of paralinguistic noises consists of **vocalizations.** These are identifiable noises that are turned on and off at perceivable and relatively short intervals. They are, nonetheless, separate from language sounds. One category of vocalizations is **vocal characterizers:** the sounds of laughing or crying, yelling or whispering, yawning or belching, and the like. Speakers "talk" through vocal characterizers, which generally indicate their attitude. If a person yawns while speaking to someone, for example, this may indicate an attitude of boredom. *Breaking,* an intermittent tensing and relaxing of the vocal musculature that produces a tremulousness while speaking, may indicate great emotion on the part of the speaker.

Another category of vocalizations consists of **vocal qualifiers.** These are of briefer duration than vocal characterizers, limited generally to the space of a single intonation, rather than over whole phrases. They modify utterances in terms of intensity (loud versus soft), pitch (high versus low), and extent (drawl versus clipping). Vocal qualifiers indicate the speaker's attitude toward specific phrases, such as "Get out!" The third category consists of **vocal segregates.** Sometimes called "*oh oh* expressions," these are somewhat like the actual sounds of language, but they do not appear in the kinds of sequences that can be called words. Examples of vocal segregates that are familiar to many people are such substitutes for language as *shh, uh-uh,* or *uh-huh.* Unlike such paralinguistic sounds as sobs, giggles, and screams, "*oh oh* expressions" are conventional, learned, and far more variable from culture to culture.

LINGUISTIC CHANGE

Of the various approaches to linguistics, *descriptive linguistics* is concerned with registering and explaining all the features of a particular language at any one time in its history. This approach concentrates, for example, on the way modern French or Spanish functions now, as if it were a separate system, consistent within itself, without any reference to historical reasons for its development. Yet languages, like the rest of culture, have histories.

A second approach, *historical linguistics,* by contrast, investigates relationships between earlier and later forms of the same language, antecedents in older languages for developments in modern ones, and questions of relationships between languages. Historical linguists, for example, attempt to identify and explain the development of early medieval spoken Latin into later medieval French and Spanish by investigating both natural change in the original language and the influence of contacts with invaders from the north. No conflicts exist between historical and descriptive linguists; the two approaches are recognized as interdependent. Even a modern language is constantly changing; consider, for example, the changed meaning of the word *gay* in English, which today is used to refer to homosexual persons. Its meaning in the title of the 1942 play *Our Hearts Were Young and Gay* illustrates the word's changing usage. Such changes occur according to principles that can be established only historically.

Historical linguists have achieved considerable success working out the genealogical relationships between different languages, and these are reflected in classification schemes. For example, English is one of a number of languages classified in the Indo-European **language family** (see Figure 4.1). This family is subdivided into 11 subgroups, which reflect the long period

---

Vocalizations.   Identifiable paralinguistic noises turned on and off at perceivable and relatively short intervals. **> Vocal characterizers.**   In paralanguage, sound productions such as laughing or crying that humans "speak" through. **> Vocal qualifiers.**   In paralanguage, sound productions of brief duration that modify utterances in terms of intensity. **> Vocal segregates.**   In paralanguage, sound productions that are similar to the sounds of language but do not appear in sequences that can be properly called words. **> Language family.**   A group of languages ultimately descended from a single ancestral language.

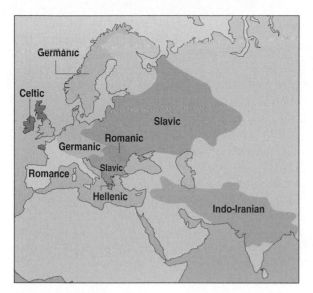

FIGURE 4.1
The Indo-European languages.

(8000 years or so) of **linguistic divergence** from an ancient unified language (referred to as Proto-Indo-European) into separate "daughter" languages. English is only one of a number of languages in the Germanic subgroup (see Figure 4.2); all are more closely related to one another than to the languages of any other subgroup of the Indo-European family. The same is true of French, which is one of the Romance subgroups, along with Italian, Spanish, Romanian, and so on (Figures 4.1, 4.2). So, in spite of the differences among them, the languages of one subgroup share certain features when compared to other subgroups. As an illustration, the word for *father* in the Germanic languages always starts with an *f* or closely related *v* sound (Dutch *vader,* German *Vater,* Gothic *Fadar*). Among the Romance languages, by contrast, the comparable word always starts with a *p* (French *père,* Spanish and Italian *padre*) and all are derived from the

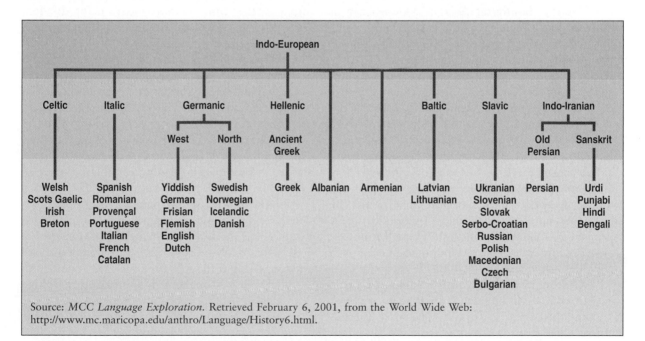

Source: *MCC Language Exploration.* Retrieved February 6, 2001, from the World Wide Web: http://www.mc.maricopa.edu/anthro/Language/History6.html.

FIGURE 4.2 The Indo-European language family.
English is one of a group of languages in the Germanic subgroup of the Indo-European family, and French is one of the languages in the Romance subgroup. This simplified diagram shows its relationship to other languages in the same subgroup. The root was Proto-Indo-European, a language spoken by a people who spread westward over Europe, bringing with them both their customs and their language.

Linguistic divergence.   The development of different languages from a single ancestral language.

Latin *pater.* The original Indo-European word for *father* was *p'tēr,* so in this case, the Romance languages have retained the earlier pronunciation, whereas the Germanic languages have diverged.

Historical linguists have successfully described the changes that have occurred as languages diverged from more ancient parent languages. They also have developed a means of estimating when certain migrations, invasions, and contacts of peoples have taken place, on the basis of linguistic similarities and differences. The concept of linguistic divergence is used to guess when one group of speakers of a language separated from another group. Anthropologists use the methods and knowledge of historical linguistics as a supplement to archaeological investigations of the early pre-contact histories of nonliterate peoples. The study of shifts in language forms has provided critical clues, for instance, in our understanding of the development and expansion of Austronesian language groups over the past 9000 years from their early homeland in Southeast Asia to Madagascar in the west and Polynesia in the east. A more complicated technique, known as **glottochronology**, was developed by Swadesh and Lees in the early 1950s to try to date the divergence of related languages, such as Latin and Greek, from an earlier common language. The technique is based on the assumption that changes in a language's **core vocabulary**—pronouns, lower numerals, and names for body parts and natural objects—change at a more or less constant rate. By applying a logarithmic formula to two related core vocabularies, linguists should be able to determine how many years the languages have been separated. Although not as precise as this might suggest, glottochronology provides a useful way to estimate when languages may have separated.

While many of the changes that have occurred in the course of linguistic divergence are well known, their causes are not. One force for linguistic change is borrowing from another language, something speakers readily do when in a position to do so; but if borrowing were the sole force for change, linguistic differences would become less pronounced over time. By studying modern languages in their cultural settings, linguistic anthropologists can begin to understand the forces for change. One such force is novelty, pure and simple. Humans tend to admire the person who comes up with a new and clever idiom, a new and useful word, or a particularly stylish pronunciation, so long as these do not seriously interfere with communication. Indeed, in linguistic matters, complexity tends to be admired, while simplicity seems dull. Hence, about as fast as a language is simplified, purged of needlessly complex constructions or phrases, new ones arise.

Group membership also plays a role in linguistic change. Part of this change is functional: Professions, sects, or other groups in a society often need special vocabularies to communicate effectively about their special interests. Beyond this, special vocabularies may serve as labelling devices; those who use such vocabularies are set off as a group from those who do not. Here, we have the paradox of language acting to *prevent* communication, in this case between members of different groups. Such linguistic barriers serve to create a strong sense of group identity.

When a military officer speaks of "incontinent ordinance" and "collateral damage," a physician of "exsanguination," a dentist of the "oral cavity," or an anthropologist of "the structural implications of matrilateral cross-cousin marriage," they express, in part at least, their membership in a profession and their command of its language. For insiders, professional terminology reinforces their sense of belonging to a select in-group; to outsiders it often seems an unneeded and pretentious use of "bafflegab" where perfectly adequate and simple words would do as well. Whether needed or not, professional terminology does serve to differentiate language and to set the speech of one group apart from that of others. Therefore, it is a force for stylistic divergence.

Pronunciation differences between groups may be regarded in the same light as vocabulary differences. In a class-structured society, for example, members of the upper class may try to keep their pronunciation distinct from that of

---

Glottochronology.   In linguistics, a method of dating divergence in branches of language families. **> Core vocabulary.** In language, pronouns, lower numerals, and names for body parts and natural objects.

lower classes. An example of a different sort involves coastal communities in Maine, in particular, although it may be seen to varying degrees elsewhere along the New England coast. In the past, people in these communities developed a regional dialect with a pronunciation style quite distinct from those of "inlanders." More recently, as outsiders have moved into these coastal communities, either as summer people or as permanent residents, the traditional coastal style has come to identify those who adhere to traditional coastal values, as opposed to those who do not. In English Canada, accents tend to be fairly uniform from coast to coast.[5] Variation does exist, of course; for example, recent immigrants to Canada speak English with an accent, but by the second generation these accents tend to disappear. Exceptions to this homogeneity, somewhat similar to the New England example, are evident in the Atlantic provinces, rural Ontario, and Newfoundland. Newfoundlanders use sounds and vocabulary separate from mainland Canada, although as the generations pass, these linguistic differences are diminishing.

One other far-reaching force for linguistic change is **linguistic nationalism,** an attempt by whole countries to proclaim their independence by purging their vocabularies of "foreign" terms. This phenomenon is particularly characteristic of the former colonial countries in Africa and Asia today. It is by no means limited to those countries, however, as shown by periodic French-Canadian attempts to purge their language of such anglicisms as *le hamburger*. In an effort to further protect the endangered French language, Quebec's government passed the French Language Charter, Bill 101, in 1976.[6] Bill 101 declared French the only language of Quebec, and soon became the emblem of linguistic nationalism for French Canadians. Among other things,

this bill requires that all public signs be in French, that immigrant children must attend French schools, and that businesses over a certain size must be able to conduct their business in French. The nature of Quebec's struggle for language equality and official bilingualism is explored in Monica Heller's Original Study on pages 112–114 of this chapter. Also in the category of linguistic nationalism are revivals of languages, long out of common use, by ethnic minorities and sometimes even whole countries. In the latter group is the successful revival of Hebrew as Israel's first language, although not without a bitter campaign against its competitor, Yiddish. In Canada, aboriginal language conservation among First Nations, Métis, and Inuit peoples is a matter of great concern and urgency. The 1991 census revealed that only 17 percent of the aboriginal population claimed an aboriginal tongue.[7] Most of the 53 distinct aboriginal languages in Canada, with the possible exception of Cree and Ojibwa in the Algonquian language family and Inuktitut in the Aleut-Eskimo language family, are in danger of extinction because they are no longer taught at home from birth. Since language retention is a strong component of cultural identity, the aboriginal peoples of Canada are fearful, and rightfully

---

[7]Drapeau, L. (1998). Aboriginal languages: Current status. In J. Edwards (Ed.), *Language in Canada*. Cambridge, UK: Cambridge University Press.

To offset the rapid disappearance of aboriginal languages in Canada, aboriginal language training programs are being established.

---

[5]Chambers, J.K. (1998). English: Canadian varieties. In J. Edwards (Ed.), *Language in Canada*. Cambridge, UK: Cambridge University Press.

[6]Genesee, F. (1998). French immersion in Canada. In J. Edwards (Ed.), *Language in Canada*. Cambridge, UK: Cambridge University Press.

Linguistic nationalism. The attempt by ethnic minorities, and even countries, to proclaim independence by purging their languages of foreign terms or reviving unused languages.

Anthropology **Applied**

Visual Anthropology and Ethnographic Film

Anthropologists have long recognized the research and educational value of visual media, in particular, ethnographic films. Franz Boas and Margaret Mead readily adopted this medium to ethnographically record the lives of little-known indigenous peoples around the world. Historically, ethnographic films were used to visually present detailed and objective records of cultures, but more recently ethnographic films have been used to tell the story of a group of people, in some cases a story that otherwise would be lost. Outstanding series, such as *The Disappearing World*, bring the lives of exotic peoples to the attention of Western viewers. This form of media, then, becomes a vehicle for culture.

One of the most influential early ethnographic filmmakers was Asen Balikci, professor of anthropology at the University of Montreal until his retirement in 1994. Following several years (1957–1965) of fieldwork in the Canadian Arctic, where he studied the Pelly Bay Netsilingmiut (Netsilik) Inuit, Balikci returned in 1963 to make a series of films on the traditional lives of the Netsilik Inuit before Europeans arrived in Canada. The series was made possible through grants from the National Science Foundation and the Ford Foundation (U.S.), and in association with the National Film Board of Canada.

The films were originally designed to eliminate the ethnocentrism prevalent in U.S. history and social sciences courses through a comparative study of world cultures. The Inuit were chosen as the first study group because North Americans had particularly simplistic and naive ideas about the Inuit. In charge of film content, Asen Balikci set out to change this perception by showing the Inuit in their traditional life as highly organized hunters who had adapted with great ingenuity to a harsh environment. Balikci chose to reconstruct the annual migration cycle of the Netsilik from traditional times, before contact with Europeans and the acquisition of rifles for hunting. Balikci studied Netsilik subsistence strategies, settlement patterns, technology, and organization, providing detail in the film about how they caught salmon and hunted seals and caribou.

Spending 13 gruelling months in the field, overcoming the elements and other hardships and accidents, Balikci and the crew shot close to 600 rolls of film and ended up with 10 hours' worth of an integrated series of films, known as the *Netsilik Eskimo*. As a result of budget constraints and the failure of the public, educators, and politicians to grasp the educational value of such media, the series was removed from American grade 5 curricula. The American public seemed unable to deal with a realistic picture of how the Inuit really lived; rather, they preferred dramatizations and romanticized views of happy-go-lucky, primitive sport hunters. This type of "white-washing" of the facts, ignoring realities such as tuberculosis epidemics, high infant mortality rates, and hunger, is evident in many of the ethno-documentaries available on television today.

Balikci believes that visual anthropology, although still in its infancy and often misused and neglected, has much to offer in our search for understanding human cultures. Visual anthropology also provides opportunities for people who in the past were the subject of ethnographic films to use media to present their worldview, as a form of ethnic self-assertion. Regardless of other uses, ethnographic film in an academic setting is a valuable teaching tool, as it can show in one scene what could never be adequately described in a thousand words.

Source: Balikci, A. (1989). Anthropology, film and the Arctic peoples: The first Forman Lecture. *Anthropology Today, 5* (2), 4–10.

so, that 19th-century assimilation policies may come to pass in the 21st century. Attempts to revitalize aboriginal languages are hampered by the sheer size of Canada and by the fact that aboriginal linguistic enclaves are scattered throughout the country, surrounded by English- or French-speaking people. Yet ongoing efforts to develop aboriginal language curriculum materials, educational programs, and a national policy on aboriginal languages are meeting with some success, and a recent resurgence of interest in their mother tongue by aboriginal youth offers some hope.

As with First Nations groups, for ethnic minorities the retention of traditional languages is important for their sense of identity and self-worth. For Canadian Buddhists, protecting linguistic traditions also aids in maintaining strong ethnic ties. By continuing to use their traditional languages in religious services, festivals, and other gatherings, they keep their languages and their cultures alive. The picture is not so bright for the Acadians. Official bilingualism in Canada has helped the Acadians preserve their language heritage, thus slowing the process of assimilation, but fewer young Acadians speak French every year. Canadian statistics tell the grim story: In 1996, 242 410 people claimed French as their mother tongue, but in 2001, only 236 665 people did so.[8] As discussed earlier, much of this language loss can be traced to the economic realities of Acadians, who often have to leave their French communities for employment.

A prime means that states use to assert their dominance over minorities living within their borders is to suppress their languages. A good illustration was the policy pursued in Canada in the early 20th century of taking First Nations children away from their parents and putting them in residential schools, where use of aboriginal languages was absolutely forbidden and punished with physical abuse and humiliation. In the mid-20th century the Canadian federal government began to ease up on its assimilation policies. However, it was not until the 1970s that First Nations children attending band-operated schools could receive instruction in their tradi-

tional aboriginal language. And although the 1982 Canadian Charter of Rights and Freedoms offers vague reference to aboriginal languages, the Assembly of First Nations (AFN) is seeking official status for their languages with constitutional recognition and legislative protection.[9]

In the 1970s and 1980s, the British Columbia Provincial Museum was the only museum in North America with a Linguistics Division devoted to recording and preserving First Nations languages. Dr. Barbara Efrat, the provincial linguist at the time, set up an accession system so that although the Linguistics Division is now gone, First Nations peoples can still access tape recordings of their elders speaking their native languages and telling stories.

North American aboriginal languages are not the only languages in danger; indeed, linguistic diversity is seriously threatened around the world.[10] Of the 6800 extant languages in the world today, nearly half are spoken by less than 2500 people. Linguist Michael Krause at the Alaskan Native Language Center estimates that only 600 of the world's languages are presently safe from extinction, meaning children are still learning them at home and in school. Language loss is not a new phenomenon; at the dawn of the 15th century, approximately 15 000 languages were spoken. Since then, wars, genocides, legal bans, and European expansion and assimilation agendas have resulted in the disappearance of more than half of these languages. The process continues today; most of the 250 indigenous languages in Australia are nearing extinction (of the 50 aboriginal languages in Queensland most have fewer than 20 speakers), most South American languages were wiped out following the Spanish conquest, in Africa 54 languages are dead and another 116 are near extinction, and in Asia half the native languages are spoken by fewer than 10 000 speakers.

Nor is Europe immune, despite the dominance of its languages around the world: Manx, once spoken on the Isle of Man, became extinct

---

[8]Statistics Canada. (2003, August 11). 2001 Census: Population by mother tongue, provinces and territories. *The Daily*. Retrieved August 11, 2003, from the World Wide Web: http://www.statcan.ca/english/Pgdb/demo18a.htm.

[9]Drapeau, L. (1998). Aboriginal languages: Current status. In J. Edwards (Ed.), *Language in Canada*. Cambridge, UK: Cambridge University Press.

[10]The following statistics and information on language loss are taken from Sampet, P. (2001). Last words. *World Watch*, *14* (3).

in 1974 when its last speaker died, and when Turkish farmer Tefvik Esenc died in 1992, Ubykh, a Caucasus language with the highest number of consonants ever recorded, died also. The loss of so many languages is a form of cultural impoverishment; we are losing not only linguistic diversity but also the links to our past. As we have already seen, language provides clues to human history, to the migrations and contacts of people in the past, and like the loss of biodiversity, the disappearance of languages and their vocabularies deprives us of a great deal of the human experience, both past and present.

In many human societies, it is not unusual for people to be fluent in two, three, or even four languages, but to become so it is important to begin learning these languages as children. In Canada, this recognition led to the establishment of French immersion programs across the country. Rather than spending a few minutes each day learning French, these students are immersed in the French language for most of their instructional day. Parents and students alike have enthusiastically embraced French immersion programs, with more than 300 000 students enrolled by 1994.[11] Multicultural language schools that attempt to conserve other heritage languages, such as Italian, Mandarin, Greek, and Ukrainian, also have become increasingly popular in Canada.

---

[11]Genesee, F. (1998). French Immersion in Canada. In J. Edwards (Ed.), *Language in Canada*. Cambridge, UK: Cambridge University Press.

Not everyone agrees with the benefits of linguistic diversity. In the United States, for example, proponents of an "English only" national policy argue that multilingualism is divisive and often cite the example of French separatism in Canada. What they do not cite are examples such as the former Yugoslavia or Northern Ireland, both instances where speaking a single language has not prevented violent fighting between factions. Nor do they mention countries like Finland, where three official languages are spoken, or Switzerland, where four exist without people being at one another's throats. The fact is, where linguistic diversity is divisive, it is often *because* of official policies in favour of monolingualism.

LANGUAGE IN ITS CULTURAL SETTING

As the preceding discussion suggests, language is not simply a matter of combining sounds according to certain rules to come up with meaningful utterances. It is important to remember that languages are spoken by people, who are members of societies, each of which has its own distinctive culture. Individuals tend to vary in the ways they use language, and influences include social variables such as class, ethnicity, status, and outside influences like the media. Moreover, people choose words and sentences to communicate meaning,

Canada has embraced official bilingualism, reflected here by students enrolled in a French immersion program.

and what is meaningful in one culture may not be in another. In other words, our use of language affects, and is affected by, the rest of our culture.

The whole question of the relationships between language and other aspects of culture is the province of **ethnolinguistics,** an outgrowth of both ethnology and descriptive linguistics, which has become almost a separate field of inquiry. Ethnolinguists are concerned with every aspect of the structure and use of language that has anything to do with society, culture, and human behaviour.

Language and Thought

An important ethnolinguistic concern of the 1930s and 1940s was the question of whether language might actually determine other aspects of culture. Do we see and react differently to the colours blue and green, with different cultural symbolism for each colour, only because our language has different names for these two neighbouring parts of the unbroken colour spectrum? When anthropologists noticed that some cultures, such as the Coast Salish of southwestern British Columbia, lump together blue and green with one name, they began to wonder. American linguist Edward Sapir had earlier formulated the problem, and his student Benjamin Lee Whorf, drawing on his experience with the Hopi language, developed a full-fledged theory, sometimes called the **Sapir-Whorf hypothesis.** Whorf proposed that a language is not simply an encoding process for voicing ideas and needs but, rather, is a shaping force, which, by providing habitual grooves of expression that predispose people to see the world in a certain way, guides their thinking and behaviour. The problem is a little like the old question of the chicken or the egg. Some later formulations of Whorf's theory about which came first, thinking and behaviour or language, have since been criticized as both logically unsound and not amenable to any experimentation or proof. The idea's primary value is that it draws attention to the relationships between language and the rest of culture. For example, how strong is the connection between aboriginal language retention and cultural survival?

The opposite point of view is that language reflects reality. In this view, because language mirrors cultural reality, as the latter changes, so too will language. Some support for this is provided by studies of blue-green colour terms. It has been shown that eye pigmentation acts to filter out the shorter wavelengths of solar radiation. Colour vision is thus limited by a reduced sensitivity to blue and confusion of the short visible wavelengths. The effect shows up in colour-naming behaviour, where green may be identified with blue, blue with black, or both green and blue with black. The severity of the visual limitation, as well as the extent of the lumping of colour terms, depends on the density of eye pigmentation characteristic of the people in a given society.

These findings do not mean language merely reflects reality, any more than thinking and behaviour are determined by language. The truth is more as anthropologist Peter Woolfson has put it:

> Reality should be the same for us all. Our nervous systems, however, are being bombarded by a continual flow of sensations of different kinds, intensities, and durations. It is obvious that all of these sensations do not reach our consciousness; some kind of filtering system reduces them to manageable propositions. The Whorfian hypothesis suggests that the filtering system is one's language. Our language, in effect, provides us with a special pair of glasses that heightens certain perceptions and dims others. Thus, while all sensations are received by the nervous system, only some are brought to the level of consciousness.[12]

---

[12]Woolfson, P. (1972). Language, thought, and culture. In V.P. Clark, P.A. Escholz, & A.F. Rosa (Eds.), *Language* (p. 4). New York: St. Martin's Press.

Ethnolinguistics. The study of the relation between language and culture. **> Sapir-Whorf hypothesis.** The hypothesis, proposed by linguist B.L. Whorf, that states that language, by providing habitual grooves of expression, predisposes people to see the world in a certain way and thus guides their thinking and behaviour.

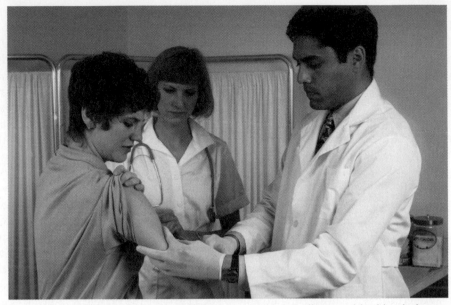

The ability of language to influence the way we think is illustrated by bland phrases such as "you are going to feel some pressure" before the doctor sticks the needle in.

Linguists have found that although language is generally flexible and adaptable, once a terminology is established, it tends to perpetuate itself and to reflect and reveal the social structure and a group's common perceptions and concerns. For example, English is richly endowed with words having to do with computers—the technology, software, and function. Computer metaphors abound, as when we speak of "downloading" information, going "online," and opening "windows" using an "icon" or "button." We search for informative "sites," update our "address book," and cannot survive without our "mouse." An observer from an entirely different culture could understand a great deal about the importance of computer technology in our lives simply from what we have found necessary to name and how we talk. Similarly, anthropologists have noted that the language of the Nuer, a nomadic people of southern Sudan, is rich in words and expressions having to do with cattle; not only are more than 400 words used to describe cattle, but also Nuer boys actually take their names from them. Thus, by studying the language, we can determine the importance of cattle to Nuer culture, attitudes toward cattle, and the whole etiquette of human and cattle relationships.

A people's language does not, however, prevent them from thinking in new and novel ways. If this new way of thinking leads to important changes in common perceptions and concerns, then language can be expected to change accordingly. Politically correct language, or more preferably, sensitive language, is a reflection of new ways of thinking through language use. We can demonstrate respect and sensitivity for cultural groups by using their choice of a name, rather than a name given by some colonial power; for example, Inuit instead of Eskimo, First Nations instead of Indian, Ju/'hoansi instead of Bushmen or !Kung. We can also use expressions that consider the feelings of others, such as hearing or visually challenged, and gender-inclusive terms such as humankind.

Kinship Terms

In the same connection, anthropologists have paid considerable attention to the way people name their relatives, as we will see in Chapter 9. In English we have terms to identify brother, sister, mother, father, grandmother, grandfather, granddaughter, grandson, niece, nephew, mother-in-law, father-in-law, sister-in-law, and brother-in-law. Some people also distinguish first and second cousin and great-aunt and great-uncle. Is this the

Regna Darnell

Language is the hallmark of our species. It is upon language that human culture itself depends. – Regna Darnell

Regna Darnell is a renowned Canadian anthropologist and linguist. Her field-work among the First Nations peoples of Canada has shed light on the interdependence and dynamics of language and culture.

Darnell's distinguished 30-year career has focused on many aspects of linguistics and culture, from a historical, symbolic, and ethnographic perspective. She is fluent in several First Nations languages, including Slavey, Cree, and Mohawk, and versed in their cultures. During her time among the Cree of northern Alberta and Saskatchewan she explored language acquisition and bilingualism, and the relationship of language and culture. She developed a course in Cree language and culture that is now taught by native speakers at the School of Native Studies. In collaboration with Anthony L. Vanek, a Slavic linguist, she examined language attitudes and second-language teaching for maintenance of ethnic language among the Doukhobors of southern British Columbia and northern Saskatchewan. Darnell has also worked abroad, studying the cross-cultural typologies of languages in West Africa. Currently

she is conducting research on First Nations and Canadian national identity. In 2000 Darnell received the Hellmuth Prize for achievement in research; she was the first woman to be presented with this award.

Darnell is a faculty member at the University of Western Ontario, where she also serves as director of the Centre for Research and Teaching of Canadian Native Languages. She has published extensively on First Nations languages and culture, as well as on the history of anthropology. Her recent publications include *Edward Sapir: Linguist, Anthropologist, Humanist* (1990) and *Invisible Genealogies: A History of Americanist Anthropology* (2000).

Sources:

The University of Western Ontario, Department of Anthropology. (2001). *Meet Regna Darnell*. Retrieved January 13, 2001, from the World Wide Web: http://publish.uwo.ca/~rdarnell/home.htm.

The University of Western Ontario, Regna's C.V. page. (2000). *Regna Darnell* curriculum vitae. Retrieved January 13, 2001, from the World Wide Web: http://publish.uwo.ca/~rdarnell/CV-1.htm.

---

only possible system for naming relatives and identifying relationships? Obviously not. We could have separate terms, as some cultures do, for younger and older brothers, for mother's sister and father's sister, and so on. What we can describe in English with a phrase, if pressed to do so, other languages make explicit from the outset, and vice versa: A number of languages use the same word to denote both a brother and a cousin, and a mother's sister also may be called by the same term as the mother.

What do kinship terms reveal? They certainly can provide a good idea of how the family is structured, what relationships are considered especially important, and sometimes what attitudes toward relationships may prevail. Caution is required, however, in drawing conclusions

from kinship terms. Just because English speakers do not distinguish linguistically between their mother's parents and their father's parents (both are simply grandmother and grandfather), does that mean they do not know or care about which is which? Certainly not. Nevertheless, nonanthropologists, when confronted with a kinship system that applies the same term for father's brother to father, frequently make the mistake of assuming "these people don't know who their own father is."

Social Dialects

In our previous discussion of linguistic change, phonological and vocabulary differences among groups were noted as important forces for linguistic change. Varying forms of a language

So important are cattle to the Nuer of southern Sudan that they have more than 400 words to describe them.

similar enough to be mutually intelligible are known as **dialects,** and the study of dialects is a concern of **sociolinguistics.** Technically, all dialects are languages—they have nothing partial or sublinguistic about them—and at the point two dialects become distinctly different languages is roughly where speakers of one are almost totally unable to communicate with speakers of the other. Boundaries may be psychological, geographic, social, or economic, and they are not always very clear. Regional dialects frequently have a transitional territory, or perhaps a buffer zone, where features of both are found and understood, as between regions in China. Of the many languages spoken in China, some are offshoots or dialects of Mandarin, while others, like Cantonese and Tibetan, are totally different, originating in other language families, reflecting the ethnic diversity of Chinese people. From a fairly young age, all school children are taught standard Beijing Mandarin, and the language of government and nonlocal business is Mandarin. However, owing to China's enormous size and diverse geography, there are numerous differences in the way people speak Mandarin. These variations are based partly on the linguistic patterns of local languages influencing the way certain sounds are made. The "shr" sound of a Beijing resident turns into a "si" sound for a resident of Guangzhou (Canton). People who speak standard Mandarin will be understood anywhere they travel in China, but they will have some difficulty understanding people in regions where the common dialect is Sichaunese or Shanghaiese.

A classic example of the kind of dialect that may set one group apart from others within a single society is one spoken by many inner-city African Americans. Technically known as African-American Vernacular English, it often has been referred to as Black English and (more recently) as Ebonics.

Unfortunately, a widespread perception among upper- and middle-class Euro-North Americans and African Americans alike is that this dialect is somehow substandard or defective, which it is not. A basic principle of linguistics is that the selection of a prestige dialect—in this case, what we may call Standard English as opposed to

Dialects.   Varying forms of a language that reflect particular regions or social classes and that are similar enough to be mutually intelligible. **> Sociolinguistics.**   The study of the structure and use of language as it relates to its social setting.

Gender **Perspectives**

Gender in Language

Throughout history, humans have handled the relationship between men and women in different ways, and here again language can be revealing. In Japanese, for example, men and women vary their word choices depending on whom they are speaking with and the perceived status and respect of the listener. In English, words spoken by or about women imply, sometimes subtly and sometimes not, a lesser status. For example, behaviour described as "forceful" for a man might be described as "pushy" for a woman. Or, while a man "passes out" (falling directly to the ground), a woman "faints" (as if giving way to weakness). While a man is "a fighter," a woman is "spunky" or "feisty," words suggestive of lesser power. In numerous ways the traditional inequality of men and women in North American society receives linguistic expression.

Sexist language perpetuates stereotypes of women and their place in society. Take the word *housewife*. The word suggests that domestic chores are the exclusive burden of females; it gives females the idea that they were born to keep house and teaches males they should expect laundry, cooking, and housecleaning services from the women in their life. Another favourite is *mankind*. In this case, the word *man* or *mankind* contrives to keep women invisible by representing everyone, and yet not women. The generic pronoun *he* serves the same purpose. Advocates of gender-neutral language have promoted forms such as *person* and *people* and *he* or *she* to replace *man, he,* and *his*. The title *Ms.,* to replace *Miss* and *Mrs.,* is an attempt by women to gain an identity of their own, regardless of their marital status. Recent word suggestions, such as *herstory* for history and *sportsoneship* for sportsmanship, are attempts to rewrite the English language to be more gender inclusive, yet they have met with derision and obstinacy. Negative stereotypes about men are also perpetuated using language: Women are "sensitive," men are "wimpy." We also reflect gender bias by using derogatory terms to describe men and women within a homosexual context, such as "girlie" for a gentle man, "butch" for a strong woman.

Language reflects the values and beliefs of a culture, and it can also reflect changes in those values and beliefs. In Western society we hold dear the ideal of marriage and the family. Value-laden terms such as *old maid* and *spinster* show our inherent disapproval of women who do not fulfill these traditional roles, while terms such as *bachelor* for unmarried men suggests an entirely different status. Yet, as men and women became more equal in the workforce and in the home, these terms gave way to new words, such as the more gender-neutral *singles*.

The English language reflects a long-standing ideology of male dominance in Western societies. Although on the surface we resolutely endorse gender equality, by using language that demeans women or men and essentially trivializes their existence, we continue to perpetuate stereotypes and reinforce gender bias in our society. The issue of gender bias in language is not a feminist issue; it is a societal issue.

Sources:

Miller, C., & Swift, K. (2000). One small step for genkind. In E. Ashton-Jones, G.A. Olson, & M.G. Perry (Eds.), *The gender reader* (2nd ed., pp. 289–300). Needham Heights, MA: Allyn and Bacon.

Nilsen, A.P. (2000). Sexism in English: A 1990s update. In E. Ashton-Jones, G.A. Olson, & M.G. Perry (Eds.), *The gender reader* (2nd ed., pp. 301–312). Needham Heights, MA: Allyn and Bacon.

Ebonics—is determined by accidental extralinguistic forces and is not dependent on indirect virtues of the dialects themselves. In fact, African-American Vernacular English is a highly structured mode of speech, capable of expressing anything its speakers care to express, often in extremely creative ways (as in "rapping"). Many of its distinctive features stem from the retention of sound patterns, grammatical devices, and even words of the West African languages spoken by the ancestors of today's African Americans. Compared with the richness of Ebonics, the

ORIGINAL STUDY

Speak *bilingue*?

Monica Heller
University of Toronto

In many parts of Canada, someone who speaks only English can under-standably arrive at the conclusion that French–English bilingualism is a matter of zones—French in some places, English in others—and without too much effort, the twain do not have to meet except perhaps in the virtual worlds of channel-hopping or product labelling. In some parts of Canada, even people who speak only French can live an almost monolingual life, if it were not for the fact that English does in the end dominate and touches almost everybody one way or another. But language borders are as fictive as national borders, as messy and as complicated. Scratch the surface, and you find many people who are themselves bilingual and many others who, while monolingual, nonetheless find their lives affected by the fact that the relationship between speakers of French and speakers of English is one of the structuring principles of the organization of Canadian society.

Sometimes this is pure fun. Bilinguals tell the wildest jokes (unfortu-nately, they are the only ones who understand them). One of my favourites was reported to me by a kindergarten teacher. One of the five-year-olds in her class came up to her to ask: *Qu'est-ce que «je m'en fiche» veut dire?* ("What does 'je m'en fiche' [I don't care] mean?"). Being a teacher who believes in self-directed learning rather than the transmission model, she instructed him to find out for himself. A while later, he came back and announced that he had found the answer: *Ca veut dire «je m'en poissonne»!* Seeing her puzzled look (she had learned English relatively late in life), he spelled it out for her: "*Fiche*, fish, *poisson . . .* " and fell on the floor laugh-ing. Now not everyone in Canada can do this; those who do use it to great effect, and not just to amuse themselves and each other. Such performances also serve (albeit largely unconsciously) as markers of the special place that bilinguals occupy astride the language border, and may help them deal with some of the tensions that can arise there.

Which brings me to the part that is perhaps not so amusing: French–English bilingualism can also be a domain of competition and conflict. First, there are many people, of many different language backgrounds, and them-selves frequently bilingual or multilingual, who sincerely believe that being monolingual is the best way for individuals or societies or both. Often this perspective is connected to a sense that realism dictates recognizing the language of power (in this case, English) for what it is, and making sure that everyone has equal access to it. It can also be connected to a com-mitment to achieving equity through identity—that is, giving everyone a fair chance by making sure everyone is fundamentally the same. But it can also be connected to the fear that dominant groups often feel about the ways in which difference can threaten their power.

Then there are the questions that apply to those who in principle agree that speaking both French and English is a good thing. How to explain why parents in Calgary line up all night to enroll their children in French immer-sion? Or why francophones in Quebec argue about when to introduce Eng-lish in school? What about fights in francophone minority communities over whether to have bilingual or French-only programs, and how much French students and parents should speak in order for students to be admitted to their schools? Or the tensions in the federal civil service between anglo-phones who feel they have made a commitment to learning French, only to find that their francophone workmates won't speak to them in French, and francophones who don't understand why they should act as unpaid language teachers on the job when they themselves learned English before they were in the job market? Why would a 17-year-old francophone in Toronto, talking about English speakers in French immersion, say, *«Les anglophones nous ont tout pris, maintenant ils veulent nous prendre notre langue»* ("The anglophones have taken everything from us, now they want to take our language")?

Clearly, for many people in Canada, French–English bilingualism is an important resource, one which they believe gives them a head start in life, whether in education, in the job market, or simply in terms of enriching life experiences. The problem is that this resource is not equally distributed; some people get access to it from birth, in their families or neighbourhoods, while others must rely on schools or the media. But a more fundamental problem has to do with who will count as the best, or the real, bilinguals. And for many francophones it is frustrating to see the one advantage that came from being in a minority position being eroded by anglophone access to the same advantage. In other words, underlying many of these tensions is a competition between anglophones and francophones, understood as distinct social groups, over access to the resource of bilingualism, in the service of gaining or maintaining a position in Canadian society in which life conditions will be good.

But we must also note competition within these groups. Among anglophones, as mentioned earlier, not everyone agrees that it is important to speak French. Even among those who do strive for some form of bilingualism, there is disagreement about what the nature and extent of that bilingualism should be. Among francophones, it may be difficult to find people who deny the importance of English, but there are struggles over how to articulate the relationship between the two—that is, over how to become and to be bilingual.

Two competing views of bilingualism dominate the debate, for both groups. One is a view that is usually held by schools and other agencies or individuals who accord themselves, or are accorded, the authority to pronounce on such matters. This view (which can be seen to originate in 19th-century European ideas about the link between unified nations, states, cultures, and languages) holds that the best, indeed perhaps the only, real bilingualism is a kind of double monolingualism. Such speakers can act as though they were both monolingual speakers of English and monolingual speakers of French.

But as any bilingual will tell you, keeping your languages separate is not such an easy task, and, besides, doing so cuts out all those hysterically funny bilingual jokes that keep popping unbidden into your brain. Instead, many bilinguals (more often those who learned their languages outside school, or who are far from the realms of power and prestige in Canadian society, and therefore mainly working-class francophones) mix their languages. Most of them accept others' judgement of this practice as low-status; people will say they know they "don't sound too intelligent" when they talk like that, or that their French is "bad." Nonetheless, the practice persists, in a form of minority resistance and ethnoclass solidarity, the importance of which should not be underestimated. Middle-class anglophones who mix their languages, on the other hand, often confer upon the practice a mark of prestige; in any case, they also know that they can turn in a perfectly good monolingual performance, at least in English, when they need to. For them, French is not imposed, and they are in a position to define the value of their own performances. These two competing views of bilingualism are mainly about class relations, and about the ways in which language and ethnicity crosscut them.

At the same time, relations across ethnoclasses are a daily occurrence in some parts of Canada, ones which have to be conducted on an ongoing basis, and which many people feel add something to the intensity of the pleasure of life. This is a comment one hears often enough in Montreal, probably the place in Canada where you find the most discussion about these matters. But what is also common in Montreal is a strategy that emerged at least 25 years ago, and that allows everyday life to go on in a city where it is usually impossible to know what kind of person you are speaking to, and even less what their language politics are likely to be. *Bonjour*, hello? May I help you, *puis-je vous aider*? Bilingual talk in service encounters is increasingly routine, and helps people in business make sure that the customer is always right.

Now this has just been about English and French. Let's throw Inuktitut and Cree into this mix, and Italian and Bengali. The relevance of the French–English binary categorization may go the way of the overwhelming 19th- and early 20th-century relevance of religious distinctions between Catholics and Protestants. More and more Canadians not only speak French and English, but have some knowledge of, or feel some authentic tie to, many other languages. One nation, one language, one identity: This is a constellation that is increasingly not only impossible for many, but also not particularly interesting. People can stake claims to many identities, and do not always link language to all or any of them.

Through the lens of bilingualism we can see the changes in Canadian society, what matters to whom, and why. We may not all share the same visions of our country, we may not all want to go about our lives the same way, but we ignore each other at our peril. Speak *bilingue*?

Standard English dialect lacks certain sounds; contains some unnecessary sounds that others may serve for just as well; doubles and drawls some of its vowel sounds in unusual sequences that are difficult to imitate; lacks a method of forming an important tense (the habitual); requires more ways than necessary to indicate tense, plurality, and gender; and does not mark negatives so as to make a strong negative statement.

Because their dialect differs so much from Standard English and has been stigmatized so often, speakers of African-American Vernacular English frequently find themselves at a disadvantage outside their communities. In schools African-American children often have been judged by teachers as deficient in verbal skills and even have been diagnosed—quite wrongly—as "learning impaired." The great challenge for U.S. schools is to find ways to teach these children how to use Standard English in situations where it is to their advantage to do so, without denigrating them or affecting their ability to use their community dialect.

In Scotland, Scots English is recognized in the schools as a valid and valued way of speaking, and it is used in teaching Standard English. As a consequence, individuals become skilled at switching back and forth between the two dialects, depending on the situation. Without being conscious of it, we all do something similar when we switch from formal to informal speech, depending on where we are and with whom we

Martin Luther King, Jr. Part of his effectiveness as a civil rights leader was his skill at code switching between Standard and African-American Vernacular English.

are speaking. The process of changing from one level of language to another as the situation demands, whether from one language to another or from one dialect of a language to another, is known as **code switching,** and it has been the subject of a number of sociolinguistic studies.

Pidgin and Creole Languages

Code switching is also evident in pidgin and creole languages. **Pidgin** languages arise out of the necessity to communicate when people speaking different languages come into close and prolonged contact. A pidgin language combines, in a simplified form, the syntax, vocabulary, and grammar (e.g., prepositions omitted) of several languages. Pidgin formation is most often linked to trade and colonialism, where a single group dominates one or more groups.

After generations of use, pidgin languages may transform into **creole** languages, which possess more complex grammars and are sometimes considered the mother tongue of the speakers. A

creole develops among children who are taught a pidgin as their first language. An example of a well-established creole language is French Creole, spoken today in several regions of the Caribbean. French Creole is a mixture of 17th-century French vocabulary, Western African syntax, and elements from American aboriginal, Anglo-Saxon, and Hispanic languages.[13] In Haiti 8 million people speak French Creole as their mother tongue. According to Milan Kundera, French Creole was born during "the shaping of a violent civilizational process mixing elements from Europe, Africa, America, and later Asia. Creole is the bitter-sweet result of the colonial era."[14] French Creole is relatively poor in vocabulary (e.g., to express abstract concepts), but when spoken is rich with images and humour that give the language a colour and deepness. It is through oral literature that Creole comes into its own: The songs; mixed stories of European and African legends; fairy tales and stories featuring animals (Brere Rabbit and Uncle Remus); jokes; riddles; and humorous images express the true nature of French Creole.

THE ORIGINS OF LANGUAGE

The realization of language's central importance to human culture leads inevitably to speculation about how language might have begun. The origin of human language has long been a popular subject, and some reasonable and many not-so-reasonable ideas have been proposed: Exclamations became words, sounds in nature were imitated, or people simply got together and assigned sounds to objects and actions. With so little concrete evidence regarding the origin of human languages, most explanations amounted to little more than speculation. The result was a

[13]Multimania. (n.d.). *French Creole: A language and a culture.* Retrieved June 21, 2001, from the World Wide Web: http://www.multimania.com/fdl/e-kreyol.htm.
[14]Ibid.

Code switching. The process of changing from one level of language to another. **> Pidgin.** A language that combines and simplifies elements (vocabulary, syntax, and grammar) of two or more languages. **> Creole.** A more complex pidgin language that has become the mother tongue of a significant population.

reaction against such speculation, exemplified by the ban the Société de Linguistique de Paris imposed in 1866 against papers on linguistic origins. Today researchers have more evidence to work with—better knowledge of primate brains, new studies of primate communication, more information on the development of linguistic competence in children, more human fossils that can be used to tentatively reconstruct ancient brains and vocal tracts, and a better understanding of early hominine ways of life. Researchers still cannot prove how and when human language developed, but they can speculate much less wildly than was once the case.

Attempts to teach nonhuman primates to speak like humans have not been successful. In one famous experiment in communication that went on for seven years, the chimpanzee Viki learned to voice only a few words, such as *up, mama,* and *papa.* When researchers changed tactics and taught chimps and gorillas to use Ameslan-American Sign Language, they met with much greater success. Psychologists Allen and Beatrice Gardner began teaching American Sign Language, used by the hearing impaired, to their young chimpanzee Washoe, the first of several who have since learned to sign. With vocabularies of more than 400 signs, chimps have shown they can transfer each sign from its original referent to other appropriate objects and even pictures of objects. Their vocabularies include verbs, adjectives, and words such as *sorry* and *please.* Furthermore, they can string signs together properly to produce original sentences, even inflecting their signs to indicate person, place, and instrument. More impressive still, Washoe has been observed spontaneously teaching her adopted offspring Loulis how to sign by deliberately manipulating his hand. For five years, humans refrained from signing when in sight of Loulis, while he learned no fewer than 50 signs. Today, Loulis and Washoe live with three other signing chimpanzees, all of whom have shown via remote videotaping that they use signs to communicate among themselves when no humans are present.

Other chimpanzees have been taught to communicate by other means. One named Sarah learned to converse using pictographs—designs such as squares and triangles—on brightly coloured plastic chips. Each pictograph stands for a noun or a verb. Sarah also can produce new sentences of her own. Another chimpanzee, Lana, learned to converse via a computer with a keyboard somewhat like that of a typewriter, but with symbols rather than letters. One of the most adept with this system is a bonobo named Kanzi, who, rather than being taught by a human, learned it as an infant from its mother and soon went on to surpass her abilities.

Gorillas and orangutans also have been taught American Sign Language with results that replicate those obtained with chimps. As a consequence, there is now a growing consensus that all of the great apes can develop language skills at least to the level of a two- to three-year-old human.[15] Not only are comprehension skills similar, but so is acquisition order: What and where, what-to-do and who, as well as how questions are acquired in that order by both apes and humans. Like humans, apes are capable of referring to events removed in time and space, a phenomenon known as **displacement** and one of the distinctive features of human language.

In view of an ape's demonstrated abilities in sign language, it is not surprising that a number of anthropologists, psychologists, and other linguists have shown new interest in an old hypothesis, that human language began as a gestural, rather than vocal, system. Certainly, the potential to communicate through gestures must have been as well developed among the earliest human ancestors as it is among today's apes.

One of the most difficult problems for students dealing with the origin of language is the origin of syntax (sentence formation), which was necessary to enable our ancestors to articulate and communicate complex thought. Here, a look at the physical nature of gestures is helpful, for, in fact, they can be construed not just as words but also as sentences. This is illustrated with the modern gesture meaning *seize*: The hand begins

[15]Miles, H.L.W. (1993). Language and the orangutan: The old "person" of the forest. In P. Cavalieri & P. Singer (Eds.), *The Great Ape Project* (p. 46). New York: St. Martin's Press.

Displacement.   The ability to refer to objects and events removed in time and space.

fully open or slightly bent, the elbow is slightly flexed, and the upper arm rotates at the shoulder to bring the forearm and hand across the body until the moving hand closes around the upright forefinger of the other hand. This is not just the word *seize* but also a complete transitive sentence with a verb and a direct object or, in semantic terms, an agent, an action, and a patient.[16] In this case, the sign and what is signified are clearly related, suggesting that syntax could have its origin in signs that mimic what they stand for.

Another conceptual problem involves the shift from manual gestures to spoken language. Two facts to keep in mind here are that (1) the manual signs of a sign language are typically accompanied by facial gestures, and (2) just as a sign is the outcome of a particular motor act, so is speech the outcome of a series of motor acts, in this case concentrated in the mouth and throat. In other words, *all* language, signed or spoken, can be analyzed as gesture. Furthermore, research on hearing-impaired users of American Sign Language suggests that the brain areas critical for speech may be critical to signing as well. Thus, continuity exists between gestural and spoken language, and the latter could have emerged from the former through increasing emphasis on finely controlled movements of the mouth and throat. This scenario is consistent with the appearance of neurological structures underlying language in the earliest representatives of the genus *Homo* and the steady enlargement of the human brain *before* the vocal tract alteration that allows us to speak the way we do.

The advantage of spoken over gestural language to a species increasingly dependent on tool use for survival is obvious. To talk with their hands, people must stop whatever else they are doing with them; speech does not interfere with that. Other benefits include ability to talk in the dark, past opaque objects, or among speakers whose attention is diverted. Just when the changeover to spoken language occurred is not known, although all would agree that spoken languages are at least as old as anatomically modern *Homo sapiens*. What's more, no anatomical evidence exists to support arguments that Neanderthals and other representatives of archaic *H. sapiens* were incapable of speech. Perhaps its emergence began with *Homo erectus*, the first human ancestors to live in regions with cold climates. The ability to plan ahead for changes in seasonal conditions was crucial for survival and would not have been possible without a grammatically structured language, either gestural or vocal. We do know that having the use of fire, *H. erectus* would not have had to cease all activity when darkness fell. Extrapolating from this, what do we do when sitting around a camp fire—talk! We also know that the vocal tract and brain of *H. erectus* were intermediate between that of *H. sapiens* and the earlier *Australopithecus*. It may be that the changeover from gestural to spoken language was a driving force in these evolutionary changes.

The once popular search for a truly primitive language spoken by a living people that might show the processes of language just beginning or developing now has been abandoned. The reason is that no such thing as a primitive language exists in the world today, or even in the recent past. So far, all human languages that have been described and studied, even among people with something approximating a Stone Age technology, are highly developed, complex, and capable of expressing infinite meanings. The truth is, people have been talking in this world for an extremely long time, and every known language, wherever it is, now has a long history and has developed subtleties

Far from being "simple" or "primitive," the languages of nonliterate people are often the opposite. The complexity of Ojibwa and Cree distinctions between animate and inanimate has challenged linguistic anthropologists.

---

[16]Armstrong, D.F., Stokoe, W.C., & Wilcox, S.E. (1994). Signs of the origin of syntax. *Current Anthropology, 35,* 355.

and complexities that do not permit any label of "primitivism." What a language may or may not express is not a measure of its age but of its speakers' way of life, reflecting what they want or need to share and communicate with others.

CHAPTER SUMMARY

Anthropologists need to understand the workings of language, because it is language that enables people in every society to share their experiences, concerns, and beliefs, in the past and in the present, and communicate these to the next generation. Language makes communication of infinite meanings possible by employing sounds or gestures that, when combined according to certain rules, result in meanings intelligible to all speakers. Linguistics is the modern scientific study of all aspects of language. Phonetics focuses on the production, transmission, and reception of speech sounds, or phonemes. Phonology studies the sound patterns of language to extract the rules that govern the way sounds are combined. Morphology is concerned with the smallest units of meaningful combinations of sounds—morphemes—in a language. Syntax refers to the principles with which phrases and sentences are built. The entire formal structure of a language, consisting of all observations about its morphemes and syntax, constitutes its grammar.

Human language is embedded in a gesture-call system inherited from our primate ancestors that serves to "key" speech, providing the appropriate frame for interpreting linguistic form. The gestural component of this system consists of body motions used to convey messages; the system of notating and recording these motions is known as kinesics. The call component is represented by paralanguage, consisting of extralinguistic noises involving various voice qualities and vocalizations. Proxemics is the study of culturally defined use of space as a form of communication, and touch communicates through physical contact.

Descriptive linguistics registers and explains the features of a language at a particular time in its history. Historical linguistics investigates relationships between earlier and later forms of the same language. A major concern of historical linguists is to identify the forces behind the changes that have occurred in languages in the course of linguistic divergence. Historical linguistics also provides a means of roughly dating certain human migrations, invasions, and contacts with other people. Efforts to save endangered languages are evident in many parts of the world; one way to do so is through bilingual education programs.

Ethnolinguistics deals with language as it relates to society, the rest of culture, and human behaviour. Some linguists, following Benjamin Lee Whorf, have proposed that language shapes the way people think and behave. Others have argued that language reflects reality. Although linguists find language flexible and adaptable, they have found that once a terminology is established, it tends to perpetuate itself and to reflect much about the speakers' beliefs and social relationships. Kinship terms, for example, help reveal how a family is structured, what relationships are considered close or distant, and what attitudes are held toward relationships. Similarly, gender language reveals how the men and women in a society relate to one another.

A social dialect is the language of a group of people within a larger group, all of whom may speak more or less the same language. Sociolinguists are concerned with whether dialect differences reflect cultural differences. They also study code switching—the process of changing from one level of language to another as the situation demands.

One theory of language origins is that our human ancestors, with their hands freed by their bipedalism, began using gestures as a tool to communicate and implement intentions within a social setting. With the movement of *Homo erectus* out of the tropics, the need to plan for the future in order to survive seasons of cold temperatures likely required structured sentences to communicate information about events removed in time and space. By the time archaic *Homo sapiens* appeared, emphasis on finely controlled movements of the mouth and throat had probably given rise to spoken language.

All languages that have been studied, including those of people from small-scale foraging cultures, are complex, highly developed, and able to express a wide range of experiences.

QUESTIONS FOR CRITICAL THOUGHT

1. Music and the visual arts often are spoken of as if they have their own "language." Is this a language in the same sense as spoken or written language? Would your interpretation change if you distinguished between improvised music (such as some jazz) and written and rehearsed music (such as classical or pop music)? between highly formal, professional painting and a child's scribblings? What do music and the visual arts communicate to an audience?

2. How does your vocabulary reflect your interests? your opinions? the groups and culture you belong to? How does your language change in the classroom? when you are shopping or are with your family? Is your vocabulary larger or smaller than five years ago? 15 years ago? Do you use any specialized vocabulary, for example, because of a job, hobby, or a special interest in sports or music?

3. Do you know of any new languages? If so, how did they originate? What is new about them—vocabulary? grammar? syntax? How might they differ from an "older" language such as English? Can languages die? Are Latin and Sanskrit dead?

4. Do you try to use politically correct or sensitive language? Why or why not? How can your choice of words reflect your attitude toward others? How can your choice of words affect others? Explain.

5. What impression does an individual convey when he or she slouches around, avoiding eye contact? What impression does an individual convey when he or she purposefully strides into a room, head up, smiling in greeting? Do you judge people by these nonverbal messages? Explain.

6. What examples of gender bias or sexual orientation bias in your language can you identify? What does the use of these words tell you about attitudes regarding gender and sexual orientation in our society? What does it tell you about the people who use these terms?

7. Try invading someone's personal space in a social setting. Note how this person responds to your behaviour. Carry on a conversation with someone without using any body language or paralanguage. How difficult was it for you to communicate, and how much of your message was lost?

INTERNET RESOURCES

French Language
http://uni.ca/cdhowe4.html
Addresses the issues related to French-language retention and Quebec dissatisfaction with the status quo.

Canadian Bilingualism
http://canadaonline.about.com/cs/bilingualism
This site provides two good links to discussions of Canadian bilingualism issues.

Aboriginal Language Initiative
http://firstnationhelp.com/ali
This site looks at First Peoples heritage, language, and culture and provides a discussion of attempts to revitalize aboriginal languages. Offers links to other information on First Nations culture.

Origins of Language
http://emuseum.mnsu.edu/cultural/language/chimpanzee.html
A discussion of the origins of human language, including chimpanzee communication.

http://www.nsf.gov/sbe/nuggets/021/nugget.htm
A good site addressing the biological nature of language ability.

Primate Use of Language
http://www.pigeon.psy.tufts.edu/psych26/language.htm
This extensive site discusses recent research on primate ability to acquire language. Several projects are described.

Chimpanzee Communication

http://kroeber.anthro.mankato.msus.edu/cultural/language/chimpanzee.html

Discusses chimp communication and insight into the origin of language.

World Languages

http://kroeber.anthro.mankato.msus.edu/cultural/langauge/index.shtml

Provides links to many world languages and audio clips of native speakers of each language.

Tonal Language

http://kroeber.anthro.mankato.msus.edu/cultural/language/tonal.html

A look at tonal languages—the use of pitch to signal different meaning—in Southeast Asia and Africa.

Whorf-Sapir Hypothesis

http://kroeber.anthro.mankato.msus.edu/cultural/language/whorf.html

An examination of the Whorf-Sapir hypothesis, which suggests that language influences culture.

SUGGESTED READINGS

Birdwhistell, R.L. (1970). *Kinesics and context: Essays in body motion communication*. Philadelphia: University of Pennsylvania Press.

Kinesics was first delineated as an area for anthropological research by Birdwhistell, so this book is particularly appropriate for those who wish to know more about the phenomenon.

Bonvillain, N. (2000). Language, culture, and communication: The meaning of messages (3rd ed.). Upper Saddle River, NJ: Prentice Hall.

A discussion of language and the meaning of symbolic messages.

Eastman, C.M. (1990). *Aspects of language and culture* (2nd ed.). Novato, CA: Chandler and Sharp.

The bulk of this book is devoted to the subjects of worldview, ethnography of communication, nonverbal behaviour, animal communication, discourse pragmatics, conversational analysis, semiotics, and ethnicity. A single chapter deals with linguistics as a field tool.

Edwards, J. (Ed.). (1998). *Language in Canada*. Cambridge, UK: Cambridge University Press.

This comprehensive book provides a contemporary account of the linguistic and cultural state of affairs in Canada, including conflicts and tension evident today. The articles are divided into four main categories: French language issues, English language issues, aboriginal language issues, followed by a province-by-province examination of specific linguistic circumstances.

Gardner, R.A., Gardner, B.T., & Van Cantfort, T.E. (Eds.). (1989). *Teaching sign language to chimpanzees*. Albany, NY: State University of New York Press.

In 10 jargon-free chapters, easily accessible to the interested layperson as well as professionals, the methods and results of the Gardners and their students are laid out in great detail. Psychologists and anthropologists who reviewed the book agree it represents a milestone in ape language research and, as one put it, should be read by all interested in the evolution of human behaviour.

Hickerson, N.P. (1980). *Linguistic anthropology*. New York: Holt, Rinehart and Winston.

A description and explanation of what anthropological linguistics is all about, written so beginning students can understand it.

Jebwab, J. (2000). *Ethnic identification and heritage language in Canada*. Montreal: Éditions Images.

A brief examination of Canada's multiethnic and multilingual nature. Although full of statistics, this book will provide readers with a clear picture of the linguistic and cultural dynamics of Canadian society, and the current state of heritage languages in Canada.

Ruhlen, M. (1994). *The origin of language: Tracing the evolution of the mother tongue.* New York: John Wiley and Sons.

Scholarly in substance but written for a popular audience, this book is a good intro-duction to comparative linguistics for beginning anthropology students. With an evolutionary theme, it cuts through the difficult problems of our linguistic ancestors with plausible though still controversial results.

CNN TODAY VIDEOS

Lost Language (CNN Cultural Anthropology, vol. 1, 2:11)
This segment looks at a group of Native people attempting to preserve its native language.

English Only (CNN Cultural Anthropology, vol. 1, 2:04)
This segment looks at the controversy surrounding the English-only movement.

Singapore Singlish (CNN Cultural Anthropology, vol. 4, 2:33)
In a country of diverse languages, English words are merging with other languages to form a unique language.

Gender Talks (CNN Cultural Anthropology, vol. 4, 2:27)
Women learn different communication skills for the workplace.

Ancient Egyptian Language (CNN Cultural Anthropology, vol. 5, 2:18)
We can read ancient Egyptian hieroglyphics, but what did the language sound like? Linguists and archaeologists fear that these sounds may be lost forever.

Language Lineage (CNN Cultural Anthropology, vol. 5, 2:18)
This segment looks at the origin of modern languages and linguists' theories about the way different languages developed and spread around the globe.

Snaps (CNN Cultural Anthropology, vol. 5, 2:30)
This amusing segment looks at snapping, the "art of verbal warfare," and shows how snapping allows young people to trade insults instead of punches.

Terror Language (CNN Cultural Anthropology, vol. 6, 2:35)
The U.S. National Security Agency and the FBI are in desperate need of linguists proficient in Arabic and other foreign languages. The Bush administration proposes a Linguistics Reserve Corps to help alleviate the crisis.

Chapter 5

Making a Living

A Ju/'hoansi woman in southern Africa gathers food. The basic business of culture is securing the survival of those who live by its rules, and so the study of subsistence is an important aspect of anthropological study.

Chapter Preview

1. What Is Adaptation?

Adaptation refers to the interaction process between changes an organism makes in its environment and changes the environment makes in the organism. This kind of two-way adjustment is necessary for the survival of all life forms, including humans.

2. How Do Humans Adapt?

Humans adapt through the medium of culture as they develop ways of doing things compatible with the resources they have available to them and within the limitations of the environment they live in. Humans have used various strategies to fulfill their needs; these adaptations are known as patterns of subsistence. These adaptations may be remarkably stable for long periods of time.

3. What Sorts of Adaptations Have Humans Achieved through the Ages?

Food foraging is the oldest and most universal type of human adaptation. To it we owe such important elements of social organization as the sexual division of labour, food sharing, and a home base as the centre of daily activity. Domestication of plants and animals began to develop in some parts of the world between 9000 and 11 000 years ago. Horticulture—the cultivation of domestic plants with simple hand tools—made possible a more stationary way of life. Under pastoralism—reliance on raising herds of domestic animals—nomadism continued, but new modes of interaction with other peoples developed. As early as 6000 years ago in some places, intensive agriculture produced sufficient food to support urban populations. Mechanized agriculture is a technologically complex form of intensive agriculture that, today, is challenging modern agriculturalists' ability to maintain the system.

CHAPTER OUTLINE

Adaptation

The Food-Foraging Way of Life

Gender Perspectives: Gender Autonomy in
   Foraging Groups

The Food-Producing Way of Life

Anthropology Applied: Agricultural
   Development and the Anthropologist

Mechanized Agriculture

Several times today you will interrupt your activities to eat or drink. You may take this very much for granted, but if you went totally without food for as long as a day, you would begin to feel the symptoms of hunger: weakness, fatigue, headache. After a month of starvation, your body would probably never repair the damage. A mere week to 10 days without water would be enough to kill you.

All living beings, and people are no exception, must satisfy certain basic needs in order to stay alive. Among these needs are food, water, and shelter. Humans may not "live by bread alone," but nobody can live for long without any bread at all, and no creature can survive for long if its relations with its environment are random and chaotic. Living beings must have regular access to a supply of food and water and a reliable means of obtaining and using it. People have an overwhelming advantage over other creatures: We have culture. If our meat supply dwindles, we can turn to a vegetable, such as the soybean, and process it to taste like meat. When our tools fail, we replace them or invent better ones. Even when our stomachs are incapable of digesting food, we can predigest food by boiling or puréeing. We are, however, subject to the same needs and pressures as all living creatures, and it is important to understand human behaviour from this point of view. The crucial concept that underlies such a perspective is *adaptation*, that is, the way humans adjust to their environments to fulfill their needs.

Over the course of human history people have adopted various strategies to acquire their basic needs, like food; these adaptations are known as **patterns of subsistence**. Anthropologists have identified five patterns of subsistence, including foraging (hunting and gathering), pastoralism, horticulture, intensive agriculture, and mechanized agriculture (industrialism). Suggesting that all people have operated under one of these five subsistence strategies is somewhat misleading; there is a great deal of diversity in the way people adapt to one environment or another. The Ju/'hoansi of the Kalahari Desert in Africa and the historic Blackfoot of western Canada are good examples of this diversity: Both are consid-

ered foragers, yet both developed distinctly different ways of making a living. We will examine the foraging practices of these two groups later in this chapter. Even within the same cultural groups, there can be variations in their subsistence strategies from region to region. Moreover, any one group may practise more than one subsistence strategy, although one form usually dominates.

Since culture is integrated, the subsistence patterns that groups follow will influence every other aspect of their culture, from community size and permanence of settlements to marriage customs and kinship. As an example, hunter-gatherers, such as the Assiniboine, lived in small nomadic bands in order to follow the vast herds of bison that roamed the Canadian prairies before Europeans arrived.

In this chapter we will briefly survey the subsistence patterns practised by humans, and the social behaviours affected by, and affecting, these patterns. The following discussion emphasizes foraging practices, in part because this subsistence pattern is likely unfamiliar to many students, and also because it is the oldest pattern: Most peoples of the world were, at one time, foragers.

ADAPTATION

The adaptation process establishes a moving balance between the needs of a population and the potential of its environment. The Tsembaga highlanders of New Guinea, who support themselves chiefly through **horticulture**—the cultivation of crops carried out with simple hand tools—illustrate this process.[1] Although they also raise pigs, they eat them only under conditions of illness, injury, warfare, or celebration. At such times the pigs are sacrificed to ancestral spirits, and their

---

[1]Rappaport, R.A. (1969). Ritual regulation of environmental relations among a New Guinea people. In A.P. Vayda (Ed.), *Environment and cultural behavior* (pp. 181–201). Garden City, NY: Natural History Press.

Patterns of subsistence.   Food-procuring strategies.   **> Horticulture.**   Cultivation of crops using hand tools such as digging sticks or hoes.

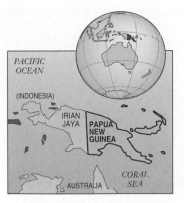

flesh is ritually consumed by the people involved in the crisis. (This guarantees a supply of high-quality protein when it is most needed.)

In precolonial times the Tsembaga and their neighbours were bound together in a unique cycle of pig sacrifices that served to mark the end of hostilities between groups. Frequent hostilities were set off by a number of ecological pressures, with pigs playing a significant role. Since very few pigs normally were slaughtered and their food requirements were great, they could very quickly eat a local group out of house and home. The need to expand food production to support the prestigious but hungry pigs put a strain on the land, which was best suited for farming.

A clear reminder that despite human technological advances, natural disasters such as forest fires can still cause considerable damage to human habitation and economic activities. Shown here is one of the fires near Kelowna, British Columbia, that engulfed the region in 2003.

Therefore, when one group had driven another off its land, hostilities ended, and the new residents celebrated their victory with a pig festival. Many pigs were slaughtered, and the pork was widely shared among allied groups. Even without hostilities, festivals were held whenever the pig population became unmanageable, every five to 10 years, depending on the groups' success at farming. Thus the cycle of fighting and feasting maintained balance among humans, land, and animals.

Adaptation also refers to the interaction process between changes an organism makes in its environment and changes the environment makes in the organism. Humans are particularly influential on their environment, causing a range of changes through a process known as **anthropogenesis.** Humans have adapted to a range of environments, including anthropogenic ones. The spread of the gene for sickle-cell anemia is a case in point. Long ago, in the tropics of central Africa, a genetic mutation appeared in human populations, causing the manufacture of red blood cells that take on a sickle shape under conditions of low oxygen pressure. Since persons who receive a gene for this trait from each parent usually develop severe anemia and die in childhood, selective pressure was exerted against the spread of this gene in the local gene pool. Then slash-and-burn horticulture was introduced into this region, creating a change in the natural environment by removal—through cutting (slashing) and burning—of the natural vegetative cover. This form of anthropogenesis was conducive to the breeding of mosquitoes that carry the parasite causing falciparum malaria. When transmitted to humans, the parasites live in the red blood cells and cause a disease that is always debilitating and very often fatal. Individuals who received the gene for the sickle-cell trait from only one parent, however (receiving one "normal" gene from the other), turned out to have a natural defence against the parasite. The gene's presence caused only some of the cells to take on a sickle shape; when those cells circulated through the spleen, which routinely screens out all damaged or worn red blood cells, the infected cells and the parasites

Anthropogenesis. The process whereby ecosystems are influenced or altered by humans.

Although the Blackfoot, Crow, and Hidatsa shared the same environment—the North American Plains—their cultures were quite different. Before Europeans arrived, the Blackfoot Confederacy lived as nomadic bison hunters on the northern Plains of Canada. Farther south, the Hidatsa, also Plains peoples, engaged in an agricultural economy. Some groups, such as the Crow and Sioux, who were agriculturalists in earlier times, later abandoned their gardens for the more exciting life of a nomadic Plains hunter.

along with them were destroyed. Since these individuals did not succumb to malaria, they were favoured by selection, and the sickling trait became more and more common in the population. Thus, while people changed their environment, their environment also changed them. Nor is this an isolated example; analogous forms of hereditary anemias that protect against malaria followed the spread of farming from southwest Asia and Southeast Asia as well.

Sickle-cell and similar anemias are an example of the relativity of any adaptation. In malarial areas, the genes responsible for these conditions are adaptive for human populations, even though some individuals suffer as a result of their presence. In nonmalarial regions, however, they are highly maladaptive, for not only do such genes confer no advantages on human populations living under such conditions, but some individuals die as a result of their presence.

Although environments do not determine culture, they do present certain possibilities and limitations. Consider the example of a group of lakeside people who live off fish. The fish in turn live off smaller organisms, which in turn consume green plants; plants liberate minerals from water

and mud and, with energy from sunlight, transform them into proteins and carbohydrates. Dead plant and animal matter is decomposed by bacteria, returning chemicals to the soil and water. Some energy escapes from this system in the form of heat. Evaporation and rainfall constantly recirculate the water. People add chemicals to the system in the form of their wastes, and, if they are judicious, they may help to regulate the balance of animals and plants.

Some anthropologists have borrowed the ecologists' concept of **ecosystem.** An ecosystem is composed of both the physical environment and the organisms living within it. The system is bound by the activities of the organisms, as well as by such physical processes as erosion and evaporation.

Human ecologists generally are concerned with detailed microstudies of particular human ecosystems; they emphasize that all aspects of human culture must be considered, not just the most obvious technological ones. The Tsembaga's attitude toward pigs and the cycle of sacrifices have important economic functions; outsiders may see them in this way, but the Tsembaga do not. They are motivated by their belief in the power and needs of their ancestral spirits.

Ecosystem.   A system, or a functioning whole, composed of both the physical environment and the organisms living within it.

Shown here are Plains Cree equestrian hunters, driving bison into a buffalo pound. Plains groups, such as the Blackfoot, Plains Cree, Assiniboine, and Sarcee, developed similar cultures, as they adapted to similar environmental conditions.

Although the pigs are consumed *by* the living, they are sacrificed *for* ancestors. Human ecosystems often must be interpreted in cultural terms.

Adaptation also must be understood from a historical point of view. The Ojibwa, who once lived on the northern shores of lakes Huron and Superior, provide a good example.[2] In their original home, they lived in small family units for most of the year, hunting moose, deer, bear, and beaver, and gathering plant foods. During the fall months, the Ojibwa fished, in the spring they tapped maple trees for maple syrup, and in the summer they harvested wild rice along the edges of the lakes. This type of subsistence enabled the Ojibwa to live a fairly sedentary and abundant lifestyle.[3]

After the arrival of Europeans, the Ojibwa were one of the first groups to actively engage in the lucrative fur trade, and by the beginning of the 18th century, many Ojibwa had been lured westward, into eastern Saskatchewan and Manitoba, in search of new trapping lands. Here, they readily adopted the Plains nomadic lifestyle, becoming bison hunters and accepting Plains

rituals such as the Sun Dance into their culture. The Plains Ojibwa, also known as Saulteaux, did not completely abandon their woodlands heritage. They tended to live on the edge of the Plains, preferring the parkland environment. They returned to the forests to collect maple sugar each spring, and continued to fish, although most other nomadic hunters of the Plains scorned such food. The Plains Ojibwa also retained their Midewiwin (Grand Medicine Society) curing rituals, and soon became famous throughout the Plains for their conjuring powers and love charms. Cultural borrowing was not entirely one-way; the Ojibwa introduced their Woodlands floral designs to the Plains groups. In moving from one environment to another, and in evolving from one way of life to another, the Ojibwa were able to capitalize on existing cultural capabilities to flourish in their new situation while still retaining valued elements of their own culture.

Once a satisfactory adaptation is achieved, the culture may enjoy long periods of relative stability. For example, by 3500 B.C., a way of life had evolved in northwestern New England and southern Quebec that was well attuned to the environmental conditions of the times.[4] Since

[2]McMillan, A.D. (1988). *Native peoples and cultures of Canada. An anthropological overview* (pp. 140–141). Vancouver: Douglas and McIntyre.

[3]Friesen, J.W. (1997). *Rediscovering the First Nations of Canada* (p. 85). Calgary: Detselig.

[4]Haviland, W.A., & Power, M.W. (1994). *The original Vermonters* (Rev. and exp. ed.). Hanover, NH: University Press of New England.

Saying that a society is stable is not saying that it is changeless. These northwest coastal Kwakwaka'wakw (Kwakiutl) are descendants of people who maintained a stable way of life for thousands of years, even though they frequently incorporated new elements into their culture. Even today, hundreds of years after the Kwakwaka'wakw's first contact with Europeans, many traditional values and practices endure.

those conditions remained more or less stable for the next 5000 years or so, it is understandable that people's lifeways also remained stable. This does not mean change was entirely absent. Periodically, people refined and enhanced their way of life—for example, improving hunting methods by replacing spears and spear throwers with bows and arrows; replacing containers made from animal hides, wood, or bark with pottery vessels; improving transportation by replacing heavy and cumbersome dugouts with sturdy yet lightweight birchbark canoes; and increasing yields by supplementing the products of hunting, gathering, and fishing with limited cultivation of corn, beans, and squash. In spite of these changes, the aboriginal peoples of the region retained the basic structure of their culture and tended toward a balance with their resource base well into the 17th century, when they had to adjust to pressures associated with Europeans moving into North

America. Such long-term stability by no means implies "stagnation," "backwardness," or "failure to progress"; rather, it indicates success. Had people's long-term physical and psychological needs not been met, the culture never would have endured as it did for thousands of years.

THE FOOD-FORAGING WAY OF LIFE

Today, perhaps a quarter of a million people—less than 0.00005 percent of the world population of over 6 billion—support themselves chiefly through hunting, fishing, and gathering wild plant foods. Yet, before the domestication of plants and animals, which began a mere 10 000 years ago, all people supported themselves through some combination of wild plant collection, hunting, and fishing. Of all the people who have *ever* lived, 90 percent have been food foragers, and it was as food foragers that we became truly human, acquiring the basic habits of dealing with one another and with the world around us that still guide the behaviour of individuals, communities, and nations today. Thus, if we want to know who we are and how we came to be, if we want to understand the relationship between environment and culture, and if we want to comprehend the institutions of the food-producing societies that have arisen since the development of farming and animal husbandry, we should turn first to the oldest and most universal of fully human lifestyles, the food-foraging adaptation. The beginnings of food foraging were examined in Chapter 3.

When food foragers had the world to themselves some 10 000 years ago, they had their pick of the best environments. These areas have long since been appropriated by agriculture and, more recently, by industrial societies. Today, most food foragers are found only in the world's marginal areas—the frozen Arctic tundra, deserts, and inaccessible forests.

Some have assumed that a food-foraging life was difficult and that people had to struggle just to stay alive. Behind this view lies the Western notion of progress, which, although widely accepted as a fact of nature, is actually nothing more than a culturally conditioned bias. This bias predisposes us to see what is new as generally preferable to what is old and to read human history as a more-or-less steady climb up an evolutionary ladder of progress. Thus, many assume that because food foraging is much older than industrial society and requires less technology, then it must be inferior to modern adaptations. Hence, food-foraging societies are referred to as "primitive," "backward," or "undeveloped," labels economists, politicians, and other members of industrial or would-be industrial societies use to express their superiority. In reality, food-foraging societies were and are highly developed, but in a way quite different from industrial societies.

Detailed studies have revealed that life in food-foraging societies was far from "solitary, poor, nasty, brutish, and short," as philosopher Thomas Hobbes asserted more than 300 years ago. Rather, food foragers' diets were well balanced and ample, and they were far less likely to experience severe famine than farmers. While their material comforts were limited, so were their needs and desires. They also had plenty of leisure time for concentrating on family ties, social life, and spiritual development. The Blackfoot Confederacy (Piegan, Blood, and Siksika people) is an excellent historical example of a Canadian food-foraging group who had adapted well to their ecosystem. Their primary food source was the huge bison herds (numbering in the thousands before Europeans arrived) roaming the Great Plains of southern Alberta and northern Montana.

Even today, food foragers who live on marginal lands lead less ardous lives than we assume. The Ju/'hoansi people of southern Africa's Kalahari Desert—scarcely what we would call a "lush" environment—obtain in an average workweek of about 20 hours a diet that surpasses internationally recommended levels of nutrients. Add the time spent making and repairing equipment, and the total workweek rises to just over 23 hours, while the equivalent of Western housework adds another 19 hours. The grand total, just over 42 hours (44.5 for men, 40.1 for women), is still less than the time spent on the job (currently 41 hours for manufacturing jobs, just under 44 hours for white-collar jobs), on maintenance tasks, and on housework in North America today.[5] Their lives are rich in human warmth and aesthetic experience, displaying a balance of work and love, ritual, and play many of us might envy. Small wonder some anthropologists have gone so far as to label foragers "the original affluent society." The Ju/'hoansi are not exceptional among food foragers today; we can only wonder about the level of affluence their ancient counterparts who lived in lusher environments achieved with more secure and plentiful supplies of food.

All modern food foragers have had some degree of interaction with neighbours whose ways of life often differ radically from their own. The Ju/'hoansi, for example, have interacted for at least 2000 years with Bantu farmers who keep

---

[5]Cashdan, E. (1989). Hunters and gatherers: Economic behavior in bands. In S. Plattner (Ed.), *Economic anthropology* (pp. 23–24). Stanford, CA: Stanford University Press.

Food foraging has by no means disappeared, even in industrial societies such as Canada and the United States. Some people forage occasionally for pleasure, as William A. Haviland and his brother-in-law are shown doing in the photo at the left—gathering wild mussels. Some, such as commercial fishers, like the Kwakwaka'wakw of British Columbia, forage full time.

cattle and sheep. Likewise, the food-foraging Mbuti of the Republic of Congo's Ituri rain forest live in a complex patron–client relationship with their neighbours, Bantu- and Sudanic-speaking peoples who are agriculturalists. They exchange meat and other products of the forest for farm produce and manufactured goods. During part of the year, they live in their patron's village and are incorporated into his kin group, even to the point of allowing him to initiate their sons.

Although some modern food foragers, such as the Mbuti, have continued to maintain traditional ways while adapting to neighbours and traders, various other groups turned to this way of life after giving up other modes of subsistence. Some, such as the Cheyenne of the Great Plains, were once farmers, while others, such as some of the San of southern Africa, have at times been farmers and at others pastoral nomads. Nor are such transformations only of the past. In the 1980s, when a world economic recession led to the abandonment of many sheep stations in the Australian outback, a number of aboriginal people returned to food foraging, thereby emancipating themselves from dependency on the government.

An important point that emerges from the preceding discussion is this: People in the world today who subsist by hunting, fishing, and gathering wild plants are not following an ancient way of life because they do not know any better; they are doing it either because they have been forced by circumstances into a situation where

foraging is the best means of survival or because they simply prefer to live this way. In many cases, they find such satisfaction in living the way they do that, like the Hadza of northern Tanzania, they go to great lengths to avoid adopting other ways of life.[6] The fact is, foraging constitutes a rational response to particular ecological, economic, and sociopolitical realities. Moreover, for at least 2000 years, a need has existed for specialist "commercial" hunter-gatherers to supply the wild forest commodities that have helped feed east–west trade since ancient times.[7]

Characteristics of Food Foragers

Mobility and Technology

Food foragers are by definition people who do not farm or practise animal husbandry. Hence, they must live where food sources are available, usually necessitating frequent movement. Such mobility is not aimless wandering but is done within a fixed territory or home range. Some groups, such as the Ju/'hoansi, who depend on the reliable and highly drought-resistant mongongo nut, may keep to fairly fixed annual routes

[6]Hawkes, K., O'Connell, J.F., & Blurton Jones, N.G. (1997). Hadza women's time allocation, offspring provisioning, and the evolution of long postmenopausal life spans. *Current Anthropology, 38,* 552.

[7]Stiles, D. (1992). The hunter-gatherer "revisionist" debate. *Anthropology Today, 8* (2), 15.

Richard B. Lee

Richard B. Lee (Ph.D., University of California, Berkeley) is internationally known for his studies of hunting and gathering cultures, particularly the Ju/'hoansi San of the Kalahari Desert in Botswana, with whom he has worked since 1963. Lee's fieldwork among the Ju/'hoansi challenged the prevailing view that hunter-gatherers lived precarious existences, constantly struggling to survive. Lee discovered that, like most foragers, the Ju/'hoansi enjoyed well-balanced diets and a surprising amount of leisure time.

Lee's ethnographies, most notably *Man the Hunter* (1968), *The !Kung San* (1979), and *The Dobe Ju/'hoansi* (1993), demonstrate the broad scope of socio-cultural anthropology, covering such diverse topics as language, subsistence strategies, kinship, marriage, social control, and belief systems. Lee's remarkable piece "Eating Christmas in the Kalahari," featured in Chapter 1 of this text, has helped to enlighten countless students to the perils of ethnographic fieldwork.

Currently professor of anthropology at the University of Toronto and co-author of this text, Lee has

Richard Borshay Lee (second from right, standing) with the Honourable Royal J.K. /ui/o/oo (standing, far left), Ju/'haan member of Namibian parliament, August 2001.

also studied foragers in Tanzania, Alaska, Australia, northern Russia, and parts of the Canadian subarctic. His most recent research has focused on the interaction of AIDS, political economy, and the politics of culture and health in southern Africa. Along with Irven DeVore, he is co-founder of the Kalahari Research Group, an assembly of scholars who have conducted fieldwork among the San peoples. In 1999 Lee edited, with Richard H. Daly, *The Cambridge Encyclopedia of Hunters and Gatherers*, a major source for this text.

Sources:

Lee, R.B. (1993). About the author. In G. Spindler & L. Spindler (Eds.), *The Dobe Ju/'hoansi: Case Studies in Cultural Anthropology* (2nd ed.). Toronto: Harcourt Brace.

Social-Cultural Anthropology at University of Toronto. (2000, December). *Biography of Richard B. Lee.* Retrieved January 27, 2001, from the World Wide Web: http://www.utoronto.ca/anthropology/Faculty/lee.htm.

and cover only a restricted territory. Others, such as the Great Plains Blackfoot, had to cover a wider territory; in this case, their route was determined by the seasonal movements of the bison herds. The mobility of food-foraging groups may also depend on the availability of water, as among the Ju/'hoansi.

Hunting styles and equipment also may play a role in determining population size and movement. Some Mbuti hunt with nets. This requires the cooperation of seven to thirty families; consequently, their camps are relatively large. The camps of Mbuti who hunt with bow and arrow number from three to six families. Too many archers in the same locale means each must travel a great distance daily to keep out of another's way. Only during midsummer do the archers collect into larger camps for religious ceremonies,

matrimonial arrangements, and social exchange. At this time the bowmen turn to communal hunts. Without nets they are less effective than their neighbours, and only when the net hunters are widely dispersed in the pursuit of honey (and not competing for meat) can the archers come together and still hunt.

In the past, the composition and size of Canadian First Nations social groups varied regionally and seasonally. The Maritime Mi'kmaq, for example, traditionally lived in winter camps composed of a few related families. They hunted seal, beaver, moose, and caribou, while in the summer, when the resources were more plentiful, especially fish, they formed bands of several hundred people. Similarly, the Ojibwa of eastern Canada lived in small family bands for most of the year, hunting bear, deer, and moose, only assembling in larger units in late spring and summer at their favourite fishing sites. The Cree, who traditionally inhabited subarctic lands, lived in small social groups, constantly on the move searching for scarce resources. The Montagnais and Naskapi (Innu) of eastern Quebec and Labrador also congregated and dispersed depending on the season. They lived in winter hunting camps composed of several related nuclear families; in the summer these small groups emerged from the woods and gathered on the shores of lakes to fish.[8]

Camp Organization

Another characteristic of the food-foraging adaptation is the small size of local groups, which usually include fewer than 100 people. Although no completely satisfactory explanation of group size has yet been offered, it seems certain that both ecological and social factors are involved. Among those suggested are the **carrying capacity** of the land, or the number of people the available resources can support at a given level of food-getting techniques, and the **density of social relations,** or roughly the number and intensity of interactions among camp members. More people means a higher social density, which, in turn, means more opportunities for conflict. Population size may also be dependent on a group's understanding of the environment, spiritual components, and cultural preferences.

Both carrying capacity and social density are complex variables. Carrying capacity involves not only the immediate presence of food and water but also the tools and work necessary to secure them, as well as short- and long-term fluctuations in their availability. Social density involves not only the number of people and their interactions but also the circumstances and quality of those interactions, as well as the mechanisms for regulating them. A mob of a hundred angry strangers

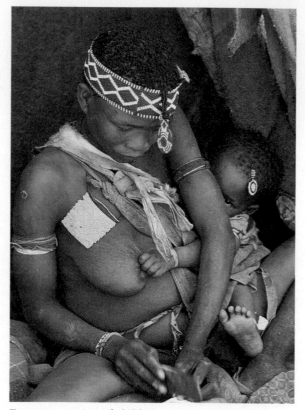

Frequent nursing of children over as many as four or five years acts to suppress ovulation among food foragers such as the Ju/'hoansi. As a consequence, women give birth to relatively few offspring at widely spaced intervals.

has a different social density than the same number of neighbours enjoying themselves at a block party.

Among food-foraging populations, social density always seems in a state of flux as people spend more or less time away from camp and as they move to other camps, either on visits or more permanently. Among the Ju/'hoansi, exhaustion of local food resources, conflict within the group, or the desire to visit friends or relatives living elsewhere may cause people to leave one group for another. As Richard Lee notes: "Ju love to go visiting, and the practice acts as a safety valve when tempers get frayed. In fact, the Ju usually move, not when their food is

---

[8]McMillan, A.D. (1988). *Native peoples and cultures of Canada: An anthropological overview* (pp. 128–137). Vancouver: Douglas and McIntyre.

Carrying capacity.   The number of people the available resources can support at a given technological level.
> Density of social relations.   Roughly the number and intensity of interactions among the members of a camp or other residential unit.

exhausted, but rather when only their patience is exhausted."[9] The ratio of children to adults may also contribute to fluctuating membership. If a camp has so many children as to create a burden for the working adults, some young families may be encouraged to join others where fewer children live. Conversely, groups with few children may actively recruit families with young children in order to ensure the group's survival. Redistribution of people, then, is an important mechanism for regulating social density, as well as for ensuring that the size and composition of local groups are suited to local variations in resources.

Band membership among the Blackfoot was also fluid. Because of limited resources, the people broke into smaller groups in early November to winter in protected areas away from the harsh winds and deep snow.[10] In the spring, they left their camps and followed the bison as they began drifting away from their winter habitat. The scattered bands reassembled in the summer for communal hunts and to celebrate the Sun Dance. In the fall, they killed large numbers of bison cows, preserving most of the meat for the long winter months. Thus, Blackfoot movement patterns were dependent on the seasonal availability of food resources and weather conditions.

In addition to seasonal or local adjustments, food foragers must make long-term adjustments to resources. Most food-foraging populations seem to stabilize at numbers well below the carrying capacity of their land. In fact, the home ranges of most food foragers could support from three to five times as many people as they typically do. In the long run, it may be more adaptive for a group to keep its numbers low, rather than to expand indefinitely and risk destruction by a sudden and unexpected natural reduction in vital food resources such as water. The population density of food-foraging groups rarely exceeds one person per 2.5 square kilometres, a very low density, even though their resources could usually support greater numbers.

How food-foraging peoples regulate population size relates to how they care for their children. Typically, mothers nurse their infants several times each hour, even at night, over a period of as many as four or five years. The constant stimulation of the mothers' nipples suppresses the hormones that promote ovulation, making conception unlikely, especially if their work keeps them physically active and they do not have large stores of body fat to draw on for energy.[11] By continuing to nurse for several years, women give birth only at widely spaced intervals, and the total number of offspring remains low.

Division of Labour

Although much has been written on the theoretical importance of hunting for shaping the supposedly competitive and aggressive nature of the human species, most anthropologists are unconvinced by these arguments. To be sure, warlike food-foraging people are known, but their behaviour is most often a response to pressure from expansionist states, a recent phenomenon in human history (see Chapter 11). In the absence of such pressures, food-foraging peoples are remarkably unaggressive and place more emphasis on cooperation than they do on competition. Division of labour, which is a crucial component of social organization and cooperation, has been observed in all human societies and is probably as old as human culture.

The hunting and butchering of large game and the processing of hard or tough raw materials are almost universally masculine occupations. Women's work, by contrast, usually consists of gathering and processing a variety of vegetal foods, as well as other domestic chores. Historically, this pattern appears to have its origin in an earlier era, when males, who were twice the size of females, got meat by scavenging from the carcasses of dead animals, butchered it with stone tools, and shared it with females. The latter, for their part, gathered wild plant foods, probably using digging sticks and carrying devices made of soft, perishable materials. Hunting live animals gradually replaced scavenging as a source of meat and the biological

[9]Lee, R. (1993). *The Dobe Ju/'hoansi* (p. 65). Fort Worth, TX: Harcourt Brace.

[10]Ewers, J.C. (1985). *The horse in Blackfoot Indian culture.* Washington, DC: Smithsonian Institute Press.

[11]Small, M.F. (1997). Making connections. *American Scientist, 85,* 503.

Food foragers like the Korowai have a division of labour in which women gather and prepare food and the men hunt, whereas in pastoral groups such as the Kurds (discussed later in this chapter), women are responsible for tending the herds and carrying out such chores as milking the ewes.

differences between the sexes were reduced to minor proportions; however, the essence of the original division of labour was maintained.

Among food foragers today, the work of women is no less arduous than that of men. Ju/'hoansi women, for example, may walk as many as 10 kilometres a day two or three times a week to gather food, carrying not only their children but also, on the return home, anywhere from 7 to 15 kilograms of food. Still, they do not have to travel quite so far afield as do men on the hunt, nor is their work usually quite so dangerous. Finally, their tasks require less rapid mobility, do not need complete and undivided attention, and are readily resumed after interruption. All of this is compatible with the biological differences that remain between the sexes. Certainly women who are pregnant, or have infants to nurse, cannot as easily travel long distances in pursuit of game as men can. In addition to wide-ranging mobility, the successful hunter also must be able to rapidly mobilize high bursts of energy. Although some women certainly can run faster than some men, in general men can run faster than women, even when the latter are not pregnant or encumbered with infants. Because human females must be able to give birth to infants with relatively large heads, their pelvic structure differs from that of human males to a greater degree than the male/female structures differ among most other species of mammals. As a consequence, the human female is not as well equipped as the human male for rapid and prolonged mobility.

On the Canadian Northern Plains, men and women tended to work together as a team—the men hunted bison and other animals, such as antelope, and the women gathered berries, tubers, and other plant foods found close to camp. Blackfoot men used several resourceful techniques for hunting bison: They lured the animals between drive lanes of stone or brush and down a hillside into a pound (heavy corral) built of logs and branches, or they drove the bison over a steep cliff. The men then cut each carcass into five or six manageable pieces and hauled them to a nearby processing area, where they butchered and processed the meat. Besides gathering plant foods (such as wild turnips, nuts, and many varieties of berries) to supplement their diets, Blackfoot women were responsible for the everyday functioning of the camp: food preparation, childcare, and sewing. They also excelled at the complex task of tanning hides; indeed, they gained status within their community from their skills as tanners. The hides were used to make clothing, moccasins, and tipi covers. Blackfoot women were also gifted artists, painting designs on their tipis and clothing, and decorating their clothing and moccasins with quillwork and beads.

The men and women worked together after a successful hunt, stripping hides off the carcasses, extracting marrow from the long bones, and collecting sinews for later use. Some of the meat was roasted or boiled, then used immediately; the rest was dried, then pounded into powder, and mixed with melted bison fat and wild cherry-berries to

Gender **Perspectives**

Gender Autonomy in Foraging Groups

Although some researchers have argued that men in traditional foraging groups dominate and control women through such practices as arranging marriages and excluding women from decision-making processes, the ethnographic literature suggests otherwise.

Foraging groups exhibit a great deal of variability in their marriage practices. For example, not all groups arrange marriages for their young people, and even in those that do, both parents have a say in choosing a prospective spouse; in fact, women often possess a great deal of influence over these decisions. A Ju/'hoansi first marriage, when the youths tend to be fairly young, is arranged, but for subsequent marriages both men and women may choose their own partners. If a marriage is an unhappy one, the woman can return home, ending the marriage. In most cultural systems, a young groom is wise to get on the good side of his future mother-in-law; otherwise, the marriage might not take place. When an Ojibwa man met a woman he wished to marry, he had to prove to her family, especially the mother, that he was a good hunter and provider. Thus, even though marriage arranging has been viewed as wife-exchange organized by the men, in reality women exert a great deal of control through such practices as mother-in-law relationships, divorce rights, and choosing their own partners.

In subsistence activities, hunter-gatherers leave decision making regarding men's work to the men, and women's work to the women, thereby allowing the experts in each area to make the decisions. As for group decisions, both age and gender play a significant role. For example, older men and women in the Evenki culture of eastern Eurasia coordinate activities within the community. Even among the Netsilik Inuit, where the majority of the food resources comes from hunting, and the men make decisions about when and where to move, the women strongly influence their husbands' decisions and maintain autonomy and high status within their own domains. Women are also valued for their skill in making warm winter clothing and boots. Without this ability, the men would perish when out hunting. Young Inuit men defer to older men, and young women defer to older women, and while males rule the household, they are careful not to interfere with women's work and to always defer to their elderly grandmothers.

In many foraging groups the men consistently seek wisdom and approval from the women; consensus and discussion between both genders were and still are typical decision-making practices in foraging groups.

Sources:

Endicott, K.L. (1999). Gender relations in hunter-gatherer societies. In R.B. Lee & R. Daly (Eds.), *The Cambridge encyclopedia of hunters and gatherers.* Cambridge, UK: Cambridge University Press.

Friesen, J.W. (1997). *Rediscovering the First Nations of Canada.* Calgary: Detselig.

McMillan, A.D. (1988). *Native peoples and cultures of Canada: An anthropological overview.* Vancouver: Douglas and McIntyre.

make pemmican.[12] Interestingly, the Blackfoot hardly ever ate fish, a food they found distasteful.

After the horse arrived on the Plains in the mid-18th century, hunting bison became easier and more efficient, and pedestrian hunters became mounted or equestrian hunters.[13] Unfortunately, the great bison herds disappeared from the Plains in 1884, ending a successful subsistence strategy.

---

[12]Kidd, K.E. (1937, reprinted 1986). *Blackfoot ethnography.* Archaeological Survey of Alberta, No. 8.

[13]McMillan, A.D. (1988). *Native peoples and cultures of Canada: An anthropological overview* (pp. 128–137). Vancouver: Douglas and McIntyre.

The nature of women's work in food-foraging societies is such that women can do it while taking care of children. They also can do it in company with other women, which helps alleviate the monotony of the work. In the past, the cultural gender biases of European and North American anthropologists caused them to underestimate the contributions the food-gathering activities of women made to the survival of their group. We now know that modern food foragers may obtain 60 to 70 percent of their diets from plant foods, with perhaps some fish and shellfish women provide (the exceptions tend to be food foragers living in the far north, where plant foods are not available for much of the year).

Although women in food-foraging societies may spend some time each day gathering plant food, men do not spend all or even the greatest part of their time hunting. The amount of energy expended in hunting, especially in hot climates, is often greater than the energy return from the kill. Too much time spent searching out game actually might be counterproductive. Energy itself is derived primarily from plant carbohydrates, and it is usually the female gatherer who brings in the bulk of the calories. A certain amount of meat in the diet, though, guarantees high-quality protein that is less easily obtained from plant sources, for meat contains exactly the right balance of all the amino acids (the building blocks of protein) the human body requires. No single plant food does this, and in order to get by without meat, people must hit on exactly the right combination of plants to provide the essential amino acids in the correct proportions.

Food Sharing

Another important characteristic of foragers is the sharing of food between adults, something quite rare among nonhuman primates. It is easy enough to see why sharing takes place, with women supplying one kind of food and men another. Among the Ju/'hoansi, women have control over the food they collect and can share it with whomever they choose. Men, by contrast, are constrained by rules that specify how much meat is to be distributed and to whom. Thus, a hunter has little effective control over the meat he brings into camp. For the individual hunter, meat sharing is really a way of storing it for the future; his generosity, obligatory though it might be, gives him a claim on the future

kills of other hunters. As a cultural trait, food sharing has the obvious survival value of distributing resources needed for subsistence. For example, in the Blackfoot culture, the leader distributed meat and hides, giving each family what they needed to survive.

A final distinctive feature of the food-foraging economy is the importance of the camp as the centre of daily activity and the place where food sharing actually occurs. Historically known food-foraging people live in camps of some permanence, ranging from the dry-season camps of the Ju/'hoansi that serve for the entire winter to the wet-season camps of the Hadza, oriented to berry picking and honey collecting, that serve for a few weeks at most. Moreover, human camps are more than sleeping areas; people are in and out all day, eating, working, and socializing in camps to a greater extent than any other primates, and this is the place where food is shared.

David Damas examined the Copper Inuit seal-sharing practices in the early 1970s.[14] He found a system based on seal-sharing partnerships, whereby a hunter was obligated to share certain portions of the seal to predetermined partners, identified as the heart partner, flipper partner, and so forth.

> After the hunter secured a seal he generally tied it to one of his hunting dogs, who towed it back to the village. The various hunters of the village who were to receive shares sent sons, daughters, or wives to the successful hunter's house and waited in the passageway of the house while the seal was being flensed and dismembered. Each in turn present his skin bucket through the doorway, speaking the name of the partner he represented, and the housewife would award the heart, liver, front flipper, etc., depending upon which partnership was involved.[15]

If not all the hunter's partners were in the camp at that time, he could keep those portions for his family, or, as more usually happened, he would send some of the meat and fat to other villagers who were not formal partners. This structured, formal sharing system was used exclusively when

[14]Damas, D. (1972). Central Eskimo systems of food sharing. *Ethnology, 11,* 220–240.
[15]Ibid., p. 223.

hunting ringed seals. More informal, less structured sharing took place when a bearded seal was killed. Here, men of the village visited the hunter's home and quickly sliced off portions they desired, the action often becoming something of a knife-wielding competition or, according to Damas, a test of bravery and manhood as the knives flew.

Egalitarian Society

An important characteristic of the food-foraging society is its egalitarianism. Food foragers are usually highly mobile, and, lacking animal or mechanical transportation, they must be able to travel without many encumbrances, especially on food-getting expeditions. The average weight of an individual's personal belongings among the Ju/'hoansi, for example, is just under 11 kilograms. The material goods of food foragers must be limited to the barest essentials, which include implements for hunting, gathering, fishing, building, and making tools, cooking utensils, traps, and nets. They have little chance to accumulate luxuries or surplus goods, and the fact that no one owns significantly more than others helps to limit status differences. Age and sex are usually the only sources of significant status differences.

It is important to realize that status differences by themselves do not imply any necessary inequality, a point that all too often has been misunderstood, especially where relations between men and women are concerned. In traditional food-foraging societies, nothing necessitates special deference of women to men. To be sure, women may be excluded from some rituals males participate in, but the reverse is also true. Moreover, the fruits of women's labour are not controlled by men but by the women themselves. Nor do women sacrifice their autonomy, even in societies in which male hunting, rather than female gathering, brings in the bulk of the food. Such was the case among the Montagnais and Naskapi (Innu) people of Labrador. The hunt was overwhelmingly important in their society. For their part, women manufactured clothing and other necessities but provided much less of the food than is common among food foragers. Until recently, women as well as men could be shamans. Nevertheless, women were excluded from ritual feasts having to do with hunting, but men were excluded from ritual feasts held by women. Thus each sex carried out its own activi-

ties, with neither meddling in the activities of the other. Early missionaries to the Montagnais and Naskapi as well as other North American First Nations groups lamented that men had no inclination to make their wives obey them and worked long and hard to convince the First Nations men that civilization required men to impose their authority on women.

Food foragers make no attempt to accumulate surplus foodstuffs, often an important source of status in agrarian societies. This does not mean, however, they live on the verge of starvation. Their environment is their storehouse, and, except in the coldest climates (where a surplus must be stored to see people through the lean season) or in times of acute ecological disaster, some food is always to be found in a group's territory. Because food resources are typically distributed equally throughout the group, no one achieves the wealth or status that hoarding might bring. In such a society, wealth is a sign of deviance rather than a desirable characteristic.

The food forager's concept of territory contributes as much to social equality as it does to the equal distribution of resources. Most groups use home ranges where access to resources is open to all members: What is available to one is available to all. If a Mbuti hunter discovers a honey tree, he has first use rights; but when he has taken his share, others have a turn. In the unlikely possibility he does not take advantage of his discovery, others will. No one owns the tree; the system is first come, first served.

Although most food foragers own little property, an interesting exception developed on the Great Plains after 1730, when the Blackfoot acquired horses. The fairly egalitarian nature of their culture altered in significant ways. Horses soon became the most valuable possession of the Blackfoot hunters; marriages and alliances were made with the exchange of horses. With horse ownership (a form of property) came social distinctions and the beginnings of a class system.

The food-forager pattern of generalized exchange, or sharing without any expectation of a direct return, also serves the ends of balancing resource distribution and social equality. A Ju/'hoansi man or woman spends as much as two-thirds of his or her day visiting others or receiving guests; during this time, many exchanges of gifts occur. Refusing to share—hoarding—would be morally wrong. By sharing whatever is at hand, the Ju/'hoansi achieve social levelling and assure their right to share in others' windfalls.

We will conclude this section as we began it, emphasizing the remarkable diversity found within foraging groups, both in the past and the present, and their propensity to readily adopt new technologies and practices as their circumstances changed. The same can be said for food-producing societies.

▲▼▲▼▲▼▲▼▲▼▲▼▲▼▲▼▲▼▲▼▲▼▲▼▲▼▲▼▲

THE FOOD-PRODUCING WAY OF LIFE

The transition from food forager to food producer that began between 9000 and 11 000 years ago in several parts of the world (Figure 5.1) has been termed revolutionary. By changing the way they provided for their subsistence, people changed the very nature of human society.

Just why this change occurred is one of the important questions in anthropology. Since food production by and large requires more work than food foraging; is more monotonous; promotes larger, more complex communities in which diseases easily mutate and spread; and is generally associated with intensive competition for resources such as land, it is unlikely people planned to

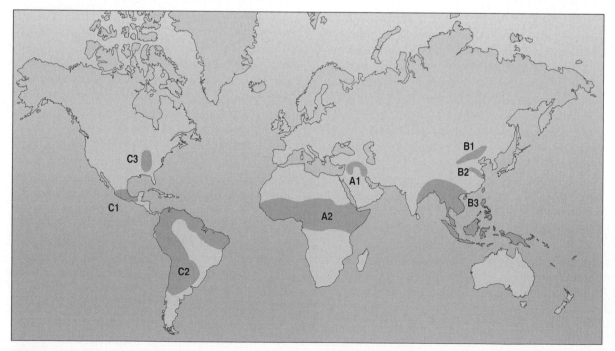

FIGURE 5.1

Early plant and animal domestication occurred in such widely scattered places as southwest Asia (A1), central Africa (A2), north China (B1), southcentral China (B2), South and Southeast Asia (B3), Mesoamerica (C1), South America (C2), and eastern North America (C3).

become food producers. Initially, it appears food production arose as a largely unintended by-product of existing food-management practices. By chance, these food-management practices promoted the development of new varieties of particular plants and animals, which came to take on increasing importance for people's subsistence. Food production probably did not provide much more food at the beginning, but it helped even out the seasonal fluctuations in wild resources and brought a heretofore unknown predictability to life.

The Settled Life of Farmers

Whatever the causes, one of the most significant correlates of this new way of life was the development of permanent settlements where families of farmers lived together, staying near their gardens. The task of food production lent itself to a different kind of social organization; the hard work of some group members could provide food for all, thus freeing some people to devote their time to inventing and manufacturing the equipment needed for a new sedentary way of life. Harvesting and digging tools, pottery for storage and cooking, clothing made of woven textiles, and housing made of stone, wood, or sun-dried bricks were some of the results of this combination of new sedentary living conditions and altered division of labour.

While it supports larger and more sedentary populations than food foraging, farming generally requires longer and more monotonous work.

The transition also brought important changes in social structure. At first, social relations were egalitarian and hardly different from those that prevailed among food foragers. As settlements grew, however, and large numbers of people began to share the same important resources, such as land and water, society became more elaborately structured. Multifamily kinship groups such as lineages, which people belong to by virtue of descent from a common ancestor but which do not commonly play a large part in the social order of food foragers, were probably the organizing units. As will be discussed in Chapter 9, they provide a convenient way to handle the distinctive problems of land use and ownership that arise in food-producing societies.

Humans adapted to this new settled life in a number of ways. Some people became horticultural—small communities of gardeners working with simple hand tools and using neither irrigation nor the plow. Horticulturists usually cultivate several varieties of crops together in small gardens they have cleared by hand. Because these gardeners typically use a given garden plot for only a few years before abandoning it in favour of a new one, horticulture may be said to constitute an *extensive* form of agriculture. Production is for subsistence, rather than to produce a surplus for sale; however, the politics of horticultural communities commonly involve periodic feasts, when substantial amounts of produce and other gifts are given away to gain prestige. Such prestige is the basis for the political power of leaders, who play important roles in production, exchange, and resource allocation.

One of the most widespread forms of horticulture, especially in the tropical forests of Mesoamerica, South America, and Southeast Asia, is slash and burn, or **swidden farming**. In slash-and-burn horticulture, the natural vegetation is manually cut down, allowed to dry, and then burned. Crops are quickly planted in the ash, thus fertilizing the nutrient-poor soil. After one to three years, the plot is abandoned and the natural vegetation is allowed to grow back. Use of fire to clear vast tracts of Amazonian or Indonesian forest for cattle raising and other

Swidden farming. An extensive form of horticulture in which the natural vegetation is cut, the slash is subsequently burned, and crops then are planted among the ashes.

development schemes has led many people to see slash-and-burn farming in a negative light. In fact, it is an ecologically sophisticated and sustainable way of raising food when carried out under the right conditions: low population densities and adequate amounts of land. Only when pursued in the absence of these conditions does the practice lead to environmental degradation and destruction. Properly carried out, swidden farming mimics the diversity of the natural ecosystem; moreover, growing several crops together in the same field makes them less vulnerable to pests and plant diseases than growing single crops. Not only is the system ecologically sound, but it is far more energy efficient than farming as carried out in countries such as Canada and the United States, which requires more energy input than comes out of the system. By contrast, for every unit of energy expended, slash-and-burn farming produces between 10 and 20 units in return.

Technologically more complex than horticulture is **intensive agriculture.** Intensive agricultural practices usually result in far more alteration of the landscape and ecology than those of horticulturalists. Intensive agriculturalists use irrigation, fertilizer, and equipment like wooden or metal plows that harnessed draft animals pull. Intensive agriculturalists can grow sufficient food to provide not just for their own needs but for those of various full-time specialists as well. This surplus may be sold for cash, or it may be coerced out of the farmers through taxes or rent paid to landowners. These landowners and other specialists typically reside in substantial towns or cities where political power is centralized in the hands of a socially elite class of people. The distinction between horticulturalist and intensive agriculturalist is not always an easy one to make. For example, the Hopi of the North American southwest traditionally employed irrigation in their farming while using simple hand tools. Moreover, they produced for their own immediate needs and lived in towns without centralized political government.

Although we tend to think of people as either food foragers or food producers, there are numerous examples of people like the Iroquois, shown here, who rely on a mix of wild and domesticated resources. The Iroquois were swidden farmers, growing corn, squash, sunflowers, tobacco, and beans, but they also hunted, fished, and gathered wild plant foods.

As food producers, people have developed several major crop complexes: two adapted to seasonal uplands and two to tropical wetlands. In the dry uplands of southwest Asia, for example, they time their agricultural activities with the rhythm of the changing seasons, cultivating wheat, barley, flax, rye, and millet. In the tropical wetlands of Southeast Asia, rice and tubers such as yams and taro are cultivated. In the Americas, people have adapted to environments similar to those of the Old World but have cultivated different plants. Maize, beans, squash, and the potato are typically grown in drier areas, whereas manioc is extensively grown in the tropical wetlands.

Pastoralism: The Bakhtiari

Before continuing our discussion of agriculture, we should examine one of the more striking examples of human adaptation to the environment, that of **pastoralism.** Pastoralists live in societies that view animal husbandry as the proper way to make a living and consider movement of all or part of the society a normal and natural way of life. This cul-

---

Intensive agriculture. Large-scale cultivators employing fertilizers, irrigation, equipment, and draft animals.
> Pastoralism.   A subsistence strategy that relies on domesticated herd animals, and usually requires seasonal movement to pastures.

This swidden plot in Chiapas, Mexico, shows what such gardens look like after slash has been burned but before the crops have begun to grow. Although it looks destructive, if properly carried out, swidden farming is an ecologically sound way of growing crops in the tropics.

tural aspect is vitally important, for although some (but not all) pastoral nomads are dependent on nearby farmers for some of their supplies, and may even earn more from nonpastoral sources than from their own herds, the concept of nomadic pastoralism remains central to their identities. These societies are built around a pastoral economic specialization but imbued with values far beyond just doing a job. This distinguishes them from North American ranchers, who likewise have a pastoral economic specialization but identify culturally with a larger society.[16] It also sets them apart from food foragers, migrant farm workers, corporate executives, and others who are nomadic but not pastoralists.

Pastoralism is an effective way of living in places that are too dry, too cold, too steep, or too rocky for farming, such as the arid grasslands that stretch eastward from North Africa through the Arabian Desert, across the plateau of Iran and into Turkestan and Mongolia. In Africa and southwest Asia alone, more than 21 million people follow pastoral nomadic ways of life. One group living in this belt of arid lands is the Bakhtiari, a fiercely

independent people who live in the south Zagros Mountains of western Iran, where they tend herds of goats and fat-tailed sheep.[17] Although

[16]Barfield, T.J. (1984). Introduction. *Cultural Survival Quarterly, 8,* 2.

[17]Material on the Bakhtiari is drawn mainly from the following: Barth, F. (1960). Nomadism in the mountain and plateau areas of south west Asia. *The problems of the arid zone* (pp. 341–355). Paris: UNESCO; Coon, C.S. (1958). *Caravan: The story of the Middle East* (2nd ed., Chap. 13). New York: Holt, Rinehart and Winston; Salzman, P.C. (1967). Political organization among nomadic peoples. *Proceedings of the American Philosophical Society, III,* 115–131.

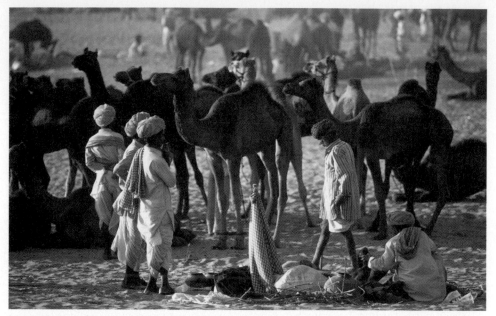

Pastoral nomadism is an adaptation that works in many parts of the world that are too hot, too cold, or too dry for farming. Shown here are Middle Eastern camel herders.

some of the Bakhtiari own horses and most own donkeys, they use these only for transport; the animals these people's lives revolve around are the sheep and goat.

The harsh, bleak environment dominates the lives of the Bakhtiari: It determines when and where they move their flocks, the clothes they wear, the food they eat, and even their dispositions—they have been called "mountain bears" by Iranian townspeople. In the Zagros are ridges that reach altitudes of 3600 to 4200 metres. Their steep, rocky trails and escarpments challenge the hardiest and ablest climbers; jagged peaks, deep chasms, and watercourses with thunderous torrents also make living and travelling hazardous.

The pastoral life of the Bakhtiari revolves around two seasonal migrations to find better grazing lands for the flocks. Twice a year the people move: in the fall from their summer quarters in the mountains and in the spring from their winter quarters in the lowlands. In the fall, before the harsh winter comes to the mountains, the nomads load their tents and other belongings on donkeys and drive their flocks down to the warm plains that border Iraq in the west; grazing land here is excellent and well watered in the winter. In the spring, when the low-lying pastures dry up, the Bakhtiari return to the mountain valleys,

where a new crop of grass is sprouting. For this trek, they split into five groups, each containing about 5000 individuals and 50 000 animals.

The return trip north is dangerous because the mountain snows are melting and the gorges are full of turbulent, ice-cold water. This long trek is further impeded by the kids and lambs born in the spring, just before migration. In the mountain passes, the Bakhtiari must make their way through slippery, unmelted snow, enduring biting winds. The stronger men often carry their children and the newborn animals on their shoulders down to the lush mountain valley. During each migration the people may cover as many as 300 kilometres, and the trek can take weeks, because the flocks travel slowly and require constant attention. The nomads have fixed routes and a somewhat definite itinerary; generally, they know where they should be and when they should be there. On the drive the men and boys herd the sheep and goats, while the women and children, along with the tents and other equipment, ride the donkeys.

Sheep and goats are central to Bakhtiari subsistence. The animals provide milk, cheese, butter, meat, hides, and wool, which is woven into clothes, tents, storage bags, and other essentials by the women or sold in towns. The people also engage in very limited horticulture; they own lands that contain orchards, and the nomads consume the fruit or sell it to townspeople. The division of labour is according to sex. The men, who take great pride in their marksmanship and horsemanship, engage in limited hunting on horseback, but their chief task is the tending of the flocks. The women cook, sew, weave, care for the children, and carry fuel and water.

The Bakhtiari have their own system of justice, including laws and a penal code. They are governed by tribal leaders, or *khans*, men who are elected or inherit their office. Because men own and control the livestock, women lack control of the economy and are relegated to the domestic sphere. This prominence of men in both economic and political affairs is common among pastoral nomads; theirs is very much a man's world. Thus, women typically occupy subordinate positions vis-à-vis men, even though elderly women eventually may gain a good deal of power. Most of the Bakhtiari *khans* grew wealthy when oil was discovered in their homeland around the start of the 20th century, and many of them are well educated, having attended Iranian or foreign universities. Despite this, and although some of them own houses in cities, the *khans* spend much of their lives among their people.

Intensive Agriculture and Nonindustrial Cities

With the intensification of agriculture, some farming communities grew into cities (Figure 5.2), where some individuals began to specialize in activities other than farming. Thus, craft specialists such as carpenters, blacksmiths, sculptors, basketmakers, and stonecutters contributed to the vibrant, diversified life of the city.

Unlike horticulturalists and pastoralists, city dwellers are only indirectly concerned with adapting to their natural environment. Far more important is the need to adapt to living with and getting along with their fellow urbanites. To an important degree, this is true as well for the farmers who provide the city dwellers with their food. Under the political control of an urban elite, much of what the farmers do is governed by

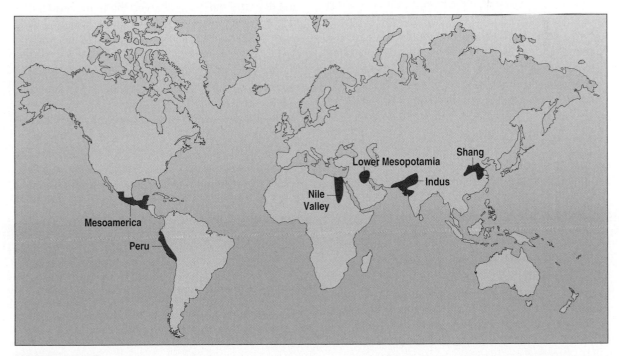

FIGURE 5.2

Locations of early state-level societies. Those of North and South America developed independently of those in Africa and Asia. Chinese civilization may have developed independently of southwest Asian (including the Nile and Indus) civilization.

Anthropology **Applied**

Agricultural Development and the Anthropologist

High up in the Andes mountains of South America lies the vast intermontane plain known as the Bolivian Altiplano. On this plain, not far from where the modern countries of Bolivia, Chile, and Peru meet, is Lake Titicaca, the world's highest navigable body of water. A kilometre or so from this lake's south end stands the elaborate, monumental architecture of Tiwanaku, one of the most impressive archaeological sites in the region that, 500 years ago, constituted the southern quarter of the Inca Empire. Today, the region is a bleak and barren landscape, where some 20 000 Aymara struggle for survival.

We now know Tiwanaku was a major city, inhabited during its Classic Period (A.D. 375 to 725) by between 20 000 and 40 000 people. Another 200 000 or so people lived in the surrounding Titicaca basin, all under the political control of Tiwanaku, a true imperial city that controlled a vast empire centuries before the Incas were anything but a relatively insignificant people living in the mountains north of Tiwanaku. Its political control stretched well beyond the Altiplano into northern Chile and southern Peru, where administrative centres, satellite cities, and even colonies were established.

To support the huge population of the Altiplano, Tiwanaku carried out massive land reclamation, constructing an extensive system of raised and ridged fields where hardy crops could be intensively grown. These fields have been studied by anthropologist Alan Kolata of the University of Chicago. Built up to a height of 1 to 1.5 metres, the constituent materials of cobblestones, clay, gravel, and topsoil were carefully layered to prevent the buildup of crop-killing salt that leaches into the ground. Between the fields ran canals that filled with groundwater. These 1.5-metre-wide trenches were oriented to soak up the maximum amount of solar heat during the day, thus acting as a kind of solar sump. One reason Altiplano agriculture today is so difficult is because of periodic frost; as much as 90 percent of a harvest can be lost as a result. In Tiwanaku times, however, the heat stored in the canals radiated over the fields' surface, raising the ambient temperatures as much as 2°C or 3°C, which is more than enough to prevent frost. In addition, the canals functioned as fertilizer factories. Organic sediments that settled in the canals could be scooped out at the end of each growing season and dumped on the fields, thereby renewing their fertility.

Having figured out how the system worked, in 1988 Kolata began to put his knowledge to work in the service of the Aymara farmers living in the region today.[1] In selected communities, Kolata has secured the cooperation of native farmers by guaranteeing a harvest, even if their experimental fields fail. Planting onions, beets, and potatoes, they have increased their yields significantly; not only do they get up to twice as many potatoes per plant, for instance, but also the potatoes are bigger and of better quality. Moreover, the farmers do not have to use scarce funds for fertilizer, since canal muck is free, and they are not causing pollution through use of chemical fertilizer.

By reintroducing an ancient technology that was lost following disintegration of the Tiwanaku empire some 1000 years ago, Kolata is now improving the quality of life for countless Aymara, reversing the poor harvests that have driven many men from the Altiplano to valleys south and east, where coca is grown to be turned into cocaine. Given the technique's success, Kolata predicted that, by the end of the 1990s, the ancient raised-field technology would be widely used not just in Bolivia but also in many other parts of South and Central America where it is suitable.

---

[1]Straughan, B. (1996). The secrets of ancient Tiwanaku are benefitting today's Bolivia. In W.A. Haviland & R.J. Gordon (Eds.), *Talking about people* (2nd ed., pp. 76–78). Mountain View, CA: Mayfield.

economic forces they have little, if any, control over. Urbanization brings with it a new social order: Marked inequality develops as society becomes stratified and people are ranked according to their gender, the kind of work they do, or the family they are born into. As social institutions cease to operate in simple, face-to-face groups of relatives, friends, and acquaintances, they become more formal and bureaucratic, with specialized political institutions.

Urbanization led to several other innovations. Writing was invented, trade intensified and expanded, the wheel and the sail were invented, and metallurgy and other crafts were developed. In many early cities, monumental buildings, such as royal palaces and temples, were built by thousands of men, often slaves taken in war; these feats of engineering still amaze modern architects and engineers. The inhabitants of these buildings—the ruling class composed of nobles and priests—formed a central government that dictated social and religious rules; in turn, the merchants, soldiers, artisans, farmers, and other citizens carried out the rules.

Aztec City Life

The Aztec empire, which flourished in Mexico in the 16th century, is a good example of a highly developed urban society among non-Western peoples.[18] The capital city of the empire, Tenochtitlán (modern-day Mexico City), was located in a fertile valley 2133 metres above sea level. Its population, along with that of its sister

city, Tlatelolco, was about 200 000 in 1519, when Cortes first saw it. This makes it five times more populous than London at the same time. The Aztec metropolis sat on an island in the middle of a lake, which has since dried up, and two aqueducts brought in fresh water from springs on the mainland. A 16-kilometre dike rimmed the eastern end of the city to prevent nearby salty waters from entering the lake around Tenochtitlán.

As in the early cities of southwest Asia, the foundation of Aztec society was intensive agriculture. Corn was the principal crop. Each family, allotted a plot of land by its lineage, cultivated any of a number of crops, including beans, squash, gourds, peppers, tomatoes, cotton, and tobacco. Unlike Old World societies, only a few animals were domesticated; these included dogs and turkeys (both for eating). Many of the crops were grown around Tenochtitlán in artificially constructed plots in the shallow waters of the surrounding lake. Canals between these *chinampas* not only facilitated transport but were also a source of water plants used for heavy mulching. In addition, muck rich in fish feces was periodically dredged from the canals and spread over the gardens to maintain their fertility. Because they were incredibly productive as well as sustainable, *chinampas* still can be found today at Xochimilco on the outskirts of Mexico City.

Aztec agricultural success provided for an increasingly large population and the diversification of labour. Skilled artisans, such as sculptors, silversmiths, stone workers, potters, weavers, feather workers, and painters, could make good livings by pursuing their crafts exclusively. Since religion was central to the Aztec social order, these craftspeople were engaged continuously in the manufacture of religious artifacts, clothing, and decorations for buildings and temples. Other nonagricultural specialists included some of the warriors, the travelling merchants or *pochteca,* the priests, and the government bureaucracy of nobles.

As specialization increased, both among individuals and cities of the Aztec empire, the market became an extremely important economic and social institution. In addition to the daily markets in each city, larger markets were held in the various cities at different times of year. Buyers and sellers travelled to these from the far reaches of

---

[18]Most of the following information is taken from Berdan, F.F. (1982). *The Aztecs of central Mexico.* New York: Holt, Rinehart and Winston.

Model of the centre of Tenochtitlán, the Aztec capital city.

the empire. The market at Tlatelolco was so huge that the Spanish compared it to those of Rome and Constantinople. At the Aztec markets, barter was the primary means of exchange. At times, however, cacao beans, gold dust, crescent-shaped knives, and copper were used as a kind of currency. In addition to its obvious economic use, the market served social functions: People went there not only to buy or to sell but also to meet other people and to hear the latest news. The other major economic institution, trade networks between the Aztec capital and other cities, brought goods such as chocolate, vanilla beans, and pineapples into Tenochtitlán.

The Aztec social order was stratified into three main classes: nobles, commoners, and serfs. The nobles, among whom gender inequality was most marked, operated outside the lineage system on the basis of land and serfs the ruler allotted them from conquered peoples. The commoners were divided into lineages they were dependent on for land. Within each of these lineages, those more closely related to the lineage founder had higher status than those whose kinship was more distant. The third class in Aztec society consisted of serfs bound to the land and porters employed by merchants as carriers. Lowest of this class were the slaves. Some voluntarily had sold themselves into bondage; others were captives taken in war.

The Aztecs were governed by a semidivine king, whom a council of nobles, priests, and leaders chose from among candidates of royal lineage. Although the king was an absolute monarch, the councillors advised him on affairs of state. Government officials oversaw various functions, such as maintenance of the tax system and the courts of justice, management of government storehouses, and control of military training.

The typical Aztec city was rectangular and reflected the way the land was divided among the lineages. In the centre was a large plaza containing the temple and the house of the city's ruler. At Tenochtitlán, with a total area of about 52 square kilometres, a huge temple and two lavish palaces stood in the central plaza, also called the Sacred Precinct. Surrounding this area were other ceremonial buildings belonging to each lineage.

As in a modern city, housing in Tenochtitlán ranged from squalid to magnificent. On the outskirts of the city, on *chinampas*, were the farmers' huts, built of wooden posts, thatched straw, and wattle plastered with mud. In the city proper were the houses of the middle class—graceful, multiroomed, single- and two-storey stone and mortar buildings, each surrounding a flower-filled patio and resting on a stone platform for protection against floods. It is estimated that Tenochtitlán had about 60 000 houses. The focal

The modern industrial city is a very recent human development, although its roots lie in preindustrial cities. Shown here is the industrial city of Toronto.

points of the city were the *teocallis,* or pyramidal temples, where religious ceremonies, including human sacrifice, were held.

The palace of the emperor Moctezuma boasted numerous rooms for attendants and concubines, a menagerie, hanging gardens, and a swimming pool. Since Tenochtitlán sat in the middle of a lake, it was unfortified and connected to the mainland by three causeways. Communication among different parts of the city was easy, and people could travel either by land or by water. A series of canals, with footpaths beside them, ran throughout the city. The Spaniards who came to the Aztec capital reported that thousands of canoes plied the canals, carrying passengers and cargo around the city; these Europeans were so impressed by the communication network that they called Tenochtitlán the Venice of the New World.

MECHANIZED AGRICULTURE

Mechanized or industrial **agriculture** is a form of intensive agriculture that relies on complex technological and production practices rather than human power. This versatile form of agriculture exhibits characteristics and faces challenges not as evident in intensive agriculture.[19] Mechanization

[19]Barlett, P.F. (1989). Industrial agriculture. In S. Plattner (Ed.), *Economic anthropology.* Stanford, CA: Stanford University Press.

of the farm operation has resulted in larger farms, using less human labour and more machinery, and the intensive use of fertilizers, insecticides, and other chemicals to ensure maximum yields. The downside of using complex machinery and chemical treatments is the added expense of purchasing equipment and chemicals, the consumption of large amounts of energy, and the inevitable environmental damage, such as water pollution from pesticides and fertilizer runoff. Hybrid plants and genetic enhancement of seeds have also increased production. However, in recent years there has been growing concern over possible health risks associated with genetically altered foods.

In countries such as Canada, government agencies control the purchase of land, marketing and pricing systems, subsidization payments, taxation, quotas, and production. This government intervention has drastically reduced the mechanized agriculturalist's autonomy, and often interferes with farming as a successful enterprise.

The Canadian Family Farm

More than a century ago immigrants from other countries began flooding the Canadian prairies, bringing with them agricultural expertise and courageous determination to build a better life for their families. Canadian farming practices

Complex machinery, such as the combines shown here on a Saskatchewan farm, lighten the workload and enable agriculturalists to open up larger farms.

Mechanized agriculture. Large-scale agriculture dependent on complex technology and biotechnology rather than human power to increase production.

Family-run grain farms, such as the one shown here, are fast becoming a thing of the past as young people seek employment in urban centres rather than brave the uncertainties of farming.

have changed drastically since that time, farm size has grown, and agriculture has become increasingly dependent on complex machinery, chemical fertilizers, and irrigation systems. But the essence of Canadian agriculture still remains the family farm: strongly independent, family-owned and -operated enterprises.

Division of labour on Canadian family farms tends to be gender specific. The men operate the farm equipment, ready the fields for seeding, care for livestock, and take off the harvest, while women manage the household chores, prepare meals, and grow gardens. If the need arises,

however, women often help with "male duties," feeding livestock, driving grain trucks, and picking up machine parts in town. Children, too, begin helping on the farm at an early age; they operate farm equipment well before they reach adulthood, care for younger children, plant and weed gardens, and so on.

Family farms were successful, thriving industries until the mid-1970s, but in recent years, farmers have faced seemingly insurmountable obstacles: low commodity prices; European and American subsidies; rising expenses and increasing debt; fears of environmental contamination and ecological disturbance; and government unwillingness to provide meaningful assistance. These problems are wreaking havoc on Canadian agriculture and threatening the demise of the family farm and the depopulation of rural Canada. Statistics tell the story: In 1976 Canada had 338 552 farms; by 1986 this number had fallen to 293 089, and in 1996 only 276 548 viable farms still remained in Canada.[20] If the family farm disappears, it will be an incalculable loss for all of Canadian society.

---

[20]The Canadian Federation of Agriculture. (1998, March). *The Canadian farm*. Retrieved April 11, 2001, from the World Wide Web: http://www.cfa-faca/farms-e.htm; Census of Agriculture. (2001, February 22). *History of the Census of Agriculture*. Retrieved April 11, 2001, from the World Wide Web: http://142.206.72.65/06_011_e.htm.

CHAPTER SUMMARY

To meet their requirements for food, water, and shelter, people must adjust their behaviour to suit their environment. This adjustment, which involves both change and stability, is a part of adaptation. Adaptation means a moving balance exists between a society's needs and its potential. Adaptation also refers to the interaction between an organism and its environment, with each causing changes in the other. Human ecosystems, which tend to be anthropogenic, must be considered in terms of all aspects of culture.

Humans have adapted to their environments through patterns of subsistence—the way we fulfill our basic needs. The food-foraging way of life, the oldest and most universal type of subsistence,

requires that people move their residence according to changing food sources; thus local group size is kept small. General characteristics of food foragers include a nomadic way of life; small, mobile camps; food sharing; sexual division of labour; and egalitarianism.

The reason for the transition from food foraging to food production, which began about 11 000 to 9000 years ago, was likely the unforeseen result of increased management of wild food resources. One correlate of the food-producing revolution was the eventual development of permanent settlements as people practised horticulture using simple hand tools. One common form of horticulture is slash and burn, or swidden farming. Intensive agriculture, a more complex activity, requires irrigation, fertilizers, and draft animals. Pastoralism is a means of subsistence that relies on raising herds of domesticated animals, such as cattle, sheep, and goats. Pastoralists are usually nomads, moving to different pastures as required for grass and water.

Cities developed as intensified agricultural techniques created a surplus, freeing individuals to specialize full time in other activities. Social structure became increasingly stratified with the development of cities, and people were ranked according to gender, the work they did, and the family they were born into. Social relationships grew more formal, and centralized political institutions were formed. In some parts of the world, intensive agriculture has evolved into mechanized or industrial agriculture, a system plagued by economic, environmental, political, and social problems in the 21st century.

We should not conclude that the sequence from food-foraging to horticultural/pastoral to intensive agricultural to nonindustrial urban and then industrial societies is inevitable. Food foraging, horticultural, pastoral, nonindustrial, and industrial urban societies are all highly evolved adaptations, each in its own particular way.

QUESTIONS FOR CRITICAL THOUGHT

1. Is change always adapative? What are examples of nonadaptive change within North American culture?

2. The Incas of South America did not have or widely use the wheel or the concept of zero. Does this mean Incan culture might have been nonadaptive?

3. Is cultural change or increasing technical complexity the same as progress? Why or why not? Do you believe in human "progress"? If so, in what sense do we progress?

4. Can large-scale, technologically advanced societies and small-scale societies coexist? Under what circumstances could they coexist?

5. If global warming causes dramatic climate changes, how might we adapt? For example, if the temperatures increase and the moisture levels decrease, what adaptations will agriculturalists have to make? Will we be able to adapt?

6. If the Canadian family farm disappears, how will this affect the economic and social life of all Canadians?

7. In North America, our reliance (some would say overreliance) on technology makes us vulnerable if this technology fails us. As a case in point, the August 2003 blackout in eastern North America affected 50 million people. Have we become too reliant on advanced technology? What happens if this technology fails us (e.g., what would happen if we no longer had access to gasoline for our vehicles)? Are there ways for us to avoid or reduce the impact of technology failures?

INTERNET RESOURCES

Horticulture—The Swidden Ecosystem
http://www.nusantara.com/heritage/swid/index.html
A small site with pictures displaying the six stages of swidden horticulture described in the site.

Foragers
http://www.kalaharipeoples.org/documents/Mobility.htm

A short paper on the mobility strategies among foraging groups in the eastern and northeastern Kalahari Desert.

http://www.abdn.ac.uk.chags9/11gardner.htm
A summary of how foragers around the world handle environmental and subsistence knowledge.

Hunter-Gatherers

http://www.heritage.nf.ca/aboriginal/beothuk.html

A comprehensive site that covers many aspects of the now extinct Beothuk people's culture.

http://www.chass.utoronto.ca/~coupland/ANT310/lectures/HGtheory.htm

This site briefly describes and compares hunter-gatherer ways of life.

Ju/'hoansi

http://www.ucc.uconn.edu/~epsadm03/kung.html

This site summarizes the main aspects of Ju/'hoansi life.

Blackfoot People

http://ccins.camosun.bc.ca/~conklin/pages/martin/html/blackfoot.htm

A small site that includes pictures, maps, and descriptions of the dress, food, location, housing, language, religion, art, and ceremonies of the Blackfoot people.

Canadian Agriculture

http://www.angelfire.com/ns/canadianagriculture/frame.html

An extensive site with information on many aspects of Canadian agriculture, such as marketing, policies, imports, and exports, as well as the past, present, and future of agriculture in Canada.

SUGGESTED READINGS

Bates, D.G., & Plog, F. (1991). *Human adaptive strategies*. New York: McGraw-Hill.

> This book takes an ecological approach to understanding human cultural diversity. A chapter each is devoted to hunting-and-gathering, horticultural, pastoral, intensive agricultural, and industrial societies, with a final chapter devoted to change and development. Theoretical issues are made easy to grasp through the use of readable ethnographic cases.

Friesen, J.W. (1999). *First Nations of the Plains: Creative, adaptable and enduring*. Calgary: Detselig.

> This book provides an in-depth look at aboriginal people of the Plains after contact with Europeans. Cultural groups are examined from a geographical, historical, and cultural perspective. Highly recommended for students of aboriginal culture.

Lee, R.B. (2003). *The Dobe Ju/'hoansi* (3rd ed.). Toronto: Nelson Thomson Learning.

> One of the pivotal case studies in anthropology, this ethnography features the Dobe Ju/'hoansi foragers of the Kalahari Desert. Based on years of ethnographic fieldwork, this very readable ethnography introduces us to the lives of the Ju/'hoansi. It also brings us up to the present, discussing the challenges, such as the HIV/AIDS epidemic, faced by the Ju/'hoansi in the modern world.

Lee, R.B., & Daly, R. (Eds.). (1999). *The Cambridge encyclopedia of hunter-gatherers*. Cambridge, UK: Cambridge University Press.

> This impressive work presents ethnographic research on diverse hunting-and-gathering peoples around the world, including several aboriginal groups in Canada. The book is divided into two parts: The first part contains more than 50 case studies, written by experts on hunter-gatherer peoples; the second part contains essays on prehistory, social life, gender, music and art, health, religion, and indigenous knowledge.

Lustig-Arecco, V. (1975). *Technology: Strategies for survival*. New York: Holt, Rinehart and Winston.

> Although the early anthropologists devoted a good deal of attention to technology, the subject fell into neglect early in the 20th century. This is one of the few more recent studies of the subject. The author's particular interest is the technoeconomic adaptation of hunters, pastoralists, and farmers.

McMillan, A.D. (1988). *Native peoples and cultures of Canada: An anthropological overview*. Vancouver: Douglas and McIntyre.

This book is an up-to-date overview of Canada's aboriginal people, from a cultural, historical, and social perspective. The information is clearly presented and covers numerous topics, serving as an excellent resource for students.

Schrire, C. (Ed.). (1984). *Past and present in hunter gatherer studies*. Orlando, FL: Academic Press.

This collection of papers demolishes many myths (including several held by anthropologists) about food-foraging societies. Especially recommended is the editor's introduction, "Wild Surmises on Savage Thoughts."

CNN TODAY VIDEOS

Buffalo (CNN Cultural Anthropology, vol. 1, 2:29)
This video clip examines the importance the buffalo continues to play in Lakota culture.

Brazil's Dying Tribe (CNN Cultural Anthropology, vol. 1, 2:34)
Former nomadic tribes living in southern Brazil are forced onto reservations. There, with increasing poverty and their traditional customs curtailed, young members of the tribe are increasingly committing suicide.

Life on the Edge: The Town of Churchill (CNN Cultural Anthropology, vol. 3, 5:00)
Seventeenth-century English explorers founded the town of Churchill on Hudson Bay. The town, mainly inhabited by native peoples, is enjoying new prosperity thanks to a large influx of tourists and a growing appreciation of native arts and crafts.

Disgusting Foods (CNN Cultural Anthropology, vol. 4, 2:50)
A lighthearted look at how foods, thought to be delicacies in one culture, are looked upon as uneatable in another culture.

South Africa Endangered (CNN Cultural Anthropology, vol. 5, 2:27)
This segment explores the conflict between the preservation of an endangered South African forest and the needs of local people who depend on the forest for their livelihood.

Chapter 6

Economic Systems :

The fundamental characteristic of the market in non-Western societies is that it always means a literal marketplace, where actual goods are exchanged. At this market in Luxor, Egypt, people exchange items they have produced for things they need but can only get from others.

Chapter Preview

1. How Do Anthropologists Study Economic Systems?

Anthropologists study how goods are produced, distributed, and consumed in the context of the total culture. Although they have borrowed theories and concepts from economists, most anthropologists feel principles derived from the study of Western market economies have limited applicability to economic systems where people do not produce and exchange goods for profit.

2. How Do Economies Work?

Every human culture has a division of labour by age and sex, with some additional craft specialization. Land and other valuable resources usually are controlled by groups of relatives, such as bands or lineages, or by private ownership. Production takes place in the quantity and at the time required, and most goods are consumed by the group that produces them. Levelling mechanisms ensure that no one accumulates significantly more goods than anyone else.

3. How and Why Are Goods Exchanged?

People exchange goods through reciprocity, redistribution, and market exchange. *Reciprocity* involves the exchange of goods and services of roughly equivalent value, and it is often undertaken for ritual purposes or in order to gain prestige. *Redistribution* requires some sort of centralized authority and/or religious elite to collect and then reallocate resources in the form of either goods or services. *Market exchange* in nonindustrial societies means going to a specific place for direct exchange of goods. *Consumption*, meaning the food and beverage we intake and the resources we use, is the third component of any economic system.

CHAPTER OUTLINE

Economic Anthropology

Resources

Distribution and Exchange

Original Study: Reciprocity on Skid Row

Consumption

Economics, Culture, and the World of Business

Gender Perspectives: Women and Economic
    Development

Anthropology Applied: Anthropology and the
    World of Business

Every group of people, each distinct culture, and all societies operate within an **economic system** that regulates the production, distribution, and consumption of goods. Obviously, our earlier discussion of subsistence patterns is an important part of any economy. Yet economic systems encompass far more than we have covered so far. This chapter will examine the systems of exchange, redistribution, and consumption.

ECONOMIC ANTHROPOLOGY

Studying the economies of nonliterate peoples is where we are most apt to fall prey to interpreting anthropological data in terms of our own technologies, our own sense of work and property, and our own determination of what is rational. Take, for example, the following statement from a respected economics textbook: "In all societies, the prevailing reality of life has been the inadequacy of output to fill the wants and needs of the people."[1] This ethnocentric assertion fails to realize that in many cultures people's wants are maintained at levels that can be fully and continuously satisfied, without jeopardizing the environment. Goods and services are produced in the quantity and at the time required, and to do more than this makes no sense at all. Thus, no matter how hard people may work when hard work is called for, at other times they will have available hours, days, or even weeks on end to devote to "unproductive" (in the Western economic sense) activities. To Western observers, such people are apt to appear lazy; "instead of disciplined workers, they are reluctant and untrained laborers."[2] If the people happen to be hunters and gatherers, even the hard work is likely to be misinterpreted. In Western culture hunting is defined as a "sport"; hence, the men in food-foraging groups often are perceived as spending virtually all of their time in "recreational pursuits," while the women are seen as working themselves to the bone. This perception was evident when Europeans encountered First Nations hunter-gatherers, who appeared somewhat lazy and casual about acquiring resources. What these early explorers did not realize is that traditional hunting-and-gathering First Nations cultures were present-oriented, survival-centred societies.[3] When they required meat, they hunted to fill their current needs, and when they required plant foods, they gathered what they needed. People such as the Mi'kmaq were not given to storing food in anticipation of the future, except for foods such as dried fish to sustain them for short periods. On the other hand, First Nations groups on Canada's Pacific coast preserved and stored large quantities of berries, shellfish, and fish, using such techniques as sun- and wind-drying and smoking. The foods were often packed in carved, red cedar bentwood boxes to be consumed or distributed during the winter season, when they devoted most of their time to ceremonial life.

The point here is that to understand how the schedule of wants or demands of a given society is balanced against the supply of goods and services available, it is necessary to introduce a noneconomic variable—the anthropological variable of culture. In any given economic system, economic processes cannot be interpreted without culturally defining the demands and understanding the conventions that dictate how and when they are satisfied. The fact is, the economic sphere of behaviour is *not* separate from the social, religious, and political spheres and thus not free to follow its own purely economic logic. To be sure, economic behaviour and institutions can be analyzed in purely economic terms, but to do so means ignoring crucial noneconomic considerations.

As a case in point, we may look briefly at yam production among the Trobriand Islanders, who inhabit a group of coral atolls that lie north of New Guinea's eastern end.[4] Trobriand men spend

Example of culture influencing

---

[1]Heilbroner, R.L., & Thurow, L.C. (1981). *The economic problem* (6th ed., p. 327). Englewood Cliffs, NJ: Prentice-Hall.

[2]Ibid., p. 609.

[3]Friesen, J.W. (1997). *Rediscovering the First Nations of Canada*. Calgary: Detselig.

[4]Weiner, A.B. (1988). *The Trobrianders of Papua New Guinea*. New York: Holt, Rinehart and Winston.

Economic system.   The production, distribution, and consumption of goods.

a great deal of their time and energy raising yams, not for themselves or their own households but to give to their sisters and married daughters. The purpose of this yam production is not to provision the households they are given to, because most of what people eat they grow for themselves in gardens where they plant taro, sweet potatoes, tapioca, greens, beans, and squash, as well as breadfruit and banana trees. The reason a man gives yams to a woman is to show his support for her husband and to enhance his own influence.

Once received by the woman, they are loaded into her husband's yam house, symbolizing that he is a man of power and influence in his community. Some of these yams he may use to purchase a variety of things, including arm shells, shell necklaces and earrings, pigs, chickens, and locally produced goods such as wooden bowls, floor mats, lime pots, and even magic spells. Some he must use to discharge obligations, presenting yams to the relatives of his daughter's husband when she marries or making required payments following the death of a member of his lineage. Finally, any man who aspires to high status and power must show his worth by organizing a yam competition, where he gives away huge quantities of yams to invited guests. As anthropologist Annette Weiner explains: "A yam house, then, is like a bank account; when full, a man is wealthy and powerful. Until yams are cooked or they rot, they may circulate as limited currency. That is why, once harvested, the usage of yams for daily food is avoided as much as possible."[5]

By giving yams to his sister or daughter, a man not only expresses his confidence in the woman's husband, but he also makes the latter indebted to him. Although the recipient rewards the gardener and his helpers by throwing a feast, at which they are fed cooked yams, taro, and ample pieces of pork, this in no way pays off the debt. Nor does the gift of a stone axe blade (another valuable in the Trobriand system), which may reward an especially good harvest. The debt can be repaid only in women's wealth, which consists of bundles of banana leaves and skirts made of the same material dyed red.

Trobriand Island men devote a great deal of time and energy to raising yams, not for themselves but to give to others. These yams, which have been raised by men related through marriage to a chief, are about to be loaded into the chief's yam house.

Although the bundles are of no utilitarian value, extensive labour is invested in their production, and large quantities of them, along with skirts, are regarded as essential for paying off all the members of other lineages who were close to a recently deceased relative in life and who assisted with the funeral. Also, the wealth and vitality of the dead person's lineage is measured by the quality and quantity of the bundles and skirts so distributed. Because a man has received yams from his wife's brother, he is obligated to provide his wife yams for purchasing the necessary bundles and skirts, beyond those she has produced, to help with payments following the death of a member of her lineage. Because deaths are unpredictable, a man must have yams available for his wife when she needs them. This, and the fact she may require all of his yams, acts as an effective check on a man's wealth.

[5]Ibid., p. 86.

Richard F. Salisbury   (1926–1989)

Canadian anthropology has benefited from the wisdom, intelligence, and dedication of many outstanding anthropologists, but none more respected and admired than Dr. Richard Salisbury. An economic anthropologist, and champion of applied anthropology, he is best remembered for his lifelong commitment to the study and resolution of social problems among aboriginal peoples.

Salisbury's academic career began at Cambridge University, where he studied modern languages and anthropology. His doctoral research took him to New Guinea, where he studied economic change among the highlands peoples. After completing his Ph.D. at the Australian National University in 1955, Salisbury taught at the University of California, Berkeley, before joining the faculty at McGill University in 1962. At McGill, Salisbury worked diligently to build one of the major centres of applied anthropology in North America.

Salisbury was a public anthropologist at heart; he felt that anthropological studies belonged to the study group and the public, rather than to academics and government agencies. He urged aboriginal peoples to take an active role in the decision-making processes that affected their communities. His unique style of dialogue between developers and aboriginal groups now serves as a model for planning and development in many parts of the world.

In the 1970s Salisbury turned his attention to social and economic development in the Canadian north. Between 1971 and 1983 he served as an intermediary with the James Bay Cree as they struggled to halt a hydroelectric project on their traditional hunting lands. In his last book, *A Homeland for the Cree,* published in 1986, Salisbury expressed pride and satisfaction that the Cree had successfully blocked the Quebec hydro project, using their own ingenuity.

Salisbury was a favourite among his students, many of whom have gone on to teach and carry out research around the world. He also gave of himself to professional organizations and government agencies. During his career he served as president of the Northeastern Anthropological Association, the Canadian Sociology and Anthropology Association, and the Society for Applied Anthropology in Canada, and in 1974 he was elected a Fellow of the Royal Society of Canada.

Among Dr. Salisbury's many published works, including 10 books, *From Stone to Steel* (1962) established his reputation as an economic anthropologist. In this work, he analyzed social transformation among the Siane people of New Guinea during the 1950s.

Dr. Bruce Trigger sums up Richard Salisbury's contributions with a most apt tribute: Dr. Salisbury believed that "no scholar has the right to force his or her ideas on anyone else. Yet his example of unremitting labour, intellectual honesty, and generosity challenged all who knew him to work harder, produce more, and discover inner talents that otherwise might have gone to waste. Few scholars have a record of enduring social and academic contributions to rival those that Salisbury made to his adopted country."

Source: A tribute to Richard F. Salisbury, FRSC, by Bruce G. Trigger, FRSC, for the Royal Society of Canada, published in *Transactions*, 1989, Fifth Series, Volume IV, pp. 419–423.

Like people the world over, the Trobriand Islanders assign meanings to objects that make the objects worth far more than their cost in labour or materials. Yams, for example, establish long-term relationships that lead to other advantages, such as access to land, protection, assistance, and other kinds of wealth. Thus, yam exchanges are as much social and political transactions as they are economic transactions. Banana leaf bundles and skirts, for their part, are symbolic of the political state of lineages and of their immortality. In their distribution, which is related to rituals associated with death, we see how men in Trobriand society are ultimately dependent on women and their valuables. So important are these matters to the Trobrianders that even in the face of Western money, education, religion, and law, these people remain as committed today as in the past to yam cultivation and the production of women's wealth. Viewed in terms of Western economics, these activities appear to make little sense, but viewed in terms of Trobriand values and concerns, they make a great deal of sense.

In any examination of world economic systems, it is also important to point out that, unlike in the past, contemporary small-scale cultures do not operate in isolation; today each group of people is connected to a larger economic system, namely the market economy, and a political organization, the state. Small-scale economic systems often coexist within this larger economic sphere, although at times they may also come into conflict.

RESOURCES

In every culture customs and rules govern the kinds of work done, who does the work, who controls the resources and tools, and how the work is accomplished. Raw materials, labour, and technology are the productive resources a social group may use to produce desired goods and services. The rules surrounding the use of these resources are embedded in the culture and determine the way the economy operates.

Patterns of Labour

Every human culture has a division of labour based on sex and age categories. Dividing by sex increases the chances that learning necessary skills will be more efficient, since only half the adult skills need be learned by any individual. Dividing labour by age provides sufficient time for developing those skills.

Sexual Division of Labour

Whether men or women do a particular job varies from group to group, but work is likely to be set apart as the responsibility of either one sex or the other. Tasks most often regarded as "women's work" tend to be carried out near home. The tasks most often regarded as "men's work" tend to require physical strength, rapid mobilization of high bursts of energy, frequent travel away from home, and high levels of risk and danger. However, plenty of exceptions occur, as in cultures where women regularly carry burdensome loads or put in long hours of hard work cultivating crops in the fields. As mentioned earlier, on

Often, work that is considered inappropriate for men (or for women) in one culture is performed by them in another. Here, a laundryman works in Bangalore, India, and women work on construction.

Canadian family farms, women often work alongside the men, driving grain trucks and combines or picking up spare parts in town. They do this work on top of their regular household duties—seasonal gardening and preserving (canning, freezing, pickling), cooking hearty meals, and raising children. Before the advent of sophisticated farm machinery, their duties were even more physically challenging. In the 19th-century kingdom of Dahomey, in West Africa, thousands of women served as warriors for the Dahomean king and in the eyes of some observers were better fighters than their male counterparts. Archaeological evidence indicates female warriors were present among the Vikings, and among the Abkhasians of Georgia women were trained in weaponry until quite recently. In modern guerilla uprisings, women frequently fight. Clearly, the sexual division of labour cannot be explained simply as a consequence of male strength, male expendability, or female reproductive biology.

Instead of looking for biological imperatives to explain the sexual division of labour, a more productive strategy is to examine the kinds of work men and women do in the context of specific cultures to see how the work relates to other cultural and historical factors. Researchers find three configurations, one featuring flexibility and sexual integration, another involving rigid segregation by sex, and a third combining elements of the other two.[6] The flexible/integrated pattern is exemplified by people such as the Ju/'hoansi and is seen most often among food foragers and subsistence farmers. In such cultures, both sexes perform up to 35 percent of activities with approximately equal participation, while tasks deemed appropriate for one sex may be performed by the other, without loss of face. Boys and girls grow up in much the same way, learn to value cooperation over competition, and learn to interact with one another on a relatively equal basis.

Sexually segregated cultures rigidly define almost all work as either masculine or feminine, so men and women rarely engage in joint efforts of any kind. In such cultures, it is inconceivable someone would do something considered the work of the opposite sex. This pattern is frequently found in pastoral nomadic, intensive agricultural, and industrial societies, where men's work keeps them outside the home for much of the time. Thus, boys and girls alike are raised primarily by women, who encourage compliance in their charges. At some point, however, boys undergo a role reversal to become men. To do this they must prove their masculinity through assertions of male superiority, and hence authority over women.

In the third, or dual sex, configuration, men and women carry out their work separately, but the relationship between them is one of balance rather than inequality. Although competition is a prevailing ethic, each sex manages its own affairs, and the interests of both men and women are represented at all levels. Thus, as in sexually integrated cultures, neither sex exerts dominance over the other. The dual sex orientation was common among First Nations peoples whose economies were based on subsistence farming, as well as among several West African kingdoms, including the Dahomeans.

Age Division of Labour

Dividing labour according to age is also typical of human cultures. Among the Ju/'hoansi, children are not expected to contribute to subsistence until they reach their late teens. The Ju/'hoansi equivalent of "retirement" comes somewhere around the age of 60. Elderly people are not expected to contribute much food. However, older men and women alike play an essential role in spiritual matters; freed from food taboos and other restrictions that apply to younger adults, they may handle ritual substances considered dangerous to those still involved with hunting or having children. By virtue of their old age, they also remember things that happened far in the past. Thus, they are repositories of accumulated wisdom and can suggest solutions to problems younger adults have never before had to face. Thus, they are far from being unproductive members of society.

In some food-foraging cultures, women do continue to make a significant contribution to provisioning in their older years. Among the Hadza of Tanzania, their contribution is critical to their daughters, whose foraging abilities are

---

[6]Sanday, P.R. (1981). *Female power and male dominance: On the origins of sexual inequality* (pp. 79–80). Cambridge, UK: Cambridge University Press.

In nonindustrial societies, households produce much of what they consume. Among the Maya, men work in the fields to produce foods for the household; women prepare the food and take care of other chores that can be performed in or near the house.

significantly impaired when they have new infants to nurse. Lactation is energetically expensive, while holding, carrying, and nursing an infant interferes with the mother's foraging efficiency. Those most affected are a woman's weaned children who are not yet old enough to forage effectively for themselves. The problem is overcome, however, by the foraging efforts of grandmothers, whose time spent foraging is greatest when their infant grandchildren are youngest and their weaned grandchildren receive the least food from their mothers.[7]

In many nonindustrial cultures, children may make a greater contribution to the economy in terms of work and responsibility than is common in modern North America. In Maya communities in southern Mexico and Guatemala, young children look after their younger brothers and sisters and help with housework. Girls begin to make a substantial contribution to household work by age 7 or 8 and by age 11 are constantly busy grinding corn, making tortillas, fetching wood

and water, sweeping the house, and so on. Boys are given small tasks, such as bringing in the chickens or playing with a baby; by age 12, they are carrying toasted tortillas to the men working in the fields and returning with loads of corn.[8]

Similar situations are not unknown in industrial societies. In Naples, Italy, children play a significant role in the economy. At a young age, girls begin to take on responsibilities for housework, freeing their mothers and older sisters to earn money for the household. Nor is it long before girls are apprenticed to neighbours and kin, who teach them skills that enable them, by age 14, to enter a small factory or workshop. The wages earned are typically turned over to the girls' mothers. Boys, too, are apprenticed at an early age, although they may achieve more freedom from adult control by becoming involved in various street activities not available to girls.[9] On North American grain farms, young boys are

[7]Hawkes, K., O'Connell, J.F., & Blurton Jones, N.G. (1997). Hadza women's time allocation, offspring, provisioning, and the evolution of long postmenopausal life spans. *Current Anthropology, 38,* 551–577.

[8]Vogt, E.Z. (1990). *The Zinacantecos of Mexico: A modern Maya way of life* (2nd ed., pp. 83–87). Fort Worth, TX: Holt, Rinehart and Winston.

[9]Goddard, V. (1993). Child labor in Naples. In W.A. Haviland & R.J. Gordon (Eds.), *Talking about people* (pp. 105–109). Mountain View, CA: Mayfield.

This Thai girl exemplifies the use of child labour in many parts of the world, often by large corporations. Even in Western countries, child labour plays a major economic role.

expected to work alongside their fathers as soon as they are able; the school calendar is set around this tradition.

The use of child labour has become a matter of increasing concern as large corporations rely on the manufacture of goods in the world's poorer countries. Although reliable figures are hard to come by, there are likely some 15 million indentured child labourers in South Asia alone, including some as young as four years old. Each year, Western countries import millions of dollars worth of products children manufacture, ranging from rugs and carpets to clothing and soccer balls.[10]

Invariably, discussions concerning child labour laws ignore the harsh realities of life in many countries. When officials or charitable groups, usually funded through Western agencies, remove a child from a "job," they are often taking away a family's main source of income. In addition, these agencies fail to consider whether there is an infrastructure in place to help families survive if child labour is banned. In other words, what will happen to the child who used to earn a wage—will he or she end up on the streets begging, and what about the family whose only source of income came from their child "lucky" enough to work in a carpet factory?

Cooperation

Cooperative work groups are found in nonliterate as well as literate and in nonindustrial as well as industrial societies. Often, if the effort involves the whole community, a festive spirit permeates the work. Jomo Kenyatta, the anthropologist who later became a respected statesman and "father" of an independent Kenya, described the time of enjoyment after a day's labour in his country:

> If a stranger happens to pass by, he will have no idea that these people who are singing and dancing have completed their day's work. This is why most Europeans have erred by not realizing that the African in his own environment does not count hours or work by the movement of the clock, but works with good spirit and enthusiasm to complete the tasks before him.[11]

Among the Ju/'hoansi, women's work is frequently highly social. About three times a week, they go out to gather wild plant foods away from the camp. They usually go out in groups, talking loudly all the while. This not only turns what might otherwise seem a monotonous task into a social occasion, but it also causes large animals— potential sources of danger—to move elsewhere.

In most human societies, the basic cooperative unit is the household. It is a unit of both production and consumption; only in industrial societies have these two activities been separated. The Maya farmer, unlike his North American counterpart (but like subsistence farmers everywhere), is not so much running a commercial enterprise as he is a household. He is motivated by a desire to provide for the welfare of his own family; each family, as an economic unit, works as a group for its own good. Cooperative work may be undertaken outside the household for other reasons,

[10]It's the law: Child labor protection. (1997, November/December). Peace and Justice News, 11.

[11]Herskovits, M. (1952). Economic anthropology: A study in comparative economics (2nd ed., p. 103). New York: Knopf.

although not always voluntarily. It may be part of fulfilling duties to in-laws, or it may be performed for political officials or priests by command, or as a means of binding a community together, such as neighbourhood "barn raisings" and quilting bees common in rural Canada earlier in the century and community harvesting, still practised today. Thus, institutions of family, community, religion, and the state all may act as organizing elements that define the nature and condition of each worker's cooperative obligations.

Craft Specialization

In nonindustrial societies, each person in the society has knowledge and competence in all aspects of work appropriate to his or her age and sex. In modern industrial societies, by contrast, more specialized tasks are performed and no individual can begin to learn them all. Yet even in non-industrial societies some specialization of craft occurs. This is often minimal in food-foraging societies, but even here the arrow points of one man may be in some demand because of his particular skill at making them. Contemporary First Nations groups are enjoying a resurgence of their traditional crafts, such as bead and quillwork. These crafts provide extra income for specialists and an opportunity to pass traditional skills on to the next generation.

Among people who produce their own food, specialization is more apt to occur. In the Trobriand Islands, if a man wanted stone to make axe blades, he had to travel some distance to an island where the kind of stone was quarried; clay pots, however, were made by people living on yet another island.

One example of specialization is afforded by the Afar people of Ethiopia's Danakil Depression. Afar men are salt miners. It is mined from the crust of an extensive salt plain in the north part of the depression, and to get it is a risky and difficult business. The heat is extreme during the day, with shade temperatures between 60°C and 68°C not unusual. Shade is not found on the salt plain, however, unless a shelter of salt blocks is built. Nor is there food or water for man or beast. To add to the difficulty, until recently the Muslim Afars and the Christian Tegreans, highlanders who also mine salt, were mortal enemies.

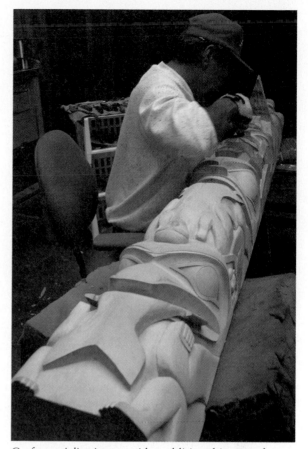

Craft specialization provides additional income for First Nations and Inuit craftspeople. Shown here is Haida carver Wilfred Stevens, Queen Charlotte Islands, British Columbia.

Successful mining, then, requires specialized skills in planning and organization, as well as physical strength and the will to work under the most trying conditions.[12] Pack animals to carry the salt have to be fed in advance, for carrying sufficient fodder for them interferes with their ability to carry salt. Food and water must be carried for the miners, who usually number 30 to 40 per group. Travel is planned to take place at night to avoid the intense heat of day. Finally, timing is critical: A party has to return to sources of food and water before these supplies are too long exhausted and before the animals are unable to continue farther.

[12]Mesghinua, H.M. (1966). Salt mining in Enderta. *Journal of Ethiopian Studies, 4* (2); O'Mahoney, K. (1970). The salt trade. *Journal of Ethiopian Studies, 8* (2).

In industrial societies, people do not have unrestricted access to the means of production, nor do they generally produce directly for their own consumption. Instead, they work for strangers, often at monotonous tasks done in a depersonalized setting.

Control of Land

All cultures have regulations that determine the way land resources are allocated. Food foragers determine who can hunt game and gather plants and where these activities take place. Horticulturists decide how their farmland is to be acquired, worked, and passed on. Pastoralists require a system that determines rights to watering places and grazing land, as well as the right of access to land they move their herds over. Intensive agriculturalists must have some means of determining title to land and access to water supplies for irrigation. In industrialized Western societies, a system of private ownership of land and rights to natural resources generally prevails.

In nonindustrial societies, land is often controlled by kinship groups such as the lineage or band, rather than by individuals. Among the Ju/'hoansi, each band of anywhere from 10 to 30 people lives on roughly 650 square kilometres of land, which they consider their territory. These territories are defined not in terms of boundaries but in terms of water holes located within them. The land is "owned" by those who have lived the longest in the band, usually a group of brothers and sisters or cousins. Their ownership, however, is more symbolic than real. They cannot sell (or buy) land, but outsiders must ask their permission to enter the territory. To refuse such permission, though, would be unthinkable.

The practice of defining territories on the basis of core features, be they water holes, distinctive landscape features where ancestral spirits are thought to dwell (as among Australian Aborigines), watercourses (as among First Nations of northeastern North America), or whatever, is typical of food foragers. Territorial boundaries are left vaguely defined at best. The adaptive value of this is clear: The size of band territories, as well as the size of the bands, can adjust to keep in balance with availability of resources.

Among some West African farmers, a feudal system of land ownership prevails: All land is said to belong to the head chief. He allocates it to various subchiefs, who in turn distribute it to lineages; lineage leaders then assign individual plots to each farmer. Just as in medieval Europe, these African people owe allegiance to the subchiefs and the principal chief. The people who work the land must pay taxes and fight for the chief when necessary. Yet these people do not really own the land; rather, it is a form of lease. No user can give away, sell, or otherwise dispose of a plot of land without approval from the elder of the lineage. When an individual no longer uses the allocated land, it reverts to the lineage head, who reallocates it to some other member of the lineage. The important operative principle here is that the system extends the individual's right to use land for an indefinite period, but the land is not "owned" outright. This system serves to maintain the integrity of valuable farmland, preventing its loss through subdivision and conversion to other uses.

Technology

All societies have some means of creating and allocating the tools and other artifacts used for producing goods and passed on to succeeding generations. The number and kinds of tools a group uses—which, together with knowledge about how to make and use them, constitute its **technology**—are related to the lifestyles of its members. Food foragers and pastoral nomads are apt to have fewer and simpler tools than the more sedentary farmer, in part because a great number of complex tools would decrease their mobility.

Food foragers make and use a variety of tools, and many are ingenious in their effectiveness. Some of these they make for their individual use, but codes of generosity are such that a person may not refuse giving or loaning what is requested. Thus, tools may be given or loaned to others in exchange for the products resulting from their use. For example, a Ju/'hoansi who gives his arrow to another hunter has a right to a share in any animals the hunter kills. Game is considered to "belong" to the man whose arrow killed it, even when he is not present on the hunt.

Among horticulturists, the axe, machete, and digging stick or hoe are the primary tools. Since these are relatively easy to produce, every person can make them. Although the maker has first rights to their use, when that person is not using them, any family member may ask to use them and usually is granted permission to do so. Refusal would cause people to treat the tool owner with scorn for this singular lack of concern for others. If a relative helps another raise the crop traded for a particular tool, that relative becomes part owner of the implement, and it may not be traded or given away without his or her permission.

In sedentary farming communities, tools and other productive goods are more complex and more difficult and costlier to make. Individual ownership is more absolute, as are the conditions underwhich persons may borrow and use such equipment. It is easy to replace a knife lost by a relative during palm cultivation but much more difficult to replace an iron plow or a power-driven threshing machine. Rights to the ownership of complex tools are more rigidly applied; generally, the person who has funded the purchase of a complex piece of machinery is considered the sole owner and may decide how and by whom it will be used.

Resource Depletion

The way people organize their productive activities is important to all cultures, but what happens when resources become depleted or disappear altogether? What are the social and economic implications for people who depend on these resources? The ecological crisis facing fisheries around the world and threatening the economic future of people who make their living by fishing is a case in point. Historically, the Grand Banks off Newfoundland and the eastern Newfoundland–Labrador continental shelves were among the richest fishing grounds in the world—cod being the most commercially important species. However, in the 30-year period following World War II, the cod population declined by 99 percent.[13] In 1992 the Canadian government placed a temporary moratorium on northern cod, followed in 1995 by the indefinite closure of commercial fishing around Newfoundland.[14] As a result, Newfoundland's main economic activity all but disappeared. Fish plants closed down, fishing companies sold their boats, and fishers found themselves unemployed (at a rate of 63.6 percent) and forced to rely on government compensation to survive. Some Newfoundlanders, especially younger people, have left the region in search of employment. Others have remained in their home communities, surviving through informal occupations such as gardening, making and selling preserves and crafts to tourists, gathering berries, and hunting rabbits, moose, and sea birds. With so much out-migration, the long-term viability of local communities is in question;

---

[13]Villagaria, M.G., Haedrich, R.L., & Fischer, J. (1999). Groundfish assemblages of eastern Canada examined over two decades. In D. Newell & R.E. Ommer (Eds.), *Fishing places, fishing people: Traditions and issues in Canadian small-scale fisheries.* Toronto: University of Toronto Press.

[14]Sinclair, P.R., Squires, H., & Downton, L. (1999). A future without fish? Constructing social life on Newfoundland's Bonavista Peninsula after the cod moratorium. In D. Newell & R.E. Ommer (Eds.), *Fishing places, fishing people: Traditions and issues in Canadian small-scale fisheries.* Toronto: University of Toronto Press.

Technology. Tools and other material equipment, together with the knowledge of how to make and use them.

community morale has dropped, and many people who once lived in vibrant communities now live in an atmosphere of hopelessness.

The loss of this industry is significant not just to Newfoundland and Labrador, but to Canada as well. Fishing has been a part of Canada for thousands of years; First Nations peoples living on the West Coast, such as the Kwakwaka'wakw, relied on salmon for food, trade, and ceremonial purposes. The Kwakwak'wakw continue to be fishers today. On the East Coast, groups like the Ojibwa fished for at least part of the year, and the Inuit peoples of the Arctic could not have survived in the frozen north without fish. Early European immigrants to eastern Canada readily adopted the fishing industry and maintained the tradition for another 500 years. Migratory fishing, or **marine transhumance,** gave way to small-boat family operations in the 1800s.[15] In the mid-20th century commercial fleets with high-tech equipment collected large fish harvests, and thus began marginalizing small fishers. As fish stocks dwindled, competition between fishers increased. Aboriginal fishers, with their treaty rights to fish, clashed with nonaboriginal fishers who had to contend with government-controlled quotas. Foreign fishers also encroached on the fishing grounds off the coast of Newfoundland, adding to the overexploitation of the fish stocks. Although aware of all these problems, fisheries management and conservation remained sporadic and controversial; experts could not predict whether fish stocks would recover or even why the stocks collapsed, nor have government regulations been able to control overexploitation.[16] Environmental problems such as ocean pollution

and ozone depletion put added pressures on the fish stocks. By the early 1990s fish had become smaller, there were fewer of them, and the "mother fish" that ensure the survival of a species had disappeared and groundfish stocks collapsed, resulting in the cod moratorium.

For a great many years, marine and fresh-water fisheries shaped the cultural, social, and economic lives of many people in Canada. The 1995 cod moratorium in Newfoundland was socially disruptive and continues to have a profound effect on individuals and local communities. An entire way of life, one deeply embedded in the ecology and economy of fisheries, is in danger of disappearing.

▲▽▲▽▲▽▲▽▲▽▲▽▲▽▲▽▲▽▲▽▲▽▲▽▲▽▲▽▲▽▲▽

DISTRIBUTION AND EXCHANGE

In cultures without money as a medium of exchange, the rewards for labour are usually direct. The workers in a family group consume what they harvest, they eat what the hunter or gatherer brings home, and they use the tools they themselves make. But even where no formal exchange medium exists, some distribution of goods occurs. Karl Polanyi, an economist, classified the cultural systems of distributing material goods into three modes: reciprocity, redistribution, and market exchange.[17]

Reciprocity

Reciprocity refers to a transaction between two parties whereby goods and services of roughly equivalent value are exchanged. This may involve gift giving, but in non-Western societies pure altruism in gift giving is as rare as it is in North America or any other Western society. The overriding motive is to fulfill social obligations and perhaps to gain prestige in the process. It might be best compared in North American society to

[15]Ommer, R.E. (1999). Rosie's Cove: Settlement morphology, history, economy, and culture in a Newfoundland outport. In D. Newell & R.E. Ommer (Eds.), *Fishing places, fishing people: Traditions and issues in Canadian small-scale fisheries.* Toronto: University of Toronto Press.

[16]Newell, D., & Ommer, R.E. (1999). Introduction: Traditions and issues. In D. Newell & R.E. Ommer (Eds.), *Fishing places, fishing people: Traditions and issues in Canadian small-scale fisheries.* Toronto: University of Toronto Press.

[17]Polanyi, K. (1968). The economy as instituted process. In E.E. LeClair, Jr., & H.K. Schneider (Eds.), *Economic anthropology: Readings in theory and analysis* (pp. 127–138). New York: Holt, Rinehart and Winston.

Marine transhumance. Seasonal migration of people from one marine resource to the next. **> Reciprocity.** The exchange of goods and services of approximately equal value between two parties.

someone who gives a party. The person may go to great lengths to impress others by the excellence of the food and drink served, not to mention the quality of wit and conversation of those in attendance. The expectation is that, sooner or later, the individual will be invited to similar parties by some, although perhaps not all, of the guests.

Social customs dictate the nature and occasion of exchange. When an animal is killed by a group of aboriginal hunters in Australia, the meat is divided among the hunters' families and other relatives. Each person in the camp gets a share, the size depending on the nature of the person's kinship tie to the hunters. The least desirable parts may be kept by the hunters themselves. If arguments were to arise over the apportionment, it would be because the principles of distribution were not followed properly. The hunter and his family seem to fare badly in this arrangement, but they have their turn when another man makes a kill. The giving and receiving is obligatory, as is the distribution. Such sharing of food reinforces community bonds and ensures that everyone eats. It also might be viewed as a way of saving perishable goods. By giving away part of his kill, the hunter gets a social IOU for a similar amount of food in the future.

The food-distribution practices just described for Australian aboriginal hunters constitute an example of **generalized reciprocity**. This may be defined as an exchange in which the value of

In the Canadian Arctic, Inuit hunters shared their kill, to ensure no families suffered hardship owing to a hunter's bad luck.

what is given is not calculated, nor is the time of repayment specified. Gift giving also falls into this category. So, too, does the act of a Good Samaritan who stops to help a stranded motorist or someone else in distress and refuses payment with the admonition "Pass it on to the next person in need." Most generalized reciprocity, though, occurs among close kin or people who otherwise have very close ties with one another. Typically, participants will deny that the exchanges are economic and will couch them explicitly in terms of kinship and friendship obligations. In North American society the homeless use a system of generalized reciprocity to ensure the group's survival. Christopher Hauch examines the nature of this survival mechanism in the following Original Study.

Balanced reciprocity differs in that it is not part of a long-term process. The giving and receiving, as well as the time involved, are more specific; a person has a direct obligation to reciprocate promptly in equal value for the social relationship to continue. Examples of balanced reciprocity in North American society include practices such as trading baseball cards or buying drinks when one's turn comes at a gathering of friends or associates. Examples from a non-Western culture include those anthropologist Robert Lowie related in his classic account of the Crow.[18] A woman skilled in the tanning of buffalo hides might offer her services to a neighbour who needed a new cover for her tipi. It took an expert to design a tipi cover, which required from 14 to 20 skins. The designer might need as many as 20 collaborators, whom she instructed on the sewing together of the skins and whom the tipi owner might remunerate with a feast. The designer herself would be given some kind of property by the tipi owner.

Giving, receiving, and sharing constitute a form of social security or insurance. A family contributes to others when they have the means and can count on receiving from others in time of

[18]Lowie, R. (1956). *Crow Indians* (p. 75). New York: Holt, Rinehart and Winston. (Original work published in 1935.)

Generalized reciprocity.   A mode of exchange in which the value of the gift is not calculated, nor is the time of repayment specified. **> Balanced reciprocity.**   A mode of exchange whereby the giving and the receiving are specific in terms of the value of the goods and the time of their delivery.

ORIGINAL STUDY

Reciprocity on Skid Row

Christopher Hauch

Introduction: The Myth of the Squandering Squatter

It seems that whenever a skid row resident encounters money, his first and overriding inclination is to squander it. Receiving a welfare cheque or other lump sum, such as an income-tax refund, the skid row man will commence swift and unrestrained consumption of the most frivolous, extravagant purchases, and treat himself and his companions to long episodes of inebriation. This phenomenon is known as "binge spending," and appears to be a pan–North American skid row tradition.

Considering the prevalence of poverty on skid row, the practice of binge spending seems economically irrational. Western social scientists have traditionally interpreted it as evidence of a psychopathology. The "symptom" is repeated failure to plan for the long term. This disorder, typically associated with the "culture of poverty" model, is characterized as a pathological fixation on life-in-the-present, and it is called "nondeferred gratification."

The concept of nondeferred gratification has dominated explanations of spending practices in urban poverty areas for nearly three decades. As a result, many treatment facilities for skid row alcoholics take great pains to teach money-management skills. Furthermore, most welfare departments in the United States and Canada maintain a policy of withholding aid from known practitioners of this "aberrant" spending behaviour. As a result, skid row people seldom benefit from income security programs.

Nevertheless, there may be more to binge spending than meets the distant critical eye. During several years' ethnographic research of skid row in Winnipeg, I discovered evidence suggesting that binges may provide selective advantages to their practitioners. The base for this research was the Main Street Project, a government-funded outreach program and emergency shelter.

As the study progressed, the ecology of skid row emerged as one so radically different from that of the world surrounding it that differences in behaviour became more understandable. In some ways, the adaptive pressures on residents of skid row resembled those of foraging groups like the Ju/'hoansi. Analogues to several of skid row's economic customs, including binge spending, are found in the ethnography of many foraging peoples.

Hard Work Does Not Pay

Winnipeg's skid row is similar to those found elsewhere in North America. As attested by its decaying turn-of-the-century buildings, it is the city's historic centre, the onetime nucleus of its trade. Skid row is the home of the city's poorest and most disaffiliated, among whom many drunkards and a few of the mentally ill are conspicuous. The population of skid row was defined as including all the homeless frequenters of the area during the five-year period of the study.

The population was quite homogeneous and displayed remarkable consistency over time. The most prominent characteristic was a lack of marketable skills. In Winnipeg, skid row residents tended to have marginal schooling, and were able to compete only for scarce short-term labour positions. Unskilled labour experiences dominated typical "pre-skid row" employment histories.

Almost all residents were male, most of them between the ages of 35 and 50. Three quarters of the population were First Nations men, a statistic that remained stable over the years. Of the Whites, the majority were transient labourers whose first homes had been in traditionally impoverished parts of the country.

While the demography remained stable, the turnover rate in some years was 60 percent of the entire population. First Nations residents who were able to, returned to their home reserves from time to time. Some found full-time work, or relocated to other skid rows. More fell victim to sickness, and were absorbed into an otherwise inaccessible social service support system. Others were imprisoned, and during my stay, many died. Literally, tens of thousands came and went over the few years' duration of the research.

All my informants were well acquainted with homelessness and, recounting their experiences, expressed fear at its prospects. The homeless endured sickness, injury, and death as ordinary consequences both of the severe Winnipeg winters and of violence in all its conceivable forms. No sane person would volunteer for all this suffering. The business of securing shelter and provision and, ultimately, an escape from skid row dominated daily life.

While life-threatening poverty came as no surprise, the "business" of circumventing it did. Initially, the presumption was that petty crime, social agency usage, and scavenging provided the baseline skid row subsistence. It turned out that all were indeed part of the broad repertoire of local survival strategies. Beyond that, it was discovered that the population was also a working one, almost to a man. Moreover, unlike crime, for example, which appeared to be largely against each other, and hence redistributive in nature, legitimate employment seemed by far the most common means of actually creating wealth for the society.

Steady jobs were nonexistent. Securing one usually implied the worker's departure from skid row. Everyone worked, however sporadically, for the very specialized network of casual-labour offices. Survival depended on it. It was in the structure of this skid-row-based industry that part of the explanation for local spending behaviour lay.

The men were retained by a casual-employment office, and they were both paid and dismissed at day's end. There was no job security and few of the benefits that normally attend full-time employment. This type of labour recruitment is known as "spot jobs"—the work of urban nomads.

Casual labour agents enlisted skid row men to work, offering them minimum wages. The labour of these men was then "sold"—by the day—to secondary purchasers for fees roughly equivalent to what the market hourly wage might be, were the position permanent and unionized. The secondary purchaser never had any obligation beyond the one-day contract and thus, over the long term, was able to adjust wage output closely to subtle variations in staffing requirements.

Due to the poverty prevalent on skid row, nearly all men, including the chronically ill, made at least periodic use of the market for casual labour. For the few fortunate who were hired, the jobs available varied in the extreme. Some small businesses required snow removal; others wanted flyers to be delivered or simple construction tasks to be performed. On better days, large contracts might be posted. The major rail companies, for example, are, by necessity, regular customers. A train entering Winnipeg may be required to pick up or discharge a single large load quickly. The task is labour intensive and it involves far more men than could be retained on a permanent basis.

Casual jobs were both temporary and unpleasant; in addition, they were almost invariably futureless. Labourers rarely enjoyed an opportunity to impress supervisors and ascend any single organizational hierarchy. Work was sparse and poorly paid. A review of annual income records revealed that the successful labourers earned about half the minimum wage for 52 weeks. Dependence upon casual labour was a condemnation to a clearly marginal subsistence.

How the Poor Pay More

Even so, the low incomes of skid row habitués were not alone responsible for the widespread chronic homelessness. Although modest, they were rarely much lower than those which many university students, living in residence, subsist on. And like university campuses, skid row was replete with outlets in which all manner of goods and services could be purchased at modest prices. Monthly rentals for hotels and rooming houses were low. Meals were inexpensive, as were the clothing and housewares sold in local thrift stores.

Rather, casual labour was only one of the necessary conditions for extreme poverty. Another was skid row's sheltering industry, the sum of all rented accommodations, which ironically not only profited from homelessness but actively promoted it, in certain creative ways.

Two distinct groups live on skid row—in a sense, two types of severely poor. One consists of all those who receive income in orderly, predictable disbursements. Some are elderly men, in particular those whose sole incomes derive from federal pension programs. Others are the recipients of long-term disability payments, modest trust funds, and so on. The second, larger, group consists of all those who rely on sporadic incomes. Some are full-time criminals, but by far the majority are casual labourers—the true, conspicuous skid row residents. Neither group can boast a superior average income. Yet the latter's poverty is ostensibly the deeper. Among labourers, homelessness is the norm, while steady earners, though generally doomed to squalid conditions, appear all but immune to the experience.

The paradox was explained during this study, in that each group was charged rent at a different rate. Steady earners were able to raise capital once per month. They shopped for the best accommodations that a reasonable portion of their incomes allowed for. Accordingly, skid row landlords set monthly rates that were equitable, or at least befitting of their products' characteristically substandard quality.

Casual labourers, on the other hand, were paid intermittently throughout the month. The most lucrative strategy for landlords was to charge rent with equal intermittence. No man was ever advanced a room against his agreeing to pay at that month's end. If unable to make full payment in advance, he was forced to a daily rate. On the average, daily hotel rates in the area reached up to seven times those normally paid by steady earners, or about 65 to 80 percent of a labourer's net daily income. If a labourer worked one day, then he was able to secure one day's shelter; if not, he was homeless.

Rooming houses provided no sanctuary. No daily rate was offered, and worse, tenants were required to supply damage deposits in advance of occupancy. The only remaining option was to stay at the Salvation Army hostel, which, unlike the hotels, did provide a reasonable daily rate. Those who could provide 30 days' rent in advance were entitled to a private, locked room, a place where they could store possessions. All others were crowded into dormitories where storage was impossible and theft inevitable. Whatever portable surplus a man had, be it money remaining from the day's wages or expensive belongings, was quickly lost to equally needy men. Thus, hotels were usually preferred.

Giving and Receiving

In the midst of such dire and seemingly intractable circumstances, it seems little but brutality and fierce individualism—Hobbe's "war of all against all"— could prevail. Brief visits to skid row strengthen the notion. The people we saw seemed all but inured to life's daily perils. Their society at once strikes us as tenuous and unstructured in the extreme. Penetrating skid row, however, one finds widespread evidence of altruistic behaviour. The culture contains only a few proscriptions regarding violence and there is an intense, universal commitment to philanthropy, articulated in the expression "you can't turn people down on the street."

The expression is more than a platitude: It summarizes economic life. Gestures of kindness and sharing, among men so uniformly impoverished, were routinely observed. Prior relationship is rarely a factor in the decision to give, so long as the remotest affiliation with skid row is confirmed. Such gestures are not accompanied by sentiment. No message of obligation, even to return thanks, is imposed on the receiver. Similarly, when receiving, no sense of obligation is displayed.

At first, this made for tremendously frustrating ethnography. Poverty on this scale, it was expected, would surely stimulate some sort of internal economic organization—perhaps intragroup support networks and stratification and commodity distribution rules. No such formal culture or organization existed. Goods flowed freely throughout the community, unhampered by any discernible structure. Residents provided for one another unhesitatingly in times of need. No direct mode of repayment was ever implicit in transactions: sometimes all parties presumed that they would never meet again.

Yet, there were two pervasive constants in the economy, unspoken practices that appeared to govern all exchange-related behaviour. First, while generosity was valued, severe punishments were exacted on misers. Everyone seemed aware that deprivation had the potential for occasioning great hazards, even death. On this basis, most tended to interpret hoarding as an act of extreme hostility and isolationism. Those who came upon wealth and did not share it were routinely beaten and robbed. If caught several times, they were ostracized.

The second was that skid row people were willing to tolerate prolonged asymmetrical exchange. For example, those few who were physically incapable of working, but who had not yet qualified for state aid, could be sustained for lengthy periods solely by the generosity of their fellows. In time, of course, this would tend to strain relations. Such was inevitable in so marginal an economy. Here, the remedial sanction was more subtle in nature.

Violence was never automatic; nor, after suffering near countless requests for aid, did anyone conspicuously act the miser. Instead, gossip would ignite and, feeding upon widespread discontent, would punish its victims with increasingly mean criticisms. Mental status was most frequently targeted. Longtime suppliants would suddenly earn reputations as "crazies," dangerous and unpredictable lunatics. As such a reputation swelled, so too usually did ostracism. Progressive poverty, illness, and ultimate rescue by welfare agencies, or hospitals, marked the typical downward sequence.

In essence, this was the extent of economy. On the one hand there was one overriding cultural value: that wealth ought always to be shared and that the act of sharing justifies neither complacence nor gratitude. Two powerful sanctions prevailed: one directed at enforcing the former law and another at curtailing its abuse.

At first, the system appeared disorganized, or at best, rife with cultural contradictions. In fact, these traits define a well-known economic institution: generalized reciprocity. There seems to be an almost eerie likeness between the material constraints of skid row and those found in the egalitarian foraging societies where anthropologists document generalized reciprocity.

Generalized reciprocity was likely the earliest form of human economic organization. Wherever it exists, the institution displays essentially the features described above. Most characteristically, there are no ironclad rules of private ownership. All members of the society are producers, in one specialty or another. All goods entering the society are viewed as belonging to all people. No overt mechanism exists to calculate debt or capital. No immediate reckoning of any kind occurs to figure out one's right of access in relation either to ascribed status or ostensible productivity.

At once, the system reveals a somewhat innate beneficence. Despite severely marginal ecosystems, all inhabitants contribute to the welfare of the nonproductive members as well as their own. Residents cling to one another for daily support, as sparse resources are distributed to a meagre but usually comfortable and equitable baseline.

The driving force of this arrangement is not pure altruism. Everyone is expected to both produce and distribute at least intermittently—to maintain balance over the long term. Failing this, hard sanctions are eventually brought to bear. Also, generalized reciprocity is sustained under material conditions that severely frustrate the accumulation of surplus and the appearance of social and economic stratification.

One of these conditions is the nondurability of subsistence goods. Most foraging societies tend to lack the technological means to preserve naturally occurring wealth. Most foodstuffs will spoil. Even those that do not spoil are difficult to transport over the great distances that foragers must travel. Nor, usually, can they be stored in any stationary locale in such a way as to be inaccessible to needy insects, beasts, or people. With small reserves and no concrete insurance against shortfalls, one is best served by cultivating a reputation for generosity.

So it is too on skid row, although here the analogue lies in the nature of business practices. One "buys" one's subsistence with sporadic income at prices more or less geared to a full day's earnings. Surplus is an oddity. Even if it does appear, it is almost impossible to protect it from robbery. Banking, of course, might be used. But each time one brings a portion of one's savings into the community, fellow residents in need are encountered. In such an event, there are only two options. One may refuse requests for aid and be beaten and ostracized. Or one may share in the remote hope of accumulating social credits for use at a time when the roles will be reversed.

Drunken Binges Are Shrewd Investments

Always, in a society that loathes debt, the management of windfalls is a delicate business. In his now classic research of the Ju/'hoansi, Richard Lee illustrated what turns out to be a typical solution in egalitarian societies. Successful hunters always tend to trivialize the value of a major kill. Colleagues will usually concur with the judgement and will participate only begrudgingly in the tasks of retrieving a carcass and rendering it to portions.

Analogous problems on skid row were resolved in a similar way—through binges. Upon acquiring any large amount of money, perhaps as an income-tax refund, the skid row resident found himself in the odious position of having to do something with it. Skid row offered few alternatives in such an instance: One could attempt to conceal it, only to end up beaten and robbed, or one could share—generously. These being the only choices, sharing, especially in the form of a quick and thorough binge, was clearly the wiser.

The ecology of skid row imposes certain minor stylistic differences on the solution. Whereas, for example, one might anticipate binging to be evident in a broad distribution of funds consumed at once in the form of needed commodities, the practice typically involved few people and frivolous purchases. Alcohol was especially favoured, often being the focus of days-long parties from which participants occasionally required clinical detoxification.

Further, the hosts to a sizable binge often exhibited great braggadocio. Announcing new-found wealth, the men boasted of their limitless philanthropy, distributing cash on the street, in bars, and even throwing it away and proclaiming, "It means nothing to me." Attracting a circle of friends and relatives, in short order, the generous host would vent self-aggrandizement, spending furiously as if to confirm each claim of greatness.

A comparatively large sum (for example, a $500 income-tax refund) afforded no special advantage to the individual skid row resident since it could never be saved, given the omnipresent threat of robbery. Nor was it sufficient to make possible a permanent relocation away from skid row to a place where miserliness would not have been a cultural taboo. The expression "Money means nothing to me" was an astute appraisal of the dilemma. Unlike possible analogues in smaller egalitarian societies, such windfalls are useless in meeting even the most basic immediate needs of the group, because of the great number of potential, nearby receivers.

Large windfalls had to be redistributed to many, so that no one became conspicuously wealthier than another. The giver was in a tenuous social position. He might have attempted to make like-sized donations to a few people of his choice, but this would invariably appear as the intended exclusion of those who received nothing. Besides, should one so overlooked wish to avenge violently the giver's snub, no one would come to his assistance for fear of appearing "paid off."

Binge spending was the perfect solution. Coming into a large sum, the recipient commenced a swift and indiscriminate distribution. As quickly as possible he purchased food, liquor, and gifts of myriad description, showing no preference for binge participants, but donating randomly to anyone who happened by. Further, as if abrogating publicly any subsequent obligation of receivers, the host boasted of his great generosity, impressing upon all his belief in the virtues of sharing and fellowship, and showing contempt for money. The host almost insisted that no one leave feeling in any way indebted to him. Thus, the louder his boasting the better, as those friends and relatives who heard too late of his spree to get their share could bear no grudge based on miserliness.

The use of alcohol during a binge provided an additional advantage. Often, former hosts would report having "lost a couple of days" during a binge, meaning that their memory of the episode had been impaired by sustained drinking. On occasions on which relatives protested their exclusion from binges, this would frequently be used as a defence. Often this would placate the accuser.

Binges are adaptive responses to the problem of distributing large sums on skid row. Quick wealth is an accident on skid row, one which places the recipient in great physical danger. Thus, the spontaneous spending of it is a matter of group enforcement, having no greater purpose than to afford the safest and most equitable division, and swiftest consumption.

Binges are clearly not exercises in frivolous indulgence, or evidence of the skid row people's inability to plan for the long term. A memorable skid row spending spree witnessed during the research illustrates this point. The host, V, had sustained serious and permanent injury to both legs because of an accident during casual labour. Hoping to avert a lawsuit, the purchasing industry offered, while V was still hospitalized, a single lump sum, some $3000, in compensation. V quickly agreed to the offer and, discharging himself from care at the encouragement of friends, began a long and unrestrained bout of partying in the skid row hotel district. Within a week, V was both penniless and unemployable.

The episode might well have been attributed to a lack of money-management skills and disregard for personal health. My experience with V then, and for three years subsequently, proved very much the contrary. Immediately after distributing his windfall, V applied for and received permanent welfare assistance for reasons of physical disability. Every month he received a cheque, again a lump sum. He used this to leave skid row. Although he occasionally visited the skid row area later, he was seldom observed intoxicated, or even patronizing the local taverns. Instead, given a secure income, V managed a largely sedentary style of life, living alone, and exhibiting great aptitude for budgeting a decidedly modest income.

And so it was for most people. Sudden, finite wealth invariably ordained madness, while opportunities for permanent income were more likely to result in health, as the fundamental ingredients of a working-class worldview.

Conclusions

This observation may have interesting implications for applied research and social programming. We can appreciate, for example, why counselling has usually failed whenever it was designed to restructure the patterns of spending of skid row residents. Many of the behaviours that this counselling attempted to elicit were maladaptive on skid row.

Contrary to such psychological explanations as the "culture of poverty" model, the causes of poverty on skid row are almost always material and ordinary. Many of them earned more than welfare recipients who were permanent residents of area hotels and rooming houses. Why, then, were they homeless? The simple answer is that those who relied on work paid by the day were forced to rent shelter by the day, at rates so high that periodic homelessness was inevitable.

This explains why life-threatening poverty in this setting cannot be eliminated until social programs target the basic material conditions of the local economy. This may not mean costly job-creation initiatives or across-the-board increases in income security benefits. Rather, the more effective strategies are likely to be small and local: some regulation of the local labour and housing businesses, together with flexible provisions for income security. A better understanding of the problems of skid row residents and the provision of more effective help will require much commitment, but also a sustained attention to the ecology of seemingly deviant patterns of behaviour.

References

Hauch, Christopher. 1985. *Coping Strategies and Street Life: The Ethnography of Winnipeg's Skid Row.* Winnipeg: Institute of Urban Studies.

Lee, Richard. 1979. *The !Kung San: Men, Women and Work in a Foraging Society.* New York: Cambridge University Press.

Liebow, Elliot. 1967. *Tally's Corner.* Boston: Little, Brown and Co.

Orwell, George. 1940. *Down and Out in Paris and London.* New York: Penguin.

Spradley, James. 1970. *You Owe Yourself a Drunk: An Ethnography of Urban Nomads.* Boston: Little, Brown and Co.

Wiseman, Jacqueline P. 1970. *Stations of the Lost: The Treatment of Skid Row Alcoholics.* Englewood Cliffs, NJ: Prentice-Hall, Inc.

Source: From Christopher Hauch (Senior Clinical Consultant, Mental Health Division of Manitoba Health), original essay, 1992. Reprinted with permission. (The views expressed in this essay are those of the author and do not necessarily represent the policy of Manitoba Health.)

need. A levelling mechanism is at work in the process of generalized or balanced reciprocity, promoting an egalitarian distribution of wealth over the long run.

Negative reciprocity is a third form of reciprocity exchange, in which the giver tries to get the better end of the deal. The parties involved have opposing interests, usually are members of different communities, and are not closely related. The ultimate form of negative reciprocity is to take something by force. Less extreme forms involve guile and deception or, at the least, hard bargaining. In North America, an example would be the stereotype of the car salesperson who claims a car was "driven by a little old lady to church" when in fact it was not and is likely to develop problems soon after it leaves the sales lot. Among the Navajo, according to anthropologist Clyde Kluckhohn, "to deceive when trading with foreign peoples is morally accepted."[19]

[19]Kluckhohn, C. (1972). Quoted in Sahlins, M. (1972). *Stone Age economics* (p. 200). Chicago: Aldine.

Negative reciprocity. A form of exchange whereby the giver tries to get the better of the exchange.

Canadian politics operates under a system of balanced or negative reciprocity. The business community provides financial contributions to candidates in the hopes that their contributions will influence the government, yet politicians must appear to serve all the people, not just the financial community.

Barter and Trade

Exchanges that occur within a group of people usually take the form of generalized or balanced reciprocity. When they occur between two groups, the potential for hostility and competition exists. Therefore, such exchanges may well take the form of negative reciprocity, unless some sort of arrangement has been made to ensure at least an approach to balance. *Barter* is one form of negative reciprocity, involving the exchange of scarce items from one group for desirable goods from another group. Relative value is calculated, and despite an outward show of indifference, sharp trading takes place.

An arrangement that combined elements of balanced reciprocity as well as barter existed between the Woodland and Plains Cree. For nearly two centuries the powerful Woodland and Plains Cree dominated European trade and technology from Labrador to the Great Lakes, over to Hudson Bay and westward to the Rocky Mountains.[20] The symbiotic relationship that developed between the Cree and European traders benefited both groups. The Cree became trappers, satisfying European demands for furs, in exchange for sturdy firearms and high-quality beads, blankets, pots and pans, and fabric. As intermediaries, they made huge profits bartering for robes and pelts from other First Nations groups, selling fresh bison meat to the fur trade posts, and trading goods they had acquired from Europeans to other First Nations groups.

The Assiniboine, who lived around Lake Winnipeg and Lake of the Woods, also served as intermediaries between the European fur companies and various First Nations groups. When the fur trade moved farther west, so did the Assiniboine, giving up their woodland traditions and adopting the plains lifestyle, becoming warriors and bison hunters. The arrival of guns and horses on the prairies further enhanced the Assiniboine's trading role, and by the mid-18th century they were highly regarded as traders, hunters, and guides.

Silent trade is a specialized form of barter with no verbal communication. In fact, it may involve no actual face-to-face contact at all. Such cases often have characterized the dealings

[20]Ward, D. (1995). *The people: A historical guide to the First Nations of Alberta, Saskatchewan, and Manitoba.* Saskatoon: Fifth House.

Silent trade.   A form of barter with no verbal communication.

between food-foraging peoples and their food-producing neighbours, as the former have supplied for the past 2000 or so years various commodities in demand by the world economy. The process goes something like this:

> The forest people creep through the lianas to the trading place, and leave a neat pile of jungle products, such as wax, camphor, monkeys' gall bladders, birds' nests for Chinese soup. They creep back a certain distance, and wait in a safe place. The partners to the exchange, who are usually agriculturalists . . . lay down beside it what they consider its equivalent in metal cutting tools, cheap cloth, bananas, and the like. They too discreetly retire. The shy folk then reappear, inspect the two piles, and if they are satisfied, take the second one away. Then the opposite group comes back and takes pile number one, and the exchange is completed.[21]

The reasons for silent trade can only be postulated, but in some situations trade may be silent for lack of a common language. More often it may serve to control situations of distrust so as to keep relations peaceful. In a very real sense, good relations are maintained by preventing relations. Another possibility, which does not exclude the others, is that it makes exchange possible where problems of status might make verbal communication unthinkable. In any event, it provides for the exchange of goods between groups in spite of potential barriers.

The Kula Ring

Although we tend to think of trade as something undertaken for purely practical purposes, in order to gain access to desired goods and services, not all trade is motivated by economic considerations. A classic case of this is the Kula ring, a Trobriand inter-island trading system whereby prestige items are ceremoniously exchanged. Malinowski first described the Kula in 1920, but it is still going strong today.[22] Men periodically set sail in their canoes to exchange shell valuables with their Kula partners, who live on distant islands. The valuables are red shell necklaces, which always circulate in trade in a clockwise direction, and ornate white arm shells, which move in the opposite direction (see Figure 6.1). These objects are ranked according to their size, their colour, how finely polished they are, and their particular histories. Such is the fame of some that, when they appear in a village, they create a sensation. No one man holds these valuables for very long—at most, perhaps 10 years. Holding onto an arm shell or necklace too long risks disrupting the "path" it must follow as it is passed from one partner to another.

Although men on Kula voyages may use the opportunity to trade for other goods, this is not the reason for such voyages, nor is the Kula even necessary for trade to occur. In fact, overseas trade is regularly undertaken without the exchange of shell valuables. Instead, Trobriand men seek to create history through their Kula exchanges. By circulating armbands and necklaces that accumulate the histories of their travels and names of those who have possessed them, men proclaim their individual fame and talent, gaining considerable influence for themselves in the process. Although the idea is to match the size and value of one shell for another, men draw on all their negotiating skills, material resources, and magical expertise to gain access to the strongest partners and most valuable

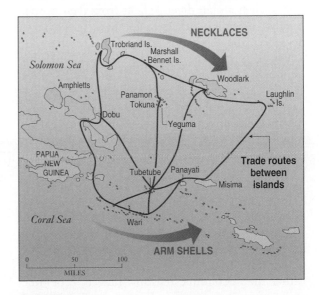

FIGURE 6.1

The ceremonial trading of necklaces and arm shells in the Kula ring encourages trade throughout Melanesia.

---

[21]Coon, C.S. (1948). *A reader in general anthropology* (p. 594). New York: Holt, Rinehart and Winston.

[22]Weiner, A.B. (1988). *The Trobrianders of Papua New Guinea* (pp. 139–157). New York: Holt, Rinehart and Winston.

These photos show Kula valuables and a canoe used for Kula voyages.

shells; thus, an element of negative reciprocity arises when a man diverts shells from their proper "paths" or entices others to compete for whatever necklaces and armbands he may have to offer. But when all is said and done, success is limited, for although a man may keep a shell for 5 or 10 years, sooner or later it must be passed on to others.

The Kula is a most elaborate complex of ceremony, political relationships, economic exchange, religion, and social integration. To see it only in its economic aspects is to misunderstand it completely. The Kula demonstrates once more how inseparable economic matters are from the rest of culture and shows that economics is not a realm unto itself. This is just as true in modern industrial societies as it is in Trobriand society; when the United States stopped trading with Cuba, Haiti, Iran, Iraq, and Serbia, it was for political rather than economic reasons. Indeed, economic embargoes are increasingly popular as political weapons both governments and special-interest groups wield. On a less political note, consider how retail activity in Canada peaks in December for a combination of religious and social, rather than purely economic, reasons.

Redistribution

In cultures with a sufficient surplus to support some sort of centralized authority, income flows into the public coffers in the form of gifts, taxes, and the spoils of war; then it is distributed again. The chief, king, or whoever the agent of redistribution may be has three motives for disposing of this income: The first is to maintain a position of superiority through a display of wealth; the second is to assure those who support the agent an adequate standard of living; and the third is to establish alliances outside the agent's territory.

The administration of the Inca empire in Peru was one of the most efficient the world has ever known, both in the collection of taxes and methods of control.[23] A census was kept of the population and resources. Tributes in goods and in services were levied. Each craft specialist had to produce a specific quota of goods from materials overseers supplied. Forced labour was used for agricultural or mining work. Forced labour was also used in public works, such as building roads and bridges throughout the mountainous terrain, aqueducts that guaranteed a supply of water, and storehouses that held surplus food. Careful accounts were kept of income and expenditures. A govern-

[23]Mason, J.A. (1957). *The ancient civilizations of Peru.* Baltimore, MD: Penguin.

In Canada, our federal income tax system collects wealth from the provinces, then redistributes this wealth in the form of equalization payments to support provincial infrastructures such as education, health care, and social services.

ment bureaucracy ensured production was maintained and commodities were distributed.

Through the activities of the centralized authority, **redistribution** took place. The ruling class lived in great luxury, but goods were redistributed to the common people when necessary. In redistribution systems the exchange is not between individuals or between groups, but, rather, products are funnelled into one source and parcelled out again as directed by a central administration. Commonly, it involves an element of coercion. Taxes are a form of redistribution in North America. People pay taxes to the government, some of which support the government itself while the rest are redistributed either in cash, to support social programs and government loans or subsidies to business, or in services, such as food and drug inspection, construction of highways, and support of the health care and education systems. With the growth of the federal deficit in the last few decades, wealth in Canada increasingly has been redistributed from middle-income taxpayers to wealthy holders of government securities. For redistribution to be possible, a society must have a centralized system of political organization, as well as an economic surplus beyond people's immediate needs.

Distribution of Wealth

In cultures where people devote most of their time to subsistence activities, gradations of wealth are small, kept that way through **levelling mechanisms** that compel people to divest themselves of wealth, keeping them from accumulating more than others, and systems of reciprocity that serve to distribute in a fairly equitable fashion what little wealth exists.

Display for social prestige, what economist Thorstein Veblen called **conspicuous consumption,** is a strong motivating force for the distribution of wealth in cultures where a substantial surplus is produced. It has, of course, long been recognized that conspicuous consumption plays a

---

Redistribution.   A form of exchange in which goods flow into a central place where they are sorted, counted, and reallocated. **> Levelling mechanism.**   A societal obligation compelling people to redistribute goods so that no one accumulates more wealth than anyone else. **> Conspicuous consumption.**   A term Thorstein Veblen coined to describe the display of wealth for social prestige.

Groups such as the Kwakwaka'wakw, on the northwest coast of British Columbia, gain prestige from giving away valuables at a potlatch.

prominent role in Western societies as individuals compete with one another for prestige. Indeed, many North Americans spend their lives trying to impress others, and this requires the display of items symbolic of prestigious positions in life. This all fits very nicely into an economy based on consumer wants:

> In an expanding economy based on consumer wants, every effort must be made to place the standard of living in the center of public and private consideration, and every effort must therefore be lent to remove material and psychological impediments to consumption. Hence, rather than feelings of restraint, feelings of letting-go must be in the ascendant, and the institutions supporting restraint must recede into the background and give way to their opposite.[24]

A form of conspicuous consumption also occurs in some nonindustrial societies. One example, more aptly termed "conspicuous generosity," is the **potlatch,** practised by First Nations groups on the northwest coast of North America, including the Nuu-chah-nulth, Coast Salish, Kwakwaka'wakw (Kwakiutl), Bella Coola, Haida, Tsimshian, and Tlingit. The potlatch is a special celebration in which the people of a community, and perhaps even more than one community, come together to enjoy elaborate feasts, ceremonial dancing and singing, speeches, and gift giving. Northwest coast peoples place great emphasis on inherited rank and privileges.[25] The potlatch serves as an opportunity for chiefs to enhance their status with public displays of generosity. The potlatch also showcases the host's

---

[24]Henry, J. (1974). A theory for an anthropological analysis of American culture. In J.G. Jorgensen & M. Truzzi (Eds.), *Anthropology and American life* (p. 14). Englewood Cliffs, NJ: Prentice-Hall.

[25]McMillan, A.D. (1988). *Native peoples and cultures of Canada: An anthropological overview.* Vancouver: Douglas and McIntyre.

Potlatch.   A special celebration in which the people of a community come together to enjoy elaborate feasts, ceremonial dancing, and gift giving. The potlatch serves as an opportunity for chiefs to enhance their status with public displays of generosity.

status by demonstrating his wealth, and it serves as an occasion to announce and display ceremonial and inherited privileges, or to transfer these privileges to an heir.[26]

An important component of the potlatch is the gift giving; in fact, in the Chinook language, the word potlatch means gift. Each guest, from the youngest child to the highest-ranking elder, receives a gift; the value of the gifts is based on the guest's rank. In this way the gift giving validates the status not only of the host but also of his guests. In former times, favourite gifts included Hudson's Bay blankets; household goods such as kettles, dishes, sewing machines, and furniture; food, especially flour; and canoes. Elders and other honoured guests might also receive some cash along with their other gifts. Today, gifts are more likely to be money; crafts, such as embroidered or crocheted doilies; housewares; clothing; and dry goods.

As mentioned, the potlatch offered an opportunity for the host to gain status from his generosity, but it also served other purposes. The spiritual component of the potlatch publicly announced and validated symbolic property, such as assuming a new name. Masked dancers, representing supernatural forces, announced these privileges through naming and ceremonial dances. The Kwakwaka'wakw, for example, traditionally held potlatches to mark critical stages in life: announcing the birth or adoption of a child, celebrating the onset of puberty or marriage, and mourning the death of a loved one. The host, often a chief, could use the potlatch as an opportunity to name a newborn child. A potlatch might be held to save face in the event of a misfortune such as the birth of a malformed child. Contemporary potlatches are held for much the same reasons, including baby showers, namings, weddings, anniversaries, special birthdays, graduations, and memorials for the dead.[27] Regardless of the reason, the host invited people to witness his generosity—the more extravagant the potlatch, the more status for the host. The quest for status never ended; participants at a potlatch

would be honour-bound to hold their own potlatch in the near future, all the while attempting to outshine everyone else's generosity, thus gaining more prestige and esteem.

Interpretations of the underlying purposes of the potlatch have varied among anthropologists. Some view the practice as competitive, especially in the past; the food and gifts laboriously accumulated over a period of months or years inevitably caused financial hardship to the hosts. This competitiveness may have occurred among some groups, such as the Kwakwaka'wakw, but in other First Nations groups, such as the Nuu-chah-nulth and Salish, this certainly was not the case. Other anthropologists recognize the social importance of the potlatch, in which gift giving and the sharing of food appears to act like a form of communication, establishing bonds and support networks between the people of the community, and even between members of more than one community. The potlatch ceremony also may have been used to ensure that other communities received adequate resources, especially during times of feast and famine. Groups enjoying an abundance of resources would be obliged to hold a potlatch to redistribute goods throughout the region. In this way the potlatch served not only as a form of economic redistribution, but also as a levelling mechanism, preventing any one group from becoming too wealthy or powerful.

Potlatches reached their heyday during the 18th and 19th centuries, although many First Nations coastal groups continue to hold potlatches today. In the late 1800s a few potlatches, known as revenge potlatches, became very competitive; wealthy rival chiefs tried to outdo each other by holding the most extravagant potlatch. These potlatches were not typical, and were in fact a response to the economic and social pressures experienced by northwest coastal peoples when Europeans arrived in their region. However, Europeans, especially missionaries, and their paternalistic governments viewed these ceremonies as wasteful in the extreme, and an obstacle to eliminating heathen practices and converting aboriginal people to Christianity. The Canadian government banned potlatches in 1884. This intervention failed to consider that the potlatch accomplished many important social, economic, and political goals for the northwest coastal peoples, and during the years potlatching

---

[26]Peabody Museum of Archaeology and Ethnology. (1999). *Gifting and feasting in the NWC potlatch/What is a potlatch?* Retrieved June 25, 2001, from the World Wide Web: http://www.peabody.harvard.edu/potlatch/potlat2.html.
[27]Ibid.

remained illegal (1884–1951), many groups secretly continued the practice.

Unlike conspicuous consumption in Western societies, the emphasis in the potlatching system was not on displaying or hoarding goods, which would make them unavailable to others, but rather on giving away the goods. In fact, today, the gift-giving part of the ceremony is called the "give-away." The potlatch served to develop economic, social, and political relationships between people, and continues to do so today. It is a way to publicly and officially recognize inheritance rights and individual status, and as a form of economic redistribution, the potlatch is a unique and appealing way to distribute goods throughout the region.

Market Exchange

To an economist, **market exchange** has to do with the buying and selling of goods and services, with prices set by the powers of supply and demand. Loyalties and values are not supposed to play a role, but they often do. Just where the buying and selling take place is largely irrelevant, so we must distinguish between market *exchange* and the *marketplace*. Although some modern market transactions do occur in a specific identifiable location—much of the trade in cotton, for example, happens in the New Orleans Cotton Exchange—it is also quite possible for North Americans to buy or sell goods without ever being on the same side of the continent as the other party. When people talk about a market in today's world, the particular place where something is sold is often not important at all. For example, think of the way people speak of a "market" for certain types of automobiles or for mouthwash. Indeed, with the advent of the Internet, a new economy, based on e-commerce, has emerged. Today's consumers have global access to goods at the "touch of their fingertips." Future implications for commercial marketplaces—for example, malls—are uncertain at this time; however, it does appear safe to say the concept of "shopping" is changing.

Until well into the 20th century, market exchange typically was carried out in specific places, as it still is in much of the non-Western world. In peasant or agrarian societies, market-

The Toronto Stock Exchange, where people are buying and selling shares in companies, even though no goods are physically present.

Market exchange.   The buying and selling of goods and services, with prices set by the powers of supply and demand.

Even in Western societies, the market is an important focus of social as well as economic activity, as typified by this farmer's market in St. Albert, Alberta.

places overseen by a centralized political authority provide the opportunity for farmers living in rural regions to exchange some of their livestock and produce for needed items manufactured in factories or the workshops of craft specialists. Thus, some sort of complex division of labour as well as centralized political organization is necessary for the appearance of markets. In the marketplace, land, labour, and occupations are not bought and sold as they are through the Western market economy. In other words, what happens in these marketplaces has little to do with the price of land, the amount paid for labour, or the cost of services. The market is local, specific, and contained. Prices are apt to be set on the basis of face-to-face bargaining (buy low and sell high is the order of the day), rather than by faceless "market forces" wholly removed from the transaction itself. Nor does some form of money need to be involved; instead, goods may be directly exchanged through some form of reciprocity between the specific individuals involved.

In non-Western societies, marketplaces have much of the excitement of a fair; they are vibrant places where an individual's senses are assaulted by a host of colourful sights, sounds, and smells. Indeed, many of the large urban and suburban malls built in Canada and other industrialized countries over the past few decades have tried to re-create, although in a more contrived manner,

some of the interest and excitement of more traditional marketplaces. In the latter, noneconomic activities may even overshadow the economic. Social relationships are as important there as they are anywhere else. As anthropologist Stuart Plattner observes, the marketplace is where friendships are made, love affairs begun, and marriages arranged.[28] Dancers and musicians may perform, and the end of the day may be marked by drinking, dancing, and fighting. At the market, too, people gather to hear news. In ancient Mexico, under the Aztecs, people were required by law to go to the market at specific intervals to keep informed about current events. Government officials held court and settled judicial disputes at the market. Thus, the market is a gathering place where people renew friendships, see relatives, gossip, and keep up with the world while procuring needed goods they cannot produce for themselves.

Although marketplaces can exist without money exchange of any sort, no one doubts that money facilitates trade. **Money** may be defined as something used to make payments for other goods and services as well as to measure their value. Its critical attributes are durability, portability, divisibility, recognizability, and fungibility (ability to substitute any item of money for any other monetary item of the same value, as when four quarters are substituted for a dollar bill). The wide range of things that have been used as money in one or another society includes salt, shells, stones, beads, feathers, fur, bones, teeth, and of course metals, from iron to gold and silver. Among the Aztecs of Mexico, both cacao beans and cotton cloaks served as money. The beans could be used to purchase merchandise and labour, although usually as a supplement to barter; if the value of the items exchanged was not equal, cacao beans could be used to make up the difference. Cotton cloaks represented a higher denomination in the monetary system, with 65 to 300 beans equivalent to one cloak, depending on the latter's quality. Cloaks

---

[28]Plattner, S. (1989). Markets and market places. In S. Plattner (Ed.), *Economic anthropology* (p. 171). Stanford, CA: Stanford University Press.

Money. Anything used to make payments for goods or labour as well as to measure their value; may be special-purpose or multipurpose.

Ancient Lydian money: the world's first coins. Lydia was located in Anatolia, which is now Turkey.

could be used to obtain credit, to purchase land, as restitution for theft, and to ransom slaves, whose value in any case was measured in terms of cloaks. Interestingly, counterfeiting was not unknown to the Aztecs—unscrupulous people sometimes carefully peeled back the outer skin of cacao beans, removed the contents, and then substituted packed earth.

Among the Tiv of West Africa, brass rods might be exchanged for cattle, with the cattle seller then using the rods to purchase slaves (the economic value of the cattle being converted into the rods and then reconverted into slaves). In both the Aztec and Tiv cases, the money in question is (or was) used only for special purposes. To a Tiv, the idea of exchanging a brass rod for subsistence foods is repugnant, and most market exchanges involve direct barter. Special-purpose monies usually have more moral restrictions on their use than do general-purpose monies, which can be used to purchase just about anything. Even the latter category, however, has limits. For example, in North America it is considered immoral, as well as illegal, to exchange money for sexual and political favours, even though infractions against these constraints occur.

In Canada and the United States, as part of a reaction to the increasingly "face-to-faceless" nature of the modern economic system, there has been something of a revival and proliferation of "flea markets" (see Figure 6.2), where anyone, for a small fee, may display and sell handicrafts, secondhand items, farm produce, and paintings in a face-to-face setting. Excitement is felt in the search for bargains and an opportunity for haggling. A carnival atmosphere prevails, with

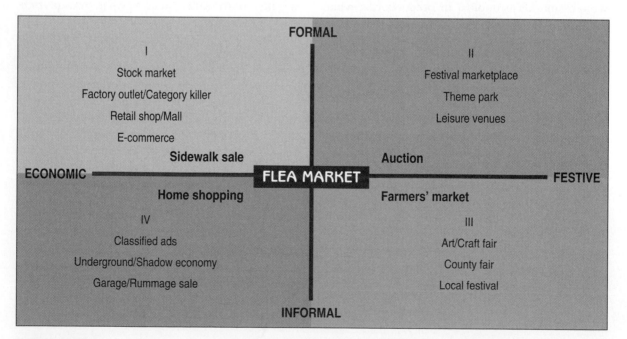

FIGURE 6.2

Marketplace structure and function may range from formal to informal and from economic to festive, as this diagram suggests.

eating, laughing, and conversation, and items even may be bartered without any cash changing hands. These flea markets, including fairs, festivals, garage sales, and farmers' markets, are similar to the marketplaces of non-Western societies.

Flea markets also raise the issue of the distinction between the informal and formal sectors of the market economy. The **informal economy** may be defined as the system whereby producers of goods and services provide marketable commodities that for various reasons escape enumeration, regulation, or other types of public monitoring or auditing. Such enterprises may encompass just about anything: market gardening, making and selling beer or other alcoholic beverages, doing repair or construction work, begging, selling things on the street, performing ritual services, lending money, dealing drugs, picking pockets, and gambling, to mention just a few. These sorts of "off the books" activities have been known for a long time but generally have been dismissed by economists as aberrant and therefore more of an annoyance than anything of importance. It is also difficult for them to track; yet, in many countries of the world, the informal economy is, in fact, more important than the formal economy. In many places, large numbers of under- and unemployed people who have only limited access to the formal sector in effect improvise as best they can various means of "getting by" on scant resources. Meanwhile, more affluent society members may evade various regulations to maximize returns and to vent their frustrations at their perceived loss of self-determination in the face of increasing government regulation.

Chinese-Canadian Contributions to the Canadian Economy

For more than a century, Canada has been a preferred destination for immigrants seeking a better life. Some have come for the stable economic and social environment, others for Canada's multiculturalism and embracing of ethnic diversity. Many people choose to immigrate to Canada because of its economic opportunities. Chinese immigrants are one of the oldest groups to make Canada their home, first coming to Canada some 130 years ago to work on the Canadian Pacific Railway. Many more have followed, with the largest wave in the 1990s, when Hong Kong Chinese immigrated to Canada in the thousands. By 1997, 1.4 million Chinese had made Canada their home.[29] They brought with them finances, skills, and an infectious entrepreneurial spirit that has revitalized cities like Vancouver and Toronto.

Chinese Canadians have contributed enormously to the Canadian economy. They have opened up small businesses, creating vibrant Chinese commercial districts. They send their children to school, and have fuelled the real estate market in large centres like Vancouver. Those who have come to Canada looking for investment and

Steve Barnett, who earned his Ph.D. in anthropology from the University of Chicago, was for several years head of a consulting firm that served several large corporations. He is now a vice president at Citibank in Long Island City, New York, where he studies long-term cultural trends in patterns of consumption worldwide.

[29]Star, M. (1997, March). Asian Canada: The economic and cultural energy that Asia immigrants are bringing may turn a green and promising land into the next California. *Transpacific, 68*, 40.

Informal economy. The production of marketable commodities that for various reasons escape enumeration, regulation, or any other sort of public monitoring or auditing.

entrepreneurial opportunities have brought enormous sums of money with them. Indeed, the economic contributions of the Hong Kong Chinese have helped sustain Canadian cities during recessionary times. Many Asian organizations also contribute significantly to Canadian charities; for example, the Tzu Chi Buddhist foundation gave a Vancouver hospital $6 million.[30]

Along with their economic contributions, Chinese Canadians have contributed to the cultural growth of Canada, introducing traditions such as dragon boat races and Chinese New Year's celebrations, which boost local economies by drawing in visitors. The introduction of ethnic foods such as dim sum has led to many Asian restaurants being opened, helping to create a cosmopolitan atmosphere in many of Canada's larger cities. Chinatowns and Chinese shopping centres in large cities offer employment to many Chinese people, including refugees who may not possess the education, skills, or necessary Canadian qualifications to find other employment.

Although Chinese immigrants, in particular immigrants from Hong Kong, make up the majority of the 3 million Asian people who have come to Canada, many other Asian groups are part of the multicultural mosaic. Japanese began coming to Canada in the 1890s to work as merchants and fishers, and today Japanese Canadians have a population of 120 000. Since the 1970s, Koreans (population 130 000 in Canada), Vietnamese (170 000), and many other Asian groups have chosen Canada for their new home and have added to the Canadian economy. Clearly, Asian migration to Canada has resulted in a tremendous expansion of the Canadian economy.[31]

[30]McLellan, J. *Buddhism in the multicultural context of Toronto, Canada: Local communities, global networks.* Retrieved August 17, 2003, from the World Wide Web: http://alcor.concordia.ca/~csaa1/porter/lectures/JanetMcLellan.html.

[31]Tian, G. (1999). *Chinese-Canadians, Canadian-Chinese coping and adapting in North America.* Queenston, ON: Edwin Mellen Press.

▲▼▲▼▲▼▲▼▲▼▲▼▲▼▲▼▲▼▲▼▲▼▲▼▲▼▲▼▲▼▲▼

CONSUMPTION

The third component of any economic system is **consumption.** Anthropologists view consumption from two perspectives. First, it is the food and beverages that we consume, and the accompanying rituals and customs. Second, it is the resources that we use or exploit in our everyday lives. Consumption serves to meet our basic needs for food, liquid, and protection from the elements (clothing and shelter); it also fulfills our wants and desires—the resources we exploit to create our tools, weapons, vehicles, art and entertainment, and numerous other materials that enrich our lives. The needs and wants of people differ from one culture to another, but all are intended to make our lives more comfortable.

Consumption habits in industrial societies have grown dramatically in recent years, as demonstrated by the 2003 blackout in eastern North America that was at least partially due to the insatiable demands of North Americans for power to fuel their technological society. This is only one example of Western overconsumption of limited world resources. The consumption demands of small-scale cultures, such as foragers, are much less; their needs are few and easily fulfilled without overexploitation of the ecosystem. In societies that have adopted new forms of production (e.g., nomadic pastoralists forced to settle in one place and become agriculturalists), people often have difficulties fulfilling their consumption needs and wants. Access to modern communication systems (e.g., television and computer networks) has increased consumer demands in developing countries, such as China, placing additional strain on already stretched resources. We will address the social inequality of access to resources in Chapter 11.

In Chapter 5 we examined the use of resources in productive activities, and earlier in this chapter we discussed the distribution and exchange of goods. These are the usual themes that occupy sociocultural anthropologists, but consumption extends beyond these, to the actual *consuming* of food and the meanings associated with this consumption. One fascinating aspect of

---

Consumption. The ingestion of food and the exploitation of available resources.

consumption is the rules of behaviour that govern the way we consume food.

Consumption Behaviour

Imagine sitting down at a table and scooping the food into your mouth with your fingers. Bad table manners? Not in many parts of the world; indeed, utensils of one kind or another are a fairly recent invention. Eating with tools likely began when hunters used their knives to cut meat from bones and then popped the meat into their mouths with the same knife.[32] Next came the spoon, made of halved gourds, seashells, or carved wood. People used these spoons to dip stew from a communal pot hanging over a fire. Status and ranking within the community determined who would dip first—usually men, then women and children. The quintessential fork did not appear until the Middle Ages, likely spreading from Italy to England and France.[33] Adoption of the fork appears to have been gender-determined: Gentlewomen carried their own forks with them at all times, while men continued to use their knives and fingers. Knives, spoons, and forks are not the only eating utensils: Millions of people use chopsticks, and others rely on their fingers, although customs associated with finger-eating vary. For example, in northern India, diners use the fingertips of their right hand, while in the south they use both hands.[34] Among the Lapps, strong coffee is a favourite beverage; it is heavily salted and consumed many times a day. The Lapps consider it appropriate behaviour to hold a lump of sugar between their teeth and suck the coffee through it.

Gestures of appreciation also vary from culture to culture, and what might be considered rude in one culture may be a sign of good manners in another. An example is slurping soup—not a sign of good manners in most North American homes, yet in Japan it shows apprecia-

tion for the cook. In Korea, leaving a spoon or chopstick in the rice is considered bad form because it symbolizes use by the dead.[35] This type of taboo is fairly common worldwide; indeed, food taboos are another important factor in the study of consumption.

Food Taboos

Because of the cultural significance of eating, many taboos have developed regarding what people can and cannot eat. For example, in the past Hawaiian women were not allowed to touch pork, coconuts, or certain kinds of fish; hence, the men cooked the food.[36] Hawaiian women could not eat with the men, and women's food was not cooked in the same oven as men's food. Similarly, Muslims and Jews prohibit eating pork, citing religious doctrine regarding cleanliness. In the Hindu religion members are not allowed to eat sacred cows. Fasting is also a part of food taboos—for example, Ukrainians eat only meatless dishes on Christmas Eve because meat is considered "heavy," while fruits and vegetables lighten the soul. A classic example of a gender-determined taboo is alcohol. Until some 40 years ago many beer parlours on the Canadian prairies had separate entrances for men and women, and others simply would not allow women on the premises unless men escorted them.

Food as Ritual and Social Interaction

Food is commonly used in rituals, such as sacrifice at religious shrines. Anthropologists have found that the connections between humans and the divine often depend on ritual transactions of food between them. The sacred nature of food is evident in Hindu pilgrimage towns, where sacred food is first offered to the deity and then consumed by the pilgrims.[37] Blessing of food figures

[32]Berry, E. (1963). Foreword. In *Eating and cooking around the world: Fingers before forks*. New York: The John Day Company.

[33]Fox, R. (n.d.). *Food and eating: An anthropological perspective*. Retrieved August 27, 2003, from the World Wide Web: http://www.sirc.org/publik/food_and_eating_3.html.

[34]Huntington, H. (2000). *How table manners become polite*. Retrieved August 27, 2003, from the World Wide Web: http://search.csmonitor.com/durable/2000/11/28/p22s1.htm.

[35]*Korean Table Manners*. Retrieved August 27, 2003, from the World Wide Web: http://www.esl-global.com/cultural_hints/manners.html.

[36]Berry, E. (1963). Foreword. In *Eating and cooking around the world: Fingers before forks*. New York: The John Day Company.

[37]Khare, R.S., & Rao, M.S.A. (1986). Introduction. In R.S. Khare & M.S.A. Rao (Eds.), *Aspects in South Asian food systems: Food, society, and culture*. Durham, NC: Carolina Academic Press.

prominently in the Ukrainian culture. At Easter, ritual foods, such as *babka* and *paska* (egg-rich Easter breads), hard-boiled eggs, and baked cheese are placed in a basket covered with a sacred cloth and taken to church to be blessed before eating.

Food also appears to play a powerful role in the formation and maintenance of social groups; people come together at social gatherings such as weddings, bar mitzvahs, and funerals to share food and enhance kinship networks and social relations. Gift giving often involves food, as when the Kwakwaka'wakw of the northwest coast of Canada hold potlatches where gifts of food are given. Potlatch feasts also augment the social bonds among the people in the community. Similarly, Ukrainian ritual foods serve to solidify ethnic identity. Ukrainians gather together on holy days and joyously consume the ritual foods, celebrating their ethnicity. Ritual foods can also symbolize status; for example, cooks renown for their ability to produce perfect *babka* or *paska* are held in high esteem within their communities.

In a pluralistic country like Canada, the study of the social constructs of food systems takes on an added dimension; ethnic food systems and the diffusion of these systems throughout Canadian society are clearly evident. Ukrainian food is an excellent example: Hardly anyone living in Canada is unaware of the culinary delights of perogies (a Canadianized version of *verenyky*), which are sold at markets and restaurants across

Canada and around the world. Thus, consumption plays an integral role in any culture's economic system.

ECONOMICS, CULTURE, AND THE WORLD OF BUSINESS

At the start of this chapter, we noted that when studying the economies of nonliterate peoples we perhaps are most apt to fall prey to our ethnocentric biases. The misunderstandings that result from our failure to overcome these biases are of major importance to us in the modern world in at least two ways. For one, they encourage development schemes for countries that, by Western economic standards, are regarded as "underdeveloped" (a comfortably ethnocentric term), schemes that all too often result in poverty, poor health, discontent, and a host of other ills. In northeastern Brazil, for example, development of large-scale plantations to grow sisal for export to the United States took over numerous small farms where peasants grew food to feed themselves. With this change, peasants were forced into the ranks of the unemployed. Because the farmers were unable to earn enough money to satisfy their minimal nutritional needs, the incidence of malnutrition rose dramatically. Similarly, development projects in Africa, designed to initiate changes in local hydrology, vegetation, and settlement patterns—and even programs aimed at reducing certain diseases—frequently have led directly to *increased* disease rates.[38] Fortunately, awareness is growing among development officials that future projects are unlikely to succeed without the expertise anthropologically trained people can bring to bear.

Second, achieving an understanding of the economic systems of other peoples that is not bound by the hopes and expectations of our own culture also has become important for corporate executives in today's world. Recognition of how embedded such systems are within the cultures of which they are parts could avoid problems of the sort a large New York City–based cosmetics man-

The consumption of food and beverages is an important social activity. In Canada, eating ethnic foods has become increasingly popular. Shown here is a Canadian family at a Japanese steak house.

[38]Bodley, J.H. (1990). *Victims of progress* (3rd ed., p. 141). Mountain View, CA: Mayfield.

ufacturer experienced. About to release an ad in Italy featuring a model holding some flowers, it was discovered the flowers were the kind traditionally given at Italian funerals. Along the same lines, the Chevrolet Nova did not sell well in Spanish-speaking countries because in Spanish "No Va" means "No Go." Anthropologists Edward and Mildred Hall describe another case of the same sort:

> José Ybarra and Sir Edmund Jones are at the same party and it is important for them to establish a cordial relationship for business reasons. Each is trying to be warm and friendly, yet they will part with mutual distrust and their business transaction will probably fall through. José, in Latin fashion, moved closer and closer to Sir Edmund as they spoke, and this movement was miscommunicated as pushiness to Sir Edmund, who kept backing away from this intimacy, and this was miscommunicated to José as coldness.[39]

When the developing countries of Africa, Asia, and South and Central America are involved, the chances for cross-cultural misunderstandings increase dramatically. The executives of major corporations realize their dependence on these countries for raw materials, they are increasingly inclined to manufacture their products in these countries, and they see their best potential for market expansion as lying outside North America and Europe. That is why business recruiters on postsecondary campuses in North America are on the lookout for job candidates with the kind of understanding of the world that anthropology provides.

The Global Economy

The cross-cultural misunderstandings examined above take on a new sense of urgency when we realize that the market economy has changed dramatically in recent years as globalization has swept the world. **Globalization** means that countries are becoming one large interdependent system of commerce, communication, and power.[40] Markets around the world have been opened to free trade, resulting in stiff competition between states for lucrative markets, skilled labour, and limited resources. A close-to-home example of globalization is the North American Free Trade Agreement (NAFTA). The basic premise of this and other agreements, such as the European Economic Union (EEU), is to remove barriers such as tariffs that restrict the movement of goods and services across political boundaries.

There are several driving forces behind globalization, and although the term was not coined until 1989, these forces were at work much earlier. Technology is one of the most influential driving forces.[41] Besides the advent of rapid and relatively inexpensive transportation to all corners of the world, which makes global economic activity easier, electronic communication systems and computerized data-processing equipment have provided almost unlimited opportunities for international commerce. The global marketplace has changed the way we do business and the way we perceive the world around us. Globalization manifests itself in consumption, such as with entertainment culture, which has seen worldwide consumer demand for all things Western, including clothes, movies, and technology. It has also changed the way we set up our work environments. People are no longer tied to a physical office, but instead can work from home using electronic equipment. Nor are they required to meet face to face with business associates—e-mail, fax, and the Internet provide fast and efficient ways of communicating, although they also can lead to increased isolation. One aspect of globalization that interests anthropologists is the domestic and transnational migration of labour

---

[39]Hall, E.T., & Hall, M.R. (1986). The sounds of silence. In E. Angeloni (Ed.), *Anthropology 86/87* (p. 65). Guilford, CT: Dushkin.

[40]Morrison, R.B., & Wilson, C.R. (2002). *Ethnographic essays in cultural anthropology: A problem-based approach.* Itasca, IL: F.E. Peacock.

[41]Lubbers, R.F.M. (1999). *The globalization of economy and society.* Retrieved August 20, 2003, from the World Wide Web: http://globus.lubpdfs/globaliz/thegloba/doc.

Globalization. The process of opening up world markets using modern technology.

In Africa, much of the farming is the job of women. Failure to accept this fact is responsible for the failure of many development schemes, since outside experts design projects that usually assume the men are the farmers.

forces.[42] For example, they consider how labour migrations affect workers' ethnic, cultural, and national identities.

Although touted as the means to eliminate economic inequalities and pave the way for the future of global economies, globalization is not without its problems. Detractors believe globalization benefits rich and powerful Westerners but provides few advantages for anyone outside this elite, and in many cases, causes a great deal of harm. Multinational corporations are increasingly moving their operations to developing countries to take advantage of cheaper labour costs, putting the economic well-being of North American workers in jeopardy. Activists protest the exploitation of developing countries, both the human toil and the damage to environments where few protective controls are in place.

The promise of prosperity for developing countries has not come to fruition; indeed, the gap between the have and have-not nations continues to grow. However, whether globalization is beneficial or harmful to societies and particular cultural groups around the world, the reality is we are becoming a global economic community, and in the coming decades we will have to learn to deal with the issues of globalization.

---

[42]Ibid.

Gender **Perspectives**
Laurel Bossen, McGill University

Women and Economic Development

Ester Boserup's pathbreaking work, *Women's Role in Economic Development*, with its demonstration of women's diverse economic roles and its stinging critique of European colonialism and development for undermining women's economic position, was published in 1970. Since then, research on women and economic development in other cultures has grown and anthropologists have contributed greatly to the study of women's work and the gendered impact of economic, commercial, and technological development (Rathgeber, 1994). They have become increasingly attuned to changing gendered divisions of labour; to women's access to income, property, and markets beyond the household; and to the diverse ways in which households, local cultures, governments, and planned development interventions affect women's ability to participate in and benefit from economic change. There is no universal pattern to these changes, as different cultures and states face specific gender challenges as their economies develop.

In Egypt, Homa Hoodfar (1997) studied the economic and social roles of poor Muslim women in Cairo, where women's labour force participation is low. Hoodfar found that Islamic marriages aided parents in negotiating financial guarantees for their daughters' marriages. A married woman was not expected to support the household monetarily, but had "an unquestioned right" to economic support from her husband in exchange for housework and childrearing. When wives earned a cash income, men were not authorized to take control over it. Thus, women's conservatism, low labour force participation, and adherence to Islamic traditions had a material basis (102). Yet when some women earned cash incomes, men reduced their household contributions, retaining more for personal consumption. As the goods and services traditionally provided by women became commercialized, "women jealously guarded or tried to salvage what the market had not yet claimed" (272). They invested time and energy in subsistence housework, in careful shopping that minimized the use of cash, and maximized the use of state-subsidized goods and services. These resourceful consumer strategies responded to changing market conditions, but did not translate into increased power for women.

Gloria Rudolf's (1999) study of small farmers in Panama found that as the economy became more commercialized, gender inequality increased. Women's ability to claim land rights became problematic as land "moved into firmer male control . . . as coffee merchants and government officials, themselves all males, made their alliances primarily with highland men" (77). Also, the spread of Christian Base Community organizations aiming to "liberate the poor" and render them a political force attracted both women and men, but established a male monopoly of leadership positions (183). Neither the state nor the church fostered organizations that strengthened women's rights.

In Guatemala, my own comparative study of women and the changing division of labour in four contrasting communities (Bossen, 1984) showed that increased commercial development did not have a uniform impact, but disproportionately expanded the range of employment options for men. Women were most disadvantaged in the better-paying formal sectors of both the rural and urban economy. Here, the long history of Hispanic conquest, military governments, and civil war also promoted male dominance within both the indigenous Maya and Hispanic populations.

Rejecting universal theories that claim capitalist development or commercialization inevitably undermine women's role in the economy, Vilia Jefremovas (2000) emphasized the importance of local gender ideology and of viewing gender as a negotiated process. Among the Sagada Igorots of North Luzon, Philippines, local ideology resisted gender stratification. Despite commercialization, land inheritance has remained bilateral. Men and women share most subsistence and domestic tasks, and cash cropping has not had a negative impact on women (133). In this area, women have been important traders since pre-colonial times (134), and still play significant roles in trade, money lending, and money management.

In China, socialist revolutionary policies of collective land ownership designed to eliminate rural inequality were in force for almost three decades (1950s to 1980s). Despite the theory that if women participated equally in farming they would gain equality with men, gender inequality persisted in lower pay, and in family, kinship, and village organization. In the reform period beginning in the 1980s, Ellen Judd (1994) noted that gender equality dropped out of official discourse. Although state policies favouring decollectivization, rural industry, and market revival appeared to be gender-neutral, the continuity of an unofficial, customary, and deeply embedded system of male dominance remained central to Chinese society and the state. Ironically, the widespread "feminization" of farming in rural China over the past two decades is not a sign of women's growing economic influence. Because land plots are very small and cannot be enlarged (village land has been contracted to households but cannot be sold to other farmers), the returns to farming are low and men are leaving farms for more lucrative nonagricultural work (Bossen, 2002).

Anthropological studies of women and economic development in different societies and cultures show that gender is intimately related to production, reproduction, and consumption. State policies, religion, and local history and customs have different and complex effects on gender. Women's opportunities to contribute and benefit from economic development and commercialization are continuously renegotiated in response to changing market opportunities interacting with state and local configurations of gender and power.

Note: Homa Hoodfar, Vilia Jefremovas, Eva Rathgeber, Ellen Judd, and Laurel Bossen are Canadian anthropologists, educated at or teaching at Canadian universities.

Sources:

Boserup, E. (1970). *Women's role in economic development.* New York: St. Martin's Press.

Bossen, L. (1984). *The redivision of labor: Women and economic choice in four Guatemalan communities.* Albany: State University of New York Press.

Bossen, L. (2002). *Chinese women and rural development.* Lanham, MD: Rowman and Littlefield.

Hoodfar, H. (1997). *Between marriage and the market: Intimate politics and survival in Cairo.* Berkeley: University of California Press.

Jefremovas, V. (2000). Women are good with money: The impact of cash cropping on class relations and gender ideology in northern Luzon, the Philippines. In A. Spring (Ed.), *Women farmers and commercial ventures: Increasing food security in developing countries.* Boulder, CO: Lynne Rienner Publishers.

Judd, E. (1994). *Gender and power in rural north China.* Stanford, CA: Stanford University Press.

Rathgeber, E. (1994). WID, WAD, GAD. Tendances de la recherche et de la pratique dans le champ du développement. In H. Dagenais & D. Piché (Eds.), *Women, feminism and development/Femmes, féminisme et développement* (pp. 77–95). Montreal: McGill–Queen's University Press for the Canadian Research Institute for the Advancement of Women.

Rudolf, G. (1999). *Panama's poor: Agents, victims, and historymakers.* Gainesville, FL: University Press of Florida.

Anthropology **Applied**

Anthropology and the World of Business

When people hear of anthropologists working for or running private-sector businesses ranging from major financial institutions to consulting firms for corporations, their reaction is usually surprise. In the public mind, anthropologists work in exotic, far-away places such as remote islands, deep forests, hostile deserts, or arctic wastes—not in the world of business. After all, when anthropology makes the pages of *The New York Times,* it is to report the "discovery" of a "last surviving Stone Age tribe," the uncovering of some ancient "lost city," or the recovery of bones of a remote human ancestor.

Not only have anthropologists found niches for themselves in the business world, but since 1972 the number going into business has grown fivefold. The reason for their success is that they have skills to offer the corporate world that other social and behavioural scientists do not. One example is the discovery of anthropology by the market-research and product industry, as reported by Susan Squires:

> The October/November 1996 issue of *Fast Company,* a magazine devoted to cutting-edge business practice, introduced its readers to the newest innovation in the market-research and design industry: ethnography. What companies in the forefront of market research and design are learning is that "nearly all the tools of conventional marketing—focus groups, customer surveys' segmentation—are designed to measure what people think. But the secret to breakthrough innovation . . . is understanding how people behave: what they do and how they live."
>
> Companies that are serious about ethnography are recruiting and hiring anthropologists like Christina Wasson, a linguist who received her Ph.D. from Yale in 1996. Wasson joined E-Lab, the company featured in the *Fast Company* article, after graduation. At E-Lab, Wasson uses methods to collect data that include participant observation, in depth interviewing, and videotaping.

> While many market research and design companies are beginning to advertise themselves as having "ethnographers" and "doing ethnography," most do not have anthropologists on staff and are not really "doing ethnography." Some of these companies would like to hire an anthropologist to legitimize their claims and improve their methods. This means that there is a potential job market for anthropologists in the market research and design area. But to be considered for available positions, the successful applicant must have some knowledge of business.
>
> Christina Wasson is a good example of the combination of skills and knowledge sought. She was recruited not only for her anthropological background but also for her business knowledge. Her dissertation, *Covert Causation: Linguistic Traces of Effective Organizational Control,* is based on lengthy fieldwork conducted at Motorola in Chicago.[1]

[1]Squires, S. (1997). The market research and product industry discovers anthropology. *Anthropology Newsletter, 38* (4), 31.

CHAPTER SUMMARY

An economic system is a means of producing, distributing, and consuming goods. Studying the economics of nonliterate, nonindustrial societies can be undertaken only in the context of the total culture. Each society solves the problem of subsisting by allocating raw materials, land, labour, and technology and by distributing goods according to its own priorities.

The work people do is a major productive resource, and the allotment of work is always governed by rules according to sex and age. Instead of looking for biological imperatives to explain the sexual division of labour, a more productive strategy is to examine the kinds of work men and women do in the context of specific societies to see how it relates to other cultural and historical factors. The cooperation of many people working together is a typical feature of both nonliterate and literate societies. Specialization of craft is important even in societies with very simple technologies. Resource depletion results in cultural, social, and economic disruption.

All societies regulate the allocation of land and its valuable resources. In nonindustrial societies, individual ownership of land is rare; generally, land is controlled by kinship groups, whereas in industrial societies private ownership is more common. The technology of a people, in the form of the tools they use and associated knowledge, is related to their mode of subsistence. Sedentary communities offer greater opportunities to accumulate material belongings, and inequalities of wealth may develop. In many such communities, though, a relatively egalitarian social order may be maintained through levelling mechanisms.

Nonliterate people consume most of what they produce themselves, but they do exchange goods. The processes of distribution include reciprocity, redistribution, and market exchange. Reciprocity is a transaction between individuals or groups, involving the exchange of goods and services of roughly equivalent value. Usually it is prescribed by ritual and ceremony.

Trading exchanges have elements of reciprocity, but they involve a greater calculation of the relative value of goods exchanged. Barter is one form of negative reciprocity whereby scarce goods from one group are exchanged for desirable goods from another group. Silent trade is a specialized form of barter with no verbal communication. A classic example of exchange between groups that involves both reciprocity and sharp trading is the Kula ring of the Trobriand Islanders.

Strong, centralized political organization is necessary for redistribution to occur. The government assesses each citizen a tax or tribute, uses the proceeds to support the governmental and religious elite, and redistributes the rest, usually in the form of public services. The collection of taxes and delivery of government services and subsidies in Canada is a form of redistribution. The potlatch is also a form of redistribution and serves as a levelling mechanism among First Nations northwest coastal peoples.

Display for social prestige is a motivating force in societies that produce some surplus of goods. In Canada, goods accumulated for display generally remain in the hands of those who accumulated them, whereas in other societies they are generally given away; the prestige comes from publicly divesting oneself of valuables, as in the potlatch ceremony of the northwest coast of British Columbia.

Exchange in the marketplace serves to distribute goods in a region. In nonindustrial societies, the marketplace is usually a specific site where produce, livestock, and material items the people produce are exchanged. It also functions as a social gathering place and a news medium. Canada's market economy provides opportunities to Chinese Canadians.

In market economies, the informal sector may become more important than the formal sector as large numbers of under- and unemployed people with marginal access to the formal economy seek to survive. The informal economy consists of economic activities that escape official scrutiny and regulation.

Consumption encompasses the resources we ingest and the resources we exploit. Meaning is given to consumption through ritual and social interaction.

The anthropological approach to economics has taken on new importance in today's world of international development and commerce. Without it, development schemes for developing countries are prone to failure, and international trade is hampered by cross-cultural misunderstandings. Globalization has brought with it many opportunities as well as many problems.

QUESTIONS FOR CRITICAL THOUGHT

1. Imagine you run a word processing service for other students or you work at a fast-food restaurant part-time. How might your personal economic valuation of your labour appear to someone from another culture with a foraging economic system? to someone from North America with a foraging economic system, such as a homeless person?

2. Do you see examples of nonindustrial forms of market exchange in your neighbourhood? Do North American consumers or sellers make use of nonindustrial forms? How and why?

3. Identify levelling mechanisms within your community, province, and country. How do these levelling mechanisms serve to redistribute goods and services to the community?

4. Do we judge people by their table manners? Can you identify some practices (e.g., belching) that are considered good manners in one culture but not in another?

5. What would happen to our economy if we experienced agricultural exhaustion (if the soil could no long support crops of any kind)? Are there alternative economies we could turn to? What social impact would an ecological disaster of this magnitude have on us?

6. Take a look around your community. How are you and the members of your community economically enriched by the presence of people from diverse ethnic backgrounds? Socially enriched?

INTERNET RESOURCES

Gifting and Feasting in the Northwest Coast Potlatch
http://www.peabody.harvard.edu/potlatch/default.html
This site provides several links that explain what a potlatch is, describe the feasting and gifting, and feature contemporary potlatches. Photos and illustrations are included in each link.

New Cultures and Economics
http://homepages.gold.ac.uk/slater
A large site addressing such topics as consumer culture and market society. Produced by Don Slater from the University of London.

Gender Inequality and Economics
http://www.unfpa.org/swp/2000/english/ch05.html
An impressive site addressing many issues relevant to students of anthropology. Consists of major topics such as "The cost of economic invisibility," "The costs of denying health care," "Maternal mortality and morbidity," "The economic cost of

HIV/AIDS," "Gender-based violence," "Psychological costs," "Education: Costs of the gender gap," "Micro-credit: Investing in women," "Demography and gender: Costs and opportunities," and "Measuring gender inequalities." Also includes several boxes on development and human rights: "Women's work is under-rewarded," and "Gender inequality in education persists."

Energy, Environment, and Sustainable Development
http://europa.eu.int/comm/research/eesd/leaflets/en
A large site with links that examine the environment, energy, and globalization from a European perspective. Numerous links to sites on topics such as quality of water, climate change, marine ecosystems, the city of tomorrow and cultural heritage, and renewable resources.

Pastoralists in Southern Africa
http://www.museums.org.za/sam/resource/arch/pastoral.htm
Extensive information on pastoralist groups in southern Africa.

SUGGESTED READINGS

Dalton, G. (1971). *Traditional tribal and peasant economies: An introductory survey of economic anthropology.* Reading, MA: Addison-Wesley.
This is just what the title says it is, by a major specialist in economic anthropology.

Freeman, M.M.R., Bogoslovskayas, L., Caulfield, R.A., Egede, I., Krupnik, I., & Stevenson, M.G. (1998). *Inuit, whaling, and sustainability.* Walnut Creek, CA: Altamira Press.
This book examines the challenges faced by Inuit whalers in today's world. It looks at the cultural conflict created between hunting peoples, who are fighting for the right to continue their traditional hunting practices, and outsiders, who believe the whales should be protected. It is also an examination of efforts to protect the ocean ecosystem and sustain whale populations. This is an excellent opportunity for students to consider both sides of the story, and perhaps develop a deeper understanding of the philosophy of hunting peoples.

Moore, J.H. (1993). *The political economy of North American Indians.* Norman and London: University of Oklahoma Press.
A collection of papers delivered at the 1988 meetings of the 12th International Congress of Anthropological and Ethnological Sciences. These discussions seek to apply a political economic approach to the study of North American aboriginal cultures. Although most

of the articles focus on U.S. cultures, there is some content directed at Canadian groups: "Natives and the development of mercantile capitalism: A new look at 'opposition' in the eighteenth-century fur trade," "Autonomy and constraint: The household economy on a southern Ontario reserve," and "The quest for Indian development in Canada: Contrasts and contradictions."

Newell, D., & Ommer, E. (Eds.). (1999). *Fishing places, fishing people: Traditions and issues in Canadian small-scale fisheries*. Toronto: University of Toronto Press.

Employing an interdisciplinary approach, the authors of these essays examine current problems in worldwide fisheries, including Canadian fisheries, and offer some direction for alternative management approaches.

Plattner, S. (Ed.). (1989). *Economic anthropology*. Stanford, CA: Stanford University Press.

This is the first comprehensive text in economic anthropology to appear since the 1970s. Twelve scholars in the field contributed chapters on a variety of issues ranging from economic behaviour in foraging, horticultural, preindustrial-state, peasant, and industrial societies to sex roles, common-property resources, informal economics in industrial societies, and mass marketing in urban areas.

CNN Today Videos

Toy Barriers (CNN Cultural Anthropology, vol. 1, 1:44)
There is a global market in industrialized countries for toys.

Russian Social Protest (CNN Cultural Anthropology, vol. 2, 1:38)
In a provincial northern Russian city, citizens face economic and social upheaval since the breakup of the old Soviet Union.

World Women's Inequality (CNN Cultural Anthropology, vol. 1, 3:54)
This segment asserts that women are of less value than men in most cultures.

Oil Spill Impacts (CNN Cultural Anthropology, vol. 5, 2:49)
A 1989 oil spill continues to impact the environment and culture of Prince William Sound's native peoples.

Chapter 7

Sex and Marriage

A Hindu wedding ceremony. In all cultures, marriage establishes a continuing sexual relationship between two individuals, backed by legal, economic, and social forces. Thus, unlike mating (which is biological), marriage is distinctly cultural.

Chapter Preview

1. What Is Marriage?

Marriage is a relationship between one or more men (male or female) and one or more women (female or male) who are recognized by the group as having a continuing claim to the right of sexual access to each other. Because gender is culturally defined, the "man" may be a female or the "woman" a male. Although in many cultures, husbands and wives live together as members of the same household, this is not true in all cultures. And although most marriages tend to involve one spouse, many cultures permit, and even regard as desirable, marriage of an individual to multiple spouses.

2. What Is the Difference between Marriage and Mating?

All animals, including humans, mate—that is, they form a sexual bond with other individuals. In some species, the bond lasts for life, but in others it lasts no longer than a single sex act. New studies of human sexuality show a remarkable diversity in sexual identity, practices, and acceptance and in control of sexual behaviour. Only marriage, however, is backed by social, legal, and economic forces. Consequently, while mating is biological, marriage is cultural.

3. Why Is Marriage Universal?

A problem universal to all human groups is the need to control sexual relations so that competition over sexual access does not introduce a disruptive, combative influence into society. The specific form marriage takes is related to who has rights to offspring, as well as how property is distributed.

CHAPTER OUTLINE

Human Sexuality

Control of Sexual Relations

Anthropology Applied: Anthropology and AIDS

Gender Perspectives: Female Genital Mutilation

Forms of Marriage

Original Study: Arranging Marriage in India

Divorce

Among the Trobriand Islanders, whose yam exchanges and Kula voyages we examined in Chapter 6, children who have reached age seven or eight begin playing erotic games with each other and imitating adult seductive attitudes. Within another four or five years they begin to pursue sexual partners in earnest, changing partners often, experimenting sexually first with one and then another. By the time they are in their mid-teens, meetings between lovers take up most of the night, and affairs between them are apt to last for several months. Ultimately, lovers begin to meet the same partner again and again, rejecting the advances of others. When the couple is ready, they appear together one morning outside the young man's house as a way of announcing their intention to be married.

For young Trobrianders, attracting sexual partners is an important business, and they spend a great deal of time making themselves look as attractive and seductive as possible. Youthful conversations during the day are loaded with sexual innuendos, and magical spells as well as small gifts are employed to entice a prospective sex partner to the beach at night or to the house where boys sleep apart from their parents. Because girls, too, sleep apart from their parents, youths and adolescents have considerable freedom to arrange their love affairs. Boys and girls play this game as equals, with neither sex having an advantage over the other.

As anthropologist Annette Weiner points out, all of this sexual activity is not a frivolous, adolescent pastime. Attracting lovers

> is the first step toward entering the adult world of strategies, where the line between influencing others while not allowing others to gain control of oneself must be carefully learned. . . . Sexual liaisons give adolescents the time and occasion to experiment with all the possibilities and problems that adults face in creating relationships with those who are not relatives. Individual wills may clash, and the achievement of one's desire takes patience, hard work, and determination. The adolescent world of lovemaking has its own dangers and disillusionments. Young people, to the degree they are capable, must learn to be both careful and fearless.[1]

The Trobriand attitude toward adolescent sexuality seems to stand in marked contrast to that of North American society. Theoretically, North Americans are not supposed to have sexual relations outside of wedlock, although, as is well known, a considerable discrepancy between theory and practice exists. Nonetheless, premarital sexual activity in North American society cannot be conducted with the openness and approval that characterizes the Trobriand situation. As a consequence, it is not subject to the kind of social pressures from the community at large that prepare traditional Trobriand youths for the adult world after marriage.

To attract lovers, young Trobriand Islanders must look as attractive and seductive as possible. The young men shown here have decorated themselves with Johnson's Baby Powder.

---

[1]Weiner, A.B. (1988). *The Trobrianders of Papua New Guinea* (p. 71). New York: Holt, Rinehart and Winston.

▲▽▲▽▲▽▲▽▲▽▲▽▲▽▲▽▲▽▲▽▲▽▲▽▲▽▲▽

HUMAN SEXUALITY

Human sexuality is a topic of considerable, albeit fairly recent, interest to anthropologists. Margaret Mead (1935) and Bronislaw Malinowski (1929) were two of the earliest anthropologists to study humans as sexual beings. However, since their pioneering work, very little anthropological attention has been turned to human sexuality. One of the difficulties anthropologists have encountered is the degree of privacy in which people hold their sexual activity. Most people are uncomfortable talking about their sex lives and their feelings concerning sexuality; this is especially true if their sexuality sits outside the "norms" of a culture, as, for example, gay or lesbian sexuality and teenage premarital sexual activity do in many cultures. Anthropologists may also experience difficulty broaching the subject because of their own uncomfortable feelings or gender barriers (e.g., females refusing to discuss their sexuality with a male stranger). Regardless of the difficulties, cross-cultural studies of human sexuality have become more common since the 1980s.

Anthropologists are finding a great deal of cultural variation in the way sexuality is viewed, practised, and controlled. Jeffrey Weeks contends that diversification of sexual practices, subcultures, and identities is characteristic of our history,[2] and to define human sexuality would require as many definitions as experiences. A woman in a lesbian relationship likely views sexuality differently than a woman in a heterosexual relationship, and a man from a small-scale society in Africa likely sees human sexuality in another light than someone from an industrial society. Why? Although human sexuality is rooted in our biological nature, it is also a cultural construct. This means our sexuality has been formed at least partly by our cultural environment and will differ from that of someone in another culture. To illustrate this point, the Mukkuvar people of south India see female sexuality as a kind of social prosperity inseparable from fertility, whereas many societies rooted in Christianity place a high value on chastity. Similar to the Trobriand Islanders, the Ju/'hoansi view sexuality among their adolescents (both heterosexual and homosexual) as natural, although they too have rules that govern this behaviour. Thus, human sexual relations are dealt with in all cultures, but in different ways.

Homosexuality

Homosexuality is common worldwide, yet anthropologists continue to grapple with a cross-cultural understanding of the many meanings attached to it.[3] Even the terminology is confusing: lesbian, gay, transgender, transsexual, bisexual, homogender, and so on. In Western cultures, homosexuality is usually defined as the desire to have sexual relations with someone of the same sex. However, this is a rather narrow definition. For example, among the Navajo, homosexuality is based more on gender and gender roles than on biological sex and anatomy.

In many cultures, both in the past and present, homosexual behaviour is looked upon as natural, and even expected. In ancient Greek and Roman societies, homosexuality was considered socially acceptable behaviour, as it is in Papua, New Guinea, where young men undergo initiation rites that include an element of homosexuality. After initiation, they are expected to partake in homosexual behaviour for a number of years before they marry and begin a heterosexual relationship. The Etero of New Guinea actually prefer homosexual relations, believing sex between males and females weakens the male and should occur only for reproductive reasons.[4]

Alternative genders, or transgenders, where biological men and women do not fit into the female or male gender, have been identified in many cultures. The "two-spirit," or *berdache*, of North America has been recorded in at least 113 aboriginal groups as geographically disparate as

[2]Connell, R.W. (1999). Making gendered people: Bodies, identities, sexualities. In M.M. Ferree, J. Locker, & B. Hess (Eds.), *Revisioning gender*. Thousand Oaks, CA: Sage.

[3]Wekker, G. (1999). What's identity got to do with it? Rethinking identity in light of the *mati* work in Suriname. E. Blackwood & S.E. Wieringa (Eds.), *Female desires: Same-sex relations and transgender practices across cultures*. New York: Columbia University Press.

[4]Kelly, R. (1976). Witchcraft and sexual relations. In P. Brown & G. Buchbender (Eds.), *Man and woman in the New Guinea Highlands*. Special Publication No. 8. Washington, DC: American Anthropological Association.

the Zuni and Cheyenne, the Ingalik of Alaska, and the Mojave of California.[5] Two-spirits may be men or women who have a dream or vision that explains and legitimizes their choice to become another gender; in this way, they represent a third and fourth gender.[6] Two-spirits may form sexual and emotional relationships with someone of their own sex. They also have important social, religious, and economic roles to fulfill—for example, female two-spirits may become hunters, warriors, or chiefs—and enjoy a special status in their community.

As mentioned earlier, the anthropological exploration of human sexuality, and even more so of homosexuality, has taken some time to develop and mature into a legitimate field of study. Of institutionalized same-sex relations among women, one of the most extensively studied is the 19th-century Chinese sisterhood in the province of Guangdon. Chinese sisterhood movements involved thousands of women who entered into sexual relations with other women and vowed before their goddess Guan Yin never to marry a man.[7] These sisterhoods, with names such as Golden Orchid Association, created support networks for women, who lived in cooperative houses where they helped one another. Following the victory of the Red Army in 1949, the sisterhoods were banned, and many of the women fled to other countries. Yet most of the early studies avoided the lesbian nature of these sisterhoods, preferring to examine other issues, such as employment.

Avoidance of all things homosexual is changing. Gloria Wekker closely examined sexual identity when she investigated the *mati* of Paramaribo, Suriname. These Creole women engage in sexual relations with men and with women, either simultaneously or consecutively.

Ethnographic studies such as Wekker's raise some interesting questions regarding homosexual behaviour and homosexual identity.[8]

CONTROL OF SEXUAL RELATIONS

Humans engage in sexual relations when it suits them and when it is deemed appropriate by their cultural mores. Many of the controls or restrictions on sexual activity involve adolescents. Males and females are biologically able to participate in sexual activity by their early teens, yet each culture possesses its own rules or guidelines of when sex is culturally permitted. Among some peoples, such as the Trobriand Islanders and the Ju/'hoansi, sexual discovery and experimentation among adolescents is acknowledged and accepted. In cultures such as these, the young are usually married soon after they reach biological maturity. Among the Masai, little girls engage in sexual play with older warriors until they reach the age of sexual maturity (the onset of first menarch). At this time, to avoid pregnancy outside marriage, the young females are circumcised and married to much older men. Conversely, many cultures strictly control sexual behaviour, especially among their adolescent females. In the Middle East, the virginity of young girls is highly prized. To this end, females are strictly controlled, secluded from the outside world, and protected from unwanted advances.

Control over gay and lesbian sexuality varies from culture to culture. Permissive cultures tend to view same-sex relationships with more tolerance than restrictive cultures, but even in such cultures, gay relationships between men are more accepted than lesbianism. A 1951 study by Clellans Ford and Frank A. Beach of male homosexuality in 76 cultures around the world found that 64 percent recognized male homosexual activity as normal and socially acceptable, as it

[5]Bonvillain, N. (1998). *Women and men: Cultural constructs of gender*. Upper Saddle River, NJ: Prentice Hall.

[6]Lang, S. (1999). Lesbians, men-women and two-spirits: Homosexuality and gender in Native American cultures. In E. Blackwood & S.E. Wieringa (Eds.), *Female desires: Same-sex relations and transgender practices across cultures*. New York: Columbia University Press.

[7]Blackwood, E., & Wieringa, S.E. (1999). Sapphic shadows: Challenging the silence in the study of sexuality. In E. Blackwood & S.E. Wieringa (Eds.), *Female desires: Same-sex relations and transgender practices across cultures*. New York: Columbia University Press.

[8]Wekker, G. (1999). "What's identity got to do with it?" Rethinking identity in light of the *mati* work in Suriname. In E. Blackwood & S.E. Wieringa (Eds.), *Female desires: Same-sex relations and transgender practices across cultures*. New York: Columbia University Press.

Anthropology **Applied**

Anthropology and AIDS

An irony of human life is that sexual activity, necessary for perpetuation of the species as well as a source of pleasure and fulfillment, also can be a source of danger. The problem lies in sexually transmitted diseases, which in recent years have been spreading and increasing in variety. Among these is acquired immune deficiency syndrome, or AIDS, although intravenous drug use and blood transfusions also contributed to its spread. Recent reports specify that 16 000 new cases of AIDS arise in the world *every day* (see Figure 7.1). What follows is A.M. Williams's account of what she and other anthropologists have to contribute to our understanding and control of this disease.

> After a decade and a half, it is hard to deny that AIDS is a pandemic experienced in significant ways at local levels. The World Health Organization (WHO) estimates 18.5 million adults are infected with HIV (the virus present in most people with AIDS) worldwide, with 4.5 million of those people diagnosed with

AIDS. While HIV and AIDS has hit areas of sub-Saharan Africa and Southeast Asia hardest, as of June 1996, the Centers for Disease Control report a cumulative total of 548 102 AIDS cases in the United States, with 343 000 deaths. Where I work in San Francisco, California, a city of less than 800 000 people, there have been 24 509 AIDS cases and 16 838 deaths from AIDS reported since 1980. Of these cases, 22 161 are among gay and bisexual men in the city.[1]

To grasp the proportions of the pandemic, public health perspectives, epidemiological models, biomedical information, and psychological interpretations are used to help figure out who is infected, who will become infected, and where these infections are most likely to occur. However, anthropology takes a different approach, one that helps to clarify the dynamic relationship between people who are infected or at risk for infection, and their social, cultural, political, and economic surroundings. Such research is important because it can provide rich explanations of why people become infected or progress rapidly in HIV disease. This in turn can

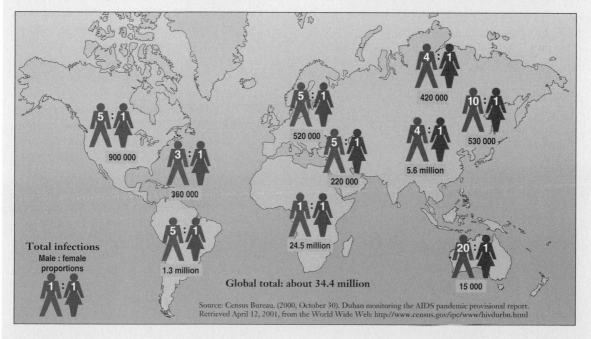

Source: Census Bureau. (2000, October 30). Duban monitoring the AIDS pandemic provisional report. Retrieved April 12, 2001, from the World Wide Web: http://www.census.gov/ipc/www/hivdurbn.html

FIGURE 7.1

Estimated global distribution of adult HIV infections, October 2000.

assist all manner of institutions in addressing a wide variety of local issues for those who need their services and support. Moreover, anthropological analyses often help describe the dynamic links between individual practices, social and cultural systems, and larger structural forces, all of which may combine in ways that encourage the problems of HIV.

Working alone or as part of teams to collect and analyze data, most anthropologists enter into an extended engagement with groups of people who are dealing with numerous aspects of HIV and AIDS. Since anthropology begins from the premise that circumstances and phenomena are complex within different populations, we employ a variety of methods and theoretical frameworks to reach our understandings. As a result, we do not develop monolithic models for explaining HIV and AIDS. For example, anthropologist Richard Parker's work in Brazil provided the formative research on sexual practices and their relationship to local systems of power and inequality needed to create more appropriate responses to the increasing spread of HIV/AIDS there. Others, like Paul Farmer, demonstrate how political economy and constructions of sickness among people in Haiti can negatively influence the quality of life of those infected in ways that encourage the further spread of the virus. And some, like Emily Martin, show that within the relationships between science, clinical research, and people affected by HIV and AIDS there emerge new concepts of body and AIDS that can reveal dynamics about society and the authoritative role of experts in shaping public awareness.[2]

These anthropological studies and many others contribute to very broad research and theoretical literature on HIV and AIDS, which can be drawn upon by community-based organizations, policymakers, and other researchers. However, some anthropologists like myself work more directly with groups and organizations on problems posed by primary prevention (preventing HIV transmission) and secondary prevention (slowing the disease's progression). Here anthropology is well suited for both formative research and con-

ducting evaluations of programs and services. As the anthropologist on a multi-disciplinary research team at the Center for AIDS Prevention Studies, University of California, San Francisco, I work directly with local gay male populations and such local AIDS organizations as the San Francisco AIDS Foundation and the STOP AIDS Project. While the team uses many strategies of inquiry, I specifically employ anthropological methods of investigation such as living and participating in the community, conducting a variety of in-depth interviews, and studying archival materials. I also rely on anthropological perspectives that require descriptions of the links between historical contexts, larger structural phenomena, and local practices and understandings.

Recently, by examining the relationship between HIV and drug use in two local groups of gay men who engage in unprotected sex, I was able to describe how groups of poorer gay male drug users in the city may be subjected to physical violence from their homophobic peers. This influences their ability to use condoms or openly seek HIV prevention education or support. At the same time, groups of more middle-class gay male drug users did not seek education or support because their social location and values encouraged them to believe that they did not need these resources because they had everything under control.[3] With a greater clarity regarding local social and cultural barriers to HIV prevention, some local HIV prevention program designers rapidly developed more culturally appropriate prevention programs for these groups of men. Because HIV and AIDS are a dynamic part of lived experiences, learning about how people conceptualize and shape their ideas and practices around the virus, selfhood, sex practices, collective life, and institutions is important. And when these concepts become part of a foundation for HIV/AIDS programs, the services are better able to respond to people's needs since the programs make better sense within the contexts of people's lived realities.

As we head into the next century, biotechnology's advances are beginning to reconfigure the HIV/AIDS pandemic. While this is good news, it also means the meanings of HIV and AIDS become more complex and difficult to navigate. Moreover, while new pharmaceutical therapies are providing hope for many enfranchised people in the West, infection rates climb and many more people remain unable to access these treatments. For most of us, culturally specific education and services will still be the most effective means to prevent infection or stem disease progression in many communities. In this light, the variety of perspectives offered by anthropology becomes even more crucial. This is because the foundations of these prevention efforts and services need to be developed with considerable understanding of how HIV and AIDS are constructed and shaped in a dynamic relationship with local complexities and concerns.

[1]*Centers For Disease Control semi-annual AIDS report (through June 1996)*. (1997). Centers For Disease Control. Atlanta, Georgia; and *AIDS monthly surveillance summary (through July 1997)*. (1997). San Francisco Department of Public Health AIDS Office, Seroepidemiology and Surveillance Branch. San Francisco, CA. The earliest circumstances for tracking HIV and AIDS were problematic, and many people today still do not know their HIV status. Therefore, the cases reported in San Francisco or anywhere in the world must be understood to be under counted.

[2]See for example, Parker, R. (1991). *Bodies, pleasures, and passions: Sexual culture in contemporary Brazil*; Farmer, P. (1992). *AIDS and accusation: Haiti and the geography of blame*; and Martin, E. (1994). *Flexible bodies: Tracking immunity in American culture—from the days of polio to the age of AIDS*.

[3]See Williams, A.M. (1996). *Sex, drugs and HIV: A sociocultural analysis of two groups of gay and bisexual male substance users who practice unprotected sex*. Unpublished manuscript.

was in ancient Greece and Rome.[9] Yet as Christianity exerted its influence worldwide, rejection of homosexuality became more common. Today, gays and lesbians in Western societies are fighting for social, economic, and political recognition.

Aside from societal controls, humans have few limitations on their sexual behaviour. Unlike other primates, a human female displays no visible signs of ovulation and may be willing to engage in sex at any time in her cycle or even when she is pregnant. In fact, among some human cultures, intercourse during pregnancy is thought to promote the growth of the fetus. Trobriand Islanders believe a child's identity comes from its mother, but it is the father's job to build up and nurture the child, which he begins to do before birth through frequent intercourse with the mother.

In Western societies, social scientists have noticed two major trends in recent years: People are increasingly developing sexual relationships outside marriage, and women are gaining greater control over their sexual lives. Regardless of these changes, just as a culture tells people what, when, and how they should eat, so does it tell them when, where, how, and with whom they should have sex.

Rules of Sexual Access

People develop rules regarding acceptable sexual behaviour that serve to control sexual relations to some extent. In Canada and the United States, the official ideology has been that all sexual activity outside of wedlock is taboo. Individuals are expected to establish a family through marriage. We may define **marriage** as a relationship between one or more men (male or female) and one or more women (female or male) recognized by society as having a continuing claim to the right of sexual access to one another.[10] With

[9]Weitz, R. (2000). What price independence? Social relations to lesbians, spinsters, widows, and nuns. In E. Ashton-Jones, G.A. Olson, & M.G. Perry (Eds.), *The gender reader*. Needham Heights, MA: Allyn and Bacon.

[10]This definition of marriage is adapted from D. Bell (1997), Defining marriage and legitimacy, *Current Anthropology, 38,* 241; and R.K. Jain (1997), Comment, *Current Anthropology, 38,* 248.

Marriage.   A relationship between one or more men (male or female) and one or more women (female or male) recognized by society as having a continuing claim to the right of sexual access to one another.

marriage, a person establishes a continuing claim to the right of sexual access to another person. Actually very few known societies—only about 5 percent—prohibit all sexual involvement outside of marriage, and even North American society has become less restrictive. Among other peoples, as we have seen, practices are quite diverse. The Nayar peoples of southern India provide an example of a traditional marriage system quite different from North American practices.[11]

The Nayar constituted a landowning, warrior caste (rather than an independent society) from southwest India. Among them, estates were held by corporations of sorts made up of kinsmen related in the female line. These kinsmen all lived together in a large household, called a *taravad*, with the eldest male serving as manager.

Three Nayar transactions are of interest here. The first, known as the *tali-tying* ceremony, occurred shortly before a girl experienced her first menstrual cycle. It involved a ceremony that joined together in a temporary union the girl with a young man. This union, which may or may not have involved sexual relations, lasted for a few days and then broke up. Neither individual had any further obligation, although the woman and her future children would mourn for the man

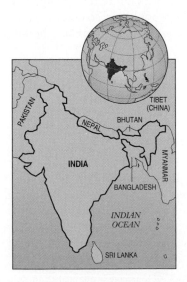

when he died. This transaction established the girl's eligibility for sexual activity with men her household approved of. With this ceremony, she officially became an adult woman.

The second transaction occurred when the woman entered into a continuing sexual liaison with an approved man. This was a formal relationship, which required the man to present her with gifts three times each year until the relationship ended. In return, the man could spend the nights with her. In spite of continuing sexual privileges, however, the man had no obligation to support his sex partner economically, nor was her home regarded as his home. In fact, she may have had such an arrangement with more than one man at the same time. Regardless of how many men were involved with one woman, this second Nayar transaction, known as the *sambandham*, clearly specified who had sexual rights to whom so as to avoid conflict.

The previous definition of marriage is universal, presumably because the problems it deals with are universal. As the Nayar case demonstrates, however, marriage need not have anything to do with starting a new family or even establishing a cooperative economic relationship between people of opposite gender.

The qualification in this definition of marriage—that the man actually may be a female or the woman actually may be a male—is an important one. It stems from the fact that gender does not automatically follow from biological sex but is culturally defined. Thus we find that in many societies, same-sex marriages are regarded as appropriate and normal in particular circumstances, even though opposite-sex marriages are far more common. We shall return to this subject later in the chapter.

In the absence of effective birth-control devices, the usual outcome of sexual activity between individuals of opposite sex is that, sooner or later, the woman becomes pregnant. When this happened among the Nayar, some man would have to formally acknowledge paternity, the third transaction. He did this by making gifts to the woman and the midwife. Although he might continue to take much interest in the child, he had no further obligations, for the child's education and support were the responsibility of the child's mother's brothers, whom the child and its mother lived with. This transaction established

[11]Haviland's interpretation of the Nayar follows W.H. Goodenough (1970), *Description and comparison in cultural anthropology* (pp. 6–11). Chicago: Aldine. It should be noted that this marriage custom has not been practised by the Nayar for many years.

In North America, gay or lesbian couples who wish to marry have met with considerable resistance, in spite of the fact that there is nothing abnormal, in any scientific sense, about such unions. In a number of other societies, same-sex marriages are regarded as perfectly appropriate.

the child's legitimacy. In this sense, it is the counterpart of the registration of births in North America that spells out parentage. In Western societies generally, the father is supposed to be the mother's husband, but he does not have to be. In 21st-century Canadian society, the child of a single mother is seldom spoken of as "illegitimate," but even if it is, the child's citizenship rights, as well as those of inheritance, are not denied. Nor does legitimacy require the father to be married to the mother. In numerous other cultural groups—for example, among the Pueblo peoples (such as the Hopi) of the North American southwest—fatherhood is utterly irrelevant to the

child's legitimacy. Legitimacy comes automatically from the mother, regardless of whether or not she is married.

The Nayar marriage system came to a gradual end in the late 19th century, owing to insidious economic, religious, and political influences. When the British gained control of the region, they dissolved the warrior caste; the men returned to their estates and became increasingly involved in the market economy, ending the corporate nature of their landholdings. Moral criticism from the British colonialists also played a part in the breakdown of the Nayar traditional marriage ceremonies. Legislation prohibiting polygyny and changing inheritance laws further eroded the practice in the 20th century. Today, the Nayar follow a monogamous marriage system.

Before we leave the Nayar, we should note that nothing in this culture is comparable to the family as we know it in North America. The group that forms the household does not include **affinal kin,** or individuals joined by a **conjugal bond** established by marriage. As will be shown in Chapter 8, a household group does not have to be a family as we know it. Among the Nayar the household is composed wholly of what we often call "blood" relatives, technically known as **consanguineal kin.** Sexual relations are with those who are not consanguineal kin and thus live in other households. This brings us to another supposed human universal, the incest taboo.

The Incest Taboo

A cultural rule that has fascinated anthropologists as well as other students of human behaviour is the **incest taboo.** This taboo prohibits sexual relations at least between parents and their offspring and usually between siblings as well. Once thought to be universal, save for a few exceptions involving siblings, the taboo has become something of a challenge for anthropologists to explain, both regarding this supposed universality and why incest is regarded as such loathsome behaviour.

Affinal kin. Relatives by marriage. **> Conjugal bond.** The bond between a man and a woman who are married. **> Consanguineal kin.** Relatives by birth—that is, "blood" relatives. **> Incest taboo.** The prohibition of sexual relations between specified individuals, usually parent–child and sibling relations at a minimum.

Gender **Perspectives**

Female Genital Mutilation

No other cultural practice has raised the ire of social activists, feminists, or the general public more than female genital mutilation (FGM), also known as female circumcision. FGM is the removal of part or all of a female's external genitalia. It can be as simple (if such a word should be used) as removing the tip of the clitoris, known as a clitoridectomy, or as invasive as excising the entire clitoris, labia minora, and labia majora, and performing infibulation—stitching the cut tissue with thorns or other sharp objects, to leave only a small opening for urine and menstrual flow. This more drastic procedure is often called pharaonic circumcision.

The origin of this custom is unclear. FGM is widespread in Africa—28 countries, both Islamic and Christian, practise some form of FGM, as well as some Middle Eastern and Far Eastern Islamic nations, such as Indonesia and Malaysia. The World Health Organization (WHO) conservatively estimates 130 million women worldwide have undergone some form of FGM. Until about 1900, clitoridectomies were practised on girls and women in Western Europe and the United States to cure everything from masturbation to frigidity.

Female birth attendants or a relative such as the child's mother, aunt, or grandmother usually perform this procedure. Babies as young as a few weeks are excised in some cultures, while in others they may not be circumcised until just before marriage, at around 15. The circumcision is performed without anaesthetic, nor are the tools (e.g., a sharp piece of glass or a stone knife) sterilized. Besides excruciating pain and terror, the young girls often experience serious physical problems following the procedure, including infection, hemorrhage, septicemia, shock, and even death. Those infibulated may experience urine and menstrual retention, bladder and bowel incontinence, and urinary tract and pelvic inflammations throughout their lives. When an infibulated woman is married, she must be cut or ripped open before intercourse, and then re-stitched following childbirth. This series of cutting and stitching continues throughout the woman's reproductive years, causing a buildup of scar tissue and frequent complications during childbirth.

Numerous reasons for continuing this practice have been offered—tradition being one. When asked, many adherents will explain it is the custom and always has been. A woman's status may be closely linked to her role as a mother and wife, and men will marry only circumcised females. Controlling women's sexual behaviour is another reason. Losing her clitoris reduces a woman's sexual pleasure, and presumably desire. Further, infibulation means a woman is "sewn up" and cannot be unfaithful, thus ensuring virginity before marriage and fidelity after marriage. Religious beliefs are also cited as an underlying reason. Many Sudanese believe that Islam commands pharaonic circumcision. Although Islamic scholars vehemently disavow this interpretation, the belief that the Prophet Mohammed commanded the practice continues to persist. For people unfamiliar with the cultural significance of this age-old custom, it is difficult to understand why anyone, especially mothers, would allow this procedure to be performed on their daughters. Janice Boddy offers the following explanation: "While the operation restrains female sexuality, this is not the purpose avowed it by women; informants assert that it is performed on young girls so as to make their bodies clean . . . smooth . . . and pure. . . . Women say a girl who has not been purified through circumcision may not marry, thus may not bear children and attain a position of respect in later years. Circumcision prepares her body for womanhood; it confers on her the right to bear children, while marriage provides her with opportunities to advance her position by giving birth."[1]

Efforts to abolish this practice have met with limited success, especially in rural areas. WHO and UNICEF have pressured governments to ban FGM, and a few African governments have complied. Others have attempted to modify the procedure or provided more sanitary conditions, with little effect. A few national women's groups have been successful in offering alternative rituals, such as Kenya's "circumcision through words." The 1995 International Conference on the Status of Women, held in Beijing, China, declared female genital mutilation a violation of human rights, and Canada and the United States have granted women political asylum based on the likelihood they or their children will face the procedure if forced to return to their homeland. However, some African feminist scholars, though they also want to see FGM abolished, take exception to the West's insensitive condemnation of this practice.

Female genital mutilation is illegal in Canada. However, as more and more people immigrate to Canada from countries where the practice is common, Canadian medical, social, and judicial officials are faced with a dilemma. Some medical personnel have advocated providing safe facilities and licensed medical staff for the surgery, to prevent needless deaths; others adamantly refuse to consider this compromise, citing human rights and legality.

Even anthropologists have difficulty reaching a consensus concerning this issue. Mary Daly calls FGM "a manifestation of planetary patriarchy," and she accuses anthropologists of ignoring or minimizing this ritual under the guise of avoiding cultural judgement. On the other hand, Janice Boddy points out that "Pharaonic circumcision is a symbolic act which brings sharply into focus the fertility potential of women by dramatically de-emphasizing their sexuality. In insisting upon circumcision for their daughters, women assert their social indispensability, an importance which is not as the sexual partners of their husbands, nor . . . as their servants, sexual or otherwise, but as the mothers of men."[2]

Certainly, FGM places anthropologists in an unenviable position: Should they ignore the fundamental principle of anthropology—cultural relativism—to protest this practice as a disregard for basic human rights and dignity? Or should they remain neutral, acting only as advisers and observers? It seems clear that genuine, lasting change must come from within the societies that practise FGM, in the form of social movements led by women, and only after the socioeconomic problems faced by these women are addressed. Outside interference will do little to eradicate this practice, and excessive pressure from foreign agencies will only create a backlash and force the practice underground.

---

[1]Boddy, J. (1989). *Wombs and alien spirits* (p. 55). Madison, WI: University of Wisconsin Press.

[2]Ibid.

Sources:

Boddy, J. (1989). *Wombs and alien spirits.* Madison, WI: University of Wisconsin Press.

Bonvillain, N. (1998). *Women and men: Cultural constructs of gender* (2nd ed., pp. 231–233). Upper Saddle River, NJ: Prentice Hall.

Daly, M. (2000). African genital mutilation: The unspeakable atrocities. In E. Ashton-Jones, G.A. Olson, & M.G. Perry (Eds.), *The gender reader* (pp. 462–485). Needham Heights, MA: Allyn and Bacon.

Gruenbaum, E. (1997). The movement against clitoridectomy and infibulation in Sudan: Public health policy and the women's movement. In C.B. Brettell & C.F. Sargent (Eds.), *Gender in cross-cultural perspectives* (2nd ed., pp. 441–452). Upper Saddle River, NJ: Prentice Hall.

Royal Australian College of Obstetricians and Gynaecologists. (1997). *Female genital mutilation.* Retrieved February 12, 2001, from the World Wide Web: http://www.ranzcog.edu.au/open/womensh/fgm.fgm1.htm.

The simplest and least satisfactory explanation is based on "human nature"—that is, some instinctive horror of incest. It has been documented that human beings raised together have less sexual attraction for one another, but by itself this "familiarity breeds contempt" argument, or **instinct explanation**, simply may substitute the result for the cause. The incest taboo ensures that children and their parents, who are constantly in intimate contact, avoid regarding one another as sexual objects. However, if an instinctive horror of incest exists, we would be hard pressed to account for the far from rare violations of the incest taboo, such as occur in Canadian society (one in three Canadian females and one in six males suffer incest abuse before age 18; 80 percent of the

---

Instinct explanation.   Sometimes known as "familiarity breeds contempt," this explanation suggests long-term association with family members discourages sexual interest.

abusers are fathers, step- or foster fathers, or another relative),[12] or for cases of institutionalized incest, such as requiring the head of the Inca empire in Peru to marry his own sister.

Various **psychoanalytical explanations** of the incest taboo have been advanced at one time or another. Sigmund Freud tried to account for it in his psychoanalytic theory of the unconscious. According to him, the son desires the mother (familiarity breeds attempt), creating a rivalry with the father. Freud called this the Oedipus complex. The son must suppress these feelings or earn the wrath of the father, who is far more powerful than he. Similarly, the attraction of the daughter to the father (the Electra complex) places her in rivalry with her mother. Thus incest avoidance would help, at least to some degree, to maintain family harmony. Freud also suggested that incest taboos prevent social stagnation, by ensuring that individuals participate in social units beyond their direct family. Some psychologists have argued that young children can be emotionally scarred by sexual experiences, which they may interpret as violent and frightening acts of aggression. The incest taboo thus protects children against sexual advances by older members of the family. A closely related theory is that the incest taboo helps prevent girls who are socially and emotionally too young for motherhood from becoming pregnant.

Early students of genetics argued that the incest taboo precluded the harmful effects of inbreeding, leading to the **genetic explanation.** Although this is so, it is also true that, as with domestic animals, inbreeding can increase desired characteristics as well as detrimental ones. Furthermore, undesirable effects show up sooner than without inbreeding, so whatever genes are

---

[12]University of Victoria Sexual Assault Centre. (1999, July 13). *Childhood sexual abuse statistics.* Retrieved March 15, 2001, from the World Wide Web: http://web.uvic.ca/~oursac/statistics.htm.

responsible for them are quickly eliminated from the population. However, a preference for a genetically different mate does tend to maintain a higher level of genetic diversity within a population, and in evolution this generally works to a species' advantage. Without genetic diversity a species cannot adapt biologically to a changing environment when and if this becomes necessary. Bronislaw Malinowski and others have suggested that if incest were practised within families, this would cause tension, competition, and conflict, resulting in an unhealthy environment for children. This **social explanation** or "peace in the family" hypothesis contends that tensions would likely interfere with normal family interactions and functions and could prove disastrous among groups like foragers who rely on cooperation to survive.

A truly convincing explanation of the incest taboo has yet to be advanced. Certainly, there are persistent hints that it may be a cultural elaboration of an underlying biological tendency toward avoidance of inbreeding. Studies of animal behaviour have shown such a tendency to be common among relatively large, long-lived, slow-to-mature, and intelligent species. Humans qualify for membership in this group on all counts. So do a number of other primates, including those most closely related to humans—chimpanzees. Although they exhibit few sexual inhibitions, chimpanzees do tend to avoid breeding with siblings and inbreeding between females and their male offspring. This suggests that the tendency for human children to look for sexual partners outside the group they have been raised in is not just the result of a cultural taboo. Studies that might seem to support this show that children raised together on an Israeli kibbutz, although not required or even encouraged to do so, almost invariably marry outside their group. In this case, however, appearances may be deceiving. There is hardly a kibbutz, for example, without a report of heterosexual relationships between adolescents who have grown up

---

Psychoanalytical explanation.   Incest taboos are an attempt by offspring to repress their sexual feelings toward their parents of the opposite gender. **> Genetic explanation.**   Inbreeding is forbidden because cultural groups recognize the potential for impaired offspring. **> Social explanation.**   Sometimes known as the "peace in the family" theory, this explanation suggests that competition over mates would interfere with normal family functions, such as acquiring adequate food resources.

Although children raised together on an Israeli kibbutz rarely marry one another, it may not be because of any instinctive desire to avoid mating with people who are close. Rather, they marry outside their group because service in the military takes them out of their kibbutz, where they meet new people, precisely when they are most likely to begin thinking about marriage.

together since infancy.[13] As for actual marriage, most Israeli youths leave the kibbutz in their late teens for service in the armed forces. Thus, they are away from the kibbutz precisely when they are most ready to consider marriage. Consequently, those most available as potential spouses often are from other parts of the country.

An even greater challenge to the "biological avoidance" theory, however, is raised by detailed census records made in Roman Egypt that conclusively demonstrate that brother–sister marriages were not only common but also preferred

by ordinary members of the farming class.[14] Moreover, anthropologist Nancy Thornhill found that, in a sample of 129 societies, only 57 had specific rules against parent–child or sibling incest (so much for the universality of the incest taboo). Twice that number, 114, had explicit rules to control activity with cousins, in-laws, or both.[15]

If indeed a biological basis for inbreeding avoidance exists among humans, it clearly is far from completely effective in its operation. Nor is its mechanism understood. Moreover, it still leaves us with questions such as these: Why do some societies have an explicit taboo while others do not? And why do some societies not only condone certain kinds of incest but even favour them?

Endogamy and Exogamy

Whatever its cause, the utility of the incest taboo can be seen by examining its effects on social structure. Closely related to prohibitions against incest are rules against **endogamy,** or marriage within a particular group of individuals (cousins and in-laws, for example). If the group is defined as an individual's immediate family alone, then cultures generally prohibit or at least discourage endogamy and practise or at least encourage **exogamy,** or marriage outside the group. Yet a society that practises exogamy at one level may practise endogamy at another. Among the Trobriand Islanders, for example, each individual has to marry outside of his or her own clan and lineage (exogamy). However, since eligible sex partners are found within their own community, village endogamy, although not obligatory, is commonly practised. This is true of the Chipewyan in northern Canada; their young people are most likely to choose a mate within the community.[16]

---

[13]Leavitt, G.C. (1990). Sociobiological explanations of incest avoidance: A critical review of evidential claims. *American Anthropologist, 92,* 973.

[14]Ibid., p. 982.

[15]Thornhill, N. (1993). Quoted in W.A. Haviland & R.J. Gordon (Eds.), *Talking about people* (p. 127). Mountain View, CA: Mayfield.

[16]Oswalt, W.H., & Neely, S. (1996). *This land was theirs: A study of North American Indians* (5th ed.). Mountain View, CA: Mayfield.

Endogamy. Marriage within a particular group or category of individuals. **> Exogamy.** Marriage outside the group.

Interestingly, considerable variation exists among societies as to which relatives are or are not covered by exogamy rules. In Europe, for example, the Catholic Church prohibits marriages to first cousins, and some U.S. states still prohibit first cousin marriages. In Canada, first cousins are allowed to marry, but marriages between uncles and nieces and aunts and nephews are prohibited.[17] In numerous other societies, first cousins are preferred spouses.

In the 19th century, Sir Edward Tylor theorized that alternatives to inbreeding were either "marrying out or being killed out, now known as the **cooperation explanation**."[18] Our ancestors, he suggested, discovered the advantage of intermarriage to create bonds of friendship. Claude Lévi-Strauss elaborated on this premise. He saw exogamy as the basis of a distinction between early hominine life in isolated endogamous groups and the life of *Homo sapiens* in a supportive society with an accumulating culture. Alliances with other groups, established and strengthened by marriage ties, make possible a sharing of culture. Building on Lévi-Strauss's work, anthropologist Yehudi Cohen suggests exogamy was an important means of promoting trade between groups, thereby ensuring access to needed goods and resources not otherwise available. Noting that incest taboos necessitating exogamy are generally most widely extended in the least complex of human societies but do not extend beyond parents and siblings in industrialized societies, he argues that as formal governments and other institutions have come to control trade, the need for extended taboos has been removed. Indeed, he suggests that this may have reached the point where the incest taboo is becoming obsolete altogether.

In a roundabout way, exogamy also helps to explain some exceptions to the incest taboo, such as that of obligatory brother and sister marriage within the royal families of ancient Egypt, the Inca empire, and Hawaii. Members of these royal families were considered semidivine, and their very sacredness kept them from marrying mere mortals. The brother and sister married so as *not* to share their godliness, thereby maintaining the "purity" of the royal line, not to mention control of royal property. By the same token, in Roman Egypt, where property was inherited by women as well as men and where the relationship between land and people was particularly tight, brother–sister marriages among the farming class acted to prevent fragmentation of a family's holdings.

The Distinction between Marriage and Mating

Having defined marriage in terms of sexual access, we must at this point make clear the distinction between systems of marriage and mating. All animals, including humans, mate—some for life and some not, some with a single individual of the opposite sex, and some with several. Mates are secured and held solely through individual effort, as opposed to marriage, which is a right society confers. Even among the Nayar, where marriage seems to involve little else than a sexual relationship, a woman's husband is legally obligated to provide her with gifts at specified intervals. Nor may a woman legally have sex with a man she is not married to. Thus, while mating is biological, marriage is cultural.

The distinction between marriage and mating may be seen by looking, briefly, at practices in contemporary North American society, where **monogamy**—the taking of a single spouse—is the only legally recognized form of marriage. Not only are other forms not legally sanctioned, but also systems of inheritance, whereby property and wealth are transferred from one generation to the next, are predicated on the institution of monogamous marriage. Mating patterns, by contrast, are frequently *not* monogamous.

---

[17]University of Manitoba. (1998, November). *Exogamy and incest prohibitions: Brian Schwimmer*. Retrieved April 12, 2001, from the World Wide Web: http://www.umanitoba.ca/anthropology/tutor/marriage/incest.html.

[18]Quoted in R.M. Keesing (1976), *Cultural anthropology: A contemporary perspective* (p. 286). New York: Holt, Rinehart and Winston.

Cooperation explanation. Forcing people outside their familial unit. **> Monogamy.** Marriage in which an individual has one spouse.

In Canada, as in most Western countries, monogamy is the only legally recognized form of marriage.

Among primates in general, monogamous mating patterns are not common. Although some smaller species of South American monkeys, a few island-dwelling populations of leaf-eating Old World monkeys, and all of the smaller apes (gibbons and siamangs) do mate for life with but one individual of the opposite sex, none of these are closely related to human beings. Nor do "monogamous" primates ever display the degree of anatomical differences between males and females characteristic of our closest primate relatives or of our own ancient ancestors. Thus it is not likely the human species began its career as one with monogamous mating patterns. Certainly, we cannot say (as some have tried to assert) the human species is, by nature, monogamous in its mating behaviour.

Common-Law Marriages

In Canada, common-law marriages or partnerships are legally recognized after a couple has been living together for one year. Common-law partnerships are defined as "the relationship between two persons who are cohabiting in a conjugal relationship, having so cohabited for a period of at least one year."[19] These couples enjoy all the rights and responsibilities of husbands and wives, including pension plans, old age security, taxation, and so on. The number of Canadians entering into common-law relationships continues to increase: Close to 1.2 million couples lived in common-law relationships in 2001, up 20 percent from 1995.[20] Quebec leads the provinces in common-law relationships. Census Canada also found that common-law families have grown more than any other type of family, with one couple in seven living common-law in 1996, compared with one in nine in 1991.

Same-Sex Marriages

Although marriage is defined in terms of a continuing sexual relationship between a man and woman, the cultural nature of gender is such that the "man" may in fact be a female or the "woman" a male. Thus, marriages between individuals of the same sex may be regarded as proper and normal. In some cases these marriages provide a way to deal with problems for which opposite-sex marriage offers no satisfactory solution. This is true for the woman/woman marriage practice sanctioned in many societies of sub-Saharan Africa, although in no society does it involve more than a small minority of all women.

The Nandi of western Kenya are a pastoral people who also do considerable farming.[21] Control of most property and the primary means of production—livestock and land—is exclusively in the hands of men and may be transmitted only to their male heirs. Since polygyny (men have more than one spouse at a time) is the preferred form of marriage, a man's property is normally divided equally among his wives for their sons to inherit. Each wife has her own house where she lives with her children, but all are under the

---

[19]Bill C-23, subsection 3(3). Retrieved March 3, 2001, from the World Wide Web: http://www.parl.gc.ca/36/2/parlbus/chambers/house/bills/government/c-23/c-23_1/90093be.html.

[20]Jacobs, M. (2002, July 17). Living together replacing "I do" for many. *Edmonton Sun*.

[21]The following is based on R.S. Obler (1980), Is the female husband a man? Woman/woman marriage among the Nandi of Kenya. *Ethnology, 19*, 69–88.

authority of the woman's husband. In such situations, the position of a woman who bears no sons is difficult; not only does she not help perpetuate her husband's male line—a major concern among the Nandi—but she has no one to inherit the proper share of her husband's property.

To get around these problems, a woman of advanced age who bore no sons may become a female husband by marrying a young woman. The purpose of this arrangement is for the wife to provide the male heirs her female husband could not. To accomplish this, the woman's wife enters into a sexual relationship with a man other than her female husband's male husband; usually it is one of his male relatives. No other obligations exist between this woman and her male sex partner, and her female husband is recognized as the social and legal father of any children born under these conditions.

In keeping with her role as female husband, this woman is expected to abandon her female gender identity and, ideally, dress and behave as a man. In practice, the ideal is not completely achieved, for the habits of a lifetime are difficult to reverse. Generally, it is in the context of domestic activities, which are most highly symbolic of female identity, that female husbands most completely assume a male identity.

The individuals who are parties to woman/woman marriages enjoy several advantages. By assuming a male identity, a barren or sonless woman raises her status considerably and even achieves near equality with men. A woman who marries a female husband is usually one who is unable to make a good marriage, often because she has lost face as a consequence of premarital pregnancy. By marrying a female husband, she too raises her status and also secures legitimacy for her children. Moreover, a female husband is usually less harsh and demanding, spends more time with her, and allows her a greater say in decision making than a male husband does. Her one prohibition is engaging in sexual activity with her marriage partner; in fact, female husbands are expected to abandon sexual activity altogether, even with their male husband, to whom they remain married even though the women now have their own wives.

This type of same-sex marriage among the Nandi is an example of a socially sanctioned practice. The same cannot be said for same-sex couples in North America, where the struggle for equality for same-sex couples has been a long and difficult road. In Canada, Bill C-23, the Modernization of Benefits and Obligations Act, passed April 11, 2000, extended the rights of common-law partnerships to same-sex couples. This means same-sex couples are viewed as common-law partnerships, enjoying the same benefits, such as pension plans and taxation. However, Bill C-23 still defines marriage as the lawful union of one man and one woman to the exclusion of all others, and some provinces, such as Alberta, passed laws to ignore any federal reference to same-sex marriages.

In December 2000, Rev. Brent Hawkes of the Metropolitan Community Church in Toronto

Since April 2000, same-sex couples in Canada have been recognized as common-law partnerships, enjoying the same benefits as their heterosexual counterparts. However, many obstacles must be overcome before true equality is achieved.

read the first "banns" for two same-sex couples wishing to get married. In keeping with Christian customs, if the banns giving notice of the intent to marry are read three Sundays in a row, then a couple can be legally married. On the second Sunday, another minister protested, calling the whole venture "lawless and godless." Reverend Hawkes overruled the protests and read the banns a third Sunday. The two couples were married on January 14, 2001, despite repeated assertions by Ontario's Consumer and Commercial Relations Minister Bob Runciman that the province would not legally recognize same-sex marriages, regardless of what the church does. This episode was only one example of a growing movement to permit same-sex couples to legally marry.

On June 10, 2003, Ontario's Court of Appeal ruled that the current definition of marriage, as between a man and a woman, was unconstitutional. The court redefined marriage as a union between two people, opening the door for gays and lesbians to legally marry in Ontario. Despite angry protests from conservative and religious quarters, Jean Chrétien and his federal government quickly announced that they accepted Ontario's definition of marriage. At the time of this writing, same-sex couples from across North America and even overseas are flocking to Ontario and British Columbia to legally marry.

In other parts of the world, the movement is also gaining strength: In 1989 Denmark recognized same-sex partnerships, essentially sanctioning gay marriages, and in April 2001 the Netherlands passed a law allowing same-sex couples to marry, giving them the same rights to adoption as heterosexual couples. By 2001 Norway, Sweden, and Iceland had recognized same-sex registered partnerships, and Italy, Israel, and Spain are considering similar legislation. Even in the United States, Vermont has passed legislation that provides same-sex couples with the legal rights, benefits, and responsibilities of heterosexual couples, Hawaii allows adults who cannot legally marry to register as domestic partners, and California is considering legalizing civil unions between same-sex couples.[22]

Those opposed to same-sex marriage frequently argue that marriage has always been between one man and one woman and that only heterosexual relations are normal. Yet, as we have seen, neither assertion is true. Anthropologists have documented same-sex marriages in many human groups, where they are regarded as acceptable under appropriate circumstances. As for homosexual behaviour, it is quite common in the animal world (including among humans).[23] The only difference between humans and other animals is that humans specify when, where, how, and with whom it is appropriate.

▲▽▲▽▲▽▲▽▲▽▲▽▲▽▲▽▲▽▲▽▲▽▲▽▲▽▲▽▲

FORMS OF MARRIAGE

Monogamy is the form of marriage North Americans are most familiar with. It is also the most common, but for economic rather than social and moral reasons. A man must be fairly wealthy to afford **polygyny,** or marriage to more than one wife. Among the Kapauku of western New Guinea, the ideal is to have as many wives as possible, and a woman actually urges her husband to spend money on acquiring additional wives.[24] She even has the legal right to divorce him if she can prove he has money for bride-prices and refuses to remarry. As we saw in Chapter 2, wives are desirable because they work in the fields and care for pigs, by which wealth is measured, but not all men are wealthy enough to afford bride-prices for multiple wives.

---

[22]CBC News. Indepth Backgrounder. (2001). *The fight for gay rights: Canada timeline: Owen Woods.* (p. 2). Retrieved March 3, 2001, from the World Wide Web: http://cbc.ca/news/indepth/background/gayrights.html.

[23]Kirkpatrick, R.C. (2000). The evolution of human homosexual behavior. *Current Anthropology, 41,* 384.

[24]Pospisil, L. (1963). *The Kapauku Papuans of west New Guinea.* New York: Holt, Rinehart and Winston.

Polygyny.   The marriage custom in which a man has two or more wives simultaneously; a form of polygamy.

Janice Boddy

Janice Boddy (Ph.D., UBC) is a professor of anthropology at the University of Toronto. Boddy's research topics range from gender roles and constructs, anthropology of "the body," ritual and religion, feminist theory, social organization and social change, to identity politics. However, it is her research into the meaning of ritual practices such as female circumcision that has given Boddy an international reputation.

Boddy's work on female circumcision has provided students and the general public with an insightful, balanced interpretation of this very difficult gender issue. Her 1989 publication *Wombs and Alien Spirits* is considered a valuable contribution to the ethnographic literature on female circumcision. In this anthropological examination of the Zar cult in northern Sudan, Boddy provides a thought-provoking discussion of why the practice of female circumcision occurs and why it continues even in the face of international condemnation. She urges colleagues, government officials, and the general public to reserve condemnation of the practice until we understand the underlying meanings and values that maintain this tradition. Unlike many contemporary anthropologists, Boddy touts the value of cultural relativism, especially when dealing with such a sensitive issue, as a necessary first step toward a true universalism, not just a Western universalism.

Her most recent publication, "Violence Embodied? Female Circumcision, Gender Politics and Cultural Aesthetics," in *Rethinking Violence Against Women* (1998), provides an "awe-inspiring analysis of circumcision in a cultural context."[1] (Rajani, 2001). In this article Boddy examines female genital mutilation using a Sudanese case study, but more important, she also examines the nature of Western moral imperialism and its claims to cultural superiority. She questions the Western agenda to impose moral ideals on other cultures in the name of universal basic human rights.

In her current work, Boddy is examining the failure of the British administration in colonial Sudan to eradicate the practice of pharaonic circumcision. Her approach is both historical and anthropological, examining the motives, methods, and assumptions of colonial agents who undertook to reform "women's customs."

----

[1]Rajani, A. (2001). *FGM bibliography*. Retrieved June 26, 2001, from the World Wide Web: http://www.scar.utoronto.ca/~97rajani/biblio.html.

Sources:

Department of Anthropology, University of Toronto. (2001). *Janice Boddy*. Retrieved June 26, 2001, from the World Wide Web: http://www.scar.utoronto.ca/acad/bios/data/boddy.html.

Rajani, A. (2001). *FGM bibliography*. Retrieved June 26, 2001, from the World Wide Web: http://www.scar.utoronto.ca/~97rajani/biblio.html.

Among the Turkana, a pastoral nomadic people of northern Kenya, the number of animals at a family's disposal is directly related to the number of adult women available to care for them. The more wives a man has, the more women there are to look after the livestock and the more substantial are the family's holdings. Thus, it is not uncommon for a man's first wife to search for another woman to marry her husband. Again, a substantial bride-price is required for marriage, and only men of wealth and prominence can afford more than one wife.

Although monogamy may be the most common form of marriage around the world, it is not the most preferred. That distinction goes to polygyny, which is favoured by about 80 to 85 percent of the world's societies. Even in North America thousands of people in the Rocky Mountains live in polygynous households. In spite of its illegality, regional law enforcement officials have adopted a "live and let live" attitude toward polygyny. Nor are those involved in such marriages uneducated. One woman—a lawyer and one of nine co-wives—expresses her attitude as follows;

> I see it as the ideal way for a woman to have a career and children. In our family, the women can help each other care for the children. Women in monogamous relationships don't have that luxury. As I see it, if this life style didn't already exist, it would have to be invented to accommodate career women.[25]

Polygyny is particularly common in cultures that support themselves by growing crops and where women do the bulk of the farmwork. Under these conditions, women are valued both as workers and as childbearers. Because the labour of wives in polygynous households generates wealth and little support is required from husbands, the wives have a strong bargaining position within the household. Often, they have considerable freedom of movement and some economic independence from the sale of crops. Commonly, each wife within the household lives with her children in her own dwelling, apart from her co-wives and husband who occupy other houses within a larger household compound (note that the terms *house* and *household* need not be synonymous; a household may consist of several houses together, as here). Because of this residential autonomy, fathers are usually remote from their sons, who grow up among women. This is the sort of setting conducive to the development of aggressiveness in adult males, who must prove their masculinity. As a consequence, a high value is often placed on military glory, and one reason for going to war is to capture women, who then may become a warrior's co-wives. This wealth-increasing pattern is found in its fullest elaboration in sub-Saharan Africa, although it is known elsewhere as well (the Kapauku are another case). Moreover, it is still intact in the world today, because its wealth-generating properties at the household level make it an economically productive system.[26]

---

[25]Johnson, D. (1996). Polygamists emerge from secrecy, seeking not just peace but respect. In W.A. Haviland & R.J. Gordon (Eds.), *Talking about people* (2nd ed., pp. 129–131). Mountain View, CA: Mayfield.

[26]White, D.R. (1988). Rethinking polygyny: Co-wives, codes and cultural systems. *Current Anthropology, 29,* 529–572.

In cultures practising wealth-generating polygyny, most men and women do enter into polygynous marriages, although some can do this earlier in life than others. This practice is made possible by a female-biased sex ratio and/or by a mean age at marriage for females significantly below that for males (this creates a cohort of women looking for husbands larger than the cohort of men looking for wives). By contrast, in cultures where men are more heavily involved in productive work, generally only a small minority of marriages are polygynous. Under these circumstances, women are more dependent on men for support, so they are valued as childbearers more than for the work they do. This is commonly the case in pastoral nomadic societies where men are the primary owners and tenders of livestock. This makes women especially vulnerable if they prove incapable of bearing children, which is one reason a man may seek another wife. Another reason for a man to take on secondary wives is to demonstrate his high position. But where men do most of the productive work, they must work exceptionally hard to support more than one wife, and few actually do so. Usually, it is the exceptional hunter, a male shaman ("medicine man") in a food-foraging culture, or a particularly wealthy man in an agricultural or pastoral society who is most apt to practise polygyny. When he does, it is usually of the *sororal* type, with the co-wives being sisters. Having already lived together before marriage, the sisters continue to do so with their husband, instead of occupying separate dwellings of their own.

Although not all that common, polygyny was also evident among First Nations groups, particularly on the northern Plains of Canada. In the 17th century, expansion of the fur trade and an influx of horses onto the Plains led to a new economic order that required changes in traditional marriage patterns. Equestrian hunters, such as the Blackfoot, were able to kill many bison in a short period of time. However, the hides had to be tanned fairly quickly or they lost their value and could not be sold. This was too much work for any one woman. Thus hunters took more than one wife. "The more wives a man had, the more women's labour he controlled. His wives provided him with additional children whose labour he also managed. Sons helped in hunting and raiding, and daughters aided their mothers in tanning hides."[27] To this end, polygyny on the Plains was viewed as an economic feature of production, rather than a social construct.

Although monogamy and polygyny are the most common forms of marriage in the world today, other forms do occur, however rarely. **Polyandry,** the marriage of one woman to two or more men simultaneously, is known in only a few societies, perhaps in part because men's life expectancy is shorter than women's, and male infant mortality is high, so a surplus of men in a society is unlikely. Where sex ratios are balanced, many women are likely to remain unmarried. Another reason for polyandry's rarity is that it limits a man's descendants more than any other pattern. Fewer than a dozen societies are known to have favoured this form of marriage, but they involve people as widely separated from one another as the eastern Inuit, Marquesan Islanders of Polynesia, and Tibetans. In Tibet, where inheritance is in the male line and arable land is limited, the marriage of brothers to a single woman averts the danger of constantly subdividing farmlands among all the sons of any one landholder. Unlike monogamy, it also restrains population growth, thereby avoiding increased pressures on resources. Finally, it provides the household with an adequate pool of male labour. For tripartite economies of farming, herding, and trading, trifraternal polyandry is highly valued, as it allows the three brothers who are co-husbands to pursue all three options at once.[28]

Group marriage, in which several men and women have sexual access to one another, also occurs rarely. Even in recent communal groups, among young people seeking alternatives to traditional marriage, group marriage seems a transitory phenomenon, despite the publicity it garners.

Shown here is a polyandrous family, a woman with her two husbands.

The Levirate and the Sororate

If a husband dies, leaving a wife and children, it is often the custom that the wife marries one of the brothers of the dead man. This custom, called the **levirate,** not only provides social security for the widow and her children but also is a way for the husband's family to maintain their rights over her sexuality and her future children: It acts to preserve relationships previously established. When a man marries the sister of his dead wife, it is called the **sororate.** In societies that have the levirate and sororate, the relationship between the two families is maintained even after a spouse's death, and in such cultures, an adequate supply of brothers and sisters is generally ensured by the structure of the kinship system (discussed in Chapter 9), whereby individuals North Americans would call "cousins" are classified as brothers and sisters.

---

[27]McMillan, A.D. (1988). *Native peoples and cultures of Canada: An anthropological overview* (pp. 140–141). Vancouver: Douglas and McIntyre.

[28]Levine, N.E., & Silk, J.B. (1997). Why polyandry fails. *Current Anthropology, 38,* 375–398.

Polyandry.   The marriage of one woman to two or more men simultaneously. **> Group marriage.**   Marriage in which several men and women have sexual access to one another. **> Levirate.**   The marriage custom whereby a widow marries a brother of her dead husband. **> Sororate.**   The marriage custom whereby a widower marries his dead wife's sister.

Serial Monogamy

A form of marriage increasingly common in North American society today is **serial monogamy**, whereby the man or the woman marries or lives with a series of partners in succession. Currently, close to 40 percent of first marriages in Canada end in divorce, and some experts project that two-thirds of recent marriages will not last.[29] Upon dissolution of a marriage, the children more often than not remain with the mother. This pattern is an outgrowth of one sociologists and anthropologists first described among people living in the West Indies and low-income urban African Americans in the United States. Early in life, women begin to bear children by men who are not married to them. To support herself and her children, a woman must look for work outside the household, but to do so she must seek help from other kin, most commonly her mother. As a consequence, households are frequently headed by women (on the average, about 32 percent are so headed in the West Indies). After a number of years, however, an unmarried woman usually does marry a man, who may or may not be the father of some or all of her children. Under poverty conditions, where this pattern has been most common, women are driven to seek this male support, owing to the difficulties of supporting themselves and their children while fulfilling their domestic obligations. This pattern is also evident among urban First Nations women in Western Canada.

In North America, with the increasing necessity for women to seek work outside the home, and rising divorce rates, serial monogamy is becoming more common among middle-class people. In most divorce cases, it is the women who assume responsibility for any children; almost one in every five children in Canada lived with a lone parent in 1996, four out of five of those children with a female parent.[30] Frequently isolated from kin or other assistance, women in single-parent households (which now outnumber nuclear family households) commonly find it difficult to cope. Within a year following divorce, the standard of living for women drops dramatically, whereas that of men *increases*. To be sure, fathers of children are usually expected to provide child support, but failure of fathers to live up to their obligations is far from rare. One solution for unmarried women is to marry (often, to remarry) to get the assistance of another adult.

Choice of Spouse

The Western egalitarian ideal that an individual should be free to marry whomever he or she chooses is an unusual arrangement, certainly not one that is universally embraced. However desirable such an ideal may be in the abstract, it is fraught with difficulties and likely contributes to the apparent instability of marital relationships in modern North American society. Part of the problem is the emphasis placed on the importance of youth and glamour, especially of women and romantic love. Female youth and beauty are perhaps most glaringly exploited by the women's fashion, cosmetics, and salon industries, but movies, television, and the recorded-music business generally do not lag far behind, nor do advertisements for cigarettes, beer, automobiles, and a host of other products that make liberal use of young, glamorous women. As anthropologist Jules Henry once observed, "even men's wear and toiletries could not be marketed as efficiently without a young, pretty woman looking at a man wearing a stylish shirt or sniffing at a man wearing a deodorant."[31] By no means are all North Americans taken in by this, but it does influence marriage decisions, based on trivial and transient characteristics. In contrast, in most other parts of the world, marriage and the establishment of a family are considered far too important to be left to the whims of young people. The marriage of two individuals expected to spend their whole lives together and raise their children together is

---

[29]Stacey, J. (1990). *Brave new families* (pp. 15, 286, n. 46). New York: Basic Books.

[30]Statistics Canada. (2001). *Families, households and housing*. Retrieved March 3, 2001, from the World Wide Web: http://www.statcan.ca/english/pgdb/people/famili.htm.

[31]Henry, J. (1966). The metaphysic of youth, beauty, and romantic love. In S. Farber & R. Wilson (Eds.), *The challenge to women*. New York: Basic Books.

Serial monogamy. A marriage form in which a man or a woman marries or lives with a series of partners in succession.

incidental to the more serious matter of making allies of two families through the marriage bond. Marriage involves a transfer of rights between families, including rights to property and rights over the children, as well as sexual rights. Thus, marriages tend to be arranged for the economic and political advantage of the family unit.

Arranged marriages are not commonplace in North American society, but they do occur. Well into the 20th century, young Canadian women, especially in rural regions, found themselves "matched" to a male neighbour in need of someone to keep house and help with farmwork. Arranged marriages still occur in Canada, particularly among first-generation immigrants from India. Among ethnic minorities, they may serve to preserve traditional values people fear might otherwise be lost. Among families of wealth and power, marriages may be arranged by segregating their children in private schools and carefully steering them toward "proper" marriages. The following Original Study illustrates how marriages may be arranged in societies where such practices are commonplace.

ORIGINAL STUDY

Arranging Marriage in India

Serena Nanda

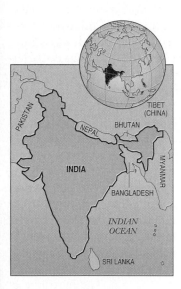

Sister and doctor brother-in-law invite correspondence from North Indian professionals only, for a beautiful, talented, sophisticated, intelligent sister, 5'3", slim, M.A. in textile design, father a senior civil officer. Would prefer immigrant doctors, between 26–29 years. Reply with full details and returnable photo.

A well-settled uncle invites matrimonial correspondence from slim, fair, educated South Indian girl, for his nephew, 25 years, smart, M.B.A., green card holder, 5'6". Full particulars with returnable photo appreciated.

—Matrimonial Advertisements, India Abroad

Six years [after my first field trip] I returned to India to again do fieldwork, this time among the middle class in Bombay (now known as Mumbai), a modern, sophisticated city. From the experience of my earlier visit, I decided to include a study of arranged marriages in my project. By this time I had met many Indian couples whose marriages had been arranged and who seemed very happy. Particularly in contrast to the fate of many of my married friends in the United States who were already in the process of divorce the positive aspects of arranged marriages appeared to me to outweigh the negatives. In fact, I thought I might even participate in arranging a marriage myself. I had been fairly successful in the United States in "fixing up" many of my friends, and I was confident that my matchmaking skills could be easily applied to this new situation, once I learned the basic rules. "After all," I thought, "how complicated can it be? People want pretty much the same things in a marriage whether it is in India or America."

An opportunity presented itself almost immediately. A friend from my previous Indian trip was in the process of arranging for the marriage of her eldest son. In India there is a perceived shortage of "good boys," and since my friend's family was eminently respectable and the boy himself personable, well educated, and nice looking, I was sure that by the end of my year's fieldwork, we would have found a match.

The basic rule seems to be that a family's reputation is most important. It is understood that matches would be arranged only within the same caste and general social class, although some crossing of subcastes is permissible if the class positions of the bride's and groom's families are similar. Although dowry is now prohibited by law in India, extensive gift exchanges took place with every marriage. Even when the boy's family do not "make demands," every girl's family nevertheless feels the obligation to give the traditional gifts, to the girl, to the boy, and to the boy's family. Particularly when the couple would be living in the joint family— that is, with the boy's parents and his married brothers and their families, as well as with unmarried siblings—which is still very common even among the urban, upper-middle class in India, the girl's parents are anxious to establish smooth relations between their family and that of the boy. Offering the proper gifts, even when not called "dowry," is often an important factor in influencing the relationship between the bride's and groom's families and perhaps, also, the treatment of the bride in her new home.

In a society where divorce is still a scandal and where, in fact, the divorce rate is exceedingly low, an arranged marriage is the beginning of a lifetime relationship not just between the bride and groom but between their families as well. Thus, while a girl's looks are important, her character is even more so, for she is being judged as a prospective daughter-in-law as much as a prospective bride. Where she would be living in a joint family, as was the case with my friend, the girl's ability to get along harmoniously in a family is perhaps the single most important quality in assessing her suitability.

My friend is a highly esteemed wife, mother, and daughter-in-law. She is religious, soft-spoken, modest, and deferential. She rarely gossips and never quarrels, two qualities highly desirable in a woman. A family that has the reputation for gossip and conflict among its womenfolk will not find it easy to get good wives for their sons. Parents will not want to send their daughter to a house in which there is conflict.

My friend's family were originally from North India. They had lived in Bombay, where her husband owned a business, for forty years. The family had delayed in seeking a match for their eldest son because he had been an Air Force pilot for several years, stationed in such remote places that it had seemed fruitless to try to find a girl who would be willing to accompany him. In their social class, a military career, despite its economic security, has little prestige and is considered a drawback in finding a suitable bride. Many families would not allow their daughters to marry a man in an occupation so potentially dangerous and which requires so much moving around.

The son had recently left the military and joined his father's business. Since he was a college graduate, modern, and well traveled, from such a good family, and, I thought, quite handsome, it seemed to me that he, or rather his family, was in a position to pick and choose. I said as much to my friend.

While she agreed that there were many advantages on their side, she also said, "We must keep in mind that my son is both short and dark; these are drawbacks in finding the right match." While the boy's height had not escaped my notice, "dark" seemed to me inaccurate; I would have called him "wheat" colored perhaps, and in any case, I did not realize that color would be a consideration. I discovered, however, that while a boy's skin color is a less important consideration than a girl's, it is still a factor.

An important source of contacts in trying to arrange her son's marriage was my friend's social club in Bombay. Many of the women had daughters of the right age, and some had already expressed an interest in my friend's son. I was most enthusiastic about the possibilities of one particular family who had five daughters, all of whom were pretty, demure, and well educated. Their mother had told my friend, "You can have your pick for your son, whichever one of my daughters appeals to you most."

I saw a match in sight. "Surely," I said to my friend, "we will find one there. Let's go visit and make our choice." But my friend held back; she did not seem to share my enthusiasm, for reasons I could not then fathom.

When I kept pressing for an explanation of her reluctance, she admitted, "See, Serena, here is the problem. The family has so many daughters, how will they be able to provide nicely for any of them? We are not making any demands, but still, with so many daughters to marry off, one wonders whether she will even be able to make a proper wedding. Since this is our eldest son, it's best if we marry him to a girl who is the only daughter, then the wedding will truly be a gala affair." I argued that surely the quality of the girls themselves made up for any deficiency in the elaborateness of the wedding. My friend admitted this point but still seemed reluctant to proceed.

"Is there something else," I asked her, "some factor I have missed?" "Well," she finally said, "there is one other thing. They have one daughter already married and living in Bombay. The mother is always complaining to me that the girl's in-laws don't let her visit her own family often enough. So it makes me wonder, will she be that kind of mother who always wants her daughter at her own home? This will prevent the girl from adjusting to our house. It is not a good thing." And so, this family of five daughters was dropped as a possibility.

Somewhat disappointed, I nevertheless respected my friend's reasoning and geared up for the next prospect. This was also the daughter of a woman in my friend's social club. There was clear interest in this family and I could see why. The family's reputation was excellent; in fact, they came from a subcaste slightly higher than my friend's own. The girl, who was an only daughter, was pretty and well educated and had a brother studying in the United States. Yet, after expressing an interest to me in this family, all talk of them suddenly died down and the search began elsewhere.

"What happened to that girl as a prospect?" I asked one day. "You never mention her any more. She is so pretty and so educated, what did you find wrong?"

"She is too educated. We've decided against it. My husband's father saw the girl on the bus the other day and thought her forward. A girl who 'roams about' the city by herself is not the girl for our family." My disappointment this time was even greater, as I thought the son would have liked the girl very much. But then I thought, my friend is right, a girl who is going to live in a joint family cannot be too independent or she will make life miserable for everyone. I also learned that if the family of the girl has even a slightly higher social status than the family of the boy, the bride may think herself too good for them, and this too will cause problems. Later my friend admitted to me that this had been an important factor in her decision not to pursue the match.

The next candidate was the daughter of a client of my friend's husband. When the client learned that the family was looking for a match for their son, he said, "Look no further, we have a daughter." This man then invited my friends to dinner to see the girl. He had already seen their son at the office and decided that "he liked the boy." We all went together for tea, rather than dinner—it was less of a commitment—and while we were there, the girl's mother showed us around the house. The girl was studying for her exams and was briefly introduced to us.

After we left, I was anxious to hear my friend's opinion. While her husband liked the family very much and was impressed with his client's business accomplishments and reputation, the wife didn't like the girl's looks. "She is short, no doubt, which is an important plus point, but she is also fat and wears glasses." My friend obviously thought she could do better for her son and asked her husband to make his excuses to his client by saying that they had decided to postpone the boy's marriage indefinitely.

By this time almost six months had passed and I was becoming impatient. What I had thought would be an easy matter to arrange was turning out to be quite complicated. I began to believe that between my friend's desire for a girl who was modest enough to fit into her joint family, yet attractive and educated enough to be an acceptable partner for her son, she would not find anyone suitable. My friend laughed at my impatience: "Don't be so much in a hurry," she said. "You Americans want everything done so quickly. You get married quickly and then just as quickly get divorced. Here we take marriage more seriously. We must take all the factors into account. It is not enough for us to learn by our mistakes. This is too serious a business. If a mistake is made we have not only ruined the life of our son or daughter, but we have spoiled the reputation of our family as well. And that will make it much harder for their brothers and sisters to get married. So we must be very careful."

What she said was true and I promised myself to be more patient, though it was not easy. I had really hoped and expected that the match would be made before my year in India was up. But it was not to be. When I left India my friend seemed no further along in finding a suitable match for her son than when I had arrived.

Two years later, I returned to India and still my friend had not found a girl for her son. By this time, he was close to thirty, and I think she was a little worried. Since she knew I had friends all over India, and I was going to be there for a year, she asked me to "help her in this work" and keep an eye out for someone suitable. I was flattered that my judgement was respected, but knowing now how complicated the process was, I had lost my earlier confidence as a matchmaker. Nevertheless, I promised that I would try.

It was almost at the end of my year's stay in India that I met a family with a marriageable daughter whom I felt might be a good possibility for my friend's son. The girl's father was related to a good friend of mine and by coincidence came from the same village as my friend's husband. This new family had a successful business in a medium-sized city in central India and were from the same subcaste as my friend. The daughter was pretty and chic; in fact, she had studied fashion design in college. Her parents would not allow her to go off by herself to any of the major cities in India where she could make a career, but they had compromised with her wish to work by allowing her to run a small dress-making boutique from their home. In spite of her desire to have a career, the daughter was both modest and home-loving and had had a traditional, sheltered upbringing. She had only one other sister, already married, and a brother who was in his father's business.

I mentioned the possibility of a match with my friend's son. The girl's parents were most interested. Although their daughter was not eager to marry just yet, the idea of living in Bombay—a sophisticated, extremely fashion-conscious city where she could continue her education in clothing design—was a great inducement. I gave the girl's father my friend's address and suggested that when they went to Bombay on some business or whatever, they look up the boy's family.

Returning to Bombay on my way to New York, I told my friend of this newly discovered possibility. She seemed to feel there was potential but, in spite of my urging, would not make any moves herself. She rather preferred to wait for the girl's family to call upon them. I hoped something would come of this introduction, though by now I had learned to rein in my optimism.

A year later I received a letter from my friend. The family had indeed come to visit Bombay, and their daughter and my friend's daughter, who were near in age, had become very good friends. During that year, the two girls had frequently visited each other. I thought things looked promising.

Last week I received an invitation to a wedding: My friend's son and the girl were getting married. Since I had found the match, my presence was particularly requested at the wedding. I was thrilled. Success at last! As I prepared to leave for India, I began thinking, "Now, my friend's younger son, who do I know who has a nice girl for him . . . ?"

Further Reflections on Arranged Marriage

The previous essay was written from the point of view of a family seeking a daughter-in-law. Arranged marriage looks somewhat different from the point of view of the bride and her family. Arranged marriage continues to be preferred, even among the more educated, Westernized sections of the Indian population. Many young women from these families still go along, more or less willingly, with the practice, and also with the specific choices of their families. Young women do get excited about the prospects of their marriage, but there is also ambivalence and increasing uncertainty, as the bride contemplates leaving the comfort and familiarity of her own home, where as a "temporary guest" she has often been indulged, to live among strangers. Even in the best situation, she will now come under the close scrutiny of her husband's family. How she dresses, how she behaves, how she gets along with others, where she goes, how she spends her time, her domestic abilities—all of this and much more—will be observed and commented on by a whole new set of relations. Her interaction with her family of birth will be monitored and curtailed considerably. Not only will she leave their home, but with increasing geographic mobility, she may also live very far from them, perhaps even on another continent. Too much expression of her fondness for her own family, or her desire to visit them, may be interpreted as an inability to adjust to her new family, and may become a source of conflict. In an arranged marriage, the burden of adjustment is clearly heavier for a woman than for a man. And that is in the best of situations.

In less happy circumstances, the bride may be a target of resentment and hostility from her husband's family, particularly her mother-in-law or her husband's unmarried sisters, for whom she is now a source of competition for the affection, loyalty, and economic resources of a son or brother. If she is psychologically or even physically abused, her options are limited, as returning to her parents' home or getting a divorce is still very stigmatized. For most Indians, marriage and motherhood are still considered the only suitable roles for a woman, even for those who have careers, and few women can comfortably contemplate remaining unmarried. Most families still consider "marrying off" their daughters as a compelling religious duty and social necessity. This increases a bride's sense of obligation to make the marriage a success, at whatever cost to her own personal happiness.

The vulnerability of a new bride may also be intensified by the issue of dowry that, although illegal, has become a more pressing issue in the consumer conscious society of contemporary urban India. In many cases, where a groom's family is not satisfied with the amount of dowry a bride brings to her marriage, the young bride will be harassed constantly to get her parents to give more. In extreme cases, the bride may even be murdered, and the murder disguised as an accident or a suicide. This also offers the husband's family an opportunity to arrange another match for him, thus bringing in another dowry. This phenomenon, called dowry death, calls attention not just to the "evils of dowry" but also to larger issues of the powerlessness of women as well.

Sources:

Nanda, S. (1992). Arranging a marriage in India. In P.R. DeVita (Ed.), *The naked anthropologist* (pp. 139–143). Belmont, CA: Wadsworth.

Nanda, S. (2000). Arranging a marriage in India. In P.R. DeVita (Ed.), *Stumbling toward truth: Anthropologists at work* (pp. 196–204). Prospect Heights, IL: Waveland Press.

Cousin Marriage

In some cultures, preferred marriages are those in which a man marries his father's brother's daughter. This is known as **patrilateral parallel-cousin marriage.** Although not obligatory, such marriages have been favoured historically among Arabs, the ancient Israelites, and also in ancient Greece and traditional China. All of these societies are hierarchical in nature; that is, some people have more property than others, and although male dominance and descent are emphasized, property of interest to men is inherited by daughters as well as sons. Thus, when a man marries his father's brother's daughter (or from the woman's point of view, her father's brother's son), property is retained within the male line of descent. In these cultures, generally speaking, the greater the property, the more this form of parallel-cousin marriage is apt to occur.

Matrilateral cross-cousin marriage—that is, of a man to his mother's brother's daughter or of a woman to her father's sister's son (a cross cousin is the child of a mother's brother or a father's sister)—is a preferred form of marriage in a variety of societies ranging from food foragers (Australian Aborigines and the Haida of

---

Patrilateral parallel-cousin marriage. Marriage of a man to his father's brother's daughter or of a woman to her father's brother's son (i.e., to a parallel cousin on the paternal side). **> Matrilateral cross-cousin marriage.** Marriage of a woman to her father's sister's son or of a man to his mother's brother's daughter (her cross cousin on the paternal side, his cross cousin on the maternal side).

Marriage is a means of creating alliances between groups of people. Since such alliances have important economic and political implications, the decision cannot be left in the hands of two young and inexperienced people. Shown here is an East Indian bride, whose marriage has been arranged between her parents and those of the groom.

Canada's Queen Charlotte Islands) to intensive agriculturists (such as among various peoples of South India). Among food-foraging peoples, who inherit relatively little property, such marriages help establish and maintain ties of solidarity between social groups. The young men of the Tlingit, living on the northwest coast of British Columbia and southwestern Alaska, traditionally preferred **patrilateral cross-cousin marriage.** Marriage to a close relative kept wealth within the family and enabled individuals to marry someone of equal rank.[32] In agricultural communities, however, the transmission of property is an important determinant. Cultures that trace descent exclusively in the female line, for instance, usually pass property and important rights from a man to his sister's son; under cross-cousin marriage, the sister's son is also the man's daughter's husband.

Marriage Exchanges

In the Trobriand Islands, when a young couple decide to get married, they sit in public on the veranda of the young man's adolescent retreat, where all may see them. Here they remain until the bride's mother brings the couple cooked yams, which they then eat together, making their marriage official. This is followed a day later by the presentation of three long skirts to the bride by the husband's sister, a symbol that the sexual freedom of adolescence is now over. This is followed by a large presentation of uncooked yams by the bride's father and her mother's brother, who represent both her father's and her own lineages.

Meanwhile, the groom's father and mother's brother—representing his father's and his own lineages—collect such valuables as stone axe blades, clay pots, money, and the occasional Kula shell to present to the young wife's maternal kin and father. After the first year of the marriage, during which the bride's mother continues to provide the couple's meals of cooked yams, each of the young husband's relatives who provided valuables for his father and mother's brother to present to the bride's relatives will receive yams from her maternal relatives and father. All of this gift giving between the lineages the husband and wife belong to, as well as those of their fathers, serves to bind the four parties together so that people respect and honour the marriage and to

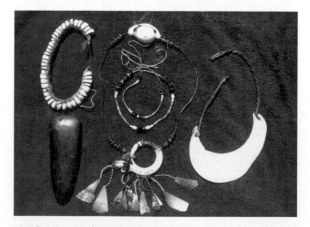

Heirlooms, such as the shell necklaces and bracelets shown above, were given as marriage gifts by a Trobriand groom's family to the bride's family.

---

[32]Oswalt, W.H., & Neely, S. (1996). *This land was theirs: A study of North American Indians* (5th ed., p. 258). Mountain View, CA: Mayfield.

Patrilateral cross-cousin marriage.   Marriage of a man to his father's sister's daughter.

create obligations for the woman's kin to take care of her husband in the future.

As among the Trobriand Islanders, marriages in many human groups are formalized by some sort of economic exchange. Among the Trobrianders, this takes the form of a gift exchange, as just described. Far more common is **bride-price,** sometimes called bride wealth. This involves payments of money or other valuables to a bride's parents or other close kin. This usually happens in cultural groups where the bride will become a member of the household where her husband grew up; this household will benefit from her labour, as well as the offspring she produces. Thus, her family must be compensated for their loss.

Not only is bride-price *not* a simple "buying and selling" of women, but also the bride's parents may use the money to buy jewellery or household furnishings for her or to finance an elaborate and costly wedding celebration. It also contributes to the stability of the marriage, because it usually must be refunded if the couple separate. Other forms of compensation are an exchange of women between families—"my son will marry your daughter if your son will marry my daughter"— or **bride service,** a period of time during which the groom works for the bride's family.

In a number of cultures more or less restricted to the western, southern, and eastern margins of Eurasia, where the economy is based on intensive agriculture, women often bring a **dowry** with them at marriage. A form of dowry in Canada is the custom of the bride's family paying the wedding expenses. In effect, a dowry is a woman's share of parental property that, instead of passing to her upon her parents' death, is distributed to her at the time of her marriage. This does not mean she retains control of this property after marriage. In a number of European countries, for example, a woman's property falls exclusively under her husband's control. Having benefited by what she has brought to the marriage, however, he is obligated to look out for her future well-being, even after his death. Thus, one

In many African societies, bride-price takes the form of cattle, which are paid by the groom's family to the bride's family.

of the functions of dowry is to ensure a woman's support in widowhood (or after divorce), an important consideration in a society where men carry out the bulk of productive work and women are valued for their reproductive potential, rather than for the work they do. In such societies, women incapable of bearing children are especially vulnerable, but the dowry they bring with them at marriage helps protect them against desertion. Another dowry function is to reflect the economic status of the woman in societies where differences in wealth are important. Thus, the property a woman brings with her at marriage demonstrates that the man is marrying a woman whose standing is on a par with his own. It also permits women, with the aid of their parents and kin, to compete through dowries for desirable (that is, wealthy) husbands.

Marriage itself is an important form of economic exchange, in essence creating affinal alliances between two kin groups. The bride-price

Bride-price. Compensation the groom or his family pays to the bride's family on marriage. **> Bride service.** A designated period after marriage when the groom works for the bride's family. **> Dowry.** Payment of a woman's inheritance at the time of her marriage, either to her or to her husband.

In some societies when a woman marries, she receives her share of the family inheritance (her dowry), which she brings to her new family (unlike bride-price, which passes from the groom's family to the bride's family). Shown here are Slovakian women carrying the objects of a woman's dowry.

and dowry discussed above symbolize these affinal ties, as well as the responsibilities that come with them. Thus, marriage alliances enhance each kin group's chance of survival and create a cooperative support network between large kin groups.

DIVORCE

Like marriage, divorce in non-Western cultures is a matter of great concern to the couple's families. Since marriage is more often an economic than a religious matter, divorce arrangements can be made for a variety of reasons and with varying degrees of difficulty.

Among the Gusii of Kenya, sterility or impotence were grounds for a divorce. Among the Chenchu of Hyderabad and certain First Nations of northern Canada, divorce was discouraged after children were born, and couples usually were urged by their families to settle their differences. By contrast, in the southwestern United States, a Hopi woman might divorce her husband at any time merely by placing his belongings outside the door to indicate he was no

longer welcome. Divorce was fairly common among the Yahgan, who lived at the southernmost tip of South America, and was seen as justified if the husband was considered cruel or failed as a provider.

Divorce in these societies seems familiar and even sensible, and, in one way or another, the children are taken care of. An adult unmarried woman is almost unheard of in most non-Western cultures; a divorced woman soon remarries. Economic considerations are often the strongest motivation to marry. On the island of New Guinea, a man does not marry because of sexual needs, which he can readily satisfy out of wedlock, but because he needs a woman to make pots and cook his meals, to fabricate nets, and to weed his plantings. A man without a wife among the Australian Aborigines is in an unsatisfactory position, since he has no one to supply him with food or firewood.

Although divorce rates may be deemed high in some non-Western cultures, they have become so high in the West as to cause many North Americans to worry about the future of marriage and the family in the contemporary world. Undoubtedly, the causes of divorce in North

America are many and varied. Among them are the trivial and transient characteristics we have already mentioned that marriages may all too easily be based upon. Beyond this, a North American marriage is supposed to involve an enduring, supportive, and intimate bond between a woman and a man, full of affection and love. In this relationship, people are supposed to find escape from the pressures of the competitive workaday world, as well as from the legal and social constraints that so affect their behaviour outside the family. Yet in a society where people are brought up to seek individual gratification, where this often is seen to come through competition at someone else's expense, and where women traditionally have been expected to be submissive to men, it should not come as a surprise to find that the reality of marriage in North America does not always live up to the ideal. Harsh treatment and neglect of spouses—usually of wives by husbands—in North America is neither new nor rare; furthermore, people are more tolerant of violence directed against spouses and

children than they are of violence against outsiders. As anthropologists Collier, Rosaldo, and Yanagisako have observed, "a smaller percentage of homicides involving family members are prosecuted than those involving strangers. We are faced with the irony that in our society the place where nurturance and noncontingent [unconditional] affection are supposed to be located is simultaneously the place where violence is most tolerated."[33] However, what has happened in recent years is that people have become less inclined toward moral censure of those—women especially—who seek escape from unsatisfactory marriages. No longer are people as willing to "stick it out at all costs" no matter how intolerable the situation may be. Thus, divorce is increasingly exercised as a sensible reaction to marriages that do not work.

[33]Collier, J., Rosaldo, M.Z., & Yanagisako, S. (1982). Is there a family? New anthropological views. In B. Thorne & M. Yalom (Eds.), *Rethinking the family: Some feminist problems* (p. 36). New York: Longman.

CHAPTER SUMMARY

Among primates, the human female is unique in her ability to engage in sexual behaviour whenever she wants to or whenever her culture tells her it is appropriate, irrespective of whether or not she is fertile. Although such activity may reinforce social bonds between men and women, competition for sexual access also can be disruptive, so every culture has rules that govern such access. The near universality of the incest taboo, which forbids sexual relations between parents and their children, and usually between siblings, long has interested anthropologists, but a truly convincing explanation of the taboo has yet to be advanced. Related to incest are the practices of endogamy and exogamy. Endogamy is marriage within a group of individuals; exogamy is marriage outside the group. Cultures that practise exogamy at one level may practise endogamy at another. Community endogamy, for example, is a relatively common practice.

Although defined in terms of a continuing sexual relationship between a man and woman, marriage should not be confused with mating. Although mating occurs within marriage, it often

occurs outside of it as well. Unlike mating, marriage is backed by social, legal, and economic forces. In Canada, legally recognized common-law relationships, in which partners enjoy all the benefits of marriage, have become increasingly common. Same-sex couples in Western society are struggling to have same-sex marriages legalized.

In some cultures, marriage arrangements exist between individuals of the same sex. An example is woman/woman marriage as practised in many African cultures. Such marriages provide a socially approved way to deal with problems for which marriages between individuals of the opposite sex offer no satisfactory solution.

Monogamy, or the taking of a single spouse, is the most common form of marriage, primarily for economic reasons. A man must have a certain amount of wealth to afford polygyny, or marriage to more than one wife at the same time. Yet in cultures where women do most of the productive work, polygyny may serve as a means of generating wealth for a household. Although few marriages in a given community may be polygynous, it is regarded as an appropriate, and even preferred, form of marriage in the majority of the world's cultures. Since few communities have a surplus of men, polyandry, or the custom of a woman having several husbands, is uncommon. Also rare is group marriage, in which several men and several women have sexual access to one another. The levirate ensures the security of a woman by providing that a widow marry her husband's brother; the sororate provides that a widower marry his wife's sister. Serial monogamy means that a man or woman marries a series of partners. In recent decades, this pattern has become increasingly common among middle-class North Americans as individuals divorce and remarry.

In Canada and the United States and many of the other industrialized countries of the West, marriages run the risk of being based on an ideal of romantic love that emphasizes youthful beauty. In no other parts of the world would marriages based on such trivial and transitory characteristics be expected to work. In non-Western cultures economic considerations are of major concern in arranging marriages. Love follows rather than precedes marriage. The family arranges marriages in cultures where it is the most powerful social institution, binding two families as allies.

Preferred marriage partners in many cultures are particular cross cousins or, less commonly, parallel cousins on the paternal side. Cross-cousin marriage is a means of establishing and maintaining solidarity between groups.

In many human groups, marriages are formalized by some sort of economic exchange. Most common is bride-price, the payment of money or other valuables from the groom's to the bride's kin; this is characteristic of cultures where the women both work and bear children for the husband's family. Bride service occurs when the groom is expected to work for a period for the bride's family. A dowry is the payment of a woman's inheritance at the time of marriage to her or her husband; its purpose is to ensure support for women in cultures where men do most of the productive work and women are valued for their reproductive potential alone.

Divorce is possible in all cultures, although reasons for divorce as well as its frequency vary widely from one group to another. In North America, factors contributing to the breakup of marriages include the trivial and transitory characteristics some marriages are based on and the difficulty of establishing a supportive, intimate bond in a culture where people are brought up to seek individual gratification, often through competition at someone else's expense, and where women traditionally have been expected to be submissive to men.

QUESTIONS FOR CRITICAL THOUGHT

1. Why do the forms and rules surrounding marriage vary so much across cultures? Does this variation weaken or reinforce the anthropological understanding of marriage? Why or why not?

2. Assuming marriage is a cross-cultural institution, why don't all humans marry? Why is marriage prohibited for certain categories of people, as in the case of Roman Catholic and Eastern Orthodox priests and nuns?

3. What socioeconomic changes might come about if same-sex marriages are legalized in Canada? If polygyny and polyandry were legalized? Do you think legalization of same-sex marriages threatens marriage and the family? Why or why not?

4. Should anthropologists become actively involved in the struggle to end female genital mutilation? If no, why not? If yes, what role(s) should they play? How do they reconcile their responsibilities as professional anthropologists with their responsibilities as human beings?

INTERNET RESOURCES

BBC News—Female Circumcision Clampdown Call

http://news.bbc.co.uk/hi/english/health

The BBC appears to deal with the issue of female circumcision fairly frequently, for example, on November 22, 2000, and December 23, 1998. This site addresses moves by the U.K. government to block the practice in the U.K. There are also links to other sites that have information on female genital mutilation.

Female Genital Mutilation

http://www.icrh.org/areas/fgm.html

This home page offers links to numerous pages dealing with female genital mutilation, particularly in Europe. Some topics include medical aspects, a list of education materials, and female genital mutilation among migrants in Europe.

http://www.amnesty.org/ailib/intcam/femgen/fgm1.htm

An extensive explanation of the different types of FGM procedures and the physical and psychological effects of the practice.

AIDS Pandemic Provisional Report

http://www.census.gov/ipc/www/hivdurbn.html

The entire text of the Durban report. Well worth a read.

The Royal Australian College of Obstetricians and Gynaecologists—Female Genital Mutilation

http://www.ranzcog.edu.au

A comprehensive site discussing female genital mutilation. The site provides a definition and description of the procedure, including diagrams, identification of countries that practise female genital mutilation, discussion of the origin of the procedure, beliefs about female genital mutilation, and reasons given for doing the procedure. Follow the links to "women's health" and "FGM booklet."

Exogamy and Incest Prohibitions

www.umanitoba.ca/faculties/arts/anthropology/tutor/marriage/incest.html

A good source of information on exogamy, including cultural variations. Includes links to cross-cultural marriage rules, legends of Hebrew patriarchs and matriarchs, endogamy, and kinship.

The Fight for Gay Rights: Canada Timeline

http://cbc.ca/news/indepth/background/gayrights.html

This site provides a brief timeline for pivotal moments in the fight for gay rights in Canada. It also provides a "link the world" timeline.

The Kibbutz

http://www.mfa.gov.il/mfa/go.asp?mfah0gal0

An overview of the kibbutz system, some history, the way the system works, and demographic statistics.

http://i-cias.com/e.o/kibbutz.htm

A brief look at the history and organization of the kibbutz, as well as maps, charts, and a photo.

SUGGESTED READINGS

Boddy, J. (1994). *Aman, the story of a Somali girl*. Toronto: Knopf.

The story of a young Somalian girl as told to the author. Examines the issue of female genital mutilation and Aman's objections to Westerners "educating" her people about the wrongness of their customs. An enlightening glimpse into the other side of this difficult gender issue.

Bonvillain, N. (1998). *Women and men: Cultural constructs of gender* (2nd ed.). Upper Saddle River, NJ: Prentice Hall.

This book is a reliable examination of gender issues, with an emphasis on marriage practices. The book takes a cross-cultural perspective, particularly in the first part, which describes several cultural groups, including the Ju/'hoansi, Inuit, Haida, Innu, and

Iroquois. Part II again uses some cross-cultural material to discuss various issues of gender, such as gender and the body, religion, and language.

duToit, B.M. (1991). *Human sexuality: Cross cultural readings.* New York: McGraw Hill.

Of the numerous texts that deal with most aspects of human sexuality, this is the only one that gives adequate recognition to the fact that most peoples in the world do things differently from North Americans. This reader deals cross-culturally with such topics as the menstrual cycle, pair bonding, sexuality, pregnancy and childbirth, childhood, puberty, birth control, sexually transmitted diseases, sex roles, and the climacteric.

Goody, J. (1976). *Production and reproduction: A comparative study of the domestic domain.* Cambridge: Cambridge University Press.

This book is especially good in its discussion of the interrelationship between marriage, property, and inheritance. Although the text is cross-cultural in its approach, readers will be fascinated by the many insights into the history of marriage in the Western world.

Mackie, M. (1991). *Gender relations in Canada: Further explorations.* Toronto: Harcourt Brace Canada.

A comprehensive, gender-inclusive study of Canadian gender issues. Of particular relevance to students who wish to study marriage and the family, the book examines the family as a primary agent of gender socialization.

Ramu, G.N. (Ed.). (1989). *Marriage and the family in Canada today.* Scarborough, ON: Prentice-Hall.

This book presents a succinct examination of emerging trends in courtship, marriage, family, and related issues in Canada. Major theoretical frameworks are discussed in detail.

CNN Today Videos

Incest Abuse (CNN Cultural Anthropology, vol. 4, 2:14)
This segment looks at the universal taboo of incest.

Gay Partnership Rights in Britain (CNN Cultural Anthropology, vol. 6, 2:07)
Rights of a lesbian couple are compared to those of a heterosexual married couple in Great Britain. The two couples discuss their partnerships and differing rights given to them by the government.

Queen Noor (CNN Cultural Anthropology, vol. 6, 5:40)
CNN news anchor Paula Zahn interviews Queen Noor of Jordan. The Queen discusses the status of women in the world, her fight against honour killings in Jordan, and the war on Iraq and its potential impact upon the region.

Honor Killing in Israel (CNN Cultural Anthropology, vol. 4, 3:54)
In some Middle Eastern cultures, the banned practice of honour killing of wives, daughters, and sisters continues within the culture.

Arranged Marriage (CNN Cultural Anthropology, vol. 4, 2:07)
In India, where a tradition of arranged marriage continues, a modern twist has been the use of the Internet to help arrange marriages.

Chinese Weddings (CNN Cultural Anthropology, vol. 4, 1:39)
In modern day China, newlywed couples spend a significant portion of their income on elaborate dress and photography.

Chapter 8

Family and Household

An Australian Aborigine family group. One of the basic functions of the family is raising children.

Chapter Preview

1. What Is the Family?

The human family is a group composed of a married or common-law couple with or without children or a lone parent with dependent children. Family can take many forms, from a married or common-law couple (including same-sex couples) with children, as in North American society, to a large group composed of several brothers and sisters with the sisters' children, as in southwest India among the Nayar. The specific form that families take is related to particular social, historical, and ecological circumstances.

2. What Is the Difference between Family and Household?

Households are task-oriented residential units where economic production, consumption, inheritance, childrearing, and shelter are organized and implemented. In the vast majority of human cultures, households consist of families, even though some household members may not be relatives of the family.

3. What Are Some of the Problems of Family and Household Organization?

Although families exist to solve the problems people must deal with, the different forms that families may take are all accompanied by their own characteristic problems. Where families are small and relatively independent, as they are in North American society, individuals are isolated from the aid and support of kin and must fend for themselves in many situations. By contrast, families that include several adults within the same large household must find ways to control tensions that invariably exist among their members.

CHAPTER OUTLINE

The Family Defined
Original Study: The Ephemeral Modern Family
Functions of the Family
Gender Perspectives: The Motherhood Mandate
Family and Household
Form of the Family
Residence Patterns
Problems of Family and Household Organization
Anthropology Applied: Public Health
   Surveillance and First Nations
   Self-Government

The family, long regarded by North Americans as a core social institution, is undergoing fundamental changes. Widespread interest in the family is evident from renewed discussion of so-called traditional family values, a euphemism for two-parent, opposite-gender, legal marriages, in which the woman stays home to raise children. Yet the increasing prevalence of blended, single-parent, common-law, and same-sex families challenges the concept of a typical or traditional family.

▲▽▲▽▲▽▲▽▲▽▲▽▲▽▲▽▲▽▲▽▲▽▲▽▲▽▲▽▲▽

THE FAMILY DEFINED

Our perception of what constitutes a family is ever changing. This dynamic nature makes it difficult to create a functional definition of family. If we were to define family in terms familiar to most North Americans, as requiring fathers, mothers, and children, then we would have to say people like the Nayar of southern India (discussed in Chapter 7) did not have families. A typical definition might suggest a family is a group composed of a woman and her dependent children and at least one adult male joined through marriage or

The nuclear family, consisting of a married or common-law couple and their dependent offspring, is held up as the ideal in Canada.

blood relationship.[1] Yet, if a woman is raising her children alone, is this not a family? Or if two males are joined in a same-sex common-law relationship and they have children, either through a previous heterosexual relationship, adoption, or other means, how do we fit them into the above definition? Another possible definition of family is "a kinship group providing the nurturant socialization of their children (natural or adopted)."[2] Although more cross-culturally acceptable, this deliberately vague definition proves less than satisfactory when attempting to define "family" in today's terms. Statistics Canada defines a **family** as a married or common-law couple, whether or not they have children, and a lone parent of any marital status, living with one or more children.[3] This definition appears to best depict current family demographics in Canada. Throughout this chapter we shall endeavour to illustrate the difficulties with developing an inclusive definition of family that is not culture-bound.

In traditional times, the Nayar marriage system served to maintain a **consanguine** (or "blood") **family** consisting of a woman, dependent offspring, and the woman's brothers. In such societies, men and women marry but do not live together as members of one household. Rather, they spend their lives in the households they grew up in, with the men "commuting" for sexual activity with their wives. Economic cooperation between men and women occurs between sisters and brothers, rather than husbands and wives.

By contrast, families formed on the basis of marital or common-law ties between husband and wife are known as conjugal families. Minimally, a **conjugal family** consists of a mar-

[1]Goodenough, W.H. (1970). *Description and comparison in cultural anthropology* (p. 19). Chicago: Aldine.

[2]Ingoldsby, B.B. (1995). Family origins and universality. In B.B. Ingoldsby & S. Smith (Eds.), *Families in multicultural perspective* (p. 94). New York: The Guilford Press.

[3]Statistics Canada. (1997, October 14). 1996 Census: Marital status, common-law unions and families. *The Daily*. Retrieved March 3, 2001, from the World Wide Web: http://www.statcan.ca/daily/english/971014/d971014.htm.

Family.   A married or common-law couple with or without children, or a lone parent with dependent children.
> Consanguine family.   A family unit consisting of a woman, her dependent offspring, and the woman's brothers.
> Conjugal family.   A family consisting of one (or more) man (who may be a female) married to one (or more) woman (who may be a male) and their offspring.

ried or common-law couple (which may be a same-sex couple) with their dependent children, otherwise known as the **nuclear family.** Other forms of conjugal families include a **polygynous family** with multiple wives of a single husband and their dependent children, and a **polyandrous family,** which includes the multiple husbands of a single wife and their dependent children. Both are often lumped together under the heading of polygamous families, and both may be thought of as aggregates of nuclear families with one spouse in common.

Historical and cross-cultural studies of the family offer as many family patterns as the fertile human imagination can invent. The one considered most typical in North America, the nuclear family, is in fact no more normal or natural than any other and cannot be used as the standard for measuring other forms. Neither universal nor even common among human societies, the independent nuclear family emerged only recently in human history. Its roots go back to a series of regulations the Roman Catholic Church imposed in the 4th century A.D. that prohibited close marriages, discouraged adoption, and condemned polygyny, concubinage, divorce, and remarriage (all of which previously had been perfectly respectable, as the Old Testament of the Bible, among other sources, makes clear). Not only did this prohibition strengthen the conjugal tie between one man and one woman, at the expense of consanguineal or "blood" ties, but it also ensured that large numbers of people would be left with no male heirs. It is a biological fact that 20 percent of all couples will have only daughters, and another 20 percent will have no children at all. By eliminating polygyny, concubinage, divorce, and remarriage and by discouraging adoption, the Church removed the means for people to overcome these odds and to make sure they would have male heirs. The result of all this was to facilitate the transfer of property from families to the Roman Catholic Church, which rapidly became the largest landowner in most European countries, a position it has retained to this day. By insinuating itself into the very fabric of domestic life, heirship, and marriage, the Church gained tremendous control over the grassroots of society, enriching itself in the process.[4]

With the industrialization of Europe and North America, the nuclear family became further isolated from other kin. One reason is that industrial economies require a mobile labour force; people must be prepared to move where the jobs are, which they do most easily without excess kin in tow. The family also came to be seen as a kind of refuge from a public world people saw as threatening to their sense of privacy and self-determination.[5] Within the family, relationships were supposed to be enduring and noncontingent, entailing love and affection, based on cooperation, and governed by feelings and morality. Although families are still considered the foundation of Canadian life, the composition of these families has shifted somewhat over the last few decades. Statistics Canada identifies three family structures within Canadian society: lone-parent families (16 percent), common-law families (14 percent), and married couples or nuclear families (70 percent). As an example of evolving Canadian family structures, in 2001, 12 percent of all Canadian couples with children were step-families, and common-law families had become the fastest-growing family structure in Canadian society.[6] In addition, approximately 15 percent of the 15 200 female same-sex couples in Canada were living with children, and 3 percent of male same-sex couples were living with children.[7]

---

[4]Goody, J. (1983). *The development of the family and marriage in Europe* (pp. 44–46). Cambridge: Cambridge University Press.

[5]Collier, J., Rosaldo, M.Z., & Yanagisako, S. (1982). Is there a family? New anthropological views. In B. Thorne & M. Yalom (Eds.), *Rethinking the family: Some feminist questions* (pp. 34–35). New York: Longman.

[6]Statistics Canada. (2002, November 6). 2001 Census: Marital status, common-law unions and families. *The Daily.* Retrieved September 12, 2003, from the World Wide Web: http://www12.statcan.ca/english/census01/products/analytic/companion/fam/canada.cfm.

[7]Statistics Canada. (2003). *Canadian families and households: The proportion of "traditional" families continues to decline.* Retrieved September 18, 2003, from the World Wide Web: http://www2.statcan.ca/english/census01/products/analytic/companion/fam/canada.cfm.

Nuclear family. A married or common-law couple and their dependent children. **> Polygynous family.** A family consisting of a man and his multiple wives, along with their dependent children. **> Polyandrous family.** A family consisting of a woman and her multiple husbands, along with their dependent children.

The family as it has emerged in Europe and North America, then, is the product of particular historical and social circumstances; where these circumstances have differed, so have family forms. Thus, how men and women in other cultures live together must be studied, not as bizarre and exotic forms of human behaviour but as logical outcomes of peoples' experience living in particular times, places, and social situations.

Although the preceding discussion emphasizes North American perceptions of the family, it is important to note that the family in one form or another is a universal feature of human social organization. Likewise, the family as an institution serves the same functions cross-culturally: that of nurturing children and creating a cooperative economic unit, the household.

Although many North Americans continue to think of families as standing in opposition to the rest of society, the truth is that they are affected by, and in turn affect, the values and structure of the society they are embedded in. To clarify this, we will take a more detailed look at the changing nature of the family in the following Original Study.

ORIGINAL STUDY

The Ephemeral Modern Family

Judith Stacey

Now that the "modern" [i.e., independent nuclear] family system has almost exited from its historical stage, we can perceive how peculiar, ephemeral, and internally contradictory was this once-revolutionary gender and kinship order. Historians place the emergence of the modern [North] American family among white middle-class people in the late eighteenth century; they depict its flowering in the nineteenth century and chart its decline in the second half of the twentieth. Thus, for white Americans, the history of modern families traverses the same historical trajectory as that of modern industrial society. What was modern about upper-middle-class family life in the half century after the American Revolution was the appearance of social arrangements governing gender and kinship relationships that contrasted sharply with those of "traditional," or premodern, patriarchal corporate units.

The premodern family among white Colonial Americans, an institution some scholars characterize as "the Godly family," was the constitutive element of Colonial society. This integrated economic, social, and political unit explicitly subordinated individual to corporate family interests and women and children to the authority of the household's patriarchal head. Decisions regarding the timing and crafting of premodern marriages served not the emotional needs of individuals but the economic, religious, and social purposes of larger kin groups, as these were interpreted by patriarchs who controlled access to land, property, and craft skills. Nostalgic images of "traditional" families rarely recall their instability or diversity. Death visited Colonial homes so frequently that second marriages and blended households composed of stepkin were commonplace. With female submission thought to be divinely prescribed, conjugal love was a fortuitous bonus, not a prerequisite of such marriages. Similarly the doctrine of innate depravity demanded authoritarian parenting to break the will and save the souls of obstinate children, a project that required extensive paternal involvement in child rearing. Few boundaries between family and work impeded such patriarchal supervision, or segregated the sexes who labored at their arduous and interdependent tasks in close proximity. Boundaries between public and private life were equally permeable. Communities regulated proper

family conduct, intervening actively to enforce disciplinary codes, and parents exchanged their children as apprentices and servants.

Four radical innovations differentiate modern from premodern family life among white Americans: (1) Family work and productive work became separated, rendering women's work invisible as they and their children became economically dependent on the earnings of men. (2) Love and companionship became the ideal purposes of marriages that were to be freely contracted by individuals. (3) A doctrine of privacy emerged that attempted to withdraw middle-class family relationships from public scrutiny. (4) Women devoted increased attention to nurturing fewer and fewer children as mothering came to be exalted as both a natural and demanding vocation.

The rise of the modern American family accompanied the rise of industrial capitalist society, with its revolutionary social, spatial, and temporal reorganization of work and domestic life. The core premises and practices of the new family regime were far more contradictory than those of the premodern family order. Coding work as masculine and home as feminine modern economic arrangements deepened the segregation of the sexes by extracting men from, and consigning white married women to, an increasingly privatized domestic domain. The institutionalized subordination of these wives to their husbands persisted; indeed, as factory production supplanted domestic industry, wives became increasingly dependent on their spouse's earnings. The doctrine of separate gender spheres governing the modern family order in the nineteenth century was so potent that few married women among even the poorest of native white families dared to venture outside their homes in search of income.

The proper sphere of working-class married white women also was confined to the home. Yet few working-class families approximated the modern family ideal before well into the twentieth century. Enduring conditions of poverty, squalor, disease, and duress rivaling those in industrializing England, most immigrant and native white working-class families in nineteenth-century America depended on supplementary income. Income from women's out work, child labor, lodgers, and the earnings of employed unmarried sons and daughters supplemented the meager and unreliable wages paid to working men. Not until the post–World War II era did substantial numbers of working-class households achieve the "modern family" pattern.

If the doctrine of separate, and unequal, gender spheres limited women's domain and rendered their work invisible, it also enhanced their capacity to formulate potent moral and political challenges to patriarchy. Men ceded the domains of child rearing and virtue to "moral" mothers who made these responsibilities the basis for expanding their social influence and political rights. This and the radical ideologies of individualism, democracy, and conjugal love, which infused modern family culture, would lead ultimately to its undoing. It is no accident, historians suggest, that the first wave of American feminism accompanied the rise of the modern family.

With rearview vision one glimpses the structural fragility of the modern family system, particularly its premise of enduring voluntary commitment. For modern marriages, unlike their predecessors, were properly affairs not of the purse but of the heart. A romantic "until death do us part" commitment volunteered by two young adults acting largely independent of the needs, interests, or wishes of their kin was the vulnerable linchpin of the modern family order. It seems rather remarkable, looking back, that during the first century of the modern family's cultural ascendancy, death did part the vast majority of married couples. But an ideology of conjugal love and companionship implies access to divorce as a safety valve for failures of youthful judgment or the vagaries of adult affective development. Thus, a statistical omen of the internal instability of this form of marriage lies in the unprecedented rise of divorce rates that accompanied the spread of the modern family. Despite severe legal and social restrictions, divorce rates began to climb at least as early as the 1840s. They have continued their ascent ever since, until by the middle of the 1970s divorce outstripped death as a source of marital dissolution. A crucial component of the modern family system, divorce would ultimately prove to be its Achilles' heel.

For a century, as the cultural significance of the modern family grew, the productive and even the reproductive work performed within its domain contracted. By the end of the "modern" industrial era in the 1950s, virtually all productive work had left the home. While advances in longevity stretched enduring marriages to unprecedented lengths, the full-time homemaker's province had been pared to the chores of housework, consumption, and the cultivation of a declining number of progeny during a shortened span of years.

Those Americans, like myself, who came of age at that historic moment were encouraged to absorb a particularly distorted impression of the normalcy and timelessness of the modern family system. The decade between the late 1940s and the late 1950s represents an aberrant period in the history of this aberrant form of family life. Fueled in part, as historian Elaine May has suggested, by the apocalyptic Cold War sensibilities of the post–World War II nuclear age, the nation indulged in what would prove to be a last-gasp orgy of modern nuclear family domesticity. Three-fifths of American households conformed to the celebrated breadwinner-fulltime homemaker modern form in 1950, as substantial sectors of working-class men began at long last to secure access to a family wage. A few years later Walt Disney opened the nation's first family theme park in southern California, designed to please and profit from the socially conservative fantasies of such increasingly prosperous families.

The aberrant fifties temporarily reversed the century's steady decline in birth rates. The average age of first-time visitors to the conjugal altar also dropped to record lows. Higher percentages of Americans were marrying than ever before or since, and even the majority of white working-class families achieved coveted home ownership status. It was during this time that Talcott Parsons provided family sociology with its most influential theoretical elaboration of the modern American family, of how its nuclear household structure and complementary division of roles into female "expressive" and male "instrumental" domains was sociologically adaptive to the functional demands of an industrial society. Rare are the generations, or even the sociologists, who perceive the historical idiosyncrasies of the normal cultural arrangements of their time.

The postwar baby boom was to make the behaviors and beliefs of that decade's offspring disproportionately significant for the rest of their lives. The media, the market, and all social and political institutions would follow their development with heightened interest. Thus, a peculiar period in U.S. family history came to set the terms for the waves of rebellion against, and nostalgia for, the passing modern family and gender order that have become such prominent and disruptive features of the American political landscape. The world's first generation of childhood television viewers grew up, as I did, inundated by such weekly paeans to the male breadwinner nuclear household and modern family ideology as *Father Knows Best, Leave It to Beaver,* and *Ozzie and Harriet.* Because unusual numbers of us later pushed women's biological "clock" to its reproductive limits, many now find ourselves parenting (or choosing not to) in the less innocent age of *Thirtysomething, Kate and Allie,* and *Who's the Boss?* For beneath the sentimental gloss that the fifties enameled onto its domestic customs, forces undermining the modern family of the 1950s accelerated while those sustaining it eroded. In the midst of profamily pageantry, nonfamily households proliferated. As the decade drew to a close, the nation entered what C. Wright Mills, with characteristic prescience, termed its "postmodern period." The emergent postindustrial economy shifted employment from heavy industries to nonunionized clerical, service, and new industrial sectors. Employers found themselves irresistibly attracted to the nonunionized, cheaper labor of women and, thus, increasingly to that of married women and mothers.

One glimpses the ironies of class and gender history here. For decades industrial unions struggled heroically for a socially recognized male breadwinner wage that would allow the working class to participate in the modern gender order. These struggles, however, contributed to the cheapening of female labor that helped gradually to undermine the modern family regime. Escalating consumption standards, the expansion of mass collegiate coeducation, and the persistence of high divorce rates then gave more and more women ample cause to invest a portion of their identities in the "instrumental" sphere of paid labor. Thus, middle-class women began to abandon their confinement in the modern family just as working-class women were approaching its access ramps. The former did so, however, only after the wives of working-class men had pioneered the twentieth-century revolution in women's paid work. Entering employment during the catastrophic 1930s, participating in defense industries in the 1940s, and raising their family incomes to middle-class standards by returning to the labor force rapidly after child rearing in the 1950s, working-class women quietly modeled and normalized the postmodern family standard of employment for married mothers. Whereas in 1950 the less a man earned, the more likely his wife was to be employed, by 1968 wives of middle-income men were the most likely to be in the labor force.

Source: Stacey, J. (1990). *Brave new families* (pp. 6–11). New York: Basic Books.

▲▽▲▽▲▽▲▽▲▽▲▽▲▽▲▽▲▽▲▽▲▽▲▽▲▽▲▽▲

FUNCTIONS OF THE FAMILY

Among humans, reliance on group living for survival is a basic characteristic. We have inherited this from our primate ancestors, although we have developed it in our own distinctively human ways.

Nurturance of Children

The sexual division of labour among humans has developed beyond that of other primates. Until the recent advent of synthetic infant formulas, human females more often than not were occupied much of their adult lives with childrearing. Human infants need active "mothering" since they are helpless at birth and the period of infant dependency is quite long. Besides all this, studies have shown that human infants need more than just food and physical care if they are to develop normally. But among humans, unlike other primates, the infant's biological mother does not have to provide all this "mothering." Not only may other women provide the child with much of the attention it needs, but so may men. In many cultures children are handled and fondled as much by men as by women, and in some men are more nurturing to children than are women. Changing trends in the Canadian workforce, most notably women working outside the home, have resulted in men becoming even more involved in childrearing, and although it is not that common yet, some men are choosing to stay at home and care for their young children, enabling their wives to pursue careers.

Since cultures handle the raising and education of children in varied ways, these practices are important subjects of anthropological inquiry. Through enculturation (discussed in Chapter 2), children begin learning their culture soon after birth. Parents, and especially mothers, are the first people responsible for enculturating children. In North American society, a family ideally includes a mother and father or stepfather and the child's siblings, although this is not always the case. In other cultures the father may seldom have contact with his children in their early years; indeed, in some cultures men do not even live with the mothers of their children. In such instances, brothers of the child's mother play important roles in raising their nieces and nephews. Grandparents, other wives of the father, brothers of the father, and sisters of the mother, not to mention their children, are also key players in the enculturation process. In some societies, and Canada is a good example, professional nannies, teachers, and daycare workers are brought into the enculturation process to provide formal care and instruction.

Children learn much of what they need to know through observation and participation. Jean Briggs has studied the unique childrearing practices of the Inuit of Baffin Island. The adults use emotionally powerful questions about moral and social dilemmas to informally socialize their children. Questions such as "Why don't you kill your little brother?" encourage a child to admit to jealousy but also love for the little brother.[8] These types of dilemmas encourage children to think about how they should treat other people.

The development of self-awareness is part of the enculturation process. North American children tend to lag behind children in other cultures in self-awareness, possibly because close human contact and active stimulation of infants is curtailed in North America. North American children do not sleep with their parents; rather, they are placed in a room by themselves with little stimulation. In more traditional cultures, such as the Ju/'hoansi, infants routinely sleep with their parents, or at least their mothers. When awake they are carried most of the time, with frequent nursing. Among the Ju/'hoansi, infants are nursed four or five times an hour, for one or two minutes at a time. Overall, a 15-week-old Ju/'hoansi infant is in close contact with its mother about 70 percent of the time, compared with 20 percent for home-reared infants in mainstream Canadian society. Inuit babies and small children receive a great deal of love and attention from their mothers and other members of their families. Mothers tend to nurse their infants on demand, holding and cuddling them most of the time. In fact, Inuit infants are seldom left alone when awake. Adult Inuit rarely become angry with their children or scold them, feeling that to do so is a sign of immaturity.

The near-constant stimulation of infants in traditional cultures is important, for recent studies show that stimulation plays a key role in the "hardwiring" of the brain; stimulation is necessary for development of the neural circuitry. Nor should the role of frequent nursing be overlooked, since the longer a child is breast-fed, the higher it will score on cognitive tests and the lower its risk of having attention deficit disorder (hyperactivity). Furthermore, breast-fed children have fewer allergies, fewer ear infections, and less diarrhea, and are at less risk of sudden infant death syndrome.[9]

---

[8]Briggs, J.L. (1998). Inuit morality play: The emotional education of a three-year old. *Social and Economic Studies*, No. 67. Institute of Social and Economic Research.

[9]Dettinger, K.A. (1997, October). When to wean. *Natural History, 49.*

Gender **Perspectives**

The Motherhood Mandate

In her essay "The Motherhood Mandate," Susan Basow suggests that all "normal" women want to become mothers, that each woman experiences a deep-rooted "maternal instinct" pushing her toward this goal.[1] Women who cannot have children are pitied, and those who choose not to have children are considered lazy, selfish, and cold-hearted—unnatural women.

From an early age, little girls are socialized into becoming "good" mothers—playing house with the requisite baby dolls, toy ovens, and ironing boards—and when they are older, their first job is likely as a babysitter, now with "living dolls." Thus, their gender identity is firmly entrenched. Media, a powerful socialization tool, inundate girls and young women with images of motherhood as the perfect life choice, using idolized role models, such as movie stars and models, enthusiastically endorsing the joys of motherhood while still maintaining exciting careers, lovely homes, and a perfect size five body.

The motherhood mandate, which remains a powerful force in many secular and religious ideologies, romanticizes the state of motherhood as the only way a woman can be "fulfilled" and ignores the reality of motherhood—the endless chores, isolation, and weariness from being a mother 24/7. It ignores the heavy responsibility placed on a mother's shoulders to raise a bright, well-adjusted, happy child and the blame if this does not happen.

Once North American women become mothers, they quickly realize the true nature of motherhood. In desperation, and perhaps guilt, some adopt the media image of a supermom. The supermom can do all things and be all things to all people. Supermoms are portrayed as women with boundless energy and enthusiasm, enviable time management skills, an innate ability to nurture; they are women who have it all—career, marriage, children, community volunteer work, not to mention a sparkling clean floor. In essence, Western supermoms are a product of both the traditional and the modern world—they are "blended" mothers, still attempting to maintain the traditional values of motherhood emanating from the 1950s, while also buying into the image of a "modern" woman, one who can juggle the multiple roles of wife, mother, and career.

Casting aside the motherhood mandate and the supermom image is a difficult decision for most modern women. The desire to be a good mother, coupled with years of socialization into these roles, seems to force women to maintain this impression of motherhood. This is unfortunate because until women themselves accept the realities and limitations of motherhood, modern Western society will continue to undervalue the role of motherhood, while still setting unrealistic expectations for mothers.

---

[1]Basow, S. A. (1992). The Motherhood Mandate. In E. D. Nelson & B. W. Robinson (1999), *Gender in Canada*. Scarborough, ON: Prentice Hall Allyn and Bacon.

Source: Nelson, E.D., & Robinson, B.W. (1999). *Gender in Canada*. Scarborough, ON: Prentice Hall Allyn and Bacon.

Economic Cooperation

The economic activities of women generally have complemented those of men, even though, in some cultures, individuals may perform tasks normally assigned to the opposite sex, as the occasion dictates. Thus, men and women could share the results of their labours on a regular basis, as was discussed in Chapters 5 and 6.

An effective way both to facilitate economic cooperation between the sexes and to provide for a close bond between mother and child at the same time is through the establishment of residential groups that include adults of both sexes. The differing nature of male and female roles, as these are defined by different cultures, requires a child to have an adult of the same sex available to

Canadian men are increasingly involved in child-rearing, enabling their wives to pursue careers.

serve as a proper model for the appropriate adult role. The presence of adult men and women in the same residential group provides for this.

Well suited though the family may be for these tasks, we should not suppose it is the only unit capable of providing such conditions. In fact, other arrangements are possible, such as the Israeli kibbutz, where paired teams of male and female specialists raise groups of children. In many food-foraging groups, all adult members of a community share in the responsibilities of child-

care. Thus, when parents go off to hunt or to collect plants and herbs, they may leave their children behind, secure in the knowledge they will be looked after by whatever adults remain in the camp. Yet another arrangement may be seen among the Mundurucu, a horticultural people of South America's Amazon forest. Their children live in houses with their mothers, apart from all men until age 13, whereupon the boys leave their mothers' houses to go live with the village men.

▲▽▲▽▲▽▲▽▲▽▲▽▲▽▲▽▲▽▲▽▲▽▲▽▲▽▲▽▲▽▲
FAMILY AND HOUSEHOLD

Although it is often stated that some form of family is present in all human cultures, the Mundurucu case just cited demonstrates this is not so. In Mundurucu villages, the men all live together in one house with all boys over age 13; women live with others of their sex as well as younger boys in two or three houses grouped around the men's house. As among the Nayar, married men and women are members of separate households, meeting periodically for sexual activity.

The **household**, defined as the basic residential unit where economic production, consumption,

One alternative to the family as a childrearing unit is the Israeli kibbutz. Here, children of a kibbutz engage in a supervised session of creative play.

Household.   The basic residential unit where economic production, consumption, inheritance, childrearing, and shelter are organized and implemented; may or may not be synonymous with *family*.

Laurel Bossen

Laurel Bossen is a professor of anthropology at McGill University whose work has focused on gender and development in both Guatemala and China. Her early work, *The Redivision of Labor* (1984), is a multi-sited ethnography, one of the early anthropological studies to view Guatemalan Maya and Hispanic communities as interlinked parts of a national economy. Bossen showed that gender relations differed by ethnicity and class, comparing the impact of economic development on women in a mountain village of Mayan small farmers, a vast lowland plantation where poor Maya and Ladino migrants did seasonal work, a city squatter settlement with migrants from all over Guatemala, and a modern wealthy suburb. Her related articles examine gender discrimination on large plantations and the vulnerable position of female domestic servants.

Bossen's most recent book, *Chinese Women and Rural Development* (2002), is a path-breaking study of how village women have been affected by major political and economic transformations from the 1949 Communist Revolution through the recent reforms opening China to the global economy. Building on one of the very rare Chinese ethnographies dating from the 1930s, Bossen details both change and continuity in the lives of women and men in Lu Village, Yunnan, China. Bossen reinterprets the formerly widespread practice of Chinese footbinding as not only turning women's feet into objects of beauty, but also ensuring that girls and women had little choice but to labour long hours in commercial production of textiles (spinning and weaving) in the home. Early twentieth century globalization and industrial textile production destroyed this form of domestic labour and contributed to the end of footbinding. Bossen also examines current issues such as China's strict family-planning policy, the national shortage of women due to selective abortion, and the impact on women of changing property rights.

A celebration at the palace in the Yoruba city of Oyo, Nigeria. As is usual in societies where royal households are found, that of the Yoruba includes many individuals not related to the ruler, as well as the royal family.

inheritance, childrearing, and shelter are organized and implemented, is universally present. Among the Mundurucu, the men's house constitutes one household, and the women's houses constitute others. Although, in this case as in many, each house is in effect a household, a number of cultures have households made up of two or more houses together, as we shall see later in this chapter.

Most households in fact constitute families, although other sorts of households may be present as well. Often, a household consists of a family along with some more distant relatives of family members. Or co-residents may be unrelated, such as the service personnel in an elaborate royal household, apprentices in the household of craft specialists, or low-status clients in the household of rich and powerful patrons. In such cultures, even though people may think in terms of households, rather than families, the households are built around the latter. Thus, in the vast majority of human cultures the family is the basic core of the household.

▲▽▲▽▲▽▲▽▲▽▲▽▲▽▲▽▲▽▲▽▲▽▲▽▲▽▲▽▲▽▲▽

FORM OF THE FAMILY

As suggested earlier in this chapter, the family may take any number of forms in response to particular social, historical, and ecological circumstances. At the outset, a distinction must be made between conjugal families, which are formed on the basis of marital ties, and consanguineal families, which are not. As defined earlier, consanguineal families consist of related women, their brothers, and the women's offspring. Such families are not common; the classic case is the Nayar household group. The Nayar are not unique, however, and consanguineal families are found elsewhere—for example, among the Tory Islanders, a Roman Catholic, Gaelic-speaking fisherfolk living off the coast of Ireland. These people do not marry until they are in their late 20s or early 30s and thus experience tremendous resistance to breaking up existing household arrangements. The Tory Islanders look at it this way: "Oh well, you get married at that age, it's too late to break up arrangements that you have already known for a long time. . . . You know, I have my sisters and brothers to look after, why should I leave home to go live with a husband? After all, he's got his sisters and his brothers looking after him."[10] Because the community numbers only a few hundred people, husbands and wives are within easy commuting distance of each other.

---

[10]Fox, R. (1981, December 3). [Interview for Coast Telecourses, Inc.]. Los Angeles.

The Nuclear Family

The form of conjugal family most familiar to North Americans is the independent nuclear family, which in spite of its steady decline is still widely regarded as the "standard" in Canada and the United States. In these countries it is not considered desirable for young people to live with their parents beyond a certain age, nor is it considered the responsibility of a couple to take their aged parents into their home when the parents no longer can care for themselves. Retirement communities and nursing homes provide these services, and to take aged parents into their homes is regarded by some as not only an economic burden but also a threat to the family's privacy and independence. However, decades of government cutbacks have created a shortage of good nursing homes at the same time as Canadian seniors are living longer, which has forced more and more middle-aged adults to care for their elderly parents.

The nuclear family is also apt to be prominent in cultural groups such as the Inuit, who live in a harsh northern environment. In traditional times, during the winter season nuclear families roamed the vast Arctic wilderness in search of food. The men hunted and fished and built their shelters. The women cooked, cared for the children, and sewed and repaired their clothing. One of the wife's chores was to chew her husband's boots to soften the leather for the next day so that he could resume his search for game. The wife and her children could not survive without the husband, and life for a man was unimaginable without a wife.

Certain parallels can be drawn between the nuclear family in industrial societies and families living under especially harsh environmental conditions. In both cases, the family is an independent unit that must be prepared to fend for itself; this creates for individual members a strong dependence on one another. Minimal help is available from outside in the event of emergencies or catastrophes. When their usefulness ends, the elderly are cared for only if it is feasible. In the event of the mother's or father's death, life becomes precarious for the child. Yet this form of family is well adapted to a life that requires a high degree of geographic mobility. For the Inuit, this mobility permits the hunt for food; for North

Americans, the hunt for jobs and improved social status requires a mobile form of family unit. Nowhere is the nuclear family as isolated from other kin as it has become among most non-aboriginal North Americans.

When Inuit families are off by themselves, it is regarded as a matter of temporary expediency; when food sources are abundant or more labourers are necessary, larger social groups are formed. For example, the Netsilik Inuit congregate to watch the breathing holes during the winter sealing hunts, and the Labrador and Mackenzie Delta Inuit come together in large numbers during whaling season. Even during these times of congregation the basic family unit is the nuclear family, and each family is free to go elsewhere as they please.[11] Thus families cooperate with one another on a daily basis, sharing food and other resources, looking out for the children, and sometimes even eating together.

The sense of shared responsibility for one another's children and for the general welfare in Inuit multifamily groups contrasts with other families in North America, which are more "on their own." Canadian parents receive some help from local and federal governments, in the form of child tax credits, universal medicare, and an extensive social welfare program. However, this assistance is mainly economic, rather than emotional or physical. To be sure, families can and often do help one another out, but they are under no obligation to do so. In fact, once children reach the age of majority (18), parents have no further legal obligation to them, nor do the children to their parents. When families do have difficulty fulfilling their functions—as is increasingly the case—even if it is through no fault of their own, less support is available to them from the community at large than in most cultures, including that of the Inuit.

The Extended Family

In North America, nuclear families have not always had the degree of independence they came to have with the rise of industrialism. In an earlier more agrarian era, the small nuclear family commonly was part of a larger **extended family.** This kind of family, in part conjugal and in part consanguine, might include grandparents, mother and father, brothers and sisters, perhaps an uncle and aunt, and a stray cousin or two. All these people lived and worked together. Because members of the younger generation brought their spouses (husbands or wives) to live in the family, extended families, like consanguine families, had continuity through time. As older members died off, new members were born into the family.

Extended families are most apt to be found in cultures with an economy based on subsistence farming. Such families are important, for they provide the large labour force necessary to till the soil, tend whatever flocks are kept, and carry out other part-time economic pursuits considered necessary for existence. At the turn of the 20th century, Canadian immigrants such as Ukrainians—maintained extended family structures to provide enough labour for work on their farms. As Canada became more urbanized, these extended families gave way to nuclear families.

Changing labour patterns also can have an impact on family dynamics. Traditionally, a Chinese daughter-in-law cared for her husband's elderly parents. This custom is not nearly as evident in Chinese-Canadian families, partly because

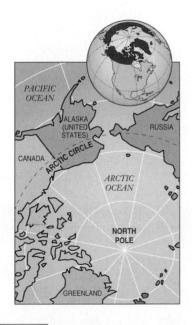

[11]McMillan, A.D. (1988). *Native peoples and cultures of Canada: An anthropological overview.* Vancouver: Douglas and McIntyre.

Extended family.   A collection of nuclear families, related by ties of blood, that live together in one household.

Among the Inuit, nuclear families such as the one shown here are the norm, although they are not as isolated from other kin as are nuclear families in the rest of Canada.

the daughter-in-law may work outside the home, and partly because many Chinese-Canadian seniors now prefer to live apart from their adult children. However, extended families in Canada have not totally disappeared; in 1996, 240 000 seniors, mostly women, lived with a daughter or son.[12]

The Maya of Guatemala and southern Mexico also live in extended family households.[13] In many of their communities, sons bring their wives to live in houses built on the edge of a small open plaza, where on one edge their father's house already stands. Numerous household activities occur on this plaza; here women may weave, men may receive guests, and children play together. The head of the family is the sons' father, who makes most of the important decisions. All family members work together for the common good and deal with outsiders as a single unit.

Extended families living together in single households were often an important social unit among the Iroquois First Nations of southern Quebec and Ontario. The Huron and Iroquois lived in extended families in villages of bark-covered longhouses, each housing several families. This extended family structure developed in response to a horticultural economy, with a mix of agriculture, wild plant gathering, fishing, and some hunting. After marriage a woman brought her husband into the home of her mother and sisters. The women worked together, planting crops of beans, corn, and squash and gathering wild plants, while their husbands cleared the lands, hunted, and fished.[14]

The 1960s saw a number of attempts by young people in Canada and the United States to reinvent a form of extended family. Their families (often called communes) were groups of unrelated nuclear families that held property in common and lived together. It is further noteworthy that the lifestyle of these families often emphasized the kinds of cooperative ties found in

[12]Health Canada. (2001). *Canada's seniors: Living with extended families*. Retrieved March 4, 2001, from the World Wide Web: http://www.hc-sc.gc.ca/seniors-aines/pub/factoids/en/no7.htm.

[13]Vogt, E.Z. (1990). *The Zinacantecos of Mexico: A modern Maya way of life* (2nd ed., pp. 30–34). Fort Worth, TX: Holt, Rinehart and Winston.

[14]McMillan, A.D. (1988). *Native peoples and cultures of Canada: An anthropological overview* (pp. 63–82). Vancouver: Douglas and McIntyre.

Extended families like this one are still found in parts of Canada, particularly among recent immigrant families.

Extended-family living arrangements are common throughout the world. Shown here is an Iroquois longhouse where several families would have lived and worked together.

rural North American extended families of old, which provided a labour pool for the many tasks required for economic survival. In some of these communes the members reverted to traditional gender roles; the women took care of the child-rearing and household chores, while the men took care of tasks outside of the household.

Same-Sex Families

Of the many forms a family can take, perhaps the most controversial is the gay or lesbian family. Same-sex families face social stigma and discrimination predicated on flawed assumptions about gay and lesbian people and their ability to be good parents. Many same-sex couples live in fear of losing custody of their children. Not being able to legally marry diminishes these family units and denies same-sex couples and their children the same status as other families. In Western societies, gay and lesbian couples with children are lobbying for the right to be recognized as legitimate family units.[15]

Opponents to same-sex families express concern regarding the impact gay and lesbian parents may have on their children's sexual, psychological, and social development. Yet fears that children raised in a same-sex family will be emotionally or physically harmed have proven groundless. In fact, there is no evidence that children in gay and lesbian families differ from other children in academic, social, or psychological health, nor are their sexual orientation and gender development affected. Much of the ignorance concerning same-sex families could be eliminated if we sought to understand them in their own right.

Same-sex families can be divided into two main categories: stepfamilies and co-parent families. In stepfamilies, children were conceived in previous heterosexual relationships, and the parent in the same-sex relationship (usually the woman) has retained custody after the breakup of the heterosexual relationship. Co-parent families exist when one or both lesbian mothers conceive a child through donor insemination, or when men have children through adoption, fostering, or surrogacy. The most prevalent same-sex families are lesbian stepfamilies. Like opposite-sex families, same-sex families exhibit a great deal of diversity based on ethnicity, age, perceived gender roles, community, and so on.

---

[15]Erera, P.I. (2002). *Family diversity: Continuity and change in the contemporary family*. Thousand Oaks, CA: Sage.

RESIDENCE PATTERNS

Where some form of conjugal or extended family is the norm, family exogamy requires that either the husband or wife, if not both, must move to a new household upon marriage. A newly married couple may adopt one of five common patterns of residence, the prime determinants of which are ecological circumstances. One option is **patrilocal residence;** as described for the Maya, a woman goes to live with her husband in the household he grew up in. Favouring this arrangement are cultures with a predominant role for men in subsistence, particularly if they own property that can be accumulated, if polygyny is customary, if warfare is prominent enough to make cooperation among men especially important, and if an elaborate political organization in which men wield authority exists. These conditions are most often found together in cultures that rely on animal husbandry and/or intensive agriculture for their subsistence. Where patrilocal residence is customary, the bride often must move to a different band or community. In such cases, her parents' family is not only losing the services of a useful family member, but they are losing her potential offspring as well. Hence, some kind of compensation to her family, most commonly bride-price, is usual.

Matrilocal residence, in which the man leaves the family he grew up with to live with his wife in her parents' household, results if ecological circumstances make the women's role predominant in subsistence. It is found most often in horticultural societies, where political organization is relatively uncentralized and where cooperation among women is important. The Iroquois provide one example; the women do the farming, control access to land, and "own" the harvest. Under matrilocal residence, men usually do not move very far from the family they were raised in, so they are available to help out there from time to time. Therefore, marriage usually does not involve compensation to the groom's family.

Members of modern Maya extended families carry out various activities on the household plaza; here, for example, women weave.

Ambilocal residence is particularly well suited to situations where economic cooperation of more people than are available in the nuclear family is needed but where resources are limited in some way. Because the couple can join either the bride's or the groom's family, family membership is flexible, and the two can live where the resources look best or where their labour is most needed. This was once the situation on the peninsulas and islands along the Maine coast, where extended family households were based on ambilocal residence. The same residential pattern is common among food-foraging peoples, such as the Mbuti of Africa's Ituri forest. Typically, a Mbuti marries someone from another band, so one spouse has in-laws who live elsewhere. Thus, if foraging is bad in their part of the forest, the couple has somewhere else to go where food may be more readily available. Ambilocality greatly enhances the Mbutis' opportunity to find food. It also provides a place to go if a dispute breaks out with someone in the band where the couple is currently living. Consequently, Mbuti camps are constantly changing their composition as people split off to live with their in-laws, while others are joining from other groups. For food foragers, who find their food in nature and who maintain an egalitarian social order, ambilocal residence

---

Patrilocal residence.   A pattern in which a married couple lives in the locality associated with the husband's father's relatives. **> Matrilocal residence.**   A pattern in which a married couple lives in the locality associated with the wife's relatives. **> Ambilocal residence.**   A pattern in which a married couple may choose either matrilocal or patrilocal residence.

Historically, Iroquoian society (e.g., Huron, Iroquois, Petan) was matrilocal; the women were the farmers, providing most of their diet, while the men hunted and fished. Even today, Iroquoian peoples maintain a matrilineal kinship system.

can be a crucial factor in both survival and conflict resolution.

Under **neolocal residence,** a married couple forms a household in an independent location. This occurs where the independence of the nuclear family is emphasized. In industrial societies such as Canada, where most economic activity occurs outside rather than inside the family and where it is important for individuals to be able to move where jobs are found, neolocal residence is better suited than any of the other patterns.

Avunculocal residence, in which a married couple goes to live with the groom's mother's brother, is favoured by the same factors that promote patrilocal residence, but only in cultures where descent through women is deemed crucial for the transmission of important rights and property. Such is the case among the people of the Trobriand Islands, where each individual is a member of a group of relatives who trace their descent through their mother, their mother's mother, and so on to the one woman all others are descended from. Each of these descent groups holds

property, consisting of hamlet sites, bush and garden lands, and, in some cases, beachfronts to which members have access rights. These properties are controlled each generation by a male chief or other leader who inherits these rights and obligations, but because descent is traced exclusively through women, a man cannot inherit these from his father. Thus, succession to positions of leadership passes from a man to his sister's son. For this reason, a man who is in line to take control of his descent group's assets will take his wife to live with the one he will succeed—his mother's brother. This enables him to observe how the older man takes care of his hamlet's affairs, as well as to learn the oral traditions and magic he will need to be an effective leader.

Although Trobriand leaders and chiefs live avunculocally, most married couples in this society live patrilocally. This allows sons to fulfill their obligations to their fathers, who helped build up and nurture them when they were small; in return, the sons will inherit personal property such as clay pots and valuable stone axe blades from their fathers. This also gives men access to

---

Neolocal residence.   A pattern in which a married couple establishes its household in a location apart from either the husband's or the wife's relatives. **> Avunculocal residence.**   A pattern in which a married couple lives with the husband's mother's brother.

This Trobriand Island chief, shown in front of his house, will be succeeded by his sister's son. Hence, men who will become chiefs live avunculocally.

land their father's descent groups control in addition to their own, enabling them to improve their own economic and political position in Trobriand society. In short, here, as in any human society, practical considerations play a central role in determining where people will live following marriage.

▲▽▲▽▲▽▲▽▲▽▲▽▲▽▲▽▲▽▲▽▲▽▲▽▲▽▲▽

PROBLEMS OF FAMILY AND HOUSEHOLD ORGANIZATION

Effective though the family may be at organizing economic production, consumption, inheritance, and childrearing, at the household level relationships within the family inevitably involve a certain amount of conflict and tension. This does not mean they may not also involve a great deal of warmth and affection. Nevertheless, at least the potential for conflict is always there and must be dealt with lest families become dysfunctional.

Different forms of families are associated with different sorts of tensions, and the means employed to manage these tensions differ accordingly.

Polygamous Families

A major source of tension within polygamous families is the potential for conflict that exists between the multiple spouses of the individual they are married to. For example, under polygyny (the most common form of polygamy), the several wives of a man must be able to get along with a minimum of bickering and jealousy. One way to handle this is through **sororal polygyny,** or marriage to women who are sisters. Presumably, women who have grown up together can get along as co-wives of a man more easily than women who grew up in different households. Another mechanism is to provide each wife with a separate apartment or house within a household compound and perhaps require the husband to adhere to a system of rotation for sleeping purposes. The latter at least prevents the husband from playing obvious favourites among his wives. Although polygyny can be difficult for the women involved, this is not always the case (recall the comments of women in polygynous marriages in the Rocky Mountains discussed in the previous chapter). In some polygynous groups, women enjoy considerable economic autonomy, and in cultures where women's work is hard and boring, polygyny allows sharing of the workload and alleviates boredom through companionship with the co-wives.

Polygynous families also may solve economic problems. Among the Hawazama pastoralists of Sudan, one wife and her children live in the nomad camp and practise animal husbandry. A second wife and her children live in a settlement, where they raise crops. Thus, each portion of the family is involved in either herding or farming, enhancing the chances of survival in a challenging environment.[16]

---

[16]Michael, B.J. (2002). Patterns of family relations. In R.B. Morrison & C.R. Wilson (Eds.), *Ethnographic essays in cultural anthropology: A problem-based approach.* Itasca, IL: F.E. Peacock.

Sororal polygyny.   A man marries several women who are sisters.

In polyandrous families, two distinctive structural characteristics may cause difficulty. One is that a woman's older husbands are apt to dominate the younger ones. The other is that, under conditions of **fraternal polyandry** (where co-husbands are brothers), the youngest brothers are likely to be considerably younger than their wives, whose reproductive years are limited. Hence, a young husband's chances of reproducing successfully are reduced, compared with older husbands. Not surprisingly, when polyandrous families break up, it is usually the younger husbands who depart. Moreover, large family groups are more prone to discord than smaller ones.[17]

Extended Families

Extended families too, no matter how well they may work, have their own potential areas of stress. Decision making in such families usually rests with an older individual, and other family members must defer to the elder's decisions. Among a group of siblings, an older one usually has the authority. Another possible problem involves in-marrying spouses, who must adjust their ways to conform to the expectations of the family they have come to live with. To combat these problems, people rely on various techniques to enforce harmony, including dependence training and the concept of "face" or "honour." Dependence training is typically associated with extended family organization and involves raising people who are more inclined to be compliant and accept their lot in life than are individuals raised to be independent (for further discussion of dependence training, visit the textbook's website at http://www.cultural2e.nelson.com). One of the many problems young people in North American society who have experimented with extended family living face is that they generally have been raised to be independent, making it hard to defer to others' wishes when they disagree.

The concept of "face" may constitute a particularly potent check on the power of senior members of extended families. Among pastoral nomads of North Africa, for example, young men can escape

Some young North Americans have attempted to re-create the extended family in the formation of communes, for example, this Langley, British Columbia, commune. These attempts sometimes run into trouble as members cope with stress associated with extended family organization they are unprepared for.

from ill treatment at the hands of a father or an older brother by leaving the patrilocal extended family to join the family of his maternal relatives, in-laws, or even an unrelated family willing to take him in.[18] Because men lose face if their sons or brothers flee in this way, they are generally at pains to control their behaviour to prevent this from happening. Women, who are the in-marrying spouses, also may return to their natal family if they are mistreated in their husband's family. A woman who does this exposes her husband and his family to scolding by her kin, again causing loss of face.

---

[17]Levine, N.E., & Silk, J.B. (1997). Why polyandry fails. *Current Anthropology, 38,* 385–387.

[18]Abu-Lughod, L. (1986). *Veiled sentiments: Honor and poetry in a Bedouin society* (pp. 99–103). Berkeley, CA: University of California Press.

Fraternal polyandry.   A woman marries several men who are brothers.

Effective though such techniques may be in cultures that stress the importance of the group over the individual, and where loss of face is to be avoided at almost any cost, not all conflict is avoided. When all else fails to restore harmony, siblings may be forced to demand their share of family assets to set up separate households, and in this way new families arise. Divorce, too, may be possible, although how easily this is accomplished varies considerably from one society to another. In cultures that practise matrilocal residence, divorce rates tend to be high, reflecting how easily unsatisfactory marriages can be terminated. In some cultures with patrilocal residence, by contrast, divorce may be all but impossible, at least for women (the in-marrying spouses). This was the case in rural Taiwan, for example, where women were raised to be cast out of their families.[19] When they married, they exchanged their dependence on fathers and brothers for absolute dependence on husbands and, later in life, sons. Without divorce as an option, to protect themselves against ill treatment women went to great lengths to develop the strongest bond possible between themselves and their sons so that the latter would rise to their mother's defence when necessary. So single-minded were many women toward developing such relationships with their sons that they often made life miserable for their daughters-in-law, who were seen as competitors for their sons' affections.

Nuclear Families

Just as extended families have built into them particular sources of stress and tensions, so too do nuclear families, especially in modern industrial societies where the family has lost one of its chief reasons for being: its economic function as a basic unit of production. Rather than staying within the fold, working with and for each other, one or both adults in a marriage must seek work outside the family. Furthermore, their work may keep them away for prolonged periods. If both spouses are employed, the requirement for workers to go where their jobs take them may pull the husband and wife in different directions.

On top of all this, neolocal residence tends to isolate husbands and wives from both sets of kin. Because clearly established patterns of responsibility no longer exist between husbands and wives, couples must work these out for themselves. Two factors make this difficult, one being women's traditional dependence on men, which has been a feature of Western society for a very long time. In spite of greater equality between men and women today, all too often the partners in a marriage do not come to it as equals. The other problem is the great emphasis North American society places on the pursuit of individual gratification through competition, often at someone else's expense. The problem is especially acute if the husband and wife grew up in households with widely divergent outlooks on life and ways of operating. Furthermore, their isolation from kin means no one is on hand to help stabilize the new marriage; for that matter, intervention of kin likely would be regarded as interference.

Isolation from kin also means that a young mother-to-be must face pregnancy and childbirth without the assistance and support of female kin. Instead, for regular advice and guidance she must turn to physicians (who are more often men than women), books, and friends and neighbours, who themselves may be inexperienced. The problem continues through motherhood, in the absence of experienced women within the family as well as a clear model for childrearing.

The impermanence of the nuclear family itself may constitute a problem, in the form of anxieties over old age. Once the children are gone, who will care for the parents in their final years? In North American society, no *requirement* exists for children to do so. North American governments have established numerous agencies and facilities to care for the elderly. In cultures where adult children have traditionally cared for their elderly parents, changing demographics and government policies may threaten this practice. China's one-child policy, put in place in 1978, was designed to reduce out-of-control population growth. However, fewer children also meant few adult children to care for the elderly. This is particularly worrisome in China, since there is no infrastructure in place to take over responsibilities once shared by large families.

---

[19]Wolf, M. (1972). *Women and the family in rural Taiwan* (pp. 32–35). Stanford, CA: Stanford University Press.

Female-Headed Families

In North America, as increasing numbers of adults have sought escape from dysfunctional nuclear families through divorce, and as young females have chosen to keep infants born outside of a marriage or common-law relationship, a dramatic rise in single-parent families headed by women has occurred. By the 1990s, nearly one-quarter of Canadian households were headed by divorced, separated, and never-married individuals.[20] In the vast majority of cases (83 percent in Canada) the children remain with their mother, who then faces the problem of having to provide for them as well as for herself. In divorce cases, fathers are usually required to pay child support, but they are not always able or willing to do this, and when they are the amount is often not sufficient to pay for all the necessary food, clothes, and medical care, let alone the cost of childcare so that the woman can seek or continue income-producing work outside the house to support herself.

As with working women who remain with their husbands, kin may not be available to look after the single mother's children, so outside help must be sought and (usually) paid for, making it even more difficult for the mother to support her family adequately. To compound the problem, women sometimes lack the skills necessary to secure more than menial and low-paying jobs, not having acquired such skills earlier as a result of raising children. Even when they do have skills, women are often not paid as much as men working at the same jobs.

Not surprisingly, as the number of single-parent families has increased, so has the number of women (and, of course, their children) who live below the poverty line. In 1996 nearly half of all female-headed families in Canada were in a low-income situation.[21] Moreover, these women and

[20]Statistics Canada. (1997, October 14). 1996 Census: Marital status, common-law unions and families. *The Daily.* Retrieved March 3, 2001, from the World Wide Web: http://www.statcan.ca/daily/english/971014/d971014.htm.

[21]Statistics Canada. (1997, October 14). 1996 Census: Families, households, living arrangements. *The Daily.* Retrieved March 4, 2001, from the World Wide Web: http://www.statcan.ca/english/pgdb/people/families/famil52a.htm.

In Canada, the elderly try to remain in their own homes as long as possible. Once they can no longer live alone, most move to retirement villas or nursing homes. Relatively few move in with their adult children.

In Canada, single mothers who are heads of households are often placed in no-win situations: if they work to support the household, they are seen as unfit mothers; if they stay home with the children, they are labelled "deadbeats."

Anthropology **Applied**

John O'Neil

Public Health Surveillance and First Nations Self-Government

Medical anthropologists John O'Neil, Joseph Kaufert, Pat Kaufert, and Kue Young at the University of Manitoba have worked closely with epidemiologists and other public health practitioners to document deteriorating health conditions and health service problems in First Nations communities for the past several decades. While this research has identified important trends in health conditions and has contributed to the development of improved health services, First Nations communities often feel alienated from the research and stigmatized by the results. Increasingly, First Nations communities have expressed a feeling of having been "researched to death" and are resistant to participating in health-related research.

Building on insights provided by the work of French philosopher Michel Foucault, this group of anthropologists has initiated a program of research that is intended to support the First Nations objective of gaining control over the technologies of public health surveillance that are fundamental elements of self-government.[1] From this theoretical perspective, "governing" requires the capacity to monitor the needs and actions of a population. For First Nations communities, these monitoring activities remain largely under the control of federal and provincial government agencies and institutions. As a result, progress toward First Nations self-government is undermined in subtle but insidious ways.

O'Neil and his colleagues are attempting to address this problem by working in partnership with First Nations authorities in Manitoba to develop First Nations public health surveillance capacity. Beginning in 1996 with the development of a longitudinal health survey and continuing with a variety of projects that examine health service data in the context of training workshops for First Nations health workers, this team opened the Manitoba First Nations Centre for Aboriginal Health Research, which provides an opportunity for First Nations authorities and university-based experts to develop health information systems that support the health policy and programming needs of First Nations and other aboriginal communities.

---

[1]O'Neil, J.D., Reading, J., & Leader, A. (1998). Changing the relations of surveillance: The development of a discourse of resistance in aboriginal epidemiology. *Human Organization, 57* (2), 230–237.

---

children are the ones most severely affected by cutbacks made in social welfare programs since 1980. The good news is that since 1996 female-headed family income has been rising, partly because of increased participation of women in the workforce.

Single-parent families are neither new nor restricted to industrialized societies such as Canada. They have been known and studied for a long time in the countries of the Caribbean basin, where men historically have been exploited as a cheap source of labour on plantations. Under such conditions, men have no power and few economic rewards; hence they are tenuously attached at best to any particular household. These are held together by women, who, as producers of subsistence foods, provide the means of economic survival for the family. Similar female-headed households are becoming increasingly common in other developing countries, too, as development projects increasingly restrict women's ability to earn a living wage.

Thus, women constitute the majority of the poor, the underprivileged, and the economically and socially disadvantaged in most of the world's societies. In developing countries, the situation has been made worse by "reforms" the International Monetary Fund (IMF) requires to renegotiate payment of foreign debts. Cutbacks in government education, health, and social programs for debt service have their most direct (and negative) impact on women and children, while further development designed to increase foreign exchange (for debt repayment and the financing of more industrialization) also comes at women's and children's expense. Meanwhile, the prices people must pay for basic life necessities increase (to cut down on unfavourable trade balances).

At the start of this chapter we posed a number of questions relating to the effectiveness of the family, as it is known today in North America, in meeting human needs. From what we have just discussed, it is obvious neolocal nuclear families impose considerable anxiety and stress on the individuals in such families. Deprived of the security and multiplicity of emotional ties found in polygamous, extended, or consanguineal families, these nuclear families find that if something goes wrong, it is potentially more devastating to the individuals involved. Yet it is also obvious that alternative forms of family and household organization come complete with their distinctive stresses and strains. To the question of which alternative is preferable, we must answer that it depends on what problems need to be overcome and what price we are willing to pay.

In North America, it is clear that the problems inherent in the "traditional" nuclear family have led to a marked decline in the percentage of households such families occupy. Meanwhile, the conditions that gave rise to these families in the first place have changed. As well, same-sex couples with children are seeking legal and public recognition for their families. So far, no single family structure or ideology has arisen to supplant the nuclear family, nor can we predict which (if any) of the alternatives will gain preeminence in the future. The only certainty is that family and household arrangements, not just in North America but throughout the world, will continue to evolve, as they always have, as the conditions to which they are sensitive continue to change.

CHAPTER SUMMARY

Dependence on group living for survival is a basic human characteristic. Nurturing children traditionally has been the adult female's job, although men also may play a role, and in some cultures men are even more involved with their children than are women. In addition to at least some childcare, women also carry out other economic tasks that complement those of men. The presence of adults of both sexes in a residential group is advantageous, in that it provides children with adult models of the same sex, from whom they can learn the gender-appropriate roles as defined in that culture.

A definition of the family that avoids Western ethnocentrism sees it as a married or common-law couple with or without children or a lone parent with dependent children. Households, which are usually families, are the basic residential units where economic production, consumption, inheritance, childrearing, and shelter are organized and implemented.

Far from being a stable, unchanging entity, the family may take any one of a number of forms in response to particular social, historical, and ecological circumstances. Conjugal families are those formed on the basis of marital ties. The smallest conjugal unit of mother, father, and their dependent children is called the nuclear family. Contrasting with the conjugal is the consanguineal family, consisting of women, their dependent children, and their brothers. The nuclear family, which became the ideal in North American society, is also found in cultures that live in harsh environments, such as the Arctic, where individual members are strongly dependent on very few people. This form of family is well suited to the mobility required both in food-foraging groups and in industrial societies where job changes are frequent. Among food foragers, however, the nuclear family is not as isolated from other kin as in modern industrial societies.

Characteristic of many nonindustrial societies is the large extended, or conjugal-consanguineal, family. Ideally, some of an extended family's members are related by blood, others are related by marriage, and all live and work together as members of one household. Conjugal or extended families are based on five basic residential patterns: patrilocal, matrilocal, ambilocal, neolocal, and avunculocal.

Different forms of family organization are accompanied by their distinctive problems. Polygamous families endure the potential for conflict among the several spouses of the individual they are married to. One way to ameliorate this problem is through sororal polygyny or fraternal polyandry. Under polyandry, an added difficulty for the youngest husbands is reduced opportunity for reproduction. In extended families, the matter of decision making may be the source of stress, resting as it does with an older individual whose views may not coincide with those of the younger family members. In-marrying spouses in particular may have trouble complying with the demands of the family they must now live in.

In neolocal nuclear families, individuals are isolated from the direct aid and support of kin, so husbands and wives must work out their own solutions to the problems of living together and having children. The problems are especially difficult in North American society, owing to the inequality that persists between men and women, the great emphasis placed on individualism and competition, and an absence of clearly understood patterns of responsibility between husbands and wives, as well as a clear model for childrearing.

In North America, single-parent families, usually headed by a woman, are becoming increasingly common, as are same-sex families. Female-headed families are also common in developing countries. Because the women in such households are hard pressed to provide adequately for themselves as well as for their children, many women in North America and abroad find themselves sinking into poverty.

QUESTIONS FOR CRITICAL THOUGHT

1. In this chapter we have examined several definitions of family. Now it is your turn. How do you define a family? What do you think might be an ideal family form for modern, urban Canadians?

2. Identify childrearing practices in your own culture that serve to mould gender identity (e.g., dress.)

3. Single-parent families are becoming increasingly common in North America. What programs might assist these families to thrive?

4. Many individuals in North America have strong feelings about families with adult members involved in a same-sex relationship. Canada is in the process of legalizing same-sex marriages, which also legitimizes same-sex families. Do you think being raised in a same-sex family would harm a child? Why or why not? In what ways are same-sex families similar to opposite-sex families? In what ways are they different?

INTERNET RESOURCES

Effect of Gender on Parental Favouritism
http://jrscience.wcp.muohio.edu/Research/HNatureProposalsArticles/TheEffectofGenderonParent.html
This research project attempted to determine whether offspring gender has an effect on parental favouritism.

Health Canada: Canada's Seniors
http://www.hc-sc.gc.ca/seniors-aines/pubs/factoids/en/ factoid.htm
Statistic snapshots of Canada's seniors. Also provides a list of related links: older seniors as Canada's fastest-growing group; criminal victimization and fear of crime among Canadian seniors. One link of particular value is "Living with extended families."

Men, Reproductive Rights, and Gender Equality
http://www.unfpa.org/swp/2000/english/ch04 .html
This United Nations site examines gender equality; men's roles and changing realities; violence; gender inequality and cultural expectations; men's support for sexual and reproductive health. An excellent resource for students of gender and the family.

Inuit Childrearing

http://anthro globe.com/bin/artdetail.cgi?id_3

Jean Briggs describes how Inuit childhood interaction moves babies into childhood and beyond.

Not Just Numbers: A Canadian Framework for Future Immigration

http://www.lgirtf.org/newsletters/Summer98

This page examines the importance of family in immigration and defines the family. Also discusses the common-law family and efforts by gays and lesbians to have the terms "spouse" and "family" redefined to meet the changing demographics of Canadian families.

Stay-at-Home Fathers

http://www.census.gov/press-release/cb97-165 .html

A U.S. census press release on how economic conditions can influence married fathers' caring for preschoolers.

Profiles of Homelessness

http://aspe.os.dhhs.gov/progsys/homeless/ profile.htm

A vast site providing key information on homelessness. Valuable links include "The face of homelessness," "The scale of contemporary homelessness," "Homelessness defined," "Characteristics of the homeless population," and "Causes of homelessness." A vital source of information for understanding the nature of homelessness.

Mormon Church History—Polygyny

http://www.ldshistory.net/pc/

A look at the history and features of polygamous families among the Mormons, including legislative history.

Canadian Medical Association Journal

http://www.cma.ca/cmaj/vol-163/ issue-5/0497a.htm

A small site that compares international infant mortality rates. Some links to related sites, including Canada's statistics.

Family, Youth, and Children

http://athena.louisville.edu/library/ekstrom/ govpubs/subjects/family/family.html

This site provides numerous links to sites on family-related issues: adoption, aging, children, family violence, marriage, military families, nurturing fatherhood, welfare, youth.

Aging

http://athena.louisville.edu/library/ekstrom/ govpubs/subjects/aging/age.html

A list of sites related to the topic of aging. Each site provides extensive information.

SUGGESTED READINGS

Briggs, J.L. (1970/1998). Inuit morality play: The emotional education of a three-year-old. *Social and Economic Studies,* No. 67. Institute of Social and Economic Research.

The book follows six months in the life of a three-year-old Inuit girl as she tries to make sense of her world. Included are touching stories of Chubby Matta, as her family gently enculturates her into Inuit social life. Of special interest to students of anthropology is the way moral questions are posed for the little girl to ponder.

Briggs, J.L. (1970). *Never in anger: Portrait of an Eskimo family.* Cambridge, MA: Harvard University Press.

This readable book is based on fieldwork Jean Briggs conducted among the Inuit living north of Hudson Bay. Her research focuses on emotional expression, in particular the handling of emotion. Her disconcerting experience of being shunned highlights some of the travails ethnographers encounter when living with a culture much different from their own.

Eichler, M. (1983). *Families in Canada today: Recent changes and their policy consequences.* Toronto: Gage.

Although somewhat dated and steeped in theoretical jargon, this book does contain an enormous amount of information on

Canadian families and changing patterns in recent decades.

Goody, J. (1983). *Development of the family and marriage in Europe*. Cambridge: Cambridge University Press.

This historical study shows how the nature of the family changed in Europe in response to regulations the Catholic Church introduced to weaken the power of kin groups and gain access to property. It explains how European patterns of kinship and marriage came to differ from those of the ancient circum-Mediterranean world and from those that succeeded them in the Middle East and North Africa.

Mandell, N., & Duffy, A. (1995). *Canadian families: Diversity, conflict and change*. Toronto: Harcourt Brace Canada.

This book explores the dynamic and tumultuous aspects of marriage and the family in Canadian society. It challenges our traditional approaches to marriage and the family, and addresses the effects of gender, race, class, sexual orientation, divorce, and violence on the family.

Ramu, G.N. (Ed.). (1980). *Courtship, marriage, and the family in Canada*. Toronto: Gage.

This book provides an introductory overview of courtship, marriage, and the family life cycle in Canada. Although somewhat dated, it still presents useful information on theoretical orientations, and it touches on several aspects of marriage, including the family, sex roles, kinship networks, divorce and remarriage, and ethnic perspectives.

Stacey, J. (1990). *Brave new families: Stories of domestic conflict in late twentieth century America*. New York: Basic Books.

Written by a sociologist, this book takes an anthropological approach to understanding the changes affecting family structure in the United States. The author concludes that "the family" is *not* here to stay, nor should we wish otherwise. For all the difficulties attendant to "the family's demise," alternative arrangements do open hopeful possibilities for the future.

Thorne, B., & Yalom, M. (Eds.). (1982). *Rethinking the family: Some feminist questions*. New York: Longman.

As anthropologists have paid more attention to how institutions and practices work from a woman's perspective, they have had to reexamine existing assumptions about families in human societies. The 12 original essays in this volume, by scholars in economics, history, law, literature, philosophy, psychology, and sociology, as well as anthropology, examine topics such as the idea of the monolithic family, the sexual division of labour and inequality, motherhood, parenting, mental illness, and relations between family, class, and state. Especially recommended is the essay "Is There a Family? New Anthropological Views."

CNN Today Video

India: Arranged Marriage (CNN Cultural Anthropology, vol. 1, 1:50)
This segment looks at the practice of arranged marriages in India.

Chapter 9

Kinship and Descent

Among people of Scottish ancestry, clan affiliation is still a matter of interest, although the importance of such kin groups has diminished. In many human cultures, however, clans and other kin groups remain strong.

Chapter Preview

1. What Are Descent Groups?

Kin groups are made up of our relatives, both consanguineal (blood) and affinal (in-laws). We organize our kin along descent groupings. A descent group is a kind of kinship group whereby being a lineal descendant of a particular real or mythical ancestor is a criterion of membership. Descent may be reckoned exclusively through men, exclusively through women, or through both.

2. What Functions Do Descent Groups Serve?

Descent groups of various kinds—lineages, clans, phratries, and moieties—are convenient devices for solving a number of problems human societies commonly confront: how to maintain the integrity of resources that cannot be divided without destruction; generating workforces for tasks that require a labour pool larger than households can provide; and allowing members of one sovereign local group to claim support and protection from members of another. Not all cultures have descent groups; in many food-foraging and industrial groups some of these problems are handled by the kindred, a group of people with a living relative in common. The kindred, however, does not exist in perpetuity, as does the descent group, nor is its membership as clearly and explicitly defined. Hence, it is generally a weaker unit than the descent group.

3. How Do Descent Groups Form?

Descent groups arise from extended family organization, as long as problems of organization exist that such groups help to solve. This is most apt to happen in food-producing groups. First to develop are localized lineages, followed by larger, dispersed groups such as clans and phratries. With the passage of time kinship terminology itself is affected by and adjusts to the kinds of descent or other kin groups important to a culture.

CHAPTER OUTLINE

Why We Study Kinship

Urban Kinship Systems in Canada

Descent Groups

Original Study: Coping as a Woman in a Man's World

Gender Perspectives: The Kinkeepers

Forms and Functions of Descent Groups

Anthropology Applied: Federal Recognition for Native Americans

Contemporary Chinese-Canadian Kinship

Kinship Terminology and Kinship Groups

All cultures have found some form of family and/or household organization a convenient way to deal with the problems human groups face: how to facilitate economic cooperation between the sexes, how to provide a proper setting for childrearing, and how to regulate sexual activity. Efficient and flexible though family and household organization may be in rising to challenges connected with such problems, the fact is many cultures confront problems beyond the coping ability of family and household organization. For one, members of one sovereign local group often need some means of claiming support and protection from individuals in another group. This can be important for defence against natural or human-made disasters; if people have the right of entry into local groups other than their own, they can secure protection or critical resources when their own group cannot provide them. For another, a group frequently needs to share rights to some means of production that cannot be divided without its destruction. This is often the case in horticultural societies, where division of land is impractical beyond a certain point. The problem can be avoided if land ownership is vested in a corporate group that exists in perpetuity. Finally, people often need some means of providing cooperative workforces for tasks that require more participants than households alone can provide.

One way of dealing with these sorts of problems is by developing a formal political system, with personnel to make and enforce laws, keep the peace, allocate resources, and perform other regulatory and societal functions. A more common way in non-industrial societies—especially horticultural and pastoral societies—is by developing kinship groups.

Our **kinship** is composed of the people we are related to—our consanguineal (blood) relatives and our affinal (through marriage) relatives. Regardless of the complexity of a culture, this kinship plays an important role in the social life of all human groups. Our kin may be divided into three groups: nominal, effective, and intimate or core kin.[1] We have little or no contact with *nominal kin,* even though we are aware of their

---

[1]Firth, R. (1956). *Two studies of kinship in London* (p. 103). London: University of London, Athlone Press.

On this altar, King Yax-Pac of the ancient Maya city of Copan portrays himself and his predecessors, thereby tracing his descent back to the founder of the dynasty. In many human groups, such genealogical connections are used to define each individual's rights, privileges, and obligations.

Kinship. The people we are related to through blood (consanguineal) and marriage (affinal).

existence. We meet *effective kin* fairly regularly, at family functions such as weddings, funerals, and reunions. We maintain continuing, close relationships with our *intimate kin,* who usually include our extended family—parents, siblings, aunts and uncles, and grandparents, both affinal and consanguineal. In Canadian society, the size of our kin group is influenced by personal choice and, to a lesser extent, proximity, gender, and class factors.[2]

In rural, preindustrial societies, kinship is the focal point of social organization; members live in close proximity and generally form economic bonds, such as ownership of land or water use rights. In urban, industrial societies, modern ideologies of individualism, privacy, nuclear family structures, and increased mobility have altered extended-family kinship systems to a degree. In addition, formal institutions such as daycare centres, banks, and schools have usurped what was formerly a family obligation.

WHY WE STUDY KINSHIP

Students often ask why they have to study kinship. The answer to this question is multifaceted. Although we may not think about our kinship network in everyday life, the fact remains that virtually everyone has kin, whether biological or adopted, and these "relatives" have a profound effect on our lives. We begin learning our kinship from birth—the way we classify our relatives seems natural and logical to us, just as other kinship systems seem to its members.

Kinship involves not only how we classify our relatives, but also how we organize our family, the support and assistance we can count on, whom we will marry, our residential patterns, and how we view our world and our future. Kinship defines our gender roles, how many children we will bear, what will happen to us when we grow old, even what faith we will practise. It is all of these things and more. Kinship is culturally diverse, and it is dynamic. When students strive to understand this diversity, they must remember that they are also seeking to understand people and their behaviour, and how this behaviour is influenced by kinship.

URBAN KINSHIP SYSTEMS IN CANADA[3]

In the early part of the 20th century, researchers assumed that urbanization and industrialization would reduce the significance of kinship in Canadian society—that nuclear families would supplant extended kin groups, and non-kin ties (i.e., friends) would become more important in our lives than kin. Supposedly, an *isolated nuclear family* structure functions more efficiently in our urban environment than an unwieldy extended family.[4] However, recent studies have disputed this isolated nuclear family hypothesis. Extended kinship ties in Canada are still fundamental to the well-being of individuals and nuclear families. Kin groups establish patterns of mutual aid, especially among parents and adult children and their families, including financial assistance, the provision of childcare during vacations, and regular gift giving. This *modified extended family*[5] does not require residential proximity or restrictive rights and obligations, maintains close emotional ties and a network of reciprocal support, and is still common in 21st-century Canadian families.

Canada is a multicultural society, strongly influenced by immigration patterns and population demographics, including ethnic, linguistic, and cultural enclaves. Early immigrants to Canada, mainly of French and British descent, were organized in a nuclear family structure, but developed strong kin ties with other relatives in Canada. Early Canadian farms were not mechanized, farmers needed human labour, and extended-family units commonly farmed collectively to supply the needed labour. Following

---

[2]Ramu, G.N. (1979). Kinship networks. In G.N. Ramu (Ed.), *Courtship, marriage, and the family in Canada* (pp. 96–114). Toronto: Gage.

[3]The following discussion is taken from Ramu, G.N. (1979). Kinship networks. In G.N. Ramu (Ed.). *Courtship, marriage, and the family in Canada* (pp. 96–114). Toronto: Gage.

[4]Parsons, T. (1943). The kinship system of contemporary United States. *American Anthropologist, 45.*

[5]Litwak, E. (1960). Occupational mobility and extended family cohesion. *American Sociological Review, 29.*

mechanization, many of these collective farming enterprises dispersed, as young people sought employment and educational opportunities in urban centres. More recent immigrants to Canada, such as Italian Canadians, tend to maintain close ties with kin in their country of origin, thanks to global transportation and communication systems, while also establishing close ties with relatives already in Canada. Neolocal nuclear families are the basic kinship unit, although other members of the extended family usually live nearby. New immigrants often substitute friends, especially of the same ethnic origin, if they do not have any family in Canada, or, as with Italian Canadians, include neighbours and friends in their kinship network. Known as **fictive kinship,** this practice is common among many Canadian people, not just recent immigrants.

In Canada, then, kinship tends to be voluntary and selective, with no strong obligations, compared with, for example, a horticultural kin group. Under normal circumstances, the nuclear family does not operate in isolation; a modified extended-family support system, involving frequent communication, visiting, and support, is available to each family. The degree of contact is not determined by geographical proximity, but rather by closeness of the individuals, with parents and adult children enjoying the most interaction.

▲▽▲▽▲▽▲▽▲▽▲▽▲▽▲▽▲▽▲▽▲▽▲▽▲▽▲▽▲

DESCENT GROUPS

A common way of organizing a society along kinship lines is by creating what anthropologists call descent groups. A **descent group** is any publicly recognized social entity requiring lineal descent from a real or mythical ancestor for membership. Members of a descent group trace their connections back to a common ancestor through parent–child links. This feature may explain why descent groups are found in so many cultures.

They appear to stem from the parent–child bond, which is built upon as the basis for a structured social group.

Descent groups clearly define membership; otherwise membership overlaps and it is not always clear where an individual's primary loyalty belongs. Membership can be restricted in a number of ways. It can be based on where people live; for example, if your parents live patrilocally, you might be assigned to your father's descent group. Another way is through choice; each individual may have a number of options. This, though, introduces the possibility of competition and conflict as groups vie for members. The most common way to restrict membership is by tracing membership through one sex. In this way, each individual is automatically assigned from the moment of birth to his or her mother's or father's group and to that group only.

Unilineal Descent

Unilineal descent (sometimes called *unilateral descent*) establishes descent group membership through the male or the female line. In non-Western cultures, unilineal descent groups are quite common. At birth, an individual is assigned membership in a specific descent group, which may be traced either by **matrilineal descent,** through the female line, or by **patrilineal descent,** through the male line.

A close relationship between the descent system and a culture's economy seems to exist. Generally, patrilineal descent predominates where the man is the breadwinner, as among pastoralists and intensive agriculturalists, where male labour is a prime factor. Matrilineal descent is important mainly among horticulturists where women are the breadwinners. Numerous matrilineal cultures are found in South Asia, one of the cradles of food production in the Old World. These include cultures in India, Sri Lanka, Indonesia, Sumatra, Tibet, South China, and many Indonesian islands. Matrilineal systems also were prominent in some

---

Fictive kinship.   Friends not biologically related, but considered part of a kin group. **> Descent group.**   Any publicly recognized social entity requiring lineal descent from a particular real or mythical ancestor for membership. **> Unilineal descent.**   Descent that establishes group membership exclusively through either the mother's or the father's line. **> Matrilineal descent.**   Descent traced exclusively through the female line to establish group membership. **> Patrilineal descent.**   Descent traced exclusively through the male line to establish group membership.

North American aboriginal groups, such as the Huron and Iroquois, and still are in parts of Africa.

In all cultures the kin of both mother and father are important components of the social structure. Just because descent may be reckoned patrilineally, for example, does not mean maternal relatives are unimportant. It simply means that, for purposes of *group membership,* the mother's relatives are excluded. Similarly, under matrilineal descent, the father's relatives are excluded for purposes of group membership. For example, we already have seen in the two preceding chapters how important paternal relatives are among the matrilineal Trobriand Islanders. Although children belong to their mothers' descent groups, fathers play an important role in nurturing and building them up. Upon marriage, the bride's and groom's paternal relatives contribute gifts, and, throughout life, a man may expect his paternal kin to help him improve his economic and political position in society. Eventually, sons may expect to inherit personal property from their fathers.

Patrilineal Descent and Organization

Patrilineal descent (sometimes called *agnatic* or *male descent*) is the more widespread of the two unilineal descent systems. The male members of a

In patrilineal and other cultures that promote the dominance of men over women, this practice sometimes goes to the extreme of inflicting physical, as well as social, disabilities on women. In earlier times, North American women often wore tight corsets, and today women wear high-heeled shoes. The result in these cases is actual physical impairment.

patrilineal descent group trace their descent through other males from a common ancestor (see Figure 9.1). Brothers and sisters belong to the

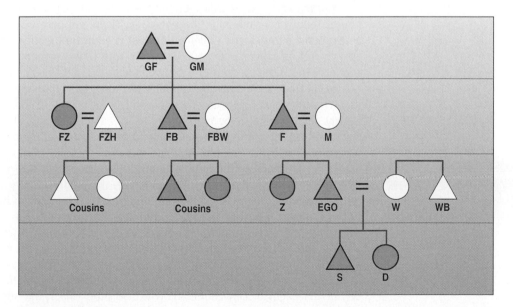

FIGURE 9.1

How patrilineal descent is traced. Only the individuals symbolized by a filled-in circle or triangle are in the same descent group as ego. The abbreviation *F* stands for father, *B* for brother, *H* for husband, *S* for son, *M* for mother, *Z* for sister, *D* for daughter, and *W* for wife.

descent group of their father's father, their father, their father's siblings, and their father's brother's children. A man's son and daughter also trace their descent through the male line to their common ancestor. In a typical patrilineal group, the responsibility for training the children rests with the father or his elder brother. A woman belongs to the same descent group as her father and his brothers, but her children cannot trace their descent through them. A woman's paternal aunt's children, for example, trace their descent through the patrilineal group of her husband.

A patrilineal culture is very much a man's world; no matter how valued women may be, they inevitably find themselves in a difficult position. Far from resigning themselves to a subordinate position, however, they actively manipulate the system to their own advantage as best they can. To learn how they may do so, the following Original Study looks more closely at the way women relate to one another in traditional Chinese society.

ORIGINAL STUDY

Coping as a Woman in a Man's World

Margery Wolf

Women in rural Taiwan do not live their lives in the walled courtyards of their husbands' households. If they did, they might be as powerless as their stereotype. It is in their relations in the outside world (and for women in rural Taiwan that world consists almost entirely of the village) that women develop sufficient backing to maintain some independence under their powerful mothers-in-law. A successful venture into the men's world is no small feat when one recalls that the men of a village were born there and are often related to one another, whereas the women are unlikely to have either the ties of childhood or the ties of kinship to unite them. All the same, shared interests, and common problems of women are reflected in every village in a loosely knit society that can when needed be called on to exercise considerable influence.

Women carry on as many of their activities as possible outside the house. They wash clothes on the riverbank, clean and pare vegetables at a communal pump, mend under a tree that is a known meetingplace, and stop to rest on a bench or group of stones with other women. There is a continual moving back and forth between kitchens, and conversations are carried on from open doorways through the long, hot afternoons of summer. The shy young girl who enters the village as a bride is examined as frankly and suspiciously by the women as an animal that is up for sale. If she is deferential to her elders, does not criticize or compare her new world unfavorably with the one she has left, the older residents will gradually accept her presence on the edge of their conversations and stop changing the topic to general subjects when she brings the family laundry to scrub on the rocks near them. As the young bride meets other girls in her position, she makes allies for the future, but she must also develop relationships with the older women. She learns to use considerable discretion in making and receiving confidences, for a girl who gossips freely about the affairs of her husband's household may find herself always on the outside of the group, or worse yet, accused of snobbery. I described in *The House of Lim* the plight of Lim Chui-ieng, who had little village backing in her troubles with her husband and his family as a result of her arrogance toward the women's community. In Peihotien the young wife of the storekeeper's son suffered a similar lack of support. Warned by her husband's parents not to be too "easy" with the other villagers lest they try to buy things on credit, she obeyed to the point of being considered unfriendly by the women of the village. When she began to have serious troubles with her husband and eventually his family, there was no one in the village she could turn to for solace, advice, and most important, peacemaking.

Once a young bride has established herself as a member of the women's community, she has also established for herself a certain amount of protection. If the members of her husband's family step beyond the limits of propriety in their treatment of her—such as refusing to allow her to return to her natal home for her brother's wedding or beating her without serious justification—she can complain to a woman friend, preferably older, while they are washing vegetables at the communal pump. The story will quickly spread to the other women, and one of them will take it upon herself to check the facts with another member of the girl's household. For a few days the matter will be thoroughly discussed whenever a few women gather. In a young wife's first few years in the community, she can expect to have her mother-in-law's side of any disagreement given fuller weight than her own—her mother-in-law has, after all, been a part of the community a lot longer. However, the discussion itself will serve to curb many offenses. Even if the older woman knows that public opinion is falling to her side, she will be somewhat more judicious about refusing her daughter-in-law's next request. Still, the daughter-in-law who hopes to make use of the village forum to depose her mother-in-law or at least gain herself special privilege will discover just how important the prerogatives of age and length of residence are. Although the women can serve as a powerful protective force for their defenseless younger members, they are also a very conservative force in the village.

Taiwanese women can and do make use of their collective power to lose face for their menfolk in order to influence decisions that are ostensibly not theirs to make. Although young women may have little or no influence over their husbands and would not dare express an unsolicited opinion (and perhaps not even a solicited one) to their fathers-in-law, older women who have raised their sons properly retain considerable influence over their sons' actions, even in activities exclusive to men. Further, older women who have displayed years of good judgement are regularly consulted by their husbands about major as well as minor economic and social projects. But even men who think themselves free to ignore the opinions of their women are never free of their own concept, face. It is much easier to lose face than to have face. We once asked a male friend in Peihotien just what "having face" amounted to. He replied, "When no one is talking about a family, you can say it has face." This is precisely where women wield their power. When a man behaves in a way that they consider wrong, they talk about him—not only among themselves, but to their sons and husbands. No one "tells him how to mind his own business," but it becomes abundantly clear that he is losing face and by continuing in this manner may bring shame to the family of his ancestors and descendants. Few men will risk that.

The rules that a Taiwanese man must learn and obey to be a successful member of his society are well developed, clear, and relatively easy to stay within. A Taiwanese woman must also learn the rules, but if she is to be a successful woman, she must learn not to stay within them, but to appear to stay within them; to manipulate them, but not to appear to be manipulating them; to teach them to her children, but not to depend on her children for her protection. A truly successful Taiwanese woman is a rugged individualist who has learned to depend largely on herself while appearing to lean on her father, her husband, and her son. The contrast between the terrified young bride and the loud, confident, often lewd old woman who has outlived her mother-in-law and her husband reflects the tests met and passed by not strictly following the rules and by making purposeful use of those who must. The Chinese male's conception of women as "narrow-hearted" and socially inept may well be his vague recognition of this facet of women's power and technique.

Source: Wolf, M. (1972). *Women and the family in rural Taiwan* (pp. 37–41). Stanford, CA: Stanford University Press.

Matrilineal Descent and Organization

In one respect, matrilineal descent is the opposite of patrilineal: It is reckoned through the female line (see Figure 9.2). The matrilineal pattern differs from the patrilineal, however, in that descent does not automatically confer authority. Thus, although patrilineal societies are patriarchal, matrilineal cultures are not matriarchal. Although descent passes through the female line and women may have considerable power, they do not hold exclusive authority in the descent group: They share it with men. These are the brothers, rather than the husbands, of the women descent is reckoned through. The adaptive purpose of the matrilineal system is to provide continuous female solidarity within the female labour pool. Matrilineal systems are usually found in farming communities where women perform much of the productive work.

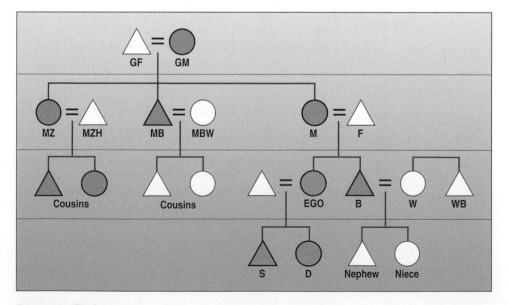

FIGURE 9.2

This diagram, which traces descent matrilineally, can be compared with that in Figure 9.1, showing patrilineal descent. The two patterns are virtually mirror images. Note that a man cannot transmit descent to his own children.

In the matrilineal system, brothers and sisters belong to the descent group of the mother's mother, the mother, the mother's siblings, and the mother's sister's children. Males belong to the same descent group as their mother and sister, but their children cannot trace their descent through them. For example, the children of a man's maternal uncle are considered members of the uncle's wife's matrilineal descent group. Similarly, a man's children belong to his wife's, but not his, descent group.

Although not true of all matrilineal systems, a common feature is the weak tie between husband and wife. The wife's brother, and not the husband/father, distributes goods, organizes work, settles disputes, administers inheritance and succession rules, and supervises rituals. The husband has legal authority not in his household but in that of his sister. Furthermore, his property and status are inherited by his sister's son, rather than by his son. Thus, brothers and sisters maintain lifelong ties with one another, whereas marital ties are easily severed. In matrilineal groups, unsatisfactory marriages are more easily ended than in patrilineal groups at least until children are born of the union.

Matrilineal clans formed the basis of Iroquoian kinship. Each clan owned a longhouse, in which the members of their clan lived. Matrilocality was preferred; typically, a longhouse consisted of an elder woman, her husband, their daughters and families, and any unmarried

sons. Senior women of matrilineages, known as "clan mothers," were held in great esteem and considered the wisest, most generous, and most good natured. They were responsible for overseeing domestic tasks in the households and allocating farmland to the women of the clan. If these senior women were opposed to the men heading off to war, they could withhold supplies; the men usually complied with their wives' and mothers' wishes. Clan mothers also played a role in selecting or demoting chiefs and advisers. The great respect shown to these clan mothers, their control over resources, and their obvious political power led early European observers to identify this culture as a matriarchy. This, however, proved inaccurate. Iroquois culture was egalitarian: Neither men nor women dominated the culture.[6]

Double Descent

Double descent, or double unilineal descent, whereby descent is reckoned both patrilineally and matrilineally at the same time, is very rare. In this system descent is matrilineal for some purposes and patrilineal for others. Generally, where double descent is reckoned, the matrilineal and patrilineal groups take action in different spheres of society.

For example, among the Yakö of eastern Nigeria, property is divided into both patrilineal line possessions and matrilineal line possessions.[7] The patrilineage owns perpetual productive resources, such as land, whereas the matrilineage owns consumable property, such as livestock. The legally weaker matrilineal line is somewhat more important in religious matters than the patrilineal line. Through double descent, a Yakö might inherit grazing lands from the father's patrilineal group and certain ritual privileges from the mother's matrilineal line.

In Iroquois society women performed many tasks, controlled resources, and wielded significant political power.

[6]Bonvillain, N. (1998). Women and men. *Cultural constructs of gender* (2nd ed.). Upper Saddle River, NJ: Prentice Hall.

[7]Forde, C.D. (1968). Double descent among the Yakö. In P. Bohannan & J. Middleton (Eds.), *Kinship and social organization* (pp. 179–191). Garden City, NY: Natural History Press.

Double descent.   A system tracing descent matrilineally for some purposes and patrilineally for others.

Gender **Perspectives**

The Kinkeepers

In most extended families, one special person takes on the responsibility of maintaining formal and informal ties with other extended-family members, keeping the lines of communication open, and offering support and comfort when needed. Typically, this kinkeeper is a female, often an older woman, who values the extended family and aims to promote solidarity among family members. She is in charge of telephoning "Aunt Mary," or more likely today, e-mailing her to catch up on the news. She sends cards and gifts to all the nieces and nephews on their birthdays, and acknowledges special occasions, such as weddings, anniversaries, and graduations. She regularly visits family members, especially shut-ins and young couples with a new baby, and organizes holiday gatherings to bring the kin together under one roof. Kinkeepers are responsible for offering emotional support to kin in crisis, for example, by taking care of sick children, and almost always become the primary caregivers for elderly parents.

The kinkeeper reminds other family members to fulfill their familial responsibilities, such as sending birthday cards and, failing that, often takes over the responsibility rather than see a family member neglected. But kinkeepers also make decisions about whether to maintain close ties with certain kin. Thus, by the very nature of their work, kinkeepers possess a certain power within their family; without their ministrations, kin ties tend to break down.

Although kinkeepers are found in every society, and in every social class, in modern Western society, kinkeepers provide many "community services" previously relegated to governmental agencies. As these government services continue to be cut back, kinkeepers are expected to pick up the slack by volunteering their unpaid labour. Women, then, are faced with competing types of work: housework, childcare, labour market work, eldercare, and kinship work.

Sources:

diLeonardo, M. (1997). The female world of cards and holidays: Women, families, and the work of kinship. In C.B. Brettel & C.F. Sargent (Eds.), *Gender in cross-cultural perspective.* Upper Saddle River, NJ: Prentice Hall.

Nelson, E.D., & Robinson, B.W. (1999). *Gender in Canada* (p. 380). Scarborough, ON: Prentice-Hall Canada.

Ramu, G.N. (1980). Kinship networks. In G.N. Ramu (Ed.), *Courtship, marriage, and the family in Canada* (p. 157). Toronto: Gage.

Ambilineal Descent

Unilineal descent provides an easy way of restricting descent group membership to avoid problems of divided loyalty and the like. A number of cultures, many of them in the Pacific and in Southeast Asia, accomplish the same task in other ways. The resultant descent groups are known as *ambilineal, nonunilineal,* or *cognatic.* **Ambilineal descent** provides a measure of flexibility not normally found under unilineal descent; each individual has the option of affiliating with either the mother's or the father's descent group.

In many of these cultures, an individual is allowed to belong to only one group at a time, regardless of how many groups he or she may be eligible to join. Thus, the group may be divided into the same sorts of discrete and separate groups of kin as in a patrilineal or matrilineal culture. Other cognatic societies, however, such as the Samoans of the South Pacific or the Bella Coola and the southern branch of the Kwakwaka'wakw of the Pacific northwest coast of North America, allow overlapping membership in a number of descent groups.

Ambilineal descent.   Descent in which the individual may affiliate with either the mother's or the father's descent group.

FORMS AND FUNCTIONS OF DESCENT GROUPS

Descent groups with restricted membership are usually more than mere groups of relatives providing warmth and a sense of belonging; in non-industrial societies they are tightly organized working units providing security and services in what can be a difficult, uncertain life. Besides acting as economic units providing mutual aid to their members, they may support the aged and infirm and help with marriages and deaths. Often, they play a role in determining who an individual may or may not marry. The descent group also may act as a repository of religious traditions, such as ancestor worship.

The Lineage

A **lineage** is a corporate descent group composed of consanguineal kin who trace descent through known links back to a common ancestor. The term is usually employed where a form of unilineal descent is the rule, but some ambilineal groups are similar.

The lineage is ancestor-oriented; membership in the group is recognized only if relationship to a common ancestor can be traced and proved. An individual may have no legal or political status except as a lineage member. Since "citizenship" is derived from lineage membership and legal status depends on it, political and religious power is derived from it as well. Important religious and magical powers, such as those associated with the cults of gods and ancestors, also may be bound to the lineage.

Because the corporate lineage endures after the deaths of members with new members continually born into it, it has a perpetual existence that enables it to take corporate actions, such as owning property, organizing productive activities, distributing goods and labour power, assigning status, and regulating relations with other groups. The lineage is a strong, effective base of social organization.

Anthropologist Peggy Reeves Sanday with members of a matrilineal clan among the Minangkabau of Sumatra gathered for a house-raising ceremony. The one adult male is the brother of the senior female leader (the woman on Sanday's left); he is the clan's male leader. Absence of other men reflects the predominance of women in this society.

Lineage.   A corporate descent group whose members trace their genealogical links to a common ancestor.

A common feature of lineages is their exogamy. This means lineage members must find their marriage partners in other lineages. One advantage of lineage exogamy is that potential sexual competition within the group is curbed, promoting the group's solidarity. Lineage exogamy also means each marriage is more than an arrangement between two individuals; it amounts as well to a new alliance between lineages. Finally, lineage exogamy supports open communication within a culture by promoting the diffusion of knowledge from one lineage to another.

The Clan

As generation succeeds generation and new members are born into the lineage, its membership may become unmanageably large or too much for the lineage's resources to support. When this happens, **fission** occurs; that is, the lineage splits into new, smaller lineages. When fission occurs, usually the members of the new lineages continue to recognize their ultimate relationship to one another. The result of this process is the appearance of a second kind of descent group, the **clan.** The term *clan* and its close relative, the *sib*, have been used differently by various anthropologists, and a certain amount of confusion exists about their meaning. The clan (or sib) will be defined here as a noncorporate descent group whose members assume descent from a common ancestor (who may be real or fictive) but are unable to trace the actual genealogical links back to that ancestor. This stems from the great genealogical depth of the clan, whose founding ancestor lived so far in the past that the links must be assumed rather than known in detail. A clan differs from a lineage in another respect: It lacks the residential unity generally—although not invariably—characteristic of a lineage's core members. As with the lineage, descent may be patrilineal, matrilineal, or ambilineal.

Because clan membership is dispersed rather than localized, it usually does not hold tangible property corporately. Instead, it tends to be more a unit for ceremonial matters. Only on special occasions will the membership gather for specific purposes. Like lineages, clans may regulate marriage through exogamy. Because of their dispersed membership, they give individuals entry rights into local groups other than their own.

Clans frequently depend on symbols—of animals, plants, natural forces, and objects—to provide members with solidarity and a ready means of identification. These symbols, called *totems,* are often associated with the clan's mythical origin and reinforce an awareness of their common descent with what the totems represent. **Totemism** was defined by British anthropologist A.R. Radcliffe-Brown as a set of "customs and beliefs by which there is set up a special system of relations between the society and the plants, animals, and other natural objects that are important in the social life."[8] Among the Haida on the west coast of Canada, important families were divided into totemic groups with such names as Bear, Killer Whale, Cannibal Spirit, Salmon, and Beaver.[9]

Phratries and Moieties

Other kinds of descent groups are phratries and moieties (see Figure 9.3). A **phratry** is a unilineal descent group composed of at least two clans that supposedly share a common ancestry, whether provable or not. Like clan individuals, phratry members cannot trace accurately their descent links to a common ancestor, although they firmly believe such an ancestor existed.

---

[8]Radcliffe-Brown, A.R. (1931). Social organization of Australian tribes. *Oceania Monographs, 1,* 29. Melbourne: Macmillan.

[9]Friesen, J.W. (1997). *Rediscovering the First Nations of Canada.* Calgary: Detselig.

Fission.   The splitting of a descent group into two or more new descent groups. **> Clan.**   A noncorporate descent group whose members claim descent from a common ancestor without actually knowing the genealogical links to that ancestor. **> Totemism.**   The belief that people are related to particular animals, plants, or natural objects by virtue of descent from common ancestral spirits. **> Phratry.**   A unilineal descent group composed of two or more clans that claim to be of common ancestry. If only two such groups exist, each is a moiety.

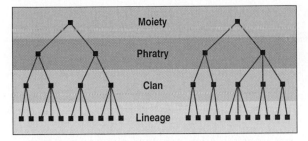

FIGURE 9.3

This diagram shows how lineages, clans, phratries, and moieties form an organizational hierarchy. Each moiety is subdivided into phratries, each phratry is subdivided into clans, and each clan is subdivided into lineages.

If the entire culture is divided into only two major descent groups, whether they are equivalent to clans or phratries or involve an even more all-inclusive level, each group is called a **moiety** (after the French word for "half"). Moiety members also believe they share a common ancestor but cannot prove it through definite genealogical links. As a rule, the feelings of kinship among members of lineages and clans are stronger than those of members of phratries and moieties. This may be due to the larger size and more diffuse nature of the latter groups.

Like clans and lineages, phratries and moieties are often exogamous and thus are bound together by marriages between their members. And like clans, they provide members rights of access to other communities. Even if a community does not include any clan members, an individual's phratry members will still be there to turn to for hospitality. Finally, moieties may perform reciprocal services for one another, as among the Mohawks and other Iroquoian nations of southern Ontario and New York State. Among them, individuals turned to members of the opposite moiety for the necessary rituals when a member of their own moiety died. Such interdependence between moieties, again, served to maintain the integrity of the entire society.

Bilateral Descent and the Kindred

Important though descent groups are in many cultures, they are not found in all cultures, nor are they the only kinds of nonfamilial kinship groups found. *Bilateral descent,* a characteristic of Western society as well as a number of food-foraging groups, affiliates a person with close relatives through both sexes; in other words, the individual traces descent through both parents, all four grandparents, and so forth, recognizing multiple ancestors. Theoretically, a person is associated equally with all consanguineal relatives on both the mother's and father's sides of the family. Thus, this principle relates an individual lineally to all eight great-grandparents and laterally to all third and fourth cousins. Since such a group is too large to be socially practical, it is usually reduced to a small circle of paternal and maternal relatives, called the **kindred.** The kindred may be defined as a group of people closely related to one living individual through both parents (see Figure 9.4).

North Americans are familiar with the kindred; those who belong are simply called relatives. It includes the relatives on both sides of the family who are seen on important occasions, such as family reunions and funerals. Most people in Canada can identify the members of their kindred up to grandparents and first, if not always second, cousins. The limits of the kindred, however, are variable and indefinite; no one can be absolutely certain which relatives to invite to important functions and which to exclude. Inevitably, situations arise that require some debate about whether to invite particular, usually distant, relatives. Kindreds are thus not clearly bounded and lack the discreteness of unilineal or ambilineal descent groups.

Because of its bilateral structure, a kindred is never the same for any two persons except siblings (brothers and sisters). Thus, no two people (except siblings) belong to the same kindred. As for the kindreds of ego's parents, these range from grandparents lineally to cousins too distant laterally for ego to know, and the same is true of ego's aunts and uncles. Thus, the kindred is not composed of people with an ancestor in common but with a living relative in common—ego. Furthermore, as ego goes through life, the kindreds he or she is affiliated with will change. When young, individuals belong to the kindreds

---

Moiety. Each group that results from a division of a society into two halves on the basis of descent. **> Kindred.** A group of consanguineal kin linked by their relationship to one living individual; includes both maternal and paternal kin.

Anthropology **Applied**

Federal Recognition for Native Americans

Esoteric though research on kinship organization may sometimes seem, it is important for the kind of applied anthropology described here by anthropologist Harald Prins.[1]

In autumn 1981, Dutch anthropologist Harald Prins drove through Maine's vast woodlands to the small town of Houlton near the Canadian border. He'd gone there to check out a job at the Association of Aroostook Indians (AAI), which needed a research and development director. Founded by a group of Indian activists in 1970 to deal with a host of serious problems, AAI served 1200 off-reservation Mi'kmaqs and Maliseets in Aroostook County. Crushed by chronic poverty and suffering from poor health, most resided in shacks or run-down apartments. Few had more than an eighth-grade education, many were alcoholics, and almost all felt victimized by racial discrimination. The AAI tried to ease their burdens by providing social services. Moreover, it tackled political problems, including reclamation of traditional rights to freely hunt, trap, and fish.

Fresh from fieldwork in the Argentine pampas and frustrated by an anthropology that had little practical use for the people being studied, Prins welcomed the opportunity to be an activist in Maine's backlands. The elders on AAI's board hired him, saying his main task was to help Aroostook Mi'kmaqs gain federal recognition as a tribal community. That would make them eligible for federal assistance (health, housing, education, and child welfare) and loan guarantees for economic development.

Prins quickly realized the difficulty of the task. A year earlier, Maine's other three Indian groups (including the Maliseet) had negotiated a land claims settlement with the U.S. government and the State of Maine, winning federal recognition and money to buy back about 300 000 acres of land. Mi'kmaqs had been left out because no one had done the research needed to ensure their inclusion. Worse, Mi'kmaqs had lost the right to put together their own claim because the settlement extinguished all aboriginal titles held by any Indian tribe to all lands in Maine.

Since Maliseets had already gained federal status as a "tribe," Prins helped Mi'kmaqs reorganize based on their ethnic identity. Newly incorporated as the Aroostook Band of Micmacs (ABM), they abandoned the AAI (which then dissolved) and set up new headquarters in Presque Isle. As staff anthropologist, Prins sought funding for ABM, worked closely with Mi'kmaq leaders to define political strategies, and helped generate broad popular support for the effort. Considering the importance of informing the public and politicians as well as government agencies about their cultural identity and their struggle for native rights, he co-produced a documentary film, *Our Lives in Our Hands* (Documentary Educational Resources, 1986), which aired on television and had dozens of public screenings. Most important, he gathered detailed ethnographic and historical documentation to address government requirements for federal recognition. Groups seeking this special status must present an elaborate document that includes (1) historical and *genealogical records* of its exis-

The Sanipass-Lafford family cluster in Chapman, Maine, represents a traditional Mi'kmaq residential kin group. Such extended families typically include grandchildren and bilaterally related family members such as in-laws, uncles, and aunts. Taken from the Sanipass family album, this picture shows a handful of members in the mid-1980s: Marline Sanipass Morey with two of her nephews and uncles.

tence as a distinct community from ancient times to the present; (2) evidence that the group has maintained political influence over its members on a continual basis; and (3) proof that its members are descendants of a tribe historically inhabiting the area.

Aroostook Mi'kmaqs faced many obstacles in meeting these requirements: (1) Band members lived widely dispersed in small family groups throughout the huge county, so they didn't fit the conventional definition of community. (2) They didn't have a clearly defined membership and lacked formally appointed political leaders. (3) Scholars had described them as "Canadian Indians" without historic ties to Maine. They did this on the basis of a widely accepted "riverine model" of tribal territoriality that tied each tribe to a particular river. Thus, Mi'kmaqs dwelling in the St. John River drainage area in northern Maine were considered recent interlopers on traditional Maliseet lands.

Several years of research yielded the data needed to counter these problems. Prins (with the help of others) unearthed genealogical documentation showing that most Mi'kmaq adults were at least "half-blood" (having two of their grandparents officially recorded as Mi'kmaq Indians). He discovered that the loosely structured ABM, with its informal system of political leadership, actually matched that of traditional Mi'kmaq hunting bands.

And, finding historical evidence that Mi'kmaqs were no strangers to northern Maine, he showed that the region fell within the aboriginal range of their ancestors who were historically allied with Maine's other three tribes in the Wabanaki Confederacy. Based on this evidence, Mi'kmaqs argued that they would have been able to claim aboriginal title to jointly used lands in the region and should not have been left out of the earlier settlement. Supported by Maine's recognized tribes, ABM convinced the state's Congressional delegation in Washington, D.C., to introduce a special bill to acknowledge their tribal status and settle their land claims. When formal hearings were held, Prins testified as expert witness for the Mi'kmaqs. In 1991 President George Bush signed the Aroostook Band of Micmacs Settlement Act into federal law. Since then, the band has received assistance available to all federally recognized tribes, plus funding to buy a 5000-acre tribal land base. Although their cultural survival is not guaranteed, Aroostook's Mi'kmaqs have witnessed vital improvements in their community.

---

[1]Harald Prins, now a professor of anthropology at Kansas State University, also serves on the land claims team of Newfoundland's Miawpukek Band of Mi'kmaqs. For further information, see his case study (1996), *The Mi'kmaq: Resistance, accommodation, and cultural survival*. Fort Worth, TX: Harcourt Brace.

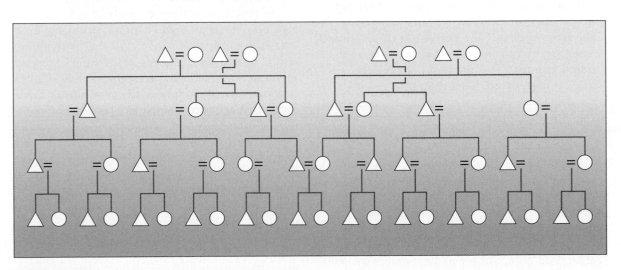

FIGURE 9.4

The kinship pattern of the kindred. These people are related not to a common ancestor but, rather, to a living relative, here the sister and brother shown at the centre of the bottom row.

Members of the groom's personal kindred shown here are his new wife, father, mother, two brothers, sister-in-law, aunt, and niece.

of their parents; ultimately, they belong to the kindreds of their sons and daughters as well as their nieces and nephews.

Thus, because of its vagueness, temporary nature, and changing affiliation, the kindred cannot function as a group except in relation to ego. Unlike descent groups, it is not self-perpetuating—it ceases with ego's death. It has no constant leader, nor can it easily hold, administer, or pass on property. In most cases, it cannot organize work, nor can it easily administer justice or assign status. It can, however, be turned to for aid, as with urban kin groups (kindreds) in Canadian society. In non-Western cultures, raiding or trading parties may be composed of kindred groups. The group is assembled, does what it was gathered to do, shares the results, and then disbands. It also can act as a ceremonial group for rites of passage: initiation ceremonies and the like. Thus, as noted, kindreds assemble only for specific purposes.

Kindreds are frequently found in industrial societies such as Canada, where mobility weakens contact with relatives. Individuality is emphasized in such societies, and strong kinship organization is usually not as important as it is among non-Western peoples. In contrast, bilateral kindred groups also may be found in societies where kinship ties are important, and in some instances they even occur alongside descent groups.

The Descent Group

Just as various types of families occur in different societies, so do various kinds of nonfamilial kin groups. Descent groups, for example, are *not* a common feature of food-foraging groups, where marriage acts as the social mechanism for integrating individuals within communities. In horticultural, pastoral, or many intensive agricultural cultures, however, the descent group usually provides the structural framework upon which the fabric of the culture rests.

Lineages arise from extended-family organization, as long as organizational problems exist that such groups help solve. All that is required, really, is that as members of existing extended families find it necessary to split off and establish new households elsewhere, they not move too far away; that the core members of such related families (men in patrilocal, women in matrilocal, and members of both sexes in ambilocal extended families) explicitly acknowledge their descent from a common ancestor; and that they continue to participate in common activities in an organized way. As these divisions proceed, lineages will develop, and these may with time give rise to clans and ultimately phratries.

Another way clans may arise is as legal fictions to integrate otherwise autonomous units. The five Iroquoian nations of what now is New York State, for example, developed clans by simply behaving as if lineages of the same name in different villages were related. Thus, their members became fictitious brothers and sisters. By this device, members of, say, a "Turtle" lineage in one village could travel to another and be welcomed in and hosted by members of another "Turtle" lineage. In this way, the Five Nations achieved a wider unity than had previously existed.

As larger, dispersed descent groups develop, the conditions that gave rise to extended families and lineages may change. For example, economic diversity and the availability of alternative occupations for individuals may conflict with the residential unity of extended families and (usually) lineages. Or, lineages may lose their economic bases if developing political institutions take control of resources. In such circumstances, lineages would be expected to disappear as important organizational units. Clans, however, might survive, if they continue to provide an important integrative function. This helps explain a clan's continued strength and vitality in North America today: They perform an integrative function among kin who are geographically dispersed as well as socially diverse but in a way that does not conflict with the mobility characteristic of North American society.

Iroquoian clans were a legal fiction that allowed people to travel back and forth between villages of the "Five Nations" in what is now New York State. This portrait, done in 1710, shows a member of the Mohawk Nation. Behind him stands a bear, which represents his clan.

Parin Dossa

Parin Dossa is an associate professor of anthropology at Simon Fraser University. Educated in Africa, Europe, and North America, her work focuses on the production of knowledge by marginal groups. Her research on Muslim women in Canada and Kenya (Lamu) is guided by three theoretical and practice-based orientations in anthropology: (1) to document the richness of people's lives while critiquing domination and human inequality; (2) to explore the question "What is social knowledge for?" using the narratives of Muslim women from the margins—the elderly, disabled, and those seeking care; and (3) to examine the question of how anthropologists can theo-rize and learn from the "telling and listening paradigm" of stories in their practice and teaching. Her current work on mental health and displacement of Iranian women looks at the process of re-authoring and reclaiming of a demedicalized mode of care.

Dossa has contributed to journals such as the *International Journal of Rehabilitation Research, International Journal on Human Development and Aging,* and *Canadian Ethnic Studies.* In addition, she has co-produced two videos: *New Voices: Ethnic Elderly in Calgary* and *Out of the Shadows: Narratives of Women with Disabilities.*

In cultures where the small domestic units—nuclear families or single-parent households—are of primary importance, bilateral descent and kindred organization are apt to result. This can be seen in modern industrial societies, in newly emerging societies in the developing world, and in many food-foraging cultures throughout the world.

▲▽▲▽▲▽▲▽▲▽▲▽▲▽▲▽▲▽▲▽▲▽▲▽▲▽▲

CONTEMPORARY CHINESE-CANADIAN KINSHIP[10]

As we have seen, kinship plays an important role in the way humans organize their lives. Kinship is also dynamic, changing as new situations and needs arise. A case in point is the way Chinese immigrants to Canada have used kinship and, in particular, clan-based associations to adjust to Canadian life (see Chapter 10 for further discussion of common-interest associations).

The history of Chinese immigration to Canada is a long and colourful one, beginning in 1858 when the Fraser River gold rush drew a small number of men to Canada. Large-scale immigration began in 1880, when 17 000 Chinese men came to western Canada to work on the final section of the Canadian Pacific Railway. During this initial immigration period, Chinese men were not allowed to bring their families with them. Instead, they lived in a married-bachelor society, while maintaining kin ties in China and sending money to help support their families. Once the railroad was completed, Chinese immigrants were no longer wanted in Canada. In 1923 a Chinese exclusion law was enacted, effectively shutting down immigration. Those already in Canada mostly settled in British Columbia, setting up laundries, grocery stores, and restaurants. Some of the more fortunate men made occasional trips back to China to visit their families, but most endured long periods of separation, which disrupted normal family relations and kinship structure and had a profound effect on the next generation of Chinese Canadians.

The Chinese claim a long history of identifying and interacting with people based on kinship ties. Indeed, many Chinese Canadians can trace their lineage to a village of origin in southeastern China. The basic social organization in these villages was a patrilineage: a corporate, residential unit of patrilineal kin, able to trace ancestry to a common male ancestor who originally founded the lineage. The villages were composed of people belonging to the same lineage, or even several lineages that occupied separate sections of the village. Exogamy ensured that multigenerational ties of intervillage cooperation and exchange were maintained. Lineages not linked by marriage were considered outsiders and were often hostile to one another. The patrilineage was based on common residence and corporate property, yet in foreign countries such as Canada, the lineage was not maintained.

Instead, Chinese immigrants organized their lives around associations, in particular clan and district associations. Clan associations were founded on the premise that all people with the same surname came from a common ancestry. Through legends, myths, and stories, members of the associations traced their descent back patrilineally to at least one ancestor. Most immigrants came from the same district in China; thus, many of the associations that sprang up were based on district origins. Both clan and district associations provided protection and economic, social, political, and cultural assistance to Chinese immigrants. In Vancouver, workers established communal rooming houses based on clan and district ties to provide mutual assistance and a social life. In essence, clan affiliation substituted for absent families. By 1923 almost 40 associations existed in Vancouver's Chinatown, mostly to protect members from systemic discrimination and to provide a sense of identity. Yet there is a distinction between clans in China and clan associations in Canada. The latter included only those with the same surname, not all resident members of the clan. In fact, clan associations were more often based on friendship than on membership in a clan.

[10]The following discussion is based on the research of Hoe, B.S. (1989). *Beyond the golden mountain: Chinese cultural traditions in Canada.* Ottawa: Canadian Museum of Civilization; Thompson, R.H. (1989). *Toronto's Chinatown: The changing social organization of an ethnic community.* New York: AMS Press; Li, P.S. (1988). *The Chinese in Canada.* Toronto: Oxford University Press; and Ng, W.C. (1999). *The Chinese in Vancouver, 1945–80: The pursuit of identity and power.* Vancouver: UBC Press.

Following World War II and the 1947 repeal of the Chinese Immigration Act, many families were reunited and the Chinese community began to stabilize. Kinship ties played an important role in this stage of immigration; most new immigrants were spouses and children sponsored by kin already living in Canada. Once in the country, new immigrants relied heavily on their kin to help them adjust to Canadian life. Even distantly related kin, tied through patrilineal and marriage relationships, cooperated with one another. Often kin ties provided employment opportunities, a place to live, and assistance in setting up a household. In some instances, kin pooled their resources to purchase a business. Again, the fact that most immigrants came from the same district and shared a common lineage or clanship ties provided a link for potential business partners. Distant kinship ties were also a source of investment, keeping distant kin in contact. As family members provided additional labour, often working in restaurants and other businesses as paid or unpaid labour, partnerships through clan ties gradually declined.

From the 1960s onward, immigration rose dramatically and an increasingly complex and diverse Chinese-Canadian community developed. Chinese families, not just individuals, flocked to Canada from Hong Kong, Taiwan, and mainland China. At the same time, Canadian-born Chinese began moving out of the Chinatowns and isolated ethnic communities and into the Anglo-Canadian social system, where they tend to live in nuclear families, although some Chinese households still contain additional people, such as an aged parent. These changes resulted in a gradual decrease in the importance of the traditional kin-based community. Today, clanship and district associations, which played such an important role in the lives of early Chinese immigrants, have little significance for new arrivals and the younger generation of Canadian-born Chinese.

KINSHIP TERMINOLOGY AND KINSHIP GROUPS

Any system of organizing people who are relatives into different kinds of groups, whether descent-based or ego-oriented, is bound to have an important effect on the ways relatives are labelled. The fact is, the kinship terminologies of other peoples are far from what Western people all too often interpret as arbitrary and even capricious ways of labelling relatives. Rather, they reflect the positions individuals occupy within their culture. In particular, kinship terminology is affected by, and adjusts to, the kinds of kinship groups that exist in a culture. However, other factors also are at work in each system of kinship terminology that help differentiate one kin from another. These factors may be sex, generational differences, or genealogical differences. In the various systems of kinship terminology, any one of these factors may be emphasized at the expense of others, and sometimes they are qualified by distinguishing younger from older individuals in a particular category or by emphasizing the sex of the person who is referring to a particular relative. But regardless of the factors emphasized, all kinship terminologies accomplish two important tasks. First, they classify similar kinds of persons into specific categories; second, they separate different kinds of persons into distinct categories. Generally, two or more kin are merged under the same term when the individuals share similar status, which then emphasizes these similarities.

Six different systems of kinship terminology result from the application of the principles mentioned: the Eskimo, Hawaiian, Iroquois, Crow, Omaha, and Sudanese or descriptive systems, each identified according to the way cousins are classified.

Eskimo System

The **Eskimo system** of kinship terminology, comparatively rare among all the world's systems, is the one used by Euro Canadians and Anglo

---

Eskimo system. A system of kinship terminology, also called the *lineal system*, that emphasizes the nuclear family by specifically identifying the mother, father, brother, and sister while lumping together all other relatives into broad categories such as uncle, aunt, and cousin.

Americans, as well as by a number of North American food-foraging peoples, including the Inuit, and other hunter-gatherer people, such as the Ju/'hoansi. The Eskimo or lineal system emphasizes the nuclear family by specifically identifying the mother, father, brother, and sister while lumping together all other relatives into a few general categories (see Figure 9.5). For example, the father is distinguished from the father's brother *(uncle),* but the father's brother is not distinguished from the mother's brother (both are called *uncle).* The mother's sister and father's sister are treated similarly, both called *aunt.* In addition, all the sons and daughters of aunts and uncles are called *cousin,* thereby making a generational distinction but without indicating the side of the family they belong to or even their sex.

Unlike other terminologies, the Eskimo system provides separate and distinct terms for each nuclear family member. This is probably because the Eskimo system generally is found in societies where the dominant kin group is the bilateral kindred, in which only immediate family members are important in day-to-day affairs. This is especially true of modern North American society, where the family is independent, living apart from, and not directly involved with, other kin except on ceremonial occasions. Thus, people in Canada distinguish between their closest kin (parents and siblings) but lump together (as aunts, uncles, cousins) other kin on both sides of the family.

Hawaiian System

The **Hawaiian system** of kinship terminology, common (as its name implies) in Hawaii and other Malayo–Polynesian-speaking areas but also found among the Coast Salish First Nations of southwestern British Columbia and among other cultures as well, is the least complex system, in that it uses the fewest terms. In the Hawaiian system all relatives from the mother's and father's side of the family, and of the same generation and sex, are referred to by the same term (see Figure 9.6). For example, mother, mother's sister, and father's sister are referred to by the same kinship term. In ego's generation, male and female kin (different sex) are distinguished by terminology, but terms for brothers and sisters are the same for cousins.

The Hawaiian system reflects the absence of strong unilineal descent and is usually associated with ambilineal descent. Because ambilineal rules allow individuals the option of tracing their ancestry back through either side of the family and members on both the father's and the mother's side are viewed as more-or-less equal, a certain degree of similarity is created among the father's and the mother's siblings. Thus, they are all simultaneously recognized as being similar relations and are merged under a single term appropriate for their sex. In like manner, the children of the mother's and father's siblings are

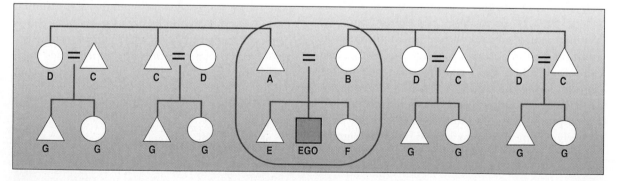

FIGURE 9.5

The Eskimo system of kinship terminology emphasizes the nuclear family (surrounded by the red line). Symbols with the same letters are referred to in the same way by ego.

Hawaiian system.   Kinship reckoning in which all relatives of the same sex and generation are referred to by the same term.

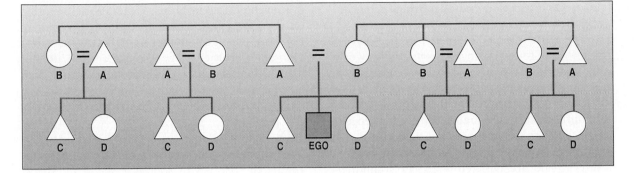

FIGURE 9.6
The Hawaiian kinship system.

related to ego in the same way brothers and sisters are, ruling them out as potential marriage partners.

Iroquois System

In the **Iroquois system** of kinship terminology, the father and father's brother are referred to by a single term, as are the mother and mother's sister; however, the father's sister and mother's brother are given separate terms (see Figure 9.7). In an individual's own generation, brothers, sisters, and parallel cousins (offspring of parental siblings of the same sex; that is, the children of the mother's sister or father's brother) of the same sex are referred to by the same terms. Cross cousins (offspring of parental siblings of opposite sex; that is, the children of the mother's brother or father's

sister) are distinguished by terms that set them apart from all other kin. In fact, cross cousins are often preferred as spouses, for marriage to them reaffirms alliances between related lineages.

Iroquois terminology, named for the Iroquois of northeastern North America, is widespread in matrilineal or double descent and emphasizes unilineal descent groups. It was, for example, the terminology in use until recently in rural Chinese society.

Crow System

In the preceding systems of terminology, some relatives were grouped under common terms, while others of the same generation were separated and given different labels or terms. In the Crow system, another variable enters the picture: The system

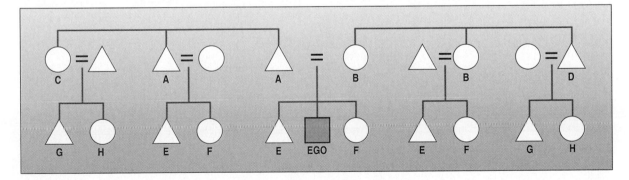

FIGURE 9.7
The Iroquois system of kinship terminology.

Iroquois system.   Kinship terminology wherein a father and father's brother are given a single term, as are a mother and mother's sister, but a father's sister and mother's brother are given separate terms. Parallel cousins are classified with brothers and sisters, while cross cousins are classified separately but (unlike Crow and Omaha kinship) are not equated with relatives of some other generation.

ignores the distinction that occurs between generations among certain kin.

The **Crow system** (named for the Crow of Montana) is found in many parts of the world. This complex system is associated with strong matrilineal descent organization, and it groups differently the relations on the father's side and the mother's side (see Figure 9.8). Cross cousins on the father's side are equated with relatives of the parental generation, while those on the mother's side are equated with ego's children's generation. Otherwise, the system is much like Iroquois terminology.

Omaha System

The **Omaha system** (named for the Omaha of Nebraska) is the patrilineal equivalent of the matrilineal Crow system. Thus, a mother and her sister are designated by a single term, the father and his brother are merged under another, and parallel cousins are merged with brothers and sisters (see Figure 9.9). Cross cousins are referred to by separate terms. A man will refer to his brother's children using the same terms as his own children, but he will refer to his sister's children using different terms. Generational merging on the mother's side is a feature of this system. For example, ego's mother's patrilineage is called "mother's brother"; age and generation do not matter. Interestingly, generational merging does not happen on the father's side, even though fathers and brothers are called by the same terms.

Sudanese or Descriptive System

The **Sudanese or descriptive system** is found among the peoples of southern Sudan in Africa. Otherwise, it is found among few of the world's societies, although it has come to replace Iroquois terminology among rural Chinese. In this system, the mother's brother is distinguished from the father's brother, who is distinguished from the father; the mother's sister is distinguished from the mother, as well as from the father's sister (see Figure 9.10). Each cousin is distinguished from all others, as well as from siblings. It is therefore more precise than any of the other systems (including that used by Anglo Canadians), which may be one reason it is so rare. In few societies are all aunts, uncles, cousins, and siblings treated differently from one another.

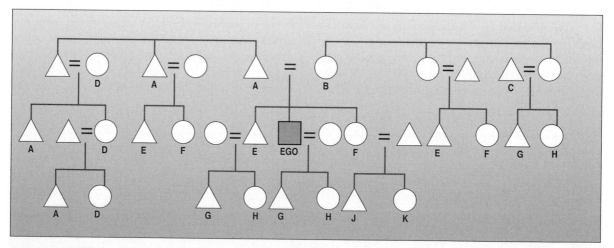

FIGURE 9.8

The Crow system is the obverse of the Omaha system, shown in Figure 9.9.

Crow system. Kinship classification usually associated with matrilineal descent in which a father's sister and father's sister's daughter are called by the same term, a mother and mother's sister are merged under another, and a father and father's brother are given a third. Parallel cousins are equated with brothers and sisters. **> Omaha system.** The patrilineal equivalent of the Crow system; the mother's patrilineal kin are equated across generations. **> Sudanese or descriptive system.** The system of kinship terminology whereby a father, father's brother, and mother's brother are distinguished from one another, as are a mother, mother's sister, and father's sister; cross and parallel cousins are distinguished from each other as well as from siblings.

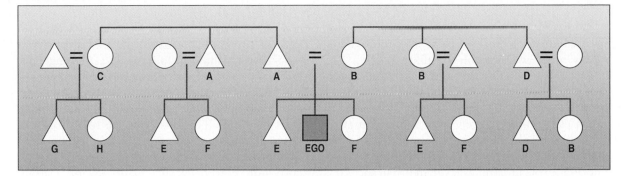

FIGURE 9.9

The Omaha kinship system.

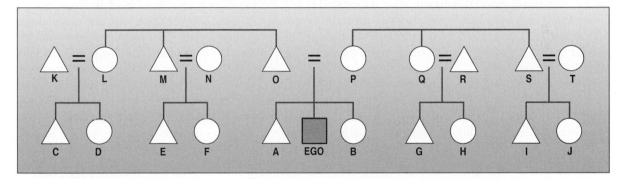

FIGURE 9.10

The Sudanese kinship system.

In matrilineal societies with Crow kinship, sisters remain close to one another throughout their lives. Such a people are the Hopi, in whose traditional housing sisters lived in adjacent rooms. Under these circumstances, very little differentiates a mother and her sister or siblings and the children of the mother's sister. The mother's brother and his children, however, live elsewhere.

CHAPTER SUMMARY

In nonindustrial cultures, kinship groups commonly deal with problems that families and households alone cannot handle: problems such as those involving protection, the allocation of property, and the pooling of other resources. As societies become larger and more complex, formal political systems take over many of these matters; however, kinship continues to play an important role in families, even in urban societies.

A common form of kinship is the descent group, which has as its criterion of membership descent from a common ancestor through a series of parent–child links. Unilineal descent establishes kin group membership exclusively through the male or female line. Matrilineal descent is traced through the female line; patrilineal, through the male.

The descent system is closely tied to a society's economic base. Generally, patrilineal descent predominates where the male is the breadwinner and matrilineal where the female is the breadwinner. Anthropologists now recognize that in all cultures the kin of both mother and father are important elements in the social structure, regardless of how descent group membership is defined.

The male members of a patrilineage trace their descent from a common male ancestor. A female belongs to the same descent group as her father and his brother, but her children cannot trace their descent through him. Typically, authority over the children lies with the father or his elder brother. The requirement for younger men to defer to older men and for women to defer to men, as well as to the women of a household they marry into, are common sources of tension in a patrilineal culture.

In the matrilineal pattern, descent is traced through the female line. Unlike the patrilineal pattern, which confers authority on men, matrilineal descent does not necessarily confer authority on women, although women usually have more of a say in decision making than they do in patrilineal cultures. The matrilineal system is common in cultures where women perform much of the productive work.

Double descent is matrilineal for some purposes and patrilineal for others. Ambilineal descent provides a measure of flexibility in that an individual has the option of affiliating with either the mother's or father's descent group.

Descent groups are often highly structured economic units that provide aid and security to their members. They also may be repositories of religious tradition, with group solidarity enhanced by worship of a common ancestor. A lineage is a corporate descent group made up of consanguineal kin who can trace their genealogical links to a common ancestor. Marriage of a group member represents an alliance of two lineages.

Fission is the splitting up of a large lineage group into new, smaller ones, with the original lineage becoming a clan. Clan members claim descent from a common ancestor but without actually knowing the genealogical links to that ancestor. Unlike lineages, clan residence is usually dispersed rather than localized. In the absence of residential unity, clan identification is often reinforced by totems, usually symbols from nature that remind members of their common ancestry. A phratry is a unilineal descent group of two or more clans that supposedly share a common ancestry. If there are but two such groups, they are called moieties.

Bilateral descent, characteristic of Western and many food-foraging cultures, is traced through both parents and recognizes several ancestors. An individual is affiliated equally with all relatives on both the mother's and father's sides. Such a large group is socially impractical and is usually reduced to a small circle of paternal and maternal relatives called the kindred.

Early Chinese immigrants relied on clan and district-based associations to assist in adjusting to life in Canada. As Canadian society became more accepting of Chinese Canadians, the need for these associations began to decline.

In any culture, rules dictate the way kinship relationships are defined. Factors such as sex and generational or genealogical differences help distinguish one kin from another. The Hawaiian system is the simplest system of kinship terminology. All relatives of the same generation and sex are referred to by the same term. The Eskimo system, used by Euro Canadians and Anglo Americans, emphasizes the nuclear family and merges all other relatives in a given generation into a few large, generally undifferentiated categories. In the Iroquois system, a single term is used for a father and his brother and another term for a mother and her sister. Parallel cousins are equated with brothers and sisters but distinguished from cross cousins. The same is true in the Omaha and Crow systems, except they equate cross cousins with relatives of other generations. The relatively rare Sudanese or descriptive system treats all aunts, uncles, cousins, and siblings as different from one another.

QUESTIONS FOR CRITICAL THOUGHT

1. How do you identify your relatives? Through direct descent? Through "adopted" or fictive descent? Through some combination? How important to you are your extended kin? How many generations of your kin can you trace?

2. When in your life has the ability to trace your descent been the most important or obvious? When are you made aware of your kin group? Do you find your kindred or a descent group more relevant to your daily life? Why?

3. How are changes in North American families altering how North Americans view descent? How do these changes contrast with those occurring in other cultures?

4. Do you think urbanization has affected your kinship networks? If yes, in what ways?

5. Identify your kinkeeper. What roles does he or she perform? What would happen to the cohesion of your extended family if you lost this kinkeeper?

6. Chinese-Canadian kinship has been drastically affected by government policies and discriminatory practices in Canada. Research your own or some other group of people to determine whether outside factors have resulted in a change in the kinship structure and form of your ethnic community.

INTERNET RESOURCES

The Nature of Kinship
http://daphne.palomar.edu/kinship/default.htm
An introduction to descent systems and family organization. This site provides several pages with an overview of kinship, descent principles, descent groups, and kin naming systems, as well as related Internet sites.

Systems of Kinship
http://www.umanitoba.ca/faculties/art/anthropology/tutor/index.html
An excellent site on kinship; explains descent kinship terminology, marriage systems, and residence rules, with many ethnographic examples.
http://www.as.ua.edu/ant/faculty/murphy/436/kinship.htm
Provides brief explanations of a vast number of kinship terms and concepts.

Kinship Chart
http://www.users.on.net/proformat/kinship.html
Have some fun and create your own kinship chart using this site.

Descent Groups
http://daphne.palomar.edu/kinship/kinship_3.htm
An examination of descent groups, descent principles, marriage rules, bilateral descent patterns, nuclear families, moieties, consanguineal relatives, and affines.

Who's a Relative? Kinship Terminology in the Middle Ages
http://kuhttp.cc.ukans.edu/kansas/orb/essays/text03.html
This site features kinship terminology in medieval Western Europe.

SUGGESTED READINGS

Blackman, M. (1992). *During my time: Florence Edenshaw Davidson, a Haida woman* (Rev. ed.). Vancouver: Douglas and McIntyre.

A very readable ethnographic account of matrilineality.

Fox, R. (1967). *Kinship and marriage in an anthropological perspective*. Baltimore: Penguin.

An excellent introduction to the concepts of kinship and marriage, this book outlines some of the methods of analysis used in the anthropological treatment of kinship and marriage. It updates Radcliffe-Brown's *African Systems of Kinship and Marriage* and features a perspective focused on kinship groups and social organization.

Ramu, G.N. (1989). *Marriage and the family in Canada today*. Scarborough, ON: Prentice-Hall Canada.

This is an updated version of *Courtship, Marriage, and the Family in Canada*. It presents significant information on the state of marriage, kinship, and the family and emphasizes emerging trends in marriage.

Schusky, E.L. (1975). *Variation in kinship*. New York: Holt, Rinehart and Winston.

This book is an introduction to kinship, descent, and residence for the beginner. A case-study approach leads the reader from basic data to generalizations, a strategy that helps remove some of the abstraction students of kinship organization sometimes find confusing.

Schusky, E.L. (1983). *Manual for kinship analysis* (2nd ed.). Lanham, MD: University Press of America.

This useful book discusses the elements of kinship, diagramming, systems classification, and descent with specific examples.

Thompson, R.H. (1989). *Toronto's Chinatown: The changing social organization of an ethnic community*. New York: AMS Press.

This community study addresses issues such as the way government policies have affected Chinese Canadians, and provides valuable information on the history and social organization of Toronto's Chinese population. Other topics include Chinese immigration, Chinese associations, and class structure, conflict, and status.

CNN TODAY VIDEOS

Multiracial Families (CNN Cultural Anthropology, vol. 5, 3:45)
As interracial marriages enter the mainstream in many parts of the United States, parents in mixed-race families look for a balance between their different cultures while their children struggle for acceptance and recognition within their communities.

Chapter 10

Social Stratification and Groupings

These children exemplify the phenomena of grouping by gender, age, and common interest, some of the means by which people may be organized into groups without recourse to kinship or descent.

Chapter Preview

1. ## What Principles, besides Kinship and Marriage, Do People Use to Organize Societies?

    People group themselves by gender, age, common interest, and position to deal with problems not conveniently handled by marriage, the family, or descent groups. In addition, certain groups within a culture may use stratification to enjoy preferential treatment for themselves at the expense of other groups.

2. ## What Are Common-Interest Associations?

    Common-interest associations are formed to deal with specific problems and range from fully voluntary to compulsory. Common-interest associations have been a feature of human societies since the advent of the first farming villages several thousand years ago, but they have become especially prominent in modern industrial or industrializing societies.

3. ## What Is Social Stratification?

    Stratification is the division of society into two or more groups of people that do not share equally in wealth, power, or prestige. Groups may be stratified based on age, gender, class, ethnicity, or race.

CHAPTER OUTLINE

Grouping by Gender

Age Grouping

Common-Interest Associations

Social Stratification

Anthropology Applied: Social Impact
    Assessment: The Berger Report

Gender Perspectives: *Purdah*

Original Study: Genocide in Rwanda

Social organization based on kinship and marriage has received an extraordinary amount of attention from anthropologists, and the subject usually is quite prominent in anthropological writing. There are several reasons for this: In one way or another, kinship and marriage operate as organizing principles in all cultures, and in the small-scale cultures anthropologists so often study, they are usually the most important organizational principles. There is, too, a certain fascination in the almost mathematical way kinship systems appear to work. To the unwary, all this attention to kinship and marriage may convey the impression that these are the only principles of social organization that really count. Yet it is obvious that other principles of social organization not only exist but also may be quite important. Principles we will examine in this chapter are grouping by gender, age, common interest, and class.

GROUPING BY GENDER

Although we differentiate between gender and sex, the two concepts are inextricably linked: Women bear children, and men place great importance on their sexual prowess. These biological functions are strongly influenced by cultural attitudes and values.[1]

A discussion of gender grouping inevitably turns to gender roles. Some division of labour along gender lines is characteristic of all human groups. Although in some cultures men and women may share tasks, and people may perform work normally assigned to the opposite sex without loss of face, in other cultures, men and women are rigidly segregated in what they do. For instance, among 17th-century Iroquoian peoples, such as the Huron of southern Ontario, society was divided into two parts consisting of sedentary women, who resided in their community year-round, and nomadic men, who were seasonally absent. The women living in villages were "blood" relatives of one another, and their job was to grow the corn, kidney beans, and squash

the Huron relied on for subsistence. Although the men built the houses and palisades that protected the villages and helped women clear the fields, their most important work was pursued at some distance from the villages. This work consisted of hunting, fishing, trading, warring, and diplomacy. As a consequence, men were transients in the villages, likely present for only brief periods.

Although masculine activities were considered more prestigious than women's labour, women were explicitly acknowledged by all as the sustainers of life. Moreover, women headed the longhouses (dwellings that matrilocal extended families occupied), descent and inheritance passed through women, and ceremonial life centred on women's activities. Although men held all leadership positions outside households, on the councils of the villages, tribes, and the league of Five Nations, the women of their lineages nominated them for these positions and held veto power over them. Thus, male leadership was balanced by female authority. Overall, the phrase "separate but equal" accurately describes relations between the sexes in Iroquoian society, with members of neither sex dominant or submissive to the other. Related to this equality seems to have been a low incidence of rape, at least among the Iroquois. Outside observers in the 19th century widely commented on an apparent absence of rape within Iroquoian communities. Even in warfare, sexual violation of female captives was virtually unheard of.

Groupings by gender are even more evident among the Mundurucu of the Amazon. Here men not only work apart from women but eat and sleep separately as well. All men from age 13 on live in a large house of their own, while women with their young children occupy two or three houses grouped around that of the men. Men associate with men, and women with women. Rather than harassment, the relationship between the sexes is one of opposition. According to Mundurucu belief, sex roles were once reversed: Women ruled over men and controlled the sacred trumpets that are the symbols of power and represent the generative capacities of women. But because women could not hunt, they could not supply the meat demanded by the ancient spirits contained within the trumpets, enabling the men to take the trumpets from the women and establishing their dominance in the process. Ever since,

[1]Eichler (1980) cited in Mackie, M. (1991). *Gender relations in Canada: Further explorations.* Toronto: Harcourt Brace.

Harassment or Intimidation Will Not Be Tolerated In This Workplace.

Please report any incidents or concerns to:

COASTAL

In industrial nations like Canada and the United States, women have been expected to tolerate unwanted sexual advances in the workplace. In recent years, laws against harassment have attempted to achieve a more egalitarian workplace.

the trumpets have been kept carefully guarded and hidden in the men's house, and no woman can see them under penalty of gang rape. Thus, Mundurucu men express fear and envy toward women, whom they seek to control by force. For their part, the women neither like nor accept a submissive status, and even though men occupy all formal positions of political and religious leadership, women are autonomous in the economic realm.

Although important differences exist, there are nonetheless interesting similarities between Mundurucu beliefs and those of traditional European (including Euro-Canadian) culture. The idea of rule by men replacing an earlier state of matriarchy (rule by women), for example, was held by many 19th-century intellectuals. Moreover, the idea that men may use force in order to control women is deeply embedded in both Judaic and Christian traditions (and even today, in spite of

changing attitudes, a Canadian woman is sexually assaulted every six minutes, and one out of four is sexually assaulted at some time in her life).[2] A major difference between Mundurucu and traditional European society is that, in the latter, women have not had control of their economic activities. Although this is now changing, women in Canada and other Western countries still have a considerable distance to go before they achieve economic parity with men.

AGE GROUPING

Age grouping is so familiar and so significant that it and gender sometimes have been called the only universal factors for determining a person's position in society. In North America today, children's first friends generally are children their own age, especially schoolmates. At specified ages, North Americans finally are allowed to do things reserved for adults, such as driving a car, voting, and drinking alcoholic beverages. As North Americans age, they are labelled "teen-agers," "middle-aged," and "senior citizens" whether they like it or not and for no other reason than their age. Ultimately, North Americans retire from their jobs at a specified age and some of them live the final years of their lives in "retirement communities," segregated from the rest of society.

Age classification plays a significant role in non-Western societies, which make a distinction among immature, mature, and elderly people. Advanced age brings with it the period of greatest respect (for women it may mean the first social equality with men); rarely are the elderly shunted aside or abandoned. The Inuit, who often are cited as a people who abandoned their aged relatives, did so only in truly desperate circumstances, when the group's physical survival was at stake. In all nonliterate cultures, the elders are the repositories of accumulated wisdom; they are the "living libraries" for their people. In keeping with this, and given their freedom from many subsistence activities, they play a major role in passing cultural traditions to their grandchildren. For a small-scale culture to cast them aside would be

---

[2]National Advisory Council on the Status of Women.

Bonnie McElhinny

Bonnie McElhinny is a professor of anthropology at the University of Toronto. Her research has focused on language, gender, and political economy. McElhinny's first major research project was a study of linguistic practices in the workplace. She examined how women learn to integrate into male-dominated workplaces, such as a police department, and how the workplace adapts to them. In this study she questioned whether female police officers adapted their speech patterns to fit into a traditionally masculine workplace or if they developed alternative speech patterns. In this case, McElhinny found that female officers tend to do both—accommodating both traditional policing practices and developing new ones. This research resulted in a book entitled *Working on Gender: Women and Gender in a Traditionally Masculine Workplace.*

Her most recent research examined cross-cultural and transnational caregiving in Canadian households. She is interested in Filipina women working as domestic workers and nannies in Toronto. McElhinny contends that domestic work creates class, cultural, and racialized ethnic differences that are shaped by global economic forces. These differences are most evident in interpersonal interactions, especially between a female employer and a female employee. McElhinny's study considers the prevailing argument that the dynamics of employer–employee relationships offer employers justifications for exploiting domestic workers, as well as giving approval for racialized ethnic identities and ranking of these workers. McElhinny is also examining this issue from the point of view of children, whose perspectives on cultural differences are just beginning to develop.

Source: University of Toronto. (n.d.). *Biography of Bonnie McElhinny.* Retrieved June 16, 2001, from the World Wide Web: http://www.chass. utoronto.ca/anthropology/faculty/bmcel.htm.

analogous to closing down all the schools, archives, and libraries in an industrial state.

In North America people rely on the written word, rather than on their elders, for long-term memory. Moreover, some people have become so accustomed to rapid change that they tend to assume the experiences of their grandparents and others of the oldest generation are hardly relevant to them in "today's world." Indeed, retirement from earning a living implies that an individual has nothing further to offer society and should stay out of the way of those who are younger. "The symbolism of the traditional gold watch is all too plain: You should have made your money by now, and your time has run out. The watch will merely tick off the hours that remain between the end of adulthood and death."[3] The status of the elderly is even more problematic because they now constitute so large (and growing) a part of the overall population. By 2026, one in every five people in Canada will be a senior, making up 21 percent of the population compared with

Age grading in modern North American society is exemplified by the educational system, which specifies that at six years of age all children must enter the first grade.

[3]Turnbull, C.M. (1983). *The human cycle* (p. 229). New York: Simon & Schuster.

In many cultures it is common for children of the same age to play, eat, and learn together, such as these Masai boys, who are gathering for the first time to receive instruction for their initiation into an age grade.

13 percent in 2000.[4] Thus, the achievement of old age seems less an accomplishment than it once did and so commands less respect. Furthermore, the elderly begin to be seen as not just unproductive but also as a serious economic burden.

In the institutionalization of age, cultural rather than biological factors are of prime importance for determining social status. All human cultures recognize a number of life stages; precisely how they are defined varies from one culture to another. Out of this recognition they establish patterns of activity, attitudes, prohibitions, and obligations. In some instances, these are designed to help the transition from one age to another, to teach needed skills, or to lend economic assistance. Often they are taken as the basis for forming organized groups. An organized class of people with membership based on age is known as an **age grade.** Entry into and transfer out of age grades may be accomplished individually, either by a biological distinction, such as puberty, or by a socially recognized status, such as marriage or childbirth.

COMMON-INTEREST ASSOCIATIONS

The proliferation of **common-interest associations,** whether out of individual predilection or community need, is a theme intimately associated with world urbanization and its attendant social upheavals. This fondness for joining common-interest associations no doubt reflects the reality that individuals often are separated by physical distance from their brothers, sisters, and age mates, which requires searching out other like-minded companions for support and friendship.

[4]Johnson, J. (2001, March 14). Saskatchewan population sinking. *The Star Phoenix*, Saskatoon.

Age grade. An organized category of people based on age; every individual passes through a series of such categories during a lifetime. **> Common-interest associations.** Associations not based on age, kinship, marriage, or territory but that result from the act of joining.

The diversity of common-interest associations is astounding. Shown here is an environmental activist organization and a dragon boat club.

Common-interest associations often have been referred to in the anthropological literature as voluntary associations, but this term is misleading. The act of joining may range from a fully voluntary act to one required by law. For example, it is not really compulsory to join a labour union, but unless potential employees do, they cannot work in a unionized organization. The term *voluntary association* really refers to associations that are not based on sex, age, kinship, marriage, or territory but that result from the act of joining. Therefore, the act often may be voluntary, but it does not have to be.

Kinds of Common-Interest Associations

The diversity of common-interest associations is astonishing. In Canada, they include women's groups like the Status of Women, business and professional women's associations, and MADD (Mothers Against Drunk Drivers); men's groups, such as the Kiwanis and Kinsmen; parent, teacher, and alumni associations; religious organizations; political parties; support groups like Alcoholics Anonymous; chambers of commerce; labour unions—the list could go on and on. Their goals may include the pursuit of friendship, recreation, and promotion of certain values, as well as governing and the pursuit or defence of economic interests. Associations such as the Tribal Unions of West Africa also serve to preserve traditional songs, history, language, and moral beliefs among

various ethnic minorities. Similar organizations have kept traditions alive among Canadian First Nations, who are undergoing a resurgence of ethnic pride despite generations of schooling designed to stamp out their cultural identity. Another significant force in the formation of associations may be a supernatural experience common to all members; the Crow Indian Tobacco Society, the secret associations of the Kwakwaka'wakw (Kwakiutl) of British Columbia with cycles of rituals known only to initiates, and the Kachina cults of the Hopi are well-known examples. Among other traditional forms of association are military, occupational, political, and entertainment groups, the Canadian Legion, and university or college clubs, not to mention sports groups and co-ops of every kind.

Men's and Women's Associations

For many years, scholars dismissed women's contributions to common-interest associations as less than men's. However, scholars of both sexes have shown this kind of thinking to be culture bound. In some cultures, women have not formed associations to the extent men have because the demands of raising a family and their daily activities have not permitted it and because men have not always encouraged them to do so. Earlier in Canada's history, when women were stuck at home in rural situations with no near neighbours, they had little chance to participate in common-interest associations. However, this also held true for men. Very quickly, as settlers moved into new

Nongovernmental organizations such as Amnesty International are common-interest associations that promote the rights of people around the world. Shown here is a press conference for Amnesty International.

regions, social clubs cropped up, to organize picnics, dances, and sliding parties as a means of alleviating the isolation and loneliness of frontier living. In a number of the world's traditional cultures, the opportunities for female sociability are so great that little need may exist for women's associations. Among the First Nations of northeastern North America (including the Five Nations Iroquois discussed earlier), the men spent extended periods off in the woods hunting, either by themselves or with a single companion. The women, by contrast, spent most of their time in and around their village, in close, everyday contact with all the other women of the community. Not only did they find many people to talk to, but they always found someone available to help with whatever tasks required assistance.

Still, as cross-cultural research makes clear, women do play important roles in associations of their own and even in those where men predominate. Among the Crow, women participated in the secret Tobacco Society, as well as in their own exclusive groups. In Sierra Leone, where once-simple dancing societies have developed under urban conditions into complex organizations, the dancing *compin* is made up of young women as well as men who together perform plays based on traditional music and dancing and raise money for various mutual-benefit causes.

Women's rights organizations, consciousness-raising groups, hospital auxiliaries, and professional organizations for women are examples of associations arising directly or indirectly out of today's social climate. If an unresolved point does exist in the matter of women's participation, it is in determining why women are excluded from associations in some cultures, while in others their participation is essentially equal to that of men.

SOCIAL STRATIFICATION

Social stratification is a system whereby some members of a society are ranked higher or lower relative to other members. It is a common and powerful phenomenon found in most of the world's cultures. Members of lower-ranked social layers or strata tend to be denied the same privileges as those in higher strata, including equal

---

Social Stratification. Institutionalized inequality resulting in some groups receiving differential access to power, wealth, and prestige.

Common-interest associations are not limited to modern industrial societies. This 1832 painting shows a Mandan Bull Dance. The Bulls were one of several common-interest groups concerned with both social and military affairs.

access to basic resources. Their restrictions and obligations, too, are usually more onerous, although members of high-ranked strata have their own set of restrictions and obligations. The way people are ranked varies, but stratification is commonly based on age, gender, class, ethnicity, or race.

Anthropologists measure the degree of stratification in a given group according to an individual's access to wealth, power, and prestige. **Wealth** may include financial resources, material possessions, wives and children, and the potential for future earnings. **Power** suggests the ability to overcome obstacles to reach personal, financial, and professional goals, and **prestige** is the social esteem others hold for an individual. Anthro-

pologists disagree over which of these dimensions of stratification is the most influential, and it is important to recognize that the way power, wealth, and prestige are perceived differs greatly cross-culturally. For example, in Canada individuals gain wealth, prestige, and, in some cases, power from professions or employment. For the Masai, a man, and by extension his family, gains wealth and prestige from the size of his family (the number of wives and children) and the size of the cattle herd his family maintains.

Social stratification is most common in **stratified societies,** where ranking and inequality among members vary, thus creating different levels of social position and quality of life. Stratified societies first arose when state-level

---

Wealth.   Accumulation of financial resources, material possessions, wives and children, and the potential for future earnings. **> Power.**   The ability to reach personal, financial, and professional goals regardless of obstacles. **> Prestige.**   The social esteem others hold for an individual. **> Stratified societies.**   Societies in which ranking and inequality among members vary.

societies, and the ensuing specialization of occupations, began some 5000 to 6000 years ago. Since then, as states have become more complex and specialized, so too has the degree of stratification. In contrast, **egalitarian cultures** such as food foragers have as many valued positions as people capable of filling them. Hence, foragers depend mostly on their abilities for positions. A poor hunter may become a good hunter if he has the ability; he is not excluded from such a prestigious position because he comes from a group of poor hunters. Poor hunters do not constitute a social stratum. Furthermore, they have as much right to a group's resources as any other members. In an egalitarian system, no one can deny a poor hunter his fair share of food, the right to be heard when important decisions are made, or anything else a man is entitled to. This situation differs markedly from the inequalities and restrictions found in stratified societies.

Theories of Stratification[5]

Fundamental to the study of social stratification is the question, why is inequality so prevalent? The **functionalist theory of stratification** suggests that inequality is necessary for the maintenance or *functioning* of complex societies, where a wide variety of professions of varying degrees of specialization are required. For example, in Canadian society we have maintenance workers, teachers, and physicians—all of them needed, yet each possessing a different status. According to this theory, to entice the best people to difficult professions that require a great deal of time (education and training) and sacrifice (personal and financial), such as the many years it takes to become a surgeon, there must be incentives at the end of the long road. Otherwise, no one would train for years to become a surgeon if they could

attain the same level of wealth, power, and prestige by working at a maintenance job.

The functionalist theory certainly has some credibility; however, it also has several weaknesses. First, in complex societies we do not always reward the professions most involved in *maintaining* society: Just how important is a hockey player as opposed to a nurse? Yet the wealth, power, and prestige attached to these two professions differ dramatically. Second, functionalists ignore barriers to achieving the high-prestige professions; ethnic minorities, women, and those from a lower socioeconomic strata often do not have the same opportunities to compete for education and high-paying employment. Third, this theory assumes that everyone is motivated to seek the highest paying, highest status jobs, when other factors such as a desire for meaningful work helping others may take precedence.

Countering the functionalist theory, the **conflict theory of stratification** emphasizes conflict between those in the upper levels of society who attempt to maintain the status quo and those in the lower levels who struggle for a more equitable division of wealth, power, and prestige. Conflict theorists contend that people in the upper levels use their influence within governments, industry, and educational and religious institutions to keep others satisfied with their lower status. The conflict theory takes its cue from the 19th-century writings of Karl Marx, who viewed the world as a constant struggle between the bourgeoisie (those who own the resources) and the proletariat (the working class). Marx believed that the bourgeoisie, with all their power, convinced the proletariat that if they failed to reach the highest echelons of society, it was their fault—they did not try hard enough. The conflict theory tends to ignore other contributing factors to failure to reach the highest levels of society, such as personal choice, ability, and effort.

Social stratification is a general term used to highlight the inequalities experienced by various groups around the world. Within this broad

[5]The following discussion is adapted from Davis, K., & Moore, W.E. (2001). Some principles of stratification. In D.B. Grusky (Ed.), *Social Stratification: Class, Race, and Gender in Sociological Perspective* (pp. 55–64). Boulder, CO: Westview Press.

Egalitarian cultures. Groups in which members enjoy equal access to resources and positions. **> Functionalist theory of stratification.** A theory suggesting that inequality is necessary to maintain complex societies. **> Conflict theory of stratification.** A theory suggesting that a power struggle takes place between the upper and lower levels of society.

category are several forms of stratification, but before we look at these, it is worth our while to examine the concept of race.

The Concept of Race

Much of the inequality found in the world today is based on the concept of race. The term **race** is commonly used to categorize groups of people according to certain biological or physical features. Even more problematic is the tendency to attribute behavioural or cultural characteristics and abilities to these "races." Although some early anthropologists considered whether biological features could influence cultural behaviour, they soon dismissed the idea, partly because the genetic variation within a human population may be greater than between populations, and partly because anthropologists like Franz Boas proved that behaviour is determined by cultural history and learning rather than physical features. (For further discussion of Franz Boas's views on equality, visit the textbook's website at http://www.cultural2e.nelson.com.) Moreover, a northern European may have more in common genetically with a Black from southern Africa than with someone from Greece or Italy, depending on what genetically based characteristics (other than skin colour) are considered. Finally, the only clear biological difference between human populations is blood type, but blood groups do not coincide with so-called racial groups. Today, anthropologists recognize that the concept of race is a cultural construct based on socioeconomic and political agendas rather than a biological reality.

The concept of race first emerged in the 18th century as a way of justifying European colonial expansion and dominance over other groups of people, in particular, Africans and aboriginal peoples, often called "people of colour." Skin colour is commonly used to distinguish races, yet pigmentation is nothing more than an adaptation to differing amounts of ultraviolent radiation. In fact, all so-called racial characteristics represent biological adaptations to environment and have nothing to do with intelligence, capabilities, or behaviour. Furthermore, because human populations have been interbreeding for many thousands of years, there are no separate races: We are all of one race—the human race. Yet some people still insist on separating humans into races and applying stereotypical traits to these groups, and then ranking or stratifying people according to superior and inferior traits.

Racial Stratification

Any examination of social stratification would be incomplete without considering the inequality surrounding the interrelated concepts of race and ethnicity. It is the differences between human groups, whether seen as racial or ethnic, that lead to social inequality, discrimination, and what has commonly become known as racism. **Racism** is the belief that one "race" is superior to another owing to biological and cultural features. Although this attitude sounds remarkably like ethnocentrism, behind racism lies exploitation. Instances of horrific racial discrimination in the 20th century are numerous, including the Holocaust of World War II, South Africa's apartheid, and the genocide in Rwanda. It is important to point out that since racial categories hold no basis, what we are really examining is ethnic prejudice and conflict. Still, the term racism is used to define these acts.

In South Africa, stratification emerged as conquerors excluded the conquered from positions of importance and restricted their access to basic resources. Shown here is the Black township outside the capital of Namibia, once ruled from South Africa.

Race.   Groups of people who are categorized based on biological and behavioural traits. **> Racism.**   The perception that some groups are biologically and culturally inferior to other groups.

Tom Jackson is representative of First Nations people who are overcoming social, economic, and political barriers to achieve recognition and success in their chosen careers.

Canada is not without is own history of racial discrimination, such as the reservation system forced on First Nations peoples, the internment of the Japanese in World War II, the enactment of exclusionary laws against the Chinese, and, more recently, the backlash against immigrants from Muslim countries. The sad fact is Canada suffers from institutionalized racism that permeates virtually every aspect of Canadian life.

First Nations peoples were stripped of their land, their traditional subsistence patterns, and their ability to support themselves, leading to poverty, loss of identity, and social problems. In a concerted effort to assimilate First Nations peoples into mainstream society, children were taken from their parents to live at residential schools where they were forced to learn the White man's ways. It has taken decades for First Nations peoples to overcome these obstacles, and only recently have they begun to acquire the resources, such as higher education, necessary to improve their economic and political situation. An increasing percentage of First Nations young people are completing high school, attending university, and assuming professional careers in law,

medicine, and business. A vibrant First Nations artistic and entertainment community has taken shape in Canada. However, like the African Americans in the United States, First Nations peoples are still disproportionately represented in the lower ranks of society.

With the exception of aboriginal peoples, no other group within Canada's borders has endured such a long history of discrimination and systemic racism as the Chinese.[6] In the 19th and 20th centuries anti-Chinese sentiments ran high in British Columbia, and although over time this attitude has been tempered by a growing social maturity and education among Canadian citizens, intolerance is still evident today.

One of the early problems was the perception that the Chinese were not permanent immigrants; rather, they were considered a short-term labour pool and were expected to return to their homeland once the need for their labour disappeared. In this early period of immigration, from 1858 to 1923, racism against the Chinese began, in large part because of difficult economic times in British Columbia and the irrational fear that the Chinese were competitors for resources. Those Chinese working on railway construction were considered a necessary evil, and were seen as little more than human horses or living pieces of machinery. Consequently, the first anti-Chinese bill was passed in 1885, soon after the Canadian Pacific Railway was finished, mostly to appease British Columbians who considered the Chinese "a public menace." Civil rights of those Chinese already in Canada were curtailed between 1875 and 1923, culminating in the 1923 Chinese Immigration Act, which excluded Chinese from immigrating to Canada and legalized the inferior status of Chinese Canadians.

Besides the legal restrictions placed on Chinese immigrants, they were also subjected to racial hostilities and attacks, as illustrated by the 1887 and 1907 anti-Chinese riots in Vancouver. Crowds of hooligans vandalized Chinese homes and tried to intimidate the Chinese into leaving. In the 1907 riot, slogans on banners read "A white Canada and no cheap Asiatic labor," and "White Canada—patronize your own race and

---

[6]The following examination of racial discrimination against Chinese Canadians is taken from Li, P.S. (1988). *The Chinese in Canada*. Toronto: Oxford University Press.

Canada." In the minds of these rioters, patriotism meant defending a White Canada. Even children were not safe from the racists: Calls for segregating Chinese children in a separate school were heard, and in 1922 Chinese children in the Victoria school system were segregated in one school, setting off a year-long boycott by Chinese parents that ended with the children returning to their regular schools.

Racism and discrimination against the Chinese were firmly entrenched in Canadian society by the time of the 1923 Chinese Immigration Act. Although this exclusionary period resulted in many social and familial hardships for Chinese immigrants, one of the most far-reaching consequences was the economic disadvantages that jeopardized their ability to earn a decent living. When they were hired, they had to settle for lower wages than Whites, and they were excluded from many occupations. The end result was many Chinese set up their own businesses, most in the service sector.

There is no doubt that discrimination against the Chinese was based on race, and exclusionary laws were aimed at the Chinese as a racial group, regardless of whether they had citizenship. Measures such as the Chinese head tax were designed to control the number of Chinese immigrating to Canada. This systematic discrimination is known as legally sanctioned or **institutionalized racism.** The underlying reason for institutionalized racism is to maintain a group of people on the margins of society, with little collective power, in order to have a ready supply of cheap labour.

Following World War II many of the discriminatory laws against Chinese Canadians were rescinded. They were allowed to vote, and the Chinese Immigration Act was repealed in 1947, partly because China had been an ally during the war and it became embarrassing to discriminate against these allies, and partly because anti-Asian sentiments had shifted toward Japanese Canadians. Even so, Chinese immigrants were still considered second-class citizens and continued to experience social, economic, and residential segregation from mainstream society. Their response to the hostility and harassment

was to retreat into their own ethnic enclaves and build isolated Chinese communities.

In 1962 the Canadian government changed the requirements for immigration, opening the borders to Chinese and other immigrants, and further adjustments to immigration policies placed all immigrants at the same level, regardless of ethnic background. Many who came to Canada after 1962 were urbanites from Hong Kong and Taiwan, with very different backgrounds than earlier immigrants from rural mainland China.

For most of their history, Chinese immigrants to Canada were subjected to legislated discrimination and exclusion. Only since 1947 have Chinese Canadians enjoyed similar civil rights to the rest of Canadians and gradually been accepted into Canadian society. Today, Chinese Canadians enjoy access to higher education and professional and technical occupations, which has led to upward mobility. However, it would be erroneous to assume that race no longer creates a barrier for Chinese Canadians. Most of their upward mobility is due to the changing socioeconomic situation in Canada, and periodic instances of discrimination remind Chinese Canadians that despite their accomplishments, they are still seen as foreigners by other Canadians. For example, a 1979 W5 broadcast suggested that foreign students in Canada were taking away university openings that should have gone to qualified Canadian students. The program showed scenes of classrooms full of Chinese students, implying that the students, regardless of nationality, were foreigners. Protests from Canadian-born Chinese and the universities they attended later forced the network to issue an apology for the distorted statistics and stereotyping of all Chinese as foreigners.

The treatment of the Chinese is impossible for us to justify in the 21st century. Yet it is explainable (though not understandable) in part. The Chinese were visibly different than Euro Canadians, they lived on the margins of Canadian society, and they exhibited some traditional behaviour that led mainstream Canadians to believe the Chinese were culturally inferior.

Institutionalized racism.   Legally sanctioned restrictions based on the ideology that Whites are biologically and socially superior to non-Whites.

Anthropology **Applied**
Michael Asch, University of Victoria

Social Impact Assessment: The Berger Report

In 1973, a consortium of multinational oil corporations made a proposal to build a pipeline along the Mackenzie River Valley in Canada's Northwest Territories to bring Alaskan oil to the lower 48 states of the United States. Concern over the impact of this project led the Canadian government in March 1974 to establish an inquiry into the social, economic, and environmental consequences of the pipeline. This one-person inquiry was undertaken by British Columbia Supreme Court Justice Thomas Berger and became known as the Mackenzie Valley Pipeline Inquiry, or the Berger Inquiry.

Berger began preliminary hearings in 1974 and completed them 20 months later in November 1976. By that time, Berger had listened to testimony from over 1000 people. Most of the testimonies were given by indigenous people in 35 communities from the entire western Arctic region. In addition, he solicited views from southern Canadians in a number of cities, and from some 300 experts in formal hearings held in Yellowknife, Northwest Territories.

Berger determined that the pipeline construction should never take place in certain environmentally sensitive areas and that the project as a whole should be delayed for 10 years so that the people in the region could become prepared to benefit from it economically and their outstanding political issues with Canada could be resolved.

A key aspect of Berger's recommendation was the contemporary economy of the Dene, or northern Athapaskan-speaking peoples, who formed a major segment of the population along the proposed pipeline route. Experts testifying for the proponents of the pipeline asserted that, through acculturation, the traditional Dene economy, which was based on hunting, fishing, trapping, and gathering, was dead or dying. Consequently, the Dene had moved off the land and into towns where, because of scarce economic opportunities, most were living in poverty. The pipeline, they argued, would provide a significant number of jobs in the construction phase and many

long-term jobs over the projected 20-year lifetime of the Alaskan oil fields. These jobs would offer incomes that would move the Dene out of their immediate poverty and provide sufficient employment over a longer term to facilitate their transition into the larger Canadian economy.

One of the anthropologists who helped Berger form his opinion was Dr. Michael Asch, then an assistant professor in the anthropology department at the University of Alberta, who had undertaken research with the Dene beginning in the late 1960s. He was asked by the Indian Brotherhood of the Northwest Territories to provide expert information on the state of the contemporary Dene economy and the factors that had contributed to the economic conditions faced by the Dene.

The argument promoted by the developers was based on acculturation theory. They believed that the Dene had moved from the bush and into towns during the 1950s and 1960s because they no longer wished to pursue a hunting and trapping economy. Asch provided a contextualized account of their economic history to counter this argument. His account indicated that the move into towns resulted largely from government policies during a time of economic depression in the price of furs. In effect, these policies required that the Dene move into town in order to gain sufficient cash through family allowance and old age pension payments so that they could continue hunting and trapping in the bush. His data and analysis demonstrated that the Dene did not move into towns voluntarily due to an abandonment of a way of life. Rather, due to economic pressure, they were forced to move into towns in order to gain sufficient income to pursue their traditional economy. To counter the argument that the traditional economy of the Dene was dead or dying, Asch provided data based on his fieldwork in Wrigley (now Pi Dze Kin) during 1969 and 1970 as well as comparable statistics from other Dene communities. This data set indicated that the hunting end of that economy produced an amount of meat per capita from small game alone that exceeded the average per capita consumption of all meat by Canadians.

Based on information provided by experts such as Asch, Berger concluded that hunting, fishing, gathering, and trapping continued to be important factors in the contemporary Dene economy. As a consequence, he recommended that a 10-year moratorium on the pipeline development was necessary not only to prepare Dene for opportunities that might be provided by the pipeline, but also to introduce methods, such as processing of furs in the north, that would help ensure the long-term survival of their traditional economy. Unfortunately, the governments of Canada and the Northwest Territories failed to follow through on Berger's recommendation.

Canadian Arctic Resources Committee. (1976). *Final argument and recommendations: The Mackenzie Valley Pipeline Inquiry*. Ottawa: Canadian Arctic Resources Committee.

Murphy, R., & Steward, J. (1968). Tappers and trappers: Parallel processes in acculturation. In R. Manners & D. Kaplan (Eds.), *Theory in Anthropology*. New York: Aldine.

Watkins, M. (Ed.). (1977). *Dene Nation: The colony within*. Toronto: University of Toronto Press.

Sources:

Berger, T. (1988). *Northern frontier, northern homeland: The report of the Mackenzie Valley Pipeline Inquiry*. Vancouver: Douglas and McIntyre.

This perception allowed most Canadians to accept the injustices imposed on the Chinese. In other words, because the Chinese were so different, Canadians felt no affinity or empathy for their lot; it was as easy to ignore them as it was to ignore the plight of Canadian aboriginals.

Class and Caste

A **social class** may be defined as a category of individuals of equal or nearly equal prestige according to the system of evaluation. The qualification "nearly equal" is important, for a certain amount of inequality may occur even within a given class. If fine distinctions are made, then many classes may be recognized. If, however, only a few general distinctions are made, then only a few classes will be recognized. Thus, some speak of North American society as divided into three classes: lower, middle, and upper. Others speak of several classes: lower lower, middle lower, upper lower, lower middle, and so forth. Canada is a class society, with labels such as upper, middle, and lower class generally tied to income levels. Thus, the class people belong to is earned through endeavour and is know as **achieved status.** Based on gender, ethnicity, and even age, Canadians

Despite their close association, the clothing worn by these two individuals and the way they interact clearly indicate they are of different social classes.

Social class.   A category of individuals who enjoy equal or nearly equal prestige according to the evaluation system.
> Achieved status.   Status an individual earns.

experience unequal access to education and employment opportunities, which often determine wealth and ensuing status.

A **caste** is a particular kind of social class with a fairly fixed or impermeable membership. Castes are strongly endogamous, and offspring are automatically members of their parents' caste. This is known as **ascribed status.** The classic case is the caste system of India. Coupled with strict endogamy and membership by descent in Hindu castes is an association of particular castes with specific occupations and customs, such as food habits and styles of dress, along with rituals involving notions of purity and impurity. The literally thousands of castes are organized into a hierarchy of four named categories, at the top of which are the priests, or *Brahmins,* the bearers of universal order and values and of highest ritual purity. Below them are the powerful—although less pure—warriors. Dominant at the local level, besides fulfilling warrior functions, they control all village lands. Furnishing services to the landowners, and owning the tools of their trade, are two lower ranking, landless caste groups of artisans and labourers. At the bottom of the system, owning neither land nor the tools of their trade, are the outcasts, or "untouchables." In India, these people are considered most impure of all, although they constitute a large labour pool at the beck and call of those controlling economic and political affairs, the landholding warrior caste.

Although some argue that the term *caste* should be restricted to the Indian situation, others find this usage much too narrow, since castelike situations are known elsewhere in the world. In South Africa, for example, although the situation is now changing, Blacks traditionally were relegated to a low-ranking stratum in society, until recently were barred by law from marrying non-Blacks, and could not hold property except to a limited degree in specified "black homelands." Most Blacks still perform menial jobs for Whites, but even the small cadre of "middle-class" Blacks that existed were until recently prohibited from living where Whites do, or even swimming in the same water or holding the hand of someone who

Outcast groups are a common feature of stratified societies; Canada and the United States, for example, have in recent years seen the growth of a castelike underclass.

is White. These restrictions resemble the concept of purity and impurity found in the Hindu caste system; in South Africa, Whites feared pollution of their purity through improper contact with Blacks.

In the United States, the importation of African slaves produced a severely disadvantaged castelike group at the bottom of the social order. Not only was it nearly impossible for such individuals to rise above this group, but also downward mobility into it was possible, owing to the belief that "a single drop of Black blood" was enough to define one as Black (a belief similar to South African concepts of purity and pollution). It has taken a long time for African Americans to move up in the class system, although the legacy persists, as they are still disproportionately represented in the low ranks of society.

Social classes are manifested in several ways. One is through **verbal evaluation**—what people say about others in their own culture. For this, anything can be singled out for attention and spoken of favourably or unfavourably: political, military, religious, economic, or professional roles; wealth and property; kinship; physical attributes; community activity; linguistic dialect; and a host of other traits. Cultures do this differently, and what may be spoken of favourably in one may be spoken of unfavourably in another

---

Caste. A special form of social class in which membership is determined by birth and remains fixed for life. **> Ascribed status.** Status people are born into. **> Verbal evaluation.** The way people in a stratified society evaluate society members.

and ignored in a third. Furthermore, cultural values may change, so something regarded favourably at one time may not be at another. This is one reason why a researcher may be misled by verbal evaluation, for what people say may not correspond completely with social reality. As an example, the official language of Egypt is Classical Arabic, the language of the Qur'an. Although it is highly valued, no one in Egypt uses this language in daily interaction; rather, it is used for official documents or on formal occasions. Those most proficient in it are not of the upper class but, rather, of the lower-middle classes. These are the people educated in the public schools (where Classical Arabic is the language of schooling) and who hold jobs in the government bureaucracy (which requires the most use of Classical Arabic). Upper-class Egyptians, by contrast, go to private schools, where they learn the foreign languages essential for success in international diplomacy, business, and industry.[7]

Social classes also are manifested through **patterns of association:** not just who interacts with whom but also how and in what context. In Western society, informal, friendly relations take place mostly within our own class. Relations with members of other classes tend to be less informal and occur in the context of specific situations. For example, a corporate executive and a janitor normally are members of different social classes. They may have frequent contact with each other, but it occurs in the setting of the corporate office and usually requires certain stereotyped behavioural patterns.

A third way social classes are manifested is through **symbolic indicators.** Included here are activities and possessions indicative of class. For example, in North American society, symbolic indicators include occupation (a garbage collector has different class status than a physician); wealth (rich people generally are in a higher social class than poor people); dress (designer or discount);

Symbolic indicators of class or caste include factors of lifestyle, such as the kind of housing we live in.

form of recreation (upper-class people are expected to play golf rather than shoot pool down at the pool hall—but they can shoot pool at home or in a club); residential location (upper-class people do not ordinarily live in slums); material possessions (e.g., car model); and so on. The fact is, all sorts of status symbols indicate class position, including such measures as the number of bathrooms in an individual's house. At the same time, symbolic indicators may be cruder reflections of class position than verbal indicators or patterns of association. One reason is that access to wealth may not be wholly restricted to upper classes, so individuals can buy symbols suggestive of upper-class status whether or not this really is their status. To take an extreme example, the head of an organized crime ring may display more of the symbols of high-class status

---

[7]Haeri, N. (1997). The reproduction of symbolic capital: Language, state and class in Egypt. *Current Anthropology, 38*, 795–816.

Patterns of association.   Whom we associate with and in what context, reflecting social class. **> Symbolic indicators.**   In a stratified society, activities and possessions indicative of social class.

than members of old, established upper-class families. For that matter, someone from an upper class may choose a simpler lifestyle than is customary. Instead of driving a Mercedes, he or she may drive a beat-up Volkswagen.

Symbolic indicators involve factors of lifestyle, but differences in life chances also may signal differences in class standing. Life is apt to be less hard for members of an upper class as opposed to a lower class. This shows up in a tendency for lower infant mortality and longer life expectancy for the upper class. Another tendency is for greater physical stature and robustness among upper-class people, the result of better diet and protection from serious illness in their juvenile years.

Mobility

All stratified societies offer at least some **mobility**, and this helps to ease the strains in any system of inequality. Even the Hindu caste system, with its ideology of tight restrictions, has a surprising amount of flexibility and mobility, not all of it associated with the recent changes "modernization" has brought to India. As a rather dramatic case in point, in the state of Rajasthan, those who own and control most of the land and who are wealthy and politically powerful are not of the warrior caste, but are of the lowest caste. Their tenants and labourers, by contrast, are Brahmins. Thus, the group ritually superior to all others finds itself in the same social position as untouchables, whereas the landowners who are the Brahmins' ritual inferiors are superior in all other ways. Meanwhile, a group of leather workers in the untouchable category, who have gained political power in India's new democracy, are trying to better their position by claiming they are Brahmins who were tricked in the past into doing defiling work. Although individuals cannot move up or down the caste hierarchy, whole groups can do so depending on claims they can make for higher status and on how well they can manipulate others into acknowledging their claims. Interestingly, the people at the bottom of India's caste system traditionally have not questioned the

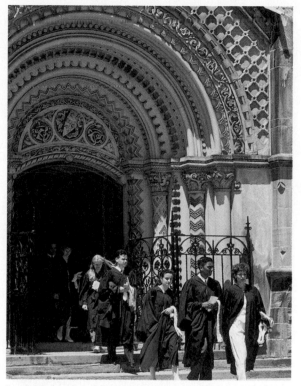

In Canada, the ability to "move up" in the system of stratification is increasingly dependent on access to higher education.

validity of the system itself so much as their particular position within it.

With their limited mobility, caste-structured groups exemplify **closed-class systems.** Those that permit a great deal of mobility are referred to as **open-class systems.** Even here, however, mobility is apt to be fairly limited. In North America, in spite of the "rags to riches" ideology, most mobility involves a move up or down only a notch, although if this continues in a family for several generations, it may add up to major changes.

The degree of mobility in a stratified society is related to the prevailing kind of family organization. In cultures where the extended family is the usual form, mobility is apt to be difficult, because each individual is strongly tied to the extended family. Hence, for a person to move up

---

Mobility. The ability to change one's class position. **> Closed-class systems.** Stratified societies that severely restrict social mobility. **> Open-class systems.** Stratified societies that permit a great deal of social mobility.

to a higher social class, his or her family must move up as well. Mobility is easier for independent nuclear families where the individual is closely tied to fewer persons. Moreover, under neolocal residence, individuals normally leave the family they were born into, and through marriage, education, occupation, and disassociation from the lower-class family they grew up in, all of which are made possible by residential mobility, individuals can more easily "move up" in society.

Gender Stratification

Gender stereotypes are preconceived ideas or guidelines about what behaviours and roles are considered feminine or masculine. It is our culture's gender stereotypes, not biological differences, that channel us into our various gender roles. Thus, gender stratification is culturally defined. It is generally recognized that the status of women varies from one culture to another. Inequality of status between males and females is known as **gender stratification.** Like social stratification, gender stratification refers to unequal access to wealth, power, and prestige. (For additional discussion of gender stratification, see the Gender Perspectives box in Chapter 1.)

Inequality between genders is manifested in numerous ways. Anthropologists measure the overall status of women within any cultural group according to the kinds of social and political positions they hold, the economic importance and cultural value attached to their work, when or how much they are required to defer to the men in their lives, and the control they have over their own bodies (e.g., the right to practise birth control). Yet such measurements do not tell the whole story, since religious, political, economic, and social factors often come into play.

Social scientists have grappled with the question of why virtually all groups have some degree of gender inequality. Two factors are generally focused on: economics and warfare. The control of production strategies and resources may be a primary factor in gender inequality. In cultures where men monopolize production, they tend to be the dominant gender, even if women contribute significantly to the family's economic well-

The burkha worn by Afghan women is seen as a symbol of female oppression by outsiders.

being. The key is *control*. The gender that controls production and distribution of a group's material goods will dominate. Even in relatively egalitarian cultures, such as food-foraging groups, men control the distribution of highly prized meat and thus have more power and a higher status. In other cultures where women have some control over the distribution of resources, they tend to enjoy more status. This explanation raises the question, why is it that men rather than women so often control production and distribution of a group's resources? The answer appears to lie in the division of labour: Women tend to spend most of their time completing domestic and childcare duties, while men spend most of their time outside the home, hunting (providing meat), clearing fields (distributing land), or working as wage earners (providing income). Although this explanation may fit with earlier times in Western society when women routinely remained in the home, it hardly fits with a hunter-gatherer lifestyle, where the women gather food outside the home as much or more than men and rely on older children or aged parents to care for small children. In contemporary Western society, women have the opportunity to work outside the domestic sphere, which has increased their status significantly, although in many cases they still do not receive the same rewards as men in the form of higher status positions and monetary compensation. For example,

---

Gender stratification. Unequal access to wealth, power, and prestige, which results in a disadvantaged, subordinate position for women.

in 1995, Canadian women who worked full-time earned 71 cents for every dollar their male counterparts earned.[8]

A second explanation suggests that men who are regularly involved in warfare, such as the Yanomami, bring their aggression home, and

women tend to defer to them. A higher value is placed on sons (future warriors), and women are viewed merely as bearers of sons or as a bargaining chip with other groups. Yet when men are at war and away from home for extended periods of time, as were the 18th-century Iroquois, the women appear to have a higher status.

The discussion of *purdah* in the following Gender Perspectives box illustrates the difficulty of measuring and interpreting gender stratification from another's perspective.

[8]Statistics Canada. (1998, May 12). *1996 Census: Sources of income, earnings and total income, and family income. The Daily.* Retrieved March 5, 2001, from the World Wide Web: http://www.statcan.ca/daily/english/980512/d980512.htm.

Gender **Perspectives**

Purdah

Hidden beneath voluminous folds of black cloth, women silently move through Muslim society, an enigmatic mystery to most Westerners. These women are observing the ancient custom of *purdah,* or female seclusion, that requires women past the age of puberty to wear a concealing chador outside the privacy of their homes. The *chador* is a loose, shapeless garment and veil that covers a woman from head to toe.

Interpretation of the Qur'an's exhortation for modest dress varies considerably. Some Muslim women believe they need only dress conservatively; others believe they must conceal their entire bodies, even to gloved hands and veiled faces. Geraldine Brooks's firsthand observations in the Cairo airport illustrate this diversity:

> Women from Pakistan, on their way to jobs in the gulf, floated by in their deliciously comfortable *salwar kameez*—silky tunics drifting low over billowing pants with long shawls of matching fabric tossed loosely over their heads. Saudi women trod carefully behind their husbands, peering from behind gauzy face veils and 360-degree black cloaks that made them look, as Guy de Maupassant once wrote, "like death out for a walk." Afghan women also wore 360-degree coverings, called *chadris*—colorful crinkly shrouds with an oblong of embroidered lattice work over the eyes. Women from Dubai wore stiff, birdlike masks of black and gold that beaked over the

nose but left their luminous, treacle-colored eyes exposed. Some Palestinians and Egyptians wore dull-colored, floor-length button through coats and white headscarves; others wore bright calf length skirts and matching scarves held in place by headbands of seed pearls.[1]

Seclusion goes beyond wearing a *chador*; under the rules of *purdah* women must be kept isolated from males to preserve their modesty. Among the Pakhtun of Swat, Pakistan, women seldom leave their homes. If they do, they are always in the company of other women or a male relative. They avoid contact with unknown men for fear others will think the meeting sexual. In earlier times, if a woman broke *purdah* she risked mutilation, such as having her nose cut off, or being killed by her husband to restore his honour. In some urban centres, such as Cairo, *purdah* is not as strictly enforced; many educated women choose modest Western clothing and a simple length of veiling, and they tend to have more freedom to visit friends and shop and generally enjoy more independence. However, a recent resurgence of *purdah* has been noted among these women as a way to reaffirm their Muslim beliefs and traditions.

Westerners tend to view *purdah* as a symbol of Middle Eastern patriarchy, female oppression, and the male supremacy ideology central to Middle Eastern male identity. This is not entirely accurate; many Muslim women wish to wear their traditional garb, even after immigrating to North America. Their *chador* is seen as a protection from the outside world, from prying eyes, and from unwanted sexual advances. Katherine Bullock found that many Muslim women view their traditional dress code as a sign of purity, modesty, a woman's Islamic identity, and "submission to god and a testament that you're Muslim." Halima, a convert to Islam, adds that Hijab (veil and scarf) symbolizes "the woman's power to take back her own dignity and her own sexuality."[2]

In Canada, a Muslim woman's right to wear traditional garb has been repeatedly challenged. In 1995 several students were expelled from a Quebec high school when they refused to remove their head scarves. Young Muslim women have reported hostile encounters with Canadians who have protested their dress, angrily accusing them of setting back the women's movement with such traditions. Muslim women appear confused by these actions, as the following statement attests: "If Canada boasts you can practice your religious freedom of thought and beliefs, if a woman believes she should wear her Hijab why shouldn't she? She's not hurting anybody, I mean if people can go down Yonge Street [Toronto] almost naked, why should her putting a scarf on her head bother people, even for that matter wearing a veil on [her] face, why should that upset somebody?"[3]

---

[1]Brooks, G. (1994). *Nine parts of desire: The hidden world of Islamic women* (pp. 21–22). New York: Anchor Books.

[2]Bullock, K. (2001). *You don't have to wear that in Canada* (pp. 1–2). Retrieved March 13, 2001, from the World Wide Web: http://www.soundvision.com/news/hijab/hjb.canada1.shtml.

[3]Ibid., p. 7.

Sources:

Brooks, G. (1994). *Nine parts of desire. The hidden world of Islamic women.* New York: Anchor Books.

Bullock, K. (2001). *You don't have to wear that in Canada.* Retrieved March 13, 2001, from the World Wide Web: http://www.soundvision.com/news/hijab/hjb.canada1.shtml.

Lindholm, C., & Lindholm, C. (2000). Life behind the veil. In E. Ashton-Jones, G.A. Olson, & M.G. Perry (Eds.), *The gender reader* (2nd ed.). Needham Heights, MA: Allyn and Bacon.

Smith, S. (1995). The world of women. In B.B. Ingoldsby & S. Smith (Eds.), *Families in multicultural perspective.* New York: The Guilford Press.

Ethnic Stratification

Whereas the concept of race is based on fallacious reasoning, ethnicity is a reliable concept. **Ethnicity** is derived from a sense of shared identity and common cultural features. Outsiders readily identify members of an ethnic group by their language, dress, cuisine, and religious practices. Ethnic groups also share a common history and territory of origin. Yet ethnicity is not fixed; it is constantly changing in reaction to new circumstances (e.g., immigration to a new country like Canada), and no ethnic group is entirely homogeneous.

Canada is a pluralistic society, with members coming from virtually every corner of the world. Ideally, when people immigrate to Canada they are free to retain their own culture while enjoying the benefits of becoming members of Canadian society. However, in reality new Canadians are expected to conform to or assimilate into the dominant culture, through language, behaviour, clothing, and so on. An individual or group who fails to do so runs the risk of being considered an outsider, or nonassimilable. A second difficulty pertains to visible minorities; because they are and always will be physically different, they always will be considered separate from "White" Canadians, regardless of how much they adapt their behaviour. Linked to these considerations is the concept of multiculturalism—that idealistic and legally sanctioned ideology. As of yet, multicultural policies in Canada have failed to eliminate racial and ethnic inequality, instead creating only superficial harmony. Nor do most ethnic groups have the power and resources to promote their cultural heritage. For example, even though

---

Ethnicity. A group of people who share a common identity, history, and territory of origin. May exhibit distinctive language, dress, cuisine, and religious practices.

language schools are common in Canada, with very few exceptions, the language of instruction in schools is either French or English.[9]

The history of Canadian immigration is rife with discrimination and ethnic intolerance. Initially, two ethnic groups moved to Canada—the French and English. Later waves of immigration brought people from eastern and southern European countries, Asia, and, more recently, the Caribbean and Latin America. Most of these groups have, to varying degrees, experienced discrimination, exploitation, and unequal access to opportunities within Canada. When Ukrainians began immigrating to Canada more than a century ago, many Canadians greeted them less than enthusiastically, some even demanding that Slavic peoples be excluded from Canada. An article that appeared in the May 13, 1901, *Winnipeg Telegram* illustrates the prevailing attitude toward Ukrainians at that time:

> That there are few people who will affirm that Slavonic immigrants are desirable settlers, or that they are welcomed by the white people of Western Canada. . . . Those whose ignorance is impenetrable, whose customs are repulsive, whose civilization is primitive, and whose character and morals are justly condemned, are surely not the class of immigrants which the country's paid immigration agents should seek to attract. Better by far to keep our land for the children, children's children, of Canadians than to fill up the country with the scum of Europe.[10]

Ukrainians, like other immigrants, were paid lower wages than other workers, and they worked in wretched and often dangerous conditions. During World War I, Ukrainians, as well as Bulgarians, Poles, Serbians, Germans, Croatians, Italians, and Jews, were declared "enemy aliens."[11]

Nearly 6000 Ukrainians were interned in one of two dozen internment camps throughout Canada between 1914 and 1920. Thousands of others had to report to the police and carry identity papers with them. Foreign language use was banned. Many lost their right to vote in the 1917 federal election, were not allowed to join the Canadian Armed Forces, and faced public persecution and discrimination. By 1918, French and English Canadians were clamouring for the deportation of all these "foreigners." The internees were used as forced labourers to develop Banff National Park and were forced to work in the mines of British Columbia, the steel mills of Ontario and Nova Scotia, and the lumber camps of northern Ontario and Quebec. The program so benefited Canadian corporations and the government that the internment continued on for two years after the end of World War I. Why was such a drastic measure taken? Was it wartime xenophobia, bigotry against a new immigrant population, or the economic benefits of a forced-labour system? Likely a combination of these factors contributed to the internment of Ukrainians and set a precedent for the 1941 internment of Japanese Canadians.[12]

Gaining acceptance in Canada has been a long struggle for Ukrainians, but today Ukrainian people have become respected, successful citizens of Canada.

Sometimes, rather than providing the basis for stratification, ethnicity comes to serve as a metaphor for what began as nothing more than class distinctions. A dramatic example of this can be found in the African state of Rwanda, where simple class distinctions were misinterpreted by Belgian colonial authorities as differences in ethnicity. Ultimately, the differences were magnified until the whole country erupted in a bloodbath, illustrating how class systems have built into them the seeds of their own destruction. In Rwanda, this happened through an intersection of class differences with the interests of particular common-interest associations.

[9]Li, P.S. (1988). *The Chinese in Canada*. Toronto: Oxford University Press.

[10]Cherney, B. (2000, October 28). *Ukrainian immigration*. Retrieved March 13, 2001, from the World Wide Web: www.mbnet.mb.ca/~rfmorris/featuring/immigration/ukrainian.immigration.html.

[11]The University of Western Ontario (1989, February 3). Ukrainians want acknowledgement of injustice: C. Gruske. *The Gazette*. Retrieved March 13, 2001, from the World Wide Web: http://www.infoukes.com/history/internment/booklet02/doc-040.html.

[12]Kakodyniak, G.W. (1998). *Internment of Ukrainians in Canada 1914–1920*. Retrieved October 19, 2003, from the World Wide Web: http://www.infoukes.com/history/internment

In any system of stratification, those who dominate proclaim their supposedly superior status, which they try to convert into respect, or at least acquiescence, from the lower status groups. As anthropologist Laura Nader points out: "Systems of thought develop over time and reflect the interests of certain classes or groups in the society who manage to universalize their beliefs and values."[13] We see this, for example, in religious ideologies that assert that the social order is divinely fixed and therefore not to be questioned. Thus, they hope members of the lower classes will thereby "know their place" and not contest their domination by the "chosen elite." If, however, this domination is contested, the elite usually control the power of the state, which they use to protect their privileged position.

[13]Nader, L. (1997). Controlling processes: Tracing the dynamic components of power. *Current Anthropology, 38*, 271.

ORIGINAL STUDY

Genocide in Rwanda

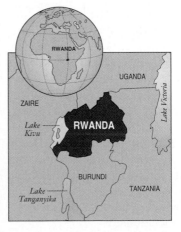

The genocide in Rwanda is a crime, perpetrated by a known group of individuals associated with two extremist parties, the National Republican Movement for Development of Democracy (MRND) and the Coalition for the Defense of the Republic (CDR). The first targets were members of opposition parties, journalists and human rights activists, both Hutu and Tutsi. As the killing spread to the rural areas, it has become a programme of genocide specifically targeted at the Tutsi, who before the killing represented about ten percent of Rwanda's seven million people. Over 200,000 have died so far [June 1994], and the killing continues. [After this piece was written, an uneasy peace was established under international supervision.]

A crime requires motive, means, and opportunity. The motive of those responsible was to continue to monopolize power and to seek a "final solution" to the political opposition, both civilian and armed. Attempts by President Juvenal Habyarimana to stall on the implementation of agreements for power sharing were not succeeding, owing to domestic and international pressure.

The primary means for perpetuating genocide is mobilization of the militias that had been established by the MRND and CDR since late 1971. Use of the civil administration to encourage ordinary people to participate in killings is a supplementary strategy. Army units, especially from the Presidential Guard, and death squads have also helped direct the killings, especially in the towns. Radio broadcasts have been used to incite the population.

The genocide against rural Tutsi in Rwanda is particularly traumatic because the killers are largely people from the same community as their victims. People are murdered by their neighbors, their schoolteachers, their local shopkeepers. Such mass mobilization of killers was necessary because of the particular nature of Rwandese society.

Rwanda has long been known as a true nation in Africa, containing three groups: Twa, Hutu and Tutsi. German and Belgian colonists characterized them as respectively aboriginal Pygmies, Bantu peasants and Nilo-Hamitic aristocrats. The truth is that they were three different strata of the same group, differentiated by occupational and political status. There is some analogy with the Indian caste system, though individuals could and did move with difficulty between the categories; and the Twa are victims of some of the worst discrimination in Africa.

Between April and August 1994, an estimated 800 000 Rwandans were killed in massacres like the one shown here.

The reciprocity in Hutu-Tutsi relations that had diluted the latter's dominance in precolonial days was destroyed by Belgian rule. Instead a rigid system of tribute and exploitation was imposed, creating deep grievances that underlie today's violence. In the northwest, formerly an anomalous region of Hutu kingdoms, the Belgians dismantled the precolonial political system, and imposed Tutsi overlords. The modern Hutu extremists—the late President Habyarimana and his clan—derive from this area.

The differences in physical stature between the groups have been widely exaggerated: it is rarely possible to tell whether an *individual* is a Twa, Hutu or Tutsi from his or her height. Speaking the same language, sharing the same culture and religion, living in the same places, they are in no sense "tribes," nor even distinct "ethnic groups."

Two things enable one to identify an individual as Twa, Hutu or Tutsi: knowledge of the person's ancestry, and the possession of an identity card which, since 1926, has by law specified which group he or she belongs to. The latter is a legacy of Belgian rule: those with ten or more cows were classified as Tutsi, those with less as Hutu—and a tiny minority of those recognized as Twa has their status as an ethnographic curiosity confirmed in perpetuity. But checking every identity card is time-consuming, and the killings needed to be carried out rapidly to be successful, so those planning the killing needed to mobilize militiamen from every community in the country, who knew every Tutsi family personally. In 1991, the government began to implement a system known as "Nyumba Kumi" (literally "ten houses")—one man from every ten houses was mobilized and armed. Such are the logistical challenges facing those who contemplate genocide.

The killers were able to practise their methods on various occasions since 1990, killing perhaps 3,000 people, mainly Tutsi. This is well documented in the 1993 report of an international human rights commission.

The opportunity was provided by a conjunction of circumstances, which allowed the hardliners to confuse the international community for sufficiently long to be able to perpetuate the crime with extraordinarily little international response. The sowing of confusion was the key to the killers' success. Because President Habyarimana himself was the first casualty, his acolytes were able to present themselves as victims of the plot, rather than the perpetrators. The deaths of ten Belgians serving on the UN force focused international attention on the plight of foreigners. The renewed offensive by the Rwandan Patriotic Front (RPF)—motivated in part by the desire to rescue Tutsi civilians from the militias—enabled the government to speak of aggression and the need for a ceasefire. But above all, the killers portrayed the situation as one of uncontrollable spontaneous ethnic violence.

Prompt international condemnation of the coup in Burundi in October 1993 prevented political extremists from seizing and holding on to power. The absence of such condemnation in Rwanda last month [May 1994] allowed the killers to carry out their task undisturbed. This was largely because the crime of genocide was misdiagnosed as a spontaneous ethnic violence. The Secretary General of the United Nations, Boutros Boutros-Ghali, spoke in late April of "Hutus killing Tutsi and Tutsi killing Hutus" and proposed sending troops to bring about a ceasefire between the (Tutsi-dominated) RPF and the (Hutu-dominated) army. This was precisely what the militias wanted: a chance to stop the RPF advance so they could complete the genocide of unarmed Tutsi away from the battle lines.

Source: de Waal, A. (1994). Genocide in Rwanda. *Anthropology Today, 10* (3), 1–2.

CHAPTER SUMMARY

All cultures group people according to gender and the division of labour associated with each gender. Age grouping is another form of association that may augment or replace kinship groupings. An age grade is a category of persons, usually of the same sex, organized by age. A specific tie is often ritually established for moving from a younger to an older age grade.

Common-interest associations are linked with rapid social change and urbanization. They are increasingly assuming the roles formerly played by kinship or age groups. In urban areas they help new arrivals cope with the changes demanded by the move from their former home to a new city. Common-interest associations are also seen in traditional cultures, and their roots are likely found in the first horticultural villages. Membership may range from voluntary to compulsory. A question that remains to be resolved is why women are barred from associations in some

cultures, while in others they participate on an equal basis with men.

In a system of social stratification people are ranked relative to one another. Those with lower ranks have limited access to wealth, power, and prestige. A stratified society exhibits the most stratification, with members experiencing varying degrees of inequality, while members of egalitarian cultures enjoy fairly equal wealth, power, and status. Human groups may be stratified in various ways, such as through gender, age, class and caste, ethnicity, and race.

Two conflicting theories attempt to explain the prevalence of stratification: the functionalist theory of stratification and the conflict theory of stratification. Functionalists believe inequalities are necessary to maintain complex societies, while conflict theorists believe there is a constant struggle between lower and upper classes. The concept of race, though erroneous, is the basis for racism or racial stratification, such as that experienced by First Nations peoples and Chinese Canadians. Racism is the belief that those designated to certain "races" are inferior to others.

Members of a class enjoy equal or nearly equal access to basic resources and prestige. Caste is a special form of social class in which membership is determined at birth and fixed for life. Endogamy is particularly marked within castes, and children automatically belong to their parents' caste. Social classes are given expression through verbal evaluation, or what people say about other people in their society; patterns of association, or who interacts with whom, how, and in what context; and symbolic indicators—activities and possessions. Open-class systems are those societies with the easiest mobility, whereas closed class systems are caste structures with limited mobility.

Gender stratification takes many forms. Anthropologists measure the degree of stratification based on gender according to the opportunities and freedoms women enjoy. Gender stratification may be due to control of resources and distribution of these resources or to the cultural organization created by constant warfare. Although race is a flawed concept, ethnicity, the shared identity of a group, is an important concept in human organization. Ethnic stratification, along with the ensuing discrimination, is common in countries like Canada, where many ethnic groups coexist.

QUESTIONS FOR CRITICAL THOUGHT

1. Are you a part of an age group as described in this chapter? If so, how does it define itself, and what are its functions?

2. Have you had an experience that made you aware of certain behaviours stemming from social stratification? Where did this occur? What was your role in the encounter? How aware of it were you at the time? Did it seem out of place, or was it an appropriate interaction?

3. Gender stratification still exists in Canada. Provide some examples of gender stratification that you have witnessed or experienced in Canadian society.

4. Research an ethnic group (preferably your own) and determine what, if any, discrimination members have experienced since immigrating to Canada. How did these immigrants overcome the limitations that discrimination placed on their lives?

INTERNET RESOURCES

Muslim Women
http://www.suite101.com
Small, but with many resources and links to related pages, this site examines the status of Muslim women from their perspective. Using the site search function will yield many interesting results: links to such topics as female genital mutilation (FGM), polygynous marriages, and the "ideal" Muslim woman. As with any site, be sure to read with a critical perspective.

Women's Issues in the Third World
http://women3rdworld.about.com/newsissues/women3rdworld/library/weekly/aa120798.htm
A large site, with many useful links on FGM, as well as links to topics such as child marriages, honour killings, and human rights.

Gender and Health
http://www.unfpa.org/swp/2000/english/ch02.html
A United Nations site addressing issues of gender inequality and discrimination harming women's health. Examines reproductive health services helping to empower women, components of reproductive health care, abortion and post-abortion care, sexually transmitted disease, female genital mutilation, reproductive health program issues, culture restrictions. Boxes include "Discrimination against girls a matter of life and death," "Honduras reduces maternal mortality," "AIDS is now the number one killer in Africa," and "Gender norms can prevent safe sex."

You Don't Have to Wear That in Canada

http://www.soundvision.com/news/hijab/hjb
.canada1.shtml

Female Muslim immigrants to Canada speak out about restrictions and discrimination they face in Canada because they choose to wear the hijab.

Ukrainian Museum of Canada

http://www.umc.sk.ca

This site offers a wealth of links to Ukrainian culture and history in Canada.

Ukrainians Want Acknowledgement of Injustice

http://www.infoukes.com/history/internment/
booklet02/doc-040.html

This article appeared in the University of Western Ontario's *Gazette*. It addresses the internment in Canada of Ukrainians during World War II and suggests that Canada should make redress.

Women: Still Something to Shout About

http://www.oneworld.org/ni/issue270/
270keynote.html

This site presents the view that widening gaps between the rich and poor are a ruthless killer, especially of women and children. An interesting summary of the rampant poverty and inequality in the world today.

The "F" Word

http://www.jenna.hennebry.com/gender.html
A brief site dedicated to various types of feminism in addition to links to other sites of interest.

The Hindu Caste System

http://www.hindubooks.org/sudheer_birodkar/
hindu_history/castevedic.html

This site provides a comprehensive, historical look at the caste system in India. Also provides links to other sites on Hinduism, Christianity, and Islam.

SUGGESTED READINGS

Bernardi, B. (1985). *Age class systems: Social institutions and policies based on age.* New York: Cambridge University Press.

This is a cross-cultural analysis of age as a device for organizing society and for distributing and rotating power.

Brooks, G. (1994). *Nine parts of desire: The hidden world of Islamic women.* New York: Anchor Books.

A refreshingly well-written, interesting book examining the lives of Muslim women. Geraldine Brooks travels through the Middle East on a journey of discovery. Her insights are remarkably objective, serving to break down many of the misconceptions Westerners have about Islamic people.

Li, P.S. (1988). *The Chinese in Canada.* Toronto: Oxford University Press.

This book provides a comprehensive, readable discussion of the lives and situations of Chinese immigrants to Canada over the course of the last 130 years. A good source for understanding the institutionalized racism Chinese Canadians have experienced in Canada.

Nelson, E.D., & Robinson, B.W. (Eds.). (1999). *Gender in Canada.* Scarborough, ON: Prentice Hall, Allyn and Bacon Canada.

A comprehensive examination of gender in Canadian society, this book will provide students with a firm grasp of issues related to gender.

Price, T.D., & Feinman, G.M. (Eds.). (1995). *Foundations of social inequality.* New York: Plenum.

This book is a collection of essays by various contributors that examines the emergence of social inequality.

Sanday, P.R. (1981). *Female power and male dominance: On the origins of sexual inequality.* Cambridge: Cambridge University Press.

In this cross-cultural study, Professor Sanday reveals the various ways male–female relations are organized in human societies and demonstrates that male dominance is not inherent in those relations. Rather, it appears to emerge in situations of stress as a result of such things as chronic food shortages, migration, and colonial domination.

CNN TODAY VIDEOS

The State of Human Rights in Central Africa (CNN Cultural Anthropology, vol. 3, 3:07)
This segment looks at the violence and ethnic conflict that erupted in the central African states of the Republic of Congo and Rwanda and the reaction or lack thereof by the Western powers to the fighting.

Egyptian Nubian Tradition (CNN Cultural Anthropology, vol. 1, 1:54)
The effects on Nubian culture following the construction of the Aswan Dam.

Japan No Romance (CNN Cultural Anthropology, vol. 1, 2:00)
This segment looks at how romantic love is expressed in the Japanese culture.

Disgusting Foods (CNN Cultural Anthropology, vol. 4, 2:50)
A lighthearted look at how foods, thought to be delicacies in one culture, are looked upon as inedible in another culture.

Chapter 11

Political Organization and the Maintenance of Order

Political organization in human cultures takes varied forms, but regardless of form, is designed to coordinate behaviour and maintain order within cultures and between cultures. Such is the case with Canadian peacekeepers sent to the former Yugoslavia in 1992–95 to ensure the distribution of relief supplies.

Chapter Preview

1. What Is Political Organization?

Political organization refers to the means a culture uses to maintain order internally and manage its affairs with other cultures externally. Such organization may be relatively uncentralized and informal, as in bands and tribes, or centralized and formal, as in chiefdoms and states.

2. How Is Order Maintained within a Culture?

Social controls may be internalized—"built into" individuals—or externalized in the form of sanctions. Built-in controls rely on deterrents such as personal shame and fear of supernatural punishment. Positive sanctions encourage approved behaviour, while negative sanctions discourage disapproved behaviour. Negative sanctions formalized and enforced by an authorized political body are called laws. Similarly, cultures do not maintain order through law alone.

3. How Is Order Maintained between Cultures?

Just as the threatened or actual use of force may maintain order within a culture, it also may manage affairs among bands, lineages, clans, or other autonomous political units. Not all cultures rely on force, because some do not practise warfare as we know it. Such cultures have views of themselves and their place in the world quite different from those characteristic of centrally organized states.

4. How Do Political Systems Obtain People's Allegiance?

Political organization cannot function without the loyalty of those it governs. To a greater or lesser extent, political organizations use religion to legitimize their power. In uncentralized systems people give loyalty and cooperation because everyone participates in making decisions. Centralized systems rely on force and coercion, although these may lessen the system's effectiveness.

CHAPTER OUTLINE

Kinds of Political Systems

Gender Perspectives: Minority Women in Canadian Politics

Political Organization and the Maintenance of Order

Original Study: Limits on Power in Bedouin Society

Social Control through Law

Anthropology Applied: Dispute Resolution and the Anthropologist

Political Organization and External Affairs

Political Systems and the Question of Legitimacy

Religion and Politics

Louis XIV proclaimed, "I am the state." With this sweeping statement, the king declared absolute rule over France; he held himself to be the law, the lawmaker, the court, the judge, jailer, and executioner—in short, the seat of all political power in France.

Louis XIV took a great deal of responsibility on his royal shoulders; had he actually performed each of these functions, he would have done the work of thousands of people, the number required to keep the machinery of a large political organization such as a state running at full steam. As a form of political organization, the 17th-century French state was not much different from those that exist in modern times. All large states require elaborate centralized structures, involving hierarchies of executives, legislators, and judges who initiate, pass, and enforce laws that affect large numbers of people.

Complex political structures are a relatively recent phenomenon. The oldest European states, for instance, are only a few hundred years old. Even today some cultural groups depend on far less formal means of organization. In these cultures, flexible and informal kinship systems with leaders who lack real power prevail. Problems, such as homicide and theft, are perceived as serious "family quarrels," rather than affairs that affect the entire community. Between these two polarities of political organization lies a world of variety, including cultures with chiefs, Big Men, or charismatic leaders and segmented tribes with multicentric authority systems. Such disparity prompts this question: What is political organization?

The term *political organization* refers to the way power is distributed and embedded in a cultural group, whether in organizing a giraffe hunt or passing legislation. In other words, political organization has to do with the way power is used to coordinate and regulate behaviour so that order is maintained. Political organization is an important component of human behaviour. However, we should resist the temptation to restrict our examination to military or police structure—this is not the only, or even the most important, aspect of political organization. Some form of political organization exists in all human groups.

KINDS OF POLITICAL SYSTEMS

Political organization is the means a human group uses to maintain social order and reduce social disorder. It assumes a variety of forms among the peoples of the world, but scholars have simplified this complex subject by identifying four basic kinds of political systems: uncentralized bands and tribes, and centralized chiefdoms and states. The following discussion is in no way meant to suggest an evolutionary "progress" from primitive to advanced political organization. Rather, each of these systems is designed to meet the needs of a population living within a specific setting.

Uncentralized Political Systems

In many non-Western cultural groups, marriage and kinship form the principal means of social organization among such peoples. The economies of these groups are of a subsistence type, and populations are typically quite small. Leaders do not have the power to force compliance with the society's customs or laws, but if individual members do not conform, they may become the target of scorn and gossip or even be ostracized. Important decisions are usually made in a democratic manner by a consensus of adults, often including women as well as men; dissenting members may decide to act with the majority, or they may choose to adopt some other course of action, if they are willing to risk the social consequences. This form of political organization provides great flexibility, which in many situations confers an adaptive advantage.

Band Organization

The **band** is a small group of politically independent, though related, families and is the least complex form of political organization. Bands are found among food foragers and other nomadic groups where people organize into politically autonomous extended-family groups that camp together, although the members of such families may frequently split into smaller groups for periods to forage for food or visit other relatives.

Band.   A small group of related households occupying a particular region that gather periodically but that do not yield their sovereignty to the larger collective.

Bands are thus kin groups, composed of men and/or women who are related (or assumed to be) and their spouses and unmarried children. Bands may be characterized as associations of related families who occupy a common (often vaguely defined) territory and who live there together, so long as environmental and subsistence circumstances are favourable. The band is probably the oldest form of political organization, since all humans were once food foragers and remained so until the domestication of plants and animals over the past 10 000 years.

In small-scale, egalitarian groups, where everyone is related to—and knows on a personal basis—everyone else and where almost everyone values "getting along," the potential for conflicts to develop is reduced. Many of those that do arise are settled informally through gossip, ridicule, direct negotiation, or mediation. In conflict resolution, the emphasis is on achieving a solution considered fair by most parties concerned, rather than conforming to some abstract law or rule. When all else fails, disgruntled individuals have the option of joining another band where they have relatives.

Decisions affecting a band are made with the participation of all its adult members, with an emphasis on achieving **consensus**, rather than a simple majority. Leaders become such by virtue of their abilities and serve in that capacity only as long as they retain the community's confidence. Thus, they have neither a guaranteed hold on their position for a specified length of time nor the power to force people to abide by their decisions. People will follow them only as long as they consider it in their best interests, and a leader who exceeds what people are willing to accept quickly loses followers.

An example of the informal nature of leadership in the band is found among the Ju/'hoansi of the Kalahari Desert. Each Ju/'hoansi band is composed of a group of families who live together, linked to one another and to the headman or, less often, headwoman through kinship. Although each band has rights to the territory it occupies and the resources within it, two or more bands may range over the same territory. The head, called the *kxau*, or "owner," is the focal point for the band's

Toma, a Ju/'hoansi headman known to many North Americans through the documentary film *The Hunters*.

Consensus. A general agreement among adult members of a group.

theoretical ownership of the territory. The headman or headwoman does not really own the land or resources but symbolically personifies the rights of band members to them. If the head leaves a territory to live elsewhere, he or she ceases to be the band's head, and people turn to someone else to lead them.

The head's chief duty is to plan when and where the group will move when resources are no longer adequate for subsistence in a particular territory. When the move begins, his or her position is at the head of the line. The leader chooses the site for the new settlement and has the first choice of a spot for his or her own fire. The head has no other rewards or duties; a head does not organize hunting parties, trading expeditions, the making of artifacts, or gift giving, nor does this leader make marriage arrangements. Instead, individuals instigate their own activities. The headman or headwoman is not a judge and does not punish other band members. Wrongdoers are judged and regulated by public opinion, usually expressed by gossip among band members. A prime technique for resolving disputes, or even avoiding them in the first place, is mobility. Those unable to get along with others of their group simply move to another group where kinship ties give them entry rights.

A similar pattern is found among North American First Nations peoples, for example, the Slavey of northern Canada. Traditionally, leaders were chosen from the most successful hunters, while senior women controlled kinship (marriage and group composition). Elders held important positions in the band; they chose the leaders and served as teachers, historians, and political advisers. Individuals with special powers provided healing and ritual services and maintained social control over the group. The band members settled their own disputes; in the case of the most serious offences, the culprit might even be banished from the band. Neighbouring groups usually enjoyed amicable relations, but if a dispute arose, band members attempted to resolve it by holding competitions and contests between medicine men, or if all else failed, they could resort to violence. As with the Ju/'hoansi, decision making was based on

consensus, and anyone unhappy with the decisions was free to "vote with their feet."[1]

Following the 1899 and 1921 treaties, chiefs and band councils were established. These early Slavey chiefs were chosen from traditional leaders, and the councillors were leaders of local bands. More recently, leaders have been elected by majority rule, which is at odds with the principles of Slavey political and social organization. In the 1960s, when megaprojects, such as the Mackenzie Valley Pipeline, threatened their territories, Slaveys allied with other Dene peoples to form the Dene Nation. The Dene Nation sought political autonomy and greater control over their traditional lands. Slavey communities in the Northwest Territories also formed a regional/Slavey organization—the Deh Cho First Nation Council. In the 1990s the Dene challenged the federal government's claim of jurisdiction over their lands.[2]

Tribal Organization

The second type of uncentralized or multicentric authority system is the **tribe,** a word that, unfortunately, is used in different ways by different people. Among the general public, it is used commonly to label any people who are not organized into states, irrespective of whether or not they constitute what anthropologists would call bands, tribes, or chiefdoms. Sometimes, the term is even applied to non-Western peoples who in fact had strongly centralized states (the Aztecs, for example), a practice no more warranted than calling the Chinese people a tribe. Historically, Europeans coined the term to contrast people they regarded as inferior with supposedly superior, "civilized" Europeans. The word often is still used in a derogatory way, as when political unrest

[1]Asch, M. (1981), as cited in R.B. Lee & R. Daly (Eds.), *The Cambridge encyclopedia of hunters and gatherers* (pp. 342–343). Cambridge, UK: Cambridge University Press.

[2]Asch, M., & Smith, S. (1999). Slavey Dene. In R.B. Lee & R. Daly (Eds.), *The Cambridge encyclopedia of hunters and gatherers* (pp. 48–49). Cambridge, UK: Cambridge University Press.

Tribe. A group of nominally independent communities occupying a specific region and sharing a common language and culture integrated by some unifying factor.

in many parts of the world is blamed on "tribalism," which is not accurate (usually, the strife is the direct consequence of the creation of multinational states that make it possible for a governing elite of one nationality to exploit others for their own benefit).[3]

So what, then, do anthropologists have in mind when they speak of tribal organization? To them, a tribal system involves separate bands or villages integrated by factors such as clans that unite people in separate communities or age grades or associations that crosscut kinship or territorial boundaries. In such cases people sacrifice a degree of household autonomy to a larger-order group in return for greater security against enemy attacks or starvation. Typically, although not invariably, a tribe has an economy based on some form of farming or herding. Since these production methods usually yield more food than

Shown here is Phil Fontaine, chief of the Assembly of First Nations.

those of the food-foraging band, tribal membership is usually larger than band membership. Compared with bands, where population densities are usually less than 1 person per square kilometre, tribal population densities always exceed 1 person per square kilometre and may be as high as 250 per square kilometre.

Each tribe consists of one or more small, autonomous local communities, which then may form alliances with one another for various purposes. As in the band, political organization in the tribe is informal and temporary. Whenever a situation requiring political integration of all or several groups within the tribe arises—perhaps for defence, to carry out a raid, to pool resources in times of scarcity, or to capitalize on a windfall that must be distributed quickly lest it spoil—they join to deal with the situation in a cooperative manner. When the problem is satisfactorily solved, each group then returns to its autonomous state.

Leadership among tribes is also informal. The Blackfoot, for example, did not think of government as something fixed and all-powerful, and leadership was not vested in a central authority. A local leader was a man respected for his wisdom and hunting prowess. His advice therefore was sought frequently, but he had no formal means of control and could not force any decision on those who asked for his help. Group decisions were made by public consensus, although the leaders attempted to persuade others through oratory skills. Among the social mechanisms that induced members to abide by group decisions were withdrawal of cooperation, gossip, criticism, and the belief that antisocial actions caused disease.

Another example of tribal leadership is the Melanesian Big Man. Such men are leaders of localized descent groups or of a territorial group. The Big Man combines a small amount of interest in his tribe's welfare with a great deal of self-interested cunning and calculation for his own gain. His authority is personal; he does not come to office in any formal sense, nor is he elected. His status is the result of acts that raise him above most other tribe members and attract to him a band of loyal followers.

Typical of this form of political organization are the Kapauku of west New Guinea. Among them, the Big Man is called the *tonowi*, or "rich one." To achieve this status, one must be male,

[3]Whitehead, N.L., & Ferguson, R.B. (1993, November 10). Deceptive stereotypes about tribal warfare (p. A48). *Chronicle of Higher Education*; Van Den Berghe, P.L. (1992). The modern state: Nation builder or nation killer? *International Journal of Group Tensions, 22* (3), 199–200.

wealthy, generous, and eloquent; physical bravery and skills in dealing with the supernatural also are frequent characteristics of a *tonowi,* but they are not essential. The *tonowi* functions as the headman of the village unit.

Kapauku culture places a high value on wealth, so it is not surprising that a wealthy man is considered successful and admirable. Yet the possession of wealth must be coupled with the trait of generosity, which in this culture means not gift giving but willingness to make loans. Wealthy men who refuse to lend money to other villagers may be ostracized, ridiculed, and, in extreme cases, actually executed by a group of warriors. This social pressure ensures that economic wealth is rarely hoarded but instead is distributed throughout the group.

Through the loans he makes, the *tonowi* acquires his political power. Other villagers comply with his requests because they are in his debt (often without paying interest), and they do not want to have to repay their loans. Those who have not yet borrowed from the *tonowi* may wish to do so in the future, so they, too, want to keep his goodwill.

Other sources of support for the *tonowi* are apprentices he has taken into his household for training. They are fed, housed, given a chance to learn the *tonowi*'s business wisdom, and given a loan to get a wife when they leave; in return, they act as messengers and bodyguards. Even after they leave his household, these men are tied to the *tonowi* by bonds of affection and gratitude. Political support also comes from the *tonowi*'s kinsmen, whose relationship brings with it varying obligations.

The *tonowi* functions as a leader in a wide variety of situations. He represents his group when dealing with outsiders and other villages; he acts as negotiator and/or judge when disputes

This Big Man from New Guinea is wearing his "official" regalia.

break out among his followers. The *tonowi* also is influential in economic and social affairs, such as setting dates for pig feasts and pig markets, and convincing others to co-sponsor a feast. The *tonowi* also may sponsor and initiate dance expeditions to other villages and initiate large projects, such as building bridges.[4]

The *tonowi*'s wealth comes from his success at pig breeding. It is not uncommon for a *tonowi* to lose his fortune rapidly as a result of bad management or bad luck with his pigs. Thus the Kapauku political structure shifts frequently; as one man loses wealth and consequently power, another gains it and becomes a *tonowi*. These changes confer a degree of flexibility on the political organization and prevent any one *tonowi* from holding political power for too long.

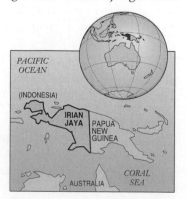

---

[4]Pospisil, L. (1963). *The Kapauku Papuans of west New Guinea* (pp. 51–52). New York: Holt, Rinehart and Winston.

Kinship Organization

In many tribal groups the organizing unit and seat of political authority is the clan, an association of people who believe themselves to share a common ancestry. Within the clan, elders or headmen regulate members' affairs and represent their clan in relations with other clans. As a group, the elders of all the clans may form a council that acts within the community or for the community in dealings with outsiders. Because clan members usually do not all live together in one community, clan organization facilitates joint action with members of other communities when necessary.

Another form of tribal kinship bond that provides political organization is the **segmentary lineage system.** This system is similar in operation to the clan, but it is less extensive and is relatively rare. The best-known examples are East African cultures such as the Somali and the Dinka or Nuer of the Sudan: pastoral nomads who are highly mobile and widely scattered over large territories. Unlike other East African pastoralists (the Maasai, for example), they lack the age-grading organization that cuts across descent group membership. Political organization among segmentary lineages is usually informal, although older tribal members may exercise some personal authority.

Among the Nuer, who number some 200 000 people living in the swampland and savanna of Sudan, at least 20 clans exist. Each is patrilineal and is segmented into maximal lineages; each of these is in turn segmented into major lineages, which are segmented into minor lineages, which in turn are segmented into minimal lineages. The minimal lineage is a group descended from one great-grandfather or great-great-grandfather.

The lineage segments among the Nuer are all equal, and no leadership or political organization exists above the level of the autonomous minimal or primary segments. The lineage's entire superstructure is an alliance, active only during conflicts between any of the minimal segments. In any serious dispute between members of different minimal lineage segments, members of all other seg-

ments take the side of the contestant they are most closely related to, and the issue is then joined between the higher-order lineages involved to address the issue. Such a system of political organization is known as *complementary* or *balanced opposition.*

Disputes among the Nuer are frequent, as they are among other groups with similar organization, and under the segmentary lineage system, they can lead to widespread feuds. This possible source of social disruption is minimized by the actions of the "leopard-skin chief," not really a chief but a holder of a ritual conciliation office. The leopard-skin chief has no political power and is viewed as standing outside the lineage network. All he can do is try to persuade feuding lineages to accept payment in "blood cattle" rather than taking another life. His mediation gives each side the chance to back down gracefully before too many people are killed, but if the participants are for some reason unwilling to compromise, the leopard-skin chief has no authority to enforce a settlement. Although the previous discussion focuses on the ethnographic present of Nuer society and political organization, the Nuer political structure described above has been severely disrupted after almost 20 years of civil war.

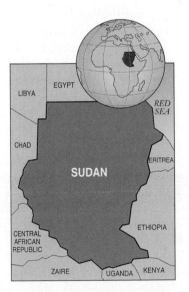

Segmentary lineage system.   A form of political organization in which a large group is broken up into clans that are further divided into lineages.

Local shamans help maintain social order in bands and tribes. Shown here is Shaman Vargas, of Indi Community, Pastaza, Ecuador.

Age-Grade Organization

Age-grade systems provide a tribe with a means of political integration beyond the kin group. Under this system, youths are initiated into an age grade, and then they pass from one age grade to another at appropriate ages. Age grades and sets cut across territorial and kin groupings and thus may be important means of political organization. Among the Tiriki of East Africa, the warrior age grade guards the country, while judicial elders resolve disputes. Between these two age grades are elder warriors, who are in a sense understudies to the judicial elders. The oldest age grade, the ritual elders, advise on matters involving the well-being of all the Tiriki people. Thus, the tribe's political affairs are in the hands of the age grades and their officers. Among East African pastoralists, those like the Tiriki with age-grading organization generally experience less feuding than those with segmentary lineage organization.

Association Organization

Common-interest associations that function as politically integrative systems within tribes are found in many areas of the world, including Africa, Melanesia, and India. A good example of association organization functioned during the 19th century among the Plains peoples of Canada. The basic Cree territorial and political unit was the band, but the men were organized into military societies, or warriors' clubs. A young man might be invited to join one of these societies when he performed a brave deed, whereupon he became familiar with the society's particular insignia, songs, and rituals. In addition to military functions, such as keeping order in the camp and on the hunt, and guarding against enemy attack, these warrior societies also performed rituals that strengthened group solidarity.

Centralized Political Systems

In bands and tribes, authority is uncentralized, and each group is economically and politically autonomous. Political organization is vested in kinship, age, and common-interest groups. Populations are small and relatively homogeneous, with people engaged mostly in the same sorts of activities throughout their lives. As populations increase and technology becomes more complex, and as specialization of labour and trade networks produce surpluses of goods, the opportunity for some individuals or groups to exercise control increases. In such groups, political authority and power are concentrated in a single individual—the chief—or in a body of individuals—the state. The state is a form of organization found in societies where each individual must interact on a regular basis with large numbers of people with diversified interests who are neither kin nor close acquaintances.

Chiefdoms

A **chiefdom** is a regional polity in which two or more local groups are organized under a single ruling individual—the chief—who is at the head

---

Chiefdom. A regional polity in which two or more local groups are organized under a single chief, who is at the head of a ranked hierarchy of people.

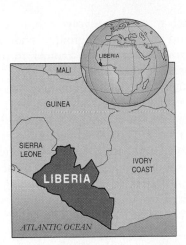

of a ranked hierarchy of people. An individual's status in such a polity is determined by his or her closeness of relationship to the chief. Those closest are officially superior and receive deferential treatment from those in lower ranks.

The office of the chief is usually hereditary, passing from a man to his own or his sister's son, depending on whether descent is reckoned patrilineally or matrilineally. Unlike the headmen in bands and lineages, the chief is generally a true authority figure, and his authority serves to unite his people in all affairs and at all times. For example, a chief can distribute land among his community members and recruit people into his military service. Chiefdoms have a recognized hierarchy consisting of major and minor authorities who control major and minor subdivisions. Such an arrangement is, in effect, a chain of command, linking leaders at every level. It serves to bind tribal groups in the heartland to the chief's headquarters, be it a mud and dung hut or a marble palace. Although chiefs inherit offices, in practice they maintain power through personal abilities and as exemplars of what is almost always seen as a semi-sacred position.

The chief controls the economic activities of his people. Chiefdoms are typically redistributive systems; the chief has control over surplus goods and perhaps even over the community labour force. Thus, he may demand a quota of rice from farmers, which he will redistribute to the entire community. Similarly, he may recruit labourers to build irrigation works, a palace, or a temple.

The chief also may amass a great amount of personal wealth and pass it on to his heirs. Land, cattle, and luxury goods produced by specialists can be collected by the chief and become part of his power base. Moreover, high-ranking families of the chiefdom may engage in the same practice and use their possessions as evidence of status.

An example of people using this form of political organization is the Kpelle of Liberia in West Africa.[5] Among them is a class of paramount chiefs, each of whom presides over one of the Kpelle chiefdoms (each of which is now a district of the Liberian state). The paramount chiefs' traditional tasks are hearing disputes, preserving order, seeing to the upkeep of trails, and maintaining "medicines." They are also salaried officials of the Liberian government, mediating between it and their people. Other rewards a paramount chief receives include a commission on taxes collected within his chiefdom, a commission for labourers furnished for the rubber plantations, a portion of court fees collected, a stipulated amount of rice from each household, and gifts from people who come to request favours and intercessions. In keeping with his exalted station in life, a paramount chief has at his disposal uniformed messengers, a literate clerk, and the symbols of wealth: many wives, embroidered gowns, and freedom from manual labour.

---

[5]Gibbs, J.L., Jr. (1965). The Kpelle of Liberia. In J.L. Gibbs, Jr. (Ed.), *Peoples of Africa* (pp. 216–218). New York: Holt, Rinehart and Winston.

A Kpelle town chief settles a dispute.

Beneath each Kpelle paramount chief are several lesser chiefs: one for each district, one for each town, and one for each quarter of all but the smallest towns. Each acts as a kind of lieutenant for his chief of the next-higher rank and also serves as a liaison between him and those of lower rank. Unlike paramount or district chiefs, who are comparatively remote, town and quarter chiefs are readily accessible to people at the local level.

Stable though the Kpelle political system may be today, traditionally chiefdoms in all parts of the world have been highly unstable. This instability happens as lesser chiefs try to take power from higher-ranking chiefs or as paramount chiefs vie with one another for supreme power. In precolonial Hawaii, for example, war was the way to gain territory and maintain power; great chiefs set out to conquer one another in an effort to become paramount chief of all the islands. When one chief conquered another, the loser and all his nobles were dispossessed of all property and were lucky if they escaped alive. The new chief then appointed his own supporters to positions of political power. As a consequence, governmental or religious administration had very little continuity.

State Systems

The **state** is the most formal of political organizations. In the state, political power is centralized in a government, which may legitimately use force to regulate the affairs of its citizens, as well as its relations with other states.

Increased food production results in increased population. Together, these lead to modification of the landscape; improvements such as irrigation and terracing, carefully managed rotation cycles, intensive competition for clearly demarcated lands, and rural populations large enough to support market systems and a specialized urban sector. Under such conditions, corporate groups that stress exclusive membership proliferate, ethnic differentiation and ethnocentrism become more pronounced, and the potential for social conflict increases dramatically. Given these circumstances, the state institu-

tions, which minimally involve a bureaucracy, a military, and an official religion, provide a means for numerous and diverse groups to function together as an integrated whole.

Although their guiding ideology purports that they are permanent and stable, the fact is, since their first appearance some 5000 to 6000 years ago, states have been anything but permanent; over the long term, they show a clear tendency toward instability and transience. Nowhere have states even begun to show the staying power exhibited by more uncentralized political systems, the longest-lasting social forms invented by humans.

An important distinction to make at this point is between **nation** and state. Today, there are roughly 181 states in the world, and most did not exist before the end of World War II. By contrast, probably about 5000 nations exist in the world today. "What makes each a nation is that its people share a language, culture, territorial base, and political organization and history."[6] Today, states commonly have living within their boundaries people of more than one nation, for example, the First Nations peoples of Canada. Rarely do state and nation coincide, although we do have some examples in Iceland, Japan, Somalia, and Swaziland. By contrast, some 73 percent of the world's states are multinational.[7]

Canada was a nation long before Europeans "discovered" this land. First Nations and Inuit peoples covered the vast expanse of this country, albeit sparsely; each nation spoke a distinctive language, and each possessed vibrant, diverse cultural traditions. Each nation occupied a loosely defined territory, with a long-standing history of occupation and adaptation to their particular environment. But the newly arrived French and English colonists refused to recognize the First

---

[6]Clay, J.W. (1996). What's a nation? In W.A. Haviland & R.J. Gordon (Eds.), *Talking about people* (2nd ed., p. 188). Mountain View, CA: Mayfield.

[7]Van Den Berghe, P.L. (1992). The modern state: Nation builder or nation killer? *International Journal of Group Tensions, 22* (3), 193.

State. In anthropology, a centralized political system with the power to coerce. **> Nation.** Communities of people who see themselves as "one people" on the basis of common ancestry, history, society, institutions, ideology, language, territory, and (often) religion.

The Royal Canadian Mounted Police (RCMP) has been a symbol of peace-keeping and authority in Canada since 1873. Shown here, in 1999, they are reenacting the 1874 march west, when 275 officers and men marched from Manitoba to southern Alberta.

Nations and Inuit peoples as true nations, regarding these groups as small nomadic bands with informal leaders, who simply did not meet the criteria for real nations.[8] Today, First Nations, Inuit, and Métis peoples are seeking recognition of their nationhood and their inherent right to self-determination. They want to regain control of their affairs and to make their own decisions concerning the preservation and development of their distinct cultures. Self-government would enable aboriginal people more control over affairs within their communities and the power to deliver programs and services, such as education, child welfare, and health care, that fit with their aboriginal values.[9]

Under section 35 of the 1982 Constitution Act, the Canadian government recognized aboriginal peoples' right to determine matters related to their culture, identity, traditions, and language, but because each nation is unique, negotiations have to be conducted on a nation-by-nation basis.

Self-government arrangements have already been settled with the Sechelt Indian Band in British Columbia, the Cree-Naskapi of Quebec, and the Yukon First Nations.[10] Métis groups also seek the power to direct and influence decisions that affect their lives. Inuit groups have taken a slightly different approach, preferring to remain within the sphere of public government. After decades of negotiations, eastern portions of the Northwest Territories separated in 1999 to form a new territory, Nunavut, for the Inuit people of the Canadian Arctic.

Western forms of political organization are state governments. Another example of a state is that of the Swazi of Swaziland, a Bantu-speaking people who live in southeast Africa.[11] They are primarily farmers, but cattle raising is more highly valued than farming: the ritual, wealth, and power of their authority system are all intricately linked with cattle. In addition to farming and cattle raising; certain people have become specialists in ritual, smithing, wood carving, and pottery. Their

[8]Friesen, J.W. (1997). *Rediscovering the First Nations of Canada.* Calgary: Detselig.

[9]Indian and Northern Affairs Canada. (2000, July 21). *Federal policy guide—Aboriginal self-government.* Retrieved March 21, 2001, from the World Wide Web: http://www.ainc-inac.gc.ca/pr/pub/sg/plcy_e.html.

[10]Ibid.

[11]Kuper, H. (1965). The Swazi of Swaziland. In J.L. Gibbs, Jr. (Ed.), *Peoples of Africa* (pp. 475–512). New York: Holt, Rinehart and Winston.

goods and services are traded, although the Swazi do not have elaborate markets.

The Swazi authority system is characterized by a highly developed dual monarchy, a hereditary aristocracy, and elaborate kinship rituals. The king and his mother are the central figures of all national activity, linking all the people of the Swazi state. They preside over higher courts, summon national gatherings, control age classes, allocate land, disburse national wealth, take precedence in ritual, and help organize important social events.

Advising the Swazi king are the senior princes, who are usually his uncles and half-brothers. Between the king and the princes are two specially created *tinsila,* or "blood brothers," who are chosen from certain common clans. These men are his shields, protecting him from evildoers and serving him in intimate personal situations. In addition, the king is guided by two *tindvuna,* or councillors, one civil and one military. The people of the state make their opinions known through two councils: the *liqoqo,* or privy council, composed of senior princes, and the *libanda,* or council of state, composed of chiefs and headmen and open to all adult males of the state. The *liqoqo* may advise the king, make decisions, and carry them out. For example, they may rule on questions about land, education, traditional ritual, court procedure, and transport.

Swazi government extends from the smallest local unit—the homestead—upward to the central administration. The head of a homestead has legal and administrative powers; he is responsible for the crimes of those under him, controls their property, and speaks for them before his superiors. On the district level, political organization is similar to that of the central government. The relationship between a district chief, however, and his subjects is personal and familiar; he knows all the families in his district. The main check on any autocratic tendencies he may exhibit rests in his subjects' ability to transfer their allegiance to a more responsive chief. Swazi officials hold their positions for life and are dismissed only for treason or witchcraft.

Political Leadership and Gender

Irrespective of cultural configuration, or type of political organization, women rarely hold positions of political leadership. Furthermore, when they do occupy publicly recognized offices, their power and authority rarely exceed those of men. Nevertheless, exceptions occur, and recent ones are Corazon Aquino (Philippines), Benazir Bhutto (Pakistan), Gro Harlem Brundtland (Norway), Indira Ghandi (India), Janet Jagan (Ghana), Golda Meir (Israel), and Margaret Thatcher (Great Britain), who do head or have headed governments. Several literary works cite female chiefs among First Nations groups. The last monarch of Hawaii and powerful queens such as Elizabeth I of England or Catherine the Great of Russia are other examples. When women do hold high office, it is often because of their relationship to men. Thus, a queen is either the wife of a reigning monarch or else the daughter of a king who died without a male heir to succeed him. Moreover, women in focal positions frequently must adopt many of the characteristics of temperament normally deemed appropriate for men in their societies. In her role as prime minister, Margaret Thatcher displayed the toughness and assertiveness that, in Western societies, have been considered desirable masculine qualities, rather than the nurturance and compliance Westerners traditionally have expected of women.

In spite of all this, in a number of societies, women regularly enjoy as much political power as men. In band societies, it is common for women to have as much say in public affairs as men, even though the latter more often than not are the nominal leaders of their groups. Among the Iroquoian nations of southern Ontario and New York State, all leadership positions above the household level were, without

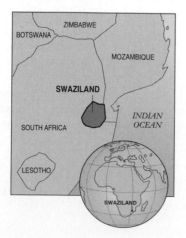

exception, filled by men. Thus they held all positions on the village and tribal councils, as well as on the great council of the league of Five Nations. Despite their power, they were beholden to women, for only the latter could appoint men to high office. Moreover, women actively lobbied the men on the councils and could remove someone from office whenever it suited them.

As these cases make clear, low visibility of women in politics does not necessarily exclude them from the realm of social control, nor does it mean men have more power in political affairs. Sometimes, though, women may play more visible roles, as in the dual-sex systems of West Africa. Among the Igbo of Nigeria, in each political unit, separate political institutions for men and women give each sex their autonomous spheres of authority, as well as an area of shared responsibility.[12] At the head of each was a male *obi,* considered the head of government though in fact he presided over the male community, and a female *omu,* the acknowledged mother of the whole community but in practice concerned with the female section. Unlike a queen (although both she and the *obi* were crowned), the *omu* was neither the *obi*'s wife nor the previous *obi*'s daughter.

Just as the Igbo *obi* had a council of dignitaries to advise him and to act as a check against any arbitrary exercise of power, the *omu* was served by a council of women in equal number to

Shown here is the Iroquois chief Joseph Brant (1742–1807). Although Iroquoian chiefs were always men, they served strictly at the pleasure of women, whose position in society was equal to that of men.

the *obi*'s male councillors. The *omu* and her councillors established rules and regulations for the community market (marketing was a women's activity) and heard cases involving women brought to her from throughout the town or village. If such cases also involved men, then she and her council would cooperate with the *obi* and his council. Widows also went to the *omu* for the final rites required to end their period of mourning for dead husbands. Since the *omu* represented all women, she had to be responsive to her constituency and would seek their approval and cooperation in all major decisions.

In addition to the *omu* and her council, the Igbo women's government included a representative body of women chosen from each quarter or section of the village or town on the basis of their ability to think logically and speak well. At the village or lineage level were political pressure groups of women who acted to stop quarrels and prevent wars.

---

[12]Okonjo, K. (1976). The dual-sex political system in operation: Igbo women and community politics in midwestern Nigeria. In N. Hafkin & E. Bay (Eds.), *Women in Africa* (pp. 45–58). Stanford, CA: Stanford University Press.

Gender **Perspectives**

Minority Women in Canadian Politics

For the most part, a narrow class of people has monopolized the political arena in Canada—typically White, affluent males—while new social groups, such as minority women, have been underrepresented. Minority women are defined as belonging to ethno-racial groups outside the two "charter" groups, the French and the English. These women face a double jeopardy: They are women and they belong to a minority group, which means they do not receive the same advantages and privileges as majority groups, in much the same way as gender-based social forces have historically kept women subordinate to men. Minority women, however, are subordinated on two fronts—as women and as minorities—and thus they face more barriers than either majority women or minority men, meaning they must deal with the limitations placed on them as a result of both gender and ethnic origin. Because of these barriers, minority women are relatively few in Canadian politics, especially at the federal level, but they are becoming a presence to reckon with.

Two models have been presented to analyze inequality within the Canadian political system. The first, known as the "similarity" model, proposes that women seeking political office in Canada must possess the same social and political resources (e.g., high educational and occupation experience)

as men do. If they meet these requirements, then the disparities should diminish. Thus, those minority women who are successful in achieving political stations will have the same qualifications as majority women and men and will have the same opportunities.

The second model suggests that minority women must surpass the standards set for majority women and men. Known as the "compensation" model, this approach recognizes the restrictive and biased nature of recruitment into the political arena, and submits that to overcome the disadvantage of being both a woman and a member of a minority group, these women must have exceptional credentials, far exceeding those of the social groups they are competing with, to overcome negative stereotypes and serious barriers.

Black's (2000) study found that minority women do have greater accomplishments relative to majority women and minority men. In addition, women, regardless of ethnic origin, tend to have greater accomplishments than men. Black found that the hurdles for women are generally higher than for men, and minority women have the added disadvantage of ethnicity, thus forcing them to achieve even greater heights in order to accomplish their goals.

Source: Black, J.H. (2000). Entering the political elite in Canada: The case of minority women as parliamentary candidates and MPs. *Canadian Review of Sociology and Anthropology, 37* (2).

In the Igbo system, then, women managed their own affairs, and their interests were represented at all levels of government. Moreover, they had the right to enforce their decisions and rules with sanctions similar to those men employed. Included were strikes, boycotts, and "sitting on a man" or woman. Political scientist Judith Van Allen describes the latter:

To "sit on" or "make war on" a man involved gathering at his compound, sometimes late at night, dancing, singing scurrilous songs which detailed the

women's grievances against him and often called his manhood into question, banging on his hut with the pestles women used for pounding yams, and perhaps demolishing his hut or plastering it with mud and roughing him up a bit. A man might be sanctioned in this way for mistreating his wife, for violating the women's market rules, or for letting his cows eat the women's crops. The women would stay at his hut throughout the day, and late into the night if necessary, until he repented and promised to mend his ways. . . . Although this could hardly have been a pleasant experience for the offending man, it was considered legitimate and no man would consider intervening.[13]

Given the high visibility of women in the Igbo political system, it may come as a surprise to learn that when the British imposed colonial rule on these people, they failed to recognize the autonomy and power those women possessed. The reason is the British were blinded by their Victorian values, which then were at their height. To them, a woman's mind was not strong enough for such supposedly masculine subjects as science, business, and politics; her place was clearly in the home. Hence, it was inconceivable women might play important roles in politics. As a consequence, the British introduced "reforms" that destroyed women's traditional forms of autonomy and power without providing alternative forms in exchange. Far from enhancing women's status, as Western people like to think their influence does, in this case, women lost their equality and became subordinate to men. Nor is the Igbo situation unusual in this regard. Historically, in state-organized societies, women usually have been subordinate to men. Hence, when states impose their control on societies where the sexes are equal to each other, the situation almost invariably changes so that women become subordinate to men.

▲▽▲▽▲▽▲▽▲▽▲▽▲▽▲▽▲▽▲▽▲▽▲▽▲▽▲▽▲▽

POLITICAL ORGANIZATION AND THE MAINTENANCE OF ORDER

Whatever form political organization may take, and whatever else it may do, it is always involved in one way or another with maintaining social order. Always it seeks to ensure that people behave in acceptable ways and defines the proper action to take when they do not. In chiefdoms and states, some sort of authority has the power to regulate the affairs of society. In bands and tribes, however, people behave generally as they are expected to, without the direct intervention of any centralized political authority. To a large degree, gossip, criti-

cism, fear of supernatural forces, and the like serve as effective deterrents to antisocial behaviour.

As an example of how such seemingly informal considerations serve to keep people in line, we may look at the Wape people of Papua New Guinea, who believe the ghosts of dead ancestors roam lineage lands, protecting them from trespassers and helping their hunting descendants by driving game their way.[14] These ghosts also punish those who have wronged them or their descendants by preventing hunters from finding game or by causing them to miss their shots, thereby depriving people of much-needed meat. Nowadays, the Wape hunt with shotguns, which the community purchases for the use of one man, whose job it is to hunt for all the others. The cartridges used in the hunt, however, are invariably supplied by individual community members. Not always is the gunman successful; if he shoots and misses, it is because the owner of the fired shell, or some close relative, has quarrelled or wronged another person whose ghost relative is securing revenge by causing the hunter to miss. Or, if the gunman cannot even find game, it is because vengeful ghosts have chased the animals away. As a proxy hunter for the villagers, the gunman is potentially subject to ghostly sanctions in response to collective wrongs by those he hunts for.

For the Wape, then, successful hunting depends on avoiding quarrels and maintaining tranquillity within the community so as not to antagonize anybody's ghost ancestor. Unfortunately, complete peace and tranquillity are impossible to achieve in any human community, and the Wape are no exception. Thus, when hunting is poor, the gunman must discover what quarrels and wrongs have occurred within his village to identify the proper ancestral ghosts to appeal to for renewed success. Usually, this is done in a special meeting where confessions of wrongdoing may be forthcoming. If not, questioning accusations are bandied about until resolution occurs, but even with no resolution, the meeting must end amicably to prevent new antagonisms. Thus, everyone's behaviour comes under public scrutiny, reminding everyone

---

[13]Van Allen, J. (1979). Sitting on a man: Colonialism and the lost political institutions of Igbo women. In S. Tiffany (Ed.), *Women in society* (p. 169). St. Albans, VT: Eden Press.

[14]Mitchell, W.E. (1973, December). A new weapon stirs up old ghosts. *Natural History Magazine*, 77–84.

of what is expected of them and encouraging everyone to avoid acts that will cast them in an unfavourable light.

Internalized Controls

The Wape concern about ancestral ghosts is a good example of internalized, or cultural, controls—beliefs so thoroughly ingrained that each person becomes personally responsible for his or her own conduct. **Cultural control** may be thought of as control by the mind, as opposed to **social control,** which involves overt coercion. Examples of cultural control also can be found in North American society; for instance, people refrain from committing incest not so much from fear of legal punishment as from a sense of deep disgust at the thought of the act and from the shame they would feel in performing it. Obviously, not all members of North American society feel this disgust, or such a high incidence of incest would not occur, especially between fathers and daughters, but, then, no deterrent to misbehaviour is ever 100 percent effective. Cultural controls are built in, or internalized, and rely on such deterrents as fear of supernatural punishment—ancestral ghosts sabotaging the hunting, for example—and magical retaliation. Like the devout Christian who avoids sinning for fear of hell, the individual expects some sort of punishment, even though no one in the community may be aware of the wrongdoing.

Externalized Controls

Because internalized controls are not wholly sufficient even in bands and tribes, every society develops customs or **sanctions** designed to encourage conformity to social norms. Sanctions are externalized controls and involve varying mixes of cultural and social control. According to Radcliffe-Brown, "A sanction is a reaction on the part of a society or of a considerable number of its members to a mode of behaviour which is thereby approved (positive sanctions) or disapproved (negative sanctions)."[15]

Jody Williams, who in 1997 was awarded the Nobel Peace Prize for her work to ban land mines. Awards such as the Nobel Prize are examples of positive sanctions, by which societies promote approved behaviour.

Sanctions operate within social groups of all sizes. Moreover, they need not be enacted into law to play a significant role in regulating peoples' behaviour:

> They include not only the organized sanctions of the law but also the gossip of neighbors or the customs regulating norms of production that are spontaneously generated among workers on the factory floor. In small scale communities . . . informal sanctions may become more drastic than the penalties provided for in the legal code.[16]

If, however, a sanction is to be effective, it cannot be arbitrary. Sanctions must be consistently applied, and the culture's members must know generally of their existence.

Social sanctions may be categorized as either positive or negative. Positive sanctions consist of

---

[15]Radcliffe-Brown, A.R. (1952). *Structure and function in primitive society* (p. 205). New York: Free Press.

[16]Epstein, A.L. (1968). Sanctions. *International encyclopedia of social sciences*, vol. 14 (p. 3). New York: Macmillan.

Cultural control. Control through beliefs and values deeply internalized in the minds of individuals. **> Social control.** Control over groups through coercion. **> Sanctions.** Externalized social controls designed to encourage conformity to social norms.

incentives to conformity, such as awards, titles, and recognition by our neighbours. Negative sanctions consist of threats, such as imprisonment, corporal punishment, or ostracism from the community for violation of social norms. One example of a negative sanction discussed earlier is the Igbo practice of "sitting on a man." If some individuals are not convinced of the advantages of social conformity, they are still more likely to obey their culture's rules than to accept the consequences of not doing so.

Sanctions also may be categorized as either formal or informal, depending on whether or not a legal statute is involved. In North America, the man who wears tennis shorts to a church service may be subject to a variety of informal sanctions, ranging from disapproving glances from the clergy to the chuckling of other parishioners. If, however, he were to show up without any pants on, he would be subject to the formal negative sanction of arrest for indecent exposure. Only in the second instance would he have been guilty of breaking the **law.**

Formal sanctions, such as laws, are always organized, because they attempt to precisely and explicitly regulate people's behaviour. Other examples of organized sanctions include, on the positive side, awards of merit, such as the Order of Canada, Citizen of the Year, and recognition for heroic deeds. On the negative side are loss of face, exclusion from social life and its privileges, seizure of property, imprisonment, and even bodily mutilation or death.

Informal sanctions emphasize cultural control and are diffuse in nature, involving spontaneous expressions of approval or disapproval by members of the community. They are, nonetheless, very effective in enforcing a large number of seemingly unimportant customs. Because most people want to be accepted, they are willing to acquiesce to the rules that govern dress, eating, and conversation, even in the absence of actual laws.

To show how informal sanctions work, we will examine them in the context of power relationships among the Bedouin of Egypt's western desert (see the following Original Study). The example is especially interesting, for it shows how sanctions act not only to control people's behav-

The Okimaw Ohci Healing Lodge in Maple Creek, Saskatchewan, is a prison for aboriginal women that incorporates traditional spiritual healing.

iour but also to keep individuals in their place in a hierarchical society.

Another agent of control in human groups, whether or not they possess centralized political systems, may be witchcraft. An individual would hesitate to offend a neighbour when that neighbour might retaliate by resorting to black magic. Similarly, individuals may not wish to be accused of practising witchcraft, so they behave with greater circumspection. Among the Azande of the Sudan, people who think they have been bewitched may consult an oracle, who, after performing the appropriate mystical rites, then may establish or confirm the identity of the offending witch.[17]

Confronted with this evidence, the accused witch usually will agree to cooperate in order to avoid any additional trouble. Should the victim die, the relatives of the deceased may choose to make magic against the witch, ultimately accepting the death of some villager both as evidence of guilt and of the efficacy of their magic. For the Azande, witchcraft provides not only a sanction against antisocial behaviour but also a means of dealing with natural hostilities and death. No one wishes

[17]Evans-Pritchard, E.E. (1937). *Witchcraft, oracles and magic among the Azande.* London: Oxford University Press.

Law.   Formal negative sanctions.

ORIGINAL STUDY

Limits on Power in Bedouin Society

Where individuals value their independence and believe in equality, those who exercise authority over others enjoy a precarious status. In Bedouin society, social precedence or power depends not on force but on demonstration of the moral virtues that win respect from others. Persons in positions of power are said to have social standing (*gíma*), which is recognized by the respect paid them. To win the respect of others, in particular dependents, such persons must adhere to the ideals of honor, provide for and protect their dependents, and be fair, taking no undue advantage of their positions. They must assert their authority gingerly lest it so compromise their dependents' autonomy that it provoke rebellion and be exposed as a sham.

Because those in authority are expected to treat their dependents, even children, with some respect, they must draw as little attention as possible to the inequality of their relationships. Euphemisms that obscure the nature of such relationships abound. For example, Sa'ádi [free tribes] individuals do not like to call Mrábit [client tribes] associates Mrábtín in their presence. My host corrected me once when I referred to his shepherds by the technical word for shepherd, saying, "We prefer to call them 'people of the sheep' [*hal il-ghanam*]. It sounds nicer." The use of fictive kin terms serves the same function of masking relations of inequality, as for example in the case of patrons and clients.

Those in authority are also expected to respect their dependents' dignity by minimizing open assertion of their power over them. Because the provider's position requires dependents, he risks losing his power base if he alienates them. When a superior publicly orders, insults, or beats a dependent, he invites the rebellion that would undermine his position. Such moments are fraught with tension, as the dependent might feel the need to respond to a public humiliation to preserve his dignity or honor. Indeed, refusal to comply with an unreasonable order, or an order given in a compromising way, reflects well on the dependent and undercuts the authority of the person who gave it.

Tyranny is never tolerated for long. Most dependents wield sanctions that check the power of their providers. Anyone can appeal to a mediator to intervene on his or her behalf, and more radical solutions are open to all but young children. Clients can simply leave an unreasonable patron and attach themselves to a new one. Young men can always escape the tyranny of a father or paternal uncle by leaving to join maternal relatives or, if they have them, affines, or even to become clients to some other family. For the last twenty years or so, young men could go to Libya to find work.

Younger brothers commonly get out from under difficult elder brothers by splitting off from them, demanding their share of the patrimony and setting up separate households. The dynamic is clear in the case of four brothers who constituted the core of the camp in which I lived. Two had split off and lived in separate households. Another two still shared property, herds, and expenses. While I was there, tensions began to develop. Although the elder brother was more important in the community at large, and the younger brother was slightly irresponsible and less intelligent, for the most part they worked various enterprises jointly and without friction.

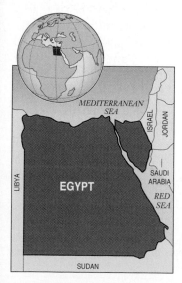

The younger brother deferred to his older brother and usually executed his decisions.

But one day the tensions surfaced. The elder brother came home at midday in a bad mood only to find that no one had prepared him lunch. He went to one of his wives and scolded her for not having prepared any lunch, asserting that his children had complained that they were hungry. He accused her of trying to starve his children and threatened to beat her. His younger brother tried to intervene, but the elder brother then turned on him, calling him names. Accusing him of being lazy (because he had failed to follow through on a promise involving the care of the sheep that day), he then asked why the younger brother let his wife get away with sitting in her room when there was plenty of work to be done around the household. Then he went off toward his other wife carrying a big stick and yelling.

The younger brother was furious and set off to get their mother. The matriarch, accompanied by another of her sons, arrived and conferred at length with the quarreling men. The younger son wished to split off from his elder brother's household; the other brother scolded him for being so sensitive about a few words, reminding him that this was his elder brother, from whom even a beating should not matter. His mother disapproved of splitting up the households. Eventually everyone calmed down. But it is likely that a few more incidents such as that will eventually lead the younger brother to demand a separate household.

Even a woman can resist a tyrannical husband by leaving for her natal home "angry" (*mughtáóa*). This is the approved response to abuse, and it forces the husband or his representatives to face the scolding of the woman's kin and, sometimes, to appease her with gifts. Women have less recourse against tyrannical fathers or guardians, but various informal means to resist the imposition of unwanted decisions do exist. As a last resort there is always suicide, and I heard of a number of both young men and women who committed suicide in desperate resistance to their fathers' decisions, especially regarding marriage. One old woman's tale illustrates the extent to which force can be resisted, even by women. Náfla reminisced:

> My first marriage was to my paternal cousin [*ibn 'amm*]. He was from the same camp. One day the men came over to our tent. I saw the tent full of men and wondered why. I heard they were coming to ask for my hand [*yukhultú fiyya*]. I went and stood at the edge of the tent and called out, "If you're planning to do anything, stop. I don't want it." Well, they went ahead anyway, and every day I would cry and say that I did not want to marry him. I was young, perhaps fourteen. When they began drumming and singing, everyone assured me that it was in celebration of another cousin's wedding, so I sang and danced along with them. This went on for days. Then on the day of the wedding my aunt and another relative caught me in the tent and suddenly closed it and took out the washbasin. They wanted to bathe me. I screamed. I screamed and screamed; every time they held a pitcher of water to wash me with, I knocked it out of their hands.
>
> His relatives came with camels and dragged me into the litter and took me to his tent. I screamed and screamed when he came into the

tent in the afternoon [for the defloration]. Then at night, I hid among the blankets. Look as they might, they couldn't find me. My father was furious. After a few days he insisted I had to stay in my tent with my husband. As soon as he left, I ran off and hid behind the tent in which the groom's sister stayed. I made her promise not to tell anyone I was there and slept there.

But they made me go back. That night, my father stood guard nearby with his gun. Every time I started to leave the tent, he would take a puff on his cigarette so I could see that he was still there. Finally I rolled myself up in the straw mat. When the groom came, he looked and looked but could not find me.

Finally I went back to my family's household. I pretended to be possessed. I tensed my body, rolled my eyes, and everyone rushed about, brought me incense and prayed for me. They brought the healer [or holyman, *f'gih*], who blamed the unwanted marriage. Then they decided that perhaps I was too young and that I should not be forced to return to my husband. I came out of the seizure, and they were so grateful that they forced my husband's family to grant a divorce. My family returned the bride-price, and I stayed at home.

Náfla could not oppose her father's decision directly, but she was nevertheless able to resist his will through indirect means. Like other options for resistance by dependents unfairly treated, abused, or humiliated publicly, her rebellion served as a check on her father's and, perhaps, more important, her paternal uncle's power.

Supernatural sanctions, which seem to be associated with the weak and with dependents, provide the final check on abuse of authority. Supernatural retribution is believed to follow when the saintly lineages of Mrábtín are mistreated, their curses causing death or the downfall of the offender's lineage. In one Bedouin tale, when a woman denied food to two young girls, she fell ill, and blood appeared on food she cooked—a punishment for mistreating the helpless. Possession, as Náfla's tale illustrates, may also be a form of resistance. . . .

All these sanctions serve to check the abuse of power by eminent persons who have the resources to be autonomous and to control those who are dependent upon them. At the same time, moreover, figures of authority are vulnerable to their dependents because their positions rest on the respect these people are willing to give them.

Source: Abu-Lughod, L. (1986). *Veiled sentiments: Honor and poetry in a Bedouin society* (pp. 99–103). Berkeley: University of California Press.

to be thought of as a witch, and surely no one wishes to be victimized by one. By institutionalizing their emotional responses, the Azande successfully maintain social order. (For more on witchcraft, see Chapter 12.)

Bernard Saladin d'Anglure

Bernard Saladin d'Anglure is internationally recognized as a pioneer in the field of Inuit studies. Born in France, Saladin d'Anglure studied in Paris and at the University of Montreal, and he later served as an assistant to world-renowned anthropologist Claude Lévi-Strauss.

On his numerous visits to Canada's north, Saladin d'Anglure gathered demographic and ethnographic material on the Inuit of Nunavik and made an award-winning documentary film about the people. Upon completion of his Ph.D., Saladin d'Anglure turned his attention to shamanism and political organization among the Inuit.

He learned to speak Inuktitut fluently, and he regularly involved the Inuit in the research he was doing, listening to their perspectives on traditional and contemporary Inuit worldviews.

In 1974 Saladin d'Anglure founded the Association Inuksiutiit Katimajiit, the primary purpose of which was to return his research data (e.g., land use maps and family trees) to the Inuit. In 1977 he established the *International Journal of Inuit Studies, Études Inuit Studies,* considered a valuable source of information on Arctic social sciences. He also founded the Inuit and Circumpolar Studies Group, Canada's leading Arctic social sciences centre.

Saladin d'Anglure is a professor of anthropology at Laval University and an avid promoter of public education. His dedication to learning about the Inuit and sharing his knowledge with the public through written, recorded, and visual media is highly valued both inside and outside the academic world.

Source: Indian and Northern Affairs Canada. (2003). *Biographical data. Bernard Saladin d'Anglure: Northern science award winner.* Retrieved September 20, 2003, from the World Wide Web: http://www.ainc-inac.gc.ca/nr/prs/j-a2003/02293bbk-e.html.

SOCIAL CONTROL THROUGH LAW

Among the Inuit of northern Canada, all offences are considered to involve disputes between individuals; thus, they must be settled between the disputants themselves. One way they may do so is through a song duel, in which they heap insults upon one another in songs specially composed for the occasion. The people's interests are represented by spectators, whose applause determines the outcome. If, however, social harmony cannot be restored—and that, rather than assigning and punishing guilt, is the goal—one or the other disputant may move to another band. Among the Inuit, the alternative to peaceful settlement is to leave the group. Ultimately, no binding legal authority exists.

In Western society, by contrast, someone who commits an offence against another person is subject to a series of complex legal proceedings. In criminal cases the primary concern is to assign and punish guilt, rather than to help the victim. The offender will be arrested by the police; tried before a judge and, perhaps, a jury; and, if the crime is serious enough, may be fined, imprisoned, or even executed. Rarely does the victim receive restitution or compensation. Throughout this chain of events, the accused party is dealt with by (presumably) disinterested police, judges, jurors, and jailers, who may have no personal acquaintance whatsoever with the plaintiff or the defendant. How strange this complicated system must seem from the standpoint of traditional aboriginal cultures. Clearly, the two systems operate under distinctly different assumptions.

Recognition of the disparities between these two systems, coupled with the disproportionate number of aboriginal people in Canadian prisons, has led government officials and First Nations leaders to consider alternative justice systems, such as sentencing circles. In sentencing circles the accused is brought before representatives of the aboriginal community who then decide what is to be done with the individual. This practice is growing, especially in the Canadian north. However, opponents of traditional sentencing circles fear that the system is not structured enough and that the community will "let the criminal off too easy" or fail to meticulously enforce any punishments mandated.

Definition of Law

Once two Inuit settle a dispute by engaging in a song contest, the affair is considered closed; no further action is expected. Would we choose to describe the outcome of such a contest as a legal decision? If every law is a sanction but not every sanction is a law, how are we to distinguish between social sanctions in general and those to which we apply the label of law?

The definition of *law* was a lively point of contention among anthropologists in the 20th century. In 1926, Malinowski argued that the rules of law are distinguished from the rules of custom in that "they are regarded as the obligation of one person and the rightful claim of another, sanctioned not by mere psychological motive, but by a definite social machinery of binding force based . . . upon mutual dependence."[18] In other words, laws exemplify social control because they employ overt coercion. An example of one rule of custom in contemporary North American society might be the dictate that guests at a dinner party should repay the person who gave the party with entertainment in the future. A host or hostess who does not receive a return invitation may feel cheated of something thought to be owed but has no legal claim against the ungrateful guest for the $22.67 spent on food. If, however, an individual was cheated of the same sum by the grocer when shopping, the law could be invoked. Although Malinowski's definition introduced several important elements of law, his failure to distinguish adequately between legal and nonlegal sanctions left the problem of formulating a workable definition of *law* in the hands of later anthropologists.

An important pioneer in the anthropological study of law was E. Adamson Hoebel, according to whom "a social norm is legal if its neglect or infraction is regularly met, in threat or in fact, by the application of physical force by an individual or group possessing the socially recognized privilege of so acting."[19] In stressing the legitimate use of physical coercion, Hoebel deemphasized the

In Western society, someone who commits an offence against someone else is subject to a series of complex proceedings in which the emphasis is on assigning and punishing guilt. In non-Western societies, by contrast, the emphasis is often on finding a solution that both parties can live with.

traditional association of law with a centralized court system. Although judge and jury are fundamental features of Western jurisprudence, they are not the universal backbone of human law. Some anthropologists have proposed that a precise definition of *law* is an impossible—and perhaps even undesirable—undertaking. When we speak of "the law," are we not inclined to fall back on our familiar Western conception of rules enacted by an authorized legislative body and enforced by the judicial mechanisms of the state? Can any concept of law be applied to the Nuer or the Inuit, for whom the notion of a centralized judiciary is virtually meaningless? How shall we categorize duels, song contests, and other socially condoned forms of self-help that seem to meet some but not all of the criteria of law? Ultimately, it is always of greatest value to consider each case within its cultural context. Nonetheless, a working definition of *law* is useful for purposes of discussion and cross-cultural comparison, and for this, *law* is adequately characterized as formal negative sanctions.

Functions of Law

In *The Law of Primitive Man* (1954), Hoebel writes of a time when the notion that private property should be generously shared was a fundamental precept of Cheyenne life. Subsequently, however, some men assumed the privilege of bor-

---

[18]Malinowski, B. (1951). *Crime and custom in savage society* (p. 55). London: Routledge.

[19]Hoebel, E.A. (1954). *The law of primitive man: A study in comparative legal dynamics* (p. 28). Cambridge, MA: Harvard University Press.

The police, shown here breaking up an unruly demonstration at the Summit of the Americas in Quebec City in 2001, have the power to use overt coercion to maintain order.

rowing other men's horses without bothering to obtain permission. When Wolf Lies Down complained of such unauthorized borrowing to the members of the Elk Soldier Society, the Elk Soldiers not only had his horse returned to him but also secured an award for damages from the offender. The Elk Soldiers then announced that, to avoid such difficulties in the future, horses no longer could be borrowed without permission. Furthermore, they declared their intention to retrieve any such property and to administer a whipping to anyone who resisted their efforts to return improperly borrowed goods.

The case of Wolf Lies Down and the Elk Soldier Society clearly illustrates three basic functions of law. First, it defines relationships among members of a culture, determining proper behaviour under specified circumstances. Knowledge of the law permits each person to know his or her rights and duties in respect to every other member. Second, law allocates the authority to employ coercion in the enforcement of sanctions. In societies with centralized political systems, such authority is generally vested in the government and its judiciary system. In cultures that lack centralized political control, the authority to employ force may be allocated directly to the injured party. Third, law functions to redefine social relations and to ensure social flexibility. As new situations arise, law must determine whether old rules and assumptions retain their validity and the extent to which they must be altered. Law, if it is to operate efficiently, must allow room for change.

In practice, law is rarely the smooth and well-integrated system described here. In any given culture, various legal sanctions may apply at various levels. Because the people are usually members of numerous subgroups, they are subject to the dictates of these diverse groups. For example, each Kapauku is simultaneously a member of a family, a household, a sublineage, and a confederacy and is subject to all their laws. In some cases it may be impossible for an individual to submit to contradictory legal indications:

> In one of the confederacy's lineages, incestuous relations between members of the same clan were punished by execution of the culprits, and in another by severe beating, in the third constituent lineage such a relationship was not punishable and . . . was not regarded as incest at all. In one of the sublineages, it became even a preferred type of marriage.[20]

Furthermore, the power to employ sanctions may vary from level to level within a given group. The head of a Kapauku household may punish a household member by slapping or beating, but the authority to confiscate property is vested exclusively in the headman of the lineage. Analogous distinctions exist in Canada among municipal, provincial, and federal jurisdictions. The complexity of legal jurisdiction makes generalization about law difficult.

Crime

As we have observed, an important function of sanctions, legal or otherwise, is to discourage the breach of social norms. A person contemplating theft is aware of the possibility of being caught and punished. Yet, even in the face of severe sanctions, individuals sometimes violate the norms and subject themselves to the consequences of their behaviour. What is the nature of crime in non-Western cultures?

Nation-states with centralized governments make a clear distinction between offences against the state and offences against individuals. *Black's Law Dictionary* tells us,

> The distinction between a crime and a tort or civil injury is that the former is a breach and violation

_____

[20]Pospisil, L. (1971). *Anthropology of law: A comparative theory* (p. 36). New York: Harper and Row.

of the public right and of duties due to the whole community considered as such, and in its social and aggregate capacity; whereas the latter is an infringement or privation of the civil rights of individuals merely.[21]

Thus, a reckless driver who crashes into another car may be guilty of a crime by endangering public safety. The same driver also may be guilty of a tort by causing damages to the other car, and the other driver may sue for their cost.

In cultures without centralized governance all offences are viewed as against members rather than against the state, rendering the distinction between crime and tort irrelevant. Indeed, a dispute between individuals may seriously disrupt the social order, especially in small groups where the number of disputants, though small in absolute numbers, may be a large percentage of the total population. Although in the past the Inuit had no effective domestic or economic unit beyond the family, a dispute between two people would interfere with the ability of members of separate families to come to one another's aid when necessary and is consequently a matter of wider social concern. The goal of judicial proceedings in most cases is to restore social harmony, instead of punishing an offender. When distinguishing between offences of concern to the community as a whole and those of concern to only a few individuals, we may refer to offences as public or private, rather than distinguishing between criminal and civil law. In this way we may avoid values and assumptions irrelevant to a discussion of systems of law.

Basically, disputes are settled in one of two ways. First, disputing parties may, via argument and compromise, voluntarily arrive at a mutually satisfactory agreement. This form of settlement is referred to as **negotiation** or, if it involves an unbiased third party's assistance, **mediation.** In bands and tribes a third-party mediator has no coercive power and thus cannot force disputants to abide by such a decision, but as a person who commands

great personal respect, the mediator frequently may effect a settlement through these judgements.

Second, in chiefdoms and states, an authorized third party may issue a binding decision that the disputing parties will be compelled to respect. This process is referred to as **adjudication.** The difference between mediation and adjudication is essentially a difference in authorization. In a dispute settled by adjudication, the disputing parties present their positions as convincingly as they can, but they do not participate in the ultimate decision making.

Although the adjudication process is not universally characteristic, every culture employs some form of negotiation to settle disputes. Often negotiation acts as a prerequisite or an alternative to adjudication. For example, in the resolution of North American labour disputes, striking workers may first negotiate with management, often with the mediation of a third party. If the state decides the strike constitutes a threat to the public welfare, the disputing parties may be forced to submit to adjudication. In this case, the responsibility for resolving the dispute is transferred to a presumably impartial judge.

In many politically centralized cultures, incorruptible supernatural, or at least nonhuman, powers are thought to make judgements through trial by ordeal. Among the Kpelle of Liberia, for example, when guilt is in doubt an ordeal operator licensed by the government may apply a hot knife to a suspect's leg. If the leg is burned, the suspect is guilty; if not, innocence is assumed. But the operator does not merely heat the knife and apply it. After massaging the suspect's legs and determining the knife is hot enough, the operator then strokes his own leg with it without being burned, demonstrating that the innocent will escape injury. The knife is then applied to the suspect. Up to this point—consciously or unconsciously—the operator has read the suspect's nonverbal cues: gestures, the degree of muscular tension, amount of perspiration, and so forth. From this the operator can judge whether or not the accused is showing enough anxiety to indicate probable guilt; in effect, a psychological stress

---

[21]Black, H.C. (1968). *Black's law dictionary*. St. Paul, MN: West.

Negotiation.   The use of direct argument and compromise by the parties to a dispute to arrive voluntarily at a mutually satisfactory agreement. **> Mediation.**   Settlement of a dispute through negotiation assisted by an unbiased third party. **> Adjudication.**   Mediation with an unbiased third party making the ultimate decision.

Anthropology **Applied**

Dispute Resolution and the Anthropologist

In an era when the peaceful resolution of disputes is increasingly valued, the field of dispute management is one of growing anthropological involvement (and employment). One practitioner is William L. Ury, an independent negotiations specialist who earned his Ph.D. at Harvard University. His 1982 dissertation was entitled *Talk Out or Walk Out: The Role and Control of Conflict in a Kentucky Coal Mine.*

At Harvard, Ury co-founded—with Roger Fisher of the law school—the program on negotiation. Together, the two also authored what has become the negotiator's "bible": *Getting to Yes: Negotiating Agreement without Giving In* (published in 1981, it has been translated into 21 languages). In 1980, Ury helped the United States and Soviet Union replace their obsolete "hot line" with fully equipped nuclear crisis centres in each capital.

Ury now runs regular workshops on dealing with difficult people and situations. Among those who have enlisted his services is the Ford Motor Company, whose 6000 top executives worldwide have taken his seminars. As one put it, "His influence on the company is incalculable. He inoculated a whole culture with a new way of looking at

things."[1] Now, Ury specializes in ethnic and secessionist disputes, including those between White and Black South Africans, Serbs and Croats, and Turks and Kurds. One of his toughest jobs has been to mediate a peace between the Russians and Chechens, a task that has brought together other adversaries from the former Soviet Union as well: Tatars, Crimeans, Moldovans, and Georgians.

In his most recent book, *Getting Past No: Negotiating Your Way from Confrontation,* Ury praises the perspective of Japan's "home-run king" who viewed opposing "pitchers" not as enemies trying to do him in but as partners offering repeated opportunities to hit another ball out of the park. In dealing with the Chechens, one of his techniques was to have them imagine the speech the Russian president could give that would help his people accept the Chechens' goal. The Russians were asked to do the same: What kind of speech could the Chechen president give that would persuade his followers to remain in the Russian Federation?

Ury and others are helping to create a culture of negotiation in a world where adversarial, win–lose attitudes are out of step with the increasingly interdependent relations among people.

[1]Stewart, D. (1997). Expanding the pie before you divvy it up. *Smithsonian, 28,* 82.

evaluation has been made. As the knife is applied, it is manipulated to either burn or not burn the suspect, once this judgement has been made. The operator easily does this manipulation by controlling how long the knife is in the fire, as well as the pressure and angle at which it is pressed against the leg.[22]

Similar to this is the use of the lie detector (polygraph). An incorruptible nonhuman agency is thought to establish who is lying and who is not, whereas in reality the polygraph operator cannot just "read" the needles of the machine.

[22]Gibbs, J.L., Jr. (1983). [Interview.] *Faces of culture: Program 18.* Fountain Valley, CA: Coast Telecourses.

One mean of psychological evaluation is the Western polygraph ("lie detector").

He or she must judge whether or not they are registering a high level of anxiety brought on by the testing situation, as opposed to the stress of guilt. Thus, the polygraph operator has much in common with the Kpelle ordeal operator.

▲▽▲▽▲▽▲▽▲▽▲▽▲▽▲▽▲▽▲▽▲▽▲▽▲▽▲▽▲▽▲

POLITICAL ORGANIZATION AND EXTERNAL AFFAIRS

Although the regulation of internal affairs is an important function of any political system, it is by no means the sole function. Another is the management of external or international affairs—relations not just between states but also between different bands, lineages, clans, or whatever the largest autonomous political unit may be. And just as threatened or actual force may be used to maintain order within a culture, it also may be used in the conduct of external affairs.

War

For thousands of years, people have engaged in a seemingly endless chain of wars and intergroup hostilities. Why do wars occur? Is the need to wage war an instinctive feature of the human personality? What are the alternatives to violence as a means of settling disputes between groups?

War is not a universal phenomenon, for in various parts of the world, people such as the Ju/'hoansi of southern Africa, the Arapesh of New Guinea, and the Hopi of North America do not practise warfare as we know it.

We have ample reason to suppose war has become a problem only in the past 10 000 years, since the development of food-production techniques and centralized states. Warfare reached crisis proportions in the past 200 years, with the invention of modern weaponry and increased direction of violence against civilian populations. In contemporary warfare, we have reached the point where casualties not just of civilians but also of *children* outnumber those of soldiers. Thus, war is not so much an age-old problem, as some have supposed, as it is a relatively recent one.

Among food foragers, with their uncentralized political systems, warfare is all but unknown, although violence emerges sporadically. Because territorial boundaries and membership of food-foraging bands are fluid and loosely defined, a man who hunts with one band today may hunt with a neighbouring band tomorrow. Warfare is further rendered impractical by the systematic interchange of marriage partners among food-foraging groups—it is likely someone in each band will have a sister, a brother, or a cousin in a neighbouring band. Moreover, absence of a food surplus does not permit prolonged combat. Where populations are small, food surpluses absent, property ownership minimal, and state organization does not exist, the likelihood of organized violence by one group against another is minimal.[23]

Despite the view of the farmer as a gentle tiller of the soil, it is among such people, along with pastoralists, that warfare becomes prominent. One reason may be that food-producing peoples are far more prone to population growth than are food foragers, whose numbers generally are maintained well below carrying capacity. This population growth, if unchecked, can lead to resource depletion, one solution to which may be seizure of some other group's resources. In addition, the commitment to a fixed piece of land inherent in farming makes such groups somewhat less fluid in their membership than food foragers. In rigidly matrilocal or patrilocal societies, each new generation is bound to the same territory, no matter how small it may be or how large the group trying to live within it.

The availability of virgin land may not serve as a sufficient detriment to the outbreak of war. Among slash-and-burn horticulturists, for example, competition for land cleared of virgin forest frequently leads to hostility and armed conflict. The centralization of political control and the possession of valuable property among farming peoples provide many more stimuli for warfare. When such groups are organized into states, the violence of warfare is most apt to result in indiscriminate killing. This development has reached its peak in modern states. Indeed, much (but not all) of the warfare observed in stateless societies (so-called tribal warfare) has been induced by states, as a reaction to their colonial expansion.[24]

[23]Knauft, B. (1991). Violence and sociality in human evolution. *Current Anthropology, 32,* 391–409.

[24]Whitehead, N.L., & Ferguson, R.B. (1993, November 10). Deceptive stereotypes about tribal warfare. *Chronicle of Higher Education,* A48.

In Mexico, as in many countries of the world, armed conflict has become commonplace as governments controlled by one ethnic group seek to control members of other once autonomous ethnic groups in order to benefit from their resources and labour. Shown here are police of the Mexican state of Chiapas, with local Maya and (in the bags) the bodies of sympathizers of the Zapatista rebel movement. The Zapatista movement is an uprising following 500 years of exploitation by the Spanish and their descendants in Mexico.

Another difference between food-gathering and food-producing populations lies in their different **worldviews.** As a general rule, food foragers tend to conceive of themselves as a part of the natural world and in some sort of balance with it. Western Abenaki hunters thought animals, like humans, were composed of both a body and a personal spirit. Thus, when beaver, muskrat, or waterfowl were killed, the hunters could not just toss their bones into the nearest garbage pit. Proper respect required that their bones be returned to the water, with a request that the species be continued. Such attitudes may be referred to as part of a **naturalistic worldview.**

The Abenakis' respect for nature contrasts sharply with the kind of worldview prevalent among farmers and pastoralists, who do not find their food in nature but impose their dominance upon it to produce food for themselves. The attitude that nature exists only for human use may be referred to as an **exploitative worldview.** With such an outlook, it is a small step from dominating the rest of nature to dominating other human groups for the benefit of one's own. The exploitative worldview, prevalent among food-producing peoples, is an important contributor to intersocietal warfare.

A comparison between the Western Abenakis and their Iroquoian neighbours to the west is instructive. Among the Abenakis, warfare was essentially a defensive activity. These food foragers, with their naturalistic worldview, believed they could not operate in someone else's territory, since they did not control the necessary supernatural powers. Furthermore, operating far below carrying capacity, they had no need to prey upon

---

Worldviews.   The conceptions, explicit and implicit, an individual or a group has of the limits and workings of its world. **> Naturalistic worldview.**   The belief that humans are merely one part of the natural world. **> Exploitative worldview.**   The belief that nature exists for humans to dominate and exploit.

the resources of others. The Iroquois, by contrast, were slash-and-burn horticulturists who engaged in predatory warfare. Evidence indicates significant environmental degradation around their settlements, suggesting overutilization of resources. Although the Iroquois went to war to replace men lost in previous battles, the main motive was to achieve dominance by making their victims acknowledge Iroquoian superiority. The relation between victim and victor, however, was subjection, rather than outright subordination. The payment of tribute purchased "protection" from the Iroquois, no doubt helping to offset the depletion of resources near the village of the would-be protectors. The price of protection went further than this, though; it included constant and public ceremonial deference to the Iroquois, free passage for their war parties through the subjugated group's country, and the contribution of young men to Iroquoian war parties.

A comparison between the Iroquois and Europeans is also instructive. Sometime in the 16th century, Iroquoian nations determined to end warfare among themselves by directing their predatory activities against outsiders, rather than each other. In this way the famous League of the Iroquois came into being. Similarly, in the year 1095, Pope Urban II launched the Crusades with a speech urging European barons to end their ceaseless wars against each other and direct their hostilities outward against the Turks and Arabs. In that same speech he also alluded to the economic benefits of seizing the resources of the infidels. Although rationalized as a "holy war," the Crusades were motivated by more than religious ideology.

Although the Europeans never did "liberate" the Holy Land, at least some of them benefited from the booty obtained in battle, lending credence to the idea people could live better than they had before by locating and seizing the resources of others. Thus, the state formation that occurred in Europe in the centuries after A.D. 1000 was followed by colonial expansion into other parts of the world.

The so-called war on terrorism adds a new dimension to any discussion of warfare. Rather than fighting political entities, states dealing with terrorism must battle politico-religious factions that are intent on destroying their security. The purpose of **terrorism** is to intimidate or coerce a civilian population, to spread fear, and to manipulate governments.[25] Terrorism involves violence of some form against persons or property, such as through assassination, bombing, biological agents, and hijacking, and usually is politically motivated with a range of justifications, including ideological, religious, and nationalistic reasons. Responses to this relatively new threat include beefed-up security, loss of personal freedoms, heightened alerts, restrictive border crossings, racial profiling, and preemptive strikes on states believed to be harbouring or supporting terrorist organizations.

As the examples show, the causes of warfare are complex; economic, political, and ideological factors are all involved. With the emergence of states (not just in Europe but in other parts of the

---

[25]Arzt, D. (2003). Terrorism and terrorists. *Jurist: The Legal Education Network*. University of Pittsburgh School of Law. Retrieved September 28, 2003, from the World Wide Web: http://jurist.law.pitt.edu/terrorism/terrorism1.htm.

The world changed on September 11, 2001, when the United States came under terrorist attack.

Terrorism.   Violence against persons or property designed to elicit fear, usually based on ideological, religious, and political motivations.

world as well) has come a dramatic increase in the scale of warfare. Perhaps this is not surprising, given the state's acceptance of force as a legitimate tool for regulating human affairs and its ability to organize large numbers of people. In the modern world, we are as far (and probably farther) from the elimination of war as humanity ever has been, a fact reflected in the 120-odd shooting wars going on in the mid-1990s. Moreover, value systems seem to be as crucial as any element to the continued existence of warfare.

Canada's Role in International Peacekeeping

Although the preceding discussion might lead readers to believe otherwise, external affairs refers to more than warfare; diplomatic offices, trade relations, and international aid are all examples of enduring external affairs. In Canada, international peacekeeping is an important component of foreign policy. In 1957, Prime Minister Lester B. Pearson received the Nobel Peace Prize for his establishment of an international peacekeeping force within the United Nations Security Council. Since then, Canada has participated in numerous military peacekeeping missions, sending over 100 000 men and women on more than 40 missions. Former UN Secretary-General Boutros Boutros-Ghali stated, "Peacekeeping is a technique that expands the possibilities for both the prevention of conflict and the making of peace."[26]

The peacekeepers' roles have evolved over the years. Besides military missions to supervise ceasefires and the withdrawal of forces, the Royal Canadian Mounted Police, Elections Canada, and the Canadian Red Cross also have become involved. During the Cambodia mission in 1991–93, UN peacekeepers disarmed warring factions, repatriated refugees, upheld human rights, and organized provisional elections. In Somalia, in 1992–93, peacekeepers ensured the equitable distribution of relief supplies, and in 2003, Canadian soldiers went to Afghanistan to help the people rebuild their country.

---

[26]Backgrounder. (2001). *Canada and peacekeeping* (p. 2). Retrieved March 20, 2001, from the World Wide Web: http://www.dfait-maeci.gc.ca/peacekeeping/back-e/asp.

Canadian peacekeepers are a reflection of Canada's fundamental belief in peace not war, dialogue not bullets.

Peacekeepers are also peacebuilders—they work to reestablish normal life in war-torn countries. For example, in Rwanda, Canadian troops opened airports and restored communications systems, in Haiti the RCMP trained a local police force, and in Afghanistan peacekeepers are working to restore vital services, for example, digging wells in the rural areas for clean, safe water. The primary goal of peacekeeping is to establish conditions in troubled societies that enable the people to resolve their differences and build a better future. By convincing people to lay down their weapons and settle their grievances without violence, peacekeepers seek to accomplish what the United Nations was established to do.[27]

▲▽▲▽▲▽▲▽▲▽▲▽▲▽▲▽▲▽▲▽▲▽▲▽▲▽▲▽▲▽▲

POLITICAL SYSTEMS AND THE QUESTION OF LEGITIMACY

Whatever form a culture's political system may take and however the people may go about their business, it must find some way to obtain the people's allegiance. In uncentralized systems, where every adult participates in all decision making, loyalty and cooperation are freely given, since each person is considered a part of the political system. As the group grows larger, however, and the organization becomes more formal, the problems of obtaining and keeping public support become greater.

In centralized political systems, increased reliance is placed on coercion as a means of social control. The reliance on force, however, tends to lessen the effectiveness of a political system. For example, the staff needed to apply force often must be large and may itself grow to be a political power. The emphasis on force may create resentment from those it is applied to, which lessens cooperation. Thus, police states are generally short-lived; most groups choose less-extreme forms of social control.

Also basic to the political process is the concept of legitimacy, or the right of political leaders to rule. Like force, legitimacy is a form of support for a political system; unlike force, legitimacy is based on the values a particular culture believes

In a democratic country such as Canada, legitimacy comes through elections that grant representatives of the people the power to make decisions on their behalf.

most important. For example, among the Kapauku the legitimacy of the *tonowi*'s power comes from his wealth; the kings of Hawaii and of England and France were thought to have a divine right to rule; and the head of the Dahomey state of West Africa acquires legitimacy through his age, as he is always the oldest living male.

Legitimacy grants the right to hold, use, and allocate power. Power based on legitimacy, a form of cultural control, may be distinguished from power based on force alone (social control): Obedience to the former results from the belief obedience is "right"; compliance to power based on force results from fear of the deprivation of liberty, physical well-being, life, and material property. Thus, power based on legitimacy is symbolic and depends not on any intrinsic value but on the positive expectations of those who recognize and accede to it. If the expectations are not met regularly (if the head of state fails to deliver "economic prosperity" or the leader is continu-

---

[27]Ibid., p. 6.

ously unsuccessful in preventing horse or camel theft), the legitimacy of the recognized power figure is minimized and may collapse altogether.

RELIGION AND POLITICS

Religion is intricately connected with politics. Religious beliefs may influence laws: Acts people believe to be sinful, such as incest, are often illegal as well. Frequently, it is religion that legitimizes the political order.

In both industrial and nonindustrial societies, belief in the supernatural is reflected in the political organization. The effect of religion on politics was perhaps best exemplified in medieval Europe.

Holy wars were fought over the smallest matter; labour was mobilized to build immense cathedrals in honour of the Virgin and other saints; and kings and queens ruled by "divine right," pledged allegiance to the pope, and asked his blessing in all important ventures, were they marital or martial. In the pre-Columbian Americas the Aztec state was a religious state, or theocracy, that thrived in spite of more-or-less constant warfare carried out to procure captives for human sacrifices to assuage or please the gods. In Peru the Inca emperor proclaimed absolute authority based on the proposition he was descended from the sun god. Modern Iran was proclaimed an "Islamic republic," and its first head of state was the most holy of all Shiite Muslim holy men.

In many regions of the world, religion and politics are inextricably bound up in hostilities between opposing groups. Such is the case with Israelis and Palestinians in their long-standing struggle.

CHAPTER SUMMARY

Political organization and control are the ways power is distributed and embedded in cultures. Through political organization, cultures maintain social order, manage public affairs, and reduce social disorder. No group can live together without persuading or coercing its members to conform to agreed-upon rules of conduct. To properly understand a culture's political organization, we need to view it in the light of its ecological, social, and ideological context.

Four basic types of political systems may be identified: uncentralized bands and tribes, and centralized chiefdoms and states. The band, characteristic of food-foraging and some other nomadic groups, is an association of politically independent but related families or households occupying a common territory. Informal control is maintained by public opinion in the form of gossip and ridicule. Band leaders are older men, or sometimes women, with personal authority.

The tribe is composed of separate bands or other social units tied together by such unifying factors as descent groups, age grading, or common interest. With an economy usually based on farming or herding, the tribe's population is larger than that of the band, although family units within the tribe are still relatively autonomous and egalitarian. As in the band, political organization is transitory, and leaders have no formal means of maintaining authority.

Chiefdoms are ranked cultures in which every member has a position in the hierarchy. Status is determined by the individual's position in a descent group and distance of relationship to the chief. Power is concentrated in a single chief whose true authority serves to unite his community in all matters. The chief may accumulate great personal wealth, which enhances his power base and which he may pass on to his heirs.

The most centralized of political organizations is the state. It has a central power that can use force to administer a rigid code of laws and to maintain order, even beyond its borders. A large bureaucracy functions to uphold the central power's authority. Typically, a state is a stratified society where economic functions and wealth are distributed unequally. Although thought of as stable and permanent, it is, in fact, inherently unstable and transitory. States differ from nations, which are communities of people who see themselves as "one people" with a common culture but who may or may not have a centralized form of political organization.

Historically women have rarely held important positions of political leadership. Nonetheless, in a number of cultures, women have enjoyed political equality with men, as among the Iroquoian tribes of southern Ontario and New York State. Under centralized political systems, women are most apt to be subordinate to men, and when states impose their control on cultures marked by sexual egalitarianism, the relationship changes so that men dominate women.

Two kinds of cultural control exist: internalized and externalized. Internalized controls are self-imposed by individuals. These are purely cultural in nature, as they are built into the people's minds. They rely on such deterrents as personal shame, fear of divine punishment, and magical retaliation. Although bands and tribes rely heavily on them, internalized controls are generally insufficient by themselves. Every culture develops externalized controls, called sanctions, that mix cultural and social control. Positive sanctions, in the form of rewards or recognition, involve the position a culture or a number of its members take toward approved behaviour; negative sanctions, such as threat of imprisonment, corporal punishment, or "loss of face," reflect societal reactions to disapproved behaviour.

Sanctions also may be classified as either formal, including actual laws, or informal, involving norms but not legal statutes. Formal sanctions are organized and reward or punish behaviour through a rigidly regulated social procedure. Informal sanctions are diffuse, involving immediate reactions of approval or disapproval by individual community members to a compatriot's behaviour. Other important agents of social control are witchcraft beliefs and religious sanctions.

Law serves several basic functions. First, it defines relationships among a group's members, thus dictating proper behaviour under different circumstances. Second, law allocates authority to employ coercion to enforce sanctions. In centralized political systems, this authority rests with the government and court system. In uncentralized systems, this authority is given directly to the injured party. Third, law redefines social relations and aids its own efficient operation by ensuring that it allows for change.

Western societies clearly distinguish offences against the state, called crimes, from offences against individuals, called torts. In uncentralized systems, all offences are against individuals. A dispute may be settled in two ways: negotiation and adjudication. All human groups use negotiation to settle individual disputes. In negotiation the parties to the dispute reach an agreement themselves, with or without the help of a third party. In adjudication, not found in some societies, an authorized third party issues a binding decision.

Political systems also attempt to regulate external affairs, or relations between politically autonomous units. In doing so they may resort to the threat or use of force, but they also may attempt to maintain the peace through such organizations as peacekeepers.

War is not a universal phenomenon, since some cultures do not practise warfare as Westeners know it. Usually, these are small-scale cultures that have some kind of naturalistic worldview. International terrorism is adding a new dimension to the concept of warfare.

Religion is so intricately woven into the life of the people in both industrial and nonindustrial countries that its presence is inevitably felt in the political sphere. To a greater or lesser extent, most governments the world over use religion to legitimize political power.

QUESTIONS FOR CRITICAL THOUGHT

1. In this chapter we read about the use of informal *sanctions* (as opposed to formalized, codified *laws*) to control individual behaviour in a group. What are examples of such sanctions? How do they operate in large societies that do have more codified laws? Are the two necessarily in total accord?

2. In many countries the press has taken on the role of watching and reporting on the behaviour of powerful individuals. How can this serve as a sanction? What are the potential benefits of such publications and broadcastings? the potential drawbacks?

3. Do informal sanctions operate in Canadian society? If so, how effective are they at various levels of our political organization?

4. Canada has generally maintained a "peace not war" ideology, as evidenced by its role in international peacekeeping forces. Do you agree or disagree with this statement? Provide reasons for your answer.

5. Our Canadian legal system is increasingly criticized for failing to solve the crime problem in Canada. Is this criticism justified? In what ways? How might the system be changed to provide more of a deterrent to criminal activity?

6. Will the measures taken by the United States and other countries successfully combat terrorism? What do you think are the underlying reasons for international terrorism?

INTERNET RESOURCES

Aboriginal Self-Government
http://www.ainc-inac.gc.ca/pr/pub/sg/plcy_e.html
This comprehensive site highlights the concept of self-government, policy framework, negotiations, mechanisms for implementation, existing treaties and land claim agreements, and the various approaches to self-government.

Aboriginal Self-Government

http://www.parl.gc.ca/information/library/
prbpubs/962-e.htm

A comprehensive site discussing many aspects of aboriginal self-government, including approaches, evolution, arrangements, and chronology.

Canada and Peacekeeping

www.dfait-maeci.gc.ca/peacekeeping/back-e.asp

This site examines Canada's peacekeeping roles and commitments, as well as recent changes in its roles.

Assembly of First Nations

http://www.afn.ca

A huge site with extensive links to related pages. Includes links to programs, press releases, and current events.

Ethnic Cleansing in Armenia

http://www.genocide.am/karabakh/caroline/
index.htm

A comprehensive site that examines the historical, political, religious, and social issues linked to the present-day genocide taking place in Armenia.

Ending Violence against Women and Girls

http://www.unfpa.org/swp/2000/english/ch03
.html

A United Nations site addressing the issues of gender-based violence in cultures around the world. Several boxes include "Women's attackers seldom punished in Pakistan" and "Killings in Sweden spark debate about domestic violence." Other topics include "Trafficking in women and girls," "Honour killings," and "Impact on reproductive health."

Nation, State, and Economy

http://www.mises.org/nsande.asp

An extensive site reviewing the essence of nationalism, with links to Prussia and Austria.

Political Anthropology

http://home.cc.umanitoba.ca/~umdudgeo/
polianth.html

A political anthropology of traditional ecological knowledge (TEK) in the Canadian subarctic. Topics include Cree land tenure and resources management practices, and the politics of TEK.

SUGGESTED READINGS

Bothwell, R. (1998). *Canada and Quebec: One country, two histories.* Vancouver: UBC Press.

This book addresses the relationship and sources of misunderstanding between Quebec and the rest of Canada through interviews with politicians, journalists, and academics, such as Jean Chrétien, Ovide Mercredi, Lise Bissonnette, Graham Fraser, Michael Bliss, and Ramsay Cook. Through personal accounts and opinions, readers will become acquainted with the critical issues facing Canadian unity.

Frideres, J.S. (1998). *Aboriginal peoples of Canada: Contemporary conflicts* (5th ed.). Scarborough, ON: Prentice Hall Allyn and Bacon Canada.

This comprehensive book traces the changes in aboriginal–White relations from first contact to the present day. The book covers such diverse topics as colonialism, treaties and land claims, and self-government.

Gordon, R.J., & Meggitt, M.J. (1985). *Law and order in the New Guinea highlands.* Hanover, NH: University Press of New England.

This ethnographic study of the resurgence of tribal fighting among the Mae-Enga addresses two issues of major importance in today's world: the changing nature of law and order in "underdeveloped" countries and the nature of violence in human societies.

Johnson, A.W., & Earle, T. (1987). *The evolution of human societies, from foraging group to agrarian state.* Stanford, CA: Stanford University Press.

Although written as a synthesis of economic and ecological anthropology, this is also a book on the evolution of political organization in human societies. Proceeding from family-level up through state organization, the authors discuss nine levels, illustrating each with specific case studies, and specify the conditions that give rise to each level.

McGlynn, F., & Tuden, A. (Eds.). (1991). *Anthropological approaches to political behavior*. Pittsburgh, PA: Pittsburgh Press.

A diverse collection of essays taken from previous editions of the journal *Ethnology*. These articles serve to highlight various theoretical concerns in political anthropology, and provide valuable insight into political behaviour, power, and action.

McRoberts, K. (1997). *Misconceiving Canada: The struggle for national unity*. Toronto: Oxford University Press.

A very readable examination of the struggle for national unity in Canada. In addition to providing political analysis, McRoberts examines from a historical perspective the issues of unity facing Canadians.

CNN TODAY VIDEOS

The Politics of Reconciliation: Cambodia and the Khmer Rouge (CNN Cultural Anthropology, vol. 3, 2:30)
This segment examines how the Cambodian people are attempting to come to a civil resolution of the harsh period of dominance by the Khmer Rouge.

Russian Social Protest (CNN Cultural Anthropology, vol. 2, 1:38)
In a provincial northern Russian city, citizens face economic and social upheaval since the breakup of the old Soviet Union.

Yugoslavia History (CNN Cultural Anthropology, vol. 2, 2:12)
This segment follows the development of the multiethnic Yugoslavia from World War II through the death of its postwar leader Tito. It provides background for the tragic recent developments in the Balkans.

A Glimpse Inside Afghanistan (CNN Cultural Anthropology, vol. 3, 1:26)
This short, offbeat clip of a motorcycle stuntman inside Afghanistan throws light on the restriction on public display imposed by the Muslim fundamentalist rulers of the country.

The Promising Future of a Central American Nation: Guatemala (CNN Cultural Anthropology, vol. 3, 1:53)
Democracy and freedom are slowly taking root inside Guatemala, a Central American country that has known mostly dictatorship and civil unrest until recently.

Caste Killings in India (CNN Cultural Anthropology, vol. 6, 2:10)
A boyfriend and girlfriend are hanged because their families are from different castes. Few people in and around the village condemn the killings. Social activists in India say a global forum must act now.

Chapter 12

Religion and the Supernatural

Ritual is religion in action, and trance, dance, and sacrifice are frequently part of ritual. Shown here is a Balinese cremation ritual.

Chapter Preview

1.   What Is Religion?

Religion may be regarded as the beliefs and patterns of behaviour by which humans try to deal with what they view as important problems that cannot be solved with known technology or organizational techniques. To overcome these limitations, people turn to the manipulation of supernatural beings and powers.

2.   What Are Religion's Identifying Features?

Religion consists of various rituals—prayers, songs, dances, offerings, and sacrifices—people enact to manipulate supernatural beings and powers to their advantage. These beings and powers may consist of gods and goddesses, ancestral and other spirits, or impersonal powers. In all human groups certain individuals are skilled at dealing with these beings and powers and assist other members in their ritual activities. A body of myths rationalizes or "explains" the system in a manner consistent with people's experience in the world in which they live.

3.   What Functions Does Religion Serve?

Whether or not a particular religion accomplishes what people believe it does, all religions serve a number of important psychological and social functions. They reduce anxiety by explaining the unknown and making it understandable, as well as provide comfort in the belief that supernatural aid is available in times of crisis. They sanction a wide range of human conduct by providing notions of right and wrong, setting precedents for acceptable behaviour, and by transferring the burden of decision making from individuals to supernatural powers. Through ritual, religion may enhance the learning of oral traditions. Finally, religion plays an important role in maintaining social solidarity.

CHAPTER OUTLINE

The Anthropological Approach to Religion

The Practice of Religion

Original Study: Healing among the Ju/'hoansi of the Kalahari

Gender Perspectives: Menstrual Taboo

Religion, Magic, and Witchcraft

Anthropology Applied: Aboriginal Men and Traditional Healing in Canadian Prisons

The Functions of Religion

Religion and Cultural Change

According to the Iroquois origin myth, the earth was once covered with water and shrouded in darkness; only water animals lived there. Then the Great Spirit commanded his pregnant daughter, Sky Woman, to bring light to the world below. He wrapped her in light and dropped her through a hole in the sky. Waterfowl rose to cushion Sky Woman's descent, and muskrat brought dirt from the seabed to make dry land for Sky Woman. Turtle rose to hold the land in place as it spread and grew larger, until the land became the size it is today. Sky Woman gave birth to a daughter; in time this daughter met a man, who placed two arrows within her. The daughter bore twins; the good twin was called Sapling. The evil twin, called Flint, killed his mother during his birth. In grief, Sapling created the sun from his mother's face; Flint made darkness to drive the sun west. Sapling brought the moon and stars from his mother's breast, and created mountains and rivers; Flint jumbled the mountains and made the rivers crooked. Sapling planted forests and fruit trees; Flint sent storms to tear at the land. Sapling then made humans, and planted maize and tobacco; Flint made monsters, weeds, and vermin. Sapling defeated Flint and banished him to an underground cave, though Flint still sends out wicked spirits, ensuring good and evil are in all things.

There are more than 40 versions of this Iroquois origin myth, but regardless of the account, this myth conveys several interwoven themes of central importance to the Iroquois. The myth por-

trays the constant struggle between good and evil—the Iroquois world is composed of good, but always tainted with evil. The main character of this myth is a woman, exemplifying the importance of women in Iroquois communities—women are the source of all life and sustenance. The myth also describes the interdependence of all things in nature—waterfowl, muskrat, and turtle all helped save Sky Woman, the mother of humankind. The twins are a reflection of the duality in Iroquois social organization; the twins lived in the same lodge for a while, facing each other across a fire, similar to traditional Iroquois living arrangements, and the Iroquois village is divided into two halves of a moiety.[1]

To those of other religious persuasions, such beliefs may seem, at best, irrational and arbitrary, but in fact they are neither. The Iroquois religion is not only logical and socially functional but also the very model of Iroquois social organization. The culture is divided into two independent moieties, each with its own economy, rituals, and authority. An individual is introduced into one of these moieties (which in this case are *not* based on kinship), and his or her membership is regularly reinforced through a series of ceremonies that reaffirm the balance and reciprocity between men and women and between moieties. The rites of birth and death are shared by the whole community; a deceased individual's moiety immediately begins to grieve, while the other moiety offers condolences and organizes the burial.[2]

Iroquois religion enters into virtually every aspect of Iroquois life and culture. It is the basis of the simultaneously dualistic and unified worldview of the individual Iroquois. It provides numerous points of mediation so that the two moieties can continue to exist together as a single community. It sanctifies the community by linking its origin with the realm of the supernatural, and it offers divine sanction to *rites of passage* that soften life's major transitions. By providing an afterworld that is the mirror image of human society, it answers the question of death in a manner that reinforces social structure. In short, Iroquois religion provides a solid foundation for the stability and continuity of Iroquois culture.

The origin or creation myth often exemplifies the interdependence of all things in nature. Shown here is Sky Woman's descent to earth, helped by Turtle and Geese.

[1]Snow, D.R. (1994). *The Iroquois*. Cambridge, MA: Blackwell.

[2]Ibid.

All religions fulfill numerous social and psychological needs. Some of these—the need to confront and explain death, for example—appear to be universal; indeed, we know of no group of people anywhere on the face of the earth who, for an extended history, have been without religion. Unbound by time, religion gives meaning to individual and group life, drawing power from "the time of the gods in the Beginning" and offering continuity of existence beyond death. It can provide the path by which people transcend their arduous earthly existence and attain, if only momentarily, spiritual selfhood. The social functions of religion are no less important than the psychological ones. A traditional religion reinforces group norms, provides moral sanctions for individual conduct, and furnishes the substratum of common purpose and values upon which the equilibrium of the community depends.

In the 19th century, the European intellectual tradition gave rise to the idea that science ultimately would destroy religion by showing people the irrationality of their myths and rituals. Indeed, many still believe that as scientific explanations replace those of religion, the latter will wither on the vine. This has not happened. Not only do traditional mainline religions continue to thrive, but also fundamentalist religions are experiencing a strong resurgence, for example, Islamic fundamentalism in countries such as Algeria and Iran; Jewish fundamentalism in Israel; and Hindu fundamentalism in India. Christian fundamentalism is represented in evangelical denominations. Other religions continue to grow in Canada as well, including Islam (a rise from 253 000 in 1991 to 579 600 in 2001), Buddhism (163 000 in 1991 to 300 300 in 2001), and Hinduism (157 000 in 1991 to 297 200 in 2001),[3] not to mention the various "New Age" options. Yet, religious affiliation has taken a nosedive in many parts of Europe, where people presumably face similar dilemmas, and the Canadian census demonstrates a dramatic decline in church attendance in most parts of Canada in the last

50 years, especially in Quebec.[4] Some parts of the country have become quite polarized in religious

Far from causing the death of religion, the growth of scientific knowledge, by producing new anxieties and raising new questions about human existence, may have contributed to the continuing practice of religion in modern life. North Americans continue to participate in traditional religions, such as Judaism (top), Islam (middle), and Christianity (bottom).

---

[3]Statistics Canada. (2001). *Population by religion, 1981 and 1991 Censuses, Canada.* Retrieved March 25, 2001, from the World Wide Web: http://www.statcan.ca/english/pgdb/people/population/demo32.htm; and Statistics Canada. (May 13, 2003). *2001 Census: Analysis series. Religion in Canada.* Retrieved October 28, 2003, from the World Wide Web: http://www12.statcan.ca/english/census01/products/analytic/companion/rel/pdf/96f0030xie2001015.pdf.

---

[4]Statistics Canada. (2001). *Population by religion, 1981 and 1991 Censuses, Canada.* Retrieved March 25, 2001, from the World Wide Web: http://www.statcan.ca/english/pgdb/people/population/demo32.htm.

attitudes. For example, British Columbia has the largest concentration of people with no religious affiliation, and country-wide the number of Canadians reporting no religious affiliation has risen to 16 percent, or 4.8 million people.

Science, far from destroying religion, may have contributed to the creation of a veritable religious boom. Science has fostered this boom by removing many traditional psychological props while creating, in its technological applications, a host of new problems: threat of nuclear catastrophe; epidemic health scares; unease about the consequences of new developments in biotechnology, such as the cloning of animals, production of new strains of genetically engineered organisms, and the ability to store human sperm and eggs for future fertilization; fear of loss of economic security as machines replace workers; and fear of loneliness in a society that isolates us from our kin and places impediments in the way of establishing deep and lasting friendships, to list but a few issues

New developments in biotechnology, such as cloning, which produced the sheep Dolly, have been a source of new anxieties. Answers to these anxieties are often sought in religion.

people now must deal with. In the face of these new anxieties, religion offers social and psychological support.

The continuing strength of religion in the face of Western rationalism clearly reveals it is a powerful and dynamic force in society. Although anthropologists are not qualified to pass judgement on the metaphysical truths of any particular religion, they can show how each religion embodies a number of "truths" about humans and society.

THE ANTHROPOLOGICAL APPROACH TO RELIGION

Anthropologist Anthony F.C. Wallace defined **religion** as "a set of rituals, rationalized by myth, which mobilizes supernatural powers for the purpose of achieving or preventing transformations of state in man and nature."[5] Behind this definition is a recognition that people, when they cannot "fix" through technological or organizational means serious problems that cause them anxiety, try to do so through the manipulation of supernatural beings and powers. To do so requires ritual, which Wallace sees as the primary phenomenon of religion, or "religion in action." Religion reduces anxiety and keeps confidence high, which serves to keep people in some sort of shape to cope with reality. It is this that gives religion its survival value.

Religion, then, may be regarded as the beliefs and patterns of behaviour by which people try to control aspects of their world otherwise beyond their control. Since no known culture, including those of modern industrial societies, has achieved complete certainty in controlling the universe, religion is a part of all known cultures. However, considerable variability exists. On the one hand there are food-foraging peoples, whose technological ability to manipulate their environment is limited and who tend to see themselves more as

---

[5]Wallace, A.F.C. (1966). *Religion: An anthropological view* (p. 107). New York: Random House.

Religion.   A set of rituals, rationalized by myth, that mobilizes supernatural powers to achieve or prevent transformations of state in people and nature.

part, rather than masters, of nature. This is what we referred to in Chapter 11 as a naturalistic worldview. Among food foragers religion is apt to be inseparable from the rest of daily life. It also mirrors and confirms the egalitarian nature of social relations in their cultures, in that individuals do not plead for aid to high-ranking deities the way members of stratified societies do. On the other hand are Western societies, with their ideological commitment to overcoming problems through technological and organizational skills. Here religion is less a part of daily activities and is restricted to specific occasions. Moreover, with its hierarchy of supernatural beings—for instance, God, the angels, and the saints of Christianity—it reflects and confirms the stratified nature of the society in which it is embedded.

Even so, variation exists between these two extremes. Religious activity may be less prominent in the lives of social elites, who see themselves as more in control of their own destinies, than it is in the lives of peasants or members of lower classes. Among the latter, religion may afford some compensation for a subordinate position in society. Yet religion is still important to the elite in that it rationalizes the system in such a way that people are not as likely to question the existing social order as they might otherwise. After all, with hope for a better existence after death, people may be more willing to put up with a disadvantaged position in life. Thus, religious beliefs serve to influence and perpetuate conceptions, if not actual relations, between different classes of people.

THE PRACTICE OF RELIGION

Much of religion's value comes from the activities its practice calls for. Participation in religious ceremonies may bring a sense of personal transcendence—a wave of reassurance, security, and even ecstasy—or a feeling of closeness to fellow participants. Although the rituals and practices of religions vary considerably, even rites that seem strange and exotic to us serve the same basic social and psychological functions.

Supernatural Beings and Powers

One of the hallmarks of religion is a belief in supernatural beings and forces. When attempting to control by religious means what cannot be controlled in other ways, humans turn to prayer, sacrifice, and other religious rituals. This presupposes

The huge public participation in the funeral of Pierre Elliot Trudeau, as in all collective rituals, created a sense of communion that encouraged a belief in shared values.

a world of supernatural beings who have an interest in human affairs and to whom people may turn for aid. We divide these beings into three categories: major deities (gods and goddesses), ancestral spirits, and other spirit beings. Although the variety of deities and spirits humans recognize is tremendous, we can make certain generalizations.

Gods and Goddesses

Gods and goddesses are the greatest and most remote beings. They are seen as controlling the universe, or, if several are recognized (known as **polytheism**), each has charge of a particular part of the universe. Such was the case of the gods and goddesses of ancient Greece: Zeus was lord of the sky, Poseidon was ruler of the sea, and Hades was lord of the underworld and the dead. Besides these three brothers were a host of other deities, female as well as male, each similarly concerned with specific aspects of life and the universe.

Pantheons, or collections of gods and goddesses such as those of the Greeks, are common in non-Western states. Since states usually have grown through conquest, their pantheons often have developed as local deities of conquered peoples were incorporated into the official state pantheon. Although creators of the present world may be included, this is not always the case; the Greeks, to cite but one example, did not include them. Another frequent feature of pantheons is the presence of a supreme deity, who may be all but totally ignored by humans. The Aztecs of Mexico, for instance, recognized a supreme pair to whom they paid little attention. After all, being so remote, the deities were unlikely to be interested in human affairs. The sensible practice, then, was to focus attention on less-remote deities who were more directly concerned with human matters.

Whether or not a people recognize gods, goddesses, or both has to do with how men and women relate to one another in everyday life. Generally speaking, cultures that subordinate women to men define the godhead in exclusively masculine terms. For example, in the Greek pantheon, the goddess Hera is usually identified as consort to Zeus; she is portrayed as a jealous,

petty wife, and Aphrodite, goddess of love, exists to bring pleasure to men. Male godheads are found among those with economies based on the herding of animals or intensive agriculture carried out by men, who as fathers are distant and controlling figures to their children.

Goddesses, by contrast, are apt to be most prominent in groups where women make a major contribution to the economy and enjoy relative equality with men and where men are more involved in their children's lives, as in farming communities. As an illustration, the early Hebrews, like other pastoral nomadic tribes of the Middle East, described their god in masculine, authoritarian terms. By contrast, goddesses played central roles in religious ritual and the popular consciousness of the region's agricultural peoples. Associated with these goddesses were concepts of light, love, fertility, and procreation. Around 1300 B.C., the Hebrew tribes entered the land of Canaan and began to practise agriculture, requiring them to establish a new kind of relationship with the soil. As they became dependent on rainfall and the rotation of seasons for crops and concerned about fertility, they adopted many of the Canaanite goddess cults. Although diametrically opposed to the original Hebrew cult, belief in the Canaanite goddesses catered to the human desire for security by seeking to control the forces of fertility in the interest of people's well-being.

Later on, when the Israelite tribes sought national unity in the face of a military threat by the Philistines and when they strengthened their identity as a "chosen people," the goddess cults lost out to followers of the old masculine tribal god. This ancient masculine-authoritarian concept of god has been perpetuated down to the present, not just in the Judaic tradition but also by Christians and Muslims, whose religions stem from the old Hebrew religion. As a consequence, this masculine-authoritarian model has played an important role in perpetuating a relationship between men and women in which the latter traditionally have been expected to submit to the "rule" of men at every level of Jewish, Christian, and Islamic society.

Polytheism.   Belief in several gods and/or goddesses (as contrasted with monotheism—belief in one god).
> Pantheon.   A collection of gods and goddesses.

The patriarchal nature of Western society is expressed in its theology, in which a masculine God gives life to the first man, as depicted here on the ceiling of the Sistine Chapel. Only after this is the first woman created from the first man.

Ancestral Spirits

A belief in ancestral spirits is consistent with the widespread notion that human beings are made up of two parts, a body and some kind of vital spirit. For example, the Penobscot maintained that each person had a personal spirit that could detach itself and travel about apart from the body, while the latter remained inert. Given such a concept, the idea of the spirit being freed from the body by death and having a continued existence seems quite logical.

Where a belief in ancestral spirits exists, these beings frequently are seen as retaining an active interest and even membership in society. In Chapter 11, for instance, we saw how ghost ancestors of the Wape acted to provide or withhold meat from their living descendants. Like living persons, ancestral spirits may be benevolent or malevolent, but no one is ever quite sure what their behaviour will be. The same feeling of uncertainty—"How will they react to what I have done?"—may be displayed toward ancestral spirits that tends to be displayed toward people of

a senior generation who hold authority over individuals. Beyond this, ancestral spirits closely resemble living humans in their appetites, feelings, emotions, and behaviour. Thus, they reflect and reinforce social reality.

A belief in ancestral spirits of one sort or another is found in many parts of the world, especially among people with unilineal descent systems. In several such African cultures, the concept is especially elaborate. Ancestral spirits frequently behave like humans. They are able to feel hot, cold, and pain, and they may be capable of dying a second death by drowning or burning. They even may participate in family and lineage affairs, and seats will be provided for them, even though the spirits are invisible. If they are annoyed, they may send sickness or even death. Eventually, they are reborn as new members of their lineage, and, in groups that hold such beliefs, adults need to observe infants closely to determine just who has been reborn.

Deceased ancestors were also important in the patrilineal society of traditional China. For the gift of life, a boy was forever indebted to his parents, owing them obedience, deference, and a comfortable old age. Even after their death, he had to provide for them in the spirit world, offering food, money, and incense to them on the anniversaries of their births and deaths. In addition, people collectively worshipped all lineage ancestors periodically throughout the year. This society even regarded the birth of sons as an obligation to the ancestors, because this ensured the latter's needs would continue to be attended to even after their own sons' death. To satisfy ancestors' needs for descendants, a man might marry a girl who had been adopted into his family as an infant to be raised as a dutiful wife for him, even when this arrangement went against the wishes of both parties. Furthermore, a man would force his daughter to marry a man against her will. In fact, a female child was raised to be cast out by her natal family yet might not find acceptance in her husband's family for years. Not until after death, when her soul was carried in a tablet and placed in the shrine of her husband's family, was she an official member of it. As a consequence, once a son was born to her, a woman worked long and hard to establish the strongest possible tie between herself and her son to ensure she would be looked after in life.

Strong beliefs in ancestral spirits are particularly appropriate in a culture of descent-based groups with their associated ancestral orientation. More than this, though, these beliefs provide a strong sense of continuity that links the past, present, and future.

Animism

One of the most widespread beliefs about supernatural beings is **animism,** which sees nature as animated by all sorts of spirits. In reality, the term masks a wide range of variation. Animals and plants, like humans, all may have their individual spirits, as may springs, mountains, stones, weapons, ornaments, and so on. In addition, the woods may be full of a variety of unattached or free-ranging spirits. Generally speaking, though, they are less remote from people than gods and goddesses and are more involved in daily affairs. They may be benevolent, malevolent, or neutral.

First Nations artists carved these images of people, animals, and animal tracks into rock in Petroglyphs Provincial Park, near Mephton, Ontario.

They may be awesome, terrifying, lovable, or even mischievous. Since they may be pleased or irritated by human actions, people are obliged to be concerned about them.

Animism is typical of those who see themselves as a part of nature rather than superior to it. This takes in most food foragers, including most North American aboriginal groups, as well as food-producing peoples who recognize little difference between a human life and that of any growing thing. Among such societies, gods and goddesses are relatively unimportant, but the woods are full of all sorts of spirits. Gods and goddesses, if they exist at all, may be seen as having created the world and perhaps making it fit to live in, but it is spirits whom individuals turn to for curing, who help or hinder the shaman, and whom the ordinary hunter may meet when off in the woods.

Animatism

Although supernatural power is often thought of as being vested in supernatural beings, it does not have to be. Some Melanesians, for example, think of *mana* as a force inherent in all objects. It is not in itself physical, but it can reveal itself physically. A warrior's success in fighting is not attributed to his own strength but to the *mana* contained in an amulet that hangs around his neck. Similarly, a farmer may know a great deal about horticulture, soil conditioning, and the correct time for sowing and harvesting but nevertheless depends on *mana*

Animism.   A belief in spirit beings thought to animate nature.

Robin Ridington

Robin Ridington is professor emeritus of anthropology at the University of British Columbia. During his long and illustrious career, Ridington has explored the worlds of North American hunter-gatherers, in particular, the Omaha and Beaver First Nations. In the course of his research, he became interested in such diverse topics as cosmology, history, and artistic endeavours.

Ridington began his fieldwork with the Beaver First Nations of the Peace River region in 1964. His personal journey of discovery as he studied these people has provided many anthropologists with food for thought. Ridington struggled with his preconceived ideas about academic research and the abstract, and the objective nature of going into the field to "study" a cultural group. His insights have helped other anthropologists realize that ethnographic research is a collaborative endeavour, and that the end result should present both the anthropologist's and the study group's experiences. Early in his career, Ridington recognized the importance of using a people's own name; the Beaver First Nation's name for themselves is Dane-zaa ("real people").

Ridington's understanding of Dane-zaa myths, dreams, and visions has provided extraordinary insight into their thought world. "I came to learn, that events can take place only after people have known and experienced them in myths, dreams, and visions. Even their concept of person is different from ours. In Dane-zaa reality, animals, winds, rocks, and natural forces are people."[1] In his narrative ethnography *Trail to Heaven* (1988), Ridington reveals the complex belief systems of the Dane-zaa, often using unedited narratives in the Dane-zaa's own words.

In his 1990 book, *Little Bit Know Something: Stories in the Language of Anthropology,* Ridington raises the voices of the Dane-zaa, but he attempts to blend their voices with the voices of anthropology. More recently, Ridington, together with his Omaha friend and brother, Dennis Hastings, wrote the story of the Omaha people, their struggle to survive after the buffalo disappeared, and their spiritual renewal in the present, in the award-winning *Blessing for a Long Time: The Sacred Pole of the Omaha Tribe* (1997).

Now retired from UBC, Ridington is pursuing his interest in audio and visual media. Along with sociologist Jillian Ridington, he is working on a computer-based genealogy for the Doig River First Nation. He has transferred his archive of audio and visual images to digital format for the local First Nations, and he is collaborating with the Dane-zaa to produce CDs of Dane-zaa music and videos in the Beaver language, and documenting traditional and contemporary oral histories.

---

[1]Ridington, R. (1988). *Trail to heaven: Knowledge and narrative in a northern native community* (p. xi). Vancouver: Douglas and McIntyre.

---

for a successful crop, often building a simple altar to this power at the end of the field. If the crop is good, it is a sign the farmer has in some way appropriated the necessary *mana*. Far from being a personalized force, *mana* is abstract in the extreme, a power lying always just beyond reach of the senses. As R.H. Codrington described it, "Virtue, prestige, authority, good fortune, influence, sanctity, luck are all words which, under certain conditions, give something near the meaning. . . . *Mana* sometimes means a more than natural virtue or power attaching to some person or thing."[6] This concept of impersonal power also was widespread among North American First Nations. The Iroquois called it *orenda*, to the Sioux it was *wakonda*, and to the Algonquians it was *manitu*.

R.R. Marett called this concept of impersonal power **animatism.** The two concepts, animatism

---

[6]Quoted by Leinhardt, G. (1960). Religion. In H. Shapiro (Ed.), *Man, culture, and society* (p. 368). London: Oxford University Press.

Animatism.   A belief that the world is animated by impersonal supernatural powers.

(which is inanimate) and animism (a belief in spirit beings), are not mutually exclusive. They often are found in the same culture, as in Melanesia, and also in the North American First Nations groups just mentioned.

People attempting to comprehend beliefs in supernatural beings and powers that others recognize frequently ask how such beliefs are maintained. In part, the answer is through manifestations of power. This means, given a belief in animatism and/or the powers of supernatural beings, a person is predisposed to see what appear to be results of the application of such powers. For example, if a Melanesian warrior is convinced of his power because he possesses the necessary *mana* and he is successful, he is likely to interpret this success as proof of the power of *mana*. "After all, I would have lost had I not possessed it, wouldn't I?" Beyond this, because of his confidence in his *mana*, he may be willing to take more chances in his fighting, and this indeed could mean the difference between success or failure.

Failures, of course, do occur, but they can be explained. Perhaps a prayer was not answered because a deity or spirit was still angry about some past insult. Or perhaps our Melanesian warrior lost his battle—the obvious explanation is that he was not as successful in bringing *mana* to bear as he thought, or else his opponent had more of it. In any case, humans generally emphasize successes over failures, and, long after many of the latter have been forgotten, tales will be told of striking cases of the workings of supernatural powers.

Another feature that tends to perpetuate beliefs in supernatural beings is that the beings have attributes people are familiar with. Allowing for the fact that supernatural beings are in a sense larger than life, they generally are conceived of as living the way people do and as having the same sorts of interests. For example, the Penobscot people believed in a quasi–human being called Gluskabe. Like ordinary mortals, Gluskabe travelled about in a canoe, used snowshoes, lived in a wigwam, and made stone arrowheads. The gods and goddesses of the ancient Greeks experienced familiar human lusts and petty jealousies. Such features serve to make supernatural beings believable.

Myths

The role of mythology in maintaining beliefs should not be overlooked. **Myths** are explanatory narratives that rationalize religious beliefs and practices. Myths invariably focus on human existence: where humans and everything in our world came from, why we are here, and where we are going. They are symbolic expressions of meaning. Myths depict and describe an orderly universe and set the stage for orderly behaviour. To Euro Canadians and European Americans, the word *myth* immediately conjures up the idea of a story about imaginary events, but the people responsible for a particular myth do not see it that way. To them myths are true stories, analogous to historical documents in modern North American culture, for example, the Inuit myth of Sedna, the sea goddess of the Inuit. When Sedna's angry bird husband brought on a violent storm, Sedna's desperate father threw her from their boat. She clung to the side of the boat, but her father cut off her fingers, joint by joint, and she sunk to the bottom of the sea, where she remains today. Sedna's fingers became the sea animals that Inuit now hunt.[7]

All societies have myths; in literate cultures, this mythology is written down, such as in the Judaic and Christian account of creation in the Bible's Book of Genesis. In nonliterate cultures myths are maintained through oral histories or stories. Myths invariably are full of accounts of the doings of various supernatural beings and thus serve to reinforce belief in them.

Studying mythology in nonliterate cultures presents its own challenges. Mathias Guenther, professor of sociology and anthropology at Wilfrid Laurier University, has studied the trickster in Ju/'hoansi mythology, yet he readily admits this is a difficult task because of the ambiguity of these beliefs. The Ju/'hoansi trickster is a mythological and spiritual being that changes its identity and appearance from lewd prankster to divine creator, goblin to god, human to jackal, and goes by many names. Yet for all his ambiguity, the trickster creates understanding and order within the Ju/'hoansi world:

---

[7]Blodgett, J. (1988). Whale bone. In *Inuit art: An anthology* (p. 31). Winnipeg: Watson and Dwyer.

Myth. A sacred narrative explaining how the world came to be in its present form.

As creator, as well as culture hero, he may bring into the world beings, things, and conditions of importance to nature and humankind, as well as structure and order. Thanks to his creative acts or antics there is now fire and cooking, the rivers and water holes of the Kalahari, the vocal sounds and body patterns of some animals, healing medicine and trance arrows, rain magic, and the knowledge of procreation (as well as death).[8]

Religious Specialists

Priests and Priestesses

In all human cultures there exist individuals whose job it is to guide and supplement the religious practices of others. Such individuals are highly skilled at contacting and influencing supernatural beings and manipulating supernatural forces. Their qualification for this is that they have undergone special training. In addition, they may display certain distinctive personality traits that particularly suit them for their job. Cultures with the resources to support full-time occupational specialists give the role of guiding religious practices and influencing the supernatural to the **priest** or **priestess.** He or she is the socially initiated, ceremonially inducted member of a recognized religious organization, with a rank and function that belong to him or her as the tenant of an office others have held before. The sources of power are the culture and the institution the priest or priestess functions within.

The priest, if not the priestess, is a familiar figure in Western societies; he is the priest, minister, pastor, rector, rabbi, or whatever the official title may be in an organized religion. With the Judaic, Christian, and Islamic god defined in masculine-authoritarian terms, it was not surprising that traditionally men have filled the most important positions in these religions. Only in cultures where women make a major contribution to the economy and goddesses as well as gods are recognized are female religious specialists likely to be found.

----

[8]Guenther, M. (1999). *Tricksters and trancers* (p. 101). Bloomington and Indianapolis, IL: Indiana University Press.

Shamans

Shamans are part-time religious specialists who acquired religious power individually, usually in solitude and isolation, when the Great Spirit, the Power, the Great Mystery, or whatever is revealed to them. These people become the recipients of certain special gifts, such as healing or divination; when they return to their community, they frequently are given another kind of religious role, that of the **shaman** or medicine person. (For further discussion of the healing skills of shamans, see Chapter 14).

Typically, a person becomes a shaman by passing through difficult stages commonly set forth in many myths. These stages are often thought to involve torture and violent dismemberment of the body; scraping away of the flesh until the body is reduced to a skeleton; substitution of the viscera and renewal of the blood; a period spent in the land of the dead, during which the shaman is taught by the souls of dead shamans and other spirit beings; and an ascent to a sky realm. Among North American Plains peoples, any man could become a shaman, since no ecclesiastical organization provided rules and regulations to guide religious consciousness. The search for shamanistic visions was pursued by many adult Plains aboriginal males, who would engage in bodily deprivation, even self-torture, to

Shown here is Reggie Crowshoe, a First Nations medicine person, at the Sundial Medicine Wheel in Alberta.

Priest or **Priestess.**   A full-time religious specialist.   **> Shaman/medicine person.**   A part-time religious specialist who has unique power acquired through his or her initiative; such individuals are thought to possess exceptional abilities for dealing with supernatural beings and powers.

induce such visions. Not all seekers were granted a vision, but failure carried no social stigma. Although those who claimed supernatural vision would be expected to manifest some special power in battle or wealth, the sincerity of the seeker carried the essential truth of the experience.

The shaman is essentially a religious entrepreneur who acts on behalf of some human client, often to effect a cure or foretell some future event. To do so, the shaman intervenes to influence or impose his or her will on supernatural powers. The shaman can be contrasted with the priest or priestess, whose "clients" are the deities. Priests and priestesses frequently tell people what to do; the shaman tells the supernatural what to do. In return for services rendered, the shaman may collect a fee—fresh meat, yams, or a favourite possession. In some cases, the added prestige, authority, and social power attached to the shaman's status are reward enough.

When a shaman acts for a client, he or she may put on something of a show—one that heightens the basic drama with a sense of danger. Frequently, the shaman must enter a trancelike state, in which he or she experiences the sensation of travelling to the spirit world, seeing and interacting with spirit beings there. The shaman tries to impose his or her will on these spirits, an inherently dangerous contest, considering the superhuman powers spirits are usually thought to possess. One example of this is afforded by the trance dances of the Ju/'hoansi of Africa's Kalahari Desert (see the following Original Study). Among these people shamans constitute, on average, about half the men and a third of the older women in any group. The most common reasons for their going into trance are to bring rain, to control animals, and—as in the present example—to heal the sick (always an important activity of shamans, wherever they are found).

ORIGINAL STUDY

Healing among the Ju/'hoansi of the Kalahari

One way the spirits affect humans is by shooting them with invisible arrows carrying disease, death, or misfortune. If the arrows can be warded off, illness will not take hold. If illness has already penetrated, the arrows must be removed to enable the sick person to recover. An ancestral spirit may exercise this power against the living if a person is not being treated well by others. If people argue with her frequently, if her husband shows how little he values her by carrying on blatant affairs, or if people refuse to cooperate or share with her, the spirit may conclude that no one cares whether or not she remains alive and may "take her into the sky."

Interceding with the spirits and drawing out their invisible arrows is the task of (Ju/'hoansi) healers, men and women who possess the powerful healing force called *n/um* (the Ju/'hoansi equivalent of *mana*). N/um generally remains dormant in a healer until an effort is made to activate it. Although an occasional healer can accomplish this through solo singing or instrumental playing, the usual way of activating n/um is through the medicinal curing ceremony or trance dance. To the sound of undulating melodies sung by women, healers dance around and around the fire, sometimes for hours. The music, the strenuous dancing, the smoke, the heat of the fire, and the healers' intense concentration cause their n/um to heat up. When it comes to a boil, trance is achieved.

At this moment the n/um becomes available as a powerful healing force, to serve the entire community. In trance, a healer lays hands on and ritually cures everyone sitting around the fire. His hands flutter lightly beside each person's head or chest or wherever illness is evident; his body trembles; his breathing becomes deep and coarse; and he becomes coated with a thick sweat—also considered to be imbued with power. Whatever

Ju/'hoansi healers, when
entering trance, are assisted by
others among the trance
dancers.

"badness" is discovered in the person is drawn into the healer's own body
and met by the n/um coursing up his spinal column. The healer gives a
mounting cry that culminates in a soul-wrenching shriek as the illness is cat-
apulted out of his body and into the air.

While in trance, many healers see various gods and spirits sitting just
outside the circle of firelight, enjoying the spectacle of the dance.
Sometimes the spirits are recognizable—departed relatives and friends—at
other times they are "just people." Whoever these beings are, healers in
trance usually blame them for whatever misfortune is being experienced by
the community. They are barraged by hurled objects, shouted at, and
aggressively warned not to take any of the living back with them to the village of the spirits.

To cure a very serious illness, the most experienced healers may be
called upon, for only they have enough knowledge to undertake the dangerous spiritual exploration that may be necessary to effect a cure. When
they are in a trance, their souls are said to leave their bodies and to travel
to the spirit world to discover the cause of the illness or the problem. An
ancestral spirit or a god is usually found responsible and asked to reconsider.
If the healer is persuasive and the spirit agrees, the sick person recovers. If
the spirit is elusive or unsympathetic, a cure is not achieved. The healer may
go to the principal god, but even this does not always work. As one healer
put it, "Sometimes, when you speak with God, he says, 'I want this person
to die and won't help you make him better.' At other times, God helps; the
next morning, someone who has been lying on the ground, seriously ill,
gets up and walks again."

These journeys are considered dangerous because while the healer's
soul is absent his body is in half-death. Akin to loss of consciousness, this
state has been observed and verified by medical and scientific investigators.
The power of other healers' n/um is all that is thought to protect the healer
in this state from actual death. He receives lavish attention and care—his
body is vigorously massaged, his skin is rubbed with sweat, and hands are
laid on him. Only when consciousness returns—the signal that his soul has
been reunited with his body—do the other healers cease their efforts.

Source: Shostak, M. (1983). *Nisa: The life and words of a !Kung woman*
(pp. 291–293). New York: Vintage.

The importance of shamanism in any culture
should not be underestimated. For individual
members, it promotes, through the drama of performance, a feeling of ecstasy and release of tension. It provides psychological assurance, through
the manipulation of supernatural powers and
spirits otherwise beyond human control, of such
things as invulnerability from attack, success at
love, or the return of health. In fact, a frequent
reason for a shamanistic performance is to cure
illness. Although the treatment may not be med-
ically effective, the state of mind induced in the
patient may be critical to his or her recovery.

What shamanism provides for people, then,
is a focal point of attention. This is not without
danger to the shaman. Someone with so much
skill and power has the ability to work evil as
well as good and so is potentially dangerous. The
group may interpret too much nonsuccess from a
shaman as evidence of malpractice and may drive
out or even kill the shaman. Likewise, the shaman
may help maintain social control through the
ability to detect and punish evildoers.

Rituals and Ceremonies

Although not all rituals are religious in nature (graduation ceremonies in North America, for example), those that are religious play a crucial role in religious activity. Religious ritual is the means through which individuals relate to the sacred; it is religion in action, although the activities associated with ritual are variable, including prayer, song, sweatbaths, offerings, and sacrifice. Not only is ritual a means for reinforcing a group's social bonds and for relieving tensions, it is also one way important events are celebrated and crises, such as death, are made less socially disruptive and less difficult for individuals to bear. Anthropologists have classified several types of ritual, among them **rites of passage,** which pertain to stages in the individual's life cycle, and **rites of intensification,** which occur during a crisis in the life of the group, serving to bind individuals together.

Rites of Passage

In one of anthropology's classic works, Arnold Van Gennep analyzed the rites of passage that help individuals through the crucial crises of their lives, such as birth, puberty, marriage, parenthood, advancement to a higher class, occupational specialization, and death.[9] He found it useful to divide ceremonies for all of these life crises into three stages: **separation, transition,** and **incorporation.** The individual first would be ritually removed from the culture as a whole, then isolated for a period, and finally incorporated back into the group in his or her new status.

Van Gennep described the male initiation rites of Australian Aborigines. When the elders decide the time for the initiation, the boys are taken from the village (separation), while the women cry and make a ritual show of resistance. At a place distant from the camp, groups of men

from many villages gather. The elders sing and dance, while the initiates act as though they are dead. The climax of this part of the ritual is a bodily operation, such as circumcision or the knocking out of a tooth. Anthropologist A.P. Elkin says,

> This is partly a continuation of the drama of death. The tooth-knocking, circumcision or other symbolical act "killed" the novice; after this he does not return to the general camp and normally may not be seen by any woman. He is dead to the ordinary life of the tribe.[10]

In this transitional stage, the novice may be shown secret ceremonies and receive some instruction, but the most significant element is his complete removal from the community. In the course of these Australian puberty rites, the initiate must learn the lore all adult men are expected to know. The trauma of the occasion is a pedagogical technique that ensures he will learn and remember everything; in a nonliterate culture, the perpetuation of traditions requires no less, so effective teaching methods are necessary.

---

[9]Van Gennep, A. (1960). *The rites of passage.* Chicago: University of Chicago Press.

[10]Elkin, A.P. (1964). *The Australian Aborigines.* Garden City, NY: Doubleday/Anchor Books.

Rites of passage.   Rituals, often religious in nature, marking important stages in the lives of individuals, such as birth, marriage, and death. **> Rites of intensification.**   Religious rituals enacted during a group's real or potential crisis. **> Separation.**   In rites of passage, the ritual removal of the individual from society. **> Transition.**   In rites of passage, a stage where the individual is isolated following separation and prior to incorporation into society. **> Incorporation.**   In rites of passage, reincorporation of the individual into society in his or her new status.

On his return to the culture (incorporation) the novice is welcomed with ceremonies, as though he had returned from the dead. This alerts the members to the individual's new status—that people can expect him to act in certain ways and in return they must act in appropriate ways toward him. The individual's new rights and duties are thus clearly defined. He is spared, for example, the problems of North American teenagers, a time when an individual is neither adult nor child but a person whose status is ill-defined.

In the Australian case just cited, boys are prepared not just for adulthood but also for *manhood*. Fortitude is considered an important masculine virtue, and the pain of tooth-knocking or circumcision helps instill this trait in initiates. In a similar way, female initiation rites help prepare Mende girls in West Africa for womanhood. After they have begun to menstruate, the girls are secluded for weeks, or even months. There they discard the clothes of childhood, smear their bodies with white clay, and dress in brief skirts and many strands of beads. Shortly after entering this transitional stage, they undergo female circumcision (previously discussed in the Gender Perspectives box in Chapter 7). Until their incorporation back into the community, they are trained in the moral and practical responsibilities of potential childbearers by experienced women in the Sande association, an organization the initiates will belong to once their training has ended. This training is not all harsh, however, for it is accompanied by a good deal of singing, dancing, and storytelling, and the initiates are very well fed. Thus, they acquire both a positive image of womanhood and a strong sense of sisterhood. Once their training is complete, a medicine made by brewing leaves in water is used for a ritual washing, removing the magical protection that has shielded them during the period of their confinement.

Mende women emerge from their initiation as women in knowledgeable control of their sexuality, eligible for marriage and childbearing. The pain and danger of the surgery, endured in the context of intense social support from other women, serves as a metaphor for childbirth, which may well take place in the same place of seclusion, again with the support of Sande women. It also has been suggested that, symbolically, excision of the clitoris (as the female version of the male penis) removes sexual ambiguity.[11] Once it is done, a woman *knows* she is "all woman." Thus we have symbolic expression of gender as something important in people's cultural lives.

The traditional Plains sun dance (sometimes called the thirsting dance) is also a rite of passage. In traditional times, Plains aboriginal groups held the religious ceremony during the summer solstice, when all the bands assembled. Although each cultural group developed its own customs, some commonalities in the basic ritual can be discerned. An individual had to sponsor the ceremony: Among the Blackfoot and Sarcee, a virtuous woman might vow to sponsor a ceremony if she suffered a personal crisis such as illness in the family; among the Plains Cree and Ojibwa, a man promised to hold a sun dance if he returned safely from a battle; for the Assiniboine, the sun dance was an act of worship.[12]

The ritual began with the building of a ceremonial lodge. While the sponsor fasted, the warriors cut down a suitable tree for the sacred centre pole. They then constructed a circular lodge made of leafy branches around the pole. Plains Cree and Ojibwa built a "thunderbird nest" of branches at the top of the pole, and hung offerings from it. Once the lodge was finished, the dancing began. The dancers danced to the rhythm of chanted prayers, blowing on eagle-bone whistles, and never taking their eyes off the centre pole. They danced for days, going without food, water, or

Shown here is a traditional sun dance lodge of the Blood First Nations.

[11]MacCormack, C.P. (1977). Biological events and cultural control. *Signs, 3,* 98.

[12]Friesen, J.W. (1999). *First Nations of the Plains: Creative, adaptable, enduring.* Calgary: Detselig.

Gender **Perspectives**

Menstrual Taboo

Once a month, women the world over have a menstrual period. This is normal and natural, yet no other biological function elicits such confused feelings and varied reactions as the menstrual cycle. For anthropologists, the most compelling aspect of menstruation is the seemingly universal menstrual taboo. Cross-cultural observations suggest that menstrual blood and menstruating women are considered dangerous, even offensive to the rest of a community. A ban on sexual intercourse, limits on contact with other people, rules against touching men's ritual gear, avoidance of handling or preparing food, and seclusion in a hut—these are all taboos imposed on women during their menstrual cycle. But do these taboos symbolize gender inequality and oppression of women, or do they suggest something entirely different?

Feminists, as well as some anthropologists, have used menstrual taboos to support the notion of universal male dominance and oppression of women—that men fear menstruating women and therefore impose restrictions on women's movements and activities in order to assure men's continued dominance. Isolation in a "menstrual hut" is often cited as a sign of lower status for women. This perspective ignores other factors, such as the role of religious beliefs. In addition, cross-culturally, and even within single cultures, menstrual taboos are highly variable. Rather than protecting a community from feminine evil, some cultural groups seem far more concerned with protecting a woman's vulnerable, procreative spirit. Among Buddhists in Sri Lanka,[1] women's menstruation is considered a threat to cosmic purity, so they are isolated; to Sri Lankan Catholics, menstruation is a sign of a woman's vulnerability, making isolation desirable. Their rituals, though similar in nature, mean something quite different to each group.

As for the menstrual hut, rather than a sign of oppression, it might also symbolize a sanctuary. Women of Mogmog Island in the Pacific atoll of Ulithi[2] spend their menstrual days in isolation, visiting with other women, resting, and weaving. They appear to enjoy the respite from hard work and from the care of children and men. Among the Kaska of western Canada[3] as well as other cultural groups, menstrual seclusion offers the women sexual autonomy and even opportunities for illicit affairs, so obviously some men do not heed the taboos. Perhaps the menstrual hut is not so much a decision of the community to segregate and suppress women, as it is a way for women to acquire some peace and relaxation.

The social functions of menstrual taboos appear to be culturally defined and specific to the needs and attitudes of each group. Some may see menstrual taboos as a way of subordinating women; others see it as a way for women to gain power and control over their lives. To suggest that menstrual taboos are a symbol of male dominance and oppression of women is perhaps partly true for some groups, but such a conclusion cannot be applied universally.

---

[1]Winslow, D. (1980). Rituals of first menstruation in Sri Lanka. *Man, 15,* 603–625 as cited in Buckley, T., & Gottlieb, A. (1988). A critical appraisal of theories of menstrual symbolism. In T. Buckley & A. Gottlieb (Eds.), *Blood magic: The anthropology of menstruation* (p. 10). Berkeley and Los Angeles: University of California Press.

[2]Patterson, C.B. (1986). In the far Pacific at the birth of nations. *National Geographic, 170* (4), 460–499, as cited in Buckley, T., & Gottlieb, A. (1988). A critical appraisal of theories of menstrual symbolism. In T. Buckley & A. Gottlieb (Eds.) *Blood magic: The anthropology of menstruation* (p. 12). Berkeley and Los Angeles: University of California Press.

[3]Honigmann, J.J. (1954). The Kaska Indians: An ethnographic reconstruction. *Publications in Anthropology* No. 51, as cited in Buckley, T., & Gottlieb, A. (1988). A critical appraisal of theories of menstrual symbolism. In T. Buckley & A. Gottlieb (Eds.), *Blood magic: The anthropology of menstruation* (p. 13). Berkeley and Los Angeles: University of California Press.

Sources:

Bonvillain, N. (1998). *Women and men: Cultural constructs of gender* (2nd ed.). Upper Saddle River, NJ: Prentice Hall.

Buckley, T., & Gottlieb, A. (1988). A critical appraisal of theories of menstrual symbolism. In T. Buckley & A. Gottlieb (Eds.), *Blood magic: The anthropology of menstruation*. Berkeley and Los Angeles: University of California Press.

sleep. Young men, in fulfillment of special vows to the Creator, had the muscles on their chests pierced and wooden skewers pushed through the wounds. Ropes, tied to the centre pole, were attached to the skewers. The men danced, and leaned back from the ropes until they tore free. The scars from this ordeal were proudly borne for the rest of their lives. The sun dance was also a time for people to strengthen their shared faith, visit friends, find spouses, gamble, and race horses.[13] Amendments to the 1876 Indian Act banned the sun dance in order to suppress aboriginal culture and hurry along assimilation policies. However, in 1951 a further amendment to the act reversed the ban on ceremonies like the sun dance. Today, the sun dance is still practised by some aboriginal peoples, such as the Crow, and is one of several expressions of traditional Crow culture.[14]

Rites of Intensification

Rites of intensification are rituals that mark occasions of crisis in the life of the group, rather than an individual. Whatever the precise nature of the crisis—a severe lack of rain that threatens crops in the fields, the sudden appearance of an enemy war party, the onset of an epidemic, or some other event that disturbs everyone—mass ceremonies are performed to allay the danger to the group. This unites people in a common effort so that fear and confusion yield to collective action and a degree of optimism. The balance in the relations of all concerned, which has been upset, is restored to normal, and the community values are celebrated and affirmed.

While death might be regarded as the ultimate crisis in an individual's life, it is, as well, a crisis for the entire group, particularly if the group is small. A member of the group has been lost and the group's equilibrium has been upset. The survivors, therefore, must readjust and restore balance. They also need to reconcile themselves to the loss of someone to whom they were emotionally tied. Funerary ceremonies, then, can be regarded as rites of intensification that permit the living to express in nondisruptive ways their upset over the death while providing for social readjustment. A frequent feature of such ceremonies is an ambivalence toward the dead person. Among some Melanesians, one part of the funerary rite was the eating of the dead person's flesh. This ritual cannibalism, witnessed by anthropologist Bronislaw Malinowski, was performed with "extreme repugnance and dread and usually followed by a violent vomiting fit. At the same time it is felt to be a supreme act of reverence, love and devotion."[15] This custom and the emotions accompanying it clearly reveal an ambiguous attitude toward death: On the one hand, the survivors desire to maintain the tie to the dead person, and, on the other hand, they feel disgust and fear at the transformation wrought by death. According to Malinowski, funeral ceremonies provide an approved collective means for individuals to express these feelings while maintaining social cohesiveness and preventing disruption of the culture.

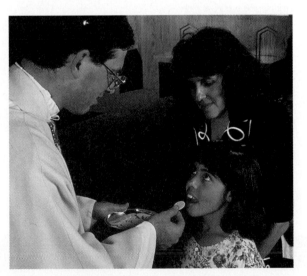

Ritual cannibalism appears in various societies in diverse forms. In Christianity, it is symbolic rather than actual, although some Christians believe the communion wafer actually becomes the body of Christ.

[13]McMillan, A.D. (1988). *Native peoples and cultures of Canada: An anthropological overview* (pp. 136–137). Vancouver: Douglas and McIntyre.

[14]Oswalt, W.H., & Neely, S. (1996). *This land was theirs: A study of North American Indians* (5th ed.). Mountain View, CA: Mayfield.

[15]Malinowski, B. (1954). *Magic, science and religion, and other essays* (p. 50). Garden City, NY: Doubleday/Anchor Books.

The performance of rites of intensification does not have to be limited to times of overt crisis. In regions where the seasons differ enough that human activities must change accordingly, they take the form of annual ceremonies. These are particularly common among horticultural and agricultural people, with their planting, first-fruit, and harvest ceremonies. For these critical times in the lives of people in such cultures, the ceremonies express a reverent attitude toward nature's forces of generation and fertility that people's very existence depends on. If all goes well, as it often does at such times, participation in a happy situation reinforces group involvement. It also serves as a kind of dress rehearsal for serious crisis situations; it promotes a habit of reliance on supernatural forces through ritual activity, which can be easily activated under stressful circumstances when it is important not to give way to fear and despair.

RELIGION, MAGIC, AND WITCHCRAFT

Among the most fascinating of ritual practices is the belief that supernatural powers can be compelled to act in certain ways for good or evil purposes by recourse to particular specified formulas. This is the classic anthropological notion of magic. Many cultures have magical rituals to ensure good crops, the replenishment of game, the fertility of domestic animals, and the avoidance or cure of illness in humans.

Although many Westerners have tried to suppress the existence of these fantastic notions in their own consciousness, they continue to be fascinated by them. Books and films about demonic possession and witchcraft are avidly devoured and discussed, and sales of Ouija boards and other occult paraphernalia like Tarot cards have increased dramatically in recent years. Thirty years ago few newspapers carried horoscope columns, but today virtually all Canadian daily newspapers regularly carry such columns. Although it is certainly true that non-Western and peasant peoples tend to endow their world quite freely with magical properties, so do many highly educated Western people. We will return to this topic later.

Queen Elizabeth II presides at the launching of a ship. Magic plays an important part in British ship-launching ceremonies, involving symbolic classification of the ship, the reincarnating power of the ship's name, and the relationship between women and ships. All play an important role in what sailors, including their officers, believe and how they act.

In the 19th century Sir James George Frazer, author of one of the most widely read anthropological books of all time, *The Golden Bough*, made a strong distinction between religion and magic. Religion he saw as "a propitiation or conciliation of powers superior to man which are believed to direct and control the course of nature and human life."[16] Magic, by contrast, he saw as an attempt to manipulate certain perceived "laws" of nature. The magician never doubts the same causes always will produce the same effects. Thus, Frazer saw magic as a sort of pseudo-science, differing from modern science only in its misconception of the nature of the particular laws that govern the succession of events.

Useful though Frazer's characterization of magic has been, anthropologists no longer accept his distinction between it and religion. Far from being separate, magical procedures frequently are part of religious rituals, and both magic and religion deal directly with the supernatural. In fact, Frazer's distinction seems to be no more than a bias of Western culture, which regards magic as quite separate from religion.

Frazer did make a useful distinction between two fundamental principles of magic. The first principle, that "like produces like," he called

---

[16]Frazer, J.G. (1931). Magic and religion. In V.F. Calverton (Ed.), *The making of man: An outline of anthropology* (p. 693). New York: Modern Library.

imitative magic. In Burma, for example, a rejected lover might engage a sorcerer to make an image of his would-be love. If this image were tossed into water, to the accompaniment of certain charms, the hapless girl would go mad. Thus, the girl would suffer a fate similar to that of her image.

Frazer's second principle was called **contagious magic**—the concept that things or persons once in contact can afterward influence one another. The most common example of contagious magic is the permanent relationship between an individual and any part of his or her body, such as hair, fingernails, or teeth. Frazer cites the Basutos of Lesotho, in southern Africa, who were careful to conceal their extracted teeth, because these might fall into the hands of certain mythical beings who could harm the owners of the teeth by working magic on them. Related to this is the custom, in Western societies, of treasuring objects that have been touched by special people.

Witchcraft

In Salem, Massachusetts, 200 suspected witches were arrested in 1692; of these, 19 were hanged and one was hounded to death. Despite the awarding of damages to descendants of some of the victims 19 years later, not until 1957 were the last of the Salem witches exonerated by the Massachusetts legislature. **Witchcraft** is an explanation of events based on the belief that certain individuals possess an innate psychic power capable of causing harm, including sickness and death. As you will see in the following examples, belief in witchcraft and fear of its practice has by no means disappeared in contemporary cultures. For example, as the Ibibio of Nigeria have become increasingly exposed to modern education and scientific training, their reliance on witchcraft as an explanation for misfortune has increased.[17] Furthermore, it is often the younger, more edu-

cated members of the Ibibio culture who accuse others of bewitching them. Frequently, the accused are the older, more traditional members; thus we have an expression of the intergenerational hostility that often exists in fast-changing traditional cultures.

Ibibio Witchcraft

Among the Ibibio, as among most peoples of sub-Saharan Africa, witchcraft beliefs are highly developed and long standing. A rat that eats up a person's crops is not really a rat but a witch that changed into one; if a young and enterprising man cannot get a job or fails an exam, he has been bewitched; and if a person becomes sick or is bitten by a snake, the reason is always the same—witchcraft. Indeed, virtually all misfortune, illness, and death are attributed to the malevolent activities of witches. The Ibibio's modern knowledge of such discoveries as the role that microorganisms play in disease has little impact; after all, it says nothing about why these were sent to the afflicted individual. Although Ibibio religious beliefs provide alternative explanations for misfortune, they carry negative connotations and do not elicit nearly as much sympathy from others. Thus, if evil befalls a person, witchcraft is a far more satisfying explanation than something such as filial disobedience or violation of some taboo.

---

[17]Offiong, D. (1985). Witchcraft among the Ibibio of Nigeria. In A. C. Lehmann & J.E. Myers (Eds.), *Magic, witchcraft and religion* (pp. 152–165). Palo Alto, CA: Mayfield.

Imitative magic. Magic based on the principle that like produces like. **> Contagious magic.** Magic based on the principle that beings once in contact can influence one another after separation. **> Witchcraft.** An explanation of events based on the belief that certain individuals possess an innate psychic power capable of causing harm, including sickness and death. Also includes beliefs and practices of benevolent magic.

Who are these Ibibio witches? They are thought to be males or females who have within them a special substance acquired from another established witch. This substance is made up of red, white, and black threads, needles, and other ingredients that a person acquires by swallowing it. From it comes a special power that causes harm, irrespective of whether its possessor intends to cause harm or not. The power is purely psychic, and Ibibio witches do not perform rites or make use of "bad medicine." It gives them the ability to change into animals, to travel any distance at incredible speed to get at their victims, whom they may torture or kill by transferring the victim's soul into an animal, which is then eaten.

To identify a witch, an Ibibio looks for any person whose behaviour is out of the ordinary, such as not being fond of greeting people; living alone in a place apart from others; charging too much for something; committing incest or adultery; walking alone at night; not showing sufficient grief upon the death of a relative or other community member; taking improper care of parents, children, or wives; and hardheartedness. Witches are apt to look and act mean and to be socially disruptive people in the sense that their behaviour exceeds the range of variance considered acceptable.

Neither the Ibibio in particular nor Africans in general are alone in attributing most malevolent happenings to witchcraft. Similar beliefs can be found in any human group, including North American cultures. As among the Ibibio, the powers (however they may be gained) are generally considered innate and uncontrollable; they result in activities that are the antithesis of proper behaviour, and persons displaying undesirable personality characteristics (however these may be defined) are generally the ones accused of being witches.

The Ibibio make a distinction between "black witches," whose acts are especially diabolical and destructive, and "white witches," whose witchcraft is relatively benign, even though their powers are thought to be greater than those of their black counterparts. This exemplifies a common distinction between what Lucy Mair, a British anthropologist, has dubbed "nightmare witches" and "everyday witches."[18] The nightmare witch is the

In North America, interest in and practice of neopagan religions, including Wicca, have grown significantly over the past 40 years, often among highly educated segments of society. Contrary to popular belief, Wicca, also know as witchcraft, is *not* concerned with working evil.

very embodiment of a culture's conception of evil, a being that flouts the rules of sexual behaviour and disregards every standard of decency. Nightmare witches, being almost literally the product of dreams and repressed fantasies, have much in common wherever they appear: The modern Navajo and the ancient Romans, like the Ibibio, conceived of witches who could turn themselves into animals and gather to feast on their victims. Everyday witches are often the community's nonconformists, who are morose, eat alone, are arrogant and unfriendly, but otherwise cause little trouble. Such witches may be dangerous when offended and retaliate by causing sickness, death, crop failure, cattle disease, or any number of lesser ills; hence people thought to be witches are treated cautiously and courteously.

The Functions of Witchcraft

Why witchcraft? We might better ask, why not? As Mair aptly observed, in a world where there are few proven techniques for dealing with everyday crises, especially sickness, a belief in witches is not foolish; it is indispensable. We do not resign ourselves to illness, and if the malady is

---

[18]Mair, L. (1969). *Witchcraft* (p. 37). New York: McGraw-Hill.

caused by a witch's hex, then magical counter-measures should cure it. Not only does the idea of personalized evil answer the problem of unmerited suffering, but it also provides an explanation for many happenings for which no cause can be discovered. Witchcraft, then, cannot be refuted. Even if we could convince a person that his or her illness was due to natural causes, the victim would still ask, as the Ibibio do, Why me? Why now? Such a view leaves no room for pure chance; everything must be assigned a cause or meaning. Witchcraft provides the explanation and, in so doing, also provides both the basis and the means for taking counteraction.

Nor is witchcraft always malevolent; even during the Spanish Inquisition, church officials recognized a benevolent variety. The positive functions of even malevolent witchcraft may be seen in many African cultures in which people believe sickness and death are caused by witches. The ensuing search for the perpetrator of the misfortune becomes, in effect, a communal probe into social behaviour.

A witch-hunt is, in fact, a systematic investigation, through a public hearing, into all social relationships involving the victim of the sickness or death. Was her husband unfaithful or her son lacking in the performance of his duties? Were her friends uncooperative, or was the victim guilty of any of these wrongs? Accusations are reciprocal, and before long just about every antisocial or hostile act that has occurred in that society since the last outbreak of witchcraft (sickness or death) is brought into the open.[19]

Through such periodic public scrutiny of everyone's behaviour, people are reminded of what their society regards as both strengths and weaknesses of character. This encourages individuals to suppress as best they can those personality traits looked upon with disapproval, for if they do not, they at some time may be accused of being a witch. A belief in witchcraft functions as a form of social control.

Psychological Functions of Witchcraft among the Navajo

The Navajo possess a detailed concept of witchcraft. Several types of witchcraft are distinguished. *Witchery* encompasses the practices of witches, who are said to meet at night to practise cannibalism and kill people at a distance. *Sorcery* is distinguished from witchery only by the methods used by the sorcerer, who casts spells on individuals using the victim's fingernails, hair, or discarded clothing. *Wizardry* is not distinguished so much by its effects as by its manner of working: Wizards kill by injecting a cursed substance, such as a tooth from a corpse, into the victim's body.

Whether or not a particular illness results from Navajo witchcraft is determined by **divination,** a magical procedure that also reveals the witch's identity. Once a person is charged with witchcraft, he or she is publicly interrogated, possibly even tortured, until there is a confession. It is believed the witch's own curse will turn against the witch once this happens, so it is expected the witch will die within a year. Some confessed witches have been allowed to live in exile.

According to Clyde Kluckhohn, Navajo witchcraft served to channel anxieties, tensions, and frustrations caused by the pressures from Anglo Americans.[20] The rigid rules of decorum among the Navajo allow little means for expressing hostility, except through accusations of witchcraft. Such accusations funnel pent-up negative emotions against individuals without upsetting the wider society. Another function of witchcraft accusations is they permit individuals to directly express hostile feelings against people toward whom they otherwise would be unable to express anger or enmity. On a more positive note, individuals strive to behave in ways that will prevent their being accused of witchcraft. Since excessive wealth is believed to result from witchcraft, individuals are encouraged to redistribute their assets among friends and relatives, thereby

[19]Turnbull, C.M. (1983). *The human cycle* (p. 181). New York: Simon & Schuster.

[20]Kluckhohn, C. (1944). Navajo witchcraft. *Papers of the Peabody Museum of American Archaeology and Ethnology,* 22 (2).

Divination. A magical procedure for determining the cause of a particular event, such as illness, or foretelling the future.

Anthropology **Applied**

James B. Waldram

Aboriginal Men and Traditional Healing in Canadian Prisons

Aboriginal men are overrepresented in Canadian prisons, both federally and provincially. In Saskatchewan, for instance, where the aboriginal population is approximately 10 percent, the aboriginal inmate population is over 40 percent. It is widely recognized that mainstream prison rehabilitation programs are less effective for aboriginal inmates, who often come from cultures very different from those of the treatment staff or who harbour long-standing, historic resentment toward those who try to change them—the legacy of more than a century of assimilationist policies.

Since the early 1980s, many aboriginal offenders have become increasingly involved in various forms of aboriginal spirituality and healing behind the walls, in an effort to reacquaint themselves with their spiritual traditions and undergo the rehabilitation that will allow them to lead productive lives upon release. The core of these programs has been the work of aboriginal elders and healers who engage in what anthropologists refer to as "symbolic healing," the construction, use, and manipulation of cultural symbols in the therapeutic process. Elements of symbolic healing can be found in all medical systems, including biomedicine. Many offenders have had little or no exposure to traditional forms of healing prior to incarceration, and the elders must engage them in a process of spiritual education. Various symbols are explained, and ceremonial and healing activities described.

One of the central symbolic systems is the sweat lodge. A healing facility common to many aboriginal groups in North America, the lodge is a dome-shaped structure constructed from tree branches and covered with a tarp to ensure an interior draped in total darkness during the ceremony. Individuals sit in a circle around a pit where heated stones are placed. Water poured on the stones creates intense heat and steam. During the ceremony, which frequently lasts for four rounds, the elders lead participants in singing, drumming, and prayer.

Individuals are free to disclose any thoughts or feelings they might have, secure in the knowledge that the lodge is a sacred place and what they say inside will not be repeated outside. Elders explain that the lodge represents the womb, and that the ceremony is a form of rebirth from which the individual emerges cleansed. Tobacco, burned inside and/or smoked in the ceremonial pipe, carries individuals' prayers to the Creator. Participation in the sweat lodge ceremony requires that the individual abstain from alcohol and drug use, a common problem within prisons. Scientists have tried to explain how the sweat lodge works, suggesting, for instance, that it may foster the release of endorphins, giving participants a euphoric feeling. The elders, however, believe that all healing comes from the Creator, and that they are simply the Creator's tools in this process.

Are these aboriginal healing programs effective? Not everyone agrees that they should exist in prison let alone that they might be beneficial. Unfortunately there are no data comparing the recidivism rates of men who have gone through these healing programs in prison. Anthropological research in prison, however, has documented some of the ways traditional healing is resulting in important behavioural changes. Many correctional staff believe that individuals working with the elders are less likely to engage in problematic behaviour while in prison, like fighting or drug abuse, and are more attentive in the mainstream programs that the prisons offer. The aboriginal inmates themselves who have become involved often present narratives documenting profound personal transformations. Individuals have been known to change from being intensely angry and violent threats to the security of the institutions to model inmates willing to work with others to further promote their healing. The elders have described many important changes they have witnessed in individuals, especially emerging patterns of altruism and respect for others. By examining the issue of therapeutic efficacy, the research has provided important information to all those involved in the rehabilitation of aboriginal inmates and has helped free up the necessary resources to allow the men to continue on their healing journeys.

Aboriginal healing programs in Canadian prisons may represent the best hope for these individuals to change the course of their lives and to reenter our communities with healthier attitudes toward themselves and others. Traditional healing works insofar as it helps these individuals understand their past as individuals and as aboriginal peoples; it reconnects them to their cultural and spiritual heritages; and it gives them both pride and hope for the future.

Source: Waldram, J.B. (1997). *The way of the pipe: Aboriginal spirituality and symbolic healing in Canadian prisons.* Peterborough, ON: Broadview Press.

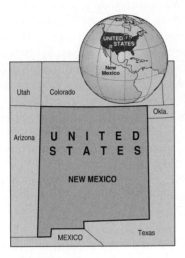

levelling economic differences. Similarly, because Navajos believe uncared-for elders will turn into witches, people are strongly motivated to take care of aged relatives. And because leaders are thought to be witches, people are understandably reluctant to go against their wishes, lest they suffer supernatural retribution.

Analyses such as these demonstrate that witchcraft, in spite of its often negative image, frequently functions in a very positive way to manage tensions within a group. Nonetheless, events may get out of hand, particularly in crisis situations, when widespread accusations may cause great suffering. This certainly was the case in the Salem witch trials, but even those pale in comparison to the 7 million accused and half a million individuals (more than 85 percent women) executed as witches in Europe from the 15th through 17th centuries. This was a time of profound change in European society, marked by a good deal of political and religious conflict. At such times, it is all too easy to search out scapegoats to blame for what people believe are undesirable changes.

Neo-Paganism

Anthropologists view renewed interest in paganism as a widespread cultural response to the decline in mainstream religions and a rising fear of pending ecological crises. Paganism is an alternative expression of spirituality that traces its roots to pre-Christian times. Modern pagan religions are referred to collectively as **neo-paganism.** Yet neo-pagan religions exhibit a great deal of variety, each religion possessing its own set of beliefs, rituals, and standards.

One of the better known and more recently revived neo-pagan religions is **Wicca.** Wicca, derived from the Anglo-Saxon word for witch, is the name given by its practitioners to the practice of witchcraft. The beliefs of most Wiccans involve elements of polytheism (worship of more than one supernatural being), and animism (recognition of the spirit values of everything in nature).[21]

Founded by Gerald Gardner in 1951, Wicca is a modern version of an ancient magical religion, although Wiccans believe their power comes from the inner self rather than the supernatural.[22] Gardner claimed to have been initiated

[21]Crowly, V. (1998). Wicca as nature religion. In J. Pearson, R.H. Roberts, & F. Samuel (Eds.), *Nature religion today: Paganism in the modern world.* Edinburgh: Edinburgh University Press.

[22]The material on Wicca is predominantly taken from Junker, K., & Vergara, V. (2001). *Religious movements homepage: Wicca.* Retrieved October 24, 2003, from the World Wide Web: http://religiousmovements.lib.virginia.edu/nrms/wicca/html.

Neo-paganism. Modern pagan religions. **> Wicca.** A neo-pagan belief system involving magic.

into the New Forest Coven in 1939, in which rituals and practices had been passed down from pre-Christian times, but he likely assembled ideas and practices from several old religions to create modern Wicca, which in turn has been revised to generate various Wiccan traditions. Wiccans are organized into covens (groups), typically led by a high priestess, although men also can lead and belong to covens. Each coven can trace its lineage, or line of teaching passed down by initiated priests and priestesses, to Gardner. Gardner recorded Wiccan beliefs, rituals, invocations, and charms in the *Book of Shadows*, to be shared only with those initiated into Wicca, but much of the history and practice of Wicca is passed down through oral traditions. A coven in Canada owns the original *Book of Shadows*.

Although traditional witchcraft, as discussed earlier, appears to be a negative force, Wicca is not concerned with doing evil or causing harm. Wicca is a "mystery" religion, requiring secret initiation rites to enter the coven, and coven members are ranked based on their level of training and skills in the craft. Wiccans believe in a balance between males and females, and worship two deities, Goddess and God. These deities appear in different forms, depending on the season; for example, there is a Corn God and a Great Mother Goddess. The covens live by three fundamental beliefs or laws. The first law, known as the Wiccan Rede, states, "An ye harm none, do what ye will." In other words, the practices of Wicca must not harm anyone. The second law, known as the Threefold Law, states that a person's deeds (good or bad) will return to the doer three times over. The third law concerns reincarnation, although there is some disagreement over the way reincarnation works. Some covens hold that a soul may continuously be reborn, others that once a soul learns all life's lessons, it earns eternal rest in Summerlands.

Ritual is an important component of Wicca. Wiccans do not have holy buildings; any place in contact with the earth will do for worship. Important symbols of Wicca are the broom, used for purifying an area before casting a circle, and the wand, cup, pentacle, and athame (a black-handled dagger), which represent the four elements: fire, water, earth, and air, respectively. Circle-casting begins with a Wiccan drawing a circle in the ground and purifying it. An altar is set up in the centre of the circle, where members perform magical and sacred rites by invoking the names of the Goddess and God and the powers of nature to create a Cone of Power. The rituals celebrate the processes of nature: conception, birth, mating, parenthood, maturation, and death.

There are three types of Wiccan gatherings: Sabbats, Esbats, and special-purpose gatherings. At special-purpose gatherings, a coven meets to deal with an issue needing immediate attention, such as casting a health spell. Most magical rites are performed at Esbats, small gatherings that correspond to the moon phases. Sabbats are large tribal festivals; in the 40 years since Wicca began in North America, a vast system of festivals and meetings has arisen.

A common misconception regarding Wicca, partly because Wiccans are referred to as witches, is that they worship Satan. Nothing could be further from the truth: Wiccans hold dear the values of truth, honesty, and integrity. They place a great deal of value on maintaining harmony with nature and are no more likely to commit evil than any other person. Wiccans in the old religion form were persecuted for centuries, particularly during the "Burning Times" in the 15th century, when the Christian Church in Europe spread misinformation about the Wiccan tradition and accused female practitioners of being Satanists. Thousands of accused witches were murdered even into the 18th century. Present-day Wiccans continue to be misunderstood, feared, and persecuted, owing in large part to ignorance about the religion. Female Wiccans also have been accused of being radical feminists, when in reality Wiccans are true feminists, believing in the equality and necessity of both males and females. Anthropologist Lauren Kendall notes, "Many witches, wizards, druids, Cabalists, and shamans . . . practice modern magic in contemporary England and the United States, where their ranks are comfortably reckoned in the tens of thousands. . . . The usual magician is ordinary, generally middle class, and often highly intelligent—a noticeable number of them have something to do with computers."[23] In Canada and the United States, Wiccan covens are

[23]Kendall, L. (1990, October). In the company of witches. *Natural History*, 92.

campaigning for their practitioners to be recognized as legitimate clergy.

Wicca is not the only form of neo-paganism gaining popularity; **reconstructionist religions** are modern-day revivals of ancient pagan religions.[24] These religions are usually polytheistic—members believe in several gods and goddesses. They also emphasize the importance of scholarship, relying on classical texts such as the Nordic Eddas to keep in touch with their cultural history. Magic tends to play a lesser role in reconstructionist religions than in Wicca. There are numerous forms of reconstructionist religions: çsatrœ (Nordic, Norse); Baltic; Celtic; Druidism; Hellenismos (Greek); Kemetism (Egyptian); and Slavic.

The Baltic reconstructionist religions of Lithuanian, Estonian, and Latvian peoples consider folklore and custom important in their practices and rituals. Through the centuries, the Baltic peoples have maintained their language, folklore, pagan beliefs, and customs. They consider nature a sacred force and value harmony within an individual, within society, and with the gods and ancestors.

Modern Druidism is a reconstruction of the wisdom, lore, and ritual of ancient Druids. Druids are polytheistic and follow a calendar based on the stages of the sun, earth, and moon. Druid lore was passed down through the ages by means of closely guarded oral history, but little is known of the ancient rites. Although neo-Druids can be either male or female, like Wicca, members are ranked based on years of training and acquired knowledge and expertise: Bards are the composers of verses and keepers of the lore; Ovates are the guardians and interpreters of the mysteries, as well as diviners. The highest ranking members are the Druids, who are advisers and authorities on worship, law, and ceremony.

Kemetism is associated with Egyptian gods and goddesses and the concept of *Ma'at* ("all") and *Netjer* ("the divine force"). The Kemetic religion is not polytheistic, although many deities are

acknowledged. It is more a monolatry—one god manifests many personalities and divinities. Kemetics have a vast array of rituals and offerings and value ancient texts and archaeological research to validate their beliefs.

Neo-pagan religions belong to an intricate system of nature religions that are finding an increasing audience among educated, successful urbanites worldwide. The reason for this acceptance of what in the past would have been considered corrupt reasoning is manifold, like the reasons for accepting other religions. As people search for answers to the "big" questions, such as the meaning of life, but also question the realities of their daily lives, neo-pagan religions are increasingly meeting their needs.

▲▽▲▽▲▽▲▽▲▽▲▽▲▽▲▽▲▽▲▽▲▽▲▽▲▽▲▽▲▽▲

THE FUNCTIONS OF RELIGION

Just as a belief in witchcraft may serve a variety of psychological and social functions, so too do religious beliefs and practices. One psychological function is to provide an orderly model of the universe. Beyond this, by explaining the unknown and making it understandable, religion reduces individuals' fears and anxieties. As we have seen, the explanations usually assume the existence of various sorts of supernatural beings and powers, which people may appeal to or manipulate. This being so, a means is provided for dealing with crises: Divine aid is, theoretically, available when all else fails.

A social function of religion is to sanction a wide range of conduct. In this context, religion plays a role in social control, which, as we saw in Chapter 11, does not rely on law alone. Right actions earn the approval of whatever supernatural powers a particular culture recognizes. Wrong actions may cause retribution through supernatural agencies. In short, by deliberately *raising* people's feelings of guilt and anxiety about their actions, religion helps keep them in line.

Religion does more than this, though; it sets precedents for acceptable behaviour. We have noted the connection between myths and religion. Usually, myths portray supernatural beings in ways that illustrate the culture's ethical code in action.

---

[24]The discussion of reconstructionist religions is taken from Walker, W. (2002). *Neo-Pagan, heathen and reconstructionist religions*. Retrieved October 23, 2003, from the World Wide Web: http://www.witchvox.com/basics/intro.html.

Reconstructionist religions.   Modern-day revivals of ancient pagan religions.

Members of the same religion may engage in, as well as suffer, persecution. In the former Yugoslavia, Roman Catholic Croats and Eastern Orthodox Serbs fought each other, while both fought Islamic Bosnians. In the Middle East, at the same time that Jews are the victims of violence from Islamic fundamentalists, Israeli security forces have directed violence against Muslims.

So it is that Napi (also known as Nanabush in other First Nations groups), the Blackfoot trickster, is portrayed in the Blackfoot myths as tricking and punishing youths who mock others, lie, are greedy, or go in for extremes of behaviour. Moreover, the specific situations serve to teach the youth of the tribe appropriate behaviour in similar circumstances. The Bible's Old and New Testaments are rich in the same sort of material. Through the models it presents and the morals it espouses, religion serves to justify and perpetuate a particular social order. Thus, in the Jewish, Christian, and Islamic traditions, a masculine-authoritarian godhead along with a creation story that portrays a woman as responsible for a fall from grace serves to justify a social order where men exercise control over women.

A psychological function also is tied up in all this. A society's moral code, since it is considered divinely fixed, lifts the burden of responsibility for conduct from the shoulders of an individual. It can be a tremendous relief to people to believe that the responsibility for the way things are rests with the gods, rather than with themselves, and that the burden of decision making can be transferred to the divine.

Religion helps maintain social solidarity within a group. Participation in rituals, coupled with a basic uniformity of beliefs, helps to bind people together and reinforce their identification with their group. Particularly effective may be their participation together in rituals, when the atmosphere is charged with emotion. The exalted feelings people may experience in such circum-

stances serve as a positive reinforcement in that they feel good as a result. Here, once again, we find religion providing psychological assurance while providing for the needs of society.

One other area where religion serves a social function is education. In our discussion of rites of passage, we noted that Australian puberty rites served as a kind of cram course in tribal lore. By providing a memorable occasion, initiation rites can enhance learning and thus help ensure the perpetuation of a nonliterate culture's knowledge and history. And as we saw in the female initiation rites among the Mende, these rituals can serve to ensure individuals have the knowledge they will need to fulfill their adult roles. Education also may be served by rites of intensification. Frequently, such rites involve dramas that portray matters of cultural importance. For example, among a food-foraging people, dances may imitate the movement of game and techniques of hunting. Among farmers a fixed round of ceremonies may emphasize the steps necessary for good crops. These rites help preserve knowledge important to a people's material well-being.

RELIGION AND CULTURAL CHANGE

Although the subject of culture change is taken up in a later chapter, no anthropological consideration of religion is complete without some mention of *revitalization movements*. In 1931, at Buka in the Solomon Islands, a religious cult suddenly emerged, its prophets predicting that a deluge would soon engulf all Whites. This would be followed by the arrival of a ship laden with European goods. The believers were to construct a storehouse for the goods and to prepare themselves to repulse the colonial police. Because the ship would arrive only after the islanders had used up all their own supplies, they ceased working in the fields. Although the cult leaders were arrested, the movement continued for some years.

This was not an isolated instance. Such "cargo cults"—and many other movements promising the resurrection of the dead, the destruction or enslavement of Europeans, and the coming of utopian riches—have sporadically appeared throughout Melanesia for a hundred years or more. Since these cults are widely separated in space and time, their similarities are apparently the result of similar social conditions. In these areas the traditional cultures of the indigenous peoples have been uprooted. Europeans, or European-influenced Melanesians, hold all political and economic power. Melanesians are employed unloading and distributing Western-made goods but have no practical knowledge of how to attain these goods.

Shown here is a member of the Raelians, a "New Age" revitalization movement that believes in the future arrival of wise space beings who will inspire a new spiritual awareness in human beings.

When cold reality offers no respite from the daily frustrations of cultural deterioration and economic deprivation, religion offers the solution.

Revitalization Movements

From the 1890 Ghost Dance of many North American aboriginals to the Mau Mau of Kenya to the "cargo cults" of Melanesia, religious reactions to European domination are so common that anthropologists have sought to formulate their underlying causes and general characteristics. Yet **revitalization movements,** as they are now called, are by no means restricted to the colonial world; in North America alone hundreds of such movements have sprung up. Among the more widely known are Mormonism, which began in the 19th century; the more recent Unification Church of the Reverend Sun Myung Moon; the Branch Davidians whose "prophet" was David Koresh; and the Heaven's Gate cult led by Marshall Herf Applewhite and Bonnie Lu Trousdale Nettles. As these four examples suggest, revitalization movements show a great deal of diversity, and some have been much more successful than others.

A revitalization movement is a deliberate effort by members of a culture to construct a more satisfying culture based on an idealized past. The movement is usually led by a visionary or messiah. The emphasis in this definition is on the reformation not just of the religious sphere of activity but also of the entire cultural system. Such a drastic solution is attempted when a group's anxiety and frustration have become so intense that the only way to reduce the stress is to overturn the entire social system and replace it with a new one.

Given the numerous sources of anxiety in North American society today, ranging from science and technology to what many regard as a breakdown of the family and morality, we may expect to see a propagation of various revitalization movements for the next few years. Although periods of 1000 years (millennia) have no relationship whatever to any astronomical cycle, numbers have their own fascination in the seemingly magical ways they can be manipulated. In

---

Revitalization movements.   Social movements, often of a religious nature, with the purpose of totally reforming a society.

In the United States, Mormonism is an example of a revitalization movement that is enormously successful in gaining acceptance in the wider society. By contrast, the Branch Davidians so antagonized elements of mainstream society that a confrontation occurred, ending with the mass immolation of many cult members.

this case, the completely arbitrary unit of 1000 years is fused with apocalyptic Christian beliefs to predict an imminent destruction of the present world. Oddly, the recent millennium change produced relatively few millenarian movements.

Anthropologist Anthony Wallace has outlined a sequence common to all expressions of the revitalization process.[25] First is the normal state of society, in which stress is low and sufficient cultural means of satisfying needs exist. Under certain conditions, such as domination by a more powerful group or severe economic depression, stress and frustration are steadily amplified; this ushers in the second phase, or the period of increased individual stress. If there are no significant adaptive changes, a period of cultural distortion follows, in which stress becomes so chronic that socially approved methods of releasing tension begin to break down. This steady deterioration of the culture may be checked by a period of revitalization, during which a dynamic cult or religious movement grips

a sizable proportion of the population. Often the movement will be so out of touch with reality that it is doomed to failure from the beginning. This was the case with the Heaven's Gate cult, because its followers self-destructed from suicide based on a conviction their spiritual essences would reunite with extraterrestrials in a spaceship that awaited them behind the tail of the Hale-Bopp comet to take them "home." This self-destruction was the case also with the Branch Davidians, when the suspicions of government authorities led to an assault on the cult's compound. In reaction, cult members committed mass suicide by deliberately immolating themselves in their headquarters.

More rarely, a movement may tap long-dormant adaptive forces underlying a culture, and an enduring religion may result. Such is the case with Mormonism. Although heavily persecuted at first and hounded from place to place, Mormons adapted to the point that their religion thrives in the United States today. Indeed, revitalization movements lie at the root of all known religions, Judaism, Christianity, and Islam included.

[25]Wallace, A.F.C. (1970). *Culture and personality* (2nd ed., pp. 191–196). New York: Random House.

CHAPTER SUMMARY

Religion is a part of all cultures. It consists of beliefs and behaviour patterns by which people try to control areas of their world otherwise beyond their control. Among food-foraging peoples, religion is a basic ingredient of everyday life. As societies become more complex, religion is less a part of daily activities and tends to be restricted to particular occasions.

Religion is characterized by a belief in supernatural beings and forces. Through prayer, sacrifice, and other religious rituals, people appeal to the supernatural world for aid. Supernatural beings may be grouped into three categories: major deities (gods and goddesses), ancestral spirits, and other sorts of spirit beings. Gods and goddesses are the greatest but most remote beings. They are usually thought of as controlling the universe or a specific part of it. Animism is a belief in spirit beings, other than ancestors, who are believed to animate all of nature. Animism is typical of peoples who see themselves as a part of nature rather than as superior to it. A belief in ancestral spirits is based on the idea that human beings are made up of a body and a soul. At death the spirit is freed from the body and continues to participate in human affairs. Animatism is a force or power directed to a successful outcome and may make itself manifest in any object. Myths serve to rationalize religious beliefs and practices.

All human cultures have specialists—priests and priestesses and/or shamans—to guide religious practices and to intervene with the supernatural world. Shamanism, with its often dramatic ritual, promotes a release of tension among members of a group. The shaman can help maintain social control.

Religious rituals reinforce social bonds. Rites of passage mark the stages in an individual's life. Rites of intensification are rituals to mark crisis occasions in the life of the group rather than the individual. They serve to unite people, allay fear of the crisis, and prompt collective action. Funerary ceremonies are rites of intensification that provide for social readjustment after the loss of the deceased. Rites of intensification also may involve annual ceremonies to seek favourable conditions surrounding critical activities such as planting and harvesting.

Ritual practices of peasant and non-Western peoples are often an expression of the belief they can force supernatural powers to act in certain ways with certain prescribed formulas. This is the classic anthropological notion of magic. Sir James Frazer differentiated two principles of magic: "like produces like," or imitative magic, and the law of contagion.

Witchcraft functions as an effective way for people to explain away personal misfortune. Even malevolent witchcraft may function positively in the realm of social control. It also may provide an outlet for feelings of hostility and frustration without disturbing the norms of the larger group. Neo-pagan religions, such as Wicca, are modern manifestations of ancient nature religions.

Religion (including magic and witchcraft) serves several important social functions. First, it sanctions a wide range of conduct by providing notions of right and wrong. Second, it sets precedents for acceptable behaviour and helps perpetuate an existing social order. Third, religion serves to lift the burden of decision making from individuals and places responsibility with the gods. Fourth, religion plays a large role in maintaining social solidarity. Finally, religion serves education. Ritual ceremonies enhance learning of tribal lore and thus help to ensure the perpetuation of a nonliterate culture.

Revitalization movements are a response by non-Western cultures to Western interference and domination. In the islands of Melanesia, these take the form of cargo cults that have appeared spontaneously at different times since the beginning of the 20th century. Anthony Wallace has interpreted revitalization movements as attempts to change the society. Regardless of where they appear, revitalization movements follow a common sequence. Islam, Judaism, and Christianity stem from such movements.

QUESTIONS FOR CRITICAL THOUGHT

1. Many have felt that with the advance of technology and Western scientific investigation, "irrational" religious beliefs gradually would fade away to be replaced by "logical knowledge." Has this been the case? Is it ever likely to occur? Why or why not?

2. What is the purpose of myths? What is their relationship to social organization? How do the functions of myths compare with those of "history" in various societies?

3. How do we in the West regard menstruation—as unclean, something to hide, "the curse," or as a natural symbol of womanhood? As a woman, do you feel comfortable discussing your menstrual cycle with men present? As a man, do you feel comfortable hearing about a woman's menstrual cycle?

4. How does spiritual revival among First Nations groups serve to strengthen their cultural identity?

5. Research a contemporary neo-pagan religion. What are the basic tenets of this religion? What purposes and needs does this religion fulfill? Why do you think neo-pagan religions are becoming increasingly popular in Western societies?

INTERNET RESOURCES

Warriors of the Amazon
http://www.pbs.org/wgbh/nova/shaman/index.html
This site provides links to other pages that tell the story of Yanomami shamans.

Religions of the World
http://www.geocities.com/athens/forum/8424/religion.html
This site contains a description of many religions, past and present, such as Mormonism, Confucianism, Christianity, and Islam, as well as worldviews such as agnosticism and atheism.

The Ute Sun Dance
http://www.southern-ute.nsn.us/culture/sun.html
A description of the sun dance in Colorado.

An Introduction to the World Religions
http://134.29.9.229/cultural/religion/index.shtml
Links to Islam, Judaism, Buddhism, Animism, Christianity, and Hinduism.

Religions of the World
http://www.wcc-coe.org/wcc/links/religs.html
Some less-studied religions, including African traditional religion, Baha'i faith, Buddhism, Hinduism, Shintoism, and Taoism.

Religion
http://www.willinet.net/~dfarnham/cultural_anthropology/religion.html
An outline by anthropologist Clifford Geertz defining religion, belief systems, religious specialists, ritual, magic and witchcraft, and sorcery.

Salem Witch Trials
http://www.salemweb.com/memorial/default.htm
A riveting account of the trial of Sarah Good for witchcraft. Also provides a link to the Witch Trials Memorial, which reminds us that these women were real people.

Wicca
http://1734.net/index2.html
An information site that introduces the ancient religion of Wicca. Should dispel some misconceptions about the religion.

http://religiousmovements.lib.virginia.edu/nrms/wicca.html
An extensive site with historical, religious, and social information on Wicca and neo-paganism.

SUGGESTED READINGS

Guenther, M. (1999). *Tricksters and trancers: Bushman religion and society.* Bloomington and Indianapolis, IL: Indiana University Press.

Although this extensive examination of Ju/'hoansi mythology and cosmology is fairly academic, there is some interesting information on Ju/'hoansi beliefs about tricksters and trancers.

Kalwet, H. (1988). *Dreamtime and inner space: The world of the shaman.* New York: Random House.

Written by an ethnopsychologist, this book surveys the practices and paranormal experiences of healers and shamans from Africa, the Americas, Asia, and Australia.

Lehmann, A.C., & Myers, J.E. (Eds.). (1993). *Magic, witchcraft and religion: An anthropological study of the supernatural* (3rd ed.). Mountain View, CA: Mayfield.

This anthology of readings is cross-cultural in scope, covering traditional as well as nontraditional themes. Well represented are both "tribal" and "modern" religions. It is a good way to discover the relevance and vitality of anthropological approaches to the supernatural.

Pearson, J., Roberts, R.H., & Samuel, G. (Eds.). (1998). *Nature religion today: Paganism in the modern world.* Edinburgh: Edinburgh University Press.

This is a well-written, fascinating look at contemporary neo-pagan religions, including Druidism, Wicca, and New Age. The articles in the book examine these religions from an anthropological, sociological, and historical perspective, and some of the contributors are practising neo-pagans.

Ridington, R. (1988). *Trail to heaven: Knowledge and narrative in a northern native community.* Vancouver: Douglas and McIntyre.

This book describes moments in the life of a northern Beaver (Dane-zaa) community from the point of view of Ridington's experiences in the community. The author reflects on the prevailing philosophy of anthropology while examining the complex belief systems of the Dane-zaa.

Wallace, A.F.C. (1966). *Religion: An anthropological view.* New York: Random House.

This is a classic textbook treatment of religion by an anthropologist who has specialized in the study of revitalization movements.

CNN TODAY VIDEOS

***Harry Potter* Witchcraft Controversy (CNN Cultural Anthropology, vol. 6, 2:43)**
A family fights against the reading of *Harry Potter* in the classroom, claiming that the books violate the separation of church and state principle and that the popular series teaches witchcraft.

Curious Cures (CNN Cultural Anthropology, vol. 4, 2:23)
In many cultures, folk remedies are still widely practised along with modern medicine.

China's Last Remaining Shamans (CNN Cultural Anthropology, vol. 2, 2:44)
The traditional languages and customs of China's many ethnic minorities were virtually wiped out during the Cultural Revolution of the 1960s.

Today the Chinese government is attempting to preserve the traditions of some of its ethnic minorities.

Ramadan Nights (CNN Cultural Anthropology, vol. 1, 1:41)
This segment looks at the many activities Islamic believers engage in after sundown during Ramadan.

Buffalo (CNN Cultural Anthropology, vol. 1, 2:29)
This video clip examines the importance the buffalo continues to play in Lakota culture.

Yugoslavia Religion (CNN Cultural Anthropology, vol. 2, 2:14)
This segment covers the religious background of the Kosovo crisis.

Chapter 13

The Arts

No known culture is without some form of art, even though that art may be applied to purely utilitarian objects. This Inuk soapstone carving, from Holman, on Victoria Island in the Northwest Territories, is one expression of the universal urge for artistic creation.

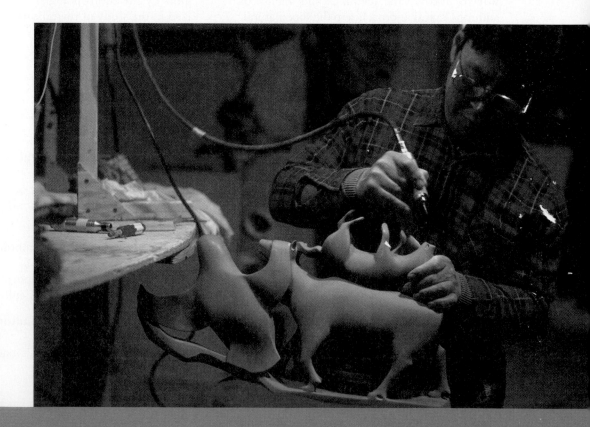

Chapter Preview

1. What Is Art?

Art is the creative use of the human imagination to interpret, understand, and enjoy life. Although the idea of art serving nonuseful, nonpractical purposes seems firmly entrenched in the thinking of modern Western peoples, in other cultures art often serves what are regarded as important, practical purposes.

2. Why Do Anthropologists Study Art?

Anthropologists have found that art reflects a people's cultural values and concerns. This is especially true of the verbal arts—myths, legends, and tales. From these the anthropologist may learn how a people order their world and may discover much about the history of a culture. As well, art, no matter the medium, may provide insights into values, benefits, and worldview and may suggest things about a people's history.

3. What Are the Functions of the Arts?

Aside from adding pleasure to everyday life, the various arts serve a number of functions. Myths, for example, set standards for orderly behaviour, and the verbal arts generally transmit and preserve a culture's customs and values. Songs, too, may do this within the restrictions musical form imposes. The visual arts provide an avenue for interpreting historical events and preserve traditional crafts. Artistic expression promotes cultural identity and a sense of pride in one's cultural heritage; this is exemplified by body art in all its forms. For many indigenous groups, such as the Inuit, artwork provides significant economic value.

CHAPTER OUTLINE

The Anthropological Study of Art

Verbal Arts

Anthropology Applied: Protecting Cultural Heritages

Original Study: The Mock Wedding: Folk Drama in the Prairie Provinces

The Art of Music

Visual Art

Gender Perspectives: On Being a Man

Body Art

Censorship

In North America, the arts often are seen as something of a frill, something to be engaged in for personal enjoyment apart from more productive pursuits or to provide pleasure for others, or both. This attitude becomes apparent whenever public funds are in short supply; on the local level, for example, in battles over school budgets, art programs are often the first to be cut. Unlike sports, which usually are supported more than the arts because they are perceived as providing skills thought to be essential to success in a competitive world, the arts are seen as nonessential: pleasurable and worthwhile but expensive, with little practical payoff. On the national level, fiscal conservatives labour to cut back government funding for the arts, on the premise the arts lack the practical importance of defence, economic, or other governmental activities. Indeed, artists and their supporters are seen as something of an elite, subsidized at the expense of hard-working "practical" people. And yet the calls to protect Canada's cultural heritage, especially in light of strong influences from U.S. media, are equally vociferous. Canada has a long tradition of public funding and support for the arts. Canadians take great pride in their visual, literary, and performing arts, and hold artistic expression as one essence of a distinct Canadian culture.

The fact is artistic behaviour is far from unimportant and is as basic to human expression as language. Just as speech is used to communicate feelings, to make statements, so too is artistic expression. And just as free speech is considered a fundamental right of all Canadians, so too is artistic freedom. Moreover, art is not created only by a special category of persons called "artists"; for example, all human beings adorn their bodies in certain ways and by doing so make a statement about who they are, both as individuals and as members of social groups. Similarly, all people tell stories, in which they express their values, their hopes, and their concerns and thus reveal much about themselves and the nature of the world as they see it. Artistic expression reflects and shapes our social structure and cultural identity, and in many cases serves to promote each cultural group's uniqueness of expression. In short, all peoples engage in artistic behaviour as they use their imagination creatively to interpret, understand, and enjoy life. What's more, they have been doing this for at least 40 000 years, if not longer. Far from a luxury afforded or appreciated by a minority of aesthetes or escapists, art is a necessary kind of social behaviour every human being participates in.

The idea of art serving nonuseful, nonpractical purposes seems firmly entrenched in the

Perhaps the oldest means of artistic expression is body decoration. Shown here are a Moroccan woman whose hands and feet are dyed with henna (to celebrate a royal wedding) and a tattooed Asian man.

thinking of modern Western peoples. Today, for example, objects from the tomb of the young Egyptian king Tutankhamen are on display in a museum, where they may be seen and admired as the exquisite works of art they are. They were made, however, to be hidden away from human eyes, where they were to guarantee the eternal life of the king and to protect him from evil forces that might enter his body and gain control over it. Or we may listen to the singing of a sea chantey purely for aesthetic pleasure, as a form of entertainment. In fact, in earlier days sea chanteys set the appropriate rhythm for performance of specific shipboard tasks, and the same qualities that make them pleasurable to listen to today served to relieve the boredom of those tasks. Such links between art and other aspects of life are common in human groups around the world.

Westerners distinguish between *fine art*—art that is expensive, produced by formally trained artists, and difficult to acquire—and *pop* or *folk art*—art that is easy to acquire, produced by ordinary people, and not that highly valued. Yet folk art continues to thrive. Because art, like any aspect of culture, is inextricably intertwined with everything else people do, it affords us glimpses into other aspects of our lives, including human values and worldviews.

To people today, making exquisite objects of gold and precious stones to place in a tomb might seem like throwing them away. Yet something similar happens when a Navajo artist creates an intricate sand painting as part of a ritual act, only to destroy it once the ritual is over. Johann Sebastian Bach did the very same thing when, almost 300 years ago, he composed his cantatas

Much of the world's art is created for functional rather than aesthetic purposes. Shown here, counterclockwise, are examples of art used in healing and blessing ceremonies (a Navajo sand painting), to express cultural identity (Carabana Festival), and for political purposes (graffiti from Katatura, Namibia).

for church services. These compositions were "throwaway" music, meant to be discarded after the services they were written for. That many of them are still performed today is something of an accident, for Bach did not compose them for posterity. In many human societies, creating the art is often of greater importance than the final product itself.

Whether a particular work of art is intended to be appreciated purely as such or to serve some practical purpose, it will in every case require the same special combination of the symbolic representation of form and the expression of feeling that constitute the creative imagination. Insofar as the creative use of the human ability to symbolize is universal and both expresses and is shaped by cultural values and concerns, it is an important subject for anthropological study.

As an activity or kind of behaviour that contributes to human well-being and that helps give shape and significance to life, art must be related to, yet differentiated from, religion. The dividing line between the two is not distinct: It is not easy to say, for example, precisely where art stops and religion begins in an elaborate ceremony involving ornamentation, masks, costumes, songs, dances, myths, and effigies. And like magic, music, dance, and other arts may be used to "enchant"—to exploit the innate or psychological biases of another person or group so as to cause them to perceive social reality in a way favourable to the interests of the "enchanter." Indeed, the arts may be used to manipulate a seemingly inexhaustible list of human passions, including desire, terror, wonder, cupidity, fantasy, and vanity.[1]

Defining art is a difficult task. In a very broad sense, art is a creative means for expressing symbolic thought, for using our human imagination to interpret, understand, and enjoy life. Art embraces many forms of symbolic expression, from the visual, performing, and literary arts as broad categories, to more specific artistic media, such as body or decorative art, painting, sculpture, folk music, square dancing, opera, oral his-

Use of art to enchant: By singing to her child, this mother soothes and at the same time promotes the kind of behaviour she wants from her child.

tories, graffiti, and poetry. We will examine some of these media later in this chapter.

What constitutes art varies, depending on factors such as audience expectations, and what is considered art in one context may be considered non-art in another. Negative reactions to forms of artistic expression often arise when the message is misunderstood. A case in point is the 1990 video "We're Talking Vulva" by Lorri Milan and Shawna Dempsey of Winnipeg. The immensely popular video has been shown on rock video stations around the world to an estimated million viewers. The video was screened at the Third International Istanbul Biennial, one of seven entries chosen to represent Canada.[2] And yet, when the same video was shown in 2001 to high school students specializing in art, parents protested.

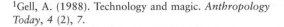

[1]Gell, A. (1988). Technology and magic. *Anthropology Today, 4* (2), 7.

[2]Medusa, M. (1994). *Shawna Dempsey and Lorri Milan.* Retrieved July 4, 2001, from the World Wide Web: http://www.oboro.net/en/exhib9394/dempsey.htm.

▲▽▲▽▲▽▲▽▲▽▲▽▲▽▲▽▲▽▲▽▲▽▲▽▲▽▲

THE ANTHROPOLOGICAL STUDY OF ART

When approaching art as a cultural phenomenon, anthropologists have the pleasant task of cataloguing, photographing, recording, and describing all possible forms of imaginative activity in any particular culture. An enormous variety of forms and modes of artistic expression exist in the world. Because people everywhere continue to create and develop in new directions, no point of diminishing returns is foreseeable for the interesting process of collecting and describing the world's ornaments, body decorations, variations in clothing, blanket and rug designs, pottery and basket styles, architectural embellishments, monuments, ceremonial masks, legends, work songs, dances, and other art forms. The collecting process, however, eventually must lead to some kind of analysis and generalizations about relationships between art and the rest of culture.

Anthropologists examine how people express their social structure and cultural patterns through art, and how these traditional artistic expressions change through time. Anthropologists studying art consider the artist who creates the art, the meaning or symbol of the art, and its importance within a culture or society. For example, the perception of status differences in Western art goes beyond the product, to the artist. Just as fine art holds a higher position in Western society than folk art, a financially successful painter or sculptor possesses more prestige than the rural woman who makes quilts and sells them at local country fairs, yet each is an artist.

A good way to begin a study of the relationships between art and the rest of culture is to examine critically some of the generalizations already made about specific arts. Since it is impossible to cover all art forms in the space of a single chapter, we shall concentrate on just a few: verbal arts, music, visual art, and body art.

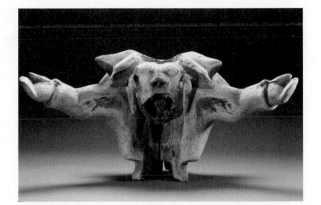

Among the Inuit, the artist does not impose his or her will on the medium, but rather seeks to help what is already there to emerge from hiding. Shown here is a whalebone carving, entitled *Shaman,* by Markosee Karpik of Pangnirtung, Nunavut, and acquired by the Art Gallery of Ontario in 1988.

▲▽▲▽▲▽▲▽▲▽▲▽▲▽▲▽▲▽▲▽▲▽▲▽▲▽▲

VERBAL ARTS

The term **folklore** was coined in the 19th century to denote the unwritten stories, beliefs, and customs of European peasantry, as opposed to the traditions of the literate elite. The subsequent study of folklore, **folkloristics,** has become a discipline allied to but somewhat independent of anthropology, working on cross-cultural comparisons of themes, motifs, genres, and structures from a literary as well as ethnological point of view. Many linguists and anthropologists prefer to speak of a culture's oral traditions and verbal arts rather than its folklore and folktales, recognizing that creative verbal expression takes many forms and that the implied distinction between folk and "fine" art is a projection of the recent attitude of European (and European-derived) cultures onto others.

The verbal arts include narratives, dramas, poetry, incantations, proverbs, riddles, word games, and even naming procedures, compliments, and insults, when these take structured and special forms. Narratives seem to be one of the

---

Folklore.   A 19th-century term first used to refer to the traditional oral stories and sayings of European peasants and later extended to traditions preserved orally in all societies. **> Folkloristics.**   The study of folklore (as linguistics is the study of language).

Anthropology **Applied**

Protecting Cultural Heritages

In these first years of the 21st century, the time is long past when the anthropologist could go out and describe small tribal groups in out-of-the-way places that had not been "contaminated" by contact with Western people. Not only do few such groups exist in the world today, but also those that do remain face strong pressures to abandon their traditional ways in the name of "progress." All too often, tribal peoples are made to forfeit their indigenous identity and are pressed into a mould that allows them neither the opportunity nor the motivation to rise above the lowest rung of the social ladder. From an autonomous people able to provide for their own needs, with pride and a strong sense of identity as a people, they are transformed into a deprived underclass with neither pride nor a sense of identity, often despised by more fortunate members of some multinational state in which they live.

The basic rights of groups of people to be themselves and to retain their distinctive cultural identities are and should be our paramount consideration and will be dealt with in the final chapter of this book. However, anthropologists have additional reasons to be concerned about the disappearance of the societies and traditions they study. For one thing, the need for information about them has become steadily more apparent. If we are ever to have a realistic understanding of that elusive thing called human nature, we need reliable data on all humans. More is involved than this, though; once a traditional society is gone, it is lost to humanity, unless an adequate record of it exists. When a culture is lost without records of it, humanity is the poorer for the loss. Hence, anthropologists have in a sense rescued many such societies from oblivion. This not only helps to preserve the human heritage, but it also may be important to an ethnic group that, having become Westernized, wishes to rediscover and reassert its past cultural identity. Better yet, of course, is to find ways to prevent the loss of cultural traditions and societies in the first place.

To the Pomo Indians of California, the art of basket making has been important for their sense of who they are since before the coming of European settlers. Recognized for their skilled techniques and aesthetic artistry, Pomo baskets—some of the finest in the world—are prized by museums and private collectors alike. Nevertheless, the art of Pomo basket making was threatened in the 1970s by the impending construction of the Warm Springs Dam–Lake Sonoma Project to the north of San Francisco. The effect of this project would be to wipe out virtually all existing habitat for a particular species of sedge essential for the weaving of Pomo baskets.

Accordingly, a coalition of archaeologists, Native Americans, and others with objections to the project brought suit in federal district court. As it happened, the U.S. Army Corps of Engineers had recently hired anthropologist Richard N. Lerner for its San Francisco District Office to advise on sociocultural factors associated with water resources programs in northwestern California. One of Lerner's first tasks, therefore, was to undertake studies of the problem and to find ways to overcome it.[1]

After comprehensive archaeological, ethnographic, and other studies were completed in 1976, Lerner succeeded in having the Pomo basketry materials recognized by the National Register of Historic Places as "historic property," requiring the Corps of Engineers to find ways to mitigate the adverse impact dam construction would have. The result was a complex ethnobotanical project developed and implemented by Lerner. Working in concert with Pomo Indians as well as botanists, Lerner relocated 48 000 sedge plants onto nearly three acres of suitable lands downstream from the dam. By the fall of 1983, the sedge was doing well enough to be harvested and proved to be of excellent quality. Since this initial harvest, groups of weavers have returned each year, and the art of Pomo Indian basket making appears to be safe for the time being.

[1]Lerner, R.N. (1987). Preserving plants for Pomos. In R.M. Wulff & S.J. Fiske (Eds.), *Anthropological praxis: Translating knowledge into action* (pp. 212–222). Boulder, CO: Westview.

easiest kinds of verbal arts to record or collect. Perhaps because they also are the most publishable, with popular appeal in North American society, they have received the most study and attention. Generally, narratives have been divided into three basic and recurring categories: myth, legend, and tale.

Myths

The word *myth,* in popular usage, refers to something that is widely believed to be true but probably is not. Actually, a true myth, as discussed in Chapter 12, provides a rationale for religious beliefs and practices. One of the most common types of myths is the origin or creation myth that explains the beginnings of all things. A typical origin myth traditional with the Western Abenaki of northwestern New England and southern Quebec follows:

> In the beginning, *Tabaldak,* "The Owner," created all living things but one—the spirit being who was to accomplish the final transformation of the earth. Man and woman *Tabaldak* made out of a piece of stone, but he didn't like the result, their hearts being cold and hard. This being so, he broke them up, and their remains today can be seen in the many stones that litter the landscape of the Abenaki homeland. But *Tabaldak* tried again, this time using living wood, and from them came all later Abenakis. Like the trees from which the wood came, these people were rooted in the earth and (like trees when being blown by the wind) could dance gracefully. [3]

Such a myth, insofar as it is believed, accepted, and perpetuated in a culture, may be said to express a worldview: the unexpressed but implicit conceptions of their place in nature and of the limits and workings of their world. Extrapolating from the details of the myth, we might conclude that the Abenaki recognize a kinship among all living things; after all, they were all part of the same creation, and humans even were made from living wood. Moreover, an attempt to make them of nonliving stone was not satisfactory. This idea of a closeness among all living things led the Abenaki to show special respect to the animals they hunted; after killing a beaver, muskrat, or waterfowl, the hunter must show respect by returning the bones to the water, with a request to continue its kind. Failure to respect animals' rights would result in their unwillingness to continue sacrificing their lives that people might live.

A characteristic of explanatory myths such as this one is that the unknown is simplified and explained in terms of the known. This myth accounts for the existence of rivers, mountains, lakes, and other features of the landscape, as well as of humans and all other living things. It also sanctions particular attitudes and behaviours. It is a product of creative imagination, and it is a work of art, as well as a potentially religious statement.

One aspect of mythology that has attracted a good deal of interest over the years is the similarity of certain themes in the stories of peoples living in separate parts of the world. One of these themes is the myth of matriarchy, or one-time rule

Raven and the First Men, by Haida artist Bill Reid, represents a First Nations creation myth.

---

[3]Haviland, W.A., & Power, M.W. (1994). *The original Vermonters: Native inhabitants, past and present* (Rev. and exp. ed., p. 193). Hanover, NH: University Press of New England.

by women. In a number of cultures, stories tell about a time when women ruled over men. Eventually, so these stories go, men were forced to rise up and assert their dominance over women to combat their tyranny or incompetence (or both). In the 19th century, a number of European scholars interpreted such myths as evidence of an early stage of matriarchy in the evolution of human culture, an idea some feminists recently have revived. Although a number of societies are known where the two sexes relate to one another as equals (Western Abenaki society was one), never have anthropologists found one where women rule over or dominate men. The interesting thing about myths of matriarchy is that they generally are found in cultures where men dominate women, but the latter have considerable autonomy.[4] Under such conditions, male dominance is insecure, and a rationale is needed to justify it. Thus, myths of men overthrowing women and taking control mirror an existing paradoxical relationship between the two sexes.

Myth making is an extremely important kind of human creativity, and the study of the myth-making process provides valuable clues to the way people perceive and think about their world.

Legends

Legends are stories told as true and set in the postcreation world. An example of a modern urban legend is the man hiding in the back seat of a young woman's car. When she stops for gas at a local gas station, late one night, a disreputable-looking gas attendant goes to great lengths to convince her to follow him into the station. Fearing for her safety, the woman repeatedly refuses. When she finally agrees, the gas attendant calls the police and the man hiding in the back seat of the car is arrested. In alternative versions the stubborn woman drives away, with the man hidden in the back seat. The heroic gas attendant calls the police, and depending on the version, the police save the woman or arrive too late. This particular legend illustrates a number of features all such narratives share: They cannot be attributed to any known author; they always exist in multiple versions, but, in spite of variation, they are told with sufficient detail to be plausible; and they tell us something about the societies they are found in. In this case, we are reminded of the dangers inherent in Western society, the reality that some people are dangerous deviants while others are unsung heroes, and the old adage, "don't judge a book by its cover."

As the preceding example shows, legends are not confined to nonliterate, nonindustrialized societies. Commonly, legends consist of pseudo-historical narratives that account for the deeds of heroes, the movements of peoples, and the establishment of local customs, typically with a mixture of realism and the supernatural or extraordinary. As stories, they are not necessarily believed or disbelieved, but they usually serve to entertain, as well as to instruct and to inspire or bolster pride in family, community, or nation.

To a degree, in literate states, the function of legends has been taken over by written history. Yet much of what passes for history, to paraphrase one historian, consists of the legends we develop to make ourselves feel better about who we are.[5] The trouble is that history does not always tell people what they want to hear about themselves, or, conversely, it tells them things they would prefer not to hear. By projecting their culture's hopes and expectations onto the record of the past, they seize upon and even exaggerate some past events while ignoring or giving scant attention to others. Although this often occurs unconsciously, so strong is the motivation to transform history into legend that states often have gone so far as to deliberately rewrite it, as when the 15th-century Aztecs, during the reign of King Itzcoatl, rewrote their history in a way more flattering to their position of dominance in ancient Mexico. So too the Louis Riel resistance,

---

[4]Sanday, P.R. (1981). *Female power and male dominance: On the origins of sexual inequality* (p. 181). Cambridge: Cambridge University Press.

[5]Stoler, M. (1982). To tell the truth. *Vermont Visions, 82* (3), 3.

Legends.   Stories told as true and set in the postcreation world.

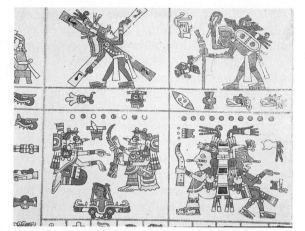

Part of an ancient Aztec manuscript. In the reign of King Itzcoatl, the Aztecs rewrote their history in a way to better glorify their past. In politically centralized states, such rewriting of history is a common practice.

a protest by the Métis in 1869 and 1885, is portrayed in Canadian history books as a treacherous uprising, rather than a desperate bid for survival in the face of encroaching European settlements. Riel and his people were resisting dispossession from their land, but to this day, thanks to history books, many Canadians still believe Riel led a treasonous rebellion against the federal government. The former Soviet Union was particularly well known for similar practices. Historians, when attempting to separate fact from fiction, frequently incur the wrath of people who will not willingly abandon what they wish to believe is true, whether or not it really is.

Legends may incorporate mythological details, especially when they make an appeal to the supernatural, and are therefore not always clearly distinct from myth. The Mwindo epic of the Nyanga people follows him through the earth, the atmosphere, the underworld, and the remote sky and gives a complete picture of the Nyanga people's view of their world's organization and limits. Legends also may incorporate proverbs and incidental tales and thus may be related to other forms of verbal art as well. A recitation of the Kambili epic of the Mande, for example, has been said to include as many as 150 proverbs.

For the anthropologist, a major significance of the secular and apparently realistic portions of legends, whether long or short, is the clues they provide to what constitutes a culture's approved or ideal ethical behaviour. The subject matter of legends is essentially problem solving, and the content is likely to include combat, warfare, confrontations, and physical and psychological trials of many kinds. Certain questions may be answered explicitly or implicitly. Do the people justify homicide? What kinds of behaviour are considered brave or cowardly? What is the etiquette of combat or warfare? Do the people honour or recognize a concept of altruism or self-sacrifice? Here again, however, pitfalls occur in the process of interpreting art in relation to life. It is always possible that certain kinds of behaviour are acceptable or even admirable, with the distance or objectivity art affords, but are not at all approved for daily life. In Euro-Canadian cultures, murderers, charlatans, and rakes sometimes have become popular heroes and the subjects of legends; however, North Americans do not approve or want to emulate the morality of characters like Billy the Kid or Jesse James.

Tales

The term **tale** is a nonspecific label for a third category of creative narratives: those purely secular, nonhistorical, and recognized as fiction for entertainment, although they may draw a moral or teach a practical lesson, as well. Consider this brief summary of a tale from Ghana, known as "Father, Son, and Donkey":

> A father and his son farmed their corn, sold it, and spent part of the profit on a donkey. When the hot season came, they harvested their yams and prepared to take them to storage using their donkey. The father mounted the donkey, and they all three proceeded on their way until they met some people. "What? You lazy man!" the people said to the father. "You let your young son walk barefoot on this hot ground while you ride on a donkey? For shame!" The father yielded his place to the son, and they proceeded until they came to an old woman. "What? You useless boy!" said the old woman. "You ride on the donkey and let your

---

Tale. A creative narrative recognized as fiction for entertainment.

poor father walk barefoot on this hot ground? For shame!" The son dismounted, and both father and son walked on the road, leading the donkey behind them until they came to an old man. "What? You foolish people!" said the old man. "You have a donkey and you walk barefoot on the hot ground instead of riding?" And so it goes. Listen: when you are doing something and other people come along, just keep on doing what you like.

This is precisely the kind of tale of special interest in traditional folklore studies. It is an internationally popular "numbskull" tale; versions of it have been recorded in India, the Middle East, the Balkans, Italy, Spain, England, and North America, as well as in West Africa. It is classified or catalogued as exhibiting a basic **motif**, or story situation—father and son trying to please everyone—one of the many thousands found to recur in world folktales. Despite variations in detail, every version has about the same basic structure in the sequence of events, sometimes called the *syntax* of the tale: A peasant father and son work together, a beast of burden is purchased, the three set out on a short excursion, the father rides and is criticized, the son rides and is criticized, both walk and are criticized, and a conclusion is drawn.

A surprising number of motifs in European and African tales are traceable to ancient sources in India. Is this good evidence of a spread of culture from a "cradle" of civilization, or is it an example of diffusion of tales in contiguous areas? Of course, purely local tales exist. Within any particular culture, anthropologists likely could categorize local types of tales: animal, human experience, trickster, dilemma, ghost, moral, scatological, nonsense tales, and so on. In West Africa there is a remarkable prevalence of animal stories, for example, with creatures such as the spider, the rabbit, and the hyena as the protagonists. Many were carried to the Americas; the Uncle Remus stories about Brer Rabbit, Brer Fox, and other animals may be survivors of this tradition.

The significance of tales for anthropologists rests partly in their distribution. The tales provide evidence of either cultural contacts or cultural isolation and of limits of influence and cultural cohesion. Debated for decades now, for example, has been the extent to which the culture of West Africa was transmitted to the southeastern United States. As far as folktales are concerned, one school of folklorists always has found and insisted on European origins; another school, somewhat more recently, points to African prototypes. Anthropologists are interested, however, in more than these questions of distribution. Like legends, tales very often illustrate local solutions to universal human ethical problems, and in some sense they state a moral philosophy. Anthropologists see that whether the tale of the father, the son, and the donkey originated in West Africa or arrived there from Europe or the Middle East, the very fact it is told in West Africa suggests it states something valid for that culture. The tale's lesson of a necessary degree of self-confidence in the face of arbitrary social criticism is therefore something that can be read into the culture's values and beliefs.

Other Verbal Arts

Myths, legends, and tales, prominent as they are in anthropological studies, turn out to be no more important than the other verbal arts. To the Awlad 'Ali Bedouin of Egypt's western desert, for

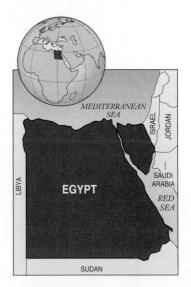

Motif. A story situation in a folktale.

The "little songs" of the Awlad 'Ali Bedouin punctuate conversations carried out while the people perform everyday chores, such as making bread, as these young women are doing. Through these "little songs," they can express what otherwise are taboo topics.

example, poetry is a lively and active verbal art, especially as a vehicle for personal expression and private communication. These people use two forms of poetry, one being the elaborately structured and heroic poems men chant or recite only on ceremonial occasions and in specific public contexts. The other is the *ghinnáwa,* or "little songs" that punctuate everyday conversations. Simple in structure, these deal with personal matters and feelings more appropriate to informal social situations, and older men regard them as the unimportant productions of women and youths. Despite this official devaluation in the male-dominated society of the Bedouin, however, they play a vital part in daily life. In their "little songs" individuals are shielded from the consequences of making statements and expressing sentiments that contravene the moral system. Paradoxically, by sharing these "immoral" sentiments only with intimates and veiling them in impersonal traditional formulas, people are allowed a sanctioned outlet for otherwise taboo thoughts or opinions. Disaster jokes serve the same function in contemporary North American society.

In all cultures the words of songs constitute a kind of poetry. Poetry and stories recited with gestures, movement, and props become drama. Drama combined with dance, music, and spectacle becomes a public celebration. The more we look at the individual arts, the clearer it becomes that they often are interrelated and interdependent. The verbal arts are, in fact, simply differing manifestations of the same creative imagination that produces music and the other arts, as can be seen in prairie mock weddings, which combine folklore, drama, and even dance to entertain on a cold prairie night (as described in the following Original Study).

ORIGINAL STUDY

The Mock Wedding: Folk Drama in the Prairie Provinces

Michael Taft, American Folklife Center

▲▽▲

Among the lesser-studied forms of Canadian folklore is folk drama. With the exception of the Newfoundland mumming sword-play—moribund for a generation or more—which has received considerable attention, most traditions of Canadian vernacular theatre remain to be explored. Among these dramatic forms is the mock wedding of the Prairie provinces.

The mock wedding is a dramatic parody in which members of a community dress as a wedding entourage and stage a marriage ceremony. Players have specific roles and there is a script in which several of the players have speaking parts. This form of folk drama is characterized by cross-dressing, bawdy behaviour, ad-libbing, and general carousing. The mock wedding is a ritual within a ritual, for it most often occurs as part of the larger community celebration of a couple's marriage or their wedding anniversary—most often a milestone event such as a 25th wedding anniversary. This drama, however, might also be part of wedding and baby showers, birthdays, community benefit concerts, or adult Halloween house-visiting.

The prairies are largely made up of small, agricultural communities, many with populations of less than one hundred families. Despite the small size of their communities (or perhaps because of it), these rural people busy themselves with an array of local functions—from wild fowl suppers and rodeos to daily get-togethers at the local café or pub. The wedding anniversary is one such occasion for the community to gather. For a couple's 25th anniversary, the community will hold a celebration in their honour, usually in the local hall or church basement. The honoured couple, surrounded by friends, neighbours, and relatives, is regaled with speeches (sometimes of the "roast" variety), gifts, poems composed in their honour by a local poet, and favourite songs sung by members of the community. Food and drink are essential elements of this celebration, and usually there is dancing, either to the music of a local band or to prerecorded music.

Unannounced and supposedly unexpected, a mock wedding procession enters the hall and takes over centre stage. Amidst laughter, jeers, and expressions of dismay, the procession arranges itself in a tableau: a minister standing before a bride and groom, surrounded by bridesmaids, parents of the mock couple, a best man or ring-bearer, sometimes a flower girl, sometimes a musician, sometimes other dramatis personae. The most striking feature of the entourage is that all female parts are played by men and all male parts are played by women.

The minister begins with a "dearly beloved" speech, a parody of the actual wedding liturgy:

> Dearly beloved we are gathered here/with many a qualm and many a fear/To join in wedlock this youthful pair/Before they are exposed to the wear and tear/Of wedded bliss and domestic wars./With dish-pan hands and scrubbing of floors/With the squawking kids and grocery bills/With burned potatoes and other ills/With bullet-like biscuits and washday dinners/And flaring tempers as hubby grows thinner/With mental cruelty and talk of divorce/And the final annulment in Reno of course./But why should I add to their mental confusion/By saying it's naught but a vain delusion?/Their dream-filled souls are happy today/So why should I steal their bliss away?/The guests are assembled, the gifts are many/So let's get on with the ceremony.[1]

Holding a telephone book, old catalogue, or perhaps a *Playboy* magazine, the minister reads the vows to the couple before pronouncing them "man and wife." The finale usually involves a post-nuptial kiss (sometimes devolving into a wrestling match) and the presentation of a bridal bouquet composed of local, noxious weeds to the honoured couple.

The drama is usually limited to this parody of a wedding, but it can also include further scenes. For example, one performance included a comic elopement scene because the honoured couple had eloped. While such a parody relates to an actual event in the lives of the anniversary couple, at least one stock scene is also part of this folk dramatic tradition: At the point when the minister asks if anyone can show why the couple should not be wed, a character playing a girlfriend—either pregnant or carrying a baby—will rush forward, causing a scene within the scene.

Like the girlfriend, most of the roles in the drama are stereotypes of typical members of a wedding: the weeping mother (sometimes carrying a roll of toilet paper to wipe her eyes); a father of the bride (usually carrying a shotgun with which to prod the groom); a ring-bearer (who may wear a suit covered with jar-sealer rings or respond to the minister's call for the ring by ringing a bell or producing a teething ring, cigar band, washer, or other gag ring). The minister (the only role that can be played by either a man or a woman) wears a funny cloak and hat, carries the aforementioned liturgical "text," and often has a jug of hooch hanging from his or her sash.

The bride and groom, however, are not so much stereotypes as caricatures of the honoured couple. In their dress, mannerisms, and stage actions, they parody known characteristics. At the same time, the minister reveals further characteristic and humorous or embarrassing events in the lives of the anniversary couple through a series of vows. For example, in one drama the groom was asked if he promised to buy his chickens from the market rather than steal them from the Hutterites, while in another drama the bride was asked if she promised to shoot the deer when she was the only one with a loaded gun. Both vows related to funny stories known within the community about the people being honoured.

The mock wedding would not be possible without a producer-director. Like the local poet, musician, raconteur, woodcarver, cake decorator, or other person with an acknowledged talent, the producer-director of mock weddings serves the community when the need arises. In almost all cases, the producer-director is a woman, and she is in charge of all aspects of the event, writing the script (she is often the local poet as well and the script is sometimes written in verse), gathering props and costumes, and selecting members of the cast. Some weeks before the couple's anniversary, friends or relatives of the couple will contact the producer-director and ask her to prepare a mock wedding. Because she must either write or, in most cases, refashion her existing script to fit the couple to be honoured, she will ask for interesting or funny stories about the couple, or specific quirks or traits of character that make them distinctive within the community; in many cases, of course, she will already have the information, since she is the couple's neighbour and most likely their friend. It is difficult to keep secrets in such small communities, and "open secrets" are grist for the producer-director's mill.

There is little difficulty in getting men to play the parts of women. While prairie society is typical of mainstream North American culture in its machismo ethic, there is a kind of reverse-machismo at work during the mock wedding. Only a "real man" can give up his dignity with good humour; only a man entirely in control of himself and entirely confident in his manliness would agree to dress in women's clothes. There are, in fact, some men who insist on being part of the production and who take pride in their roles.[2]

Any sense of lost manly dignity is counterbalanced by the men's behaviour during the performance: Much more than the women-dressed-as-men, the female impersonators engage in considerable mugging and clowning. They parody feminine stereotypes through mincing, blushing, and speaking in falsetto voices; or they assert the masculinity beneath their costumes through making their muscles bulge and strutting and swaggering in a supposedly manly fashion. They often exhibit bawdy behaviour by lifting their skirts, scratching themselves, or revealing and "redistributing" their movable breasts; and their costumes often exaggerate the female anatomy, with padding used to create grossly oversized breasts and backsides. Through this exaggerated and bawdy behaviour, the men show that they are ultimately in control. The men are not so much playing a role as playing *with* a role, and if a man were perceived to be taking his role seriously, his manliness might well be called into question.

The women act in a much more straightforward style. Since they are used to wearing men's clothes on the farm (or wearing clothes fashioned after men's styles), their costumes are not so far from their everyday dress, and they feel no need to reassure either themselves or their audience about their real-life status. But the women face other risks. Because the mock wedding is a woman's production, the women are responsible for how the drama is received by the community. Because so much of the script is derived from local gossip, the women producer-directors must know what they can and cannot include; they must know how far they can go in revealing the honoured couple to their community. They walk the fine line between good clean fun and malicious gossip. Standards of propriety vary from community to community, from couple to couple. In one drama, a vow that the bride would scratch her husband's psoriasis was considered within the bounds of good taste; in another, however, the father's shotgun was dispensed with because it was known that the woman being honoured was pregnant at the time of her marriage.

The localization and custom-fashioning of mock wedding scripts seems to be a phenomenon found mainly in the Prairie provinces. While the roots of the mock wedding go back to 19th-century Tom Thumb and women-less weddings in eastern North America,[3] they now owe little to that tradition. By comparison, the lesser, more conservative mock wedding tradition of southern Ontario relies much more on a standard, nonlocalized script.[4] While further research might reveal a more complex pattern of influence and dissemination of the greater North American wedding parody tradition, there seems to be a regional dimension to the mock wedding forms found in the prairies.

The distinctiveness of the prairie mock wedding lies in what it says about the role of women on large, modern, family-run farms. Among the most common topics of conversation among prairie farm wives is the conflict they feel between the traditional feminine roles they are expected to honour and the actual roles of farm workers they must fulfill: On a family-run farm, the women must perform many tasks ordinarily regarded as men's work. From driving grain trucks and combines, maintaining outbuildings, and slaughtering animals to keeping the accounts, women are engaged in work outside traditional female roles.

Women's concern over this necessary performance of a double role reveals itself both in conversation and in other forms of expression.[5] Perhaps because prairie people seem especially prone to use costumes as a form of expression—parades, benefit concerts, sporting events, and especially Halloween (which is an important community holiday on the prairies) all involve costumes or masks[6]—it is not so surprising that this topic should be at the centre of many mock wedding scripts. In fact, the mock wedding as a whole might be seen as a commentary on the role of women in prairie society. The very fact that women are dressed as men in the mock wedding sends the message "as farm wives, we are both women and men at the same time."

The mock wedding vows also address this topic; while some vows concern gossip, others concern the expectations of the farm wife. The minister asks the bride, "Do you promise to clean the slaughterhouse mess and not love and honour your husband any less?" and asks the groom, "Do you promise to keep her dressed in the finest of jeans, even if they are beyond your means?" And again, he asks the bride, "Wilt thou promise to tend the chickens, milk the cows, and churn the butter?" "Wilt thou promise to paint the granaries?" The mock bride's vows, however, also include all the domestic duties and traditional role expectations: "Do you promise from harvest to harvest to serve him with coffee and cake?" "Will you take him to the health spa for sexual rejuvenation?" "Will you promise to produce four children?" "Wilt thou promise to change the diapers?"

The mock wedding thus allows the women to turn the tables on the men—making *them* feel the ambivalence of having to live two roles. When men dress and act (albeit in a clownish way) as women, while still striving to maintain their manliness, they experience through the drama what their wives experience daily: the conflict of roles faced by women in a modern, agrarian culture.

[1]This quote and all others from mock wedding scripts are taken from the author's fieldwork in Saskatchewan.

[2]For a further examination of masculinity in mock weddings, see Taft, M. (1997). Men in women's clothes: Theatrical transvestites on the Canadian prairie. In Pauline Greenhill & Diane Tye (Eds.), *Undisciplined women: Tradition and culture in Canada* (pp. 131–138). Montreal/Kingston: McGill–Queen's University Press.

[3]See Stewart, S. (1984). *On longing: Narratives of the miniature, the gigantic, the souvenir, the collection* (pp. 117–125). Baltimore: Johns Hopkins University Press.

[4]See Greenhill, P. (1988). Folk drama in Anglo Canada and the mock wedding: Transaction, performance and meaning. *Canadian Drama, 14,* 172–173.

[5]For a discussion of this topic revealed in narratives, see Taft, M. (1983). *Discovering Saskatchewan folklore: Three case studies* (pp. 73–78). Edmonton: NeWest Press.

[6]For studies of prairie Halloween, see Hunter, D. (1983). No "malice in wonderland": Conservation and change in the three Halloweens of Ann Mesko. *Culture & Tradition, 7,* 36–53; and Taft, M. (1994). Adult Halloween celebrations on the Canadian prairie. In J. Santino (Ed.), *Halloween and other festivals of death and life* (pp. 152–169). Knoxville: University of Tennessee Press.

▲▽▲▽▲▽▲▽▲▽▲▽▲▽▲▽▲▽▲▽▲▽▲▽▲▽▲▽▲▽
THE ART OF MUSIC

The study of music in specific cultural settings, beginning in the 19th century with the collection of folksongs, has developed into a specialized field called **ethnomusicology.** Like the study of folktales for their own sake, ethnomusicology is both related to and somewhat independent of anthropology. Nevertheless, it is possible to sort out several concepts of interest to general anthropology from the field's various concerns.

To begin, we may ask these questions: How does music reflect a culture? What is considered important when distinguishing music from other modes of expression? What aspects of music are considered important in Western and non-Western cultures? Music is a form of communication that includes a nonverbal component: Often music transmits emotions rather than ideas. This nonverbal component of music makes it difficult to analyze. In fact, it is even difficult to agree on a definition of music, and ethnomusicologists often rely on a working definition to distinguish between "music" and that which is "musical."

Much of the early development of musicology was based on the study of Western European music, and on the elements considered important in European music (rhythm, melody,

Among food-foraging peoples, music plays an important role. Shown here is an Australian Aborigine playing a digeridoo.

and tonality). Yet these elements may not reflect the spiritual significance of African, First Nations, East Indian, or Asian music.

Early investigators of non-European music were struck by the apparent simplicity of melody and endless repetition of phrases. A great deal of non-European music was dismissed as "primitive" and formless, when in fact it was complex in structure and quite sophisticated. For example, African music, which is based on simultaneous multiple rhythmic patterns (polyrhythms), demonstrates remarkable precision. These polyrhythms are inte-

---

Ethnomusicology.   The study of a society's music in terms of its cultural setting.

Julie Cruikshank

Julie Cruikshank has documented women's oral traditions in the Yukon for more than 30 years, and has contributed enormously to the understanding of life history, oral narrative, and oral history; the value of informal storytelling; and the way narratives can challenge conventional ways of thinking.

Cruikshank has lived in northern Canada and Alaska and worked on community-based cultural documentation projects in the Yukon. She has discovered that "living narrators" in northern Canada organize accounts of their life experiences by using ancient narratives to explain contemporary events. In her recent publication, *The Social Life of Stories: Narrative and Knowledge in the Yukon Territory,* Cruikshank demonstrates how several older women taught her that they can have social lives, and that stories can have different meanings, depending on audience expectations and situations.

Cruikshank's award-winning book, *Life Lived Like a Story: Life Stories of Three Yukon Native Elders,* contains the narrative stories of three Yukon elders of Athapaskan and Tlingit ancestry: Angela Sidney, Kitty Smith, and Annie Ned. This book is innovative in that it relates the life experiences of these women from their perspective; they tell the story of their culture in their own words. Cruikshank's work is groundbreaking in that she avoids researcher intrusion and invasive theoretical perspectives—common pitfalls of anthropological studies. As one reviewer of *Life Lived Like a Story* states, "Their words stand by themselves rather than as adjuncts to anthro-pological accounts of social organization."[1] This research is also innovative in that the narrators were full collaborators in the project. Cruikshank illustrates that recording life histories, in the narrator's words, is an effective research method for interpreting and explaining cultural processes. She has set the stage for a new kind of anthropological research.

Currently, Cruikshank is a professor of anthropology at the University of British Columbia. She also holds a diploma in polar studies from the University of Cambridge.

---

[1]Dubrow, S. (1991). Book reviews in *The Canadian Journal of Native Studies, 11* (1). Retrieved July 4, 2001, from the World Wide Web: http://www.brandonu.ca/native/cjns/11.1/book_rev.pdf.

Sources:

Cruikshank, J. (n.d.). *Changing traditions in northern ethnography.* Retrieved July 3, 2001, from the World Wide Web: http://arcticcircle.uconn.edu/Museum/Anthropology/NorthernReview/cruikshank.html.

Cruikshank, J. (1992). *Oral tradition and material culture: Multiplying meanings of "words" and "things."* Retrieved July 5, 2001, from the World Wide Web: http://sapir.ukc.ac.uk/PRM/prmroot/musantob/thobrep1.html. Previously published in *Anthropology Today, 8* (3) (1992), 5–9.

UBC Reports. (1999). *Julie Cruikshank.* Retrieved July 3, 2001, from the World Wide Web: http://publicaffairs.ubc.ca/reports/99mar18/authcruiksk.html.

gral aspects of modern jazz, world music, and folk music. While much of European music employs melodic lines based on 12 equal steps, Arabic and East Indian music often uses melodic lines of 24 equal steps. Thus, the sounds may often sound "out of tune" or strange to the unaccustomed ear. However, these non-European songs evoke emotions and feelings as well as or better than European styles.

Although anthropologists do not necessarily need to untangle the complicated technical matters of music, they will want to know enough to be aware of the degree of skill involved in a performance. This allows a measure of the extent to which people in a culture have learned to practise and respond to this often important creative activity. Moreover, the distribution of musical forms and instruments can reveal much about cultural contact or isolation.

Functions of Music

Even without concern for technical matters, anthropologists can profitably investigate the function of music in human groups. First, people have expressed themselves through music for a very long time. The earliest multinote, playable musical instrument, the flute, is dated to 7000–6000 B.C. in China. Bone flutes and

Groups often express their cultural identity through music and dance. Shown here is a First Nations powwow at Chippawa Hill, Ontario.

whistles as old as 40 000 years have been found by archaeologists. Historically known food-for-aging peoples have their own form of music. In the Kalahari Desert, for example, a Ju/'hoansi hunter off by himself might play a tune on his bow simply to help while away the time. In northern New England, Abenaki shamans used cedar flutes to call game, lure enemies, and attract women. A drum with two rawhide strings stretched over it to produce a buzzing sound, thought to represent singing, gave the shaman the power to communicate with the spirit world.

Music is also a powerful identifier. Many marginalized groups have used music for purposes of self-identification, bringing the group together through their music, sometimes in an effort to counter a dominant culture's influence, or to raise their voices in social and political commentary. Examples of this include rap groups such as Public Enemy or L.L. Cool J, as well as ethnic groups sponsoring musical festivals. Canadians celebrate multiculturalism through music, for example, Ukrainian Yevshen dancers, Jewish klezmer bands, and the

Celtic folk music of the Atlantic provinces and Quebec. Potlatches and powwows encourage First Nations groups to reaffirm and celebrate their ethnic identity. Music plays an important part at these events, thus becoming closely bound to the group identity, both from without and from within the group. It should be understood, too, that these associations of music with groups are not dependent on words alone but also on tonal, rhythmic, and instrumental conventions. For example, Scottish gatherings would not be "Scottish" without the sound of the Highland bagpipes and the fiddle.

This power of music to shape identity has been recognized everywhere, with varying consequences. The English recognized the power of the bagpipes for creating an esprit de corps among the Highland regiments of the British army and encouraged it within certain bounds, even while surpressing piping in Scotland itself under the Disarming Act. Over time, the British military piping tradition was assimilated into the Scottish piping tradition, so the blend was accepted and spread by Scottish pipers. As a result, much of

Although much music performed by Scottish pipers is of English origin, it has been so thoroughly absorbed that most people think of it as purely Scottish.

the supposedly Scottish piping we hear today consists of marches written within the conventions of the English musical tradition, though shaped to fit the physical constraints of the instrument.

The English adoption of the Highland bagpipe into Scottish regiments is an instance of those in authority employing music to further a political agenda. So too in Spain, the dictator Francisco Franco (who came to power in the 1930s) established community choruses in even the smallest towns to promote the singing of patriotic songs. Similarly, in Brittany and Galicia, music is playing an important role in attempts to revive the spirits of the indigenous Celtic cultures in these regions. Indeed, Celtic dancing has developed an international reputation. But, however played or for whatever reason, music (like all art)

is an individual creative skill each of us can cultivate and be proud of, whether from a sense of accomplishment or from the sheer pleasure of performing. It is a form of social behaviour promoting a communication or sharing of feelings and life experience with other humans. Moreover, because individual creativity is constrained by the traditions of the particular group, each culture's art is distinctive and helps to define its members' sense of identity.

The social function of music is perhaps most obvious in songs, since these contain verbal text. Songs serve many purposes, entertainment being only one of them. Work songs have served to coordinate heavy or dangerous labour, such as weighing anchor and furling sail on board ships and making axe or hammer strokes, and serving to pass time and relieve tedium, such as with oyster shucking songs. Songs also have been used to soothe babies to sleep, charm animals into giving more milk, keep witchcraft at bay, advertise goods, and much more. Songs also may serve social and political purposes, spreading particular ideas swiftly and effectively by giving them a special form involving poetic language and rhythm and by attaching a pleasing and appropriate tune, be it solemn or light.

In North America numerous examples exist of marginalized social and ethnic groups attempting to gain a larger audience and more compassion for their plight through song. Familiar to Canadians are Bruce Cockburn, Buffy Sainte-Marie, Bob Dylan, and Joni Mitchell, who have supported civil and human rights causes in their music. Indeed, these performers' celebrity status led to the broader dissemination of their social and political beliefs. Such celebrity status comes from skill in performing and communicating with the intended audience. Music can often convey political messages that would never be allowed in narrative; for example, *Music for Prague 1968* by Karel Husa is a piece that portrays, through dominant rhythms and tonal colours, the Soviet invasion of Czechoslovakia in 1968.

In Australia, traditional aboriginal songs have taken on a new legal function, as they are being introduced into court as evidence of early settlement patterns. This evidence helps the Aborigines claim more extensive land ownership, thus allowing them greater authority to use the land, as well as to negotiate and profit from the

Human rights activist Buffy Sainte-Marie uses music to comment on social issues.

sale of natural resources. This had been impossible before. The British, upon their annexation of Australia, declared the land ownerless (Terra Nullius). Although the Aborigines had preserved their records of ownership in song and story, these were not admissible in the British courts. In the early 1970s, however, the Aborigines exposed the injustice of the situation, and the Australian government began responding in a more favourable, if somewhat limited, fashion, granting the claims of traditional ownership to groups in the Northern Territory. Proof of Aborigine ownership includes recordings of traditional songs indicating traditional settlement and travel patterns and land use.[6]

Music gives a concrete form, made memorable and attractive with melody and rhythm, to basic human ideas. Whether the song's content is didactic, satirical, inspirational, religious, political, or purely emotional, the important thing is that the formless has been given form and that feelings hard to express in words alone are communicated in a symbolic and memorable way that can be repeated and shared. The group is consequently united and has the sense their shared experience, whatever it may be, has shape and meaning. This, in turn, shapes and gives meaning to the community.

---

[6]Koch, G. (1997). Songs, land rights and archives in Australia. *Cultural Survival Quarterly, 20* (4).

VISUAL ART

To many Westerners, the first image that springs to mind in connection with the word *art* is some sort of visual art, be it a painting, drawing, sculpture, or totem pole. And indeed, in many parts of the world, people have been expressing their artistic talents in one way or another for a very long time—etching designs in bone or wood, gourds or pots; engraving pictures in rock and painting them on cave walls, textiles, and animal hides; and carving shapes out of stone or wood, antler and bone, or even their own bodies. As with musical art, some form of visual art is a part of every historically known human culture.

Much like verbal art and music, visual art can convey political, cultural, and social messages. A good example is graffiti tagging. Graffiti is a form of artistic expression that has become prominent in urban settings. Urban youths scratch, paint, or spray their "tags" or nicknames on the sides of buildings and vehicles—even entire subway trains. Hiphop graffiti originated in the subways of New York in the 1960s and 1970s, and continues to flourish today in many large cities around the world. Subways provided a perfect milieu for graffiti writing—a way for writers to display their work to the riding public and especially to other graffiti writers. Although graffiti writing originally began with Puerto Rican youths, graffiti

An example of graffiti art, a form of artistic expression not appreciated by everyone, yet often fulfilling social, cultural, and political needs for urban youths.

Gender **Perspectives**

On Being a Man

"Real men don't cry." "Real men don't eat quiche." We have all heard these sentiments expressed, but have you ever stopped to wonder why males must "act like a man" or "be a man?" And do men everywhere seek to be "manly"? Is there a culture of manhood? These gender images or ideals for males are as significant as those for females.

Gender images vary from one culture to another, but beneath the superficial differences lie some interesting similarities. Cross-cultural comparisons suggest that regardless of lifestyle, geographical location, or standard of living, males are required to pass a test in order to be accepted as a man. For example, the Truk fishers of the South Pacific risk their lives to maintain a manly image, engaging in dangerous activities such as deep-sea fishing in shark-infested waters to prove their manhood. They are encouraged to think strong, manly thoughts, and their youths engage in brawls, heavy drinking, and sexual conquests, again to prove their manhood. Among East African cultural groups, such as the Masai, adolescent boys must undergo ritual circumcision without flinching or crying out lest they be branded unworthy of manhood and bring shame on their lineage. Even among the peaceful Ju/'hoansi, young boys must earn their manhood— by single-handedly tracking and killing an antelope. In the Balkans, a real man is a heavy drinker, spends money freely, fights bravely, and raises a large family, thus proving his sexual prowess.

North America has not escaped this pressured manhood; indeed, popular culture, especially Hollywood films, promotes whisky-swilling, gun-toting cowboys and Rambo-style heroes who would rather die in battle than risk being labelled unmanly. Even such innocuous institutions as the Boy Scouts aim to turn little boys into strong men. These ideals, though presented in technologically complex images, are eerily similar to the Truk, Masai, and Ju/'hoansi male's quest for manhood.

Some say we socialize our boys to be tough; others suggest socialization has little to do with it. From a young age, our little boys strive to be manly, play with boys' toys like guns, wrestle, and play rough. In high school, sports jocks rule—how is the young man who would rather play a flute than hockey or football labelled? What happens to the young man who cries in disappointment after losing a basketball game? Indeed, sports have often been touted as the way to make boys into men: By succeeding at sports a young man can stake his claim to masculinity.[1]

Social scientists have put forth countless explanations to explain the seemingly universal imagery of manhood. Feminists and Marxists see the concept of manhood as a mechanism for oppressing females. Biological arguments suggest that males had to develop masculine tendencies, such as aggression and male bonding, in order to survive as hunters. Psychoanalytic theories suggest that males must defend themselves against castration anxieties. Psychological and neo-Freudian theorists focus on a young man's need to create a separate identity from his mother and defend against eternal childhood by performing a great deed. Although each has its limitations, these theories attempt to explain why males risk everything to be manly, and why "real men don't cry."

---

[1]Whitson, D. (1990). Sport in the social construction of masculinity. In M.A. Messner & D.F. Sabo (Eds.), *Sport, men and the gender order: Critical feminist perspectives.* Champaign, IL: Human Kinetics Books.

Source: Adapted from Gilmore, D.D. (1997). The manhood puzzle. In C.B. Brettell & C.F. Sargent (Eds.), *Gender in cross-cultural perspective* (2nd ed., pp. 185–197). Upper Saddle River, NJ: Prentice Hall.

---

artists today come from all socioeconomic backgrounds, are usually quite young (10 to 16 being the most common age), and are almost always males.

Earlier in this chapter we asked the question, what is art? Many people, especially government and city officials, refuse to recognize graffiti as a form of artistic expression, viewing it as vandalism rather than art. Anthropologists explore the reasons why youths write graffiti, and what motivates them to continue writing even in the face of public and government pressure. Most studies suggest that graffiti writers seek recognition, even fame. Graffiti was originally a means for members of the hiphop subculture—usually disenfranchised, impoverished youths living in decaying neighbourhoods—to feel empowered and to visibly and artistically express their resistance to authority. This art form became the voice of disaffected youth from ghettos.

In the 1990s graffiti moved beyond the subway systems into such venues as freight trains, rocks, signs, fences, and even legal walls like Phun Phactory and Halls of Fame in New York City. Graffiti has become a legitimate art form, constantly changing, but still fulfilling the need for expression.[7]

As symbolic expression, visual art may be representational, imitating nature, or abstract, drawing from natural forms but representing only their basic patterns or arrangements. Actually, the two categories are not mutually exclusive, for even the most naturalistic portrayal is partly abstract in that it generalizes from nature and abstracts patterns of ideal beauty, ugliness, or typical expressions of emotion. But between the most naturalistic and the most schematic or symbolic abstract art lies a continuum. In some of the First Nations artwork on Canada's northwest coast, for example, animal figures may be so highly stylized as to be difficult for an outsider to identify. Although the art is abstract, the artist has drawn on nature, though he or she has exaggerated and deliberately transformed some of its shapes to express a particular feeling toward them. Because the artists do these exaggerations and transformations according to the canons of northwest coast First Nations culture, their meanings are understood not just by the artist but by other community members as well.

This stylized painting on a ceremonial shirt represents a bear. Although the art of the northwest coast First Nations often portrays actual animals, they are not depicted in a naturalistic style. To identify them, we must be familiar with the conventions of this art.

Canadian Visual Art

The visual arts have flourished in Canada for millennia. From the first petroglyphs, originating some 7000 years ago, to the abstract paintings found in modern-day art galleries, Canadian art has provided artists and art lovers with a wide variety of artistic expressions. Identifying a Canadian style of art is difficult: Each region, each cultural group, and even each artist has brought a distinctive flavour to Canadian art. This diversity is also evident in the vast array of media for visual arts—from watercolours and oil paintings to prairie quilting, from Inuit sculpture to First Nations basket weaving and beading.

Although diversity characterizes contemporary Canadian art, trends over the past century reflect the manner in which Canadian cultures

---

[7]Dennant, P. (1997). *Urban expression ... urban assault ... urban wildstyle ... New York City graffiti*. Retrieved July 4, 2001, from the World Wide Web: http://www.graffiti.org/faq/pamdennant.html.

Ju/'hoansi rock paintings and engravings from southern Africa often depict animals thought to possess great supernatural power.

have influenced artistic styles. One of the earliest artists to make a lasting impression on Canada's art history was Paul Kane. Fascinated with First Nations peoples, Kane travelled westward across Canada, sketching all that he saw. His powerful watercolours and field sketches have provided a valuable record of western Canadian life in the mid-1800s. When he returned to Toronto, Kane spent six years creating a series of 100 oil paint-

Quilting is presently enjoying a revival in the Canadian prairies and Maritime provinces. This ancient craft, traced back to Egyptian times, binds people together around the world, and has even been used to honour those who have died of AIDS, symbolizing hope for a cure.

ings and wrote his pivotal work, *Wanderings of an Artist among the Indians of North America*, published in 1859.[8]

Early in the 20th century, some of Canada's most influential artists joined together to form the Group of Seven. Artists Lawren Harris, J.E.H. MacDonald, Arthur Lismer, F.H. Varley, Franz Johnston, Franklin Carmichael, and A.Y. Jackson intended to showcase the natural beauty of Canada to all Canadians through their landscape paintings. They were consumed with the belief that art "must grow and flower in the land before the country be a real home for its people."[9] The Group of Seven's 1920 exhibition at the Art Gallery of Toronto was an important moment in the history of Canadian art, representing a growing sense of nationalism and the Group's desire to capture the spirit of Canada in their paintings.[10]

[8]Our Heritage. (2001). *Who was Paul Kane?* Retrieved April 4, 2001, from the World Wide Web: http://ourheritage.net/who/kanewho.html.

[9]*Canadian Art at the McMichael. (1996–2000). The Group of Seven and their contemporaries.* Retrieved March 29, 2001, from the World Wide Web: http://www.mcmichael.com/group.htm.

[10]Ibid.

The age-old tradition of decorating eggs is an important component of Ukrainian religion. Shown here is craftsperson Annie Fedorak with a collection of Ukranian Easter eggs.

The Group of Seven's passion for Canadian scenery influenced other Canadian artists, such as Emily Carr, who spent much of her career painting fishing villages and First Nations totem poles north of Victoria, British Columbia. Carr's paintings document a bygone era: As the aboriginal world around her disintegrated, Carr's work also metamorphosed, reflecting these changes. Her paintings gained international attention when her work was included in anthropologists Marius Barbeau and Eric Brown's exhibition, *Canadian West Coast Art, Native and Modern,* at the National Gallery in 1927.[11] Following her death in 1945, Carr's work continued to gain international fame; today she is considered one of Canada's most important artists.

In the 1960s, at a time when Western society was experiencing political and social turmoil, the artistic community began questioning the very nature of art. This was a time of experimentation, alternative art forms, and increasing abstraction. By the 1970s artists recognized that the ideas rooted in art and the process of creating art were more important than the art itself. "Conceptual art often pointed to issues or the power embedded in institutions or society, raising questions and offering multiple layers of meaning rather than presenting singular, fully developed points of view."[12] Today, we continue to witness diversity in art—sculpture, painting, video, and photography—each reflecting the multiplicity of media and artists in Canada.

By the middle of the 20th century, art connoisseurs recognized the vitality of Canadian aboriginal art forms. In particular, Inuit sculpture captured the imagination of museums and art collectors the world over. Inuit art has a venerable history that can be traced back at least 4000 years. The first significant artifacts come from the Dorset culture (600 B.C.–A.D. 1000).[13] These people

Emily Carr's vibrant paintings brought the culture of the northwest coastal peoples alive.

[11]Department of Fine Arts, Okanagan University College. (1999). *Important moments in the history of Canadian visual culture: R.J. Belton.* Retrieved March 13, 2001, from the World Wide Web: http://www.ouc.bc.ca/fiar/1918_45 .html.

[12]*Modern and Contemporary Art at the McMichael. (1996–2001).* Retrieved March 27, 2001, from the World Wide Web: http://www.mcmichael.com/modern.htm.

[13]Harris Gallery. (2001). *Inuit art background.* Retrieved April 3, 2001, from the World Wide Web: http://www.harrisinuitgallery.com/artinfo.htm.

carved land and sea animals, human figures, masks, and face clusters out of bone, ivory, and wood. The Thule, believed to be the ancestors of today's Inuit, succeeded the Dorset peoples. Their art also included human and animal figures, but most of the artwork from this time featured graphic designs on objects such as combs, needle cases, harpoon toggles, and gaming pieces.[14]

Contemporary Inuit art, although still influenced by the past, is constantly evolving. In fact, the soapstone carvings so popular with contemporary art collectors around the world are a relatively recent innovation. Besides affording a sense of cultural identity and pride, Inuit artwork has become a major source of revenue for Inuit peoples, and in the process artists have earned international recognition and acclaim. Inuit artists use a variety of local materials: weathered and fossilized whalebone, walrus ivory, and caribou antler, as well as the famous soapstone. As with other Canadian art forms, Inuit art is also highly variable; each community produces its own distinctive style. Traditional themes of Arctic wildlife, Inuit hunting and family scenes, spirits, mythology, and shamanistic images remain most popular.

▲▽▲▽▲▽▲▽▲▽▲▽▲▽▲▽▲▽▲▽▲▽▲▽▲▽▲▽▲▽▲▽

BODY ART

Humans are willing to endure pain and discomfort, waste precious time and resources, and risk chastisement from more conservative sectors of society in an attempt to enhance their physical appearance—to become more attractive, distinctive, or acceptable to other members of a group.[15]

Body art can take many forms—from something as innocuous as rubbing red ochre into the hair or wearing makeup and jewellery, to the serious business of cutting intricate patterns into the skin or piercing and tattooing various body parts. Even the clothes we wear and the hairstyles we sport signify a desire for self-expression and a need to demonstrate individuality. Yet this search for personal identity also creates a sense of com-

munity or group membership with like-minded people who participate in similar body modification. Body art is not a frivolous endeavour; patterns and designs created by painting, styling, tattooing, or piercing serve as a symbolic language, a way of expressing values, beliefs, and worldview.

Because the norms of any given culture vary, forms of body modification will also vary. Body art in traditional cultures tends to remain constant and unchanging for generations, but in the West, fashions and styles can change from one season to the next. Westerners also have a choice of which styles and practices they will adopt, or whether they will adhere to any of the so-called norms, but in traditional cultures, adopting the artistic norms of the culture may not be voluntary. Thus, human appearance is a cultural construct as well as a biological creation.

Body Painting

Many cultures create colourful, imaginative human bodies through body painting and makeup. The women of New Guinea paint their faces red, blue, and white, and the Tchikrin people of Brazil paint their limbs red and their torsos black. In the Sudan, Nuba men paint their bodies white on one side and black on the other, and the women paint their bodies either red or yellow. Although body paint is more common in traditional cultures, it is also found in the West: In North America, New York's East Village punks display vividly multicoloured bodies, and in Europe, vampiric "goths" paint themselves white, with huge, black skull-like eyes and jet-black lips. This body art serves far more than an aesthetic role; it also communicates ancient mythology, represents group values and religious beliefs, and sets each group apart as visually distinct. Body painting also can mark the celebration of important events in a person's life. Among Nuba males, colours represent different age grades; only members of older age grades can wear deep yellow or jet black. The importance of body painting can differ based on gender. Nuba men spend hours applying makeup and creating intricate patterns, while the women simply apply the colour appropriate to their kinship group. This tradition exemplifies the tendency for males throughout the animal world to be more elaborately decorated than the women—the so-called peacock

---

[14]Ibid.

[15]The following discussion is predominantly taken from Polhemus, T., & Randall, H. (2000). *The customized body.* London and New York: Serpent's Tail.

Body art, such as the piercing and tatooing shown here, is a way for people to symbolically express their individuality, as well as their values, beliefs, and worldview.

syndrome. Conversely, women in the West are more decorative, but use makeup for cosmetic rather than artistic purposes. However, there are examples of Western men decorating their bodies, such as the hippies of the 1970s, who applied psychedelic and flowery designs. More recently, punks have used makeup as a medium of visual experimentation. An interesting trend is currently emerging among sports fans that can be likened to traditional body painting; football fans, for example, adorn their faces with brightly coloured designs to celebrate an important game. Thus, people paint their bodies for many reasons—to enhance their appearance, to demonstrate personal or group identity, and to celebrate religious and other rituals.

Tattooing

Tattoos are created by injecting a pigment beneath the skin. The Inuit used a sooty thread sewn through the skin with a needle to create permanent markings, while other early groups likely used bone or antler splinters dipped in berry juice. Unlike body paint, which washes off, tattoos are a permanent and usually irreversible art form.

Defining the role of tattooing can be difficult. Is tattooing a symbol of status or rebellion, a traditional marker, or a contemporary artistic expression? Is it a sign of individuality or of group identity? In fact, tattoo art is all of these and much more. In traditional cultures, tattoos often mark significant stages or rites of passage in a person's life, such as passing through puberty and into adulthood. A young Nuba girl may receive her first tattoo when her breasts grow. To most Westerners tattooing is a symbol of difference, providing visible messages of uniqueness, as in the case of goths and punks.

As an art form, tattooing has flourished in many variations around the world. One of the most intricate forms is found among the New Zealand Maori, whose *moko*, facial swirls, are chiselled into the face as a sign of cultural pride.

Tattoos traditionally afforded Maori men and women special privileges and rank. In Canada, aboriginal groups such as the Cree and Inuit also produced distinctive styles of tattooing to express links with spirit guardians.

The origins of tattooing remain unclear, although the fact that tattooing is so widely distributed suggests the custom is ancient. The 5000-year-old body of a hunter discovered in an Alpine glacier had 15 tattoos, including parallel stripes around the left wrist. Two female Egyptian mummies dated to 4000 years ago had dots and dashes tattooed on their bodies. Many consider Japanese tattooing of the Edo Period (1600–1868) to be the epitome of tattoo art. Ancient Incas, Mayas, and Aztecs also had sophisticated tattooing styles, as did the Iberians, Gauls, Goths, Teutons, Picts, Scots, and Britons. In fact, most European groups, with the exception of the Greeks and Romans, used tattooing to customize their bodies. Even early Christians and crusaders were tattooed. However, this changed when Constantine declared Christianity the official religion of the Roman Empire and banned tattooing in A.D. 325, essentially shutting down the practice until British explorers reintroduced tattooing to the West from Polynesia in the 18th century. Later, working-class men in North America embraced tattooing, and by the mid-20th century, bikers, convicts, and other marginalized groups also took up the art.

Western society faced two dilemmas in the 1960s and onward: the need for members to exhibit at least some individuality in an increasingly homogenized world, and the need to belong to a group or community. Tattooing helped satisfy both these needs: Unique tattoos made individuals feel special, and having a tattoo signified belonging to a distinct group. Flash designs (readily available standards) like peace symbols, mushrooms, marijuana leaves, and zodiac signs became the symbols of hippies and other fringe groups, much like bikers' symbols of rebellion. Gays also chose their own symbols. Thus, mainstream society as well as fringe elements took notice of the tattoo. With the advent of the women's movement, women also began getting tattoos. New sanitization regulations made tattooing safer and again more acceptable to mainstream society. By the end of the 1970s tattooing had become more of a middle-class activity, and the practice had become more professional and hence safer. Tattoo art has adopted non-Western images and styles and become more customized, becoming a real art form rather than decoration.[16] Although tattooing has enjoyed a resurgence in the West, in many other parts of the world, incessant contact with outsiders such as missionaries has endangered the role of tattooing in traditional cultures.

Body Adornment

Adorning our bodies with flowers, shells, feathers, and metals is an ancient custom found in most cultural groups around the world. Such adornment may serve to make individuals, both male and female, more attractive; it may be seen as magical (e.g., talisman) or of religious significance; it may indicate wealth (e.g., a diamond necklace, Kula shell necklace) and status (e.g., a wedding ring, chief's feather headdress); or it may assert identity.

One form of adornment is body piercing, puncturing the skin with holes for decorative reasons. The most universal site for piercing is the earlobe, closely followed by the nose and lips. Once pierced, the holes are adorned with all manner of artwork. The Masai stretch their pierced ears, inserting increasingly larger plugs and heavier jewellery. Leaders of the Amazon Kayapo stretch their bottom lip out by inserting plates the size of saucers; these are known as *labrets,* or lip plugs. These lip plugs symbolize status and manhood; among the Kayapo the labret embodies the value placed on oratory skills, just as nose piercing among some New Guinea groups denotes the importance of smell. The Inuit also had stretched labret piercings, both above and below their lips. During a blood-letting ritual, the Maya royals pierced their tongues with a stingray thorn to appease the gods and ancestors.[17]

Body piercing has now become the fastest growing body decoration in the West. Westerners have adopted numerous expressions of this art:

[16]DeMello, M. (2000). *Bodies of inscription: A cultural history of the modern tattoo community.* Durham, NC: Duke University Press.

[17]American Museum of Natural History. (n.d.). *A body arts expo.* Retrieved October 15, 2003, from the World Wide Web: http://www.coldsteel.co.uk/articles/bodyartexpo.html.

Multiple ear piercings (a way for the less adventurous to express their unique identity), and nostril, septum, lip, eyebrow, navel, nipple, and genital piercings all have become common. Although some no doubt view these extreme piercings as barbaric, in fact, they are a way for individuals to take control of their own bodies: "My body wasn't mine until I claimed it through piercing. I didn't do it for fashion. I make all my own jewellery and use it to create balance within me, that is very important. I like modifying and recreating my body in many ways, this is exciting."[18]

Painting, tattooing, and piercing are by no means the limit of our attempts to modify our bodies. Hair and nails are also expressions of beauty, power, and identity. Humans cut, braid, knot, dye, backcomb, and adorn their hair with all manner of decorative pieces, including ribbons, shells, flowers, and bones. Hairstyling is an ancient custom, one that is a universal practice in contemporary groups and can be quite intricate. For example, the Masai warriors smear their long hair with red ochre, fat, and clay, then twist it into 400 or so strands, which are then grouped as three braids and bound around long, pliant sticks. This design shows group identity and marks individual status in the group. Western examples include skinheads, who shave their heads; punks, who wear "Mohawks": and rappers, who sport razor designs. Hairstyles often communicate class; for example, the silver wigs aristocrats wore in 17th-century England were a sign of power and status.

Body art is an ancient, dynamic custom that has served to beautify, customize, and display the myriad ways humans interpret and depict their bodies. In anthropology, body art is seen as a universal feature of traditional cultures and an informative indicator of age, status, family position, and group affiliation.

▲▽▲▽▲▽▲▽▲▽▲▽▲▽▲▽▲▽▲▽▲▽▲▽▲▽▲▽▲▽
CENSORSHIP

The issue of censorship in Canada is very complex, and has to do with audience expectations and topics discussed. As visual artists eagerly embrace new media and attempt to "push the envelope," conservative factions have protested the movement into unconventional artistic expression. For example, in 1991 the National Gallery incited protests for exhibiting Jana Sterbak's dress of raw meat. The gallery was accused of wastefulness, and received threats and mail smeared with excrement. A billboard showing two women kissing under the caption "Lesbian is not a dirty word" angered some Winnipeg residents in 1992, and the showing of *Pisschrist* by controversial American artist Andreas Serrano raised the hackles of Vancouver citizens. Little Sister's gay and lesbian bookstore in Vancouver was fire-bombed and the owners have experienced major problems with Canada Customs regarding books they attempt to import. The previous examples of censorship reveal a great deal about Canadian society.

As mentioned earlier in this chapter, proponents of censorship and the funding of more "practical" endeavours are forever pressuring the federal funding agencies to cut funding to the arts, and to censor alternative artistic expressions. Nevertheless, many Canadian citizens recognize that artistic expression promotes cultural identity and a sense of pride in our cultural heritage.

---

[18]Polhemus, T., & Randall, H. (2000). *The customized body.* London and New York: Serpent's Tail.

CHAPTER SUMMARY

Art is the creative use of the human imagination to interpret, understand, and enjoy life. It stems from the uniquely human ability to use symbols to give shape and significance to the physical world for more than just a utilitarian purpose. Anthropologists are concerned with art as a reflection of people's cultural values and concerns.

Oral traditions denote a culture's unwritten stories, beliefs, and customs. Verbal arts include narratives, dramas, poetry, incantations, proverbs, riddles, and word games. Narratives, which have received the most study, have been divided into three categories: myths, legends, and tales.

Myths are sacred narratives that explain how the world came to be as it is. By describing an orderly universe, myths function to set standards for orderly behaviour. Legends are stories told as if true that often recount the exploits of heroes, the movements of people, and the establishment of local customs. Anthropologists are interested in legends because they provide clues about what constitutes model ethical behaviour in a culture. Tales are fictional, secular, and nonhistorical narratives that instruct as they entertain. Anthropological interest in tales centres in part on the fact that their distribution provides evidence of cultural contacts or cultural isolation.

The study of music in cultural settings has developed into the specialized field of ethnomusicology.

The social function of music is most obvious in songs. Like tales, songs may express a group's concerns, but with greater formalism because of the restrictions musical forms impose. Music also serves as a powerful way for a social or ethnic group to assert its distinctive identity. As well, it may be used to advance particular political, economic, and social agendas or for any one of a number of other purposes.

Visual art may be regarded as either representational or abstract, although in truth these categories represent polar ends of a continuum. Canadian visual art has exhibited a great deal of cultural diversity. Inuit art is one of the most successful examples of aboriginal art, nationally and internationally. Body art, in all its forms, is a way for people to express their individuality, group identity, and worldview. Despite the flourishing of diverse art forms in Canada, censorship and funding crises have not left the Canadian art community unscathed.

QUESTIONS FOR CRITICAL THOUGHT

1. In this chapter the Navajo tradition of sand painting is used to illustrate how sometimes the "art" is the process of creation, rather than what is produced. What other traditions stress the act over the product? Why would Western people think more in terms of the resulting object than the act of creation? What does this tell observers about Western values?

2. Why is art perceived as elitist and nonproductive in Western society? Is this a valid viewpoint? How does it differ from other cultures' opinions, and how might Western culture itself belie such a statement?

3. How does art participate in politics? Why are various art forms (music, visual and graphic arts, literature, etc.) so important to nationalist or ethnic groups existing under the influence of foreign dominant cultures?

4. How does music reflect a culture's beliefs, norms, and values? How does music evoke emotions from listeners?

5. Is censorship a necessary part of the arts? If yes, who should decide on censorship rules?

6. Should public monies be directed toward the arts in Canada? Why or why not? Is there a department of fine arts at your college or university? Does the institution have a policy on what students can exhibit?

7. Interview someone you know who has numerous body piercings or tattoos, who wears unique clothing, or who has an original hairstyle. Determine this person's reasons for choosing a particular form of body art, certain designs, particular body parts, and so on.

INTERNET RESOURCES

Paul Kane's Great Nor-West

http://www.umanitoba.ca/cm/vol2/no26/kane.html

A comprehensive examination of Paul Kane's life and work, displaying some of his paintings.

The Group of Seven and Their Contemporaries

http://www.mcmichael.com/group.htm

A good presentation of the Group of Seven's lives and work. Includes links to sites on each artist, which display some of their work in vivid colour.

Important Moments in the History of Canadian Visual Culture

http://www.ouc.bc.ca/fiar/1918_45.html

This site provides a timeline of visual art in Canada.

Modern and Contemporary Art at the McMichael

http://www.mcmichael.com/modern.htm

This site provides a brief examination of modern and contemporary art in Canada.

Inuit Art Background

http://www.harrisinuitgallery.com/artinfo.htm

This site present a brief sketch of Inuit art and its history. The site also includes photos of Inuit sculpture.

Manitoba Aboriginal Artist Archive

http://aboriginalcollections.ic.gc.ca/artist/artists/006/index.html

This site features several Manitoba artists and provides descriptions and photos of their work.

Music and Anthropology

http://www.muspe.unibo.it/period/ma/index/ma_ind.htm

The *Journal of Musical Anthropology of the Mediterranean* presents several journal articles reflecting on music. Two recent additions: "Relating the present to the past: Thoughts on the study of musical change and culture change in ethnomusicology" and "Music, ceremony and self-identity in Renaissance Venice."

Professional Weeping

http://www.research.umbc.edu/eol/5/greene

A study of professional weeping: music, affect, and hierarchy in a south Indian folk performance by Paul D. Greene. Some of the topics include funerals, oppari, and performance analysis.

Urban Expression

http://www.graffiti.org/faq/pamdennant.html

A comprehensive examination by Pamela Dennant of the roots of New York graffiti. Provides a good historical overview set within the social and political context of inner-city New York.

SUGGESTED READINGS

Dundes, A. (1980). *Interpreting folk lore*. Bloomington: Indiana University Press.

A collection of articles that assess the materials folklorists have amassed and classified, this book seeks to broaden and refine traditional assumptions about the proper subject matter and methods of folklore.

Hannah, J.L. (1988). *Dance, sex and gender*. Chicago: University of Chicago Press.

Like other art forms, dances are social acts that contribute to the continuation and emergence of culture. One of the oldest—if not the oldest—art forms, dance shares the same instrument, the human body, with sexuality. This book, written for a broad nonspecialist audience, explicitly examines sexuality and the construction of gender identities as they are played out in the production and visual imagery of dance.

Hatcher, E.P. (1985). *Art as culture: An introduction to the anthropology of art.* New York: University Press of America.

This handy, clearly written book does a nice job of relating the visual arts to other aspects of culture. Topics include "The Technological Means," "The Psychological Perspective," "Social Contexts and Social Functions," "Art as Communication," and "The Time Dimension." Numerous line drawings help the reader understand the varied art forms in non-Western societies.

Inuit art: An anthology. (1988). Introduction by Alma Houston. Winnipeg: Watson & Dwyer.

A collection of vivid photographs of Inuit artwork, coupled with descriptions of historical and contemporary Inuit art. The book features some well-known Inuit artists.

Otten, C.M. (1971). *Anthropology and art: Readings in cross-cultural aesthetics.* Garden City, NY: Natural History Press.

This is a collection of articles by anthropologists and art historians with emphasis on the functional relationships between art and culture.

Randall, H., & Polhemus, T. (1996). *The customized body.* London: Serpent's Tail.

An informative and visually stimulating examination of body art, including painting, tattooing, scarification, body piercing, makeup and jewellery, and gender modification.

CNN Today Videos

Gaza Theatre (CNN Cultural Anthropology, vol. 1, 2:05)
Looks at the interplay between Palestinian theatre and politics.

English Only (CNN Cultural Anthropology, vol. 1, 2:04)
This segment looks at the controversy surrounding the English-only movement.

Culture Crimes: Myanmar Stolen Artifacts (CNN Cultural Anthropology, vol. 3, 3:32)
A large black market exists around the world, dealing in stolen cultural artifacts and art. The segment also touches on the actions of former colonial rulers with regard to cultural artifacts.

Life on the Edge: The Town of Churchill (CNN Cultural Anthropology, vol. 3, 5:00)
Seventeenth-century English explorers founded the town of Churchill on Hudson Bay. The town, mainly inhabited by native peoples, is enjoying new prosperity thanks to a large influx of tourists and a growing appreciation of native arts and crafts.

The Mexican Bullfight (CNN Cultural Anthropology, vol. 3, 7:05)
Bullfighting has long held a central place in the culture of Mexico and other countries with a Hispanic heritage. To the lovers of the bullring, the activity has deeply held cultural values. The segment shows how animal rights activists disagree. Warning: Some viewers may find scenes of this segment objectionable.

Papua New Guinea Tourism (CNN Cultural Anthropology, vol. 5, 6:57)
Tourists visiting Papua New Guinea get a glimpse of a colourful and fascinating culture that has survived into the 21st century.

Chapter 14

The Anthropology of Health

One of the fastest-growing branches of anthropology, medical anthropology explores a wide range of topics on the interfaces of culture, the body, health, and social issues. Research takes the medical anthropologist to sites like Vancouver's Downtown Eastside, to work on harm-reduction programs and safe housing for injecting drug users.

Chapter Preview

1. What Is Medical Anthropology?

Medical anthropology places human health and illness in a cultural context, exploring cross-cultural differences in patterns of disease and in perceptions of health and illness. While an array of sciences can tell us about the biological bases of disease, medical anthropology also explores how social, cultural, political, and historical factors affect health and illness.

2. How Do Anthropologists Approach Medical Anthropology?

There are three main approaches to medical anthropology. The first, the biocultural or biomedical approach, deals with the epidemiology of health and illness: the causes of disease and patterns of distribution in populations. The second, known as the cultural interpretive or cultural constructionist approach, explores the cultural context of disease, or how cultural beliefs and perceptions affect people's health and the treatment of disease. The third, the critical medical anthropology (CMA) approach, considers the political economy and ecology of health.

3. How Does Social Inequality Affect Health and Illness?

Critical medical anthropology deals with the undeniable impact of the wider political economy on the health of individuals and communities. CMA asks how divisions of class, gender, and ethnicity affect health and how industrialization has historically affected the health of various cultures. It also considers the role pharmaceutical corporations play in the development of new drugs for certain diseases.

CHAPTER OUTLINE

The Biocultural Approach

The Cultural Interpretive Approach

Critical Medical Anthropology

Original Study: Health and Disease in One
    Culture: The Ju/'hoansi

Anthropology Applied: Vancouver's Downtown
    Eastside

Gender Perspectives: Women and Health

Contemporary Biomedicine

Medical anthropology considers three questions related to health and illness. First, how do various cultural conditions and practices affect the health of members of a given culture? Second, how do members of different cultures *conceptualize* health, illness, and healing? And third, how does the structure of society—divisions of class, gender, and ethnicity, as well as political organization—affect a people's health? These key issues in medical anthropology are dealt with by three theoretical approaches. The **biocultural approach** has its origins in the natural sciences and attempts to study the health and illness of populations by placing humans in their particular ecological and physiological settings. The **cultural interpretive approach** takes the position that health and illness are affected by how the culture views them. Thus, both approaches share an interest in the cultural context of health and disease, and both have a role to play in the understanding of human health. Finally, **critical medical anthropology** factors in the historical impact of social inequality on human health and the pervasive influence, both positive and negative, of capitalist systems.

THE BIOCULTURAL APPROACH

The biocultural approach (also called the biomedical approach) to medical anthropology stems from two core elements of the natural sciences. The first is the study of the human body and the way it functions, through research in anatomy, physiology, microbiology, genetics, biochemistry, and related sciences. The second is the study of population dynamics, through demography, epidemiology, and biostatistics—carefully collected and assessed statistics on thousands or even millions of people that reveal patterns of life, death, illness, and health. Medical anthropology brings findings from these sciences together with

key understandings of cultural and populational differences. Thus, biomedical research is placed in a richer and more nuanced cultural context.

One early biocultural study, conducted in 1962 by University of Michigan medical anthropologist James V. Neel, examined adult-onset diabetes among aboriginal peoples of North America.[1] Thanks to the pioneering research of Canadians Sir Frederick Banting (1891–1941) and Charles Best (1899–1978), the physiology and chemistry of insulin and its relation to diabetes mellitus were well understood. But a continuing mystery about the disease was why the levels of diabetes among aboriginal populations were three to five times higher than among non-aboriginals.

To answer this question, Neel had to go beyond the clinical diagnosis and treatment of the disease and place diabetes in the social and historical context of aboriginal life. In pre-Columbian times, he noted, North American aboriginals lived on foraged or farmed food that could vary greatly in quantity from season to season. Thus, they had developed a survival strategy of consuming very large quantities when food was available in anticipation of leaner times in the future. This "feast or famine" lifestyle had favoured selection for what Neel called "the thrifty genotype," an ability of the body to conserve insulin and fat stores from the season of plenty to the season of hardship.

As their traditional way of life on the land ended and they were relocated to reservations, aboriginal people switched to a steady diet high in refined carbohydrates. This meant that the physiological adaptation that had served them so well in their traditional way of life was now wildly out of synch with the now steady (if monotonous) food supply. The result has been a

---

[1]Neel, J.V. (1962). Diabetes mellitus: A "thrifty" genotype rendered detrimental by "progress"? *American Journal of Human Genetics, 14* (4), 353–362.

Biocultural approach. An approach to medical anthropology that studies how ecological and physiological conditions affect the health and disease of populations. **> Cultural interpretive approach.** The study of how cultural beliefs and perceptions of health and illness affect people's health and the treatment of disease. **> Critical medical anthropology.** A branch of medical anthropology that considers the political economy of health and the effect of social inequality on people's health.

Medical anthropology has pioneered research that seeks to explain the high rates of adult-onset diabetes observed among contemporary First Nations peoples in Canada.

tendency toward chronic overproduction of insulin, as well as high rates of obesity and other diseases of modern life. Neel's historical and cultural insight into what had been treated until then as essentially a medical problem had significant benefits for aboriginal people in terms of designing better methods of treatment and prevention. Canadian anthropologists Emoke Szathmáry and John O'Neil at the University of Manitoba and T. Kue Young at the University of Toronto have carried on and refined anthropological studies of diabetes in First Nations people, from both biological and cultural perspectives.[2]

American anthropologist Frank Livingstone of the University of Michigan also took a biocultural approach in studying sickle-cell anemia among African Americans in the 1950s.[3] As we saw in Chapter 5, people with this condition have abnormally shaped red blood cells that are unable to carry an adequate supply of oxygen to the organs, causing kidney failure, heart murmurs, and other often fatal complications. Scientists wondered why such a maladaptive gene would continue to appear in the gene pool despite its near fatal consequences.

Following his colleague Neel's lead in searching for the cultural and historical roots of the condition, Livingstone travelled to West Africa, the ancestral home of many African Americans. From the 15th to 19th centuries, irrigation agriculture had expanded in West Africa. The standing water created ideal breeding sites for malaria-carrying mosquitoes, and the disease spread rapidly. However, people who had inherited the sickle-cell gene from only one parent— the heterozygous form—not only did not develop anemia, but possessed a natural resistance to falciparum malaria. A person possessing a homozygous form of the sickle-cell gene, passed on by both parents, would develop severe, usually fatal, anemia. People lacking the gene entirely had a much higher risk of contracting malaria. This explained why the sickle-cell gene remained in the population, and also why it remained present in only a small percentage of people. The selective advantage of malarial resistance overrode the negative consequences of the anemia, and so the gene remained in the population. About 10 percent of African Americans carry the heterozygous form of the sickle cell gene, but only three-tenths of 1 percent have sickle-cell anemia. Today, African-American couples planning to marry routinely consult genetics laboratories and are screened for the sickle-cell gene.

Livingstone's cultural-genetic research into the sickle-cell gene illustrates the strength of the biocultural approach in medical anthropology. The sickle-cell gene is also found in Mediterranean populations and has recently been studied in the Greek community of Montreal to explore its effects on individuals and families.

Some biocultural medical anthropologists are engaged in an active dialogue with critical medical anthropologists and are exploring the effects of racial theories, class divisions, gender power imbalances, and ethnicity on human health and well-being. These are summarized in an important recent volume edited by Alan Goodman and Thomas Leatherman entitled *Building a New Biocultural Synthesis: Political-Economic Perspectives on Human Biology.*[4]

[2]O'Neil, J.D. (1989). Cultural and political context of patient dissatisfaction in cross-cultural clinical encounters: A Canadian Inuit study. *Medical Anthropology Quarterly, 3* (4), 325–344; Szathmáry, E.J. (1994). Non-insulin dependent diabetes mellitus among aboriginal North Americans. *Annual Review of Anthropology, 23,* 457–482; Kue Young, T. (1993). Diabetes mellitus among Native Americans in Canada and the United States: An epidemiological review. *American Journal of Human Biology, 5* (4), 399–413.

[3]Livingstone, F. (1958). Anthropological implications of sickle-cell gene distribution in West Africa. *American Anthropologist, 58,* 533–562.

[4]Goodman, A., & Leatherman, T. (Eds.). (1998). *Building a new biocultural synthesis: Political-economic perspectives on human biology.* Ann Arbor: University of Michigan Press.

THE CULTURAL INTERPRETIVE APPROACH

Given the strengths of the biomedical approach, it may be difficult to accept the view that cultural perceptions have a significant part to play in the understanding of health and illness. After all, germs are germs, and the way to cure sickness is to take the appropriate medical measures. But medical science is far from perfect in diagnosing and treating disease. As Donald Joralemon points out, medical practice in any age is strongly influenced by the social context and prejudices of the day.[5] Accepted medical knowledge and practices often turn out to be ridiculously misguided by today's standards. Two centuries ago the dominant medical opinion held that a variety of illnesses, from epilepsy to heart disease, could be traced to a single cause: masturbation. And during the 1860s in the American South, learned medical opinion proclaimed that African-American slaves' propensity to escape had nothing to do with the injustices of the system, but was a clinical condition labelled "drapetomania" that could be treated and cured.

Every society and every period of history brings its own cultural bias to bear on the encounter between humans and their health. Medical practices, even in countries that claim to be biomedically "enlightened," such as Canada and the United States, are shaped by social forces and cultural beliefs.

But there is an even more compelling reason why biomedicine alone gives us only a partial understanding of illness and how to cure it. Consider the example of fetal alcohol syndrome (FAS), a condition that can cause serious birth defects in babies whose mothers were heavy consumers of alcohol during pregnancy. Medical science can tell us about the clinical symptoms of FAS, including low birth weight, short length, small head size, muscle damage, and mental retardation. But the social ills that produced the problem—the poverty, poor home environment, and sexual abuse, the social traumas that led the mother to dull the pain of her existence even while putting the unborn child at risk—these are questions that medical science is not equipped to answer. Unravelling them is a task for the social scientist, the philosopher, or the ethicist, and the medical anthropologist can provide valuable insight.

The Three Bodies: An Approach to Culture and Health

Conventional biomedicine, as well as the pharmaceutical industry, conceives of and treats the body as existing in a Cartesian universe. In this universe, the body is regarded as a machine, which depends on the workings of its individual parts to function smoothly. If drug therapies can improve the functioning of the individual parts, then the entire physical body can be healed. In their famous essay "The Mindful Body," medical anthropologists Nancy Scheper-Hughes and Margaret Lock point out the many cultural assumptions in this model of the human body.[6] They criticize the biomedical view of the body and offer alternative ways of thinking about sickness and health, in a paradigm for use in medical anthropology that they call the "three bodies." These are

- *the individual body/self* of the lived experience of being sick (or well), drawn from phenomenology, a branch of philosophy that studies subjectivity.
- *the social body* of symbolic representation, exploring the ways in which views of the body in sickness and health are metaphors for thinking about society, and vice versa.
- *the body politic* of the political sphere, focused on power, domination, and control, a view that draws on the poststructuralist ideas of Michel Foucault.

The authors' main point is that modern biomedicine grew out of the mind–body dualism that goes back in Western thought to Aristotle and the 17th-century philosophy of René Descartes. The mind comprehends the body as an entirely separate sphere of existence, whereas under the

[5]Joralemon, D. (1999). *Exploring medical anthropology.* Boston: Allyn and Bacon.

[6]Scheper-Hughes, N., & Lock, M. (1987). The mindful body: A prolegomenon to future work in medical anthropology. *Medical Anthropology Quarterly, 1* (1). Reprinted in P. Brown (Ed.). (1998). *Understanding and applying medical anthropology* (pp. 209–210). Mountain View, CA: Mayfield.

phenomenological view of the self—the first of the three bodies the individual body is seen as enmeshed in its cultural milieu. To illustrate just how artificial the mind–body dualism can be, Scheper-Hughes and Lock tell the following story. While doing their rounds, a class of medical students is shown a patient, a woman who suffers from chronic headaches. The subject describes at length her home life, her abusive alcoholic husband, her aged mother, senile and incontinent, and her son flunking high school. As the litany of troubles goes on and on, one student leaps up impatiently and asks, "But what is the *real* cause of the headaches?"[7]

The way of thinking behind the medical student's question reveals deeply entrenched patterns of thought in which a medical problem is either wholly biological or entirely psychological. The concept of psychosomatic illness, in which symptoms are real to the patient but have no observable organic basis, relies on the mind–body dualism. Medical theorist Dr. Leon Eisenberg attempted to recognize this problem by drawing a distinction between a *disease,* which has an identifiable biological basis, and an *illness,* which is the patient's *perception* of that condition.

Scheper-Hughes and Lock point out that in cultures around the world, the mind–body dualism is by no means universal. Medical anthropologists need to find a language that enables them to understand alternative views of health and disease in other cultures. Health practices might incorporate the "balanced complementarity" view of the universe in the yin–yang of Chinese cosmology, or the idea of "oneness" with the universe in Buddhist thought.

The second body, the social body, refers to ways in which society is structured by views of the body and nature. While Western thought separates nature and culture, the natural and the supernatural, many cultures see the individual, society, nature, and the supernatural as intertwined in complex ways. Thus, social transgressions, such as breaking taboos, can affect people's health or even trigger natural disasters like hurricanes or floods. Sickness, in turn, might be seen as a sign of divine displeasure. Referring mainly to tribal societies, Scheper-Hughes and Lock write, "The body is seen as a unitary, integrated aspect of self and social relations. It is dependent on and vulnerable to, the feelings, wishes, and actions of others, including spirits and dead ancestors. The body is not understood as a vast and complex machine, but rather as a microcosm of the universe."[8] With such insight, the medical anthropologist is better equipped to understand the ways of thinking that underlie alternative forms of medical knowledge and practice, such as shamanism, spirit possession, and faith healing.

The third body, the body politic, refers to the effects on people's health of powerful societal forces, expressed through class, ethnicity, and gender. Patriarchy, for example, imposes discipline on women's bodies in the form of dress codes, prescribed body language, and, in extreme cases, body mutilation through such practices as Chinese foot binding, Victorian corsets, or contemporary breast-enlargement surgery. Michel Foucault pioneered the study of key institutions of modernity, such as the clinic, the asylum, and the prison, to show how states impose their will and shape the very bodies of their subjects.[9]

Scheper-Hughes and Lock draw on Mary Douglas's important book *Purity and Danger: An Analysis of the Concepts of Pollution and Taboo.*[10] According to Douglas, when a society feels threatened at times of war, economic uncertainty, or rapid change, it tends to expand the number of social controls through regulation and surveillance. The recent heightening of security and the restriction of civil liberties in the post-9/11 era are examples of this trend anticipated by Douglas's theory. The medical profession, in this view, plays an important role. Doctors are seen as authority figures, representing and defending one of the most powerful institutions in society. Bearing with them an aura of moral authority backed by state power, doctors become the agents of this form of domination.

A major component of Scheper-Hughes and Lock's essay is their critique of contemporary Western biomedicine. In particular, they criticize

---

[7]Ibid.

[8]Ibid.

[9]Foucault, M. (1975). *The birth of the clinic: An archaeology of medical perception.* New York: Vintage.

[10]Douglas, M. (1966/1991). *Purity and Danger: An Analysis of the Concepts of Pollution and Taboo.* London: Routledge.

How the dominant culture imposes its will on women's bodies can be seen in Chinese foot-binding practices, Victorian corsetry, and contemporary breast-enlargement surgery.

medical hegemony—the idea that the "official" theories of health and disease in biomedicine form a kind of orthodoxy, with medical doctors as the high priests. Under this system, alternative views are dismissed as not only wrong but somehow beyond the moral pale. One expression of this hegemony is the process of **medicalization,** whereby elements of social and cultural life that had existed outside the realm of medicine are reformulated as medical problems. Examples include childbirth, which until the 20th century was largely in the hands of midwives; substance abuse; hyperactivity in children; weight control; and various mental health issues, which people had formerly coped with through the support of families and kin groups, elders, and religious fig-

ures such as priests, or in tribal societies traditional healers and shamans. All of these areas have been brought under the broad umbrella of biomedicine. The process of medicalization has been driven in large part by the drug industry, whose laboratories produce drug after drug to address what in many ways are society's problems: Ritalin for hyperactive children, Botox for the aging, antidepressants for the emotionally distressed, and diet drugs for the overweight are but a few examples. There is a strong legal and financial component to medicalization as well, as society defines which conditions are illnesses, and therefore eligible for medical insurance coverage, and which are nonmedical or even criminal, such as acts committed while under the influence of alcohol.

Scheper-Hughes and Lock's ideas in "The Mindful Body" have provided a rich source of models and thinking for the cultural interpretive school of medical anthropology. As we shall see later in this chapter, their critique of medicine under capitalism has provided tools of analysis for critical medical anthropology, as well. However, these ideas are best seen as an invitation to biomedicine to engage in dialogue, rather than as a radical rejection of the biological bases of health and disease.

Shamanism

It is a basic tenet of anthropology that cultural beliefs have a great impact on health and illness, and the way people perceive the interconnection of human health and the spirit world can affect their healing. Shamanistic practices are widespread both in Western and non-Western regions. For much of human history, shamanism was the dominant form of healing, involving elaborate rituals to intercede with the spirit world and magically remove afflictions from the bodies of the sick. It wasn't until the rise of state societies that medical practice became set off from religious practices, and thus it is only in the last few hundred years that medicine has built its foundations (at least in theory) on rational and empirical evidence.

Medical hegemony.   The influence of the official medical establishment on society's views of health and illness.
> Medicalization.   The reformulation of aspects of social and cultural life, such as childbirth, as medical problems.

Margaret Lock

Margaret Lock is the Marjorie Bronfman Professor in Social Studies in Medicine, affiliated with the Social Studies of Medicine and Anthropology departments at McGill University. Trained as a cultural anthropologist with a particular interest in anthropology of the body in health and illness, Lock has carried out comparative research primarily in Japan and North America. She explores the relationship of emerging bioscientific knowledge and associated technology with the social, political, and moral order, and with subjectivity. Lock has researched the 20th-century revival of indigenous Japanese medical systems, which continue to proliferate today, and the cultural management and political meanings associated with life-cycle transitions, including adolescence, female midlife, and old age. Her book *Encounters with Aging: Mythologies of Menopause in Japan and North America*, published in 1993, won several prizes, including the Staley Prize of the School of American Research and the Wellcome Medal of the Royal Anthropological Institute of Great Britain.

Lock's most recent research focuses on people's changing conceptions of life and death, and of normalized and hybrid bodies, as technologically innovative medical practices became routine in Japan and North America. Her award-winning 2002 book, *Twice Dead: Organ Transplants and the Reinvention of Death,* explores the creation of the diagnosis of brain death to allow organs for transplant to be harvested from still living, but brain dead, bodies. Lock documents public and professional medical responses, moral and political, over the past 30 years to this new death and to the organ transplant procedure. Currently, she is investigating how molecular and population genetics are being theorized, researched, and implemented in clinical practice, and to what effect. The implications for professional and popular understanding of what are assumed to be normal and abnormal bodies, for the concept of risk and its application in everyday life, and for the "enhancement" of individuals and society are central to Lock's research. One of her objectives is to monitor the emergence of the forms of biocapitalism, the commercialization of the biological components of life, on which the new genetics depends.

Source: Adapted from McGill University. (2004). *Social Studies of Medicine.* Retrieved February 12, 2004, from the World Wide Web: http://www.mcgill.ca/ssom/#lock.

The term *shaman* came into Western languages in the late 19th century, when Russian-American anthropologist Waldemar Bogoras returned from fieldwork in eastern Siberia among the Evenk, a group of Tungus-speaking nomads who followed reindeer herds. He described a form of magical healing that certain extraordinary individuals would perform. These healers were revered by the nomads and believed to have magical powers to contact the spirit world and heal the sick. When anthropologists conducted comparative studies, they found the practices Bogoras had observed were widespread throughout the world's regions, especially among band and tribal societies but also in "advanced" industrial societies such as Korea and Japan.

Piers Vitebsky notes that, in their societies, shamans fulfill the functions of doctors and priests, as well as social workers and mystics.[11] The diversity of cultures in which shamans exist is truly astonishing. The *angakok* of the Canadian Inuit, the *curanderos* throughout Latin America, the "psychic surgeons" of the Philippines, the *n/um k'xausi* of the Ju/'hoansi—from Nepal to Mongolia and Taiwan to Peru, there are practising shamans in hundreds of cultures around the world even today (see Chapter 12).

The stock-in-trade of all shamans includes healing sickness and contacting the spirit world. Most but not all shamans enter altered states of

---

[11]Vitebsky, P. (1995). *The shaman: Voyages of the soul, trance, ecstasy, and healing from Siberia to the Amazon.* Boston: Little, Brown.

The shaman's stock-in-trade includes ritual paraphernalia like this Inuit shaman's rattle, believed to imbue the practitioner with powers drawn from the spirit world. It is deeply meaningful to both healer and patient.

consciousness, forms of trance in which they unleash their supernatural healing and other powers. In many shamanic traditions the trance gives the healer a kind of X-ray vision to see into the body to identify sickness and also to see spirits lurking in the background. Other almost universal elements of the shaman's craft include the employment of special ritual paraphernalia, sacred music, and dance.

Many but not all shamans use hallucinogenic drugs to achieve the trance state. The Yanomami of Venezuela snort the drug ebene through the nostrils and enter violent and dramatic trance states, accompanied by copious discharges of green phlegm. Ayahuasca *(Banisteriopsis caapi)* is widely used in Quechua-speaking parts of South America. Mazatec curanderos in northern Mexico use psilocybe mushrooms to enter trance, while Ju/'hoansi n/um k'xausi can achieve deep trance states without drugs. The trance can be so deep that some Ju healers can step into the coals of the fire without being burned. Firewalking is part of many other shamanic traditions and has even found its way into urban North America.

Many shamans resort to elaborate stage business and turn their healing rites into bravura performances. Scholars believe this is one of the keys to their effectiveness as healers. Claude Lévi-Strauss describes the process by drawing on the life history, collected by Franz Boas, of a young Kwakwaka-wakw man in British Columbia, who later would become the famous shaman Quesalid.[12] At first the young man is skeptical about the magical powers of the shamans and even wants to expose them as frauds. When he is invited by a senior shaman to be apprenticed to train and be initiated into the secrets of the profession, he jumps at the chance to discover their methods. One day, observing his master closely in a healing session, he notes how the shaman tricks his patient by concealing a feather in his mouth and biting his cheek to draw blood. The shaman dramatically appears to extract the blood-soaked feather from the patient's body, claiming it to be a bloody worm and the source of the illness.

Quesalid now has the evidence of deception he has been seeking, but events have moved beyond him. Another sick person has had a dream in which the young shaman-in-training healed him, and he is clamouring for Quesalid's services as a healer. Though still skeptical, Quesalid copies his master's technique with such skill that the patient declares himself cured. Success after success follows, and his fame extends throughout the region. Gradually he loses his qualms when he realizes that people believe in him and that belief effects the cure. In the end he comes to believe in himself and becomes convinced of the power of his medicine.

Does Shamanism Work?

Does shamanic healing actually heal? Or is it all in the mind of the believer? Shamanic healers face the same odds as conventional medical doctors: 99 percent of sicknesses are self-limiting. Minor colds, headaches, infections, muscular complaints, PMS, stomachaches, even serious flu—all are likely to resolve themselves without medical intervention. What medicine may do is speed recovery and shorten the duration of the illness, a not insignificant benefit.

[12]Lévi-Strauss, C. (1963). The sorcerer and his magic. In *Structural Anthropology*, vol. 1. New York: Basic Books.

In another account of shamanic healing, Lévi-Strauss addresses this question by studying the Cuna Indians living on the San Blas Islands off the Caribbean coast of Panama.[13] A shaman is called to the bedside of a woman who is going through a difficult labour. After days of contractions she is exhausted and still not fully dilated; she is in danger of losing the baby, dying herself, or both. The shaman sits by her hammock and explains to her in terms of the complex cosmology of the Cuna what is afflicting her.

The problem is with Muu, the female deity who controls women's wombs and creates the fetus. Muu has gone beyond her prescribed role and has captured the woman's *purba*, or soul. If the woman and her baby are to survive, the soul must be recaptured. An elaborate ritual is performed. The shaman carves figurines, which become his assistants and will accompany him on a difficult journey to the abode of Muu to reclaim the woman's purba.

Continuing the narrative, the shaman describes how with his assistants he mounts an expedition to find the woman's soul; it is a journey to a sacred place deep in the jungle. The way is blocked by what seems to be a dense growth of tangled vines soaked in blood. In narrow single file the men force their way into the interior, hacking a trail inch by inch, aided by magical white hats that light the way. Reaching their destination after much struggle, they find the sacred object, the purba, and convince Muu to relinquish her hold on the woman. After uttering many spells, they prepare to return to the village. Here they summon other deities, the lords of the wood-boring insects and the lords of the burrowing animals, "the clearers of the way." They return through the jungle vegetation to begin the difficult descent. The trail widens, and the shaman concludes his account by describing how he and his team finally make their way out of the jungle to safety. Soon after, the woman, who had followed the story with rapt attention and is now fully dilated, gives birth to a healthy baby.

The symbolism of the story is certainly not hard to decipher. What is perhaps remarkable is that its telling had such a profound effect. By using imagery, the shaman encouraged dilation and delivery of the baby.

What these stories convey about the power of shamanism is the importance of shared meaning between patient and healer. To believe is to participate in a deeply meaningful cultural world. To realize the importance of living in a world of coherent meanings, where things make sense, however strange they may seem to others, is to begin to understand the still largely unknown power of the mind in the healing process.

Medicine has recognized this power: In recent years some shamanistic practices have lost their marginal status and have been incorporated into mainstream biomedicine. The method the Cuna shaman used in the case of the difficult delivery is now widely adopted in the treatment of cancer in Canadian hospitals, under the label **guided imagery.** Typically, cancer patients, singly or in groups, are talked through a meditation session, in which they are asked to imagine an intense white healing light and visualize it penetrating their bodies, seeking out the site of the tumour, and through its warmth and healing goodness, shrinking the tumour. Many variants of such guided imagery are in use.[14]

Since guided imagery is used in conjunction with conventional chemo- and radiation therapy, it is difficult to know to what extent success can be attributed solely to the mental work. Although results vary, many patients report the positive nature of the experience, and some report remission of their cancers. Whatever the outcome, the technique itself is a direct adaptation of shamanistic practice, although the link may not always be acknowledged. Forms of touching and "therapeutic touch," currently in vogue as an

---

[13]Lévi-Strauss, C. (1963). The effectiveness of symbols. In *Structural Anthropology*, vol. 1. New York: Basic Books.

[14]Achterberg, J., Dossey, B., & Kolkmeier, L. (1994). *Rituals of healing: Using imagery for health and wellness.* New York: Bantam Books.

Guided imagery.   The use of visualization techniques and meditation in cancer and other treatments to encourage healing.

alternative therapy, are other examples of healing methods that have their roots in the shamanic tradition.

▲▽▲▽▲▽▲▽▲▽▲▽▲▽▲▽▲▽▲▽▲▽▲▽▲▽▲▽▲▽▲

CRITICAL MEDICAL ANTHROPOLOGY

Scheper-Hughes and Lock's concept of the three bodies, discussed above, is a wide-ranging critique of the philosophical roots of biomedicine. One part of this critique focuses on the point that without a sense of the larger political economy in which health and illness are embedded, medical anthropology can give only a partial understanding of human suffering.

The third branch of contemporary medical anthropology is critical medical anthropology (CMA), a term coined by Hans Baer and Merrill Singer in 1982.[15] CMA joins other disciplines in exploring capitalist industrialization, the emergence of a global market, and other issues in the headlines, such as militarism and human rights, that have an impact on human health and disease.

Where does CMA fit into the broader picture of medical anthropology? Early medical anthropology involved two approaches: the biocultural and the cultural interpretive. The first took the biomedical view of disease as a given and studied the underlying cultural or ecological circumstances of people's health. The second took an insider's view and looked at disease from the "native's" perspective. Both approaches are valid, and both grew out of critiques of conventional medicine. The biocultural approach argued that the forms of disease vary according to time, place, and ethnicity, and to understand disease we must understand the specific context in which it arose. The cultural interpretive approach focused on the subjective elements in medical treatment, calling into question the universality of Western biomedical views of disease.

But something was missing: Neither approach factored in the historical impact of social inequality on human health, and the perva-

sive influence, both positive and negative, of the capitalist world system.

In *Medical Anthropology and the World System,* Hans Baer, Merrill Singer, and Ida Susser note, for example, that a standard textbook in the field, *Medical Anthropology in Ecological Perspective,* presents the Tasmanian Aborigines of Australia as an example of a maladapted people, whose lack of "fitness" caused them to quickly die out.[16] Absent in this analysis is the fact that the Tasmanians had lived successfully in

[15]Baer, H.A., Singer, M., & Susser. I. (2004). *Medical anthropology and the world system: A critical perspective* (2nd ed.). Westport, CT: Bergin and Garvey.

[16]McElroy, A., & Townsend, P. (1996). *Medical anthropology in ecological perspective.* Boulder, CO: Westview.

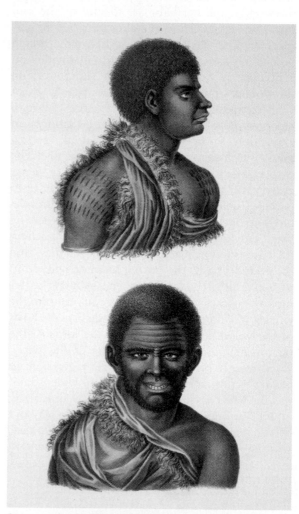

Some medical anthropologists have argued that the Tasmanian aborigines became extinct because they were maladapted. Critical medical anthropology argues that this view ignores the role that a brutal colonial conquest played in their extinction.

their island habitant for thousands of years; it wasn't until the colonial period in the early 19th century that the population collapsed, after the Tasmanians were systematically dispossessed of their land, infected with European diseases, and, in one of the most cruel chapters of European colonialism, hunted for sport. In other words, the textbook authors ignored the political economy of colonialism.

Countless examples of the applicability of CMA can be found in the anthropological literature. In *We Eat the Mines and the Mines Eat Us*, a classic study of tin mining in the Bolivian Andes, June Nash describes the many occupational hazards the miners faced.[17] These men worked underground in primitive conditions, 3658 to 4267 metres above sea level, and dealt with hazards ranging from cave-ins to accidents involving faulty equipment, flooding, and, in the long run, disabling respiratory diseases and arthritis aggravated by the shock of moving from the stifling heat underground to the damp cold of the altiplano where they lived. To explain their afflictions and give meaning to their difficult lives, the miners' etiological system involved a belief in ancient devil spirits, or *tios*, that inhabited the mines and caused disease and accidents. To appease the tios, the miners took food and alcoholic drinks down into the mineshafts and offered them to carved and painted images of the spirits.

June Nash's book gives insight into the culturally constructed images of disease and how the Bolivian miners saw their world. But beyond the cultural interpretive perspective lies a deeper meaning. While the mine management accepted the miners' high mortality rate as the cost of doing business, the miners recognized that the capitalist system that gave them their livelihood ("we eat the mines") also took their lives ("and the mines eat us"). Capitalism is here personified as a voracious and unforgiving deity. Similar beliefs are found elsewhere in Latin America. The poor agricultural labourers of the Cauca Valley of Colombia, who did backbreaking work of another kind, had a similar belief system, one also found among the Toba of Argentina.[18]

Culture and Health through History

As we contemplate the world of today, its vast disparities in wealth and power sharply reflected in patterns of health, we must ask ourselves, how did it get this way? How does human health look in the long run, say over the last 10 000 years?[19] What are the characteristic patterns of health, disease, and modes of treatment in each phase of human history? What were the health effects of major world historical transitions, such as the origins of agriculture, urbanization, colonization, and industrialization?

Anthropologists draw upon two principal sources of information in studying the health of cultures historically. First, they use the direct evidence of **paleopathology**—the study of ancient skeletal material to reconstruct age at death and cause of death, as well as health, diet, and lifestyle. In recent years scientists have developed sophisticated techniques of bone analysis to present remarkably accurate assessments of past health status.

Second, anthropologists study the health and nutrition of contemporary peoples whose way of life resembles that of times past, and who live beyond the reach of "modern" medicine. Thus, the medical study of contemporary hunters and gatherers like the Ju/'hoansi can offer useful clues to health in times past.

When anthropologists scan the history of the last 10 000 years, they identify several key stages in human political development, each accompanied by corresponding patterns of subsistence and economic organization, as we saw in Chapter 11.

---

[17]Nash, J. (1979). *We eat the mines and the mines eat us: Dependency and exploitation in Bolivian tin mines.* New York: Columbia University Press.

[18]Taussig, M. (1986). *The devil and commodity fetishism in South America.* Chapel Hill, NC: University of North Carolina Press; Gordillo, G. (2002). The breath of the devils: Memories and places of an experience of terror. *American Ethnologist, 29* (1), 33–57.

[19]Cohen, M.N. (1989). *Health and the rise of civilization.* New Haven, CT: Yale University Press.

Paleopathology.   The study of ancient skeletal material to reconstruct age at death, cause of death, and health, diet, and lifestyle.

These stages of development are separated by three main transformations or revolutions.

Before agriculture, people lived in band societies based on hunting and gathering. Around 10 000 years ago the first great transformation, often referred to as the Neolithic revolution, brought about the domestication of plants and animals. Political organization shifted to larger, more settled, and more centralized societies, commonly called tribes and chiefdoms.

The second great transformation, beginning about 5000 B.C. in the Middle East and later elsewhere, was the origin of the state and the rise of cities, sometimes called the urban revolution. This produced ever larger and more centralized polities, which were sharply divided between rich and poor.

Beginning less than 500 years ago and still underway is the third great transformation, the expansion of Europe and the rise of the industrial system of production, resulting in what we have come to call the modern world system. "Modernity" has been highly uneven in its impact on the world, with some regions and populations enjoying the benefits and others, incorporated into the world system at the bottom of the ladder, being impoverished (see Chapter 15).

Bands, tribes and chiefdoms, early states, and industrial states: What are the characteristic health conditions of each system of organization, and what are the health consequences of each of the great transformations?

Band Societies

Food-foraging societies, such as the Ju/'hoansi and Cree, tended to live in small mobile bands, with relatively egalitarian politics. Population density was low and settlements were temporary, as the people moved camp several times a year to seek game and other resources. Despite previous views of hunter-gatherers as leading a constant struggle for existence, modern research has revealed quite a different picture.[20]

Food foragers enjoyed relatively good health as measured by overall fitness. Key to their success were several factors. Their mobility and low population density meant that human and animal wastes did not have a chance to build up. Their well-documented commitment to social equality is correlated with an absence of health problems related to the social stress of living in hierarchies.

Detailed studies of the food-forager diet reveal it to be high in protein and dietary fibre, low in refined carbohydrates and sugars, and containing a diversity of vitamins and minerals. And don't forget: All the food was strictly organic. Add the exemplary activity regime, with plenty of outdoor aerobic exercise for men, women, and children, and you have a formula for healthy living that deserves careful study.

In recent years scientists have been probing the diet and lifestyle of hunter-gatherers to draw direct implications for modern humans. In *The Palaeolithic Prescription*, Boyd Eaton, Marjorie Shostak, and Mel Konner build a powerful case that modern health would be better if we consciously modelled our diet, exercise, and interpersonal relations on our Palaeolithic forebears.[21] The popular Atkins and Eades diet books have sold millions of copies on the premise that the high protein, low carb diet of our ancestors is ideal for modern living, and the consumption of fat is not the cause of obesity.

Yet there certainly was a downside to hunter-gatherer health. Hunting was a demanding and often risky way to make a living: Accidents, encounters with animals, and other hazards were significant causes of injury and death. Social mortality—death from homicide, raiding, and war—also may have been significant. Parasitic infection, especially for peoples living in tropical forests, was certainly a source of illness. Furthermore, the need for mobility and the lack of fixed living sites hastened death for the seriously ill and the infirm elderly, who would have been unable to keep up with the group's migrations.

In facing the afflictions of daily life, food foragers developed a variety of methods of treatment, including herbal remedies, massage, wound dressing, and bone-setting techniques, but the primary response to illness and misfortune was some form of shamanistic practice.

---

[20]Lee, R.B., & Daly, R.H. (Eds.). (1999). *The Cambridge encyclopedia of hunters and gatherers.* Cambridge, UK: Cambridge University Press.

[21]Eaton, B., Shostak, M., & Konner, M. (1988). *The Palaeolithic prescription: A program of diet and exercise and a design for living.* New York: Harper and Row.

Tribal Societies and Chiefdoms

The first great transformation, the domestication of plants and animals, began approximately 10 000 years ago and has been hailed as the Neolithic "great leap forward," ushering in an era of progress and advancement for humankind. The move to larger and more sedentary villages and an economy based on horticulture and livestock has been assumed by historians, archaeologists, and the public to have been a boon to humanity, offering stability of settlement and security of food supply. Chiefdoms, with the beginnings of central authority and social hierarchies, continued social trends ultimately made possible by more intensive agriculture and animal husbandry.

Given the general view that the Neolithic shift to farming and herding was a marked improvement over hunting and gathering, it came as a distinct surprise to archaeologists when a pivotal study of the health of Neolithic populations (as measured by skeletal remains) showed sharp declines in fitness when compared with the health of their Palaeolithic and Mesolithic ancestors. As George Armelagos notes, "While this scenario is appealing, the empirical evidence paints a different picture. The biological consequence of the shift from gathering and hunting to agriculture presents a much bleaker picture of health and disease. Instead of experiencing improved health, there is evidence of an increase in infection and nutritional disease."[22]

Advances in paleolopathology have shown that many diseases can be determined by examining skeletal remains. Tuberculosis, syphilis, and leprosy, for example, leave distinctive signatures on bone. Other infections leave generalized and nonspecific lesions on bone, called periosteal reactions, and nutritional deficiencies can be discerned on bone by a variety of signs. Deficiencies in the growth of long bones, for example, or changes in dental enamel give clues to shortfalls in calories or nutrients during childhood.

In a now classic study, *Paleopathology at the Origin of Agriculture,* Mark Cohen and George

Paleopathology, the study of health and disease from ancient skeletal remains, has shown that the transition from hunting and gathering to agriculture is accompanied by a relative decline in human health, not an advance.

Armelagos looked at the available studies (19 in all) comparing pre-farming archaeological populations with their Neolithic descendants.[23] Remarkably, out of the 17 studies for which the comparative data were available, 12 showed a significant drop in health status (71 percent of subjects), four others had equivocal results (24 percent of subjects showed declining health), and one showed that health status actually improved in the early stages of farming but then declined as agriculture intensified.

A number of factors had a negative impact on the health status of Neolithic farmers. With the growth in population, people began living in higher densities, fostering the transmission of disease and creating social stress. As people formed more sedentary settlements, serious problems of waste disposal arose, also leading to increased spread of disease. The change in subsistence placed further stress on people's health. With the move to agriculture, quantity increased but quality declined, and food insecurity got worse, not better. Living close to domesticated animals also led to transmission of zoonotic infections (pathogens that cross from animals to humans), as well as increased exposure to parasitic infections through helminths such as tapeworm and nematodes such as hookworm. Finally, with the

[22]Armelagos, G. (1998). Health and disease in prehistoric populations in transition. In P. Brown (Ed.), *Understanding and applying medical anthropology* (pp. 59–69). Mountain View, CA: Mayfield.

[23]Cohen, M., & Armelagos, G. (1984). *Paleopathology and the origins of agriculture.* New Haven, CT: Yale University Press.

move toward state organization, risks were borne differentially by those in higher and lower status positions. As ever larger numbers of people competed for space, intergroup violence increased, leading to what has been called the "neolithic masculinity/militarism complex."

Despite the increase in health problems, the ability of farming to increase food production led to an ever-expanding population, albeit of less healthy individuals. How did tribal peoples cope with the additional burdens of disease and social stress? Settled village horticulturalists used the same range of treatments as their hunter-gatherer predecessors: herbals, massage, and shamanistic healing. Occupational specialization also arose as shamans began to form priestly guilds.

State Societies and the Rise of Cities

The next great transformation brought about even more far-reaching changes in human society. The origin of the state roughly 5000 years ago ushered in an entirely new form of centralized, stratified political organization.[24] The rise of cities brought unprecedented numbers of people together, creating new and acute problems in maintaining sanitation, food supply, and social order. But perhaps the most striking change was the sharp rise in social inequality, as a centralized authority assumed power, along with a small privileged elite, leaving the vast majority of people to become peasants or slaves. Examples of early states include ancient Greece, Rome, Egypt, India, and China, as well as the Incas and Aztecs of the Americas.

The growing concentration of populations created more crowded conditions and easy transmission of communicable diseases. Epidemics periodically swept early cities. The widespread development of irrigation systems increased agricultural production but also fostered waterborne diseases such as schistosomiasis and wet conditions favouring the spread of malaria. The removal of waste products proved to be a major problem, as indicated by the periodic epidemics of waste-borne diseases such as cholera, plague, and typhus that swept the ancient world.

[24]Trigger, B. (2003). *Understanding early civilizations: A comparative study.* Cambridge and New York: Cambridge University Press.

The sheer size of early states and the autocratic methods of rule made them inherently unstable. Wars and civil unrest periodically overthrew dynasties and triggered periods of hardship. Frequent crop failures had the same effect: During these times, death from violence, famine, and associated diseases sharply increased.

The main issue affecting health was the continued inability to solve pressing ecological problems: how to create a stable social order that could exist within the carrying capacity of the land. This problem was so acute that demographers believe throughout the history of cities, right up until the mid-19th century, city death rates always exceeded the birth rates. The population and growth rates of cities could be maintained only by substantial annual net migration from the countryside.

The urban revolution produced a permanent division of society into classes, with vast differences in life conditions and health between elites and commoners. Archaeological studies have shown the underclass to be smaller in stature and shorter-lived than members of the elite. The latter, for their part, had problems of their own: For elites who maintained their rule through the strength of a warrior class, such as the Japanese samurai or the medieval knights of Europe, death in battle was a major hazard.

In dealing with the many illnesses and hazards that afflicted the burgeoning numbers of people, early states developed a variety of responses:

- *Rudimentary public health measures.* Ancient states could not have survived without systems of night-soil collection, careful disposal of the dead, regulation of abattoirs, quarantine measures in the event of epidemics, and regulation of the water supply.
- *The emergence of medical specialists.* Guilds of doctors, some with extensive training, and advanced medical theories arose in the ancient world to serve the elite. Some forms of medicine, including traditional Chinese medicine and Ayurvedic medicine in India, are still practised today, and some techniques, such as acupuncture, yoga, and shiatsu massage, have gained a respected foothold as alternative therapies within contemporary biomedicine.

Traditional health practitioners continue to provide treatment for illness throughout the world. Many of their treatments have been shown to have efficacy, and some have been incorporated into complementary "mainstream" medicine.

- *The development of state religion.* Much of the treatment of illness remained firmly based in religion. The rise of major religions—Buddhism, Hinduism, Confucianism, Christianity, and Islam—gave devout followers grounds for hope through faith healing.
- *Folk medicine.* For the mass of the population, traditional shamanism and herbal healing continued to be practised (and are still in use today) but were now reclassified as "folk medicine" and "folk healing."

The Industrial Revolution and the Modern World System

The rise of the modern nation state, colonization, and the processes of modernization are discussed elsewhere in this text (see Chapters 6, 11, and 15). From a public health point of view, the history of the last 500 years can be seen as the product of five interrelated strands of development:

- *The expansion of Europe and the age of colonization.* The "discovery" of the New World unleashed a major period of migration, and people from all continents mixed in melting pots as diverse as the Caribbean, Brazil, South Africa, and the streets of New York, London, and Hong Kong. Diseases brought by migrants

often had disastrous consequences for the formerly isolated aboriginals of such continents as North America and Australia. Some areas of the New World lost up to 90 percent of their population through introduced diseases such as smallpox.[25]
- *The development of the capitalist mode of production.* The reorganization of first the European and then the entire world's economy by profit-driven enterprises had major consequences, drawing millions into commodity production, often as slaves or indentured labourers, and further accentuating inequalities of wealth, power, and health between rich and poor.
- *Industrialization.* In the 19th century, the invention of the steam engine and the dramatic transition from hand production to machine production caused a truly revolutionary change in world society. The vast increase in the volume of manufactured goods initially benefited only the small number of owners, while factory workers toiled long hours in intolerable conditions. As railways and steamships were built, the volume of trade and the speed of transport between regions and continents increased, as did the speed of transmission and dispersal of disease-causing microorganisms.
- *Biomedicine.* The same social forces that produced the steam engine and advances in science also affected medical practice. The gradual development of scientific medicine after 1850 finally began to yield benefits for society at large. Public health measures cleaned up the water supply and waste disposal, and antiseptic clinical practice began to save lives in surgery and childbirth.
- *Health and social welfare.* The period from 1850 to 1950 represented the high-water mark in the fight for workers' rights. Campaigns for the right to a living wage, better working conditions, and a shorter work week were the real means by which the benefits of modern medicine were extended to workers, later to their families, and eventually to society at large.

[25]Crosby, A. (1972/2003). *The Columbian exchange: Biological and cultural consequences of 1492* (30th anniversary ed.). Westport, CT: Praeger.

These forces led to the rise of the modern welfare state and the extension of at least some of the benefits of medical innovation to the public.[26]

Health Outcomes of Modernity

What changes has modernity brought to the world order? The most obvious change is in the sheer number of people: The population recently passed the 6 billion mark, and over 300 000 babies are born every 24 hours. The world also is becoming increasingly urbanized. Tokyo; Mexico City; Bombay; Sao Paulo, Brazil; and New York already each have 15 million or more people, and a dozen more cities have topped 10 million.

Vast disparities in wealth and power characterize the human world. While in a minority of developed countries such as Canada citizens enjoy per capita annual incomes of over $28 000, billions of people in the developing world live on less than $2 a day. The Internet, biotechnology, and other advanced technologies seem to offer a glowing future, but these modern marvels are beyond most people's reach. Much of the world continues to suffer under wars, civil unrest, poverty, and oppression.

Advocates for the present social order may agree with Dr. Pangloss, the character in Voltaire's novel *Candide* (1759), who expressed the view that French society of the day was "the best of all possible worlds." But a more realistic and critical observer would acknowledge that the wonders of modern medicine and health care are unevenly distributed around the globe.

In the developed nations of western Europe, Japan, and North America, and a few well-to-do others—Australia, New Zealand, Dubai, Hong Kong, and Singapore—modernity has brought major improvements in health. Life expectancy in Canada rose from 50 years at the time of Confederation to 60 in 1931, and is almost 80

years of age today.[27] By the mid-20th century, most of the infectious diseases of the past, including smallpox, malaria, and tuberculosis, had been conquered or reduced to very low numbers in developed countries. But new threats to health came into prominence. The primary causes of death became the so-called **diseases of civilization**: heart disease, stroke, and cancer. Along with an affluent lifestyle came an epidemic of obesity. Up to half of Canadians are said to be overweight, and this has triggered many additional health problems such as diabetes. There is concern that in the 21st century some governments, following a neoliberal agenda, are moving away from the ideal of health care for all and rolling back the gains in access that earlier generations achieved.

Corporate power, hand in hand with the advertising industry, plays a significant role in modern society's health. Massive consumption of two products known to have negative health consequences—alcohol and tobacco—is sustained by heavy marketing campaigns. These problematic but perfectly legal substances have been shown to cause significant impairment of health and increased mortality in both developed and developing countries. The drive for corporate profits has sustained the tobacco industry, even in the face of mounting medical evidence of the damage smoking causes to health, a topic discussed further below.

Another well-documented consequence of the industrial system is the appearance of countless new chemicals created in manufacturing new products. Over the years, millions of tons of these chemicals have entered the water, air, and soil and found their way into the food chain. From the 1920s on, human health began to be seriously affected, but few researchers were able to identify the links between, for example, mounting rates of cancer and industrial pollution. After Rachel Carson published her groundbreaking book *Silent Spring* in 1962, the public became aware of

---

[26]Rosen, G. (1993). *A history of public health*. Baltimore, MD: Johns Hopkins University Press; Roberts, C.A., & Cox, M. (2003). *Health and disease in Britain: From prehistory to the present day*. Stroud, Gloucestershire: Sutton.

[27]Girvan, S. (Ed.). (2002). *Canadian global almanac 2003*. Toronto: John Wiley and Sons.

Diseases of civilization.   Diseases such as heart disease, stroke, and cancer that are most prevalent in affluent, industrialized countries.

just how serious the problem of pollution had become for the health of humanity and the environment.[28] This awareness has led to worldwide citizens' campaigns for environmental justice, a major branch of medical anthropology described later in this chapter.

The modern medical system has produced definite improvements in human health in the affluent countries of the world. However, medical experts believe that simple public health measures introduced without much fanfare, such as clean water supply and systems of waste management, have been the largest contributing factors to

improvements in health by eliminating infectious diseases.

While advances in drug therapies, surgical techniques, and diagnostic procedures also have extended life for millions, for many people, even the poor in affluent countries like the United States, good health care is still out of reach. Canadian activists George Manuel and Michael Posluns coined the term "fourth world" to refer to indigenous minorities inside other countries, such as First Nations peoples in Canada and the Australian Aborigines.[29] Despite living in affluent nations, indigenous minorities' health resembles that of the disadvantaged peoples of the

[28]Carson, R. (1962). *Silent spring.* Boston: Houghton Mifflin.

[29]Manuel, G., & Posluns, M. (1974). *The fourth world: An Indian reality.* New York: Free Press.

Vast disparities in health exist among and within world regions. While the countries of the First World (top left) enjoy the benefits of advanced public health care and medicine, billions in the Third World (top right) have only limited access. Since the fall of communism, the former USSR (lower left) has experienced a drop from First to Third World health status, while Fourth World indigenous minorities in Canada and the United States (lower right) have poorer health than other citizens of those countries.

developing world. Health disparities for fourth world peoples in Canada and elsewhere remain an important issue of equity and social justice.

For the billions of poor in developing countries undergoing rapid urbanization—including China, India, and other parts of Asia; African countries; and many parts of Latin America—stress-related diseases have now been added to the existing threat of epidemic disease. In parts of Asia and Africa, life expectancy is 37 to 45 years and dropping; life expectancy also is declining in Russia. On top of it all, the spread of industrialization means that pollution-related health conditions such as asthma, allergies, emphysema, and many cancers are on the rise.

The following sections detail some of the significant health consequences of social inequality in the world today. One of medical anthropology's prime directives is to document these continuing inequities in the distribution of health care, and to work with activist organizations such as Médecins Sans Frontières (Doctors Without Borders), as well as with more mainstream organizations like the Canadian Cancer Society and the Heart and Stroke Foundation, for the betterment of humanity.

ORIGINAL STUDY

Health and Disease in One Culture: The Ju/'hoansi

Richard Borshay Lee, University of Toronto

Throughout this text, reference is made to the Ju/'hoansi, one of the best-known examples of hunting-and-gathering society in anthropology.[1] Medical anthropologists have traced the health of the Ju/'hoansi during the period of great transition from the colonial to the post-colonial period. Health surveys taken in the 1960s when the Ju/'hoansi were still largely living as hunters and gatherers showed them to be relatively healthy.[2] They led active outdoor lives, the men hunting wild game and the women gathering over 100 species of wild plants. It has been estimated that women walked a total of 2000 kilometres annually, or over 5 kilometres per day, usually carrying loads of 5 to 15 kilograms. Men out hunting could walk and run up to 50 kilometres in a single day.

Analysis of the Ju/'hoansi's varied diet shows it to be well balanced in terms of vitamins and minerals, high in proteins, and very low in carbohydrates. No significant shortfalls in nutrition have been recorded, except perhaps for a moderate shortage of overall calories, leading to lower adult weight and stature than among their farming and herding neighbours. Yet the calorie deficit seems to have had no negative effect on their active lifestyle. In fact, recent research in the United States has shown that underconsumption of calories—eating less as you grow older—may be one of the keys to longevity.

Dental examinations reveal an absence of dental caries, but periodontal (gum) disease was fairly common. Fertility was low (on average, there were 4.7 live births per woman) and infant mortality quite high; in retrospective studies of births prior to 1950, close to 40 percent of babies did not survive to maturity. Nevertheless, low net fertility may have been crucial to survival, since a rapidly growing population could not have been sustained.[3] Most remarkable was the absence of symptoms associated with heart disease. Blood pressure did not rise with age, and serum cholesterol levels were among the lowest ever recorded for a human population.[4]

Apart from their healthy diet and lifestyle, what means did the Ju/'hoansi possess for diagnosing and treating illness and trauma? Like all people, the Ju/'hoansi had developed a set of beliefs and practices to face this universal human need. According to the Ju/'hoansi, supernatural forces, primarily the ghosts of ancestors who had passed on to the spirit world, caused sickness and misfortune. For complex motives these ghosts remained close to the living, hovering around the villages and bringing with them sickness and misfortune.

In response, certain gifted Ju/'hoansi took up the calling of *n/um k'xau,* or "medicine owner," the Ju/'hoan equivalent of shaman.[5] Years of training helped n/um k'xau develop the ability to enter trance, diagnose illness, and magically pull sickness from the body and cast it away (see Chapter 12). The Ju/'hoan healers also possessed an extensive pharmacopeia of herbal remedies, which they would administer as infusions or teas, or mix with fat and rub into incisions at sites on the body, as a form of subcutaneous injection. Healers rarely if ever charged a fee; their stated goal was to work for the good of the community, although when called to perform by clients from neighbouring tribes, they received a goat or other gift in payment.

With Botswana's achievement of independence in 1966, the government made efforts to entice hunter-gatherers like the Ju/'hoansi to settle in one place. By the late 1980s this had become largely accomplished, with Ju in semipermanent villages, subsisting on food from an eclectic mix of sources: government food handouts, small-scale farming and herding, receipts from wage labour and handicraft production, and even some foraging. The road into the Dobe area was rebuilt, making the area more accessible to outsiders. Frequent bans on hunting and the ready availability of food handouts led to a sharp decrease in the amount of exercise for adults and loss of a sense of purpose. In the new cash economy, alcohol consumption increased from almost zero in the 1960s to a significant portion of cash expenditures; chronic alcohol abuse had become a health and social problem for the Ju/'hoansi.

A re-examination of the people's overall health status only 20 years after the initial studies revealed dramatic changes.[6] Blood pressure now increased markedly with age, and for the first time there was evidence of hypertension and heart disease. Dental health had deteriorated, with more cavities noted. On the plus side, women (but not men) showed higher skinfold measurements, indicating more stored fat deposits, and children's height for age had increased slightly. People spoke of coping with greater social stress as a result of their sedentary, higher density lifestyle, and they expressed nostalgia for the days before stores and alcohol. These stresses, plus the lower quality diet of refined carbohydrates, probably account for the appearance of symptoms associated with diseases of civilization.

As an additional challenge to community health and well-being, HIV/AIDS began to enter the area in the 1990s. However, even though Botswana has the highest HIV-positive rates in the world (38 percent of people aged 15–49, in recent UN estimates), the Ju/'hoansi have a 75 to 90 percent lower rate than the national statistics. The combination of isolation, women's empowerment, and common sense about sex and risk probably accounts for the lower rates. Yet with the opening of the area to tourism and other traffic there is concern that this picture may change. Tuberculosis also is on the rise and is considered an even bigger health threat than AIDS, although the two often exist as co-infections.

In the first decade of the 21st century, the people of the Dobe area have undergone dramatic changes in diet and lifestyle. In some ways they have benefited from improved access to the outside world by road, two airstrips, and a radio link. They certainly make good use of the two government clinics in the area, and the seriously ill can be evacuated to hospital by air ambulance. However, perceptive Ju/'hoansi have observed that the very diseases that the clinic is treating them for, including tuberculosis and HIV/AIDS, are themselves brought in from the outside. In this sense, the gains and losses in health status are equal.

[1]Lee, R.B. (2003). *The Dobe Ju/'hoansi* (3rd ed.). Toronto: Wadsworth/Thomson Learning.

[2]Truswell, S., & Hansen, J.D.L. (1976). Medical research among the !Kung. In R.B. Lee & I. DeVore (Eds.), *Kalahari hunter-gatherers: Studies of the !Kung San and their neighbors* (pp. 166–194). Cambridge, MA: Harvard University Press.

[3]Howell, N. (2000). *Demography of the Dobe !Kung* (2nd ed.). Hawthorne, NY: Aldine-DeGruyter.

[4]Truswell, A.S., Kennelly, B.M., Hansen, J.D.L., & Lee, R.B. (1972). Blood pressures of !Kung Bushmen in northern Botswana. *American Heart Journal, 84,* 5–12.

[5]Katz, R. (1982). *Boiling energy: Community healing among the !Kung.* Cambridge, MA: Harvard University Press.

[6]Hansen, J., Dunn, D., Lee, R.B., Becker, P., & Jenkins, T. (1994). Hunter-gatherer to pastoral way of life: Effects of the transition on health, growth and nutritional status. *South African Journal of Science, 89,* 559–564.

Poverty

Poverty is one of the best predictors of poor health. A prime directive of medical anthropology is to understand health and illness not only cross-culturally but also across lines of class. Canadian epidemiologist and physician Stephen Bezruchka, now at the University of Washington, has constructed what he calls the "Health Olympics": rankings of countries by life expectancy and/or infant mortality.[30] Surprisingly, the United States, which has the world's most expensive health care, both in overall figures and cost per capita, ranked only 15th among developed countries in 1970. Despite soaring health care costs, the United States sank even further over the last 30 years and now ranks 25th, behind every other country of the developed world.

Dr. Bezruchka bypasses most of the usual suspects in seeking to explain the U.S. ranking. Diet, exercise, and even smoking, he argues, have little impact on the overall health of large groups of people. What does profoundly affect a country's ranking is social inequality. He notes, "In countries where basic goods are readily available, peo-

ples' life span depends on the hierarchical structure of their society, that is, the size of the gap between rich and poor. In societies where inequality is severe psychological stresses afflict the entire society: power, domination, coercion (if you are on top), resignation, resentment and submission (if you are on the bottom)."[31] He goes on to compare these difficult emotions with the

[31]Bezruchka, S. (2001, February 26). Is our society making you sick? *Newsweek, 143.*

Dr. Stephen Bezruchka's Health Olympics tracks the impact of social inequality on the health and well-being of nations. Like food banks users, the poor have higher rates of most chronic and infectious diseases and conditions.

[30]Bezruchka, S. (2001, February 26). Is our society making you sick? *Newsweek, 143*; Hertzman, C. (2001). Health and human society. *American Scientist, 89,* 538–545.

positive ones more common in egalitarian societies, including friendship, support, and sociability.

Japan provides an instructive example. In the 1960s Japan stood 23rd in the Health Olympics. Now it is in first place, with a life expectancy that is over three and a half years greater than in the United States. Japan achieved this increase even though twice as many Japanese men as American men smoke. Yet the Japanese have only half as many deaths caused by smoking as Americans. Bezruchka attributes the difference to Japan's more egalitarian society, noting that after World War II, Japan restructured its economy so that citizens could share more equally in the country's economic success. Japanese heads of corporations make 15 to 20 times what entry-level workers in their factories earn. But in the United States, CEOs earn almost 500 times more than entry-level workers.

Class position strongly affects health at the local, national, and global levels. A number of factors contribute to poverty, including gender (more women than men are poor); age (older people are poorer, especially women); disability; mental illness; and racial discrimination. In Canada, aboriginal people are a prominent segment of the underclass; in the United States, more African Americans occupy that position.

A key variable in the relationship between poverty and health is the strength of the social safety net: the degree to which governments have created equal-access health care systems. In *Canada Firsts,* a book addressed mainly to Americans, health and safety crusader Ralph Nader describes the Canadian health care system, with its principle of tax-supported health care for all, as one worth studying and emulating in the United States.[32] Unlike Canada, the United States provides no comprehensive health care coverage. Middle-class, white-collar workers and professionals have private health insurance, but even they can be bankrupted by medical emergencies beyond their coverage. For the 41 million Americans in 2001 without health insurance coverage of any sort, the situation is much more dire.

Homelessness

In hierarchical societies, the most vulnerable carry the greatest burden of risk of health problems. These effects are especially visible today, in Canada as well as in the United States, as governments cut social services and funding for health care. The problem of homeless people in otherwise prosperous cities is a particularly visible aspect of poverty in North America. In 2002–2003, 32 000 people used the hostel system in the city of Toronto, including 4800 children.

In hard times, there is a downward slope for people at the bottom of the wage scale. The working poor may be stuck in minimum wage jobs in nonunion workplaces where they lack job security. The unemployed, disabled, or both often have to go on welfare and are subject to harsh scrutiny by government agencies. They may face the constant decision of whether to pay the heating bill or go to the grocery store. Food banks and other private charities provide a minimal cushion.

Along with homelessness and life on the streets come more prevalent and serious health problems. Homeless children, for example, experience immunization delays, resulting in such infections as measles, and they suffer from skin diseases, anemia, malnutrition, and emotional and developmental disorders. Homeless adults are subject to high rates of trauma through accidents and violence. They also often have severe mental health and substance abuse problems, although these may be seen as both an effect and a cause of their homelessness.

Homeless people throughout North America are experiencing a major resurgence of tuberculosis, a disease that had fallen to low levels after 1945. HIV and AIDS are also very high and rising among the homeless, especially among sex workers and intravenous drug users. Dr. Ida Susser, in her pioneering study of homeless women and their health in New York City, notes that HIV may not seem to be much of a threat because homeless people's circumstances are so desperate that they don't expect to live long enough to die of AIDS.[33] (For an extended discussion of anthropology and AIDS, see Chapter 7.)

[32]Nader, R., Milleron, N., & Conacher, D. (1992). *Canada firsts.* Toronto: McClelland and Stewart.

[33]Susser, I. (1996). Construction of poverty and homelessness in US cities. *Annual Review of Anthropology, 25,* 411–435.

Anthropology **Applied**

Vancouver's Downtown Eastside

Vancouver's Downtown Eastside is an area four blocks square where the city's homeless people, drug users, and sex workers are concentrated. The area has become nationally famous for the multiplicity and seriousness of its social, legal, and medical problems, but also for the innovative approaches to these problems that community members and various levels of government have taken. The neighbourhood was one of the first in Canada to provide a needle exchange for IV drug users. Using enlightened European cities like Amsterdam as a model, the city health department opened in September 2003 a storefront where users receive clean needles and can shoot up in safety. Users also may be referred to other municipal health services if they are ready to get off the street and enter rehabilitation programs, although the severe shortage of rehab spaces limits the possibilities for constructive change.[1]

Anthropologist Dara Culhane of Simon Fraser University, along with her students, is carrying out ongoing applied research projects with a population of formerly homeless women in Vancouver's Downtown Eastside. This award-winning three-year study is funded by a grant from the Social Science and Humanities Research Council of Canada (SSHRCC). The previous NDP provincial government had allocated money to the Bridge Housing Society and the Downtown Eastside Women's Centre to convert an old building into apartments for the women, to be run as a housing cooperative. Issues that the residents have had to face include how to build a collective spirit for their new life and a sense of individual and collective responsibility. Could these most marginalized women—drug users, sex workers, and panhandlers, many of whom were HIV-positive—submit to the discipline of living collectively, respect each other's property, follow curfews, and maintain communal spaces? Could they pay their bills? More difficult was the question of whether they should be allowed to bring in drugs or male friends. Sex workers felt that since this was their means of livelihood, they should be allowed to bring in clients. Other women

Dr. Dara Culhane of Simon Fraser University has pioneered participatory-action research in Vancouver's Downtown Eastside, to provide social services urgently needed by sex workers, injecting drug users, the homeless, and other marginalized people.

in the community objected. How will the women work out these problems? As of this writing, according to Culhane, the discussions continue. But what is most important is that by obtaining housing, these women are overcoming often horrendous histories of dislocation, incarceration, and discrimination, and are taking the first tentative steps toward recovery.

Dara Culhane's work, like Ida Susser's in New York City, illustrates the value of a particular anthropological approach, called *participatory action research* (PAR), in making successful contact with and earning the trust of a highly marginalized group. Other excellent examples of this kind of anthropological work include the study of a Winnipeg homeless shelter by Rae Bridgman of the University of Manitoba and Philippe Bourgois's now-classic study of the mostly Hispanic crack dealers and their lives and families in East Harlem, New York.[2]

---

[1]Department of Sociology and Anthropology, Simon Fraser University. (2003, October). *Dr. Dara Culhane*. Retrieved February 12, 2004, from the World Wide Web: http://www.sfu.ca/sociology/01department/biographies/culhane.html.

[2]Bridgman, R. (2003). *Safe haven: The story of a woman's shelter.* Toronto: University of Toronto Press; Bourgois, P. (2003). *In search of respect: Selling crack in El Barrio* (2nd ed.). Cambridge and New York: Cambridge University Press.

Important research is underway on how homeless people articulate with the health care system. What happens, for example, to HIV-positive people in the system? Some are told of their status and given opportunities for treatment and care, while others are just sent back to the streets. It is hard to provide services to people of no fixed address. Therefore, housing the homeless is a major concern that has repercussions for many health-related issues.

Lethal but Legal: Alcohol, Tobacco, and Health

Critical medical anthropology has taken an active interest in the worldwide health impact of the production and consumption of two enormously lucrative products: tobacco and alcohol. Since the 1970s, governments have been waging the so-called war on drugs, trying to control the production and use of banned dangerous substances like cocaine and heroin. However, other substances that many consider equally dangerous to long-term human health are perfectly legal in most countries.

Alcoholic beverages were first produced when grains were harvested in the early agricultural period; their production has grown to become one of the world's largest industries. In most world cultures, drinking wine, beer, spirits, and local variants is associated with sociability, conviviality, and good times. At the same time, overconsumption can lead to a wide spectrum of negative consequences, including serious addiction, physical breakdown, and death for heavy consumers; domestic violence and the break-up of families at the community level; and millions of lost work days, lowered productivity, and strain on the justice and health care systems at the national level.

CMA has been deeply involved in studying the impact of alcohol at the family and community levels. In their paper "Why Does Juan Garcia Have a Drinking Problem?" Merrill Singer and his co-authors critique research in medical anthropology on alcohol abuse.[34] In recent years

alcoholism has been medicalized and is now regarded as a disease, subject to treatment and rehabilitation. While Singer sees this process as a positive step, he also notes that medicalization focuses on the individual, drawing attention away from the historical and social roots of the problem. Singer explores the issue using the case study of Juan Garcia (a pseudonym), a Puerto Rican man who died of alcohol-related conditions in 1971. We follow Garcia's life from birth in rural Puerto Rico in 1909 to the growing Puerto Rican community in New York after World War II. Uneducated, Garcia found it hard to find steady employment. After losing his job in 1964, he was forced to go on welfare and became an increasingly heavy drinker and abusive to his wife and family. He died alienated, impoverished, and alone.

For Puerto Rico, a longtime colony of Spain and then the United States, sugar production was the main commodity, and manufacture of rum became the economic mainstay of the island. Heavy consumption of rum was part of the culture of the thousands of men who performed back-breaking labour in the cane fields. Changes in the Puerto Rican economy put many cane workers out of work, and Juan Garcia was one of countless Puerto Ricans who migrated to New York. There he entered the lowest wage sector with the least job security. He also brought with him a deep dependency on alcohol, now aggravated by the instability of employment and a host of other social ills in the barrios of New York. Add to this the *machismo* that was part of

Merrill Singer's classic study of alcoholism and domestic violence documents the movement of migrants from the sugar cane fields of Puerto Rico to the crowded barrios of New York City.

---

[34]Singer, M., Valentin, F., Baer, H., & Jia, Z. (1992). Why does Juan Garcia have a drinking problem? *Medical Anthropology, 14* (1), 77–108. Reprinted in P. Brown (Ed.). (1998). *Understanding and applying medical anthropology* (pp. 286–302). Mountain View, CA: Mayfield.

Gender **Perspectives**

Women and Health

An important field within medical anthropology is gender and health. The subordinate status of women in most contemporary societies is being challenged. But inequalities, expressed in many ways, persist, not the least of them in the areas of health and disease. Why do the burdens of illness and responsibility for caring for the sick fall more heavily on women than on men? How does the medical profession, dominated largely by men, approach the bodies and health problems of women? How do medical textbooks, again written largely by men, represent the array of "women's diseases," ranging from breast cancer to conditions affecting reproduction and women's emotional and psychic well-being?

Barbara Ehrenreich and Deirdre English describe some of the theories about women's bodies that were part of official medicine 150, 100,

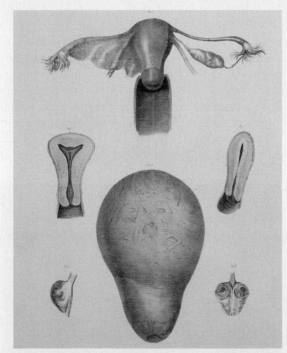

By examining old textbooks on gynecology—seemingly based on "pure" science—Emily Martin has shown that the ways in which women's reproductive processes are represented exhibit a strong overlay of male bias.

and 50 years ago but seem totally lacking in validity today.[1] In the 1870s, for example, it was believed that a woman's health was dominated by her ovaries and that the solution to many problems, ranging from tuberculosis to being oversexed (whatever that means), was ovariotomy—surgical removal of the ovaries. By 1906, over 150 000 American women had undergone this operation, until it became clear that it had little or no relation to the conditions it was supposed to cure.

The Personal Is Political

The rise of the women's health movement in the 1960s and 1970s led to a new level of consciousness about the at times difficult relationship between women and their physicians. Medical anthropologist Emily Martin brought a critical and feminist perspective to her book *The Woman in the Body,* in which she examines the cultural roots of Western biomedicine through 100 years of portrayals of women's bodies in medical textbooks.[2]

Martin points out how closely the language used to describe women's physiology corresponds to images from the wider culture of industrial production, the body being likened to a machine, a city, or a factory. According to these textbooks, if women's bodies are like factories, they are exceedingly inefficient ones. In describing the physiological processes of menstruation, for example, a typical textbook entry dating from 1983 uses negative terms such as "degenerate," "decline," "weakened," "spasms," "leak," "deteriorate," and "discharge" to describe what happens to the corpus luteum and the endometrial wall during the monthly cycle.[3] The whole process is seen as wasteful and essentially pathological. Contrast this with the description of male spermatogenesis in which the production of sperm is described in positive terms like "amazing" and "remarkable," and the author comments on the "sheer magnitude" of sperm production, even though of 100 billion sperm only one is needed to fertilize an ovum.[4] Why, Martin asks, is the female process described as "wasteful" and the male process seen as a wonder of nature?

Similarly, the process of menopause, the cessation of menstruation and ovulation in women, is seen in many textbooks as a disease, as a "failure" of hormone production, or as the "degeneration" of a formerly healthy part of the anatomy. This choice of words gained added significance when biomedicine, backed by the pharmaceutical industry, began marketing hormone replacement therapy (HRT) as a way for women to avoid these symptoms of "decline" and "degeneration" and remain young. It was even touted as a way for women to lower their chances of heart disease.

Martin conducted her research in the 1980s, when HRT was still a popular medical treatment for menopausal women. The massive marketing campaign was aided in part by metaphors that reinforced a certain view of women's bodies and a particular view of aging. In 2002, however, large-scale studies showed that the long-term health benefits of HRT were minimal and that the risk of heart disease was, if anything, elevated, not lowered. Countless Canadian women in their 50s and 60s are now struggling to decide whether to stop or continue HRT treatment.

Emily Martin's larger purpose has been to question the view that biomedicine, with its basis in "science," is somehow sealed off from the culture that surrounds it and not subject to the subtle pressures of dominant ideology. In fact, she demonstrates that biomedicine uses the language and cultural imagery of its time to describe complex biological concepts. Martin gives us a good illustration of the changing views of menstruation and menopause and of male–female differences through time. By showing the importance of understanding science against the background of its culture, Martin became a pioneer in developing feminist standpoint theory and the "science as culture" perspectives that have become an important part of critical medical anthropology.

Emily Martin's work can be seen as part of the broader women's health movement of the 1960s.[5]

Feminist medical anthropology has been grounded in the fight for a woman's right to control her own body, expressed through campaigns to make birth control more widely available and ensure a woman's right to abortion. Through much of the 20th century, even though women won the right to vote and were entering the workforce in increasing numbers, birth control information and devices such as condoms were difficult to obtain, and many women, seeking to terminate unwanted pregnancies, were forced to put themselves in the hands of illegal "back alley" abortionists. Infections and injuries often resulted, not to mention the psychic costs of stigma and secrecy.

The consciousness-raising and social activism campaign under the slogan "Every Child a Wanted Child" led to legal challenges that produced a sea change in public attitudes. The campaign produced landmark decisions in Canada and the United States, such as *Roe vs. Wade* in the U.S. Supreme Court, that confirmed a woman's right to abortion. Canada's recognition of a woman's right to control her own reproduction, as well as other rights concerning sexual activity for women and men, was summarized in the 1980s by then prime minister Pierre Elliot Trudeau in his words "The state has no place in the bedrooms of the nation."

[1]Ehrenreich, B., & English, D. (1978). *For her own good: 150 years of experts' advice to women.* New York: Anchor Books.

[2]Martin, E. (1987). *The woman in the body: A cultural analysis of reproduction.* Boston: Beacon Press.

[3]Ibid.

[4]Ibid.

[5]Boston Women's Health Book Collective. (1998). *Our bodies, ourselves for the new century: A book by and for women* (3rd ed.). New York: Simon and Schuster.

Garcia's self-image, and the recipe for disaster was complete; Garcia soon began taking out his frustrations through violence against his wife and family. Singer and his co-authors go on to document the prevalence of families like Juan Garcia's in the United States, as an undercurrent of poverty and pain against the idealized backdrop of the "good life" in America. Treating problems with alcohol such as Juan Garcia's as an individual medical problem is only a band-aid remedy. CMA argues that addressing the underlying social ills would be a more effective solution to Juan Garcia's drinking problem.

Other topics on the CMA agenda include the contradictions and issues surrounding tobacco and its health risks, and the power of the tobacco industry to market its product in spite of mounting clinical evidence of its negative health impacts. Medical anthropologists are studying how, with the drop in cigarette sales in North America, Big Tobacco is shifting its marketing pitch to the developing world. As documented by medical anthropologist Kenyon Stebbins, countries like Peru and Colombia are far less vigilant when it comes to limiting the advertising directed toward minors and printing public health messages on cigarette packs. In recent years U.S. tobacco multinationals have been earning up to half their profits from sales overseas.[35]

Environmental Health and Justice

Through the 19th and 20th centuries, as the industrial system of production grew, so did the production of pollutants. Thousands of new chemical compounds were released into the atmosphere, water, and soil and found their way into the food chain and into our bodies. For decades the industrial world celebrated its triumph over nature and the wealth of new products created. But gradually the unpaid bills for unbridled growth began to come due. Mounting levels of cancer, asthma, and birth defects led to a search for causes. And now increasingly conclusive evidence links many of these conditions to the expansion and intensification of the industrial system.

One outcome has been the growth of the environmental movement, made up of citizen activists who are defending their families and communities. A branch of medical anthropology, the **environmental justice** movement, has emerged to explore the area of environmental pollution and health. Medical anthropologist Harriet Rosenberg of York University has researched one

of the best-known cases of toxic pollution and citizen response.[36]

Just upriver from the Niagara falls is the subdivision of Love Canal, in the southeast corner of the city of Niagara Falls, New York. Dug at the turn of the 20th century, the actual canal never carried barge traffic, but from 1920 to 1945 it served as a dumpsite for toxic wastes from the nearby Hooker Chemical plant, a division of Occidental Petroleum. When the dumpsite was filled to capacity it was closed, buried under a clay cap, and covered with soil. The city government then took over the land, and in the post–World War II housing boom, built a primary school directly on top of the former dump. By the 1970s, developers had built a subdivision of over 700 homes.

The families of Love Canal, raising their children, began to notice ominous signs. Children jumping in rain puddles in the school yard found the soles of their sneakers melting away, and mothers were alarmed by the number of newborns with birth defects and by the appearance of rare cancers in older children. Asthma, allergies, skin disorders, and chronic respiratory ailments also appeared in disturbingly high numbers.

Families were demanding answers, and under the leadership of the Love Canal Homeowners Association (LCHA), they began to lobby municipal and state health authorities to address the multiplying health problems. The government response followed a pattern that has now become familiar to all environmental justice activists. There was nothing unusual about the high level of ailments, government officials insisted—this was just the usual variation around statistical norms. When the mothers of the community pressed the officials, they found their concerns dismissed as the fears of "hysterical housewives." Nevertheless, news reports spread word of the health problems and real estate values plummeted. The largely working-class families had sunk their life savings into their homes and

---

[35]Hilts, P. (1996). *Smokescreen: The truth behind the tobacco industry coverup*. New York: Addison-Wesley; Stebbins, K. (2001). "Going like gangbusters": Transnational tobacco companies making a killing in South America. *Medical Anthropology Quarterly, 15*, 147–170.

---

[36]Rosenberg, H. (1997). From trash to treasure. In J. Schneider & R. Rapp (Eds.), *Articulating hidden histories* (pp. 190–204). Berkeley: University of California Press.

Environmental justice.   A social movement in which citizen activists organize to defend against environmental threats to community health and well-being.

simply couldn't afford to abandon them and live elsewhere.

Their situation seemed hopeless until a few academics at local universities accepted the concerns of the homeowners at face value and began to conduct independent environmental studies. These studies confirmed the LCHA's worst fears: Unacceptably high levels of a list of toxins were found in the school yard and the soil of back yards, and even oozing from the walls in the basements of homes. Most prominent was dioxin, the most toxic chemical ever created, dangerous at a few parts per billion.

A young mother named Lois Gibbs took the leadership of the LCHA, and the Love Canal community rose to statewide and then national prominence as a toxic disaster area. Finally, the cumbersome government bureaucracy came to acknowledge the serious dangers to health facing the residents of Love Canal, and in 1979 president Jimmy Carter authorized relocation of residents and compensation for lost equity in their homes.[37]

The Love Canal story became a prototype for communities all over North America that faced health threats from unacknowledged sources of toxic waste, smokestack industries, and release of pollutants into the water and air. Lois Gibbs became an internationally prominent environmental crusader and founded what is now the Center for Health, Environment, and Justice, in Falls Church, Virginia. For its part, the U.S. government set aside a budgetary allocation, known as the Superfund, for the massive cleanup required to remove toxic wastes and restore sites to human use.

Similar examples of communities affected by toxic pollution in Canada include the tar ponds in Sydney, Nova Scotia, and the tainted water tragedy in Walkerton, Ontario, in which run-off from a local livestock farm infected the water supply with E. coli and cost seven people their lives in May 2000.[38] While environmental scientists conduct

This primary school, built directly on top of a toxic waste site, was at the centre of the Love Canal environmental disaster in Niagara Falls, New York. The resulting citizen protest was a key step in the formation of the environmental movement.

research in such cases to determine the level of toxic risk to humans and animals, medical anthropologists also play an important role in chronicling the social movements that spring up to fight the polluters and, at times, the governments that are slow to acknowledge the legitimacy of their concerns.

CONTEMPORARY BIOMEDICINE

Health care today is one of the largest components of affluent nations' economies. The Canadian medical establishment is a vast network of doctors and their offices; hospitals and clinics; health bureaucracies at municipal, provincial, and federal levels; and a giant manufacturing and marketing sector, including transnational pharmaceutical corporations. It is also an institution that almost every member of society is intimately acquainted with through visits to "the doctor" for an ever-expanding range of physical and nonphysical conditions. Thus, medical anthropology has turned its lens on contemporary biomedicine, examining it from a variety of perspectives.

The ethnographic method of sociocultural anthropologists is well suited to studying these complex processes. Using ethnographic techniques, anthropologists explore such topics as how doctors are trained through a dual process combining education and ideological formation;

---

[37]Gibbs, L. (1995). *Dying from dioxin: A citizen's guide to reclaiming our health and rebuilding democracy*. Boston: South End Press; Gibbs, L.M. (1998). *Love Canal: The story continues*. Gabriola Island, BC: New Society.

[38]Barlow, M., & May, E. (2000). *Frederick Street: Life and death on Canada's Love Canal*. Toronto: Harper and Row; Perkel, C. (2002). *Well of lies: The Walkerton water tragedy*. Toronto: McClelland and Stewart.

how the doctor–patient relationship unfolds given different perceptions about race, class, gender, and social position; and how medical practitioners, professing an entirely scientific and value-free position, hold views that are shaped by cultural bias.

Genetics and biogenetic engineering have been hailed as holding great promise for the future of humankind. An early achievement was the discovery of the genetic basis of a variety of health conditions, leading to the rapidly developing specialty of **genetic counselling**, screening for hereditary conditions and diseases, especially during pregnancy and childbirth. But what happens when the highly technical findings of laboratory medicine come into contact with the lay public, with women and men who are seeking good health but who need help translating the language of the lab into the language of everyday life? Rayna Rapp of New York University is a pioneer in the anthropological study of genetic counselling. In *Testing Women, Testing the Fetus,* Rapp describes observing technicians at work in the genetics laboratories, then attending counselling sessions to see how that work was explained to clients, and finally interviewing members of the public who had sought medical advice and had to make decisions in terms of their own lives and values.[39]

Amniocentesis is the main diagnostic test for fetal health. A sterile needle is inserted through the abdomen into the uterus, and a sample of amniotic fluid is withdrawn. The fluid is then tested in the lab for a variety of genetic markers, including Down syndrome, Tay-Sachs disease, and sickle-cell anemia. If any serious conditions are discovered, the client and her family have to decide whether to terminate the pregnancy or proceed to birth. Often the medical opinion favours ending the pregnancy, but the client decides to go ahead with the birth, even knowing the difficulties that lie ahead. Rapp makes the point that people bring a wide variety of beliefs and values, some cultural, some personal, and

some religious, to their encounters with medicine, and these may be sharply at odds with the seemingly rational views of the medical profession. For their part, medical professionals, through their body language or tone of voice, may unconsciously express disapproval of clients, affecting their decisions. One of Rapp's points is that medicine is not just about medical breakthroughs, providing a technical fix for all that ails us. These "magic bullets" will always meet a complex and contradictory human reality, and medicine must resist the temptation to ride roughshod over objections, and keep a sympathetic ear open to alternative viewpoints.

Other medical anthropologists are studying the growth of managed health care (HMOs) and the emergence of giant drug companies and other health care corporations as dominant players in medicine. How will they affect the future development of medicine? How will they affect which diseases are chosen for development of new remedies and which are ignored because they provide insufficient economic return? Ken Silverstein notes that the pharmaceutical industry is pouring millions into research on medicines that are essentially "lifestyle drugs," such as Viagra for erectile dysfunction and Botox for facial wrinkles, and are even devoting substantial research dollars to developing antidepressants for pets.[40] Meanwhile, ongoing diseases that take the lives of millions in developing countries, including malaria, schistosomiasis, tuberculosis, and other endemic infectious diseases, are starved for funds.

Similarly, in Canada and elsewhere, a growing proportion of health care expenditures are going toward costly high-tech medicine, in such diagnostic tools as electron microscopes and MRI scanners, while budgets for the most basic public health measures, such as a safe water supply, are being cut back. The result is scandals like the Walkerton, Ontario, water tragedy in 2000.

Roy Romanow, head of the Commission on the Future of Health Care in Canada, released his final report in 2002, in which he recommended

---

[39]Rapp, R. (1999). *Testing women, testing the fetus: The social impact of amniocentesis in America.* New York: Routledge.

[40]Silverstein, K. (1999, July 19). Millions for Viagra, pennies for diseases of the poor. *The Nation,* 13–18.

Genetic counselling. Screening for hereditary conditions and diseases, especially during pregnancy and childbirth.

revitalizing primary health care and refocusing on single-tier health care and equal access for all Canadians.[41] As this edition of the text went to press, it was still unclear to what extent the federal government would adopt Romanow's recommendations.

Medical Anthropology in Canada

Canadian researchers are conducting some of the most creative work in medical anthropology today. Earlier, we discussed the work of Margaret Lock. Lock's colleagues at McGill University and the University of Montreal have pioneered work in transcultural psychiatry. Gilles Bibeau and Ellen Corin have worked with traditional healers in the Democratic Republic of the Congo,[42] and Lawrence Kirmayer, editor of the journal *Transcultural Psychiatry,* has done recent research on several topics, including the difficult encounters between immigration authorities and refugee claimants who were tortured in their countries of origin.[43] Alan Young of the Department of Social Studies of Medicine at McGill is well known for his critical views on post-traumatic stress disorder (PTSD). In his book *Harmony of Illusions: Inventing Post-Traumatic Stress Disorder,* Young argues that PTSD is a constructed category, a psychiatric diagnosis that arose from the complex moral and scholarly debates about the Vietnam War and its effects on U.S. soldiers.[44] He uses this case study

for a broader critique of the ways in which psychiatry medicalizes diverse symptoms in order to expand the sphere of treatable illnesses, but also serve state and corporate interests.

Aboriginal health and illness is a major component of medical anthropology in Canada. On all indices, aboriginal health status is poorer than that of Canadians in general. A key text examining this inequity is *Aboriginal Health in Canada: Historical, Cultural, and Epidemiological Perspectives* (1995), by James B. Waldram, D. Ann Herring, and T. Kue Young.[45] The authors, a cultural anthropologist, a biological anthropologist, and a medical doctor–anthropologist, respectively, bring perspectives from all three approaches in medical anthropology to exploring how biology, culture, history, spirituality, politics, and the environment converge to shape disease patterns among aboriginal peoples.

Aboriginal health is also the focus of Naomi Adelson's *Being Alive Well: Health and Politics of Cree Well-Being.*[46] As a study of Cree beliefs and practices about health and healing, the book provides an excellent illustration of some of the principles discussed in this chapter. In their discussion of the social body (see pages 420–421), Scheper-Hughes and Lock point out that, in contrast to the mind–body dualism of Western science, for some peoples, the health of humans, the health of the environment, and the health of the cosmos are closely intertwined. Adelson reports that in the Cree worldview, the health of humans cannot be separated from the health of the land. For the Cree, being well is closely linked to being able to live on the land and to the health of the animal, fish, and plant populations on which they depend for subsistence. In a similar vein, the physical health of the people is bound up with their psychic and spiritual health. Adelson shows how the continuing encroachment of Euro-Canadian culture and values challenges these views, and how the dominant culture's attitudes toward difference threaten not only indigenous peoples like the Cree, but also the very survival of humankind.

[41]Commission on the Future of Health Care in Canada. (2002). *Building on values: The future of health care in Canada* (The Romanow Report). Ottawa: Government Printers.

[42]Bibeau, G. (1979). World Health Organization in encounter with African traditional medicine: Theoretical conceptions and practical strategies. In Z. Ademuwagun (Ed.), *African therapeutic systems.* Waltham, MA: Crossroads Press; Corin, E. (1998). Refiguring the person: The dynamics of effects and symbols in an African spirit possession cult. In M. Lambek & A. Strathearn (Eds.), *Bodies and persons: Comparative perspectives from Africa and Melanesia.* Cambridge, UK: Cambridge University Press.

[43]Kirmayer, L.J., Boothroyd, L., Tanner, A., Adelson, N., Robinson, E., & Oblin, C. (2000). Psychological distress among the Cree of James Bay. *Transcultural Psychiatry, 37,* 35–56.

[44]Young, A. (1995). *Harmony of illusions: Inventing post-traumatic stress disorder.* Princeton: Princeton University Press.

[45]Waldram, J.B., Herring, A., & Kue Young, T. (1995). *Aboriginal health in Canada: Historical, cultural and epidemiological perspectives.* Toronto: University of Toronto Press.

[46]Adelson, N. (2000). *Being alive well: Health and politics of Cree well-being.* Toronto: University of Toronto Press.

The physical, social, and spiritual health of a northern Cree community in an era of rapid change is the subject of Naomi Adelson's insightful monograph *Being Alive Well*.

Other topics Canadian medical anthropologists are addressing include critical studies of the biotechnology and pharmaceutical industries in Canada by Usher Fleising of the University of Calgary[47] and Janice Graham at Dalhousie University. Penny Van Esterik of York University

has done important work on social activism to counter the marketing of breast milk substitutes to women in the developing world.[48] Lisa Mitchell, influenced by the research of Emily Martin and Rayna Rapp, discussed earlier, has studied medical imaging techniques such as ultrasound and how women perceive their bodies and their fetuses.[49] Janice Boddy and Michael Lambek, at the University of Toronto, have done important work in the area of spirit possession as a form of medical practice with affinities to shamanism. Boddy studied the practice in the Sudan, Lambek on the Comoros Islands and Madagascar.[50]

Collectively, Canadian medical anthropologists are making a significant contribution to the vitality of medical anthropology in the world today.

[47]Fleising, U. (2001). In search of genohype: A content analysis of biotechnology company documents. *New Genetics and Society, 20* (3), 239–254.

[48]Van Esterik, P. (2002). *Risks, rights, and regulation: Communicating about risks and infant feeding.* Penang, Malaysia: World Alliance for Breastfeeding Action (WABA).

[49]Mitchell, L. (2001). *Baby's first picture: Ultrasound and the politics of fetal subjects.* Toronto: University of Toronto Press.

[50]Boddy, J. (1989). *Wombs and alien spirits: Women, men and the Zar cult in Northern Sudan.* Madison: University of Wisconsin Press; Lambek, M. (1993). *Knowledge and practice in Mayotte: Local discourses of Islam, sorcery, and spirit possession.* Toronto: University of Toronto Press.

CHAPTER SUMMARY

Medical anthropology began with the study of how cultural differences affect health and disease. The biocultural, or biomedical, approach, encompassing ecology, bioarchaeology, and evolution, takes medical science as a given and attempts to understand how illness expressed itself in given cultures and eras of history. Early biocultural studies examined the understanding of adult-onset diabetes among North American First Nations peoples, and the interaction of culture and genetics in the incidence of sickle-cell anemia among Africans and African Americans.

Later the field expanded to include the study of how different cultures conceptualize health and illness, and how Western medicine itself is immersed in a cultural and historical context. Rooted in the philosophical school known as phenomenology, the cultural interpretive, or cultural

constructionist, approach distinguishes between "disease," the clinical manifestation of a condition or syndrome, and "illness," the subjective sense of being sick, dealing with such difficult to define health issues as "pain" and "suffering."

The third component of the field, critical medical anthropology, arose when medical anthropologists attempted to understand the impact of larger political and economic forces, such as capitalism and industrialization, on the health of whole societies, communities, and individuals. CMA asks questions about health care for the poor within developed countries such as Canada and the United States and the more numerous and poorer developing countries. It also looks at the ways in which the economic forces of advanced capitalism shape the practice of medicine. CMA has close links to fields such as political ecology that seek to understand ways in which power relations affect humans and the environment.

Rather than being in competition, these three approaches are complementary. The point of a good analysis is to use the tools appropriate to the problem at hand. To study shamanism, the cultural interpretive approach would be the tool of choice. On the other hand, if you were interested in knowing whether a shamanic treatment was effective, you might turn to biomedical evidence for the answer. The point is that we need all three approaches, and although individual medical anthropologists may specialize in one or another approach, at their best they will not rely exclusively on just one.

As social structure evolved from bands to tribes and chiefdoms, early states, and industrial states, patterns of health and disease also changed. Contrary to expectations, as humans moved from Mesolithic (hunting and gathering) to Neolithic (farming and herding) modes of subsistence, health status declined rather than improved. The Ju/'hoansi, who transitioned from hunting and gathering to agriculture and then to incorporation into the welfare state, provide an example of a contemporary society that has undergone, in the space of decades, major changes that other societies took centuries or millennia to accomplish.

Social inequalities within and between countries have a great impact on human health: Position in the social hierarchy significantly affects life expectancy. The fact that people at the top of social hierarchies are healthier and live longer than people at the bottom is due in part to the greater stress those in subordinate positions experience, and in part to differential access to health care.

Alcohol and tobacco have devastating health repercussions for people at all levels of society. Tobacco is now known to contain substances that are both harmful and addictive. Yet the powerful tobacco lobby was able to cover up the medical evidence for over 30 years, enabling cigarettes to be advertised freely and sold to minors despite repeated cries of alarm from medical researchers and public health advocates like the Canadian Cancer Society.

Anthropologists are active as well in another branch of CMA: environmental justice, or the impact of environmental pollution on health. While research scientists determine the level of contamination by analyzing air, water, soil, and food samples, and epidemiologists determine the impact of these factors on human health, it is the role of medical anthropologists to explore the social and cultural factors that created the conditions for ecological disasters at sites such as Love Canal and Walkerton. Who profits, who pays the price, and what role government regulatory agencies play are some of the questions these researchers ask.

Medical hegemony, how medicine shapes the ways we look at the world, and medicalization, bringing into the medical sphere aspects of human behaviour that formerly lay outside it, are closely related processes that will shape the future of human health in ways we are only beginning to envision. Will medicine increasingly fall under the control of drug companies, with medical priorities driven by their agendas, or will it continue to work for the well-being of the greatest number of

Above all, medical anthropology places human health and illness in its wider social context. The 2001 Walkerton tainted water tragedy, with seven dead and hundreds sickened, was a key focus for CMA's views on health and the environment.

people? Fortunately, there are many within the field of medicine who foresee some of the looming problems and are taking steps to change course. The re-entry of midwives into the provision of birthing services; the rapid growth of complementary and alternative medical techniques such as guided imagery, and their incorporation within some medical school curricula; and the development of citizen health activism to work for better provision and more equal distribution of services are all signs of a new vitality concerning the state of biomedicine, health, and the human condition. In all these movements medical anthropology has played a constructive and critical role and will continue to do so. Given the recent flare-ups in Canada of SARS, West Nile, bovine spongiform encephalopathy, and the tainted water tragedy of Walkerton, Ontario, this branch of the field of medical anthropology will have no shortage of subject matter in years to come.

Questions for Critical Thought

1. How does medical anthropology use cultural and ecological factors affecting health and disease to expand biomedical understandings, for example in explaining such conditions as adult-onset diabetes among North American First Nations peoples, and sickle-cell anemia among Africans, African Americans, and people of Mediterranean background?

2. Medical anthropology has attempted to place Western biomedicine in its historical context. What are some cultural assumptions and biases that you believe underlie Western medicine today?

3. How does the cultural interpretive approach distinguish between "disease" and "illness"?

4. What is "critical" about critical medical anthropology? What gaps in previous versions of medical anthropology does it attempt to address?

5. How did human health change as people made the transition from hunting and gathering to agriculture? Was the Neolithic revolution a major step forward in human progress, or did the transition have a downside as well? Describe how the Ju/'hoansi illustrate the health effects of changes to subsistence patterns.

6. What are some of the specific health problems facing people who have fallen through the social safety net, such as homeless people in Canadian cities?

7. What role can anthropologists play in studying the impact of environmental pollution on health?

Internet Resources

Environmental Activism
http://www.chej.org
The Center for Health, Environment and Justice (CHEJ) in Falls Church, Vermont, was founded in 1981 by Lois Gibbs, chairperson of the Love Canal Homeowners Association. The CHEJ advises local groups of activists across North America who are fighting dumpsites or other forms of pollution threatening their communities.

Women's Health
http://www.afriendindeed.ca
Based in a women's clinic in Winnipeg, Manitoba, this newsletter is a forum for health activists focused on issues around women and menopause, including hormone replacement therapy (HRT).

Breastfeeding Issues
http://www.waba.org.my
The website for the World Alliance for Breastfeeding Action is based in Penang, Malaysia, and links a wide network of breastfeeding and child and infant health and nutrition activists.

Alcohol and Substance Abuse
http://www.health.org
This U.S. government site provides free information on alcohol and drug abuse.

Doctors Without Borders
http://www.msf.ca
Doctors Without Borders is well known and respected for its medical work in trouble spots

such as Bosnia, Rwanda, and Cambodia. This independent relief organization provides medical aid along with work on human rights.

Canadian Aboriginal Health
http://www.naho.ca

The National Aboriginal Health Organization (NAHO) was founded and is run by aboriginal people for the benefit of First Nations, Métis, and Inuit in Canada. The organization maintains 40 links to other websites of interest to medical anthropology.

Biocultural Medical Anthropology
http://citd.scar.utoronto.ca/capa

Based at the Scarborough campus of the University of Toronto, and sponsored by the Canadian Association for Physical Anthropology, this website offers a broad range of links to a spectrum of medical anthropology websites, cultural and social as well as biological.

Medical Anthropology
http://www.sfu.ca/medanth

The journal *Medical Anthropology* is based at Simon Fraser University. An excellent source of current theory and method in medical anthropology in Canada and internationally.

Vancouver's Downtown Eastside
http://web.uvic.ca/~chpc/healthandhome.htm

A report on Dara Culhane's participatory action research with women and poverty in Vancouver's Downtown Eastside.

The Walkerton Water Tragedy
http://www.cbc.ca/news/indepth/walkerton

An excellent source for information on the Walkerton water tragedy of 2000 and its aftermath. The CBC news index also provides information on other health and medical news.

SUGGESTED READINGS

Baer, H.A., Singer, M., & Susser, I. (2004). *Medical anthropology and the world system: A Critical Perspective* (2nd ed.). Westport, CT: Bergin and Garvey.

The standard introduction to critical medical anthropology, originally published in 1997, and based on a concept pioneered by Baer and Singer in 1982. It contains extensive discussion of such topics as health and the human condition; the impact on health of poverty, alcohol, tobacco, and illicit drugs such as cocaine and heroin; and the political economy of HIV/AIDS.

Brown, P. (Ed.). (1998). *Understanding and applying medical anthropology*. Mountain View, CA: Mayfield.

The major reader in medical anthropology, containing over 40 selections on every branch of the subdiscipline, including classic articles by Claude Lévi-Strauss, Nancy Scheper-Hughes and Margaret Lock, George Armelagos, and Emily Martin.

Crosby, A. (1972/2003). *The Columbian exchange: Biological and cultural consequences of 1492* (30th anniversary ed.). Westport, CT: Praeger.

Crosby's book is the definitive account of the impact the "discovery" and colonization of the New World after 1492 had on global ecology and health. It is particularly informative in detailing the introduction of European diseases into indigenous populations of the New World and describing their devastating impact.

Farmer, P. (1992). *AIDS and accusation: Haiti and the geography of blame*. Berkeley: University of California Press.

Farmer's research combines biocultural and cultural interpretive medical anthropology in a brilliant synthesis that emphasizes the politics and economics of international health care inequities. His case study of AIDS in a Haitian village is a classic in critical medical anthropology.

Garrett, L. (2000). *Betrayal of trust: The collapse of global public health*. New York: Hyperion.

An award-winning investigation into the state of public health at the turn of the millennium, and an excellent source of information about the dramatic decline in health in post-Soviet Russia and in parts of the developing world. It also documents in massive detail the up-and-down struggle for public health in the United States and the political forces at work. The chapter on the threats of biological warfare and terrorism is particularly timely.

Goodman, A.H., & Leatherman, T.L. (Eds.). (1998). *Building a new biocultural synthesis: Political-economic perspectives on human biology*. Ann Arbor: University of Michigan Press.

An important work of synthesis in which biological anthropologists attempt to apply the findings of the field to important health and social issues of the current era.

Joralemon, D. (1999). *Exploring medical anthropology*. Boston: Allyn and Bacon.

Joralemon's book is an excellent short introduction to medical anthropology from the cultural interpretive point of view. It is a particularly rich account of shamanistic healing based in part on the author's own fieldwork on healing by indigenous curanderos in Peru.

Scheper-Hughes, N., & Lock, M. (1987). The mindful body: A prolegomenon to future work in medical anthropology. *Medical Anthropology Quarterly, 1* (1).

An influential essay that attempts to ground medical anthropology in a theoretical framework that transcends the Cartesian mind–body dualism and links it to four bodies of theory: European phenomenology, symbolic anthropology, Foucaultian post-structuralism, and classical political economy.

Vitebsky, P. (1995). *The shaman*. Boston: Little Brown and Co.

An excellent brief introduction to shamanism from its prehistoric origins to its current diversity in many world regions. Strong emphasis on the elaborate belief systems articulated within shamanistic traditions.

Waldram, J.B., Herring, A., & Kue Young, T. (1995). *Aboriginal health in Canada: Historical, cultural and epidemiological perspectives*. Toronto: University of Toronto Press.

This important volume brings together much of the recent research on aboriginal health in Canada, including material on diabetes, cancer, infant and child health, and mental health and spirituality. The authors are three of Canada's leading medical anthropologists.

CNN TODAY VIDEOS

Curious Cures (CNN Cultural Anthropology, vol. 4, 2:23)

In many cultures, folk remedies are still widely practised along with modern medicine.

AIDS and Indigenous Peoples in Africa (CNN Cultural Anthropology, vol. 6, 4:04)

Drought and climate changes force a nomadic tribe, the OvaHimba of Southern Africa, to settle in order to feed their flocks—both animal and human. Men in search of jobs in the cities are exposed to HIV and are infecting many in their community. The result is a generation of grandparents raising their grandchildren due to the HIV/AIDS-related deaths of parents.

Muslim Patients (CNN Cultural Anthropology, vol. 5, 2:33)

Culturally aware nurses and hospital staff are educating the medical community about traditional Muslim behaviour and dietary restrictions in order to help Muslim patients, especially women, receive better health care.

Muslim Patients (CNN Cultural Anthropology, vol. 4, 2:33)

In the United States, Muslim women have special problems in receiving medical care due to their traditional modesty.

Chapter 15

Cultural Change and the Future of Humanity

The ability to change has always been important to human cultures. Probably at no time has the pace of change equalled that of today, as traditional peoples all over the world are pressured to "change their ways" or be "run over" by "progress." But aboriginal peoples are fighting back and gaining the world's attention. Pictured here are members of the Nisga'a Nation of British Columbia.

Chapter Preview

1. How Do Cultures Change?

The mechanisms of change are innovation, diffusion, cultural loss, and acculturation. Innovation occurs when someone within a culture discovers something new that is then accepted by other members. Diffusion is the borrowing of something from another group, and cultural loss is the abandonment of an existing practice or trait, with or without replacement. Acculturation is the massive change that comes about with the sort of intensive firsthand contact that has occurred under colonialism.

2. What Is Modernization?

Modernization is an ethnocentric term referring to a global process of change by which traditional, nonindustrial cultures seek to acquire characteristics of industrially "advanced" societies. Although modernization generally has been assumed to be a good thing, and some successes have occurred, it frequently has led to the development of a new "culture of discontent," a level of aspirations far exceeding the bounds of local opportunities. Sometimes it leads to the destruction of cherished customs and values people had no desire to abandon.

3. What Problems Will Have to Be Solved if Humanity Is to Have a Future?

If humanity is to have a future, human cultures will have to find solutions to problems posed by the increasing global disparity of wealth and power, exhaustion of fossil fuel supplies, pollution, and a growing culture of discontent. One difficulty is that, up to now, people tend to see these problems as if they were discrete and unrelated. Thus, attempts to deal with one problem, such as food and fuel shortages, are often at cross-purposes with other problems, such as an inequitable global system for the distribution of basic resources. Unless humanity gains a more realistic understanding of the "global society" that presently exists, it cannot solve the problems whose solutions are crucial for its future.

CHAPTER OUTLINE

Mechanisms of Change

Forcible Change

Rebellion and Revolution

Gender Perspectives: Reproductive Rights in Canada

Modernization

The Cultural Future of Humanity

Anthropology Applied: Aboriginal Rights in Canada

Problems of Structural Violence

Humanity's Future

Culture is the medium through which the human species solves the problems of existence, as these are perceived by members of the species. Various cultural institutions, such as kinship and marriage, political and economic organization, and religion, mesh to form an integrated cultural system. Because systems generally work to maintain stability, cultures are often fairly stable and remain so unless either the conditions they are adapted to or human perceptions of those conditions change. Archaeological studies have revealed how elements of a culture may persist for long periods. In Chapter 5, for example, we saw how the culture of the aboriginal inhabitants of northwestern New England and southern Quebec remained relatively stable for thousands of years.

Although stability may be a striking feature of many cultures, none are ever changeless, as the cultures of food foragers, subsistence farmers, and pastoralists are all too often assumed to be. In a stable culture, change may occur gently and gradually, without altering in any fundamental way the culture's underlying logic. Sometimes, though, the pace of change may increase dramatically, causing a radical cultural alteration in a relatively short period. The modern world is full of examples as diverse as the disintegration of the Soviet Union and what is happening to the aboriginal peoples of the Amazon forest as Brazil presses ahead to "develop" this vast region.

We must recognize that when anthropologists refer to culture change, they are not implying "progress," which is predominantly a nation-state concept, just as they are not suggesting that all change is adaptive. As you will see in this chapter, the so-called modernization of cultural groups has generally caused more problems than it has solved.

MECHANISMS OF CHANGE

Innovation

The ultimate source of all change is innovation: any new practice, tool, or principle that gains widespread acceptance within a group. Those that involve the chance discovery of a new principle we refer to as **primary innovations** or inventions; those that result from the deliberate applications of known principles are **secondary innovations.** The latter corresponds most closely to the West's model of change as predictable and determined, while the former involves an accidental discovery of one sort or another.

An example of a primary innovation is the discovery that the firing of clay makes it permanently hard. Presumably, accidental firing of clay occurred frequently in ancient cooking fires. An accidental discovery is of no account, however, unless someone perceives an application for it. This perception first took place about 25 000 years ago, when people began making figurines of fired clay. Pottery vessels were not made, however, nor did the practice of making objects of fired clay reach southwest Asia until sometime between 7000 and 6500 B.C., when people living there recognized a significant application of fired clay to make cheap, durable, and easy-to-produce containers and cooking vessels.

Although a culture's internal dynamics may encourage certain innovative tendencies, they may discourage others, or even remain neutral with respect to yet others. Indeed, Copernicus's discovery of the rotation of the planets around the sun and Mendel's discovery of the basic laws of heredity are instances of genuine creative insights out of step with the established needs, values, and goals of their times and places. In fact, Mendel's work remained obscure until 16 years after his death, when three scientists working independently rediscovered, all in the same year (1900), the same laws of heredity. Thus, in the context of turn-of-the-century Western culture, Mendel's laws were bound to be discovered, even had Mendel not hit upon them earlier.

Although an innovation must be reasonably consistent with a society's needs, values, and goals if it is to be accepted, this is not sufficient to assure its acceptance. Force of habit tends to be an obstacle to acceptance; people tend to stick with what they are used to, rather than adopt something new that will require some adjustment

---

Primary innovation.   The chance discovery or invention of a new principle. **> Secondary innovation.**   Something new that results from the deliberate application of known principles.

A Hopi woman firing pottery vessels. The discovery that firing clay vessels makes them indestructible (unless they are dropped or otherwise smashed) probably came about when clay-lined basins next to cooking fires in the Middle East were accidentally fired.

on their part. An example of this tendency is the continued use of the QWERTY keyboard for typewriters and computers (named from the starting arrangement of letters). Devised in 1874, the arrangement minimized jamming of type bars and was combined with other desirable mechanical features to become the first commercially successful typewriter. Yet the QWERTY keyboard has a number of serious drawbacks. The more typing done in the "home row" (second from bottom) of keys, the faster we can type, with the fewest errors and least strain on the fingers. But with QWERTY, only 32 percent of the strokes are done on the home row, versus 52 percent on the upper row and 16 percent on the (hardest) bottom row. What's more, it requires overuse of the weaker (left) hand (for the right-handed majority) and the weakest (fifth) finger.

In 1932, after extensive study, August Dvorak developed a keyboard that avoids the defects of QWERTY (see Figure 15.1). Tests consistently show that the Dvorak keyboard can be learned in one-third the time, and, once learned, typists increase their accuracy by 68 percent and their speed by 74 percent, and they experience significantly less fatigue. So why hasn't Dvorak replaced QWERTY? The answer is commitment. Because

QWERTY had a head start, by the time Dvorak came along manufacturers, typists, teachers, salespeople, and office managers were committed to the old keyboard; it was what they were used to.[1]

---

[1]Diamond, J. (1997). The curse of QWERTY. *Discover, 18* (4), 34–42.

In the face of the AIDS epidemic sweeping southern Africa, the beliefs of several million Christian Zionists, such as the one being baptized here, are highly adaptive in that they militate against the kind of sexual practices that spread the disease. That these beliefs are adaptive, however, is a consequence of, rather than a reason for, their origin.

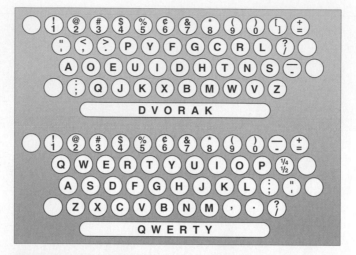

FIGURE 15.1 Dvorak and QWERTY keyboards, compared.
Although superior to the latter in virtually every way, Dvorak has
not been adopted owing to the head start enjoyed by QWERTY.

Once our reflexes become adjusted to doing something one way, it becomes difficult to do it differently. Thus, when a North American or European goes to Great Britain, learning to drive on the "wrong" side of the road is difficult.

Diffusion

When the first colonists established permanent settlements in eastern Canada, many died during the harsh winters. Many more would have frozen to death had the nearby First Nations not provided them with warm moccasins and leather clothing, and told them how to protect their homes from the fierce winter winds. And the settlers would have starved if the First Nations peoples had not told them which plants were suitable for food and medicines. The borrowing of cultural elements from one culture by members of another is known as **diffusion,** and the donor group is, for all intents and purposes, the "inventor" of that element. So common is borrowing that the late Ralph Linton, an American anthropologist, suggested that borrowing accounts for as much as 90 percent of any culture's content. People are creative about their borrowing, however, picking and choosing from multiple possibilities and sources. Usually their selections are limited to those compatible with the existing culture. Returning to our previous example, while the European colonists readily adopted First Nations' material culture to help them survive in a harsh climate, they had no interest in adopting their customs or religious beliefs; just the opposite in fact—missionaries quickly followed the fur traders and fishermen to the shores of eastern Canada, bent on converting the First Nations peoples to Christianity.

Diffusion.   The spread of customs or practices from one culture to another.

Although the tendency toward borrowing is so great it led Robert Lowie to comment, "Culture is a thing of shreds and patches," the borrowed traits usually undergo sufficient modifications to make this wry comment more colourful than critical. Moreover, existing cultural traits may be modified to accommodate a borrowed one. An awareness of the extent of borrowing can be eye-opening. Take, for example, the numerous things early European North Americans borrowed from the aboriginal peoples. Domestic plants like potatoes, avocados, corn, beans, squash, tomatoes, peanuts, manioc, chili peppers, chocolate, and sweet potatoes, to name a few, furnish a major portion of the world's food supply. In fact, North American aboriginal peoples remain the developers of the world's largest array of nutritious foods and the primary contributors to the world's varied cuisine.[2] Among drugs and stimulants, tobacco is the best known (see Figure 15.2), but others include coca in cocaine, ephedra in ephedrine, datura in pain relievers, and cascara in laxatives. Early on, European physicians recognized that North American aboriginals had the world's most sophisticated pharmacy, made from plants native to the Americas. More than 200 plants and herbs

they used for medicinal purposes have at one time or another been included in the *Pharmacopeia of the United States* or in the *National Formulary*. Varieties of cotton developed by North American aboriginals supply much of the world's clothing needs, while the woollen poncho, the parka, and moccasins are universally familiar items.

Perhaps the most powerful instruments of diffusion in the contemporary world are the U.S. media—television, radio, and literature. In Canada, efforts to maintain a distinct cultural identity separate from the United States have proved incredibly difficult owing to the pervasiveness of U.S. media. Canadians listen to U.S. music, watch U.S. television programs, and read U.S. magazines. Protective legislation to limit the influence of U.S. media has done little to slow the diffusion of U.S. culture into Canada, and some fear that Canadian culture will soon become merely a reflection of that of the United States. A similar situation exists in other parts of the world. Members of cultural groups geographically distant from the United States are constantly exposed to U.S. media, again despite the efforts of their governments to maintain their distinct and separate cultures.

Cultural Loss

Most often people tend to think of change as an accumulation of innovations: adding new things to those already there. A little reflection, however, leads to the realization that frequently the acceptance of a new innovation leads to the loss of an older one. This sort of replacement is not just a feature of Western civilization. For example, back in biblical times, chariots and carts were in widespread use in the Middle East, but by the 6th century A.D. wheeled vehicles had virtually disappeared from Morocco to Afghanistan. They were replaced by camels, not because of some reversion to the past by the region's inhabitants but because camels, used as pack animals, worked better. By the 6th century Roman roads had deteriorated, but camels, as long as they were not used to pull vehicles, were not bound to them. Not only that, their longevity, endurance, and ability to ford rivers and traverse rough ground without people having to build roads in the first place made pack camels admirably suited for the region. Finally, they were labour-saving: A wagon required a man for every two draft animals,

[2]Weatherford, J. (1988). *Indian givers: How the Indians of the Americas transformed the New World* (p. 115). New York: Ballantine.

Samuel de Champlain, the founder of Quebec, is depicted here in Georgian Bay around 1615. The first European colonists in Canada could not have survived without the help of the First Nations.

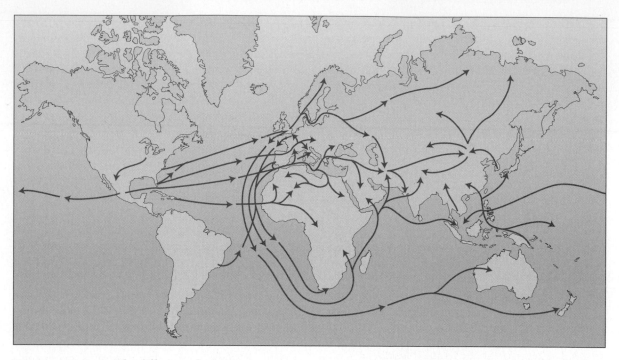

FIGURE 15.2 The diffusion of tobacco.

Having spread from the tropics of the Western hemisphere to much of the rest of North and South America, tobacco rapidly spread after 1492 to the rest of the world.

whereas a single person could manage from three to six pack camels. Stephen Jay Gould comments:

> We are initially surprised . . . because wheels have come to symbolize in our culture the sine qua non of intelligent exploitation and technological progress. Once invented, their superiority cannot be gainsaid or superseded. Indeed, "reinventing the wheel" has become our standard metaphor for deriding the repetition of such obvious truths. In an earlier era of triumphant social Darwinism, wheels stood as an ineluctable stage of human progress. The "inferior" cultures of Africa slid to defeat; their conquerors rolled to victory. The "advanced" cultures of Mexico and Peru might have repulsed Cortés and Pizarro if only a clever artisan had thought of turning a calendar stone into a cartwheel. The notion that carts could ever be replaced by pack animals strikes us not only as backward but almost sacrilegious.
>
>   The success of camels reemphasizes a fundamental theme. . . . Adaptation, be it biological or cultural, represents a better fit to specific, local environments, not an inevitable stage in a ladder of progress. Wheels were a formidable invention, and their uses are manifold (potters and millers

Although the wheel has become a symbol of progress in Western cultures, wheeled transport is not always superior to other forms. Such was the case in pre-Columbian Mexico, where wheels were used on toys but not for transport. The existence of adequate alternatives made wheeled vehicles unnecessary.

did not abandon them, even when cartwrights were eclipsed). But camels may work better in some circumstances. Wheels, like wings, fins, and brains, are exquisite devices for certain purposes, not signs of intrinsic superiority.[3]

▲▼▲▼▲▼▲▼▲▼▲▼▲▼▲▼▲▼▲▼▲▼▲▼▲▼▲▼▲▼▲▼

FORCIBLE CHANGE

Innovation, diffusion, and cultural loss all may occur among people who are free to decide what changes they will accept. Not always, however, are people free to make their own choices; frequently, changes they would not willingly make themselves have been forced upon them by some other group, usually in the course of conquest and colonialism. A direct outcome in many cases is a phenomenon anthropologists call acculturation.

Acculturation

Acculturation occurs when groups having different cultures come into intensive firsthand contact, with subsequent massive changes in the original cultural patterns of one or both groups. It always involves an element of force, either directly or indirectly. An important variable is the degree of disparity in wealth and power, who is dominant and who is submissive. It should be emphasized that acculturation and diffusion are not equivalent terms; one culture can borrow from another without being in the least acculturated.

In the course of acculturation, any one of a number of things may happen. Merger or fusion occurs when two cultures lose their separate identities and form a single culture, as expressed by the "melting pot" ideology of Anglo-American culture in the United States, although in reality the United States is no more a melting pot than any other Western country, despite the rhetoric of the ruling elite. Sometimes, though, one of the cultures loses its autonomy but retains its identity as a subculture in the form of a caste, class, or ethnic group; this is typical of conquest situa-

tions. This is certainly evident in Canada, where aboriginal peoples have endured repeated attempts to assimilate them into Euro-Canadian cultures. Canada's history of assimilating aboriginal groups is somewhat different from that of the United States—Canada used less force and violence, and more insidious methods, such as placing young children in residential schools to Europeanize them, despite the protests of their parents. These children were not allowed to speak their traditional languages; they had to dress like Europeans, eat unfamiliar foods, and learn Euro-Canadian ways. As a result, many of the children who went through the residential school system lost their traditional culture, although they never fully accepted or were accepted into Euro-Canadian mainstream society. Despite the efforts of clergy, government officials, and other "well-meaning" citizens, these assimilation plans largely failed, and today aboriginal groups retain their distinctive culture.

Extinction is the phenomenon whereby so many carriers of a culture die that those who survive become refugees living among other cultures. Examples of this may be seen in many parts of the world today, such as in Brazil's Amazon basin.

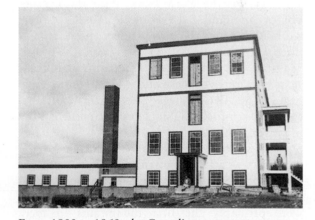

From 1900 to 1960, the Canadian government separated thousands of aboriginal children from their parents and communities and sent them to be educated under the strict discipline of the residential school system. The violent disruption this policy effected on aboriginal cultures has been implicated in many of the current problems facing aboriginal peoples in Canada.

---

[3]Gould, S.J. (1983). *Hens' teeth and horses' toes* (p. 159). New York: Norton.

Acculturation.   Major cultural changes people are forced to make owing to intensive firsthand contact between societies.

One particularly well-documented case occurred in 1968, when hired killers employed by ruthless land developers tried to wipe out several aboriginal groups, including the Cinta-Larga, using arsenic, dynamite, and machine guns from light planes, and even attacking a village when an important religious ceremony was taking place. In northern Brazil, as a conservative estimate, at least 1500 Yanomami died in the 1980s, often victims of deliberate massacres, as cattle ranchers and miners poured into their homelands. By 1990, 70 percent of the Yanomami's land in Brazil had been unconstitutionally expropriated; their fish supplies were poisoned by mercury contamination of rivers; and malaria, venereal disease, and tuberculosis were running rampant. The Yanomami were dying at an alarming rate of 10 percent a year, and their fertility had dropped off to near zero. Many villages were left with no children or old people, and the survivors awaited their fate with a profound terror of extinction.[4]

The prevailing Brazilian attitude of the time is illustrated by the government's reaction when two Kayapó and an anthropologist travelled to the United States, where they spoke with members of several congressional committees, as well as officials of the Department of State, the Treasury, and the World Bank, about the destruction of their land and way of life caused by internationally financed development projects. All three were charged with violating Brazil's Foreign Sedition Act. Fortunately, international expressions of outrage at these and other atrocities have brought positive changes from Brazilian authorities, and a more enlightened government is now in power in Brazil.

In Canada, the deliberate extinction of the Beothuk tells a similar tragic story. For many centuries the Beothuk lived in what is now called Newfoundland. Along with the Mi'kmaq, they were probably the first inhabitants to meet European explorers and fishermen, for the bountiful cod fishing grounds were in Beothuk territory. Despite early friendly relations, an unfortunate incident, in which a fishing boat fired

Once a vibrant and thriving indigenous community, the Yanomami of Brazil have suffered catastrophic decline at the hands of ranchers, miners, and ruthless land developers.

on a group of Beothuk, caused them to distrust the Europeans. As 18th-century European settlements grew more numerous they pushed the Beothuk from their traditional lands. The Beothuk fought back, raiding settlers' fishnets for food, but this only made the settlers more determined to eliminate the Beothuk. Oral tradition in Newfoundland recounts a time in 1800 when several hundred Beothuk were driven out to their favourite sealing site and shot down like animals.[5] A reduction in their food supplies, coupled with diseases like tuberculosis, eventually led to the demise of the Beothuk. The last survivors of the Beothuk were two women, Demasduwit and Shananditti, who lived with kindly settlers for the last years of their lives. We owe much of our knowledge about the Beothuk to their accounts. Shananditti, the last of the Beothuk people, died of consumption in 1829.[6]

Genocide

The Yanomami and Beothuk cases raise the issue of **genocide**—the extermination of one group of people by another.

[4]Turner, T. (1991). Major shift in Brazilian Yanomami policy. *Anthropology Newsletter, 32* (5), 1, 46.

[5]Such, P. (1978). Vanished people: The Archau Dorset and Beothuk people of Newfoundland. Cited in Friesen, J.W. (1997). *Rediscovering the First Nations of Canada* (p. 53). Calgary: Detselig.

[6]Friesen, J.W. (1997). *Rediscovering the First Nations of Canada.* Calgary: Detselig.

Genocide.   The extermination of one people by another, often in the name of "progress," either as a deliberate act or as the accidental outcome of one people's activities done with little regard for their impact on others.

Demasduwit (c. 1796–1820).

The most widely known act of genocide in recent history was the Nazi German attempt to wipe out European Jews and Roma (gypsies) in the name of racial superiority. Unfortunately, the common practice of referring to this as "*the Holocaust*"—as if it were something unique or at least exceptional—tends to blind us to the fact that this thoroughly monstrous act is simply one more example of an all too common phenomenon. From 1945 to 1987, a minimum of 6.8 million, but perhaps as many as 16.3 million, people were victims of internal (within-state) genocide, as compared to the 3.34 million people who have died in wars between different countries from 1945 to 1980.[7] Moreover, genocide continues to occur in the world today in places such as Iraq, where in 1988 the government began to use poison gas against Kurdish villagers; from 1992 to 1995, ethnic cleansing, mainly by Serb extremists, but also by Croatians and Albanian terrorists

As recent examples like the Rwandan tragedy demonstrate, genocide continues to occur in the world today, claiming more lives than war.

in Kosovo, resulted in 200 000 deaths in the wars following the breakup of Yugoslavia; and in 1994, 500 000 to 800 000 Tutsis were hacked to death by Hutus in Rwanda.[8] If such ugly practices are ever to be ended, we must gain a better understanding of them than currently exists. Anthropologists are actively engaged in this pursuit of knowledge, carrying out cross-cultural as well as individual case studies. One finding to emerge is the regularity with which religious, economic, and political interests are allied in cases of genocide.

One example (out of many) of attempted genocide in the 20th century: Hitler's Germany against Jews and Roma (gypsies), during the 1930s and the 1940s.

---

[7]Van Den Berghe, P.L. (1992). The modern state: Nation builder or nation killer? *International Journal of Group Tensions, 22* (3), 198.

[8]Megastories from OutThere News. (n.d.). *Bosnia: The psychology of genocide. What makes people mass murderers?* Retrieved April 1, 2001, from the World Wide Web: http://www.megastories.com/bosnia/genocide/genocide.htm.

Directed Change and Applied Anthropology

The most extreme cases of acculturation usually occur as a result of military conquest and displacement of traditional political authority by conquerors who know or care nothing about the culture they control. The indigenous people, unable to resist imposed changes and prevented from carrying out many of their traditional social, religious, and economic activities, may be forced into new activities that tend to isolate individuals and tear apart the integration of their cultures.

One by-product of colonial dealings with indigenous peoples has been the growth of **applied anthropology** and the use of anthropological techniques and knowledge for certain "practical" ends. Applied anthropologists bring a degree of relevancy to anthropology—their unique research methods, eclectic nature, and expertise in cultural dynamics make them valuable advocates and advisers to policymakers. In Canada, applied anthropologists offered input concerning First Nations' land claims, public policy, race relations, and economic and multinational development projects. Early in the 20th century, Diamond Jenness and Marius Barbeau

A common agent of change in many nonindustrial societies is the religious missionary. Although they see themselves as bringing enlightenment to indigenous peoples, such missionaries seek to subvert the beliefs that lie at the heart of such cultures and that make life within them meaningful.

(the latter is profiled in Chapter 2) were openly critical of government policies that excluded First Nations from decision making. Jenness and Barbeau, along with other anthropologists, protested the banning of traditional aboriginal customs, such as the northwest coast potlatch, the prairie sun dance, and the Salish guardian spirit ceremonies.

In 1939 a group of University of Toronto anthropologists and historians held a conference to discuss First Nations contemporary issues; an edited version of their work, the *North American Indian Today*, urged the federal government to develop an "Indian policy." By the 1960s applied anthropology was coming of age. Harry Hawthorn of the University of British Columbia and Marc-Adélard Tremblay of Laval University directed an ambitious collaborative study, involving 50 anthropologists, entitled *The Survey of the Contemporary Indians of Canada (1966–7)*. The study made more than 150 recommendations for meeting the economic, political, and educational needs of First Nations peoples.[9]

Today, applied anthropology in Canada has evolved into a unique form of anthropology: participatory-action research. Anthropologists, such as Joan Ryan of the Arctic Institute of North America, work closely with members of a community to solve problems. The community members conduct most of the research, own any information gathered, and determine what course of action to take.[10] This type of research is particularly relevant at a time when aboriginal peoples are attempting to regain control of their affairs.

While applied anthropologists are in some demand in international development because of their specialized knowledge of social structure and local value systems, they have to grapple with ethical dilemmas. They are bound to respect the peoples' dignity and cultural integrity, yet they

---

[9]Hedican, E.J. (1995). *Applied anthropology in Canada: Understanding aboriginal issues.* Toronto: University of Toronto Press.

[10]Ervin, A.M. (2001). *Canadian perspectives in cultural anthropology.* Scarborough, ON: Nelson Thomson Learning.

Applied anthropology.   The use of anthropological knowledge and techniques for solving "practical" problems, often for a specific "client."

Sally Weaver   *(1940–1993)*

Sally Weaver was one of Canada's leading anthropologists. She began her teaching career at the University of Waterloo in 1966, and became the first woman to receive a Ph.D. in anthropology in Canada in 1967. In 1974 she was instrumental in founding a separate association for social and cultural anthropology, the Canadian Ethnology Society, now known as the Canadian Anthropology Society.

Weaver was a student of aboriginal peoples. Her first monograph was *Medicine and Politics among the Grand River Iroquois*, written in 1972. She also studied the indigenous populations of Australia (Aborigines) and Norway (Sami). But Weaver went beyond studying aboriginal peoples; she was also their champion. She spent her life promoting justice and recognition for aboriginal peoples, tackling the misperceptions and ill-informed attitudes of Canadian federal bureaucrats toward First Nations peoples.

Weaver achieved international recognition as a scholar in applied anthropology. She is one of the few Canadian anthropologists who contributed to research on Indian Affairs, and she even tackled the "exotic tribal behaviour of the Ottawa bureaucrat."[1] Weaver believed that anthropologists had to become involved in formulating policy concerning First Nations peoples. She once stated, "Anthropologists appear to be confused about the use of anthropology in policy issues."[2] She admonished government officials, and noted that financial constraints often overrode the "needs and aspirations of people" and have become "a driving force in policy formulation."[3]

During her career at Waterloo, Weaver wrote numerous books, articles, and research papers. One of her most influential works, *Making Canadian Indian Policy: The Hidden Agenda 1968–1970* (1981), dealt with the

government's 1969 "White Paper" proposal to end its relationship with First Nations peoples. This monograph has been selected as one of the 20 best works in English in the social sciences. Shortly before her death in 1993, the Weaver-Tremblay Award in Canadian Applied Anthropology was announced in honour of her work and that of Marc-Adélard Tremblay at Laval University. The first recipient of this award was Joan Ryan.

---

[1]Abler, T.S. (1993). In Memoriam. Sally M. Weaver (1940–1993). *Anthropologica, 35* (1), 117.

[2]Weaver, S. (1985). Federal policy-making for Métis and non-status Indians in the context of native policy. *Canadian Ethnic Studies, 17*, 80–102. Cited in Hedigan, E.J. (1995). *Applied anthropology in Canada. Understanding aboriginal issues* (p. 174). Toronto: University of Toronto Press.

[3]Weaver, S. (1984). Indian government: A concept in need of a definition. In L. Little Bear, M. Boldt, & J.H. Long (Eds.), *Pathways to self-determination: Canadian Indians and the Canadian state* (p. 67). Toronto: University of Toronto Press. Cited in Hedigan, E.J. (1995). *Applied anthropology in Canada: Understanding aboriginal issues* (p. 100). Toronto: University of Toronto Press.

Sources:

Abler, T.S. (1993). In Memoriam. Sally M. Weaver (1940–1993). *Anthropologica, 35* (1).

Hedigan, E.J. (1995). *Applied anthropology in Canada: Understanding aboriginal issues.* Toronto: University of Toronto Press.

UW Gazette. (1995, December 13). Reprinted in Anthropology at Waterloo website. Retrieved April 3, 2001, from the World Wide Web: http://www.arts .uwaterloo.ca/ANTHRO/weaverpapers.html.

---

are asked for advice on how to change certain aspects of those cultures. Outside agencies, from which these requests usually come, may (or may not) have the targeted population's interests at heart. Just how far applied anthropologists should go when advising how people—especially ones without the power to resist—can be made to

embrace changes proposed for them is a serious ethical question.

Despite such difficulties, applied anthropology is flourishing today as never before. As the several Anthropology Applied boxes spaced throughout this book illustrate, anthropologists now practise their profession in many nonacademic settings,

Applied anthropologist Tekle Haile Selassie of Ethiopia speaks with women of the village of Mai Misham about water improvement systems.

both at home and abroad, in a wide variety of ways.

Revitalization Movements

A common reaction to forcible change is revitalization, a process touched on in Chapter 12. Revitalization may be viewed as a deliberate attempt by some members of a society to construct a more satisfactory culture by rapidly accepting multiple innovations. Once primary ties of culture, social relationships, and activities are broken and meaningless activity is imposed by force, individuals and groups characteristically react with fantasy, withdrawal, and escape.

REBELLION AND REVOLUTION

When the scale of discontent within a society reaches a certain level, the possibilities for rebellion and **revolution,** the toppling of a government by force—such as the Iranian Revolution, the Sandinista Revolution in Nicaragua, or the Zapatista uprising in Mexico—are high.

The question of why revolutions erupt, as well as why they frequently fail to live up to the expectations of the people initiating them, is a problem. It is clear, however, that the colonial policies of countries such as England, France, Spain, Portugal, and the United States during the 19th and early 20th centuries have created a worldwide situation in which revolution is nearly inevitable. Despite the political independence most colonies have gained since World War II, more powerful countries continue to exploit many for their natural resources and cheap labour, causing a deep resentment of rulers beholden to foreign powers and of the poverty and inequality that persist. Further discontent has been caused by the governing elite of newly independent states attempting to assert their control over fellow citizens of sharply different ethnicities or religious beliefs. Thus, in many former colonies, people have taken up arms to resist annexation and absorption by imposed state regimes run by people regarded as outsiders. While attempting to make their states into nations, governing elites of one nationality

----

Revolution.   The overthrow of a government by force.

Gender **Perspectives**

Reproductive Rights in Canada

Culture change often grows out of conflict and in contemporary democracies may be addressed by grassroots social movements. One of the most contentious issues in Canadian society has been the question of a woman's right to terminate a pregnancy. Access to safe, legal abortion has been the subject of continuous debate and has even led to violence. In the 1950s and 1960s, termination of pregnancy was extremely difficult to obtain. A woman had to go before a hospital committee, which had the discretion to determine whether the procedure would be performed under a narrow range of circumstances, such as the pregnancy being a threat to the life of the pregnant woman. The alternative, if a woman was desperate enough, was to seek an illegal "backstreet" abortion, which often resulted in serious complications and compromised health for the woman.

With the rise of the feminist movement in the 1960s, and the publication of such important works as *Our Bodies Ourselves* by the Boston Women's Health Collective (3rd ed., 1998), women grew determined to "take control of their own bodies." Active political engagement on the issue of abortion, by such groups as the Canadian Abortion

Rights Action League (CARAL), led to campaigns for clinics to provide safe abortions. Several of these opened in various provinces in the 1970s, the most famous of which were Dr. Henry Morgentaler's clinics. Opposition was vigorous; often led by religious organizations, many anti-abortion groups sprung up and began daily pickets in front of abortion clinics, so that people entering and leaving had to run a gauntlet of abuse. The anti-abortion forces recruited many people whose sincerity and integrity were not in doubt, but it also drew extremists who expressed their views by fire-bombing clinics and even assassinating doctors who performed abortions. These violent acts helped turn public opinion toward sympathy for the cause of abortion advocates. Polls in the 1970s and 1980s consistently showed that a strong majority of Canadians supported a woman's "right to choose." After years of court battles, which ended in Dr. Morgentaler's favour, the laws regarding abortion finally were repealed by Parliament and women in Canada today have largely won the right to abortion on demand, although the circumstances do vary from province to province.

Source: Canadian Abortion Rights Action League (CARAL). (2004). Retrieved January 23, 2004, from the World Wide Web: http://www.caral.ca.

---

endeavour to strip the peoples of other nations within their states of their lands, resources, and sense of identity as a people. The phenomenon is so common as to lead anthropologist Pierre Van Den Berghe to label what modern states refer to as "nation building" as, in fact, "nation killing."[11] One of the most important facts of our time is that the vast majority of the distinct peoples of the world have never consented to rule by the governments of states they find themselves

living within.[12] In many a newly emerged country, such groups feel they have no other option than to fight.

The 1950s Algerian struggle for independence from France and the long struggle of the Vietnamese people, first against French colonialism and then against the United States (1945–1975), are typical examples. Of the 120 or so armed conflicts in the world today, 98 percent are in the economically poor countries of Africa, Asia, and Central and South America, almost all

---

[11]Van Den Berghe, P. (1992). The modern state: Nation builder or nation killer? *International Journal of Group Tensions, 22* (3), 191–207.

[12]Nietschmann, B. (1987). The third world war. *Cultural Survival Quarterly, 11* (3), 3.

A leading cause of rebellion and revolution in the world today is the refusal of
governing elites to recognize the cultural, economic, and political rights of people
of other nationalities over whom the state has unilaterally asserted its authority.
The Zapatista uprising in the state of Chiapas, Mexico, recently observed the
10th anniversary of its struggle.

of which were at one time under European colonial domination. Of these wars, 75 percent are
between the state and one or more cultures within
the state's borders who are seeking to maintain or
regain control of their persons, communities,
lands, and resources in the face of what they
regard as subjugation by a foreign power.[13]

Revolutions are not always successful in
accomplishing what they set out to do. One of the
stated goals of the Chinese Revolution, for
example, was to liberate women from the oppression of a strongly patriarchal society where a
woman owed lifelong obedience to some man or
another—first her father, later her husband, and,
after his death, her sons. Although some progress
has been made, the effort overall has been frustrated by an entrenched tradition of extreme
patriarchy extending back at least 22 centuries.
With China's rapid industrialization after the
death of Mao Tse-tung in 1975, more women
began to work outside the house, but it is generally at jobs with low pay, low status, and no benefits. Indeed, the 1990s saw a major outbreak of
the abduction and sale of women from rural areas

as brides and workers. Women's no-wage
domestic labour or low-wage labour outside the
household has been essential to China's economic
expansion, which relies on the allocation of
labour by the heads of patrilineal households.[14]
Despite whatever autonomy women may achieve
for a while, they become totally dependent in
their old age on their sons. This situation shows
that the subversion of revolutionary goals, if it
occurs, is not necessarily by political opponents.
Rather, it may be a consequence of the revolutionaries' own cultural background.

Revolution is a relatively recent phenomenon, occurring only during the past 5000 years
or so. Political rebellion requires a centralized
political authority (chiefdom or state) to rebel
against, and states (if not chiefdoms) have been in
existence for only 5000 years. Obviously, then, in
societies typified by tribes and bands, and in
other nonindustrial societies lacking central
authority, rebellion or political revolution could
not have occurred.

---

[13]Ibid., 7.

[14]Gates, H. (1996). Buying brides in China—again.
Anthropology Today, 12 (4), 10.

MODERNIZATION

One of the most frequently used terms to describe social and cultural changes as they are occurring today is **modernization**. This is often defined as an all-encompassing global process of cultural and socioeconomic change, whereby developing countries seek to acquire some of the characteristics common to industrial countries. Looking closely at this definition's meaning reveals that "becoming modern" really means "becoming like us" ("us" being Canada and other industrial societies), with the very clear implication that not being like us is to be antiquated and obsolete. It is unfortunate that the term *modernization*, however ethnocentric, continues to be so widely used. Since we seem to be stuck with it, the best we can do at the moment is recognize its inappropriateness, even though we continue to use it.

Theorists who do employ the term see the process of modernization as consisting of four subprocesses. *Technological development* involves the replacement of traditional knowledge and techniques with the application of scientific knowledge from the West. With *agricultural development* comes a shift from subsistence farming to commercial farming, raising cash crops for sale rather than for home consumption, with greater reliance on markets for selling farm products and purchasing goods. *Industrialization* entails machine production driven by fossil fuels replacing hand production in the home. Finally, *urbanization* is marked by population movements from rural settlements into cities. Although all four subprocesses are interrelated, they follow no fixed order of appearance.

Modernization brings other changes in the political realm. Political parties and some sort of electoral machinery frequently appear, along with the development of a bureaucracy. In education,

Whereas most items for daily use were once made at home, almost everything we use today is the product of specialized production, as is the milk we buy in the food store.

the school system expands, literacy increases, and an indigenous educated elite develops. Religion may become less important as traditional beliefs and practices are undermined, although many countries, especially Islamic countries, are attempting to combine modernization with intensified religion. A key impact is on the traditional rights and duties connected with kinship. The strength of the extended family may weaken as more individualistic market-driven forces foster the nuclear family form. Finally, where stratification is a factor, mobility increases as who you are (ascribed status) becomes less important than what you become (achieved status).

Two other features of modernization go hand in hand with those already noted. One, **structural differentiation,** is the division of single traditional roles, which embrace two or more functions (such as political, economic, and religious functions), into two or more separate roles, each with a single specialized function. This represents a kind of fragmentation of society, which must be counteracted by new **integrative mechanisms** if the society is not to disintegrate into a number of discrete units. These new mechanisms take such

---

Modernization.   The process of cultural and socioeconomic change, whereby developing societies acquire some of the characteristics of Western industrialized societies. **> Structural differentiation.**   The division of single traditional roles, which embrace two or more functions (for example, political, economic, and religious), into two or more roles, each with a single specialized function. **> Integrative mechanisms.**   Cultural mechanisms that oppose a society's differentiation forces; in modernizing societies, they include formal governmental structures, official state ideologies, political parties, legal codes, and labour and trade unions and other common-interest associations.

forms as formal governmental structures, official state ideologies, political parties, legal codes, and labour and trade unions as well as other common-interest associations. All of these crosscut other societal divisions and thus serve to develop what political scientists have come to call *civil society*, an important concept developed particularly in the well-known theories of Italian Marxist Antonio Gramsci (1890–1937). Gramsci also developed the concept of *hegemony*, in referring to the ability of ruling elites to present their class interests in such terms that members of other classes accept their worldview as so many self-evident truths—for example, the American view that anyone can grow up to be president. Hegemony was purveyed through institutions like the educational system and the media to provide the integrative mechanism, or ideological glue, binding highly differentiated societies.

An examination of two traditional cultures that have felt the impact of modernization will help to pinpoint some of the problems such cultures have met. The cultures are the Skolt Lapps, a division of the Saami people whose homeland straddles the Arctic Circle in Norway, Sweden, Finland, and Russia, and the Shuar of Ecuador.

Skolt Lapps and the Snowmobile Revolution

The Skolt Lapps, whose homeland is in northern Finland, traditionally supported themselves by fishing and herding reindeer.[15] Although they depended on the outside world for certain material goods, the resources crucial for their system were found locally. No one was denied access to critical resources, and little social and economic differentiation existed among the people. Theirs was basically an egalitarian culture.

Of particular importance to the Skolt Lapps was reindeer herding. Indeed, herd management is central to their definition of themselves as a people. These animals were a source of meat for home consumption or for sale to procure outside goods. They were also a source of hides for shoes and clothing, sinews for sewing, and antlers and bones for making certain objects. Finally, reindeer

were used to pull sleds in the winter and as pack animals when no snow was on the ground. Understandably, the animals were the objects of much attention. The herds were not large, but without a great deal of attention, productivity suffered. Hence, most winter activities centred on reindeer.

In the early 1960s these reindeer herders speedily adopted snowmobiles (a Canadian invention) on the premise that the new machines would make herding physically easier and economically more advantageous. As early as 1967 most people had gotten rid of draft animals, and only four families were still using reindeer sleds for winter travel. Those who had not converted to snowmobiles felt disadvantaged compared with the rest.

The consequences of this mechanization were extraordinary and in part unexpected. The high cost of snowmobiles, spare parts, and fuel created a dependency on the outside world unlike anything that had previously existed. As snowmobile technology replaced traditional skills, the ability of the Lapps to determine their own survival without dependence on outsiders was lost. Accordingly, a sharp rise in the need for cash occurred. To get this, men had to regularly leave the Lapp community for wage work, or else rely on government pensions and welfare.

Was the resulting dependency on cash and outside help a price worth paying? In truth, snowmobiles made reindeer herding worse, not better. By 1971 average herd size had declined from 50 to 12, a number too small to be economically viable. The old close, prolonged, and

A Saami man slaughtering his reindeer for their meat and hides.

---

[15]Pelto, P.J. (1973). *The snowmobile revolution: Technology and social change in the Arctic.* Menlo Park, CA: Cummings.

largely peaceful relationship between herdsman and beast has changed to a noisy, traumatic relationship. Now, when men appear, they come speeding out of the woods on snarling, smelly machines that invariably chase the animals, often for long distances. Instead of aiding the reindeer in their winter food quest, helping females with their calves, and protecting them from predators, men appear either to slaughter or castrate them. Naturally enough, the reindeer have become suspicious. The result has been actual de-domestication, with reindeer scattering and running off to more inaccessible areas, given the slightest chance. Moreover, there are indications that snowmobile harassment has adversely affected reindeer birthrates. This is a classic illustration of the fact that change is not always adaptive.

This is more than just an economic problem, for in the traditional culture of this people, being a herder of reindeer is the very essence of manhood. Hence, today's nonherders are not only poor in a way they could not have been in previous times, but also they are in a sense inadequate as "men." Another consequence has been the development of a stratified society out of the older egalitarian one. Reindeer herding now has much higher start-up costs and requires skills and knowledge that were not a part of traditional culture. Those who lack the cash and skills are dependent on others if they are to participate.

The Shuar Solution

Although the Skolt Lapps have not escaped many negative aspects of modernization, the choice to modernize was essentially theirs. The Shuar (sometimes called Jivaro), by contrast, deliberately avoided modernization, until they felt they had no other option if they were to fend off the same outside forces that elsewhere in the Amazon basin have destroyed whole societies. Threatened with the loss of their land base as more and more Ecuadorian colonists intruded into their territory, the Shuar in 1964 founded a fully independent corporate body, the Shuar Federation, to take control of their own future. Recognized by Ecuador's government, albeit grudgingly, the federation is officially dedicated to promoting the social, economic, and moral advancement of its members and to coordinating development with official governmental agencies.

Since its founding, the federation has secured title to more than 96 000 hectares of communal land; has established a cattle herd of more than 15 000 head as the people's primary source of income; has taken control of their education, using their language and mostly Shuar teachers; and has established their own bilingual broadcasting station and a bilingual newspaper. Obviously, all this has required enormous changes by the Shuar, but they have been able to maintain a variety of distinctive cultural markers, including their language, communal land tenure, cooperative production and distribution, a basically egalitarian economy, and kin-based communities that retain maximum autonomy. Thus, for all the changes, they feel they are still Shuar and quite distinct from other Ecuadorians.[16]

The Shuar case shows that Amazonian nations are capable of taking control of their own destinies even in the face of intense outside pressures, *if* allowed to do so. Unfortunately, until recently, few have had that option. Prior to European invasions of the Amazon, more than 700 distinct groups inhabited the region. By 1900 in Brazil, the number was down to 270, and today something like 180 remain.[17] Many of these survivors find themselves in situations not unlike that of the Yanomami, described earlier in this chapter. Nevertheless, many of these peoples are showing a new resourcefulness in standing up to the forces of destruction arrayed against them.

Modernization and the Developing World

In the previous examples, we have seen how modernization has affected indigenous peoples in otherwise "modern" states. Elsewhere in the developing world, whole countries are in the throes of modernization. Throughout Africa, Asia, and South and Central America we are witnessing the widespread removal of economic activities—or at least their control—from the family-community setting; the altered structure of the family in the face of the changing labour market; the increased reliance of young children on parents alone for affection, instead of on the

---

[16]Bodley, J.H. (1990). *Victims of progress* (3rd ed., pp. 160–162). Mountain View, CA: Mayfield.

[17]*Cultural Survival Quarterly, 15* (4), 3. (1991).

extended family; the decline of general parental authority; schools replacing the family as the primary educational unit; the generation gap; and many other changes. The difficulty is that all this is thrust upon traditional societies so fast that they cannot adapt gradually. Changes that took generations to accomplish in Europe and North America are attempted within the span of a single generation in developing countries. In the process they frequently face the erosion of a number of dearly held values they had no intention of giving up.

Commonly, the burden of modernization falls most heavily on women. For example, the mechanization and commercialization of agriculture often involves land reforms that overlook or ignore women's traditional land rights, reducing their control of and access to resources. As a consequence, they are confined more and more to traditional domestic tasks, which, as cash cropping becomes people's dominant concern, are increasingly downgraded in value. To top it all off, the domestic workload tends to increase, because men are less available to help out, while tasks such as fuel gathering and water collection are made more difficult as common land and resources become privately owned and as wood-

lands are reserved for commercial exploitation. In short, with modernization, women frequently find themselves in an increasingly marginal position. While their workload increases, the value assigned to the work they do declines, as does their relative and absolute health, and their nutritional and educational status.

Modernization: Must It Always Be Painful?

Although most anthropologists view the changes affecting traditional non-Western peoples critically, the more widespread public opinion has been that it is good—however disagreeable the "medicine" may be, it is worth it for the people to become just like "us" (i.e., the people of Europe and North America). This view of modernization, unfortunately, is based more on Western hopes and expectations than on reality. No doubt Western peoples would like to see the non-Western world attain the "high" levels of development seen in Europe and North America, as many Japanese, South Koreans, Taiwanese, and other Asians, in fact, have done. Overlooked is the stark fact that the standard of living in the Western world is based on a rate of consumption of nonrenewable resources, in which the wealth-

An urban slum near Juarez, Mexico. All over the world, people are fleeing to the cities for a "better life," only to experience disease and poverty in such slums.

iest 20 percent of the world's population consumes 80 percent of the goods and services produced.[18] Can most of the world's peoples realistically achieve such a standard of living without seriously compromising what is left of the planet's resources and environment? Perhaps yes, but if, and only if, the countries of the West drastically cut back their own consumption of resources. So far, they have shown no willingness to do this and, in fact, are moving in the opposite direction. It is widely believed that the United States was motivated to invade Iraq in 2003 in part to gain control of that country's oil and natural gas reserves, the second largest of the world's rapidly shrinking energy reserves.

More non-Western people than ever, quite understandably, aspire to a standard of living Western countries now enjoy, even though the gap between the rich and poor people of the world is widening rather than narrowing. No longer satisfied with traditional values, people all over the world are fleeing to the cities to find a "better life," all too often to live out their days in poor, congested, and disease-infested slums in an attempt to achieve what is usually beyond their reach. Unfortunately, despite all sorts of rosy predictions about a better future, this basic reality remains.

▲▽▲▽▲▽▲▽▲▽▲▽▲▽▲▽▲▽▲▽▲▽▲▽▲▽▲▽▲▽▲▽▲▽▲

THE CULTURAL FUTURE OF HUMANITY

Whatever the biological future of the human species, culture remains the mechanism by which people solve their problems of existence. Some anthropologists have noted with concern that the problems of human existence seem to be spinning out of control, outstripping any culture's ability to find solutions. To paraphrase anthropologist Jules Henry, although cultures are "for" people, they are also "against" them.[19] As we shall see, this dilemma is now posing serious new problems for human beings. What can anthropologists tell us about future cultures?

One of the major problems with the enormous body of future-oriented literature that claims to address the many problems facing humanity is that it considers the present social order in the developed world as the best of all worlds. The goal of development, then, becomes transferring all the "benefits" of modernity uncritically to the rest of the planet. This predisposes people to think a trend that seems fine today can be projected indefinitely into the future. The danger inherent in this tendency is neatly captured in anthropologist George Cowgill's comment: "It is worth recalling the story of the person who leaped from a very tall building and on being asked how things were going as he passed the 20th floor replied 'Fine, so far.'"[20]

Another flaw is a tendency to treat subjects in isolation, without reference to pertinent trends outside an expert's field of competence. For example, agricultural planning is often predicated on the assumption that a certain amount of water is available for irrigation, whether or not urban planners or others have designs for that same water. Thus—as in the southwestern United States, where more of the Colorado River's water has been allocated than actually exists—people may be counting on resources in the future that will not, in fact, be available.

Against this background, anthropology's contribution to our view of the future is clear. With their holistic perspective, anthropologists are specialists at seeing how parts fit together into a larger whole. With their evolutionary perspective, they can see short-term trends in longer-term perspective. With more than 100 years of cross-cultural research behind them, anthropologists can recognize culture-bound assertions when they encounter them, and, finally, they are familiar with alternative ways to deal with a wide variety of problems.

One-World Culture?

In a famous treatise, *Jihad vs. McWorld* (1995),[21] social analyst Benjamin Barber contrasts the social, political, and economic forces pushing toward the development of a homogeneous world

---

[18]Sagoff, M. (1997, January–June). Do we consume too much? *The Atlantic Monthly, 279* (6), 80–96.

[19]Henry, J. (1965). *Culture against man* (p. 12). New York: Vintage Books.

[20]Cowgill, G.L. (1980). Letter. *Science, 210,* 1305.

[21]Barber, B.R. (1995). *Jihad vs. McWorld.* New York: Times Books.

culture with the persistent and powerful regional social forces that resist the idea of homogenization. The idea that a "one-world culture" is emerging is based largely on the observation that developments in communication, transportation, and trade so closely link the peoples of the world that they are increasingly wearing the same kinds of clothes, eating the same kinds of food, reading the same kinds of newspapers, watching the same kinds of television programs, and communicating directly with one another via the Internet. The continuation of such trends, so this thinking goes, should lead North Americans who travel in the year 2100 to Patagonia, Mongolia, or New Guinea to find the inhabitants living in a manner identical or similar to them. But is this so?

Certainly striking is the extent to which such items as Western-style clothing, transistor radios, Coca-Cola, and McDonald's hamburgers have spread to virtually all parts of the world, and many countries—Japan, for example—have moved a long way toward becoming "Westernized," outstripping the West in many aspects of modernity. Moreover, looking back over the past 5000 years of human history, we can see a clear-cut trend for political units to become larger and more all-encompassing while becoming fewer in number. Sociologist Charles Tilley has noted that in the year 1500 there were some 500 sovereign jurisdictions on the continent of Europe.[22] With the rise of the modern nation-state, by 1900 this number had been consolidated into fewer than 30. This trend continues with the formation of the European Union and the adoption of a common currency, the euro, by many member countries.

Could all world cultures merge into a single world political entity? One problem with such a prediction is that it ignores the one thing all large states, past and present, irrespective of other differences between them, share in common: a tendency (eventually) to come apart. Not only have the great empires of the past, without exception, broken up into smaller independent states, but countries in virtually all parts of the world today are showing a tendency to fragment. The most dramatic illustrations of this in recent years have been the breakup of the Soviet Union into a dozen smaller independent states and the fragmentation of Yugoslavia into five battered but independent republics. It also can be seen in Basque and Catalonian nationalism in Europe; Scottish, Irish, and Welsh nationalism in Britain; Tibetan nationalism in China; Kurdish nationalism in Turkey, Iran, and Iraq; Sikh separatism in India; Tamil separatism in Sri Lanka; Eritrean and Tigrean secession movements in Ethiopia; Puerto Rican nationalism in the United States; and so on—this list is far from exhaustive. Nor is Canada immune, as can be seen in First Nations' accelerating attempts to secure greater political and cultural self-determination, and in French-speaking Quebec's separatist movement. Canada has survived two Quebec sovereignty votes, one in 1980 and the most recent in 1995.

Many struggles for independence have been going on for years, such as the Karen resistance to the Burmese invasion of their territory in 1948; the takeover of Kurdistan by Iraq, Iran, and Turkey in 1925; and the even earlier Russian takeover of Chechnya. Even in relatively nonviolent cases, the stresses and strains are obviously there. In Canada, with its massive geographical size and regional disparities, there is a perceived east–west schism, in particular a western sense of alienation from the federal government located in eastern Canada. Similar stresses and strains may develop even in the absence of ethnic differences when regional interests within a large country increasingly compete.

The worldwide spread of such franchises as McDonald's is taken by some as a sign that a homogeneous world culture is developing.

---

[22]Tilley, C. (Ed.). (1975). *The formation of national states in western Europe*. Princeton, NJ: Princeton University Press.

Nunavut

On a more positive note, in 1993 the eastern half of the Canadian Northwest Territories separated to create the autonomous territory of Nunavut. Nunavut means "our land" in Inuktitut, the language of Inuit peoples. Of the 25 000 people who inhabit the 1.9 million square kilometres of eastern Arctic land, 85 percent are Inuit. The Nunavut Land Claims Agreement and the Nunavut Act, which created the territory, were signed in 1993. The agreement represents the largest aboriginal land claims settlement in Canadian history, and marks the beginning of new relations between aboriginal Canadians and the rest of Canada.[23]

On April 1, 1999, the Canadian government handed over political control of Nunavut to the Nunavut Tungavik. Key features of this agreement include title to 350 000 square kilometres, including 35 000 square kilometres with mineral rights; equal Inuit representation on wildlife, resource, and environmental management boards; the right to harvest wildlife on lands and waters throughout the Nunavut settlement area; a share of federal government royalties from oil, gas, and mineral development on Crown lands; the right to negotiate with industry for economic and social benefits from nonrenewable resource development; the right to refuse sport or commercial development; and the right to establish self-government for the Nunavut Inuit.[24]

Nunavut is governed by a territorial assembly consisting of 19 elected representative members, who may or may not be Inuit. In fact, the Inuit are not constitutionally guaranteed control of the assembly. The government is made up of specialized departments, for example, the Department of Sustainable Development, which oversees the important issue of wildlife harvesting.[25] Of equal importance is the Department of Culture, Language, Elders, and Youth, which has been given the task

of promoting cultural survival, including encouraging the use of Inuktitut in the workplace.

The creation of Nunavut came about from splintering the Northwest Territories, but rather than the fragmentation of a political entity, it heralded the beginning of self-determination and self-government for aboriginal peoples in Canada and may provide a model for future self-determination endeavours around the world.

The Rise of the Multinational Corporations

The Cold War between the Western nations, led by the United States and the Soviet Bloc, extended from the end of World War II in 1945 to 1990. It ended with the collapse of the U.S.S.R., but while the Cold War existed, the bipolar world lent a degree of stability to international relations. Both superpowers were constrained in their imperial designs by the presence of the other. In today's unipolar world, where the one remaining superpower is the United States, these restraints have been removed. The U.S. claims to global hegemony, as illustrated by its recent invasion and occupation of Iraq, put it at odds with many of its closest allies, including France, Germany, and Canada. What are some of the forces driving this unilateralism, and what can it tell us about the future of humanity?

The world's resistance to political integration seems to be offset, at least partially, by the rise of multinational corporations. These giant enterprises, many larger in scale than most of the member nations of the United Nations, are the subject of intense debate. Because the reach of corporations extends across state boundaries, some see them as a force for global unity despite the political differences that divide people. Others argue that their power and reach—including the ability to set international trade agendas—and the domination of international agencies such as the World Bank are the major obstacles to real grassroots democracy and bottom-up development for poorer nations.

Multinational corporations are not new in the world (the Hudson's Bay Company in Canada was chartered in 1670), but they were not common until the 1950s. Since then they have become a major force in the world. These modern-day giants are actually clusters of corporations of diverse

[23]Nunavut Planning Commission. (n.d.). *Land claim review.* Retrieved April 7, 2001, from the World Wide Web: http://www.arctic.ca/LUS/Nunavut.html.

[24]*Welcome to Nunavut.* (n.d.). Retrieved April 7, 2001, from the World Wide Web: http://www.polarnet.ca/polarnet/nunavut.htm.

[25]Erwin, S. (2001). *Canadian perspectives in cultural anthropology.* Toronto: Nelson Thomson Publishing.

nationality joined together by ties of common ownership and responsive to a common management strategy. Usually tightly controlled by a head office in one country, these multinationals organize and integrate production across the borders of different countries for interests formulated in corporate boardrooms, regardless of whether or not these are consistent with the interests of people in the countries where they operate. In a sense they are products of the technological revolution, for without sophisticated data-processing equipment, the multinationals could not keep adequate track of their worldwide operations.

Though typically thought of as responding impersonally to outside market forces, large corporations are in fact controlled by powerful economic elites who benefit directly from their operations. For example, in 1994, just 10 individuals helped direct 37 North American companies whose combined assets of $2 trillion rivalled those of many governments and represented nearly 10 percent of all corporate assets in U.S. "for profit" businesses. Yet the world's largest individual stockholders and most powerful directors, unlike political leaders, are unelected and are known to few people. For that matter, most people cannot even name the five largest multinational corporations.[26]

So great is the power of multinationals that they increasingly thwart the wishes of governments. Because the information these corpora-

---

[26]Bodley, J.H. (1997). Comment. *Current Anthropology, 38,* 725.

Brazil's Grand Carajas iron ore mine is an example of the kind of project states favour in their drive to develop. Not only does this introduce ecologically unsound technologies, but it also commonly has devastating effects on the people whose land is seized.

The power of corporations over individuals is illustrated by their ability to get consumers to pay, by purchasing goods such as this T-shirt, to advertise corporate products.

tions process is kept from flowing in a meaningful way to the population at large, or even to lower levels within the organization, it is difficult for governments to get the information they need for informed policy decisions. Consider how it took decades for the United States Congress to extract the information it needed from tobacco companies to decide what to do about tobacco legislation. Nor is this an isolated case. Beyond this, though, the multinationals have shown they can overrule foreign-policy decisions, as when they got around a U.S. embargo on pipeline equipment for the Soviet Union in the 1980s. Canada is not without blame; large Canadian corporations working abroad have come under increasing criticism for their actions in countries such as the Philippines, Colombia, and Angola. For example, oil revenues from a Canadian energy company, used to buy weapons in the Sudan, have been blamed for the continuation of a civil war in the region. Organizations such as the Canadian Ecumenical Jubilee Initiative (CEJI) are lobbying the Canadian government to impose restrictions and regulations on Canadian corporations and on the Export Development Corporation's activities abroad. This raises the unsettling question of whether or not the global order is determined by corporations interested only in financial profits. The recent collapse of U.S. giant corporations Enron and WorldCom amid allegations of criminal mismanagement is a warning sign of the degree to which corporations have escaped government control.

In developing countries, women have become a source of cheap labour for large corporations, as subsistence farming has given way to mechanized agriculture. Unable to contribute to their families' well-being in any other way, they have no choice but to take on menial jobs for low wages.

If the ability of multinational corporations to ignore the wishes of sovereign governments is cause for concern, so is their ability to act in concert with such governments. Here, in fact, is where their worst excesses have occurred. In Brazil, for example, where the situation is hardly unique but is especially well documented, a partnership emerged, after the military coup of 1964, between a government anxious to proceed as rapidly as possible with development of the Amazon basin and a number of multinational corporations, such as ALCOA, Borden, Union Carbide, Swift-Armour, and Volkswagen, to mention only a few, as well as major international lending institutions, such as the Export-Import Bank, the Inter-American Development Bank, and the World Bank.[27] To realize their goals, these allies introduced inappropriate technology and ecologically unsound practices into the region, converting vast tropical areas into semidesert wastelands.

The power of corporations extends far beyond governments and members of a society. Their control of television and other media, not to mention the advertising industry, gives them enormous power over the lives of millions of "ordinary" people in ways they little suspect.

In their never-ending search for cheap labour, multinational corporations more than ever have come to favour women for low-skilled assembly jobs. With the mechanization of agriculture women are less able to contribute to their families' farming. This places pressure on women to seek jobs outside the household to contribute to its support. Without education or job skills, these women find that only low-paying jobs are open to them. Corporate officials, for their part, favour young and single female workers who can be paid low wages and laid off when they marry, contributing to the emergence of a gender-segregated labour force. Higher-paying jobs, or at least those that require special skills, are generally held by men, whose workday may be shorter since they do not have additional domestic tasks to perform. Men who lack special skills—and many do—are often doomed to lives of unemployment.

---

[27]Davis, S.H. (1982). *Victims of the miracle*. Cambridge, UK: Cambridge University Press.

In sum, multinational corporations have become a major force in the world today, drawing people more firmly than ever into a truly global system of relationships. Although this brings with it potential benefits, it is also clear it poses serious new problems that now must be addressed.

Ethnic Resurgence

Despite the worldwide adoption of such items as Coca-Cola and the "Big Mac" and despite pressure for traditional cultures to disappear, it is clear that cultural diversity is still very much with us in the world today. In fact, a tendency for peoples around the world to resist modernization, or to accept it on their own terms, is strengthening. We have already alluded to the worldwide separatist movements, the success so far of the Shuar in retaining their own ethnic and cultural identity in Ecuador, and the increasing political activism of indigenous peoples throughout the world, including the recent success of Inuit peoples in Nunavut in the Canadian Arctic.

During the 1970s the world's indigenous peoples began to organize self-determination movements, culminating in the formation of the World Council of Indigenous Peoples in 1975. This council now has official status as a nongovernmental organization of the United Nations, which allows it to present the cases of aboriginal people before the world community. Leaders of this movement see their own societies as community-based, egalitarian, and close to nature and are intent upon maintaining them that way. Further credibility to their cause came when 1993–2004 was declared the Decade of Indigenous Peoples.

North Americans often have difficulty adjusting to the fact that not everyone wants to be just like they are. As children, people in Canada and the United States are taught to believe "the North American way of life" is one all other peoples aspire to, but it isn't only people such as the Shuar who resist becoming "just like us." In the world today whole countries, having striven to emulate Western ways, have become disenchanted with these ways and suddenly backed off. The most striking recent case of such a retreat from the West's vision of modernity is Iran. With

Increasingly, aboriginal peoples around the world are organizing to defend their own interests. Here, the Kayapo in Brazil protest against planned hydroelectric dams.

the overthrow of the shah, a policy of deliberate Westernization was abandoned in favour of a return to an Islamic republic out of a past "golden age," mythical though the latter may be.

Cultural Pluralism

Many regard the prospect of a homogeneous world culture with alarm, seeing instead the concept of **cultural pluralism,** in which more than one culture exists in a given society, as a far better future condition for humanity. Cultural pluralism is the social and political interaction of people with different ways of living and thinking within the same society or multinational state. Ideally, it implies a rejection of bigotry, bias, and racism in favour of respect for the cultural traditions of other peoples. In reality, it has rarely worked out quite that way. Today, many countries are plural-

Cultural pluralism.   Social and political interaction of people with different ways of living and thinking within the same society.

Sometimes, resistance to modernization takes the form of a fundamentalist reaction, as in this example of young Islamic women wearing the hijab.

Ethnic neighbourhoods, such as Chinatown in Vancouver, are evident in most major Canadian cities.

istic, or multiethnic, which makes the issues of ethnic identity and ethnic conflict of practical importance.

As mentioned in Chapter 2, Canada is one of the most culturally pluralist countries in the world; witness the vibrant diversity of cities like Vancouver, Calgary, Toronto, and Montreal. For example, Italians in Toronto, with their distinctive cultural traditions and values, exist side by side with other Torontonians. Besides tending to live in certain neighbourhoods, the Italians maintain their own language, music, religion, and restaurants. The Italians are not alone in maintaining their own way of life. An astonishing diversity of cultural groups within Canada, including Latin Americans, Middle Easterners, South and Southeast Asians, Chinese, Koreans, and Japanese, as well as Québécois and First Nations peoples, wish to keep their distinct cultural identities. In response to this ethnic and cultural diversity, the Canadian government passed the Multiculturalism Act in 1988, making Canada the first country in the world to officially adopt multiculturalism. Unless some dramatic

change in fundamental ideology occurs, Canada will remain a pluralistic country in the future.

Other familiar examples of cultural pluralism may be seen in Switzerland, where Italian, German, and French cultures exist side by side, and in Belgium, where the francophone Walloons and the Germanic-speaking Flemish have different cultural and linguistic heritages. Switzerland is one of the few countries where pluralism has worked out to the satisfaction of all parties in the arrangement, perhaps because, despite linguistic differences, German, French, Italian, and Romansch-speaking Swiss are all heirs to a common European cultural tradition. In Northern Ireland, by contrast, the existence of groups who share a common tradition has not prevented violence and bloodshed in the streets of Belfast. It is clear that no single formula can be proposed to guarantee the peaceful coexistence of cultures within countries.

In Canada the federal government has adopted an official multiculturalism policy that reflects the distinctive ethnic subcultures that make up Canada.

Ethnocentrism

The major barrier to the adoption and spread of cultural pluralism is ethnocentrism, a concept introduced in Chapter 2. To a degree, pride in one's culture is a positive attribute. To function effectively, a culture must instill the idea that its ways are "best," or at least preferable to those of other cultures. This provides individuals with a sense of loyalty to their traditions, which provide them with psychological support and bind them firmly to their group. The problem with ethnocentrism is that it all too easily can be taken as a charter for manipulating other cultures for the benefit of one's own, even though—as we saw in Chapter 11—this does not have to be the choice. When it is, however, unrest, hostility, and violence commonly result.

Global Apartheid

Ethnocentrism can be seen as the ideology behind the doctrine of apartheid, which was until the mid-1990s the official governmental policy of South Africa. Racial segregation[28] served to perpetuate the dominance of a White minority over a non-White majority through the social, economic, political, military, and cultural constitu-

---

[28]Material on global apartheid is drawn from Kohler, L. (1996). Global apartheid. Reprinted in W.A. Haviland & R.J. Gordon (Eds.), *Talking about people: Readings in contemporary cultural anthropology* (2nd ed., pp. 262–268). Mountain View, CA: Mayfield.

Shown here are Kosovar refugees fleeing their homeland, the victims of violence motivated by ethnic hatred.

tions of society. With the coming to power in 1994 of the African National Congress led by Nelson Mandela, South Africa finally threw off the political yoke of apartheid. However, the economic effects of this racialized division of society persist to the present day.

The 1990 confrontation between Mohawk warriors and the police in Oka, Quebec, was symptomatic of First Nations' frustration with slow progress toward self-government and the right to determine their political and economic destiny. Both the Quebec and South African situations reveal the willingness of governments to use their armies against people of other nationalities within their borders to promote the state's interests.

The whole world recognized the evils of apartheid. What is disturbing is that today's global society is structurally very similar—almost a mirror image of South Africa's society, even though no conscious policy of global apartheid is practised. In the world society, about three-quarters of the population live in poverty and one-quarter in relative affluence, the latter concentrated in Europe, North America, and Japan. In the world today, the poorest 75 percent of the population make do with 30 percent of the world's energy, 25 percent of its metals, 15 percent of its wood, and 40 percent of its food. The greater percentage of these and other resources goes to the richest 25 percent of the population. Life expectancy, as in South Africa, is lowest among non-Whites. Most of the world's weapons of mass destruction are owned by the United States, Russia, France, and Britain. As in South Africa, death and suffering from war and violence are distributed unequally; the world's poorest 70 percent of the population suffer more than 90 percent of violent deaths in all categories.

▲▽▲▽▲▽▲▽▲▽▲▽▲▽▲▽▲▽▲▽▲▽▲▽▲▽▲▽▲▽▲

PROBLEMS OF STRUCTURAL VIOLENCE

One of the consequences of a system of apartheid, whether official or unofficial and on the state or global level, is the phenomenon of **structural violence**: violence exerted not by weapons and

---

Structural violence. Violence exerted by situations, institutions, and social, political, and economic structures.

Anthropology **Applied**

Edward J. Hedican

Aboriginal Rights in Canada

The discipline of anthropology has had a long history of involvement in aboriginal issues in Canada. In 1884, a special committee of the British Association for the Advancement of Science was appointed to investigate the desperate plight of British Columbia's aboriginal peoples. The committee secured the services of Franz Boas four years later and, with the aid of the new Ethnographic Bureau of Canada, laid the foundation for Boas's work on the Kwakwaka'wakw (Kwakiutl) (1897) and Bella Coola (1898). Thus, much of Boas's scholarly reputation and the subsequent professionalization of anthropology in North America can be attributed to these northwest coast ethnographic origins.

The National Museum in Ottawa subsequently served as the focus for the development of anthropology in Canada. Diamond Jenness, who earned an international reputation from his ethnographic studies of the Maori in New Zealand and the northern Inuit, Carrier, and Salish, was appointed its director in 1926. Jenness's fieldwork helped him understand the problems of aboriginal peoples. He and his staff at the museum became early advocates for aboriginal rights, being especially critical of government practices that denied aboriginals consultation on policy issues.

Anthropologists played an even greater role in policy initiatives during the mid-1960s. British Columbia anthropologist Harry Hawthorn and his colleagues stated that "Indians should be regarded as 'Citizens Plus'"—that is, aboriginal people should be regarded as equal citizens and enjoy the rights attached to their special status as founding First Nations.

The 1970s were dominated by resource and northern development issues such as the James Bay hydroelectric project in Quebec (see Chapter 2) and the Mackenzie Valley Pipeline Inquiry in the Northwest Territories (see Chapter 10). Anthropologists played key roles in both of these initiatives. In this context, The James Bay Agreement [of 1975] could be seen as a laboratory for applied anthropology and its effectiveness in bringing forth the results of basic research in a legal context.

Over the following decades new organizations emerged; the Society for Applied Anthropology in Canada (SAAC, formed in 1981) and the Canadian Association for Medical Anthropology (CAMA, formed in 1982) emphasized the practical aspects of anthropological research. These associations, now largely merged under the umbrella of the Canadian Anthropology Society/Société canadienne d'anthropologie (CASCA), served to introduce a new generation of applied anthropologists to expanded research opportunities in such areas as mental health, cross-cultural studies in education, and gender issues.

One of the most significant of these research endeavours involves a long-term study of diabetes among aboriginal peoples in the Northwest Territories, headed by biological anthropologist Emoke Szathmary, currently the president of the University of Manitoba. The focus here is upon the health consequences for aboriginal peoples of resource development that destroys the forests upon which they depend for their hunting and fishing livelihoods.

Today, anthropologists are forging ahead into an uncharted future—research has begun on such topics as AIDS, genetically modified foods, and same-sex identity issues. At the turn of the 21st century, it is time for anthropologists to critically review their research as it pertains to aboriginal issues in Canada. This review should be more than just a summary of specific field reports and journal articles. It should draw upon the commonalities of the anthropological experience, thereby clarifying common goals and achievements, while identifying areas where new research is needed. Anthropologists should also seek out greater aboriginal involvement in defining the objectives and directions of applied research. A move in this direction would encourage a continued growth in the applied sector of anthropology and demonstrate further anthropology's continued vitality and adaptability in the modern world.

After years of violence and repression by Indonesian authorities, backed by the United States, the people of East Timor, a former Portuguese colony, finally achieved their United Nations-brokered independence in May 2002.

blows, but by situations, institutions, and social, political, and economic structures. A classic instance of structural violence is the economic collapse of East Asian countries in 1997. To survive, these countries had to make drastic cuts in social services, while industry downsizing and failures caused untold numbers of people to lose their jobs. As far as the victims of this economic calamity are concerned, the effect is violent, even though the cause was not the hostile act of a specific individual. The source of the violence was an anonymous structure (the economy), and this is what structural violence is all about.

The remainder of this chapter leaves insufficient space to cover all aspects of structural violence, but we can look at some aspects of particular concern to anthropologists. While other scholars consider the issue as well, anthropologists are less apt than other specialists to see these aspects of structural violence as discrete and unrelated. Thus, as synthesizers seeing the "bigger picture," they have a key contribution to make to the understanding of such persistent modern-day crises as hunger and overpopulation, environmental pollution, and widespread discontent in the world.

World Hunger

As frequently dramatized by events in various parts of Africa, a major source of structural violence in the world today is humanity's failure to provide food for all of its people. Not only is Africa declining in its capacity to feed itself, but 52 countries worldwide by 1980 were producing less food per capita than they were 10 years previously, and in 42 countries available food supplies were not adequate to provide the caloric requirements of their populations.[29] One factor contributing to this food crisis is a dramatic growth in the world's population.

Population growth is more than a simple addition of people. If it were just that, the addition of 20 people a year to a population of 1000 would double that population in 50 years; but because the added people beget more people, the doubling time is actually much less than 50 years. Hence, it took the whole of human history and prehistory for the world's population to reach 1 billion people, achieved in 1750. By 1950, world population had reached almost 2.5 billion, representing an annual growth rate of about 0.8 percent. And shortly after the turn of the millennium in 2000, it had reached 6 billion (see Figure 15.3).

The obvious question arising from the burgeoning world population is, can we produce enough food to feed all those people? The majority opinion among agriculturalists is that we can do so, but how far into the future we can do it is open to question. In the 1960s a major effort was launched to expand food production in the poor countries of the world by introducing new high-yield strains of grains. Yet despite some dramatic gains from this "Green Revolution"—India, for example, doubled its wheat crop in six years and was on the verge of grain self-sufficiency by 1970—and despite the impressive output of North American agriculture, hundreds of millions continue to face malnutrition and starvation. In Canada, meanwhile, *edible* food worth millions of dollars is thrown out every day (far more food than is sent out for famine relief), and farms are going out of business in record numbers.

The immediate cause of world hunger has less to do with food *production* than with food *distribution*. For example, millions of acres in Africa, Asia, and Latin America once devoted to subsistence farming have been given over to the raising of cash crops for export to satisfy

---

[29]Bodley, J.H. (1985). *Anthropology and contemporary human problems* (2nd ed., p. 114). Palo Alto, CA: Mayfield.

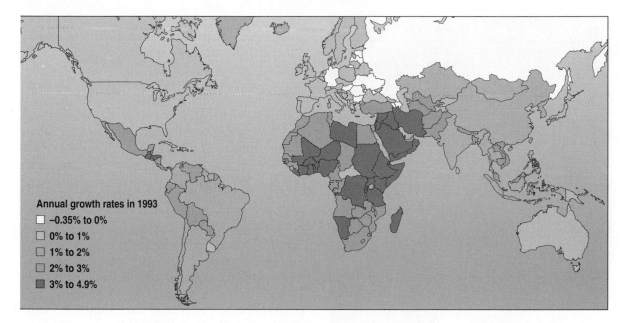

Annual growth rates in 1993
- ☐ −0.35% to 0%
- ☐ 0% to 1%
- ☐ 1% to 2%
- ☐ 2% to 3%
- ■ 3% to 4.9%

FIGURE 15.3 Population growth rates around the world.

appetites in the world's "developed" countries for products such as coffee, tea, chocolate, bananas, and beef. Those who used to farm the land for their own food needs have been forced to relocate to the cities, to sprawling urban shantytowns where unemployment is rife, or to other areas ecologically unsuited for farming. In Africa such lands often are occupied by pastoral nomads; as farmers encroach upon these, insufficient pasturage is left for livestock. The resultant overgrazing, coupled with the clearing of the land for farming, leads to increased loss of both soil and water, with disastrous consequences to nomad and farmer alike. In Brazil, which is highly dependent on outside sources of fossil fuels for its energy needs, millions of acres in the northeast were taken over for sugar production for making alcohol to fuel the vehicles in Rio. The people displaced by sugar production were given small holdings in the Amazon, where they now are being uprooted to make way for huge ranches for raising export beef.

One strategy urged upon developing countries, especially by Canadian and U.S. government officials and development advisers, is to adopt the practices that have made North American agriculture so incredibly productive. On the face of it, this seems like a good idea, but it overlooks the fact that it requires investment in expensive seeds, chemicals, and mechanization that neither small farmers nor poor countries can afford. Intensive agriculture on the Canadian model requires, in addition, enormous amounts of fossil fuels to run all the mechanized equipment. A well-known study of U.S. agriculture by the agronomist David Pimentel estimated that for every single calorie of food output produced, the equivalent of eight calories of nonrenewable fossil fuel were required to produce and distribute it.[30] By contrast, an Asian wet-rice farmer using traditional methods produces up to 300 calories for each one expended. North American agriculture is wasteful of other resources as well: about 30 pounds of fertile topsoil are ruined for every pound of food produced.[31] In the midwestern United States, about 50 percent of the topsoil has been lost over the past 100 years. Meanwhile, toxic substances from chemical nutrients and pesticides pile up in unexpected places, poisoning ground and surface waters; killing fish, birds, and other useful forms of life; upsetting natural ecological cycles; and causing major public-health

---

[30]Ibid., p. 128.

[31]Chasin, B.H., & Franke, R.W. (1983). U.S. farming: A world model? *Global Reporter, 1* (2), 10.

Hunger affects much of the world as a result of a world food system geared to satisfy an affluent minority in the world's developed nations.

problems. Despite its spectacular short-term success, serious questions arise about whether such a profligate food-production system can be sustained over the long run, even in North America.

Pollution

It is ironic that a life-sustaining activity such as food production should constitute a health hazard, but that is precisely what it becomes when agricultural chemicals poison soils and waters, and food additives (more than 2500 are or have been in use) expose people to substances that all too often turn out to be harmful. This, though, is but a part of a larger problem of environmental pollution. Industrial activities are producing highly toxic waste at unprecedented rates, and factory emissions are poisoning the air. For example, smokestack gases are clearly implicated in acid rain, which is causing damage to lakes and forests all over northeastern North America. Air containing water vapour with a high acid content is, of course, harmful to the lungs, but the health

hazard is greater than this. As surface water and groundwater become more acidic, the solubility of lead, cadmium, mercury, and aluminum increases sharply. The increase of dissolved aluminum, in particular, is becoming truly massive, and aluminum consumption has been associated with senile dementia as well as Alzheimer's and Parkinson's diseases. Today, these rank as major health problems in Canada and the United States.

Added to this is the global warming problem—the greenhouse effect—caused by the burning of fossil fuels. Although much is unknown about the extent of global warming, climatic scientists agree that it is real and its long-term effects will be harmful. Unfortunately, the response from energy interests has been similar to the campaign tobacco companies carried out for so long to convince the public that smoking was not hazardous. The former have launched a massive public relations campaign to persuade the public that global warming is not real; as a consequence, it becomes very difficult to do anything about it. While the U.S. administration of George W. Bush has outright rejected the Kyoto Accord to limit atmospheric emissions, Canada has agreed to ratify the accord. However, the province of Alberta, whose wealth is closely tied to energy revenues, has threatened to block or veto the accord.

In South America, where these tobacco crops are grown, agricultural development has caused increased malnutrition levels. As in many developing countries, modernization of agriculture has meant the conversion of land from subsistence farming to raising crops for export, making it increasingly difficult for people to satisfy their basic nutritional needs.

As with world hunger, the structural violence from pollution tends to be greatest in the poorest countries of the world, where chemicals banned in countries such as Canada are still widely used. Moreover, industrial countries have taken advantage of the lax environmental regulations of developing states to get rid of hazardous wastes. For instance, a former president of Benin (in West Africa) signed a contract with a European waste company to dump toxic and low-grade radioactive waste on the lands of his political opposition.[32] In the United States, both government and industry have tried to persuade aboriginals on reservations experiencing severe economic depression that the solution to their problems lies in allowing disposal of nuclear and other hazardous waste on their lands. In Canada, too, First Nations and government officials examined the possibility of storing radioactive wastes on reservations in the North; however, the idea was discarded.

Meanwhile, as manufacturing shifts from the developed to the developing countries of the world, a trend also encouraged by fewer safety and environmental regulations, lethal accidents such as the one in 1986 at Chernobyl, Ukraine, may be expected to increase. In that incident, a faulty reactor at a nuclear power plant released radiation, causing numerous deaths, relocation of 126 000 people, increased thyroid cancer, and damaged immune systems. Even 18 years later, increased birth defects and economic privation have plagued people living as far away as the Arctic, where Saami reindeer herds were contaminated by radioactive fallout. Indeed, development itself seems to be a health hazard; it is well known that indigenous peoples in Canada, Africa, the Pacific Islands, South America, and elsewhere were relatively free from diabetes, obesity, hypertension, and a variety of circulatory diseases until they adopted the ways of developed countries. As noted in Chapter 14, rates of these "diseases of civilization" are escalating dramatically.

Modern humanity knows the causes of pollution and realizes it is a danger to future survival. Why, then, does humanity not control this evil by which it fouls its own nest? At least part of the answer lies in philosophical and theological traditions. As we saw in Chapter 11, Western industrialized societies accept the biblical assertion that they have dominion over the earth with all that grows and lives on it, which it is their duty to subdue. These societies contribute most to global pollution. One North American, for example, consumes hundreds of times the resources of a single African, with all that implies with respect to waste disposal and environmental degradation. Moreover, each person in North America adds, on average, 20 tons of carbon dioxide (a greenhouse gas) a year to the atmosphere. In developing countries, less than 3 tons per person are emitted.[33]

A large part of the problem in this and similar situations is a human reluctance to perceive as disadvantageous the practices that previously seemed to work well. Frequently, practices carried out on a smaller scale or suited to a particular context become unsuitable when carried out on a wider scale or in altered contexts. Because they are trained to view customs in their broader context, anthropologists would seem to have an important role to play in convincing people that solutions to many problems require changed behaviour.

Population Control

Although the problems we have discussed so far may not be caused by population growth, they are certainly made worse by it. For one reason, it increases the scale of the problems; thus, the waste a small population generates is far easier to deal with than what a large one generates. For another, it often nullifies efforts people make to solve the problems, such as when increased food production is offset by increased numbers of people to be fed. Although solving the population growth problem does not by itself make the other problems go away, it is unlikely those problems can be solved unless population growth is arrested.

As our earlier look at population demonstrated, the world's population has grown enormously since the beginning of the industrial age. With the exception of European and North American populations, where birthrates are significantly lower than death rates (a balance

---

[32]*Cultural Survival Quarterly, 15* (4), 5 (1991).

[33]Broecker, W.S. (1992, April). Global warming on trial. *Natural History, 14.*

Environmental degradation is dramatically illustrated by the fires that burned out of control in Southeast Asia in 1997, causing widespread health and visibility problems from massive amounts of smoke and particulate matter in the air.

between the two is required for **replacement reproduction**), the world saw no sign of a significant decline in birthrates prior to 1976. The reason impoverished people, in particular, tended to have so many children is simple: Children are their main resource. They provide the labour needed to work farms, and they are the only source of security for the elderly; hence, having many offspring makes sense (especially if infant mortality rates are high). Historically, people were apt to limit their family size only when they became wealthy enough that their money replaced children as their main resource; at that point, children actually *cost* them money. Given this, we can see why birthrates have for so long remained high in the world's poorest countries. To those who live in poverty, children are seen as the only hope.

Nevertheless, since 1976 some encouraging signs have occurred, such as China's steep decline in birthrates. China is one of 19 developing countries where birthrates actually have dropped *below* replacement levels (Chinese birthrates and death rates balance out at about 2.1 children per woman). In much of South Asia and Central and South America (again, some of the world's poorest countries), birthrates also have declined, but far less dramatically. Examples include Bangladesh, where the rate has fallen from 6.2 to 3.4 (in just 10 years), Tunisia, where the rate has fallen from 7.2 to 2.9, and Mexico, which has moved 80 percent of the way to replacement level.[34] The tragic appearance of the AIDS epidemic in many developing countries, especially sub-Saharan Africa, has one terrible side effect: AIDS has slowed and even reversed rapid population growth, but this has been achieved at a terrible cost in human suffering.

The problem of who will care for elders in their old age is an issue for any society whose birthrates are below replacement level. The inevitable consequence is that the number of old people "explodes" relative to the number of productive people of younger age. Already countries such as Canada are beginning to worry about this. Canada has an aging population, one

---

[34]Wattenberg, B.J. (1997, November 23). The population explosion is over. *The New York Times Magazine, 60.*

Replacement reproduction. When birthrates and death rates are in equilibrium; people produce only enough offspring to replace themselves when they die.

As birthrates fall around the world, there will be a rise in the percentage of the elderly, with an attendant rise in health care costs.

requiring comprehensive health care services, pension plans, and so on, that will place an unfair burden on relatively few young, taxpaying adults.

The Culture of Discontent

Despite the difficulties, stabilization of the world's population appears to be a necessary step if the future's problems are ever to be solved. Without this, whatever else is done, the world's inability to provide enough food and distribute it equally seems inevitable. Up until about 1950, growth in the world's food supply came almost entirely from expanding the amount of cultivated land. Since then, it has come increasingly from the high-energy inputs of chemical fertilizers that new high-yield varieties of crops depend on, of pesticides and herbicides, and of fuel to run tractors and other mechanical equipment, including irrigation pumps. The source of almost all this energy is oil, yet, although the demand for food is projected to rise until at least the middle of the 21st century, oil supplies are diminishing and will surely decline over this same period. Many energy analysts are speaking of the approaching turning point of "peak oil," when fossil fuel enters a permanently downward spiral. Unless a new energy source, such as hydrogen fuel cells, replaces oil, humanity faces an energy crisis of unimaginable proportions in the future.

Insufficient food supplies are bound to result in increased structural violence in the form of higher death rates in the world's developing countries. This surely will have an impact on the developed countries, with their relatively stable populations and high living standards. It is hard to imagine how such countries could exist peacefully side by side with others experiencing high death rates and abysmally low living standards. Already, the combination of overpopulation and poverty is causing a rising tide of migration from the impoverished countries to the more affluent ones of Europe and North America, with a consequent rise of intolerance, anti-foreign sentiments, and general social unrest. Witness the public outcry (both anti-foreign and pro-compassion) when 600 desperate Chinese refugees tried to reach Canada's west coast in 1999. These refugees endured squalid conditions aboard decrepit cargo ships in the hopes of a better life in Canada, only to be met with hostility. By 2001 only a few had been granted refugee status, hundreds were deported back to China, and others are still in detention. A country as rich in resources and opportunities as Canada will continue to be a destination of choice for economic, social, and political refugees. The government and the people of Canada must decide how to deal with this issue in a compassionate and responsible manner.

Necessary though birth control may be for solving the future's problems, we have no reason to suppose it will be sufficient by itself. The result would be only to stabilize situations as they are. The problem is twofold. For the past several years, the world's poor countries have been sold on the idea they should enjoy a living standard comparable to that of the rich countries. Yet the resources necessary to maintain such a standard of living, even at moderate levels, are running out. As we saw earlier in the chapter, this situation has led to the creation of conditions of entrenched injustice and the resultant culture of resentment and protest. The problem is not just one of population growth outstripping food supplies, but also of unequal access to decent jobs, housing, sanitation, health care, and adequate police and fire protection. And it is one of steady deterioration of the natural environment as a result of increasing industrialization and overuse of the land. Displacement is one of the consequences: people on the margins redirect their legitimate anger and grievances into excessive drinking, substance abuse, petty crime, and domestic violence.

Some dramatic changes in cultural values and motivations, as well as in social institutions, are required. The emphasis on individual self-interest, materialism, and conspicuous production, acquisition, and consumption, characteristic of the world's richest countries, needs to be abandoned in favour of a more human self-image and social ethic. The source for these values can still be found in many of the world's non-Western cultures. Such values include a worldview that sees humanity as part of the natural world, rather than superior to it. Included, too, is a sense of social responsibility that recognizes that no individual, people, or state has the right to expropriate resources at the expense of others. Finally, an awareness is needed of how important supportive ties are for individuals, as is seen in kinship or other associations in the world's traditional societies. Is humanity up to the challenge? Who knows, but it appears significant changes are bound to come, one way or another.

▲▽▲▽▲▽▲▽▲▽▲▽▲▽▲▽▲▽▲▽▲▽▲▽▲▽▲▽

HUMANITY'S FUTURE

The preceding discussion may lead some readers to conclude that humanity's future is dismal indeed. It is true that we have many problems to solve, and solve them we must. But humans have always been incredibly tenacious, overcoming seemingly insurmountable obstacles to survive.

From our first tentative prehistoric steps out onto the savannas, to the roar of a space shuttle taking yet another payload to the international space station, we have overcome many hurdles, and will continue to do so.

The key to our continued survival lies in our ability and willingness to see the earth as a benevolent host, rather than a resource to exploit, and our fellow humans as partners, rather than competitors. As partners we can find equitable solutions to our problems—solutions that do not favour any one people or political regime. We are at a crossroads in human history—what we do in the next 50 years will determine the kind of existence future generations of humanity will inherit.

The greatest danger we face is apathy—a human tendency to pretend that nothing is wrong, someone else will fix it, or, even worse, there is nothing we can do. Whether we focus on environmental issues, human rights, or fair distribution of economic resources, each of us can make a difference. In the wise words of anthropologist Margaret Mead, "Never doubt that a small group of thoughtful, committed citizens can change the world. Indeed, it's the only thing that ever has."[35]

[35]National Women's History Project. (1998). *Living the legacy: The women's rights movement 1848–1998.* E. Eisenber & M. Ruthsdotter. Retrieved November 25, 2000, from the World Wide Web: http://www.legacy98.org/move-hist.html.

CHAPTER SUMMARY

Although cultures may be remarkably stable, culture change is characteristic of all cultures to a greater or lesser degree. Change may be accidental, intentional, or forced upon a people, and in outcome it may or may not turn out to be beneficial. Applied anthropology arose as anthropologists sought to provide colonial administrators with a better understanding of aboriginal cultures or to try to help indigenous people cope with outside threats to their interests.

Reactions of indigenous peoples to changes forced upon them vary considerably. Some have retreated to inaccessible places in hope of being left alone, while some others have lapsed into apathy. If a culture's values get widely out of step with reality, revitalization movements may appear. Some revitalization movements try to speed up the acculturation process to get more of the outside benefits. Others try to reconstitute a gone but not forgotten way of life. Revolutionary movements try to transform the culture from within. Rebellion differs from revolution, in that the aim is merely to replace one set of officeholders with another.

Modernization refers to a global process of cultural and socioeconomic change whereby developing societies seek to acquire characteristics of industrially "advanced" societies. The process consists of four subprocesses: technological development, agricultural development, industrialization, and urbanization. Other changes follow in the areas of political organization, education, religion, and social organization.

An example of a modernizing society is the Skolt Lapps of Finland, whose traditional reindeer-herding economy was all but destroyed when snowmobiles were adopted to make herding easier. In Ecuador, the Shuar modernized to escape the destruction visited upon many other Amazonian peoples. So far they have been successful, and others are mobilizing their resources in attempts to achieve similar success. Nevertheless, formidable forces are still arrayed against such cultures, and, on a worldwide basis, it is probably fair to say modernization has led to a deterioration, rather than improvement, of people's quality of life.

Since future forms of culture will be shaped by decisions humans have yet to make, they cannot be predicted with any accuracy. Thus, instead of trying to foretell the future, a number of anthropologists are attempting to gain a better understanding of the existing world situation so that decisions may be made intelligently. Anthropologists are especially well suited for this, owing to their experience with seeing things in context, their long-term evolutionary perspective, their ability to recognize culture-bound biases, and their familiarity with cultural alternatives.

However humanity changes biologically, culture remains the chief means by which humans try to solve their problems of existence. Some anthropologists are concerned that there is a trend for the problems to outstrip any culture's ability to find solutions. Rapid developments in communication, transportation, and world trade, some believe, will link people together to the point that a single more harmonious world culture will result. Most anthropologists are skeptical of the benefits of such a homogenized superculture in view of the recent tendency for ethnic groups to reassert their distinctive identities and to resist incorporation except on their own terms. Anthropologists also are concerned about those in power tending to treat many of the world's traditional societies as archaic and backward when they appear to stand in the way of development or "progress."

An alternative pathway is for humanity to move in the direction of cultural pluralism, where two or more cultures exist with respect for each other's differences. Some anthropologists maintain that pluralistic arrangements are the only feasible means of achieving global equilibrium and peace. A problem associated with cultural pluralism is ethnocentrism. All too often, in the name of "nation building," it has led one group to impose its control on others. Common consequences can be prolonged violent and bloody political upheavals, and even genocide.

Viewing the world today reveals a picture that is strikingly similar to South Africa's apartheid system. As a world system, global apartheid serves to maintain the dominance of a wealthy minority over a disempowered majority through the social, economic, political, military, and cultural constitution of the current "New World Order."

One consequence of any apartheid system is a great deal of structural violence exerted by situations, institutions, and social, political, and economic structures. Such violence involves problems such as overpopulation and food shortages, which anthropologists are actively working to understand and help alleviate. We face challenges to provide enough food resources to keep pace with the burgeoning population. The immediate problem, though, is not so much one of producing enough food as it is an existing food-distribution system geared to the satisfaction of appetites in the world's richest countries at the expense of those living in poorer countries.

Pollution has become a direct threat to humanity. Western peoples have protected their environments only when some crisis forces them to do so, and even at that their consumption rates continue to drive environmental degradation in other countries. Western societies have felt no long-term responsibilities toward the earth or its resources and could learn much from those non-Western peoples who see themselves as integral parts of nature.

Solving the problems of the global society depends also on lessening the gap between the living standards of impoverished and developed countries. This calls for dramatic changes in the values of Western societies, with their materialistic consumer orientation, and development of a social responsibility that recognizes that no people has a right to expropriate important resources at the expense of others. The surprising strength of recent worldwide antiwar and antiglobalization protests is a hopeful sign of change.

QUESTIONS FOR CRITICAL THOUGHT

1. Is tradition susceptible to change? What is the role of tradition in conjunction with the concept of cultural change discussed in this chapter? How important are tradition and change to a culture's health?

2. Do the benefits of modernization or globalization outweigh the harmful effects? For example, has North American free trade benefited or harmed Canada? Explain.

3. In your opinion, will continued modernization bring humanity, in the end, into a single homogeneous world culture? Does modernization mean absolute assimilation? How might tradition play a part in this process?

4. Powerful states often feel they have a responsibility to intervene in foreign affairs to speed the development of other countries or to calm political and social distress. Is this necessarily a wise idea? Even when the intentions are good, is the outcome always positive? Explain your answer.

5. Is Canada's multiculturalism beneficial or harmful to its national identity?

6. How can you and your community reduce consumption of food resources and nonrenewable resources? If every community took these measures, would it make a difference in global resources?

INTERNET RESOURCES

Yanomami Genocide

http://www.monitor.net/monitor/10-30-95/
amazongenocide.html

Gives good background information and highlights events that are devastating the Yanomami culture.

Environmental Devastation

http://www.cs.org/newdirection/voices/kenya.htm

This article explores the cultural identity, alienation, and dispossession of the Laikipia Maasai in Kenya from their ancestral lands. It addresses the impact of prolonged drought on the community.

Cultural Survival

http://www.cs.org/newdirection/voices/
dostou.htm

This article discusses a prophecy that caused the Anishnabe people to bring new balance to their lives in order to survive.

Countdown to Nunavut

http://www.islandnet.com/~jveinot/cghl/
nunavut.html

Introduces students to the new territory of Nunavut, and presents some background information on the political, economic, and social factors that went into creating this new land.

Living the Legacy: The Women's Rights Movement 1848–1998

http://www.legacy98.org/move-hist.html

A comprehensive historical, political, and social account of the women's movement from 1848 to 1998. Highly recommended for students wishing to update their knowledge of what the women's movement really stands for.

Quebec Sovereignty and Canadian National Unity

http://polisci.nelson.com/quebec.html

The 1998 Supreme Court of Canada decision on Canadian secession.

Women's Rights Are Human Rights
http://www.unfpa.org/swp/2000/english/ch06.html

A United Nations site that examines international human rights treaties and conference agreements to provide women's rights. Topics include "Human rights treaties" and "International conference consensus agreements." Boxes of note include "The right to reproductive health care" and "Action and gender equality."

Careers in Anthropology
http://www.iupui.edu/it/anthropo/careers.htm

Outlines what students can do with a degree in anthropology, and provides links to several related pages. This site is a valuable resource for students who are thinking about majoring in anthropology or who are about to graduate with an anthropology degree.

SUGGESTED READINGS

Bodley, J.H. (1985). *Anthropology and contemporary human problems* (2nd ed.). Palo Alto, CA: Mayfield.

Anthropologist Bodley examines some of the most serious problems in the world today: overconsumption, resource depletion, hunger and starvation, overpopulation, and violence and war.

Bodley, J.H. (1990). *Victims of progress* (3rd ed.). Mountain View, CA: Mayfield.

Few North Americans are aware of the devastation unleashed on indigenous peoples in the name of "progress," nor are they aware that this continues on an unprecedented scale today or of the extent to which their own society's institutions contribute to it. For most, this book will be a real eye-opener.

Davis, S.H. (1982). *Victims of the miracle.* Cambridge, UK: Cambridge University Press.

An anthropologist looks at Brazil's efforts to develop the Amazon region, the motivations behind those efforts, and their impact on indigenous peoples. Davis pays special attention to the role multinational corporations play, how they relate to the Brazilian government, and who benefits from it all.

Hedican, E.J. (1995). *Applied anthropology in Canada: Understanding aboriginal issues.* Toronto: University of Toronto Press.

This book examines anthropology's relevance in modern Canadian society. In a clear and concise manner, Hedican addresses the role of anthropology in the study of aboriginal peoples of Canada. He also provides a historical look at the development of applied anthropology, profiling some of the "greats" of Canadian anthropology.

Mackie, M. (1991). *Gender relations in Canada.* Toronto: Harcourt Brace.

This text is a comprehensive analysis of gender, including an in-depth examination of feminist perspectives and theories. Beginning with gender differences, Mackie looks at socialization agents, such as the family, peer groups, schools, religion, and the media. The book also examines social stratification, the family and aging, and avenues of change.

Miller, S. (Ed.). (1993). *State of the peoples: A global human rights report on societies in danger.* Boston: Beacon Press.

This important publication from *Cultural Survival Quarterly* systematically reports on the situation of indigenous peoples throughout the world, region by region. Also included are professional articles on critical issues affecting such diverse peoples as Bosnians and the Ju/'hoansi, all sorts of useful maps and charts, and suggested solutions to many challenges indigenous peoples face. A "must read" for anyone who is in any way concerned with the "New World Disorder."

Robbins, Richard H. (2002). *Global problems and the culture of capitalism* (2nd ed.). Boston: Allyn and Bacon.

A detailed survey of many of the issues raised in this chapter, with a thorough discussion of the historical rise of capitalism and its impact, both positive and negative, on the modern world. Chapters on environment, indigenous peoples, hunger and poverty, and resistance and rebellion offer anthropological perspectives on the problems humanity will have to face if it is to have a future.

Stannard, D.E. (1992). *American holocaust*. Oxford: Oxford University Press.

Stannard deals with 500 years of cultural change in the Americas related to the contact of European and native cultures. In doing so, he focuses on genocide, relates it to the Holocaust of World War II, and demonstrates how deeply rooted the phenomenon is in Western culture and Christianity.

CNN TODAY VIDEOS

Egyptian Nubian Tradition (CNN Cultural Anthropology, vol. 1, 1:54)
The effects on Nubian culture following the construction of the Aswan Dam.

Tokyo Fast Food (CNN Cultural Anthropology, vol. 1, 2:15)
Impact of American fast food on Japanese customs.

Toy Barriers (CNN Cultural Anthropology, vol. 1, 1:44)
There is a global market for toys in industrialized countries.

Yanomamo (CNN Cultural Anthropology, vol. 1, 2:09)
This segment looks at the impact gold mining is having on the Yanomamo.

Native Traditions in Conflict with Contemporary Values: The Whale Hunt (CNN Cultural Anthropology, vol. 2, 2:01)
The Makah Tribe of Washington has the right under their 19th treaty with the federal government to conduct an annual hunt for whales in coastal waters. Environmentalists oppose the whale hunt, leading to a conflict between the traditional ways of the Makah and contemporary social and political values.

Brazil's Dying Tribe (CNN Cultural Anthropology, vol. 2, 2:34)
Former nomadic tribes living in southern Brazil are forced onto reservations. There, with increasing poverty and their traditional customs curtailed, young members of the tribe are increasingly committing suicide.

Brazilian Indians (CNN Cultural Anthropology, vol. 4, 2:25)
Native peoples within Brazil encounter severe problems as their numbers continue to decline.

Women in Afghanistan (CNN Cultural Anthropology, vol. 5, 2:41)
For some women in Afghanistan, the Taliban's loss of power signals a time of new hope, while others—including young girls working in sweatshops—see a future of continued poverty.

Oil Spill Impacts (CNN Cultural Anthropology, vol. 5, 2:49)
A 1989 oil spill continues to impact the environment and culture of Prince William Sound's native peoples.

South Africa Endangered (CNN Cultural Anthropology, vol. 5, 2:27)
This segment explores the conflict between the preservation of an endangered South African forest and the needs of local people who depend on the forest for their livelihood.

Multiracial Families (CNN Cultural Anthropology, vol. 5, 3:45)
As interracial marriages enter the mainstream in many parts of the United States, parents in mixed-race families look for a balance between their different cultures while their children struggle for acceptance and recognition within their communities.

BIBLIOGRAPHY

8th Annual Young Scientist Conference. (n.d.). *Owen Beattie*. Retrieved October 16, 2000, from the World Wide Web: http://ftp.ei.educ.ab.ca/dept/ins/beattie.html.

Abler, T.S. (1995). In Memoriam. Sally M. Weaver (1940–1993). *Anthropologica, 35*.

Abu-Lughod, L. (1986). *Veiled sentiments: Honor and poetry in a Bedouin society*. Berkeley, CA: University of California Press.

Achterberg, J., Dossey, B., & Kolkmeier, L. (1994). *Rituals of healing: Using imagery for health and wellness*. New York: Bantam Books.

Adelson, N. (2000). Being alive well: Health and politics of Cree well-being. Toronto: University of Toronto Press.

AIDS Monthly Surveillance Summary (through July 1997). (1997). San Francisco Department of Public Health AIDS Office.

American Museum of Natural History. (n.d.). *A body arts expo*. Retrieved October 15, 2003, from the World Wide Web: http://www.coldsteel.co.uk/articles/BodyArtExpo.html.

Amiran, R. (1965). The beginnings of pottery-making in the Near East. In F.R. Matson (Ed.), *Ceramics and Man* (pp. 240–247). Viking Fund Publications in Anthropology, No. 41.

Armelagos, G. (1998). Health and disease in prehistoric populations in transition. In P. Brown (Ed.), *Understanding and applying medical anthropology* (pp. 59–69). Mountain View, CA: Mayfield.

Armstrong, D.F., Stokoe, W.C., & Wilcox, S.E. (1994). Signs of the origin of syntax. *Current Anthropology, 35*, 349–368.

Arzt, D. (2003). Terrorism and terrorists. *Jurist: The Legal Education Network*. University of Pittsburgh School of Law.

Asch, M., & Smith, S. (1999). Slavey Dene. In R.B. Lee & R. Daly (Eds.), *The Cambridge encyclopedia of hunters and gatherers* (pp. 46–50). Cambridge, UK: Cambridge University Press.

Ashton-Jones, E., Olson, G.A., & Perry, M.G. (Eds.). (2000). *The gender reader* (2nd ed.). Needham Heights, MA: Allyn and Bacon.

Backgrounder. (2001). *Canada and peacekeeping* (p. 2). Retrieved March 20, 2001, from the World Wide Web: http://www.dfait-maeci.gc.ca/peacekeepinjg/back-e/asp.

Baer, H.A., Singer, M., & Susser. I. (2004). *Medical anthropology and the world system: A critical perspective* (2nd ed.). Westport, CT: Bergin and Garvey.

Balikci, A. (1989). Anthropology, film and the Arctic peoples: The first Forman Lecture. *Anthropology Today, 5* (2), 4–10.

Barfield, T.J. (1984). Introduction. *Cultural Survival Quarterly, 8*, 2.

Barlett, P.F. (1989). Industrial agriculture. In S. Plattner (Ed.), *Economic anthropology* (pp. 253–291). Stanford, CA: Stanford University Press.

Barlow, M., & May, E. (2000). *Frederick Street: Life and death on Canada's Love Canal*. Toronto: Harper and Row.

Barnett, H. (1953). *Innovation: The basis of cultural change*. New York: McGraw-Hill.

Barnouw, V. (1985). *Culture and personality* (4th ed.). Homewood, IL: Dorsey Press.

Barr, R.G. (1997, October). The crying game. *Natural History, 47*.

Barth, F. (1960). Nomadism in the mountain and plateau areas of south west Asia. *The problems of the arid zone* (pp. 341–355): Paris: UNESCO.

Bates, D.G., & Plog, F. (1991). *Human adaptive strategies*. New York: McGraw-Hill.

Bednarik, R.G. (1995). Concept-mediated marking in the Lower Paleolithic. *Current Anthropology, 36*, 606.

Bell, D. (1997). Defining marriage and legitimacy. *Current Anthropology, 38*, 241.

Berdan, F.F. (1982). *The Aztecs of central Mexico*. New York: Holt, Rinehart and Winston.

Berger, T. (1988). *Northern frontier, northern homeland: The report of the Mackenzie Valley Pipeline Inquiry*. Vancouver: Douglas and McIntyre.

Bernardi, B. (1985). *Age class systems: Social institutions and policies based on age*. New York: Cambridge University Press.

Berry, E. (1963). Foreword. In *Eating and cooking around the world: Fingers before forks*. New York: The John Day Company.

Bezruchka, S. (2001, February 26). Is our society making you sick? *Newsweek, 143*.

Bibeau, G. (1979). World Health Organization in encounter with African traditional medicine: Theoretical conceptions and practical strategies. In Z. Ademuwagun (Fd.), *African therapeutic systems*. Waltham, MA: Crossroads Press.

Bill C-23, subsection 3(3). Retrieved March 3, 2001, from the World Wide Web: http://www.parl.gc.ca/36/2/parlbus/chambus/house/bills/government/C-23/C-23_1/90093bE.html.

Birdwhistell, R. (1970). *Kinesics and context: Essays in body motion communication*. Philadelphia: University of Pennsylvania Press.

Black, H.C. (1968). *Black's law dictionary*. St. Paul, MN: West.

Black, J.H. (2000). Entering the political elite in Canada: The case of minority women as parliamentary candidates and MPs. *Canadian Review of Sociology and Anthropology, 37* (2).

Blackwood, E., & Wieringa, S.E. (1999). Sapphic shadows: Challenging the silence in the study of sexuality. In E. Blackwood & S.E. Wieringa (Eds.), *Female desires: Same-sex relations and transgender practices across cultures*. New York: Columbia University Press.

Blodgett, J. (1988). Whale bone. In *Inuit art: An anthology*. Winnipeg: Watson and Dwyer.

Boddy, J. (1989). *Wombs and alien spirits: Women, men and the Zar cult in Northern Sudan*. Madison: University of Wisconsin Press.

Bodley, J.H. (1985). *Anthropology and contemporary human problems* (2nd ed.). Palo Alto, CA: Mayfield.

Bodley, J.H. (1990). *Victims of progress* (3rd ed.). Mountain View, CA: Mayfield.

Bodley, J.H. (1997). Comment. *Current Anthropology, 38*, 725.

Bonvillain, N. (1998). *Women and men: Cultural constructs of gender* (2nd ed.). Upper Saddle River, NJ: Prentice Hall.

Bonvillain, N. (1998). *Women and men: Cultural constructs of gender*. Upper Saddle River, NJ: Prentice Hall.

Bonvillain, N. (2000). *Language, culture, and communication: The meaning of messages* (3rd ed.). Upper Saddle River, NJ: Prentice Hall.

Bossen, L. (1984). *The Redivision of Labour: Women and Economic Choice in Four Guatemalan Communities*. Albany, NY: State University of New York Press.

Bossen, L. (2002). *Chinese Women and Rural Development: Sixty Years of Change in Lu Village, Yunnan*. Lanham, MD: Rowman & Littlefield.

Boston Women's Health Book Collective. (1998). *Our bodies, ourselves for the new century: A book by and for women* (3rd ed.). New York: Simon and Schuster.

Bourgois, P. (2003). *In search of respect: Selling crack in El Barrio* (2nd ed.). Cambridge and New York: Cambridge University Press.

Brettell, C.B., & Sargent, C.F. (Eds.). (1997). *Gender in cross-cultural perspective* (2nd ed.). Upper Saddle River, NJ: Prentice Hall.

Bridgman, R. (2003). *Safe haven: The story of a woman's shelter.* Toronto: University of Toronto Press.

Briggs, J.L. (1998). *Inuit morality play: The emotional education of a three-year old.* Social and Economic Studies, No. 67. Institute of Social and Economic Research.

Broecker, W.S. (1992, April). Global warming on trial. *Natural History, 14.*

Brooks, G. (1994). *Nine parts of desire: The hidden world of Islamic women.* New York: Anchor Books.

Brown, P. (Ed.). (1998). *Understanding and applying medical anthropology.* Mountain View, CA: Mayfield.

Buckley, T., & Gottlieb, A. (1988). A critical appraisal of theories of menstrual symbolism. In T. Buckley & A. Gottlieb (Eds.), *Blood magic: The anthropology of menstruation* (pp. 1–53). Berkeley and Los Angeles: University of California Press.

Bullock, K. (2001). *You don't have to wear that in Canada.* Retrieved March 13, 2001, from the World Wide Web: http://www.soundvision.com/news/hijab/hjb.canada1.shtml.

Burling, R. (1993). Primate calls, human language, and nonverbal communication. *Current Anthropology, 34,* 25–53.

Cachel, S. (1997). Dietary shifts and the European Upper Paleolithic transition. *Current Anthropology, 38,* 590.

Canada and the World. (1998, January). Culture shock: Immigrants come to Canada with the hope of improving life for themselves and future generations but fitting into an entirely new culture isn't easy. *Canada and the World Backgrounder, 63* (4).

Canadian Arctic Resources Committee. (1976). *Final argument and recommendations: The Mackenzie Valley Pipeline Inquiry.* Ottawa: Canadian Arctic Resources Committee.

Canadian Art at the McMichael. (1996–2000). *The Group of Seven and their contemporaries.* Retrieved March 29, 2001, from the World Wide Web: http://www.mcmichael.com/group.htm.

Canadian Federation of Agriculture. (1998, March). *The Canadian farm.*

Retrieved April 11, 2001, from the World Wide Web: http://www.cfa-fca/farms-e.htm.

Canadian Museum of Civilization Corporation. (2001). *1965 CBC interview with Marius Barbeau.* Retrieved August 11, 2003, from the World Wide Web: http://www.civilization.ca/academ/barbeau/banaeng.html. Originally published in 1982 in the *Oracle* series (no. 44) of the National Museum of Man.

Canadian Museum of Civilization Corporation. (2001). *Marius Barbeau: I was a pioneer.* Retrieved August 11, 2003, from the World Wide Web: http://www.civilization.ca/academ/barbeau/baineng.html.

Caroulis, J. (1996). Food for thought. *Pennsylvania Gazette, 95* (3), 16.

Carson, R. (1962). *Silent spring.* Boston: Houghton Mifflin.

Cashdan, E. (1989). Hunters and gatherers: Economic behavior in bands. In S. Plattner (Ed.), *Economic Anthropology* (pp. 21–48). Stanford, CA: Stanford University Press.

Cavallo, J.A. (1990, February). Cat in the human cradle. *Natural History,* 54–60.

CBC News. Indepth Backgrounder. (2001). *The fight for gay rights: Canada timeline: Owen Woods.* Retrieved March 3, 2001, from the World Wide Web: http://cbc.ca/news/indepth/background/gayrights.html.

Census of Agriculture. (2001, February 22). *History of the census of agriculture.* Retrieved April 11, 2001, from the World Wide Web: http://142.206.72.65/06_011_e.htm.

Centers For Disease Control Semi-Annual AIDS Report (through June 1996). (1997). Centers For Disease Control. Atlanta, Georgia.

Chambers, J.K. (1998). English: Canadian varieties. In J. Edwards (Ed.), *Language in Canada* (pp. 252–272). Cambridge, UK: Cambridge University Press.

Chambers, R. (1983). *Rural development: Putting the last first.* New York: Longman.

Chasin, B.H., & Franke, R.W. (1983). U.S. farming: A world model? *Global Reporter, 1* (2), 10.

Cherney, B. (2000, October 28). *Ukrainian immigration.* Retrieved March 13, 2001 from the World Wide Web: http://www.mbnet.mb.ca/~rfmorris/Featuring/Immigration/Ukrainian.Immigration.html.

Chodorow, N. (1971). Being and doing: A cross-cultural examination of the socialization of males and females. In V. Gornick & B.K. Moran (Eds.),

Woman in sexist society. New York: Basic Books.

Clark, W.E. LeGros. (1995). *The fossil evidence for human evolution.* Chicago: University of Chicago Press.

Clark, W.E.L. (1960). *The antecedents of man.* Chicago: Quadrangle Books.

Clay, J.W. (1996). What's a nation? In W.A. Haviland & R.J. Gordon (Eds.), *Talking about people* (2nd ed., p. 188). Mountain View, CA: Mayfield.

Cohen, M., & Armelagos, G. (1984). *Paleopathology and the origins of agriculture.* New Haven, CT: Yale University Press.

Cohen, M.N. (1989). *Health and the rise of civilization.* New Haven, CT: Yale University Press.

Cohen, R., & Middleton, J. (Eds.). (1967). *Comparative political systems.* Garden City, NY: Natural History Press.

Collier, J., Rosaldo, M.Z., & Yanagisako, S. (1982). Is there a family? New anthropological views. In B. Thorne & M. Yalom (Eds.), *Rethinking the family: Some feminist questions* (pp. 25–39). New York: Longman.

Commission on the Future of Health Care in Canada. (2002). *Building on values: The future of health care in Canada* (The Romanow Report). Ottawa: Government Printers.

Conaty, G.T. (1995, May). Economic models and Blackfoot ideology. *American Ethnologist, 22* (2), 403–409.

Connell, R.W. (1999). Making gendered people: Bodies, identities, sexualities. In M.M. Ferree, J. Locker, & B. Hess (Eds.), *Revisioning gender.* Thousand Oaks, CA: Sage.

Coon, C.S. (1948). *A reader in general anthropology.* New York: Holt, Rinehart and Winston.

Coon, C.S. (1954). *The story of man.* New York: Knopf.

Coon, C.S. (1958). *Caravan: The story of the Middle East* (2nd ed.). New York: Holt, Rinehart and Winston.

Cooper, A., Poinar, H.N., Pääbo, S., Radovcic, J., Debénath, A., Caparros, M., Barroso-Ruiz, C., Bertranpetit, J., Nielsen-March, C., Hedges, R.E.M., & Sykes, B. (1997). Neanderthal genetics. *Science, 277,* 1021–1024.

Corin, E. (1998). Refiguring the person: The dynamics of effects and symbols in an African spirit possession cult. In M. Lambek & A. Strathearn (Eds.), *Bodies and persons: Comparative perspectives from Africa and Melanesia.* Cambridge, UK: Cambridge University Press.

Cowgill, G.L. (1980). Letter. *Science, 210,* 1305.

Crane, L.B., Yeager, E., & Whitman, R.L. (1981). *An introduction to linguistics*. Boston: Little, Brown.

Crocker, W.H., & Crocker, J. (1994). *The Canela: Bonding through kinship, ritual, and sex*. Fort Worth, TX: Harcourt Brace.

Crosby, A. (1972/2003). *The Columbian exchange: Biological and cultural consequences of 1492* (30th anniversary ed.). Westport, CT: Praeger.

Crowly, V. (1998). Wicca as nature religion. In J. Pearson, R.H. Roberts, & F. Samuel (Eds.), *Nature religion today: Paganism in the modern world*. Edinburgh: Edinburgh University Press.

Cultural Survival Quarterly, 15 (4), 38 (1991).

Culture shock: Immigrants come to Canada with the hope of improving life for themselves and future generations but fitting into an entirely new culture isn't easy. (1998, January). *Canada and the World Backgrounder, 63* (4), 20–24.

Dalton, G. (1971). *Traditional tribal and peasant economics: An introductory survey of economic anthropology*. Reading, MA: Addison-Wesley.

Daly, M. (2000). African genital mutilation: The unspeakable atrocities. In E. Ashton-Jones, G.A. Olson, & M.G. Perry (Eds.), *The gender reader* (pp. 462–485). Needham Heights, MA: Allyn and Bacon.

Damas, D. (1972). Central Eskimo systems of food sharing. *Ethnology, 11*, 220–240.

Davis, S.H. (1982). *Victims of the miracle*. Cambridge, UK: Cambridge University Press.

de Waal, A. (1994). Genocide in Rwanda. *Anthropology Today, 10* (3), 1–2.

de Waal, F. (1996). *Good natured: The origins of right and wrong in humans and other animals*. Cambridge, MA: Harvard University Press.

DeMello, M. (2000). *Bodies of inscription: A cultural history of the modern tattoo community*. Durham, NC: Duke University Press.

Dennant, P. (1997). *Urban expression ... urban assault ... urban wildstyle ... New York City graffiti*. Retrieved July 4, 2001, from the World Wide Web: http://www.graffiti.org/faq/pamdennant .html.

Department of Sociology and Anthropology, Simon Fraser University. (2003, October). *Dr. Dara Culhane*. Retrieved February 12, 2004, from the World Wide Web: http://www.sfu.ca/ sociology/01department/biographies/ culhane.html.

Dettinger, K.A. (1997, October). When to wean. *Natural History*, 49.

Diamond, J. (1997). The curse of QWERTY. *Discover, 18* (4), 34–42.

di Leonardo, M. (1997). The female world of cards and holidays: Women, families, and the work of kinship. In C.B. Brettell & C.F. Sargent (Eds.), *Gender in cross-cultural perspective* (pp. 340–350). Upper Saddle River, NJ: Prentice Hall.

Douglas, M. (1966/1991). *Purity and Danger: An Analysis of the Concepts of Pollution and Taboo*. London: Routledge.

Drapeau, L. (1998). Aboriginal languages: Current status. In J. Edwards (Ed.), *Language in Canada* (pp. 144–159). Cambridge, UK: Cambridge University Press.

Dundes, A. (1980). *Interpreting folk lore*. Bloomington, IN: Indiana University Press.

duToit, B.M. (1991). *Human sexuality: Cross cultural readings*. New York: McGraw-Hill.

Eastman, C.M. (1990). *Aspects of language and culture* (2nd ed.). Novato, CA: Chandler and Sharp.

Eaton, B., Shostak, M., & Konner, M. (1988). *The Paleolithic prescription: A program of diet and exercise and a design for living*. New York: Harper and Row.

Ehrenreich, B., & English, D. (1978). *For her own good: 150 years of experts' advice to women*. New York: Anchor Books.

Elkin, A.P. (1964). *The Australian Aborigines*. Garden City, NY: Doubleday/Anchor Books.

Ember, C.J., & Ember, M. (1996). What have we learned from cross-cultural research? *General Anthropology, 2* (2), 5.

Ember, C.R., & Ember, M. (1985). *Cultural anthropology* (4th ed.). Englewood Cliffs, NJ: Prentice-Hall.

Endicott, K.L. (1999). Gender relations in hunter-gatherer societies. In R.B. Lee & R. Daly (Eds.), *The Cambridge encyclopedia of hunters and gatherers* (pp. 411–418). Cambridge, UK: Cambridge University Press.

Epstein, A.L. (1968). Sanctions. *International encyclopedia of social sciences, 14* (p. 3). New York: Macmillan.

Erera, P.I. (2002). *Family diversity: Continuity and change in the contemporary family*. Thousand Oaks, CA: Sage.

Erwin, A.M. (2000). *Canadian perspectives in cultural anthropology*. Scarborough, ON: Nelson Thomson Learning.

Evans-Pritchard, E.E. (1937). *Witchcraft, oracles and magic among the Azande*. London: Oxford University Press.

Ewers, J.C. (1985). *The horse in Blackfoot Indian culture*. Washington, DC: Smithsonian Institute Press.

Falk, D. (1989). Ape-like endocast of "Ape Man Taung." *American Journal of Physical Anthropology, 80*, 335–339.

Farmer, P. (1992). *AIDS and accusation: Haiti and the geography of blame*. Berkeley: University of California Press.

Fedigan, L. (1982). *Primate paradigms: Sex roles and social bonds*. Montreal: Eden Press.

Feit, H.A. (1995). Hunting and the quest for power: The James Bay Cree and Whitemen in the 20th century. In R.B. Morrison & C.R. Wilson (Eds.), *Native peoples: The Canadian experience* (2nd ed.). Toronto: McClelland and Stewart.

Feit, H.A. (1999). James Bay Cree. In R.B. Lee & R. Daly (Eds.), *The Cambridge encyclopedia of hunters and gatherers*. Cambridge, UK: Cambridge University Press.

Firth, R. (1956). *Two studies of kinship in London*. London: University of London, Athlone Press.

Fleising, U. (2001). In search of genohype: A content analysis of biotechnology company documents. *New Genetics and Society, 20* (3), 239–254.

Forde, C.D. (1950). *Habitat, economy, and society*. New York: Dutton.

Forde, C.D. (1968). Double descent among the Yakö. In P. Bohannan & J. Middleton (Eds.), *Kinship and social organization* (pp. 179–191). Garden City, NY: Natural History Press.

Foucault, M. (1975). *The birth of the clinic: An archaeology of medical perception*. New York: Vintage.

Fox, R. (1967). *Kinship and marriage in an anthropological perspective*. Baltimore: Penguin.

Fox, R. (1968). *Encounter with anthropology*. New York: Dell.

Fox, R. (1981, December 3). [Interview for Coast Telecourses, Inc.]. Los Angeles.

Fox, R. (n.d.). *Food and eating: An anthropological perspective*. Retrieved August 27, 2003, from the World Wide Web: http://www.sirc.org/publik/ food_and_eating_3.html.

Frazer, J.G. (1931). Magic and religion. In V.F. Claverton (Ed.), *The making of man: An outline of anthropology* (pp. 693–713). New York: Modern Library.

Freeman, L.G. (1992). *Ambrona and Torralba: New evidence and interpretation*. Paper presented at the 91st Annual Meeting of the American Anthropological Association, Chicago.

Fried, M. (1967). *The evolution of political society: An essay in political anthropology*. New York: Random House.

Friesen, J.W. (1997). *Rediscovering the First Nations of Canada*. Calgary: Detselig.

Friesen, J.W. (1999). *First Nations of the plains: Creative, adaptable, enduring*. Calgary: Detselig.

Frye, M. (1983). Sexism. In *The politics of reality* (pp. 17–40). New York: The Crossing Press.

Gardner, R.A., Gardner, B.T., & Van Cantfort, T.E. (Eds.). (1989). *Teaching sign language to chimpanzees*. Albany, NY: State University of New York Press.

Gates, H. (1996). Buying brides in China—again. *Anthropology Today, 12* (4), 10.

GCS Research Society. (1996). *Biruté Galdikas: Anthropologist*. Retrieved November 25, 2000, from the World Wide Web: http://www.science.ca/scientists/Galdikas/galdikas.html.

Geertz, C. (1984). Distinguished lecture: Anti-relativism. *American Anthropologist, 86,* 263–278.

Gell, A. (1988). Technology and magic. *Anthropology Today, 4* (2), 6–9.

Genesee, F. (1998). French immersion in Canada. In J. Edwards (Ed.), *Language in Canada* (pp. 305–326). Cambridge, UK: Cambridge University Press.

Gibbs, J.L., Jr. (1965). The Kpelle of Liberia. In J.L. Gibbs, Jr. (Ed.), *Peoples of Africa* (pp. 197–240). New York: Holt, Rinehart and Winston.

Gibbs, J.L., Jr. (1983). [Interview.] *Faces of culture: Program 18*. Fountain Valley, CA: Coast Telecourses.

Gibbs, L. (1995). *Dying from dioxin: A citizen's guide to reclaiming our health and rebuilding democracy*. Boston: South End Press.

Gibbs, L.M. (1998). *Love Canal: The story continues*. Gabriola Island, BC: New Society.

Gilmore, D.D. (1997). The manhood puzzle. In C.B. Brettell & C.F. Sargent (Eds.), *Gender in cross-cultural perspective* (2nd ed., pp. 185–197). Upper Saddle River, NJ: Prentice Hall.

Girvan, S. (Ed.). (2002). *Canadian global almanac 2003*. Toronto: John Wiley and Sons.

Goddard, V. (1993). Child labor in Naples. In W.A. Haviland & R.J. Gordon (Eds.), *Talking about people* (pp. 105–109). Mountain View, CA: Mayfield.

Goodall, J. (1986). *The chimpanzees of Gombe: Patterns of behavior*. Cambridge, MA: Belknap Press.

Goodall, J. (1990). *Through a window: My thirty years with the chimpanzees of Gombe*. Boston: Houghton Mifflin.

Goodenough, W. (1990). Evolution of the human capacity for beliefs. *American Anthropologist, 92,* 597–612.

Goodenough, W.H. (1970). *Description and comparison in cultural anthropology*. Chicago: Aldine.

Goodman, A., & Leatherman, T. (Eds.). (1998). *Building a new biocultural synthesis: Political-economic perspectives on human biology*. Ann Arbor: University of Michigan Press.

Goody, J. (1983). *The development of the family and marriage in Europe*. Cambridge, MA: Cambridge University Press.

Gordillo, G. (2002). The breath of the devils: Memories and places of an experience of terror. *American Ethnologist, 29* (1), 33–57.

Gordon, R.J., & Megitt, M.J. (1985). *Law and order in the New Guinea Highlands*. Hanover, NH: University Press of New England.

Gould, S.J. (1983). *Hens' teeth and horses' toes*. New York: Norton.

Gould, S.J. (1996). *Full house: The spread of excellence from Plato to Darwin*. New York: Harmony Books.

Goulet, J.A. (1996, December). The 'berdache'/'two-spirit': A comparison of anthropological and native constructions of gendered identities among the northern Athapaskans. *Journal of Royal Anthropological Institute, 2,* 683–701.

Gruenbaum, E. (1997). The movement against clitoridectomy and infibulation in Sudan: Public health policy and the women's movement. In C.B. Brettell & C.F. Sargent (Eds.), *Gender in cross-cultural perspectives* (2nd ed., pp. 441–452). Upper Saddle River, NJ: Prentice Hall.

Guenther, M. (1999). *Tricksters and trancers* (p. 101). Bloomington and Indianapolis, IL: Indiana University Press.

Haeri, N. (1997). The reproduction of symbolic capital: Language, state and class in Egypt. *Current Anthropology, 38,* 795–816.

Hale, H. (1883). The Tutelo tribe and language. *Proceedings of the American Philosophical Society, 21* (114).

Hall, E.T., & Hall, M.R. (1986). The sounds of silence. In E. Angeloni (Ed.), *Anthropology 86/87* (pp. 65–70). Guilford, CT: Dushkin.

Hannah, J.L. (1988). *Dance, sex and gender*. Chicago: University of Chicago Press.

Hansen, J., Dunn, D., Lee, R.B., Becker, P., & Jenkins, T. (1994). Hunter-gatherer to pastoral way of life: Effects of the transition on health, growth and nutritional status. *South African Journal of Science, 89,* 559–564.

Harris Gallery. (2001). *Inuit art background*. Retrieved April 3, 2001, from the World Wide Web: http://www.harrisinuitgallery.com/artinfo.htm.

Hatch, E. (1983). *Culture and morality: The relativity of values in anthropology*. New York: Columbia University Press.

Hatcher, E.P. (1985). *Art as culture: An introduction to the anthropology of art*. New York: University Press of America.

Hauch, C. (1995). Reciprocity on skid row. In J.L. Chodkiewicz (Ed.), *Peoples of the past and present: Readings in anthropology*. Toronto: Harcourt Brace.

Haviland, W.A., & Power, M.W. (1994). *The original Vermonters: Native inhabitants, past and present* (Rev. and exp. ed.). Hanover, NH: University Press of New England.

Hawkes, K., O'Connell, J.F., & Blurton Jones, N.G. (1997). Hadza women's time allocation, offspring provisioning, and the evolution of long postmenopausal life spans. *Current Anthropology, 38,* 551–577.

Health Canada. (2001). Canada's seniors: Living with extended families. Retrieved March 4, 2001, from the World Wide Web: http://www.hc-sc.gc.ca/seniors-aines/pub/factoids/en/no7.htm.

Hedigan, E.J. (1995). *Applied anthropology in Canada. Understanding aboriginal issues*. Toronto: University of Toronto Press.

Heilbroner, R.L., & Thurow, L.C. (1981). *The economic problem* (6th ed.). Englewood Cliffs, NJ: Prentice-Hall.

Henry, J. (1965). *Culture against man*. New York: Vintage Books.

Henry, J. (1966). The metaphysics of youth, beauty, and romantic love. In S. Farber & R. Wilson (Eds.), *The challenge of women*. New York: Basic Books.

Henry, J. (1974). A theory for an anthropological analysis of American culture. In J.G. Jorgensen & M. Truzzi (Eds.), *Anthropology and American life* (p. 14). Englewood Cliffs, NJ: Prentice-Hall.

Hern, W. (1992, December). Family planning, Amazon style. *Natural History, 101* (12).

Herskovits, M.J. (1952). *Economic anthropology: A study in comparative economics* (2nd ed.). New York: Knopf.

Hertzman, C. (2001). Health and human society. *American Scientist, 89,* 538–545.

Hickerson, N.P. (1980). *Linguistic anthropology*. New York: Holt, Rinehart and Winston.

Hilts, P. (1996). *Smokescreen: The truth behind the tobacco industry coverup*. New York: Addison-Wesley.

Hoe, B.S. (1989). *Beyond the golden mountain: Chinese cultural traditions in Canada*. Ottawa: Canadian Museum of Civilization

Hoebel, E.A. (1954). *The law of primitive man: A study in comparative legal dynamics*. Cambridge, MA: Harvard University Press.

Hoebel, E.A. (1972). *Anthropology: The study of man* (4th ed.). New York: McGraw-Hill.

Howell, N. (2000). *Demography of the Dobe !Kung* (2nd ed.). Hawthorne, NY: Aldine-DeGruyter.

Huntington, H. (2000). *How table manners become polite*. Retrieved August 27, 2003, from the World Wide Web: http://search.csmonitor.com/ durable/2000/11/28/p22s1.htm.

Indian and Northern Affairs Canada. (2000, July 21). *Federal policy guide— Aboriginal self-government*. Retrieved March 21, 2001, from the World Wide Web: http://www.ainc-inac.gc.ca/pr/ pub/sg/plcy_e.html.

Indian and Northern Affairs Canada. (2003). *Biographical data. Bernard Saladin d'Anglure: Northern science award winner*. Retrieved September 20, 2003, from the World Wide Web: http://www.ainc-inac.gc.ca/nr/prs/ j-a2003/02293bbk-e.html.

Ingoldsby, B.B. (1995). Family origins and universality. In B.B. Ingoldsby & S. Smith (Eds.), *Families in multicultural perspective* (pp. 36–58). New York: The Guilford Press.

It's the law: Child labor protection. (1997, November/December). *Peace and Justice News, 11*.

Jacobs, M. (2002, July 17). Living together replacing "I do" for many. *The Edmonton Sun*.

Jain, R.K. (1997). Comment. *Current Anthropology, 38*, 248.

Johanson, D., & Shreeve, J. (1989). *Lucy's child: The discovery of a human ancestor*. New York: Avon.

Johnson, A.W., & Earle, T. (1987). *The evolution of human societies, from foraging group to agrarian state*. Stanford, CA: Stanford University Press.

Johnson, D. (1996). Polygamists emerge from secrecy, seeking not just peace but respect. In W.A. Haviland & R.J. Gordon (Eds.), *Talking about people* (2nd ed., pp. 129–131). Mountain View, CA: Mayfield.

Johnson, J. (2001, March 14). *Saskatchewan population sinking. The Star Phoenix*, Saskatoon.

Johnson, L.M. (2002). Indigenous knowledge as a basis for living in local environments. In R.B. Morrison & C.R. Wilson (Eds.), *Ethnographic essays in cultural anthropology: A problem-based approach*. Itasca, IL: F.E. Peacock.

Jolly, A. (1991). Thinking like a Vervet. *Science, 251*, 574.

Joralemon, D. (1999). *Exploring medical anthropology*. Boston: Allyn and Bacon.

Joyce, C. (1991). *Witnesses from the grave: The stories bones tell*. Boston: Little, Brown.

Junker, K., & Vergara, V. (2001). *Religious movements homepage: Wicca*. Retrieved October 24, 2003, from the World Wide Web: http://religiousmovements.lib.virginia .edu/nrms/wicca/html.

Kakodyniak, G.W. (1998). *Internment of Ukrainians in Canada 1914–1920*. Retrieved October 19, 2003, from the World Wide Web: http:// www.infoukes.com/history/internment.

Katz, R. (1982). *Boiling energy: Community healing among the !Kung*. Cambridge, MA: Harvard University Press.

Keesing, R.M. (1976). *Cultural anthropology: A contemporary perspective*. New York: Holt, Rinehart and Winston.

Kelley, J.H., & Williamson, R.F. (1996, January). The positioning of archaeology within anthropology: A Canadian historical perspective. *American Antiquity, 61* (1), 5–20.

Kelly, R. (1976). Witchcraft and sexual relations. In P. Brown & G. Buchbender (Eds.), *Man and woman in the New Guinea Highlands*. Special Publication No. 8. Washington, DC: American Anthropological Association.

Kendall, L. (1990, October). In the company of witches. *Natural History, 92*.

Khare, R.S., & Rao, M.S.A. (1986). Introduction. In R.S. Khare & M.S.A. Rao (Eds.), *Aspects in South Asian food systems: Food, society, and culture*. Durham, NC: Carolina Academic Press.

Kidd, K.E. (1937, reprinted 1986). *Blackfoot ethnography*. Archaeological Survey of Alberta, No. 8.

Kirkpatrick, R.C. (2000). The evolution of human homosexual behavior. *Current Anthropology, 41*, 384.

Kirmayer, L.J., Boothroyd, L., Tanner, A., Adelson, N., Robinson, E., & Oblin, C. (2000). Psychological distress among the Cree of James Bay. *Transcultural Psychiatry, 37*, 35–56.

Kluckhohn, C. (1944). *Navajo witchcraft*. Cambridge, MA: Harvard University Press.

Kluckhohn, C. (1944). Navajo witchcraft. *Papers of the Peabody Museum of American Archaeology and Ethnology, 22* (2).

Knauft, B. (1991). Violence and sociality in human evolution. *Current Anthropology, 32*, 391–409.

Koch, G. (1997). Songs, land rights and archives in Australia. *Cultural Survival Quarterly, 20* (4).

Kohler, L. (1996). Global apartheid. Reprinted in W.A. Haviland & R.J. Gordon (Eds.), *Talking about people: Readings in contemporary cultural anthropology* (2nd ed., pp. 262–268). Mountain View, CA: Mayfield.

Korean Table Manners. Retrieved August 27, 2003, from the World Wide Web: http://www.esl-global.com/ cultural_hints/manners.html.

Kue Young, T. (1993). Diabetes mellitus among Native Americans in Canada and the United States: An epidemiological review. *American Journal of Human Biology, 5* (4), 399–413.

Kuper, H. (1965). The Swazi of Swaziland. In J.L. Gibbs, Jr. (Ed.), *Peoples of Africa* (pp. 475–512). New York: Holt, Rinehart and Winston.

Lambek, M. (1993). *Knowledge and practice in Mayotte: Local discourses of Islam, sorcery, and spirit possession*. Toronto: University of Toronto Press.

Lang, S. (1999). Lesbians, men-women and two-spirits: Homosexuality and gender in Native American cultures. In E. Blackwood & S.E. Wieringa (Eds.), *Female desires: Same-sex relations and transgender practices across cultures*. New York: Columbia University Press.

Le Clair, E., & Schneider, H.K. (Eds.). (1968). *Economic anthropology: Readings in theory and analysis*. New York: Holt, Rinehart and Winston.

Leach, E. (1982). *Social Anthropology*. Glasgow: Fontana Paperbacks.

Leavitt, G.C. (1990). Sociobiological explanations of incest avoidance: A critical review of evidential claims. *American Anthropologist, 92*, 971–993.

Lee, R.B. (1993). *The Dobe Ju/'hoansi* (2nd ed.). Orlando, FL: Harcourt Brace.

Lee, R.B. (2003). *The Dobe Ju/'hoansi* (3rd ed.). Toronto: Wadsworth/Thomson Learning.

Lee, R.B., & Daly, R. (Eds.). (1999). *The Cambridge encyclopedia of hunters and gatherers* (pp. 1–19). Cambridge, UK: Cambridge University Press.

Lehmann, A.C., & Myers, J.E. (Eds.). (1993). *Magic, witchcraft and religion: An anthropological study of the supernatural* (3rd ed.). Mountain View, CA: Mayfield.

Leinhardt, G. (1960). Religion. In H. Shapiro (Ed.), *Man, culture, and* society (pp. 382–401). London: Oxford University Press.

Lenski, G. (1966). *Power and privilege: A theory of social stratification.* New York: McGraw-Hill.

Leonard, W.R. (2003). Food for thought. *Scientific American, 13* (2), 62–71.

Leonard, W.R., & Hegman, M. (1987). Evolution of P3 morphology in *Australopithecus afarensis. American Journal of Physical Anthropology, 73,* 41–63.

Lerner, R.N. (1987). Preserving plants for Pomos. In R.M. Wulff & S.J. Fiske (Eds.), *Anthropological praxis: Translating knowledge into action* (pp. 212–222). Boulder, CO: Westview.

Lessem, D. (1995–1996). Interview with Biruté Galdikas. In E. Angeloni (Ed.), *Physical anthropology 95/96* (4th ed., pp. 77–85). Guilford, CT: Dushkin.

Lett, J. (1987). *The human enterprise: A critical introduction to anthropological theory.* Boulder, CO: Westview.

Levine, N.E., & Silk, J.B. (1997). Why polyandry fails. *Current Anthropology, 38,* 375–398.

Lévi-Strauss, C. (1963). The effectiveness of symbols. In *Structural Anthropology,* vol. 1. New York: Basic Books.

Lévi-Strauss, C. (1963). The sorcerer and his magic. In *Structural Anthropology,* vol. 1. New York: Basic Books.

Lewin, R. (1987). Four legs bad, two legs good. *Science, 235,* 969.

Lewin, R. (1987). The earliest "humans" were more like apes. *Science, 236,* 1062–1063.

Lewis-Williams, J.D., Dowson, T.A., & Deacon, J. (1993). Rock art and changing perceptions of Southern Africa's past: Ezeljagdspoort reviewed. *Antiquity, 67,* 273–291.

Li, P.S. (1988). *The Chinese in Canada.* Toronto: Oxford University Press.

Lindholm, C., & Lindholm, C. (2000). Life behind the veil. In E. Ashton-Jones, G.A. Olson, & M.G. Perry (Eds.), *The gender reader* (2nd ed., pp. 451–461). Needham Heights, MA: Allyn and Bacon.

Linton, R. (1936/1964). *The study of man: An introduction.* New York: Appleton.

Litwak, E. (1960). Occupational mobility and extended family cohesion. *American Sociological Review, 29.*

Livingstone, F. (1958). Anthropological implications of sickle-cell gene distribution in West Africa. *American Anthropologist, 58,* 533–562.

Lowie, R.H. (1935/1956). *Crow Indians.* New York: Holt, Rinehart and Winston.

Lubbers, R.F.M. (1999). *The globalization of economy and society.*

Retrieved August 20, 2003, from the World Wide Web: http://globus/lubpdfs/globaliz/thegloba/doc.

Lustig-Arecco, V. (1975). *Technology strategies for survival.* New York: Holt, Rinehart and Winston.

MacCormack, C.P. (1977). Biological events and cultural control. *Signs, 3,* 93–100.

Mackie, M. (1991). *Gender relations in Canada: Further explorations.* Toronto: Harcourt Brace.

MacNiel, R. (1982). *The right place at the right time.* Boston: Little, Brown.

Magnarella, P.J. (1974). *Tradition and change in a Turkish town.* New York: Wiley.

Mair, L. (1969). *Witchcraft.* New York: McGraw-Hill.

Malinowski, B. (1922). *Argonauts of the western Pacific.* New York: Dutton.

Malinowski, B. (1951). *Crime and custom in savage society.* London: Routledge.

Malinowski, B. (1954). *Magic, science and religion, and other essays.* Garden City, NY: Doubleday/Anchor Books.

Mandell, N., & Duffy, A. (2000). *Canadian families. Diversity, conflict, and change.* Toronto: Harcourt Brace.

Manuel, G., & Posluns, M. (1974). *The fourth world: An Indian reality.* New York: Free Press.

Martin, E. (1987). *The woman in the body: A cultural analysis of reproduction.* Boston: Beacon Press.

Martin, E. (1994). *Flexible Bodies: Tracking immunity in American culture—from the days of polio to the age of AIDS.* Boston: Beacon Press.

Mason, J.A. (1957). *The ancient civilizations of Peru.* Baltimore, MD: Penguin.

Maybury-Lewis, D. (1984). The prospects for plural societies. 1982 Proceedings of the American Ethnological Society.

Maybury-Lewis, D. (1993, Fall). A new world dilemma: The Indian question in the Americas. *Symbols,* 17–23.

McCafferty, S.D., & McCafferty, G.G. (1994, April). Engendering tomb 7 at Monte Alban: Respinning an old yarn. *Current Anthropology, 35* (2), 143–166.

McElroy, A., & Townsend, P. (1996). *Medical anthropology in ecological perspective.* Boulder, CO: Westview.

McGill University. (2004). *Social Studies of Medicine.* Retrieved February 12, 2004, from the World Wide Web: http://www.mcgill.ca/ssom/#Lock.

McKenna, J.J. (1997, October). Bedtime story. *Natural History,* 50.

McLellan, J. (2002). *Many petals of the lotus: Five Asian Buddhist communities in Toronto.* Toronto: University of Toronto Press.

McLellan, J. (2003). *Buddhism in the multicultural context of Toronto, Canada: Local communities, global networks.* Retrieved August 17, 2003, from the World Wide Web: http://alcor.concordia.ca/~csaa1/porter/lectures/JanetMcLellan.html.

McMillan, A.D. (1988). *Native peoples and cultures of Canada: An anthropological overview.* Vancouver: Douglas and McIntyre.

Medusa, M. (1994). *Shawna Dempsey and Lorri Milan.* Retrieved July 4, 2001, from the World Wide Web: http://www.oboro.net/en/exhib9394/dempsey.htm.

Mellars, P. (1989). Major issues in the emergence of modern humans. *Current Anthropology, 30,* 349–385.

Merriam, A.P. (1964). *The anthropology of music.* Chicago: Northwestern University Press.

Mesghinua, H.M. (1966). Salt mining in Enderta. *Journal of Ethiopian Studies, 4* (2).

Michael, B.J. (2002). Patterns of family relations. In R.B. Morrison & C.R. Wilson (Eds.), *Ethnographic essays in cultural anthropology: A problem-based approach.* Itasca, IL: F.E. Peacock.

Miles, H.L.W. (1993). Language and the orangutan: The old "person" of the forest. In P. Cavalieri & P. Singer (Eds.), *The great ape project* (pp. 42–57). New York: St. Martin's Press.

Miller, C., & Swift, K. (2000). One small step for genkind. In E. Ashton-Jones, G.A. Olson, & M.G. Perry (Eds.), *The gender reader* (2nd ed., pp. 289–300). Needham Heights, MA: Allyn and Bacon.

Mitchell, L. (2001). *Baby's first picture: Ultrasound and the politics of fetal subjects.* Toronto: University of Toronto Press.

Mitchell, W.E. (1973, December). A new weapon stirs up old ghosts. *Natural History Magazine,* 77–84.

Modern and Contemporary Art at the McMichael. (1996–2001). Retrieved March 27, 2001, from the World Wide Web: http://www.mcmichael.com/modern. htm.

Morrison, R.B., & Wilson, C.R. (2002). *Ethnographic essays in cultural anthropology: A problem-based approach.* Itasca, IL: F.E. Peacock.

Mowat, F. (1959). *The desperate people.* Boston: Little, Brown.

Multimania. (n.d.). *French Creole: A language and a culture.* Retrieved June 21, 2001, from the World Wide

Web: http://www.multimania.com/fdl/
e-kreyol. html.

Murphy, R., & Steward, J. (1968). Tappers and trappers: Parallel processes in acculturation. In R. Manners & D. Kaplan (Eds.), *Theory in anthropology*. New York: Aldine.

Nader, L. (1981, December). [Interview for Coast Telecourses, Inc.]. Los Angeles.

Nader, L. (1997). Controlling processes: Tracing the dynamic components of power. *Current Anthropology, 38*, 714–715.

Nader, R., Milleron, N., & Conacher, D. (1992). *Canada firsts*. Toronto: McClelland and Stewart.

Nanda, S. (1992). Arranging a marriage in India. In P.R. DeVita (Ed.), *The naked anthropologist* (pp. 139–143). Belmont, CA: Wadsworth.

Nash, J. (1979). *We eat the mines and the mines eat us: Dependency and exploitation in Bolivian tin mines*. New York: Columbia University Press.

Nash, M. (1966). *Primitive and peasant economic systems*. San Francisco: Chandler.

National Women's History Project. (1998). *Living the legacy: The women's rights movement 1848–1998*. E. Eisenber & M. Ruthsdotter. Retrieved November 25, 2000, from the World Wide Web: http://www.legacy98.org/move-hist.html.

National Women's History Project. (1998). *The women's movement in Canada*. Retrieved November 25, 2000, from the World Wide Web: http://130.15.62.164/Projects/squeezebox days/newfeminism.html.

Neel, J.V. (1962). Diabetes mellitus: A "thrifty" genotype rendered detrimental by "progress"? *American Journal of Human Genetics, 14* (4), 353–362.

Nelson, E.D., & Robinson, B.W. (1999). *Gender in Canada*. Scarborough, ON: Prentice Hall Allyn and Bacon.

Newell, D., & Ommer, R.E. (1999). Introduction: Traditions and issues. In D. Newell & R.E. Ommer (Eds.), *Fishing places, fishing people: Traditions and issues in Canadian small-scale fisheries*. Toronto: University of Toronto Press.

Ng, W.C. (1999). *The Chinese in Vancouver, 1945–80: The pursuit of identity and power*. Vancouver: UBC Press.

Nietschmann, B. (1987). The third world war. *Cultural Survival Quarterly, 11* (3), 1–16.

Nilsen A.P. (2000). Sexism in English: A 1990s update. In E. Ashton-Jones, G.A. Olson, & M.G. Perry (Eds.), *The gender reader* (2nd ed., pp. 301–312). Needham Heights, MA: Allyn and Bacon.

Nunavut Planning Commission, (n.d.). Land claim review. Retrieved April 7, 2001, from the World Wide Web: http://www.arctic.ca/LUS/Nunavut.html.

O'Barr, W.M. & Conley, J.M. (1993). When a juror watches a lawyer. In W.A. Haviland & R.J. Gordon (Eds.), *Talking about people* (2nd ed., pp. 42–45). Mountain View, CA: Mayfield.

O'Mahoney, K. (1970). The salt trade. *Journal of Ethiopian Studies, 8* (2).

O'Neil, J.D. (1989). Cultural and political context of patient dissatisfaction in cross-cultural clinical encounters: A Canadian Inuit study. *Medical Anthropology Quarterly, 3* (4), 325–344.

O'Neil, J.D., Reading, J., & Leader, A. (1998). Changing the relations of surveillance: The development of a discourse of resistance in aboriginal epidemiology. *Human Organization, 57* (2), 230–237.

Obler, R.S. (1980). Is the female husband a man? Woman/woman marriage among the Nandi of Kenya. *Ethnology, 19*, 69–88.

Offiong, D. (1985). Witchcraft among the Ibibio of Nigeria. In A.C. Lehmann & J.E. Meyers (Eds.), *Magic, witchcraft and religion* (pp. 152–165). Palo Alto, CA: Mayfield.

Okonjo, K. (1976). The dual-sex political system in operation: Igbo women and community politics in midwestern Nigeria. In N. Hafkin & E. Bay (Eds.), *Women in Africa* (pp. 45–58). Stanford, CA: Stanford University Press.

Ommer, R.E. (1999). Rosie's Cove: Settlement morphology, history, economy, and culture in a Newfoundland outport. In D. Newell & R.E. Ommer (Eds.), *Fishing places, fishing people: Traditions and issues in Canadian small-scale fisheries*. Toronto: University of Toronto Press.

Oswalt, W.H. (1972). *Habitat and technology*. New York: Holt, Rinehart and Winston.

Oswalt, W.H., & Neely, S. (1996). *This land was theirs: A study of North American Indians* (5th ed.). Mountain View, CA: Mayfield.

Otten, C.M. (1971). *Anthropology and art: Readings in cross-cultural aesthetics*. Garden City, NY: Natural History Press.

Our Heritage. (2001). *Who was Paul Kane?* Retrieved April 4, 2001, from the World Wide Web: http://ourheritage.net/Who/KaneWho.html.

Overholt, C., Anderson, M.B., Cloud, K., & Austin, J.E. (Eds.). (1985). Women in development: A framework for project analysis. In *Gender roles in development projects. A case book* (pp. 3–16). West Hartford, CT: Kumarian Press.

Parades, J.A., & Purdum, E.J. (1990). Bye, bye Ted . . . *Anthropology Today, 6* (2), 9–11.

Parker, Richard. (1991). *Bodies, pleasures, and passions: Sexual culture in contemporary Brazil*. Boston: Beacon Press.

Parsons, T. (1943). The kinship system of contemporary United States. *American Anthropologist, 45*.

Peabody Museum of Archaeology and Ethnology. (1999). *Gifting and feasting in the NWC potlatch/What is a potlatch?* Retrieved June 25, 2001, from the World Wide Web: http://www.peabody .harvard.edu/potlatch/potlat2.html.

Peacock, J.L. (1986). *The anthropological lens: Harsh light, soft focus*. New York: Cambridge University Press.

Pelto, P.J. (1973). *The snowmobile revolution: Technology and social change in the Arctic*. Menlo Park, CA: Cummings.

Perkel, C. (2002). *Well of lies: The Walkerton water tragedy*. Toronto: McClelland and Stewart.

Plattner, S. (1989). Markets and market places. In S. Plattner (Ed.), *Economic anthropology* (pp. 171–208). Stanford, CA: Stanford University Press.

Polanyi, K. (1968). The economy as instituted process. In E.E. LeClaire, Jr., & H.K. Schneider (Eds.), *Economic anthropology: Readings in theory and analysis* (pp. 122–167). New York: Holt, Rinehart and Winston.

Polhemus, T., & Randall, H. (2000). *The customized body*. London and New York: Serpent's Tail.

Pope, G. (1988, October). Bamboo and human evolution. *Natural History, 98*, 56.

Pospisil, L. (1971). *Anthropology of law: A comparative theory*. New York: Harper and Row.

Pospisil, L. (1963). *The Kapauku Papuans of West New Guinea*. New York: Holt, Rinehart and Winston.

Price, T.D., & Feinman, G.M. (Eds.). (1995). *Foundations of social inequality*. New York: Plenum.

Prins, H. (1996). *The Mi'kmaq: Resistance, accommodation, and cultural survival*. Fort Worth, TX: Harcourt Brace.

Progenix Corporation. (1998). *The history of ginseng in the United States*. Retrieved March 12, 2001, from the World Wide Web: http://progenixcorp .com/ushistory.html.

Radcliffe-Brown, A.R. (1931). Social organization of Australian tribes. *Oceania Monographs, 1*, 29. Melbourne: Macmillan.

Radcliffe-Brown, A.R. (1952). *Structure and function in primitive society*. New York: Free Press.

Rains, P. (2000). Pretty in punk: Girls' resistance in a boys' subculture. (Review). *The Canadian Review of Sociology and Anthropology, 37* (ii), 113.

Rajani, A. (2001). *FGM bibliography*. Retrieved June 26, 2001, from the World Wide Web: http://www.scar .utoronto.ca/~97rajani/biblio.html.

Ramu, G.N. (1979). Kinship networks. In G.N. Ramu (Ed.), *Courtship, marriage, and the family in Canada* (pp. 96–114). Toronto: Gage.

Rapp, R. (1999). *Testing women, testing the fetus: The social impact of amniocentesis in America*. New York: Routledge.

Rappaport, R.A. (1969). Ritual regulation of environmental relations among a New Guinea people. In A.P Vayda (Ed.), *Environment and cultural behavior* (pp. 181–201). Garden City, NY: Natural History Press.

Reina, R. (1966). *The law of the saints*. Indianapolis, IN: Bobbs-Merrill.

Reynolds, V. (1994). Primates in the field, primates in the lab. *Anthropology Today, 10* (2), 3–5.

Rice, P.C. (1997). Paleoanthropology 1996—Part II. *General Anthropology, 3* (2), 10.

Ridington, R. (1988). *Trail to heaven: Knowledge and narrative in a northern native community*. Vancouver: Douglas and McIntyre.

Roberts, C.A., & Cox, M. (2003). *Health and disease in Britain: From prehistory to the present day*. Stroud, Gloucestershire: Sutton.

Rohner, R.P., & Bettauer, E.C. (1986). *The Kwakiutl Indians of British Columbia*. Prospect Heights, IL: Waveland Press.

Rosen, G. (1993). *A history of public health*. Baltimore, MD: Johns Hopkins University Press.

Rosenberg, H. (1997). From trash to treasure. In J. Schneider & R. Rapp (Eds.), *Articulating hidden histories* (pp. 190–204). Berkeley: University of California Press.

Royal Australian College of Obstetricians and Gynaecologists. (1997). *Female genital mutilation*. Retrieved February 12, 2001, from the World Wide Web: http://www.ranzcog.edu.au/open/ womensh/fgm/fgm1.htm.

Ruhlen, M. (1994). *The origin of language: Tracing the evolution of the mother tongue*. New York: John Wiley and Sons.

Sagoff, M. (1997, January–June). Do we consume too much? *The Atlantic Monthly, 279* (6), 80–96.

Sahlins, M. (1972). *Stone age economics*. Chicago: Aldine.

Salzman, P.C. (1967). Political organization among nomadic peoples. *Proceedings of the American Philosophical Society*, III, 115–131.

Sampet, P. (2001). Last words. *World Watch, 14* (3).

Sanday, P.R. (1981). *Female power and male dominance: On the origins of sexual inequality*. Cambridge, UK: Cambridge University Press.

Scheper-Hughes, N., & Lock, M. (1987). The mindful body: A prolegomenon to future work in medical anthropology. *Medical Anthropology Quarterly, 1* (1).

Schrire, C. (Ed.). (1984). *Past and present in hunter-gatherer studies*. Orlando, FL: Academic Press.

Schusky, E.L. (1975). *Variation in kinship*. New York: Holt, Rinehart and Winston.

Schusky, E.L. (1983). *Manual for kinship analysis* (2nd ed.). Lanham, MD: University Press of America.

Sheets, P. (1987). Dawn of a new stone age in eye surgery. In R.J. Sharer & W. Ashmore (Eds.), *Archaeology: Discovering our past* (pp. 230–231). Palo Alto, CA: Mayfield.

Shostak, M. (1983). *Nisa: The life and words of a !Kung woman*. New York: Vintage.

Silverstein, K. (1999, July 19). Millions for Viagra, pennies for diseases of the poor. *The Nation*, 13–18.

Sinclair, P.R., Squires, H., & Downton, L. (1999). A future without fish? Constructing social life on Newfoundland's Bonavista Peninsula after the cod moratorium. In D. Newell & R.E. Ommer (Eds.), *Fishing places, fishing people: Traditions and issues in Canadian small-scale fisheries*. Toronto: University of Toronto Press.

Singer, M., Valentin, F., Baer, H., & Jia, Z. (1992). Why does Juan Garcia have a drinking problem? *Medical Anthropology, 14* (1), 77–108.

Small, M.F. (1997). Making connections. *American Scientist, 85, 503*.

Smith, S. (1995). The world of women. In B.B. Ingoldsby & S. Smith (Eds.), *Families in multicultural perspective* (pp. 253–259). New York: The Guilford Press.

Snow, D.R. (1994). *The Iroquois*. Cambridge, MA: Blackwell.

Social-Cultural Anthropology at University of Toronto. (2000, December). *Biography of Richard B. Lee*. Retrieved January 27, 2001, from the World Wide

Web: http://www.utoronto.ca/ anthropology/Faculty/lee.htm.

Spradley, J.P. (1979). *The ethnographic interview*. New York: Holt, Rinehart and Winston.

Spuhler, J.N. (1979). Continuities and discontinuities in anthropoid-hominid behavioral evolution: Bipedal locomotion and sexual reception. In N.A. Chagnon & W. Irons (Eds.), *Evolutionary biology and human social behavior* (pp. 454–461). North Scituate, MA: Duxbury Press.

Squires, S. (1997). The market research and product industry discovers anthropology. *Anthropology Newsletter, 38* (4), 31.

Stacey, J. (1990). *Brave new families*. New York: Basic Books.

Star, M. (1997, March). Asian Canada: The economic and cultural energy that Asia immigrants are bringing may turn a green and promising land into the next California. *Transpacific, 68, 40*.

Statistics Canada. (1997, October 14). 1996 Census: Families, households, living arrangements. *The Daily*. Retrieved March 4, 2001, from the World Wide Web: http://www.statcan.ca/ english/Pgdb/People/Families/famil52a .htm.

Statistics Canada. (1997, October 14). 1996 Census: Marital status, common-law unions and families. *The Daily*. Retrieved March 3, 2001, from the World Wide Web: http://www.statcan.ca/ Daily/English/971014/d971014.htm.

Statistics Canada. (1998, May 12). 1996 Census: Sources of income, earnings and total income, and family income. *The Daily*. Retrieved March 5, 2001, from the World Wide Web: http://www .statcan.ca/Daily/English/980512/ d980512.htm.

Statistics Canada. (2001). *Families, households and housing*. Retrieved March 3, 2001, from the World Wide Web: http://www.statcan.ca/english/Pgdb/ People/famili.htm.

Statistics Canada. (2001). *Population by religion, 1981 and 1991 Censuses, Canada*. Retrieved March 25, 2001, from the World Wide Web: http://www.statcan.ca/english/Pgdb/ People/Population/demo32.htm.

Statistics Canada. (2002, November 6). 2001 Census: Marital status, common-law unions and families. *The Daily*. Retrieved September 12, 2003, from the World Wide Web: http://www12.statcan .ca/English/censs01/Products/Analytic/ companion/fam/Canada.cfm.

Statistics Canada. (2003). *Canadian families and households: The proportion of "traditional" families continues to decline*. Retrieved September 18, 2003, from the World Wide Web:

http://www2.statcan.ca/english/census01/Products/Analytic/companion/fam/canada.cfm.

Statistics Canada. (2003, August 11). 2001 Census: Population by mother tongue, provinces and territories. *The Daily.* Retrieved August 11, 2003, from the World Wide Web: http://www.statcan.ca/english/Pgdb/demo18a.htm.

Statistics Canada. (2003, May 13). *2001 Census: Analysis series. Religion in Canada.* Retrieved October 28, 2003, from the World Wide Web: http://www12.statcan.ca/English/census01/products/analytic/companion/rel/pdf/96F0030XIE2001015.pdf.

Stebbins, K. (2001). "Going like gangbusters": Transnational tobacco companies making a killing in South America. *Medical Anthropology Quarterly, 15,* 147–170.

Stewart, D. (1997). Expanding the pie before you divvy it up. *Smithsonian, 28,* 82.

Stiles, D. (1992). The hunter-gatherer "revisionist" debate. *Anthropology Today, 8* (2), 13–17.

Stoler, M. (1982). To tell the truth. *Vermont Visions, 82* (3), 3.

Straughan, B. (1996). The secrets of ancient Tiwanaku are benefitting today's Bolivia. In W.A. Haviland & R.J. Gordon (Eds.), *Talking about people* (2nd ed., pp. 76–78). Mountain View, CA: Mayfield.

Strum, S.C., & Fedigan L. (2000). *Primate encounters: Models of science, gender, and society.* Chicago: University of Chicago Press.

Suárez-Orozoco, M.M., Spindler, G., & Spindler, L. (1994). *The making of psychological anthropology II.* Fort Worth, TX: Harcourt Brace.

Such, P. (1978). Vanished people: The Archau Dorset and Beothuk people of Newfoundland. Cited in Friesen, J.W. (1997). *Rediscovering the First Nations of Canada* (p. 53). Calgary: Detselig.

Susser, I. (1996). Construction of poverty and homelessness in US cities. *Annual Review of Anthropology, 25,* 411–435.

Szathmáry, E.J. (1994) Non-insulin dependent diabetes mellitus among aboriginal North Americans. *Annual Review of Anthropology, 23,* 457–482.

Taussig, M. (1986). *The devil and commodity fetishism in South America.* Chapel Hill, NC: University of North Carolina Press.

The Francophone Connection. (2002). *The Acadians of Nova Scotia.* Retrieved August 13, 2003, from the World Wide Web: http://www.francophonie.gc.ca/communit/ne_shtml.

Thompson, R.H. (1989) *Toronto's Chinatown: The changing social organization of an ethnic community.* New York: AMS Press.

Thorne, B., & Yalom, M. (Eds.). (1982). *Rethinking the family: Some feminist questions.* New York: Longman.

Thornhill, N. (1993). Quoted in W.A. Haviland & R.J. Gordon (Eds.), *Talking about people* (p. 127). Mountain View, CA: Mayfield.

Tian, G. (1999). *Chinese-Canadians, Canadian-Chinese coping and adapting in North America.* Queenston, ON: Edwin Mellen Press.

Together They Stay a World Apart. (1998). *Smithsonian Magazine 29* (8).

Trigger, B. (2003). *Understanding early civilizations: A comparative study.* Cambridge and New York: Cambridge University Press.

Trigger, B.G. (n.d.). *A tribute to Richard F. Salisbury.* The Royal Society of Canada.

Truswell, A.S., Kennelly, B.M., Hansen, J.D.L., & Lee, R.B. (1972). Blood pressures of !Kung Bushmen in northern Botswana. *American Heart Journal, 84,* 5–12.

Truswell, S., & Hansen, J.D.L. (1976). Medical research among the !Kung. In R.B. Lee & I. DeVore (Eds.), *Kalahari hunter-gatherers: Studies of the !Kung San and their neighbors* (pp. 166–194). Cambridge, MA: Harvard University Press.

Turnbull, C.M. (1983). *The human cycle.* New York: Simon & Schuster.

Turner, T. (1991). Major shift in Brazilian Yanomami policy. *Anthropology Newsletter, 32* (5), 1, 46.

University of Manitoba. (1998, November). *Exogamy and incest prohibitions: Brian Schwimmer.* Retrieved April 12, 2001, from the World Wide Web: http://www.umanitoba.ca/anthropology/tutor/marriage/incest.html.

University of Toronto. (1988). *Barbeau, Marius. Barbeau Papers: Northwest Coast Files.* Retrieved August 11, 2003, from the World Wide Web: http://www.library.utoronto.ca/robarts/microtext/collection/pages/barbpaps.html.

University of Toronto. (2001). *A brief history of anthropology at the University of Toronto.* Retrieved June 20, 2001, from the World Wide Web: http://www.chass.utoronto.ca/anthropology/history.htm.

University of Victoria Sexual Assault Centre. (1999, July 13). *Childhood sexual abuse statistics.* Retrieved March 15, 2001, from the World Wide Web: http://www.uvic.ca/~oursac/statistics.htm.

University of Western Ontario, Department of Anthropology. (2001). *Meet Regna Darnell.* Retrieved January 13, 2001, from the World Wide Web: http://publish.uwo.ca/~rdarnell/home.htm.

University of Western Ontario, Regna's C.V. page. (2000). *Regna Darnell curriculum vitae.* Retrieved January 13, 2001, from the World Wide Web: http://publish.uwo.ca/~rdarnell/CV-1.htm.

University of Western Ontario. (1989, February 3). Ukrainians want acknowledgement of injustice: C. Gruske. *The Gazette.* Retrieved March 13, 2001, from the World Wide Web: http://www.infoukes.com/history/internment/booklet02/doc-040.html.

Van Allen, J. (1979). Sitting on a man: Colonialism and the lost political institutions of Igbo women. In S. Tiffany (Ed.), *Women in society* (pp. 163–187). St. Albans, VT: Eden Press.

Van Den Berghe, P.L. (1992). The modern state: Nation builder or nation killer? *International Journal of Group Tensions, 22* (3), 191–207.

Van Esterik, P. (2002). *Risks, rights, and regulation: Communicating about risks and infant feeding.* Penang, Malaysia: World Alliance for Breastfeeding Action (WABA).

Van Gennep, A. (1960). *The rites of passage.* Chicago: University of Chicago Press.

Vayda, A. (Ed.). (1969). *Environment and cultural behavior: Ecological studies in cultural anthropology.* Garden City, NY: Natural History Press.

Villagaria, M.G., Haedrich, R.L., & Fischer, J. (1999). Groundfish assemblages of eastern Canada examined over two decades. In D. Newell & R.E. Ommer (Eds.), *Fishing places, fishing people: Traditions and issues in Canadian small-scale fisheries.* Toronto: University of Toronto Press.

Vitebsky, P. (1995). *The shaman: Voyages of the soul, trance, ecstasy, and healing from Siberia to the Amazon.* Boston: Little, Brown

Voget, F.W. (1975). *A history of ethnology.* New York; Holt, Rinehart and Winston.

Vogt, E.Z. (1990). *The Zinacantecos of Mexico: A modern Maya way of life* (2nd ed.). Fort Worth, TX: Holt, Rinehart and Winston.

Waldram, J.B., Herring, A., & Kue Young, T. (1995). *Aboriginal health in Canada: Historical, cultural and epidemiological perspectives.* Toronto: University of Toronto Press.

Walker, W. (2002). *Neo-pagan, heathen and reconstructionist religions.* Retrieved October 23, 2003, from the World Wide

Web: http://www.witchvox.com/basics/intro.html.

Wallace, A.F.C. (1966). *Religion: An anthropological view*. New York: Random House.

Wallace, A.F.C. (1970). *Culture and personality* (2nd ed.). New York: Random House.

Ward, D. (1995). *The people: A historical guide to the First Nations of Alberta, Saskatchewan, and Manitoba*. Saskatoon: Fifth House.

Watkins, M. (Ed.). (1977). *Dene Nation: The colony within*. Toronto: University of Toronto Press.

Wattenberg, B.J. (1997, November 23). The population explosion is over. *The New York Times Magazine*, 60.

Weatherford, J. (1988). *Indian givers: How the Indians of the Americas transformed the New World*. New York: Ballantine.

Weiner, A.B. (1988). *The Trobrianders of Papua New Guinea*. New York: Holt, Rinehart and Winston.

Weitz, R. (2000). What price independence? Social relations to lesbians, spinsters, widows, and nuns. In E. Ashton-Jones, G.A. Olson, & M.G. Perry (Eds.), *The gender reader*. Needham Heights, MA: Allyn and Bacon.

Wekker, G. (1999). What's identity got to do with it? Rethinking identity in light of the *mati* work in Suriname. In E. Blackwood & S.E. Wieringa (Eds.), *Female desires: Same-sex relations and transgender practices across cultures*. New York: Columbia University Press.

Welcome to Nunavut. (n.d.). Retrieved April 7, 2001, from the World Wide Web: http://www.polarnet.ca/polarnet/nunavut.htm.

Werner, D. (1990). *Amazon journey*. Englewood Cliffs, NJ: Prentice-Hall.

White, D.R. (1988). Rethinking polygyny: Co-wives, codes and cultural systems. *Current Anthropology, 29*, 529–572.

Whitehead, N., & Ferguson, R.B. (Eds.). (1992). *War in the tribal zone*. Santa Fe: School of American Research Press.

Whitehead, N.L., & Ferguson, R.B. (1993, November 10). Deceptive stereotypes about tribal warfare. *Chronicle of Higher Education*, A48.

Whitson, D. (1990). Sport in the social construction of masculinity. In M.A. Messner & D.F. Sabo (Eds.), *Sport, men and the gender order: Critical feminist perspectives*. Champaign, IL: Human Kinetics Books.

Wickwire, W. (1993, Fall). Women in ethnography: The research of James A.

Teit. *American Society for Ethnohistory, 40* (4), 539–567.

Williams, A.M. (1996). *Sex, drugs and HIV: A sociocultural analysis of two groups of gay and bisexual male substance users who practice unprotected sex*. Unpublished manuscript.

Williamson, R.K. (1995). The blessed curse: Spirituality and sexual difference as viewed by Euro-American and Native American cultures. *The College News, 17* (4).

Wolf, M. (1972). *Women and the family in rural Taiwan*. Stanford, CA: Stanford University Press.

Wolpoff, M. (1996). *Australopithecus*: A new look at an old ancestor. *General Anthropology, 3* (1), 2.

Woolfson, P. (1972). Language, thought, and culture. In V.P. Clark, P.A. Escholz, & A.F. Rosa (Eds.), *Language*. New York: St. Martin's Press.

Young Alberta Book Society. (1998). *Owen Beattie*. Retrieved October 16, 2000, from the World Wide Web: http://www.culturenet.ucalgary.ca/yabs/beattieo.html.

Young, A. (1995). *Harmony of illusions: Inventing post-traumatic stress disorder*. Princeton: Princeton University Press.

INDEX

The Abenaki. *See* Western Abenaki people

The Abkhasians of Georgia, 158

Aboriginal peoples (the Americas). *See also* First Nations peoples
adult-onset diabetes, 418–419
fishing, 164
language, diversity of, 83–84
language conservation, 103–105
Native Americans, federal recognition for, 274–275
"pre-contact" period, 10
as term, 7

Aboriginal rights, 479

Aborigines (Australia)
Arnhem Land study, 27
cousin marriage, 223–224
language, near extinction of, 105
male initiation rites, 366–367
music, 403–404
social customs, and exchange, 165

Abu-Lughod, L., 334–336

Abwunza, Judith, 22

The Acadians, 40, 105

Acculturation, **459–460**

Acheulian tradition, **76–77**

Achieved status, **302**

Adaptation, 47–52
anatomical adaptation, 63–66
anthropogenesis, 125
behaviour, 66–68
cultural changes, 51–52
described, 47–51, 124
evolution through, 62–63
food-foraging adaptation, 128–138
functions of culture, 51
historical perspective, 127
horticulture, 124
intensive agriculture, 140, 143–147
meaning of, 62
mechanized agriculture, 147–148
natural selection, 62
pastoralism, 140–143
patterns of subsistence, 124
process of, 124–128
relativity of, 51
stability, periods of, 127–128

Adelson, Naomi, 445

Adjudication, **340**

Adolescent sexuality, 198, 199, 200

The Afar people, 161

Affinal kin, **205**

Africa
droughts in, 52
hunger in, 480

African-Americans
sickle-cell anemia, 419
Vernacular English, 110–114

Age, and cultural variations, 37–39

Age division of labour, 158–160

Age grade, **293**

Age-grade organization, 324

Age grouping, 291–293

Agnatic descent, 265–266

Agricultural development, 467

Agriculture
development and applied anthropology, 144
intensive agriculture. *See* Intensive agriculture
mechanized agriculture, 147–148

AIDS, 201–203

Alcohol, and health, 439–442

Alternative genders, 199–200

Ambilineal descent, **270**

Ambilocal residence, **248**

American Sign Language, 92, 116

Anatomical adaptation, 63–65

Anatomically modern peoples, 82–86

Ancestral spirits, 359–360

Androcentric bias, 26, 47. *See also* Gender perspectives

Animal communication, 92, 116

Animatism, 360–362, **361**

Animism, **360**

Anthropogenesis, **125**

Anthropology, **4**
applied anthropology. *See* Applied anthropology
archeology, 7, 8–11
biological anthropology, 7, 8
Canadian anthropology, 5–6
contemporary life, relevance in, 30
cultural anthropology. *See* Sociocultural anthropology
development of, 4–7
as discipline, 7–24
economic anthropology, 154–157
educator, role as, 30
ethical issues, 29–30
forensic anthropology, 8, 9
of gender, 26
and the humanities, 28
linguistic anthropology, 7, 11
medical anthropology. *See* Medical anthropology
and other disciplines, 28–29
vs. other social sciences, 25–27
paleoanthropology, 8
primatology, 8
and science, 24–28
sociocultural anthropology. *See* Sociocultural anthropology
subfields of, 8f
terminology, 6–7

Apartheid, 303, 478

Applied anthropology, **12**
aboriginal healing in Canadian prisons, 374–375
aboriginal rights in Canada, 479
agricultural development, 144
AIDS/HIV, 201–203
Berger report, 301–302
business world, 190–191
cultural heritages, protection of, 390

described, 7, 12
and directed change, 462–464
dispute resolution, 341
ethnographic film, 104
forensic anthropology, 9
James Bay Cree and Northern Quebec Agreement, 38
Native Americans, federal recognition for, 274–275
public health surveillance, in First Nations communities, 254
social impact assessment, 301–302
stone tools for modern surgeons, 84
Vancouver's Downtown Eastside, 438
visual anthropology, 104

The Arapesh, 342

Arcand, Bernand, 6

Archeology, 7, 8–11, 27

Armelagos, George, 429

Aroostook Mi'kmaqs, 274–275

Arranged marriages, 218–223

Artistic expression, 386

Arts
anthropological study of, 389
body art, 409–412
censorship, 412
definition, difficulty of, 388
fine art *vs.* folk art, 387
music, 400–404
Upper Paleolithic culture, 82–83
verbal arts, 389–395
visual art, 404–409

Asch, Michael, 301

Ascribed status, **303**

Assembly of First Nations, 105

The Assiniboine, 174

Association organization, 324

Athapaskan-speaking peoples, 301–302

Australopithecus, **71**–72, 72f

Avunculocal residence, **249**

Awlad 'Ali Bedouin, 394–395

The Aymara, 144

The Aztecs, 54, 145–147, 181, 347

Bach, Johann Sebastian, 387–388

Baer, Hans, 426

The Bakhtiari, 141–143

Balanced reciprocity, **165**

Balikci, Asen, 104

Baltic reconstructionist religions, 377

Band, **318**

Band organization, 318–320, 429

Banting, Sir Frederick, 418

Bantu farmers, 129–130

Barbeau, Marius, 6, 21, 46

Barber, Benjamin, 471–472

Barnett, Steve, 183n

Barter, 174–175

Basic needs, 124

Basow, Susan, 241

The Basutos, 371

Beach, Frank A., 200
Beattie, Owen, 9
The Bedouin, 334–336, 394–395
Behaviour, adaptation through, 66–68
The Bella Coola, 270
The Beothuk, extinction of, 460
Berdache, 199–200
Berger report, 301–302
Best, Charles, 418
Bezruchka, Stephen, 436–437
Bias
    androcentric bias, 26, 47. *See also*
        Gender perspectives
    ethnocentrism, 54
    First Nations people, early accounts
        of, 24
    gender bias. *See* Gender perspectives
    in medicine, 420
Bibeau, Gilles, 445
Biesele, Megan, 93n
Bilateral descent, 273–276
Bilingualism, 105, 112–114
Binder, Nick, 97n
Biocultural approach, **418**–420
Biological anthropology, 7, **8**
"Biological avoidance" theory, 208,
    209
Biomedical approach, 418–420, 431
Biomedicine, contemporary, 443–446
Black English, 110–114
The Blackfoot
    band membership, fluidity of, 133
    division of labour, 134–135
    ecosystem, adaptation to, 129
    horses, and egalitarianism, 138
    informal leadership, 321
    mobility, 131
    Napi, the trickster, 378
    polygyny, 215–216
    pre-contact culture, 126n
"Blood" ties, 234, 235
Boas, Franz, 13, 30, 104, 298, 424
Boddy, Janice, 206, 207, 214, 446
Body adornment, 411–412
Body art
    body adornment, 411–412
    body painting, 409–410
    described, 409
    forms of, 409
    tattooing, 410–411
Body language. *See* Gesture-call system
Body painting, 409–410
Body piercing, 411–412
Borgoras, Waldemar, 423
Borrowing of cultural elements,
    456–457
Boserup, Ester, 189
Bossen, Laurel, 189–190, 243
Bound morpheme, **95**
Boyle, David, 6
Brahmins, 303, 305
The brain
    hominine, 71
    Homo erectus, 76
    Homo habilis, 73, 74
    Neanderthals, 80
    primates, 65
    Sahelanthropus tchadenisis, 70

toolmaking, impact of, 76
    Upper Paleolithic peoples, 82
Brant, Joseph, 329n
Brazil, extinction in, 459–460
Breaking, 100
Breton, Yvan, 21
Bride-price, **225**
Bride service, **225**
Briggs, Jean, 240
Brooks, Geraldine, 307
Bullock, Katherine, 308
Business world, 186–191

Canada. *See also* North America
    aboriginal rights, 479
    aging population in, 484–485
    arranged marriages, 218
    the Beothuk, extinction of, 460
    bilingualism in, 105
    biomedicine, contemporary,
        443–446
    Chinese-Canadians. *See* Chinese-
        Canadians
    common-interest associations, diver-
        sity of, 294
    common-law marriages, 211
    cultural heritage, protection of, 386
    distinct cultures in, 37
    divorce in, 217
    ethnic food systems, 186
    extended families, 245–246
    family patterns in, 235
    Famous Five, 42
    fictive kinship, 264
    fisheries, and ecological crises,
        163–164
    flea markets, 182–183
    French Canadians. *See* Quebec
    French immersion programs, 106
    gender wage gap, 306–307
    Group of Seven, 407–408
    immigration, history of, 309
    international peacekeeping role,
        345–346
    medical anthropology in, 445–446
    minority women in politics, 330
    multicultural society, 263–264
    pluralistic nature of society, 41, 308
    political system, inequality within,
        330
    Prairies, folk drama in, 396–399
    racial discrimination, 299
    religious affiliation statistics, 356
    reproductive rights, 465
    seniors in, 292–293
    social class, 302–304
    subcultures in, 41
    Ukrainians in, 309
    urban kinship systems, 263–264
    visual art in, 406–409
    women's movement, 42–43
Canadian anthropology, development
    of, 5–6
Canadian Charter of Rights and
    Freedoms, 105
Canadian family farm, 147–148, 158
Cannibalism, 369
Cargo cults, 379

Carrying capacity, **132**
Caste, **303**, 305
Cave art, 83
Censorship of the arts, 412
Centralized political systems
    chiefdoms, 324–326
    coercion, reliance on, 346
    described, 324
    state systems, 326–328
    trial by ordeal, 340–341
Ceremonies, 366–370
Chador, 307–308
Change. *See* Cultural change
Charest, Paul, 21
The Chenchu, 226
The Cheyenne, 130, 338–339
Chiefdoms, **324**–326, 429–430
Childrearing. *See also* Children
    enculturation process, 240
    food-foraging peoples, 133, 136
    the Inuit of Baffin Island, 240
Children
    as casualties of war, 342
    child labour, 160
    eldercare and, 252
    enculturation, 240
    in industrial societies, 159–160
    infant contact, 240
    the Ju/'hoansi, 158
    legitimacy, 205
    in nonindustrial cultures, 159
    nursing of, 240
    nurturance of, in families, 239–240
    as resource, 484
    self-awareness, development of, 240
Chimpanzees
    behaviour, 66–68
    food sharing, 75
    language, 92, 116
    siblings, avoidance of breeding
        with, 208
China
    abduction and sale of women, 466
    ancestral spirits, 359–360
    declining birth rates, 484
    dialects in, 110
    one-child policy, 252
    refugees from, 485
    sisterhood movements, and homo-
        sexuality, 200
    women, and economic development,
        190
    women, study of, 243
Chinese-Canadians
    contemporary kinship, 278–279
    contributions to Canadian economy,
        183–184
    family dynamics, changing,
        245–246
    immigration, history of, 278
    racial discrimination, 299–302
Chinese Immigration Act, 279, 300
Chinese Revolution, 466
The Chipewyan, 209
Chrétien, Jean, 213
The Cinta-Larga, 460
Cities, rise of, 430–431
Civil society, 468

Clan, 272
Clan mothers, 269
Classical Arabic, 304
Closed-class systems, 305
Clovis peoples, 84, 86
Co-sleeping, 23
Code switching, 115
Codrington, R.H., 361
Cognatic descent, 270
Cohen, Mark, 429
Cohen, Yehudi, 210
Common-interest associations, 293
    diversity of, 294
    kinds of, 294–295
    men's associations, 294–295
    as political system, 324
    women's associations, 294–295
Common-law marriages, 211
Communes, 246–247
Communication. See Language
Conflict theory of stratification, 297
Conjugal bond, 205
Conjugal family, 234–235
Consanguine family, 234, 235
Consensus, 319
Conspicuous consumption, 177–179
Constitution Act (1982), 327
Consumption, 184
    behaviour, 185
    food taboos, 185
    and globalization, 187
    industrial societies, 184
    ritual, 185–186
    social interaction, 186
Contagious magic, 371
Control
    cultural control, 332
    externalized controls, 332–336
    and gender inequality, 306
    over homosexuality, 200–203
    internalized controls, 332
    of land, 162
    law, 333
    political organizations, 331–337
    population control, 483–485
    sanctions, 332–333
    over sexual relations, 200
    social control, 332, 337–342
    witchcraft, 333–336, 373
Conventional gestures, 98
Cooperation explanation, 210
Cooperative work groups, 160–161
Core vocabulary, 102
Corin, Ellen, 445
Corporate lineage, 271
Crabtree, Don, 84
Craft specialization, 161
The Cree, 132, 174, 324, 327, 445
Creole language, 115
Crime, 339–342
Criminal justice system, 337
Critical medical anthropology, 418
    alcohol, 439–442
    capitalist system, 431–432
    chiefdoms, 429–430
    cities, rise of, 430–431
    culture, historical study of health of,
        427–432

described, 426–427
environmental health, 442–443
food-foraging societies, 428
homelessness, 437–439
human political development, stages
    of, 427–428
Industrial Revolution, 431–432
modernity, health outcomes of,
    432–443
poverty, 436–439
state societies, 430–431
tobacco, 439–442
tribal societies, 429–430
CRM archeology, 12
Cross-cultural comparisons, 23–24
The Crow, 126n, 165, 295, 369
Crow system, 281–282
Crowshoe, Reggie, 363n
Cruikshank, Julie, 401
Csonka, Yvon, 21–22
Culhane, Dara, 438, 438n
Cults, 379–380
Cultural anthropology. See
    Sociocultural anthropology
Cultural change
    acculturation, 456–460
    cultural loss, 457–459
    described, 51–52
    diffusion, 456–457
    directed change, 462–464
    forcible change, 459–464
    genocide, 460–461
    innovation, 454–455
    mechanisms of change, 454–459
    modernization, 467–471
    rebellion, 464–466
    and religion, 378–380
    revitalization movements, 464
    revolution, 464–466
Cultural control, 332
Cultural future
    apathy, 486
    cultural pluralism, 476–477
    ethnic resurgence, 476
    ethnocentrism, 478
    flaws with future-oriented literature,
        471
    global apartheid, 478
    multinational corporations, 473–476
    one-world culture, prospect of,
        471–472
    structural violence. See Structural
        violence
Cultural heritage, 386, 390
Cultural interpretive approach, 418
    body politic, 421
    described, 420
    mind-body dualism, 420–421
    shamanism, 422–426
    social body, 421
    "three bodies" paradigm, 420–422
Cultural loss, 457–459
Cultural pluralism, 476–477
Cultural relativism, 54–55
Cultural resource management
    (CRM), 12
Cultural variations
    described, 37–39

exogamy, 210
gay and lesbian sexuality, control
    over, 200–203
sexuality, 199
Culture, 36
    and adaptation, 47–52
    and change, 51–52
    characteristics of, 36–45
    communication systems, depend-
        ence on, 93
    concept of, 36
    dual sex, 158
    and economics, 186–190
    enculturation, 43–44
    ethnocentrism, 54
    evaluation of, 53–56
    and fieldwork, 46–47
    flexible/integrated, 158
    and food, 43
    functions of, 51
    health of, historical study, 427–432
    and the individual, 52–53
    integration of, 44–45
    language. See Language
    learned, 43–44
    meat eating, 73–76
    sexually segregated, 158
    shared ideals, values and standards,
        36–43
    and society, 37, 52–53
    stone toolmaking, 73–75, 76–77
    subculture, 39–41
    success of, measurement, 55–56
    symbols, basis in, 44
    uniqueness of, 62
Culture bound, 12
Culture shock, 36
The Cuna Indians, 425

Dahomey (West Africa), 158
Daly, Mary, 207
Damas, David, 136–137
The Dane-zaa, 22
Darnell, Regna, 109
De Waal, A., 310–312
Death penalty, 54
The Dene, 301–302, 320
Density of social relations, 132
Descent groups, 264
    ambilineal descent, 270
    bilateral descent, 273–276
    clan, 272
    described, 264
    development of, 276–278
    double descent, 269
    forms and functions of, 271–278
    kindred, 273–276
    lineage, 271–272
    matrilineal descent, 264–265,
        268–269
    moiety, 273
    patrilineal descent, 264, 265–266
    phratry, 272–273
    totems, 272
    unilineal descent, 264–269
Descriptive linguistics, 11, 100
Descriptive system, 282, 283f

Developing world, and modernization, 469–470
Dialects, **110–115**
Diffusion, **456–457**
The Dinka, 323
Directed change, 462–464
Discontent, culture of, 485–486
Diseases of civilization, **432**
Displacement, **116,** 485
Dispute resolution, 340–341
Distribution and exchange
   market exchange, 180–183
   modes of distribution, 164
   reciprocity, 164–173
   redistribution, 176–180
   social customs, role of, 165
Divination, **373**
Division of labour
   age division of labour, 158–160
   Canadian family farms, 148, 158
   food-foraging societies, 133–136
   sexual division of labour, 157–158
Divorce, 217, 226–227, 252, 253
Dolphins, and language, 92
Dorset culture, 408–409
Dossa, Parin, 21, 277
Double descent, **269**
Dowry, **225**
Druidism, 377
Dual sex cultures, 158
Dvorak, August, 455
Dvorak keyboard, 455, 456f

East Asian financial crisis, 480
Eaton, Boyd, 428
Ebonics, 110–114
Ecological crises, 163–164
Economic anthropology, 154–157
Economic development, 186, 189–190
Economic systems, **154**
   consumption, 184–186
   descent system, relationship with, 264–265
   distribution and exchange. *See* Distribution and exchange
   informal economy, 183
   money, 181–182
   resources, 157–164
   Trobriand Islanders, 154–156
Economics
   and business world, 186–190
   cross-cultural misunderstandings, 187
   and culture, 186–190
   global economy, 187–188
Ecosystem, **126,** 129
Edwards, Henrietta Muir, 42
Efrat, Barbara, 105
Egalitarian cultures, 137–138, **297,** 319
Ego-oriented groups, 273–276
Egypt, official language of, 304
Ehrenreich, Barbara, 440
Eisenberg, Leon, 421
Elders, 291–292
Electra complex, 208
Enculturation, 26, **43–44,** 240
Endogamy, **209–210**

English, Deirdre, 440
Environmental health, 442–443, 482–483
Environmental justice, **442–443**
Errano, Andreas, 412
Esenc, Tefvik, 106
Eskimo system, **279–280**
The Etero, 199
Ethical issues, 29–30
Ethnic minorities, and language retention, 105
Ethnic resurgence, 476
Ethnic stratification, 308–310
Ethnicity, **308**
Ethnocentrism, **54,** 154, 478
Ethnography, **13**
   biomedicine, study of, 443–444
   contemporary domestic issues, focus on, 21
   fieldwork, importance of, 14–21
   fieldwork, new directions in, 22–23
   film, 104
   holistic perspective, 14
   informants, 14
   natural science techniques, 25
   participant observation, 13–14
   postmodernist perspective, 22
   result of fieldwork, 27
Ethnohistory, **13,** 24
Ethnolinguistics, **107–115**
Ethnology, **13,** 23–24
Ethnomusicology, **400**
Europe
   family patterns, 235–236
   intellectual tradition in 19th century, 355
   witches, execution of, 375
European Economic Union (EEU), 187
Europeans
   Crusades, 344
   derogatory connotations in names, 6–7
   "savage" or "barbarian," application of label, 4–5, 39–40
The Evenk, 423
Exchange. *See* Distribution and exchange
Exogamy, 46–47, **209–210,** 248, 272
Exploitative worldview, **343**
Extended family, **245–247,** 251–252, 263
Extinction, 459–460

"Face," concept of, 251, 267
Family, **234**
   communes, 246–247
   conjugal family, 234–235
   consanguine family, 234, 235
   definitions of, 234–236
   economic cooperation, 241–242
   extended family, 245–247, 251–252, 263
   female-headed families, 253–255
   forms of, 244–247
   functions of, 239–242
   historical and cross-cultural studies of, 235
   and households, 242–244

   nuclear family, 235, 244–245, 252, 263
   nurturance of children, 239–240
   polyandrous family, 235
   polygynous family, 235, 250–251
   residence patterns, 248–250
   same-sex families, 247
   universality of, 236
Family farms, 148, 158
Family organization problems
   extended families, 251–252
   female-headed families, 253–255
   nuclear families, 252
   polygamous families, 250–251
Farmer, Paul, 202
Fedigan, Linda, 8, 74
Feit, Harvey A., 38
Female circumcision, 206–207
Female-headed families, 217, 253–255
Feudal land system, 162
Fictive kinship, **264**
Fieldwork
   culture, study of, 46–47
   ethnographic. *See* Ethnography
   physical bias in, 74
Fire, use of, 77–78, 80
Firewalking, 424
First Nations peoples. *See also*
   Aboriginal peoples (the Americas);
   specific groups
   aboriginal rights, 479
   anthropologists and advocacy, 6
   artwork, 406, 408–409
   and assimilation, 459
   biases in early accounts, 24
   common-interest associations, 295
   crafts, 161
   culture, disruption of, 52
   dual sex culture, 158
   health and illness, 445
   informal leadership, 320
   old age pensions, impact of, 14–21
   overrepresentation in justice system, 337
   polygyny among, 215–216
   potlatch, 178–180
   public health surveillance, 254
   racial discrimination, 299
   recognition of, 326–327
   residential schools, 105, 459
   sentencing circles, 337
   social groups, variations in size and composition of, 131–132
   sun dance, 367–369
   traditional healing in Canadian prisons, 374–375
   two-spirits, 199–200
   women-headed households, 217
Fisheries, and ecological crises, 163–164
Fission, **272**
Flea markets, 182–183
Fleising, Usher, 446
Flexible/integrated cultures, 158
Folk medicine, 431
Folklore, **389**
Folkloristics, **389**
Fontaine, Phil, 321n

Food
    borrowed from First Nations peoples, 457
    distribution of, and world hunger, 480–481
    manners, differences in, 185
    as ritual, 185–186
    sharing of, 75, 136–137
    as social interaction, 186
    taboos, 185
Food-foraging societies
    animism, 360
    camp, importance of, 136
    camp organization, 132–133
    characteristics of, 130–138
    childrearing, 133, 136
    described, 129
    division of labour, 133–136
    ecosystem, adaptation to, 129
    egalitarian society, 137–138
    food sharing, 136–137
    gender autonomy, 135
    generalized exchange, 138
    health, 428
    interaction with non-foraging neighbours, 129–130
    land, control of, 162
    long-term adjustments to resources, 133
    marriage practices, variability in, 135
    mobility, 130–132
    modern food foragers, 129–130
    older women, 158–159
    as "original affluent society," 129
    population size, regulation of, 133
    religion, 357
    silent trade, 175
    social density, 132–133
    specialist "commercial" hunter-gatherers, 130
    technology, 130–132
    territory, concept of, 137
    tools, 163
    war, lack of, 342
Food-producing societies
    early plant and animal domestication, 138f
    early state-level societies, 143n
    health, 429–430
    intensive agriculture, 143–147
    mechanized agriculture, 147–148
    pastoralism, 140–143
    permanent settlements, development of, 139–140
    silent trade, 175
    swidden farming, 139–140
    urbanization, 145
    warfare and, 342
Foraging. See Food-foraging societies
Forcible change, 459–464
Ford, Clellans, 200
Forensic anthropology, 8, 9
Form classes, 95
Formal sanctions, 333
Fossey, Dian, 8, 69, 74
Foucault, Michel, 254
Frame substitution, 95

Franklin Expedition, 9
Fraternal polyandry, 251
Frazer, Sir James George, 370–371
Free morphemes, 95
French Canadians. See Quebec
French Creole, 115
French-English bilingualism, 105
Freud, Sigmund, 208
Frye, Marilyn, 97
Functionalist theory of stratification, 297
Fundamentalist religions, 355–356

Galdikas, Biruté, 8, 69, 74
Garbage Project (University of Arizona), 10–11, 10n, 47
Garcia, Juan, 439–441
Gardner, Allen, 116
Gardner, Beatrice, 116
Gardner, Gerald, 375–376
Gay relations. See Homosexuality
Gender, 26
    and common-interest associations, 294–295
    cultural variations, 37
    gender signals, differences in, 96–97
    grouping by, 290–291
    inequality, 306–307
    and political leadership, 328–331
    wage gap, 306–307
Gender perspectives
    anthropology of gender, 26
    Canadian women's movement, 42–43
    economic development, and women, 189–190
    female genital mutilation (FGM), 206–207
    foraging groups, gender autonomy in, 135
    health, and women, 440–441
    kinkeepers, 270
    language, 111
    manhood, universal imagery of, 405
    menstrual taboo, 368
    minority women in Canadian politics, 330
    "motherhood mandate," 241
    primatology, gender bias in, 74
    purdah, 307–308
    reproductive rights in Canada, 465
Gender stratification, 306–307
Generalized reciprocity, 165
Genetic counselling, 444
Genetic explanation (incest taboo), 208, 209
Genocide, 310–312, 460–461
Gesture-call system
    conventional gestures, 98
    cultural similarities and variations, 98
    described, 96
    gestures of appreciation of food, 185
    kinesics, 96–98
    paralanguage, 99–100
    proxemics, 99
    spoken language, shift to, 117

    touch, 98
Global apartheid, 478
Global warming, 482
Globalization, 187–188
Glottochronology, 102
Gods and goddesses, 358
Goldschmidt, Walter, 55
Goodall, Jane, 8, 66, 69, 74
Gordon, Robert, 14
Gould, Stephen Jay, 80, 458–459
Graffiti, 404–406
Graham, Janice, 446
Grammar, 95
Gramsci, Antonio, 468
Greenhouse effect, 482
Group marriage, 216
Group membership, and linguistic change, 102
Group of Seven, 407–408
Groups. See Social organization
Guenther, Mathias, 362
Guided imagery, 425
The Gusii, 226

The Hadza, 130, 136, 158–159
The Haida, 223–224, 272
Hale, Horatio, 11
Hall, Edward, 187
Hall, Mildred, 187
Hardenbergh, Firmon, 84
Hauch, Christopher, 165, 166–173
Haviland, William A., 130n
Hawaiian system, 280–281
The Hawazama, 250
Hawkes, Rev. Brent, 212–213
Healing, 364–365, 374–375, 424–426
Health. See also Medical anthropology
    alcohol, 439–442
    capitalist system, 431–432
    chiefdoms, 429–430
    cities, rise of, 430–431
    contemporary biomedicine, 443–446
    and culture through history, 427–432
    diseases of civilization, 432
    environmental health, 442–443
    fetal alcohol syndrome (FAS), 420
    folk medicine, 431
    in food-foraging societies, 428
    genetic counselling, 444
    guided imagery, 425
    and homelessness, 437–439
    of indigenous minorities, 433–434
    Industrial Revolution, 431–432
    managed health care, 444
    medical specialists, emergence of, 430
    modernity, outcomes of, 432–443
    and pollution, 482
    and poverty, 436–439
    and religion, 431
    rudimentary public health measures, 430
    and social class, 437
    and social safety net, 437
    and social welfare, 431–432

state societies, 430–431
tobacco, 439–442
tribal societies, 429–430
and women, 440–441
Health Olympics, 436–437
Hedican, Edward J., 479
Hegemony, 468
Heller, Monica, 103, 112–114
Henry, Jules, 217
The Hidatsa, 126n
Hindu caste system, 303, 305
Historic archaeologists, **10**
Historical linguistics, 100–102
Historical linguists, **11**
History, rewriting of, 392–393
HIV, 201–203
Hoebel, E. Adamson, 338
Holism, 23
Holistic perspective, **14**
Holocaust, 461
Hominid family, 70
Hominines, **70**
   Ardipithecus, 70
   Australopithecus, 71–72, 72f
   earliest fossils, 71f
   erect bipedal posture, 71
   first hominines, 70–73
   Homo erectus, 76–79
   Homo habilis, 73–76
   Homo sapiens. See Homo sapiens
   intelligence, 71
   Sahelanthropus tchadenisis, 70
   size, 71
Homo erectus, **76**–79
Homo habilis, **73**–76
Homo sapiens, **79**
   anatomically modern peoples,
      82–86
   archaic *Homo sapiens,* 79–81
   Mousterian tools, 80–81
   the Neanderthals, 80–81
   Solo River skulls, 79–80
   Upper Paleolithic peoples, 82–86
Homosexuality
   control over, 200–203
   cross-cultural understanding of,
      199–200
   recognition of, 200–203
   same-sex families, 247
   same-sex marriages, 211–213
"Honour," concept of, 251
Hoodfar, Homa, 189
The Hopi, 140, 226, 342
Horticulture, **124**
   land, control of, 162
   matrilineal descent, 264
   slash-and-burn, 125, 139–140
   tools, 163
Household, **242**–244
Housework, 23
Human ancestors
   Eve hypothesis, 81
   evidence of, 69–70
   fire, 77–78
   first hominines, 70–73
   food-foraging peoples, 76
   Homo erectus, 76–79
   Homo habilis, 73–76

Homo sapiens. See Homo sapiens
   hunting, 78
   meat eating, significance of, 73–76
   multiregional hypothesis, 81
   scavengers for food, 75
   stone toolmaking, significance of,
      73–75, 76–77
   transitional characteristics, 79
Human culture. *See* Culture
Human Relations Area Files (HRAF),
   23–24
Human rights, and cultural relativism,
   54–55
Human sexuality. *See* Sex and sexuality
Humanistic side of anthropology, 28
Humanity's future. *See* Cultural future
Humans
   closest living relatives of, 69
   first primates, evolutionary develop-
      ment of, 62–63
   Primate Order, 62
   roots of, 62
   stereoscopic colour vision, 64
Hunger, 480–482
Hunter-gatherers. *See* Food-foraging
   societies
The Huron, 246, 290
The Hutterites, 39
The Hutu, 310–312, 461

The Ibibio, 371–372
The Igbo, 329–331
Imitative magic, **371**
Immigrants and immigration
   Asian migration, 184
   Canadian immigration, history of,
      309
   Chinese-Canadian contributions to
      Canadian economy, 183–184
   Chinese immigration, history of,
      278
   culture shock, **36**–37
   kinship ties, 264
The Inca, 176–177
Incest taboo, **205**
   exceptions, among royal families,
      210
   genetic explanation, 208, 209
   instinct explanation, 207
   psychoanalytic explanations, 207
   social explanation, 208
Incorporation, **366**
Independence, struggles for, 464–466,
   472
India
   arranged marriages in, 218–223
   caste system in, 303, 305
   motifs in European and African
      tales, 394
Indigenous peoples. *See also*
   Aboriginal peoples (the Americas)
   extinction, intended, 459–460
   as "fourth world," 433–434
   self-determination movements, 476
Individuals, and culture, 52–53
Indo-European language family,
   100–101, 101f

Industrial Revolution, and health,
   431–432
Industrial societies. *See also* North
   America
   children, 159–160
   conspicuous consumption, 178
   consumption, 184
   craft specialization, 161
   kindred, 276
   kinship, 263
   land, control of, 162
Industrialization, 431, 467
Inequality. *See* Social inequality; Social
   stratification
Infibulation, 206
Informal economy, **183**
Informal sanctions, 333
Informants, **14**
Innovation, 454–455
Instinct explanation (incest taboo),
   207
Institutionalized racism, **300**
Integration, 44–45
Integrative mechanisms, **467**–468
Intensive agriculture, **140**
   Aztec city life, 145–147
   fossil fuel use, 481
   land, control of, 162
   and nonindustrial cities, 143–147
   patrilineal descent, 264
Internalized controls, 332
International affairs, 342–346
International Monetary Fund
   "reforms," 254–255
The Inuit
   advanced age in, 291
   artwork, 408–409
   body piercing, 411
   childrearing practices, on Baffin
      Island, 240
   dispute settlement, 337
   infant contact, 240
   nuclear family, 244–245
   Nunavut, 327, 473
   Pelly Bay Netsilingmiut Inuit, 104
   recognition of, 327
   self-government and, 327
   tattooing, 410
   women and decision making, 135
The Iroquois
   clans, and legal fiction, 276–278
   extended families, 246
   gender division of labour, 290
   leadership, and men, 328–329
   matrilineal clans, 269
   matrilocal residence, 248
   moieties, interdependence between,
      273
   origin myth, 354
   warfare, 344
Iroquois system, **281**
Isolated nuclear family structure, 263
Israeli kibbutz, 208–209

James Bay Cree and Northern Quebec
   Agreement, 38
Japan, and Health Olympics, 437
Japanese Edo Period tattoos, 411

Jefremovas, Vilia, 189
Jenness, Diamond, 6
Johnson, Leslie Main, 22
Joralemon, Donald, 420
The Ju/'hoansi
 adolescent sexuality, 199
 affluence, 129
 age division of labour, 158
 average workweek, 129
 "Eating Christmas in the Kalahari"
  (Lee), 15–20
 fieldwork among, 131
 food sharing, 136
 generalized exchange, 138
 healing, 364–365, 424
 health and disease, 434–436
 infant contact, 240
 informal leadership, 319–320
 interaction with neighbours,
  129–130
 land, control of, 162
 marriage practices, 135
 meaning of name, 53
 mongongo nut, dependence on,
  130–131
 music, 402
 names for, 7
 social density, fluctuations in,
  132–133
 tools, exchange of, 163
 trance dances, 364
 trickster, 362–363
 war, lack of, 342
 water, availability of, 131
 women's work, 134, 160
Judd, Ellen, 190

Kane, Paul, 407
The Kapauku Papuans (New Guinea),
 44–45, 213, 215, 321–322, 339, 346
The Kaska, 368
The Kayapó, 411, 460
Kemetism, 377
Kendall, Lauren, 376
Kenyatta, Jomo, 160
Kindred, **273–276**
Kinesics, **96–98**
Kinkeepers, 270
Kinship, **262**
 affinal kin, 205
 conjugal bond, 205
 contemporary Chinese-Canadian
  kinship, 278–279
 descent groups. *See* Descent groups
 effective kin, 263
 fictive kinship, 264
 intimate kin, 263
 kindred, 273–276
 nominal kin, 262–263
 role of, 262–263
 sanguineal kin, 205
 study of, 263
 terms, 108–109
 urban kinship systems in Canada,
  263–264
Kinship organization, 323
Kinship terminologies
 Crow system, 281–282

 described, 279
 Eskimo system, 279–280
 Hawaiian system, 280–281
 Iroquois system, 281
 Omaha system, 282, 283f
 Sudanese (descriptive) system, 282,
  283f
Kirmayer, Lawrence, 445
Kluckhohn, Clyde, 36, 173, 373
Kolata, Alan, 144
Konner, Mel, 428
The Kpelle, 325–326, 340
Krause, Michael, 105
Kroeber, A.L., 36
Kula ring, 175–176
Kundera, Milan, 115
The Kwakwaka'wakw (Kwakiutl),
 128n, 130, 164, 179, 186, 270, 424
Kyoto Accord, 482

Labour
 child labour, 160
 cooperative work groups, 160–161
 craft specialization, 161
 division of labour. *See* Division of
  labour
Lafitau, Joseph-François, 5
Lambek, Michael, 446
Land, control of, 162
Language, **92**
 bilingualism, 105, 112–114
 code switching, 115
 colour, 107
 core vocabulary, 102
 creole language, 115
 in cultural setting, 106–115
 culture, transmission of, 44
 dialects, 109–115
 displacement, 116
 Egypt, official language of, 304
 extinction of languages, 105–106
 gender in, 111
 gesture-call system, 96–100
 grammar, 95
 kinship terms, 108–109
 linguistic change, 100–106
 monolingualism, 106
 morphology, 94–95
 nature of language, 93–95
 nonverbal communication, 96–100
 origins of, 115–118
 phonology, 94
 pidgin language, 115
 primitive language, search for,
  117–118
 Sapir-Whorf hypothesis, 107
 sensitive language, 108
 sexist language, 111
 sign language, 92
 signal, 92
 sound and shape of, 94–95
 spoken language, shift to, 117
 symbols, 92
 syntactic units of, 95
 syntax, 95, 116–117
 and thought, 107–109
Language family, **100**
The Lapps, 185

Law, **333**
 anthropological study of, 338
 definitions of, 338
 functions of, 338–339
Leach, Sir Edmund, 21
Leblanc, Lauraine, 41
Lee, Richard B., 6, 14, 15–20, 22,
 131, 133–134, 434
Legends, **392–393**
Legislated discrimination, 300
Legitimacy, and politics, 346–347
Lesbian relations. *See* Homosexuality
Levelling mechanisms, **177**
Lévi-Strauss, Claude, 210, 424, 425
Levirate, **216**
Lie detector (polygraph), 341–342
Lineage, **271–272**
Lineal system, 279–280
Linguistic anthropology, 7, **11**
Linguistic changes
 borrowing from other languages,
  102
 causes, 102
 description of, 102
 extinction of languages, 105–106
 group membership, 102–103
 linguistic divergence, 101–102
 linguistic nationalism, 103–105
Linguistic divergence, **101–102**
Linguistic nationalism, **103–105**
Linguistic origins, 115–118
Linguistics, **93**
 described, 93–94
 descriptive linguistics, 100
 glottochronology, 102
 historical linguistics, 100–102
Linton, Ralph, 456
Livingstone, Frank, 419
Lock, Margaret, 420–422, 423, 426,
 445
Love Canal, 442–443
Lowie, Robert, 165

Magic, 370–377
Mair, Lucy, 372
Male descent, 265–266
Malinowski, Bronislaw, 46–47, 175,
 199, 338, 369
The Maliseets, 274
Managed health care, 444
Manuel, George, 433
Marx, 105–106
The Maori, 410–411
Marett, R.R., 361
Marine transhumance, **164**
Market exchange, **180–183**
Market forces, 181
Marketplace, 180, 181
Marriage, **203**. *See also* Sexual rela-
 tions
 arranged marriages, 218
 bride-price, 225
 bride service, 225
 common-law marriages, 211
 conjugal bond, 205
 cooperation explanation, 210
 cousin marriage, 223–224
 definitions of, 203, 204, 213

dowry, 225
as economic exchange, 224–226
endogamy, 209–210
exogamy, 209–210
foraging groups, 135
forms of, 213–226
fraternal polyandry, 251
group marriage, 216
incest taboo, 205–209
Islamic marriages, 189
Israeli kibbutz, 208–209
levirate, 216
vs. mating, 210–211
matrilateral cross-cousin marriage, 223–224
monogamy, 210–211, 213, 214
North American marriage, 226–227
patrilateral cross-cousin marriage, 224
patrilateral parallel-cousin marriage, 223
polyandry, 216
polygyny, 204, 205, 211–212, 213, 214–216
same-sex marriages, 211–213
serial monogamy, 217
sororal polygyny, 250
sororate, 216
spouse, choice of, 217–218
Martin, Emily, 202, 440–441, 446
Marx, Karl, 297
The Masai, 200, 296, 411, 412
Mate selection, 217–218
Mati (Paramaribo, Suriname), 200
Mating, *vs.* marriage, 210–211
Matriarchy, myth of, 391–392
Matrilateral cross-cousin marriage, 223–224
Matrilineal descent, 264–265, 268–269
Matrilocal residence, 248
The Maya, 25, 159, 160–161, 246, 248, 411
The Mbuti, 130, 131, 137, 248–249
McClung, Nellie, 42
McElhinny, Bonnie, 292
McFarlane, Len, 84
McGhee, Robert, 11
McIlwraith, Thomas F., 6
McKinney, Louise, 42
Mead, Margaret, 104, 199
Mechanisms of change, 454–459
Mechanized agriculture, 147–148
Mediation, 340
Medical anthropology
aboriginal health and illness, 445
biocultural approach, 418–420
in Canada, 445–446
critical medical anthropology, 418.
See also Critical medical anthropology
cultural interpretive approach, 418, 420–426
described, 418
shamanic medicine, 422–426
"three bodies" paradigm, 420–422
Medical hegemony, 422
Medicalization, 422

Medicine person, 363–365
The Melanesians, 321, 360–362, 362, 369, 379
Men
manhood, universal imagery of, 405
rule by men, 291
as scavengers, 75
Mende women, 367, 378
Men's associations, 294–295
Men's work
in foraging societies, 133–135
sexual division of labour, 157–158
Menstrual taboo, 368
The Métis, 327
Migratory fishing, 164
The Mi'kmaqs, 131, 274–275
Minority women in Canadian politics, 330
Mitchell, Lisa, 446
Mobility of food foragers, 130–132, 305–306
Modernization, 467
and developing world, 469–470
integrative mechanisms, 467–468
pain of, 470–471
the Schuar, 469
Skolt Lapps, and snowmobile revolution, 468–469
structural differentiation, 467–468
subprocesses of, 467
women and, 470
Modernization of Benefits and Obligations Act, 212
Modified extended family structure, 263
The Mohawks, 273
Moiety, 273
Money, 181–182
Monogamy, 210–211, 213, 214
The Montagnais, 132, 137
Morgentaler, Henry, 465
Morphemes, 94–95
Motif, 394
Mousterian tools, 80–81
Multinational corporations, 473–476
The Mundurucu, 242–243, 290–291
Murdock, George Peter, 23–24
Murphy, Emily, 42
Music
flute, 401–402
functions of, 401–404
as identifier, 402–403
non-European music, 400–401
political agenda and, 403
social function of, 403
study of, 400
Muslim women, 189, 307–308
Myths, 362–363, 391–392

Nader, Laura, 30, 310
Nader, Ralph, 437
Nagata, Judith, 21n
Names, derogatory connotation of, 6–7
Nanda, Serena, 218–223
The Nandi, 211–212
Nash, June, 427
The Naskapi (Innu), 132, 137

Nation, 326
Natural selection, 62
Naturalistic worldview, 343
The Navajo, 173, 199
Navajo witchcraft, 373–375
The Nayar, 204, 205, 210, 234, 244
The Neanderthals, 80–81
Neel, James V., 418–419
Negative reciprocity, 173
Negotiation, 340
Neo-paganism, 375–377
Neolithic farmers, 429–430
Neolocal residence, 249
Nobel Prize, 332n
Nonindustrial societies
children, 159
conspicuous consumption, 178–179
intensive agriculture, 143–147
kinship, 263
labour in, 161
land, control of, 162
Nonunilineal descent, 270
Nonverbal communication. *See* Gesture-call system
North America. *See also* Industrial societies
age grouping, 291, 292
and the arts, 386–387
the arts, perception of, 386
body decoration, 410
body piercing, 411–412
family in, 235, 236–237
family organization problems, 252
female-headed families, 253
labour dispute resolution, 340
marriage, 226–227
nuclear family, 244
religion and, 357
self-awareness, development of, 240
and tattooing, 411
North American Free Trade Agreement (NAFTA), 187
The Nuba, 409
Nuclear family, 235, 244–245, 252, 263
The Nuer, 108, 323
Nunavut, 327, 473

Oedipus complex, 208
The Ojibwa, 127, 131–132, 135, 164
Oka confrontation, 30n
Old Stone Age, 73
Oldowan tools, 73
Omaha system, 282, 283f
One-world culture, prospect of, 471–472
O'Neil, John, 419
Open-class systems, 305

Paganism, 375
The Pakhtun, 307
Paleoanthropology, 8, 429
Paleolithic, 73
Paleopathology, 427
Pantheons, 358
Parades, Anthony, 54
Paralanguage, 99
described, 99

vocalizations, 100
voice qualities, 99–100
Parker, Richard, 202
Parlby, Irene, 42
Participant observation, **13–14**, 28, 29
Pastoralism, **140–143**, 162, 215, 251, 264
Patrilateral cross-cousin marriage, **224**
Patrilateral parallel-cousin marriage, **223**
Patrilineal descent, 264, 265–266
Patrilocal residence, **248**
Patterns of association, **304**
Patterns of subsistence, **124**
    described, 124
    food-foraging societies, 128–138
    horticulture, 124
    intensive agriculture, 140, 143–147
    mechanized agriculture, 147–148
    pastoralism, 140–143
"Peace in the family" hypothesis, 208
Peacekeepers', 345–346
Pearson, Lester B., 345
The Penobscot, 362
Pharaonic circumcision, 206
Phonemes, **94**
Phonetics, **94**
Phonology, 94
Phratry, **272–273**
Pidgin language, **115**
Pimental, David, 481
Plattner, Stuart, 181
Pluralistic societies, **41**
Pokotylo, David, 84
Polanyi, Karl, 164
Political organization
    and external affairs, 342–346
    externalized controls, 332–336
    internalized controls, 332
    key stages of development, 427–428
    leadership, and gender, 328–331
    and maintenance of order, 331–337
    meaning of, 318
    political systems. *See* Political systems
    and religion, 347
    and war, 342–345
Political systems
    centralized political systems, 324–328
    "compensation" model, 330
    described, 318
    legitimacy, 346–347
    "similarity" model, 330
    uncentralized political systems, 318–324
Pollution, 482–483
Polyandrous family, **235**
Polyandry, **216**
Polygraph, 341–342
Polygynous family, **235**, 250–251
Polygyny, 204, 205, 211–212, **213**, 214–216
Polytheism, **358**
The Pomo Indians, 390
Population control, 483–485
Population growth, 480
Pospisil, Leopold, 45

Potlatch, 178–180, 402
Poverty
    and health, 436–439
    homelessness, 437–439
    skid row, 166–173
    social safety net, 437
Power, **296**
Prehistoric archaeologists, 10
Prestige, **296**
Priestesses, **363**
Priests, **363**
Primary innovations, **454**
Primate dentition, 63–64
Primate Order, **62**
Primates
    anatomical adaptation, 63–66
    arboreal existence, 64, 65
    behaviour, adaptation through, 66–68
    brain, 65
    chimpanzee behaviour, 66–68
    evolution, 62–63
    food, sharing of, 75
    language and, 116
    mating patterns, 211
    sense organs, 64
    sign language, 92
    skeleton, 65–66
Primatology, 8, 74
Prins, Harald, 274
Proxemics, 99
Psychoanalytic explanations (incest taboo), 208
Public health surveillance, in First Nations communities, 254
Punk subcultures, 40–41
Purdah, 307–308
Purdum, Elizabeth D., 54

Quebec
    French Canadian culture, 21
    linguistic nationalism, 103
    separatist movement, 41
Quinn, Naomi, 74
QWERTY keyboard, 455, 456f

Race, concept of, 298
Racial stratification, 298–302
Racism, **298–302**
Radcliffe-Brown, A.R., 272, 332
Ramphele, Mamphela, 7n
Rapp, Rayna, 444, 446
Rathje, William, 10, 10n
Rebellion, 464–466
Reciprocity, **164**
    balanced reciprocity, 165
    barter, 174–175
    generalized reciprocity, 165
    Kula ring, 175–176
    negative reciprocity, 173
    silent trade, 174–175
    trade, 174–175
Reconstructionist religions, **377**
Redistribution, **177**
    described, 176–177
    potlatch, 178–180
    wealth, 177–180
Regional dialects, 110

Religion, **356**
    anthropological approach to, 356–357
    and cultural change, 378–380
    function of, 355
    functions of, 377–380
    fundamentalist religions, 355–356
    and health, 431
    and magic, 370–377
    neo-paganism, 375–377
    and politics, 347
    polytheism, 358
    practice of, 357–370
    priests and priestesses, 363
    psychological function, 378
    reconstructionist religions, 377
    religious specialists, 363–365
    revitalization movements, 378–380
    rites of intensification, 366, 369–370
    rites of passage, 366–369
    rituals and ceremonies, 366–370
    and science, 356
    shamans, 363–365
    and social control, 377–378
    supernatural beings and powers, 357–363
    Wicca, 375–377
    and witchcraft, 371–375
Replacement reproduction, **484**
Replication, 27
Reproductive rights, 465
Residence patterns
    ambilocal residence, 248
    avunculocal residence, 249
    matrilocal residence, 248
    neolocal residence, 249
    patrilocal residence, 248
Resources
    depletion of, 163–164
    labour, 157–161
    land, 162
    technology, 162–163
Revitalization movements, 378–380, 464
Revolution, **464–466**
Ridington, Robin, 22, 361
Riel, Louis, 392–393
Rites of intensification, **366**, 369–370
Rites of passage, **366–369**
Rituals, 366–370
Rock art, 82–83
Romanow, Roy, 444–445
Rosenberg, Harriet, 442
Rudolf, Gloria, 189
Rwanda (Africa), 309, 310–312, 461
Ryan, Joan, 462

The Sagada Igorots, 189
Saladin d'Anglure, Bernard, 337
Salisbury, Richard F., 156
Same-sex relations. *See also* Homosexuality
    same-sex families, 247
    same-sex marriages, 211–213
The Samoans, 270
The San, 130
Sanctions, **332–333**

Sanguineal kin, **205**
Sapir, Edward, 6, 46, 107
Sapir-Whorf hypothesis, **107**
Scheper-Hughes, Nancy, 420–422, 426
The Schuar, 469
Science
    and anthropology, 24–28
    and religion, 356
Scots English, 114–115
The Sechelt Indian Band, 327
Secondary innovations, **454**
Segmentary lineage system, **323**
Selassie, Tekle Haile, 464n
Self-awareness, development of, 240
Separation, **366**
Serial monogamy, **217**
Sex and sexuality
    adolescent sexuality, 198, 199, 200
    alternative genders, 199–200
    anthropologic study of, 199
    cultural variation in, 199
    and effect of culture, 53
    homosexuality, 199–200
    transgenders, 199–200
Sexist language, 111
Sexual access, 203–205
Sexual division of labour, 157–158.
    See also Division of labour
Sexual relations. *See also* Marriage
    controls on, 200
    divorce, 226–227
    homosexual relations, 200–203
    incest taboo, 205–209
    intercourse during pregnancy, 203
    major trends, 203
    pregnancy, as outcome, 204–205
    sexual access, rules of, 203–205
Sexually segregated cultures, 158
Shaman, **363–365**
Shamanism, 422–426
Sheets, Payson, 84
Shostak, Marjorie, 365, 428
Sickle-cell anemia, 125–126, 419
Sierra Leone, *compin* in, 295
Sign language, 92, 116
Signal, **92**
Silent trade, **174–175**
Silverstein, Ken, 444
Singer, Merrill, 426, 439
Single-parent families, 17, 253–255
The Sioux, 126n
Skid row, 166–173
Skolt Lapps, and snowmobile revolution, 468–469
Slash-and-burn horticulture, 125, 139–140
The Slavey, 320
Smart, Jasmine, 21n
Smart, Josephine, 21n
Social acceptance, 53
Social anthropology. *See* Sociocultural anthropology
Social class, **302**
    achieved status, 302
    ascribed status, 303
    caste, 303
    closed-class systems, 305
    and health, 437

manifestation of, 303–305
    open-class systems, 305
    patterns of association, 304
    symbolic indicators, 304–305
    verbal evaluation, 303–304
Social control, **332**
    crime, 339–342
    and religion, 377–378
    through law, 337–342
Social density, 132
Social dialects, 109–115
Social explanation (incest taboo), **208**
Social impact assessment, 301–302
Social inequality. *See also* Social stratification
    health consequences of, 434–443
    homelessness, 437–439
    poverty, 436–439
Social organization
    age grouping, 291–293
    common-interest associations, 293–295
    descent. *See* Descent groups
    family. *See* Family
    gender grouping, 290–291
    kinship. *See* Kinship
    marriage. *See* Marriage
    social stratification. *See* Social stratification
Social stratification, **295**. *See also* Social inequality
    conflict theory of stratification, 297
    egalitarian cultures, 297
    ethnic stratification, 308–310
    functionalist theory of stratification, 297
    gender stratification, 306–307
    measurement of degree of, 296
    mobility, 305–306
    power, 296
    prestige, 296
    race, concept of, 298
    racial stratification, 298–302
    social class, 302–305
    stratified societies, 296–297
    theories, 297–298
    wealth, 296
Social structure, **37**
Society, **37**, 52–53
Sociocultural anthropology, **12**
    described, 7, 12–13
    ethnography, 13–23
    ethnohistory, 13, 24
    ethnology, 13, 23–24
    worldwide comparisons, 27–28
Sociolinguistics, **11, 110**
The Somali, 323
Sororal polygyny, **250**
Sororate, **216**
South Africa, 303, 478
Spouse, choice of, 217–218
Squires, Susan, 191
Stacey, Judith, 236–239
The state, **326**
State systems, 326–328, 430–431
Stebbins, Kenyon, 442
Sterbak, Jana, 412
Stratification. *See* Social stratification

Stratified societies, **296–297**. *See also* Social stratification
Structural differentiation, **467–468**
Structural violence, **478**
    and culture of discontent, 485–486
    East Asian financial crisis, 480
    pollution, 482–483
    population growth, 483–485
    world hunger, 480–482
Strum, Shirley, 74
Subculture, **39–41**
Sudanese (descriptive) system, **282, 283f**
Sun dance, 367–369
Supernatural beliefs
    ancestral spirits, 359–360
    animatism, 360–362
    animism, 360
    described, 357–358
    gods and goddesses, 358
    magic, 370–377
    myths, 362–363
    and political organization, 347
    witchcraft, 333–336, 371–375
Susser, Ida, 426, 437
The Swazi, 327–328
Swidden farming, **139–140**
Switzerland, cultural pluralism in, 477
Symbolic indicators, **304–305**
Symbols, 44, **92**
Syntax, 95, 116–117
Szathmàry, Emoke, 419

Taft, Michael, 396–399
Taiwan, rural women in, 266–268
Tales, **393–394**
The Tasmanians, 426–427
Tattooing, 410–411
The Tchikrin, 409
Technological development, 467
Technology, **163**
    early hominines. *See* Tools and toolmaking
    food foragers, 130–132
    and globalization, 187
    as resource, 162–163
Teit, James A., 13
Terminology, 6–7
Terrorism, **344**
Thirsting dance, 367–369
"Three bodies" paradigm, 420–422
The Thule, 409
Tibet, polyandry in, 216
Tin mining, study of, 427
The Tiriki, 324
The Tiv, 182
Tiwanaku, 144
Tobacco, and health, 439–442
Toma (Ju/'hoansi headman), 319n
Tomb 7 (Monte Alban), 26
Tonowi, 321–322
Tools and toolmaking
    Acheulian tradition, 76–77
    atlatl, 82
    burin, 82
    diversification, 77
    earliest identifiable tools, 73–74
    food-foraging societies, 163

Homo erectus, 76–77
Homo habilis, 73–75
human brain, evolution of, 76
hunting, 78–79, 80–81
Mousterian tools, 80–81
Neanderthals, 80–81
obsidian scalpels, 84
Oldowan tools, 73–74
significance of, 74
stone, 73–74
surgeons, stone tools for, 84
Upper Paleolithic peoples, 82
Totemism, **272**
Touch, **98**
Trade, 174–175
Transgenders, 199–200
Transition, **366**
Tremblay, Marc-Adélard, 6, 21, 462
Trial by ordeal, 340–341
Tribal organization, 320–322,
429–430
Tribe, **320**
Trigger, Bruce, 156
Trobriand Islanders
adolescent sexuality, 198
exogamy, 46–47
intercourse during pregnancy, 203
Kula ring, 175–176
marriage exchanges, 224–225
marriage rules, 209
residence patterns, 249–250
specialization, 161
women, importance of, 48–50
yam production, 154–156
The Tsembaga, 124–125, 126–127
The Turkana, 214
The Tutsi, 310–312, 461
Two-spirits, 199–200
Tylor, Sir Edward Burnett, 36, 210

Ubykh, 106
Ukrainian immigrants, 309
Uncentralized political systems
age-grade organization, 324
association organization, 324
band organization, 318–320
described, 318
kinship organization, 323
segmentary lineage system, 323
tribal organization, 320–322
Unilateral descent. *See* Unilineal
descent
Unilineal descent, **264**
double descent, 269
economy, relationship with,
264–265
matrilineal descent, 264–265,
268–269
patrilineal descent, 264, 265–266
phratry, 272–273
United States. *See also* North America
African slaves, importation of, 303

flea markets, 182–183
health care in, 436, 437
media, and diffusion, 457
"melting pot" ideology, 459
Native Americans, federal recognition for, 274–275
"Untouchables," 303
Upper Paleolithic peoples, **82**
art, 82–83
Clovis peoples, 84, 86
intelligence, 82
peopling the New World, 83–86
specialization, 82
spread of, 84–85
Urban kinship systems in Canada,
263–264
Urban legends, 392
Urbanization, 145, 430–431, 467
Ury, William L., 341

Van Allen, Judith, 330–331
Van Den Berghe, Pierre, 465
Van Esterik, Penny, 446
Van Gennep, Arnold, 366
Vancouver's Downtown Eastside, 438
Vanek, Anthony L., 109
Veblen, Thorstein, 177
Verbal arts
described, 389–391
folklore, 389
legends, 392–393
myths, 391–392
poetry and songs, 394–395
tales, 393–394
Verbal evaluation, **303**–304
The Vikings, 158
Visual anthropology, 104
Visual art
Canadian, 406–409
described, 404
function of, 404–405
graffiti, 404–406
Vitebsky, Piers, 423
Vocal characterizers, **100**
Vocal qualifiers, **100**
Vocal segregates, **100**
Vocalizations, **100**
Voice qualities, **99**–100
Voluntary associations, 293

Waldram, James B., 374
Wallace, Anthony F.C., 356, 380
Wanuskewin Heritage Park
(Saskatchewan), 10n
The Wape, 331, 359
War, 342–345, 465–466
Wealth, 177–180, **296**
Wealth-generating polygyny, 215
Weaver, Sally, 463
Weeks, Jeffrey, 199
Weiner, Annette B., 48–50, 198
Wekker, Gloria, 200

West African farmers, 162
Western Abenaki people, 24, 343,
391, 402
Western societies. *See* North America
White, Leslie, 44
Whorf, Benjamin Lee, 107
Wicca, 372, **375**–377. *See also*
Witchcraft
Williams, A.M., 201
Williams, Jody, 332n
Wilson, Sir Daniel, 4, 5
Witchcraft, **371**
and control, 333–336, 373
divination, 373
everyday witches, 372
functions of, 372–373
the Ibibio, 371–372
nightmare witches, 372
psychological functions, among
Navajo, 373–375
Salem, Massachusetts, 371, 375
Wolf, Margery, 266–268
Wolf, Naomi, 43
Women. *See also* Gender perspectives
economic activities of, 241
and economic development,
189–190
and female genital mutilation
(FGM), 206–207
female-headed families, 217,
253–255
and health, 440–441
and housework, 23
Kenyan women, and female power,
22
matriarchy, myth of, 391–392
menstrual taboo, 368
and political leadership, 328–331
purdah, 307–308
sexual relations, control of, 200
in Taiwan, 266–268
Trobriand women, 48–50
and wealth-generating polygyny,
215
Women's associations, 294–295
Women's health movement, 440–441
Women's movement, 42–43
Women's work
in food-foraging societies, 133–136
sexual division of labour, 157–158
Woolfson, Peter, 107
World hunger, 480–482
Worldviews, 343

The Yakö, 269
The Yanomami, 307, 424, 460
Young, Alan, 445
Young, T. Kue, 419
The Yukon First Nations, 327

Zapatista movement, 343n, 466n
The Zapotec, 30

PHOTO PERMISSIONS

TEXT PERMISSIONS